THE ILLUSTRATED
DICTIONARY
OF
WESTERN
LITERATURE

Michael Legat

THE ILLUSTRATED

DICTIONARY

OF

WESTERN

LITERATURE

CONTINUUM · NEW YORK

1987
THE CONTINUUM PUBLISHING COMPANY
370 Lexington Avenue, New York, N.Y. 10017

Printed in Spain

Library of Congress Cataloging-in-Publication Data

Legat, Michael, 1923-
   The illustrated dictionary of Western literature/Michael Legat.
     p.   cm.
   ISBN 0-8264-0393-X
   1. Literature--Dictionaries.   I. Title.
PN41.L34 1987
803--dc 19   87-19991
                                                    CIP

This book was designed and produced by BLA Publishing Limited,
East Grinstead, Sussex, England

A member of the **Ling Kee Group**
LONDON · HONG KONG · TAIPEI · SINGAPORE · NEW YORK

Contents

Introduction

THIS BOOK is intended not only for students of literature but also for the general reader, whether he or she is an *aficionado* of the 'classics' or prefers to pick up the latest bestseller. As Samuel Johnson said, 'The chief glory of every people arises from its authors,' and here is a celebration, and in essence a history, of that glory, as manifested in the Western world.

The Dictionary consists primarily of a list of authors – novelists, playwrights, poets, biographers, historians, philosophers, naturalists, essayists, etc., including some whose work is popular rather than of great literary significance. The concentration has been unashamedly on writers of British, Irish, or United States origin, but all the major European authors are included, together with some from Africa, South America, Australia, Canada and the Caribbean. Since it is a dictionary of *Western* literature, writers from the Middle and Far East have been excluded. The entries vary in size; naturally, the maximum space available has been given to the giants of literature, with some assessment of their individual achievement and the inclusion of all their principal publications, but even in the shorter entries as much biographical detail as possible is given, together with mention of the author's major work or works.

Other entries include 'movements' and influential associations – for example, Existentialism, or the Bloomsbury Group – definitions of literary terms such as allegory, drolls and parody, and short articles on comedy, the novel, the sonnet, and the like. Many major literary works of all kinds have also been given separate entries, with their dates of publication and, in most cases, a brief description of their contents.

The period covered by the Dictionary ranges from the eighth century BC, when the works of Homer are believed to have been written, to the present day, represented by such authors as Alexander Solzhenitsyn, Saul Bellow, Doris Lessing, Norman Mailer, Kingsley Amis and V.S. Naipaul.

The compiler of such a volume as this, covering so huge a subject, is faced with a number of problems, the most thorny of which are who and what to include, how much space to devote to each entry, and who and what to leave out. It is, of course, especially difficult to decide which contemporary authors are of sufficient importance to merit inclusion, and in many cases I have made a personal selection. I should, however, like to pay tribute to my editors for much helpful advice in this context, and, indeed, throughout the preparation of the book. If your favourite author is not included, or is given briefer mention than you think is due, I ask for your indulgence. At the same time, I would claim that this Dictionary is remarkably comprehensive in scope, and includes much information not to be found elsewhere in one volume.

Mention must also be made of the two Appendices. The first gives examples of different forms of verse, which could not conveniently have been included in the text. The second lists all the major authors in the book in chronological order, thus enabling the reader to see at a glance, for instance, who were Shakespeare's important contemporaries, not only in England, but in sixteenth- and early seventeenth-century Europe.

Finally, although this is primarily a work of reference, I have tried to make it not only accurate and informative but also readable and entertaining (and in this last respect, at least, the splendid illustrations should prove an adequate compensation for any failure on my part). It is my hope that the Dictionary may introduce the reader to many previously unfamiliar authors, and perhaps persuade him or her to seek out their work.

M.L.

Acknowledgements

GRATEFUL ACKNOWLEDGEMENT is made to the following for permission to reproduce illustrations. Care has been taken to trace the ownership of the illustrations included and to make full acknowledgement for their use. If any errors or omissions have occurred, they will be corrected in subsequent editions, provided notification is sent to the publisher.

ABBEY THEATRE
ANGUS McBEAN
AQUARIUS PHOTO LIBRARY
ART RESOURCE, NY
BARBARA EDWARDS
BBC HULTON PICTURE LIBRARY
BODLEIAN LIBRARY
BRIDGEMAN ART LIBRARY
BRITISH LIBRARY
BRONTË SOCIETY
DICKENS HOUSE MUSEUM
DULWICH COLLEGE
ESSEX INSTITUTE, SALEM, MASS
FITZWILLIAM MUSEUM
FOTOMAS INDEX
IMOGEN CUNNINGHAM TRUST
JARROLD, NORWICH
KOBAL COLLECTION
LAMBETH PALACE LIBRARY
MANDER AND MITCHESON
MANSELL COLLECTION
MARY EVANS PICTURE LIBRARY
NATIONAL PORTRAIT GALLERY, LONDON
NOVOSTI PRESS AGENCY
NATIONAL TRUST PHOTOGRAPHIC LIBRARY
PENGUIN BOOKS
POPPERFOTO
ROBERT FROST LIBRARY
SCALA/ART RESOURCE, NY
SMITHSONIAN INSTITUTION
TALBOY FILE, AUSTIN HISTORY CENTER
TASS
TATE GALLERY
THE TRUSTEES OF AMHERST COLLEGE, MASS
TOPHAM PICTURE AGENCY
WEIDENFELD AND NICOLSON ARCHIVES

A

Aaron's Rod A novel by D.H. Lawrence, telling of Aaron Sisson, who deserts his family and his job in the coal-mines for a high-flying life as a flautist. It was first published in 1922.

Abbey Theatre The Abbey Theatre was opened in Dublin in 1904, thanks to the generous patronage of Miss A.E. Horniman. From the time of its first production, which consisted of short plays by W.B. Yeats and Lady Gregory, it was a showcase for Irish dramatists. Their work undoubtedly stimulated all forms of Irish literature, and the theatre can therefore be said to have exercised beyond itself, as it were, a major influence. Notable among the major playwrights whose work was first produced at the Abbey are J.M. Synge, Sean O'Casey, Lennox Robinson and St John Ervine, as well as Yeats himself. The theatre was not without its troubles in the early years: a production in 1907 of Synge's *The Playboy of the Western World* caused riots, and in 1909 *The Shewing Up of Blanco Posnet* by G. Bernard Shaw was presented amid considerable controversy and threats — fortunately not fulfilled — of censorship. Eventually such problems vanished, and the importance of the Abbey's contribution to Irish literature was recognized in 1925 by a grant from the newly-formed state of Erse, making it the first government-sponsored theatre in the English-speaking world. Nationalist sentiments later brought about the writing and performance of many plays in Eire. The original theatre was destroyed by fire in 1951, but productions continued elsewhere until a new building was opened in 1966, and the Abbey continues to thrive.

Abbot, The A novel by Sir Walter Scott, first published in 1820. It is a sequel to *The Monastery*.

A scene from *The Field* by John B. Keane at the Abbey Theatre.

Abelard with Héloïse. Shortly after their passionate elopement, her enraged father Canon Fulbert caused Abelard to be castrated. Héloïse, a young girl twenty-one years his junior, entered a convent and Abelard became a monk. Over the years they expressed their devotion in many tragic love letters, which later inspired Alexander Pope's 'Epistle of Eloisa to Abelard'. A synod at Soissons in 1121 denounced Abelard's teaching on the Trinity as heresy. Condemned by the Council of Sens in 1140, he died on his way to Rome to defend himself. Abelard was buried at Paraclete, the religious hermitage and sisterhood he had given to Héloïse during his lifetime. Twenty-two years later, Héloïse died and was buried beside him.

Abelard, Peter (1079–1142) Born in Brittany, Peter Abelard was a theologian and dialectician, who became renowned for the philosophical lectures he gave in Paris. His brilliant career was cut short by an indiscreet love affair with his pupil Héloïse, which resulted in his castration at the hands of a group led by Héloïse's enraged father. Abelard spent the remainder of his life as a monk, writing, among other works, his *Introduction ad Theologiam*, which was a transcript of many of the lectures he had given, and the autobiographical *Historia Calamitatum*. Although separated from Héloïse, Abelard remained devoted to her, and the lovers carried on a celebrated correspondence until his death.

Abercrombie, Lascelles Lascelles Abercrombie, a Professor of English Literature, published his first volume of verse, *Interludes in Poems*, in 1908. This was followed by several other collections of poetry, a number of verse plays, and various works of literary criticism. He contributed to the first book of *Georgian Poetry*, published in 1912.

Abrahams, Peter (1919–) Novelist, poet and journalist Peter Abrahams was born in a Johannesburg slum. He published a first volume of verse, *A Black Man Speaks of Freedom*, in 1940. Emigrating to England, he wrote a number of highly-regarded novels, including *Mine Boy* and *Wild Conquest*. *The View from Coyoba*, a more recent major novel, was published in 1985. He is now resident in Jamaica, where he is prominent in local media.

Absalom, Absalom! A novel by William Faulkner, first published in 1936. Set in nineteenth-century Mississippi, it is the Gothic story of Thomas Sutpen, a ruthless slave-owner, and of his final destruction.

Absalom and Achitophel An allegorical, political and satirical poem by John Dryden, first published in 1681.

Abse, Dannie (1923–) A practising doctor of medicine, Daniel Abse was born in Cardiff, Wales. He has successfully published novels, a number of plays, and a charming autobiography, *A Poet in the Family*, but he is best known and much admired as a poet. The first of many volumes of verse, *After Every Green Thing*, appeared in 1949, and *Collected Poems 1948–1976* was published in 1977. More selections have followed, including, in 1986, *Ask the Bloody Horse*.

Absentee, The A novel by Maria Edgeworth, originally written as a play, first published in 1812.

Achebe, Chinua (1930–) Born in Nigeria, the son of a teacher in a missionary school, Chinua Achebe was educated at the University College of Ibadan. After some work in broadcasting he devoted himself, with very considerable success, to an academic career, and has taught at universities in the United States as well as holding a professorship at the University of Nigeria. He has written and published volumes of poetry, essays and short stories, but has been widely regarded as a major novelist ever since the publication in 1958 of *Things Fall Apart*, which was followed by other well-received novels interpreting, often satirically, the emergence of modern Africa.

Ackland, Rodney (1908–) An English dramatist, whose work was often seen during the 1930s, but which never attained great popularity, despite its high quality. *Strange Orchestra* and *After October*, produced in 1931 and 1936 respectively, are Rodney Ackland's best plays, and demonstrate the approach to drama which earned him the title of 'the English Chekhov'.

Actes and Monuments Popularly known as *The Book of Martyrs*, the full title of this immensely long, anti-Roman Catholic history of the Christian church by John Foxe is *Actes and Monuments of these latter and perillous Dayes, touching matters of the Church, wherein are comprehended and described the great Persecution and horrible Troubles that have been wrought and practised by the Romishe Prelates, speciallye in this Realme of England and Scotland, from the yeare of our Lord a thousande to the time now present. Gathered and collected according to the true Copies and Wrytinges certifactorie as well as the Parties themselves that Suffered, as also out of the Bishop's Registers, which were the Doers thereof, by John Foxe*. It was first published in English in 1563, having previously appeared in Latin, and a number of amended editions followed both during the author's lifetime and posthumously.

Adam Bede A novel by George Eliot, which established her reputation when it was first published in 1859.

Adams, Andy (1859–1935) Andy Adams, a native of Indiana, worked for many years on Texas cattle ranches and later as a miner in Colorado during the gold rush. He wrote a number of books, which were based on his own experiences and were remarkable for their realistic approach. *The Log of a Cowboy*, the best known of these, was first published in 1903.

Adams, Henry (1838–1918) Henry Brooks Adams was the grandson of President John Quincy Adams and the great-grandson of President John Adams. He was born in Boston, Massachusetts, and after completing his education at Harvard he spent the period of the Civil War in England, working under his father, the United States minister in London. He returned in 1870 to Harvard, where he spent seven years teaching history. He had already published many articles and essays, and these continued to appear. Devoting himself to writing, he produced, among other works, two volumes on the Swiss-born politician Albert Gallatin, and two novels, the first of which, *Democracy*, came out anonymously, and the second, *Esther*, under the pseudonym of Frances Snow Compton. After his wife's suicide in 1885, he travelled widely, and several books were inspired by these journeys. He wrote a huge nine-volume *History of the United States during the Administrations of Thomas Jefferson and James Madison*, which was published during the period 1889–91. His autobiography, *The Education of Henry Adams*, which appeared in 1907, is highly critical of the education he received, which he said did not fit him to live in what he termed the 'multiverse' of the twentieth century.

Adcock, Fleur (1934–) Kareen Fleur Adcock, the well-known New Zealand poet, moved to England in 1963. Regarded as one of the most talented of modern poets and noted for the irony of her work, she has published several collections of verse since *The Eye of the Hurricane* appeared in 1964. Her *Selected Poems* was published in 1983 and *The Incident Book* in 1986. She has also edited *The Oxford Book of Contemporary New Zealand Poetry*.

Addison, Joseph (1672–1719) Born in Wiltshire, England, the son of the Dean of Lichfield, Joseph Addison was educated at Charterhouse and Oxford. He distinguished himself as a scholar – Dryden thought highly of his Latin poems – and eventually became a fellow of Magdalen College, Oxford. Various writings, including *An Address to King William*, earned him a 'pension', or grant, of three hundred pounds a year, and this enabled him to travel in Europe from 1699 until 1703. When he returned to England he published a long poem, *The Campaign*, which celebrated Marlborough's victory at Blenheim. He also began a political career, becoming a Member of Parliament in 1708 and receiving preferment from the Whig government then in office. He remained in Parliament during the period of Tory government from 1810 to 1812, and when the Whigs returned was appointed Chief Secretary for Ireland. Meanwhile, he had renewed his friendship with

Portrait by Sir Godfrey Keller of the witty essayist and playwright Joseph Addison. A member of Parliament from 1708, he became Secretary of State in 1717.

Richard Steele, whom he had first met when at school and, through him, became a member of the Kit-Cat Club. In 1709, Steele started *The Tatler*, a periodical each number of which was largely devoted to a single essay, and Addison was soon sharing in the writing of these. In 1711, he founded, jointly with Steele, a similar magazine, *The Spectator*, and wrote for it two hundred and seventy-four of the essays for which he is famous. The subjects ranged widely, only political matters being eschewed, and the liveliness, humour and elegance of style of his writing made his work extremely popular. Such periodicals tended to be short-lived, running for only a year or two, and Addison's later journalistic contributions appeared in *The Freeholder*, which was first issued in 1715. As well as being an essayist, Addison was a playwright, and he enjoyed an immense success with his verse tragedy, *Cato*, which had a Prologue by Alexander Pope, and was produced in 1713 at Drury Lane. A later comedy in prose, *The Drummer, or the Haunted House*, produced in 1716, did not repeat this triumph. His political career continued to advance, and in 1716 he was appointed a Lord Commissioner of Trade. In the same year he married the Countess of Warwick. In 1717 he became Secretary of State, but was not considered a success in this position. He retired from government office in the following year, though remaining a Member of Parliament until his death. Granted a substantial pension, he nevertheless continued to write, and now contributed to a periodical entitled *Old Whig*. His final year of life was marked by acrimony: his writings were increasingly politically prejudiced, and his relationship with Steele became strained as a result. He also incurred the enmity of his former admirer, Pope. Nothing, however, can tarnish his reputation as an essayist of wit and unsurpassed stylistic brilliance. He died in London, and was buried in Westminster Abbey.

Adonais A poem in fifty-five Spenserian stanzas by Percy Bysshe Shelley. Written at Pisa, it is an elegy for John Keats, in which Shelley not only laments the poet's tragic death but expresses his anger at the harshness of Keats' critics. It ends with a strong affirmation of belief in Keats' immortality. Considered by many to be Shelley's finest work, *Adonais* was first published in 1821.

Advancement of Learning, The A philosophical treatise by Francis Bacon, written in English and first published in 1605.

Aelfric (*c*.955–*c*.1010) An English monk, later to become Abbot at Eynsham, Aelfric is considered to be the greatest prose stylist writing in Old English. Much of his output is still extant, notably the religious works *Catholic Homilies* and *Lives of the Saints*, and, in the educational field, his Latin Grammar and *Colloquy*, a series of dialogues intended to demonstrate the art of conversation in Latin. He also translated the first seven books of the Bible into the vernacular.

Aella, Songe toe A pseudo-medieval lyric poem by Thomas Chatterton, who subsequently used the same character in his verse tragedy, *Aella*.

Aeneid, The An epic by the great Latin poet Virgil, recounting the adventures of the Trojan hero Aeneas. It includes the fall of Troy and the love affair between Aeneas and Dido, Queen of Carthage, and ends with Aeneas founding the city of Rome.

Aeschylus (525–456BC) Aeschylus is often regarded as the father of Greek tragedy because of the major innovation which he introduced in the construction of plays. Previously the presentation had been restricted to a single actor and a chorus, and by breaking with this convention Aeschylus increased the importance of the dialogue and thereby created an opportunity for much deeper characterization and greater dramatic tension than had previously been possible. The drama was henceforth free to develop into much more than the formal semi-religious ceremony which it had been. Aeschylus was born into a noble Athenian family and spent some years of his young manhood as a soldier. He was the earliest of the three great Athenian dramatists (the others being Sophocles and Euripides). His first plays were seen in Athens when he was twenty-six, and his successful career as a tragic dramatist lasted for more than forty years. He did not win the annual competition for tragedy until 484BC, fifteen years after his debut, and perhaps this was in part due to the innovative quality of his work. After 484, however, the outstanding quality of his tragedies was apparently recognized, for he was awarded the prize many times more in the remaining years of his life, and at that period was clearly the most respected of the Attic writers. He is believed to have written some ninety plays, but unfortunately only seven of them are still extant: *Prometheus Bound*, *The Suppliants*, *The Seven Against Thebes*, *The Persians* and the trilogy known as the *Oresteia*, which was his last work, consisting of *Agamemnon*, *Chorphoroe* and *Eumenides*. Although their form is not always easy for modern playgoers to appreciate to the full, the dramatic excitement of the plots and the grandeur and beauty of the language which Aeschylus used can still speak to us across the centuries.

Orestes and the Furies. This dramatic fourth century BC illustration of the story of Orestes is thought to depict a scene from Aeschylus' play *Eumenides*.

Aesop (?620–560BC) Our knowledge of Aesop, the supposed author of Greek fables, is scanty. His place of birth is uncertain, but it is known that he died at Delphi. The main source of information is the Greek historian Herodotus, who states that he was a slave who lived in the sixth century BC. It is unlikely that Aesop was in fact the originator of the fables, which probably belonged to a much older tradition of oral story-telling. It is equally improbable that he wrote them down, but the possibility remains that he was a story-teller who collected and made a speciality of such pieces.

A woodcut from Caxton's *Aesop*, one of the earliest illustrated books.

Aesthetic movement 'Art for art's sake' was the creed of the Aesthetic movement, which flourished briefly and extravagantly in England in the 1880s, largely under the influence of the Pre-Raphaelites. Oscar Wilde was prominent among its members, and he and the Movement's sentimental ideals of beauty were widely satirized, as, for example, in the Gilbert and Sullivan operetta, *Patience*.

Agamemnon A tragedy by Aeschylus, the first part of the trilogy, the *Oresteia*, in which the Trojan hero Agamemnon is murdered by his wife Clytemnestra.

Agate, James (1877–1947) James Evershed Agate was the most celebrated English theatre critic of his day. Apart from his dramatic criticism and a number of novels, his principal literary work was *Ego*. The nine volumes of this autobiography in diary form were published between 1935 and 1948, and are still read today for their lively picture of theatrical and literary London.

Agee, James (1909–55) American novelist, poet and writer of screenplays, James Agee was born in Knoxville, Tennessee, and educated at Harvard. His first book of poems, *Permit me Voyage*, was published in 1934. His most memorable work was *A Death in the Family*, a novel based in part on his own experiences which was published in 1957.

Age of Innocence, The A novel by Edith Wharton, set in New York in the 1870s, first published in 1920.

Age of Reason, The An essay on deism by Thomas Paine, first published in two parts in 1793 and 1794, and as a whole in 1795.

Agnes Grey The first of Anne Brontë's two novels, telling the story of a governess. It was published in 1847 under the pseudonym Acton Bell.

Agnon, S.Y. (1888–1970) Samuel Yosef Czaczkes, who was born in Galicia, adopted the surname Agnon following the publication of his first story *Agunot*. Resident for many years in Israel, he wrote a large number of novels. The first of them was *And the Crooked Shall Be Made Straight*, published in 1916, and the best known are perhaps *A Guest for the Night* and *A Bridal Canopy*. He was the joint winner, with Nelly Sachs, of the Nobel Prize for Literature in 1966.

Aiken, Conrad (1889–1973) Conrad Potter Aiken was born in Savannah, Georgia, and educated at Harvard. He published the first of several volumes of poetry, *Earth Triumphant*, in 1914, and his *Selected Poems* was awarded a Pulitzer Prize in 1929. Although primarily regarded as a poet, he was also a novelist, short story writer and critic. Much of his work reflects his deep interest in psychology. He spent many years of his life in England, where his daughters, Joan Aiken and Jane Aiken Hodge, are both successful writers.

Ainsworth, William Harrison (1805–82) Born in Manchester, England, William Harrison Ainsworth was, in his time, a widely-read author of historical adventure novels, many of them presenting a colourful and highly romantic picture of underworld characters such as Dick Turpin, the highwayman, who was the hero of his first book, *Rookwood*. Other novels covered several centuries of life in the north of England. In addition to *Rookwood*, the best known of his books are *Jack Sheppard*, *Old St Paul's* and *The Lancashire Witches*. For many years he edited various popular periodicals, including his own *Ainsworth's Magazine*.

Alabaster, William (1567–1640) A poet writing in Latin, William Alabaster, or Arblastier, was born at Hadleigh, Suffolk, England, and educated at Westminster School and Cambridge. He became a priest, and lived a not uneventful life. He sailed with the Earl of Essex on an expedition to Spain, and while there became a Roman Catholic, for which crime he spent two years imprisoned in the Tower of London. In 1607, while in exile in Antwerp, he published *Apparatus in Revelationem Jesu Christi*, a work which was condemned by the Roman church as heretical, and later he was again imprisoned, but this time in Rome and by the Inquisition. He escaped to England, returned to Protestantism and became a chaplain to James I. Much of his poetry was in sonnet form, and certain of his works were extravagantly praised: Edmund Spenser considered his unfinished epic on Queen Elizabeth I to be matchless, while Dr Johnson said of his tragedy, *Roxana*, that it was the best Latin verse written in England before Milton.

A la recherche du temps perdu The long sequence of novels by Marcel Proust, best known in English as *Remembrance of Things Past*, published between 1913 and 1927. Reflecting the Paris *salons* of the 1890s, it looks with despair on the emphemeral quality of human life. Its analytical method influenced many later novelists.

Alastor, or the Spirit of Solitude A poem by Percy Bysshe Shelley, published in 1816 and often considered to be his first major work.

Albee, Edward (1928–) Edward Franklin Albee, who was born in Washington, DC, and educated at Columbia University, leaped to international fame when his first full-length play, *Who's Afraid of Virginia Woolf?*, was performed in 1962. He had previously attracted notice with a number of one-act plays, including *The Zoo Story* and *The American Dream*. Many more plays have followed, among them *Tiny Alice, A Delicate Balance* and *Seascape*. The last two of these both won the Pulitzer Prize, in 1966 and 1975 respectively.

Alcestis A tragedy by Euripides, concerned with the devotion of the Queen of Pherae in Thessaly, who agreed to die in place of her husband, King Admetus.

A scene from *The Alchemist*, Ben Jonson's famous story of an elaborate confidence trick.

Alchemist, The Among Ben Jonson's finest works, this comedy was first performed in 1610 and published in 1612.

Alcott, Bronson (1799–1888) Amos Bronson Alcott, a native of Connecticut, was a teacher and, as an associate of Thoreau and Emerson, a member of the Transcendental movement. He published a number of books, mostly on educational subjects.

Although he was respected as an educationalist, he was somewhat improvident, and his family was for long dependent on the earnings as a writer of his daughter Louisa M. Alcott.

Alcott, Louisa M. (1832–88) Louisa May Alcott was born in Philadelphia, Pennsylvania. She wrote her first book, *Flower Fables*, at the age of sixteen, though it was not published until 1855. By 1860 she was writing regularly for the magazine *Atlantic Monthly*. *Hospital Sketches*, which appeared in 1863, was based on her experiences during a short period as a nurse during the Civil War, and a novel, *Moods*, was published two years later. In 1867 she became the editor of a magazine for children, *Merry's Museum*. *Little Women* was published in two parts in 1868 and 1869, and brought her immediate fame and fortune. She wrote many other novels, including sequels to *Little Women*, but often in more adult vein, and also produced short stories, poetry and plays. She was much concerned with such social issues as women's suffrage.

A coloured illustration from an early edition of *Little Women*.

A late tenth-century miniature of St Aldhelm.

Aldhelm, St (*c*.639–709) Aldhelm was a man of noble birth who entered the church as a monk and rose to become Abbot of Malmesbury. In 1705 he was consecrated as Bishop of Sherborne. He is believed to have been the first Englishman to write Latin verse, and is said also to have been popular in his time as a vernacular poet. His Anglo-Saxon poetry has not, however, survived, and his only works now known are all in Latin, including a number of letters, among which is his most celebrated work, *De Septenario*, which contains one hundred and one riddles in hexameters.

Aldington, Richard (1892–1962) Novelist and biographer Richard Edward Godfree Aldington achieved immediate success with his first novel, *Death of a Hero*, published in 1929. He wrote a number of other novels, poetry and essays, and published a number of translations, but made more impact with his highly critical biographies of D.H. Lawrence and T.E. Lawrence. These were *Portrait of a Genius, But ...*, published in 1950, and *Lawrence of Arabia: a biographical enquiry*, which came out in 1955. Both books caused much controversy. In 1913 he married the American poet and novelist Hilda Doolittle.

Aldiss, Brian (1925–) Brian Wilson Aldiss was born in Norfolk, England. He is one of the most distinguished of British science fiction writers, and his trilogy *Helliconia Spring*, *Helliconia Summer* and *Helliconia Winter*, published in 1982, 1983 and 1985, is a major achievement. A prolific author, Brian Aldiss has also written in other genres, including essays, criticism, travel and straight fiction, of which a recent example is the novella *Ruins*, published in 1986.

Aldrich, Thomas Bailey (1836–1907) Born in Portsmouth, New Hampshire, Thomas Bailey Aldrich was a poet, novelist and short story writer. Many volumes of his lyric verse were published between 1856 and 1900. His early novel, *The Story of a Bad Boy*, based largely on his own experiences, was published in 1870, and was followed by several other works of fiction, often set in his native town. Bailey was also a successful journalist, and eventually rose to edit various magazines, including, for a nine-year period, the *Atlantic Monthly*.

Aleixandre, Vicente (1900–84) The Spanish poet Vicente Aleixandre Merlo was a leading member of the group known as the 1927 Generation, which came to prominence during the 1920s. He was born in Seville and educated at Madrid University. His first book, published in 1928, was *Ambito*. Nearly thirty other volumes followed, notable among which are *Sombra del paraiso*, in 1944, and *Poesias Completas*, in 1960. He was awarded the Nobel Prize for Literature in 1977.

Alexander's Feast, or The Power of Music A long poem by John Dryden, first published in 1697.

Alexandrian Library, The A collection of manuscripts gathered at Alexandria under the Ptolomies, who reigned in Egypt from 330 to 30BC and maintained the city as a centre of culture. The library is supposed to have contained some four hundred thousand works, though some authorities put the figure as high as seven hundred thousand. Unfortunately, the collection disappeared during various sieges and sackings of Alexandria.

Alexandria Quartet, The Lawrence Durrell's sequence of four novels, set in Alexandria during the 1930s, which established his reputation. The four volumes are: *Justine*, published in 1957, *Balthazar* and *Mountolive*, both published in 1958, and *Clea* published in 1960.

alexandrine The term used to describe a line consisting of six iambic feet (see *metre*). The form is used in French heroic verse – for instance, in the plays of Racine – and sometimes occurs in English poetry to vary the more usual five-footed line.

Alfred the Great (848–900) Alfred succeeded to the throne of Wessex in 871. He had already spent some years fighting the invading Danes, and the struggle was to continue until 896. Only then was he able to devote himself to such tasks as the building of a navy, the passing of new laws, and the dissemination of literature in the vernacular, the last of which he largely achieved by bringing scholars to his court and himself joining them in translating from the Latin major works of religion, philosophy and history. Alfred also initiated and inspired the preparation of the *Anglo-Saxon Chronicle*, and it has been suggested that he wrote some parts of it, especially those which deal with his own campaigns and other events of his reign.

Alger, Horatio (1834–99) Horatio Alger was born in Revere, Massachusetts. Strictly brought up and educated for the Church, he threw up his career and went to France, where he lived a life of some dissipation. Repenting, he returned to the United States, and became a Unitarian minister in 1864. Later he was appointed chaplain to the Manhattan Newsboys' Lodging House. He published more than a hundred and twenty books, and achieved enormous popularity and sales with his highly moral stories of poor boys, including the series which appeared under the titles *Ragged Dick, Tattered Tom* and *Luck and Pluck.*

Algren, Nelson (1909–81) Born in Detroit, Nelson Agren chronicled in his novels the seamy side of life in Chicago. He published his first novel in 1935, but it was his best-known work, *The Man with the Golden Arm*, appearing in 1949, which brought him popular acclaim. The novel, which was concerned with drug addiction, won the National Book Award in 1949. *A Walk on the Wild Side*, published in 1955, was also very successful. He has also written many short stories, travel books, and some non-fiction.

Alice's Adventures in Wonderland The classic story for children by Lewis Carroll, first published in 1865 with illustrations by Sir John Tenniel.

allegory A term used for material which the reader is intended to understand as referring to persons or events other than those directly described. There is usually a desire on the part of the author who uses allegory to instruct or to criticize, and this device frequently allows a greater measure of entertainment for the reader, and at the same time a sharper pointing of the moral. Allegories have been written through the ages, Dante's *Divine Comedy* and Orwell's *Animal Farm* are but two examples.

Allen, Grant (1848–99) Charles Grant Blairfindie Allen was born in Canada, but spent most of his life in England. He began his career as a writer of philosophical and scientific works, but turned to fiction and published his first novel in 1884. The sensationalism of a later story, *The Devil's Die*, which appeared in 1888, brought him popular success. From this time on he produced new books at the rate of almost two a year. The most successful of them was *The Woman Who Did*, a fictional polemic in support of oppressed womanhood. It was published in 1895 and was considered to be scandalous in its frankness.

All For Love, or The World Well Lost A verse tragedy by John Dryden, first performed and published in 1678.

alliteration A literary device in which two or more words beginning with the same letter are placed next or so close to one another that the similarity of sound is apparent, as in 'Round and round the rugged rock the ragged rascal ran'. Alliteration was much used in Old and Middle English poetry, and indeed may be considered as one of the principal devices which distinguish poetry from prose.

All My Sons A play by Arthur Miller. First seen in 1947, it established his reputation.

All's Well that Ends Well A comedy by William Shakespeare. Probably first performed in 1603 or 1604, it was published in 1623. It tells of Helena's love for Bertram, Count of Rousillon, which is complicated by the machinations of the braggart Parolles.

Almayer's Folly Joseph Conrad's first novel, published in 1895.

Ambassadors, The A novel by Henry James, in which Mrs Newsome sends a number of friends to Paris in the hope of persuading her son to return home. It was first published in 1903.

A lithograph of the prolific novelist Grant Allen by the famous portrait painter Sir William Rothenstein, dated 1897. In 1895, a few years before his death, he scandalised society by his forthright argument in support of disadvantaged women in his novel *The Woman Who Did*.

Ambler, Eric (1909–) Born in London and educated at London University, Eric Ambler is regarded as one of the most distinguished of thriller-writers. His best known books include *Epitaph for a Spy*, first published in 1938, and *The Mask of Dimitrios*, which appeared the following year.

Amelia Henry Fielding's last novel, first published in 1751. It tells of the marital difficulties of Amelia and William Booth.

American, The A novel by Henry James, first published in volume form in 1877. It tells of a rich American who visits Paris and becomes involved with a French aristocratic family.

American Magazine, The The first magazine ever published in the British Colonies in North America. Three issues only appeared, between January and March 1741.

American Notes A highly unfavourable account by Charles Dickens of his visit to the United States in 1842, in which year the book was published.

American Senator, The A novel by Anthony Trollope, first published in 1877.

American Tragedy, An Theodore Dreiser's finest novel, first published in 1925. Based on a true-life murder case, it tells of Clyde Griffiths and his unheeding search for success.

Amis, Kingsley (1922–) Kingsley William Amis was born in London and educated at the City of London School and at Oxford. He embarked on an academic career, but, after he had published two volumes of poetry, the immediate success of his first novel, *Lucky Jim*, which appeared in 1954, eventually allowed him to write as a full-time occupation. *Lucky Jim* has been followed by a large number of successful novels, including *That Uncertain Feeling*, published in 1955, *One Fat Englishman*, published in 1963, and *Jake's Thing*, published in 1978. A more recent novel, *The Old Devils*, won the Booker Prize in 1986. A prolific writer, Amis has also published two 'James Bond' books, under the pseudonym Robert Markham, and has produced much journalism, some of which has been collected in book form. Other volumes of verse have also appeared, and in 1979 he brought out his *Collected Poems 1944–1979*. Regarded as one of the 'angry young men' at the time when *Lucky Jim* was first published, Amis is now an establishment figure, though much of his work is still concerned, beneath the wit and the polished prose, with strongly-felt protestation. His son, Martin Amis, is also a successful novelist.

Amoretti A group of eighty-eight sonnets by Edmund Spenser, believed to have been inspired by his love for his second wife. The poems were first published in 1595.

Amory, Thomas (*c*.1691–1788) The notably eccentric Thomas Amory was born in Ireland and educated at Trinity College, Dublin. He studied medicine briefly, and then devoted himself to writing. He is remembered for two books, *Memoirs containing the Lives of Several Ladies of Great Britain; a History of Antiquities &c* (which in fact concentrated on the life of one lady only) and *The Life and Opinions of John Buncle, Esquire*. Both are rambling works, in which narrative is often subordinated to descriptions of travels and dissertations on a variety of subjects.

Amphitryon A comedy by John Dryden, first performed and published in 1690.

Anatomy of Melancholy, The A supposedly medical work by Robert Burton, first published in 1621, this book covers an extraordinarily wide range of knowledge and is filled with entertaining anecdotes. Its full title is *The Anatomy of Melancholy, What it Is; With all the Kindes, Causes, Symptomes, Prognostickes, and Several Cures of it; in Three Maine Partitions with their Severall Sections, Members and Subsections, Philosophically, Medicinally, Historically, Opened and Cut up, by Democritus Junior*.

Ancient Mariner, The Rime of the A long poem by Samuel Taylor Coleridge, first published in 1798, when it appeared in *Lyrical Ballads*, of which Coleridge and William Wordsworth were joint authors.

Andersen, Hans Christian (1805–75) The son of a shoemaker, Hans Christian Andersen was born in Odense, Denmark. He received little education, and at the age of fourteen went to Copenhagen with the hope of becoming an opera singer. Failing in this endeavour, he became a dancing pupil at the Royal Theatre, and attracted the attention of King Frederick VI, who offered him a free place at a grammar school. He did not enjoy school, but continued his education until 1827. Five years earlier, when he was only seventeen, he had published his first book, *The Ghost at Palnatoke's Grave*, and now he began to write in earnest. He attracted some attention in 1829 with a book entitled *A Journey on Foot from Holman's Canal to the East Point of Amager*, but it was not until 1835 that he achieved real success with his novel, *The Improvisatore*. In the same year the first part of his celebrated *Fairy Tales* appeared, further instalments being published in 1836 and 1837. On their first appearance, these were not immediately successful, but sales soon began to grow, and before long the stories and their author had become immensely popular. Andersen was able to indulge his penchant for travel; his triumphant visit to England in 1847 resulted in a friendship with Charles Dickens, who expressed great admiration for his work. For the rest of his life, Andersen continued to produce more of his *Fairy Tales*, publishing them

An illustration by Edmund Dulac to Hans Christian Andersen's famous fairy tale *The Little Mermaid*.

at intervals until 1872. They have been greatly loved and widely translated, and have been adapted into many different forms – rewritten for small children and made into plays, screenplays and even cartoons. The stories have, of course, completely overshadowed Andersen's other works, which included novels, plays and travel books, and which are largely unknown in the English-speaking world.

Anderson, Maxwell (1888–1959) The son of a Baptist minister, Maxwell Anderson was born in Atlantic, Pennsylvania, and educated at the University of North Dakota and Stanford University, California. He began a career as a teacher before deciding to write for his living and becoming a journalist. He achieved his first success in the theatre with *What Price Glory*, a play about the First World War written in collaboration with Laurence Stallings, which was presented in 1924. Three years later, *Saturday's Children*, of which he was the sole author, was the first in the long list of plays which brought Anderson not only commercial success but a reputation as a playwright of considerable literary quality. *Both Your Houses*, first seen in 1933, received a Pulitzer Prize. A number of his plays were written in blank verse, beginning with *Elizabeth the Queen*, produced in 1930, and he used this form for his best-known play, *Winterset*. The fact that he had dared to write a contemporary play in blank verse about gangsters seemed shocking to some in 1935, when *Winterset* was first produced, but the critics were vastly outnumbered by those who admired the work. Among his other major successes, many of which were adapted for the screen, were *Wingless Victory*, *Key Largo*, *The Eve of Saint Mark* and *Anne of the Thousand Days*.

Anderson, Sherwood (1874–1941) Sherwood Anderson was born in Camden, Ohio. He received comparatively little education, and for many years had no settled occupation. After fighting in the American-Spanish War of 1898, he drifted from job to job, until he decided to go into the advertising business in Chicago. There he began to write, and his first published work was a story, 'Sister', which was printed in the *Little Review*. It was immediately apparent that he had a natural talent. His first book, *Windy McPherson's Son*, was published when he was forty-two. A second novel, *Marching Men*, came out in 1917, and a volume of verse, *Mid-American Chants*, the year after. In 1919, *Winesburg, Ohio* appeared, and this collection of linked short stories, set in a small town in the American Mid-West, established Anderson's reputation. The stories were written in a very informal style, but the characters and incidents which were depicted with such unrelenting realism had been brilliantly chosen to produce a study which was both vivid and penetrating. Anderson wrote and published a number of other collections of short stories and several novels. It is interesting to note that *Many Marriages*, a novel published in 1921, was awarded the Dial Prize of $2,000, a not inconsiderable sum at that time, but the book is now less highly regarded than some of his others, such as *Tar, A*

The innovative American novelist Sherwood Anderson.

Midwest Childhood. Sherwood's naturalism was regarded as a literary innovation of considerable importance, and it had a marked effect on several of the writers who followed him, including William Faulkner and Ernest Hemingway.

Anelida and Arcite An incomplete poem by Geoffrey Chaucer, of which two sections exist. Scholars are uncertain of the date at which it was written.

Angel in the House, The A poem in four parts, extoling marriage, by Coventry Patmore, published between 1854 and 1862.

Angelou, Maya (1928–) American dancer, singer, Black activist and academic, Maya Angelou was born in St Louis. She has published several volumes of poetry, including *And Still I Rise*, but is best known for her autobiographical books, *I Know Where the Caged Bird Sings*, *Singin' and Swingin' and Gettin' Merry Like Christmas*, *The Heart of a Woman* and *All God's Children Need Travelling Shoes*, published between 1969 and 1986.

Angel Pavement A novel by J.B. Priestley, first published in 1930.

Anglo-Norman literature After the Norman Conquest of England in 1066, French was the language not only of the royal court but also of government and of the legal system, and this usage continued until the fourteenth century. Over the years, the language was altered by local influences, and the many versions of French that resulted, some more corrupt than others, are known as Anglo-Norman. Much of the literature of the period was written in Anglo-Norman, and the output was large – there were epics and romances, histories and chronicles, text-books, and especially religious works, which included psalters, lives of the saints, and other devotional books. As a language, Anglo-Norman still survives today in certain legal terms and in the 'Oyez! Oyez!' used by town criers.

Anglo-Saxon Chronicle, The A history of events in England from the arrival of Christianity up to the middle of the twelfth century. It was written, over a period of some two hundred years, by monks working in a number of centres, of which the most important were Canterbury, Winchester and Peterborough. Seven manuscripts exist, each differing to some extent in its contents. The *Chronicle* is especially noted for its accounts of the Saxon invasion of Britain led by Hengist and Horsa, the wars of Cynewulf, king of Wessex, against the Welsh, and the long struggles of Alfred the Great to repel the Danes. It is believed that the compilation of various existing records and the continuation of the history were initiated by King Alfred, and he may also have worked on the sections relating to his own campaigns. Intended as an on-going history, it was continued until 1154 and the death of King Stephen, and includes an account of that monarch's unhappy reign. Written in Old and Middle English, the *Chronicle* is of great importance, not only as an historical record, but as the first history of a Western European country in its own language. Surprisingly, perhaps, it contains, in the parts covering the tenth and eleventh centuries, a number of poems, the most famous of which is the account of the Battle of Brunanburh, which took place in 937.

A page from the Anglo-Saxon Chronicle which depicts the Anglo-Saxon kings and records their deeds. The record shown tells of Athelstan's victory at Brunanburh in 937.

Anglo-Saxon literature The writings in Anglo-Saxon or Old English which were produced in England from the time of the Saxon invasions of the fifth century up to the early part of the twelfth century are referred to as Anglo-Saxon literature. (The terms Anglo-Saxon and Old English, though originally drawing a geographical and political distinction, have become virtually interchangeable.) Until the time of Alfred the Great, who lived from 848 to 900, Latin was still the language used by most authors, whether writing prose or poetry. But in the later years of his reign, Alfred gathered scholars at his court, and fostered the use of the vernacular as vigorously as he could, himself undertaking a number of translations and initiating work on the *Anglo-Saxon Chronicle*. A rich literature resulted. However, Anglo-Saxon writings existed long before Alfred the Great, even if not so plentifully, and the most important single literary work of this whole age which is still extant is *Beowulf*, a long narrative poem in heroic style. Scholars differ as to the date when it was written; the earliest copy is a tenth-century manuscript, but it may well have been first composed some four hundred years earlier. Various other fragments of verse also survive, usually narrative rather than lyric in content. Under strong Germanic influence, Anglo-Saxon poetry was mostly written in four-footed trochaic lines, with much use of alliteration, the device which at that time was seen as an essential element of verse. Since those persons who were able to read and write were principally priests and monks, most literary work of the period was religious in character, and prominent among the writers of prose are Aelfric, Abbot of Eynsham, and Archbishop Wulfstan of York, both of whom used this early form of English for their collections of homilies. The influence of Latin and the Celtic speech of the Ancient Britons was already bringing flexibility to the language, and some of those qualities were present which would later flower into greatness when much of the vocabulary of Norman French had been absorbed and adapted. In the meantime, Anglo-Saxon writings, whether in poetry or prose, were distinguished in their stylistic richness and vigour.

Animal Farm An allegorical novel by George Orwell, first published in 1945. The satire is directed against Communist Russia, showing the corrupting influence of power when the pig Napoleon (representing Stalin) imposes his tyranny on the other farm animals.

Anna Christie A drama by Eugene O'Neill, in which a prostitute attempts to escape from degradation. It was first produced in 1921.

Anna Karenina A novel by Leo Tolstoy, first published in parts between 1873 and 1876. Anna, wife of Karenin, falls desperately in love with Count Wronsky, and is ultimately driven to suicide.

Annales Cambriae A manuscript written in Latin during the second half of the tenth century, the *Annales Cambriae* is the oldest record of the early history of Wales still in existence. It is of particular interest in that it contains the first known reference to King Arthur, the sixth-century soldier who was later to be elevated to the status of a legendary hero, the central figure in a mythology embroidered in the poems of Chrétien de Troyes and later appearing in many guises in the works of Malory, Tennyson, T.H. White and others.

Annus Mirabilis A poem by John Dryden commemorating 1666, the year of the British war against the Dutch and of the Great Fire of London. It was first published in 1667.

Anouilh, Jean (1910–) Born in Bordeaux, the prolific dramatist Jean Anouilh was highly successful in France before 1939, but it was largely after the Second World War that he wrote his best plays and became widely known to English-speaking audiences. His work, which includes such successful pieces of Gallic charm as *Ring Round the Moon* and *The Waltz of the Toreadors* and the

Jean Anouilh, with Marie Dubois, at the gala performance of Vadim's film *La Ronde* based on one of his books.

historical dramas *Poor Bitos*, *The Lark* and *Becket*, has been enjoyed in English translation for some forty years.

Anstey, F. (1856–1934) F. Anstey was the pseudonym used by Thomas Anstey Guthrie. He wrote many novels, mostly humorous in vein, and contributed regularly to *Punch*. He is now remembered solely for *Vice Versa*, the novel in which pompous Mr Bultitude has to change places with his schoolboy son. This early book was so successful that its author was able to abandon his legal career and devote himself to writing.

Antigone A tragedy by Sophocles. Antigone, the daughter of Oedipus and Jocasta, is condemned by King Creon to be buried alive for daring, against his orders, to bury the body of her brother Polynices.

Antiquary, The A novel by Sir Walter Scott, first published in 1816. Scott himself preferred this book to all his others.

Antony and Cleopatra A tragedy by William Shakespeare, telling of the passion between the Roman general, Marc Antony, and Cleopatra, Queen of Egypt. It was first produced about 1607 and published in 1623.

aphorism Originally referring to a statement of scientific principles, the term has come to mean a short and often witty saying or adage, which compresses a great deal of meaning into a few words. Many of Oscar Wilde's most celebrated lines can be described as aphorisms. For example, 'All women become like their mothers. That is their tragedy. No man does. That's his.'

Apocrypha, The The term given to those books of the Old Testament which, although included in the Septuagint (the Greek translation dating from the third century BC) and the Vulgate (St Jerome's Latin translation, completed in 404), were excluded from editions of the Bible produced by the Protestants at the time of the Reformation. They were not written in Hebrew and were therefore not accepted as genuine by the Jews. The books are: Esdras 1 and 2, Tobit, Judith, additional parts of Esther, The Wisdom of Solomon, Ecclesiasticus, Baruch, the Song of the Three Holy Children, the History of Susannah, Bel and the Dragon, the Prayer of Manasses, and Maccabees 1 and 2.

Apologie for Poetrie, An An essay by Sir Philip Sidney, often known as *The Defence of Poesie*, first published in 1595.

Apuleius (Second century BC) The Roman philosopher and writer Lucius Apuleius was born in North Africa, the son of a well-to-do government official. He became a lawyer, and travelled widely before returning to Tripoli. He wrote a number of books and tracts, but his most famous work is his *Metamorphoses*, more often called *The Golden Ass*. It consists of a collection of stories, often ribald, relating the adventures of the young hero, who has been changed into an ass. Some of the tales were later used by Boccaccio and others.

Aquinas, St Thomas (*c.*1225–74) The son of the Count of Aquino, Thomas Aquinas was born near Naples, Italy. He became a Dominican monk, and was celebrated as a lecturer and a statesman for the Church. Considered the prince of scholastic theologians, he produced many religious works, including his masterpiece, the *Summa Theogica*, a huge work which, although it was unfinished at his death, sets forth much of the doctrine which is still largely accepted by the Roman Catholic Church today.

Arabian Nights Entertainments, or The Thousand and One Nights An ancient collection of stories which came originally from Arabia, Persia and India. Several earlier renditions into English had appeared by the nineteenth century, but Sir Richard Burton's unexpurgated version, appearing between 1885 and 1888, became the standard translation.

Aragon, Louis (1897–1982) A French poet who also wrote a number of novels, Louis Aragon published his first volume of poetry, *Feu de Joie*, in 1920. His work was successful in France, and was translated into English. He belonged originally to the Surrealist school, but later abandoned that movement. During the Second World War he rose to fame as the best and most widely read of the French Resistance poets, four collections of his work being published between 1941 and 1945.

Arbuthnot, John (1667–1735) Born in Kincardineshire, Scotland, the son of a minister, John Arbuthnot began his career as a mathematician, but later became a doctor and was eventually appointed physician to Queen Anne. He wrote several mathematical and medical treatises and many pamphlets. A collection of some of the latter, under the title *History of John Bull*, appeared in 1712. At about that time he became a friend of Jonathan Swift and Alexander Pope, and with them joined the Scriblerus Club. He was the principal author of the satirical work produced by members of the club, *The Memoirs of the Extraordinary Life, Works, and Discoveries of Martinus Scriblerus*, which was published in 1741, after Arbuthnot's death.

Arcadia, The A prose romance by Sir Philip Sidney, *The Arcadia* also includes poems at the end of its sections. It was first published posthumously in the year 1590.

Archer, Jeffrey (1940–) English businessman and politician, Jeffrey Howard Archer was educated at Wellington School and Brasenose College, Oxford. He turned to writing as a means of escaping from bankruptcy, and was immediately inordinately successful with his first novel, *Not a Penny More, Not a Penny Less*, published in 1975. His books, which include *First Among Equals* and *A Matter of Honour*, first published in 1984 and 1985 respectively, have found an enormous public, though literary critics generally view them with contempt.

Arden, John (1930–) Born in Barnsley, Yorkshire, John Arden is a crusading playwright, whose works have all contained a strong social message. *Serjeant Musgrave's Dance*, which is concerned with the corrupting effect of violence and was first produced in 1959, and *The Workhouse Donkey*, which deals with local politics and was seen in 1963, are his best-known dramas. His first novel was published in 1982.

Areopagitica Subtitled *A Speech of Mr John Milton for the liberty of unlicenc'd printing, to the Parlament of England*, this discourse was first published in

1644. Inspired by the fact that an attempt had been made to suppress his recent writings in favour of divorce, Milton produced an impassioned argument against all censorship and in particular against the ordinances which decreed that no book could be printed without a licence. 'As good almost kill a man,' he wrote, 'as kill a good book: who kills a man kills a reasonable creature, God's image; but he who destroys a good book, kills reason itself, kills the image of God, as it were in the eye.' The speech was ultimately successful in its object of regaining freedom of speech.

Aretino, Pietro (1492–1556) Arezzo in Tuscany was the birthplace of Pietro Aretino, and he took his surname from that town. He was illegitimate, and began his life in poverty, but his talent and his native wit later brought him to the favour of the Pope, the King of France, and various princes and noblemen. He wrote a tragedy and five comedies, and numerous poems and other short works. The outrageous and often bawdy nature of his work was both a passport to fame and the cause of much offence. Aretino appears to have been well-known to many English writers of the sixteenth and seventeenth centuries, many of whom borrowed from his works.

Aristophanes (c.448–380BC) The fourth of the great Athenian dramatists, Aristophanes was born during the last years of Aeschylus' life, and was a younger contemporary of Sophocles and Euripides. However, whereas the first three were tragedians, Aristophanes was a comic poet. The comedies of that period were generally satirical in content and their authors and audiences saw them as a vehicle through which criticism of public matters could be expressed. Aristophanes was considered an innovator since the satire in his plays was aimed directly and unsparingly at major personages of the time, rather than at types. This very specific content did not, however, result in plays of purely local interest, and the importance of Aristophanes in literature does not rest solely on his innovations or, indeed, on his antiquity. The contemporary references in his plays can sometimes make them difficult to understand, but the general quality of his poetry, especially in the lyrical passages, is of the highest order. He produced his first comedy, *The Banqueters*, in 427BC. He is believed to have written more than forty plays in all, but unfortunately only eleven of these have survived. In order of writing, they are: *The Archarnians, The Knights, The Clouds, The Wasps, The Peace, The Birds, The Lysistrata, The Thesmophoriazusae, The Frogs, The Ecclesiazusae* and *The Plutus*. These eleven plays received their first performances over a period of thirty-eight years, from 425 to 388BC. Aristophanes had three sons, Philippus, Araros and Nicostratus, all of whom themselves became comic poets.

Aristotle (384–322BC) The great Greek philosopher Aristotle was born at Stagira in Northern Greece, the son of a physician to the king of Macedonia. At the age of eighteen he went to Athens, and there studied under Plato for a period of twenty years. Later he became tutor to Alexander the Great, a position which he occupied for seven years. Returning to Athens in 335 at the age of fifty, he opened an open-air school in the Lyceum, just outside the city. It was familiarly known as 'the Peripatetics', apparently because of Aristotle's penchant for walking up and down as he delivered his lectures. His teachings there were to make him famous, not only in his own time, but for all centuries. The range of subjects covered at the school was extremely wide, including poetry, politics and zoology, as well as Aristotelian philosophy, which, based on the belief that all things have their separate individuality, was quite different from that of Plato. Aristotle wrote a very large number of treatises on all these matters, of which *Ethics*, *Politics* and *Poetics* are the most familiar. In translation, his writings and beliefs exercised enormous influence on the medieval world, and continued to be regarded with the highest esteem until the eighteenth century, when other views gained ascendancy.

A bust of the Greek philosopher Aristotle, who, in direct conflict with Plato, founded the science of logic.

Arlen, Michael (1895–1956) Michael Arlen was the pseudonym of Dikran Kuyumjian, who was born in Bulgaria but educated in Britain. His best-seller, *The Green Hat*, which reflected sophisticated society in the 1920s, was published in 1924.

Arms and the Man A comedy by G. Bernard Shaw, first performed in 1894 and published in 1898. It was adapted into the musical, *The Chocolate Soldier*.

Arnold, Matthew (1822–88) Matthew Arnold was the son of Dr Thomas Arnold, the headmaster of Rugby School so warmly depicted by Thomas Hughes in *Tom Brown's Schooldays*. He was born at Laleham, near Staines, England, and was educated at Winchester, Rugby and Balliol College, Oxford. His vocation as a writer was manifest at an early age, and his first published work was the poem 'Alaric at Rome', written while he was at Rugby, where it won him a prize. In 1843, while at Balliol, he won the Newdigate Prize with his poem 'Cromwell'. His first complete book of poetry, *The Strayed Reveller, and other poems*, did not appear until 1849, but a further collection, *Empedocles on Etna, and other poems*, came out in 1852, the authorship of both volumes being attributed to the single initial 'A'. In the following year his *Poems*, published for the first time under his full name, included both 'Sohrab and Rustum' and the much-loved 'The Scholar-Gypsy'. Meanwhile, in 1851, after working for Lord Lansdowne as his private secretary, followed by a very brief period spent as a teacher at Rugby, he had been appointed an Inspector of Schools, and his employment in this capacity was to continue until 1886. In addition to travelling in the course of his duties to all parts of England, he was sent by the government three times, in 1859, 1865 and 1886, to study the educational methods used in France, Germany, Holland and other European countries, and his reports brought about lasting effects, especially in the improvement of English secondary education. The reports themselves were published under such titles as *The Popular Education of France, with Notices of that of Holland and Switzerland*. Although busily employed in the field of education, he was able to accept the position of Professor of Poetry at Oxford when it was offered to him in 1857, and, despite his other commitments, he held this chair for ten years. He continued to write poetry, publishing his classical tragedy, *Merope*, in 1858, and bringing out *New Poems*, which included the elegy 'Thyrsis', in 1867. But from 1860 onwards Arnold devoted himself more often to prose, publishing several volumes of his lectures and of essays on literary, religious and general subjects, including *Essays in Criticism, On the Study of Celtic Literature*,

A portrait of the poet and essayist Matthew Arnold by George Watts, dated 1880.

Culture and Anarchy: an Essay in Political and Social Criticism, Friendship's Garland: being the Conversations, Letters and Opinions of the late Arminius Baron von Thunder-ten-Tronckh, Literature and Dogma: an Essay towards a Better Apprehension of the Bible, and, of course, many writings on educational matters. In 1883 he went on a lecture tour of the United States, which resulted in the publication of *Discourses in America*. Long before then he had become the most highly respected and influential critic of his time, and his attacks on the materialistic society in which he lived, and on its Philistinism and parochialism, were not without effect on his contemporaries or on later writers. Matthew Arnold has been considered by some critics to be more felicitous in his prose than in his poetry; certainly, the essays are exemplary in their style, structured with exact craftsmanship, and illumined by their urbane wit. But, even though he may not have been in the first rank of poets, to denigrate his work in that field is to ignore in it the same grace and polish that he brought to his prose.

Asch, Sholem (1880–1957) Of Polish birth, Sholem Asch emigrated to the United States in 1914 and lived there for the rest of his life. He continued to write, however, in Yiddish and German. He produced a large number of novels and some plays. Among his best-known novels are *Uncle Moses, Chaim Lederer's Return* and *Judge Not*, which were reissued together in 1938. Later work included *East River*, published in 1946, and a group of biblical novels such as *The Nazarene* and *The Prophet*, published in 1939 and 1955 respectively.

Ascham, Roger (1515-68) A brilliant classical scholar, Roger Ascham was born in Yorkshire, England, and educated privately in the house of Sir Humphry Wingfield, Speaker of the House of Commons, and later at Cambridge. Sir Humphry introduced the boy to archery and fostered his interest in the sport, and in 1545 Ascham published *Toxophilus: The Schole of Shootinge Conteyned in Two Books*, a treatise on archery in dialogue form. Dedicated to Henry VIII, it earned a royal pension for its author, and it may well have been the popularity of this book which brought him his appointment as tutor to the Princess Elizabeth, with whom he conversed in Latin and in Greek, both of which he spoke and wrote fluently. After travelling in Europe, he became Latin Secretary to the Roman Catholic queen, Mary I, despite the fact that he was a Protestant, and when Elizabeth succeeded to the throne he continued in this position. He ended his life in poverty, but it is not certain whether this was because of his love of gambling and cock-fighting or because he had to provide for a large family. *The Scholemaster: Or Plaine and Perfite Way of Teachyng Children the Latin Tong*, his major work, in which he argues for a humane approach to the education of young people, was published in 1570, after his death. Ascham's simplicity of style had a considerable effect on many other writers in English.

Ashbery, John (1927–) Born in Rochester, New York, and educated at Harvard, Columbia and New York universities, John Lawrence Ashbery has worked in publishing and as an art critic. He published his first volume of poetry, *Turandot and other poems*, in 1953, and has followed this with over a dozen more collections, including *A Wave*, which appeared in 1984, and *Selected Poems*, published in 1986. He has also published three plays and a novel, *A Nest of Ninnies*, written in collaboration with James Schuyler.

Ashford, Daisy (1881–1972) At the age of nine, Daisy Ashford wrote *The Young Visiters*, a short and hilarious novel which has enjoyed immense popularity since its first publication in 1919. It has been rumoured that J.M. Barrie, who wrote a Preface for that first edition, was in fact the author, but it is doubtful whether anyone but a nine-year-old could have produced so unself-conscious a parody of adult behaviour. Many other books by young children have appeared, usually depending for their charm on the naive view of the world presented by their authors — *O Ye Jigs and Juleps* by Virginia Cary Hudson is a splendid American example — but none has matched *The Young Visiters* in humour or construction or in its enduring ability to delight.

A photograph of the ingenious writer Isaac Asimov, the 'father' of science fiction.

Asimov, Isaac (1920–) Isaac Asimov was born near Smolensk, Russia, and came to the United States with his parents at the age of three. A biochemist, he is also one of the world's foremost science fiction writers, and has won the Hugo Award four times. His best known books include *I, Robot*, published in 1950, *Fantastic Voyage*, which appeared in 1966, and the many books in the 'Foundation' series, which began with a trilogy, published between 1951 and 1953, and has continued regularly since. Asimov has also edited numerous collections of science fiction stories, and has written non-fiction books on scientific subjects.

Aspern Papers, The A story by Henry James, first published in *The Atlantic Monthly* in 1888, and later used as the title story for a collection.

Astrophel and Stella A sequence of 108 sonnets, interspersed with 11 songs, by Sir Philip Sidney, first published in 1591.

As You Like It A comedy by William Shakespeare, set in the Forest of Arden, where an exiled Duke holds court, and his daughter, Rosalind, is wooed and won by Orlando. It was first produced about 1599 and published in 1623.

Atalanta in Calydon A verse drama by Algernon Swinburne, which established its author's reputation when it was first published in 1865.

Atlantic Monthly, The An American magazine devoted to literature, the arts and politics, founded in 1857 by James Russell Lowell, its first editor, and Oliver Wendell Holmes. Originally very much a New England magazine, its interest and appeal broadened over the years, and it became and remains a leading national periodical.

Atom, The History and Adventures of an A satire on British politics and politicians, first published in 1769 and attributed to Tobias Smollett, though some doubts remain as to whether he did in fact write it. If he did not, then the author remains unknown.

Attic Pertaining to Attica, a district of Greece, of which the capital is Athens. The word 'Attic' is often considered as interchangeable with 'Athenian'. The Attic form of Greek, as used by early Athenian orators and writers, was noted for its elegance and lucidity. The phrase, 'Attic salt', still used occasionally today, means wit of a dry, refined and well-turned character.

Atwood, Margaret (1939–) The well-known Canadian poet and novelist Margaret Atwood was born in Ottawa. She published the first of several volumes of poetry, *The Circle Game*, in 1960, and has also written literary criticism. Her first, award-winning novel was *The Edible Woman*, published in 1969. Since then her fiction has appeared regularly and includes *Surfacing*, in 1972, *Lady Oracle*, in 1976, *Life Before Man*, in 1979, *Bodily Harm*, in 1982, and *The Handmaid's Tale*, in 1985.

Aubrey, John (1626–97) Born near Malmesbury, England, John Aubrey was educated at Malmesbury and at Trinity College, Oxford. For a time he studied law, but abandoned it, and eventually became a noted antiquary. His *Miscellanies*, a collection of stories about dreams and ghosts, was published in 1696, but his other writings, including some topographical works, did not appear until after his death. The *Brief Lives*, for which he is famous, a splendid gallimaufry of portraits, anecdotes, opinions and odd thoughts, was first seen in print as late as 1813, and it was not until the mid-twentieth century that an unexpurgated edition was readily available.

Auchincloss, Louis (1917–) Louis Stanton Auchincloss began by writing under the pseudonym Andrew Lee. He made his reputation with fiction which examined a sophisticated section of American society, presenting it with the detached precision that he might well use in his profession as a lawyer. His novels include *The Indifferent Children*, published in 1947, and *The Great World and Timothy Colt*, which appeared in 1956, while among more recent works are *The Book Class* and the historical novel, *Exit Lady Masham*, both published in 1984. Some reviewers believe *Diary of a Yuppie*, which came out in 1986, to be his finest work.

Auden, W.H. (1907–73) Born in York, England, the youngest son of a doctor, Wystan Hugh Auden was educated at Gresham's School in Norfolk and at Christ Church, Oxford. He came to notice as a poet while still at Oxford, where he became friendly with Louis MacNeice, Stephen Spender, Cecil Day-Lewis and Christopher Isherwood, all of whom at that time adhered strongly to radically left-wing views. T.S. Eliot was enthusiastic about Auden's work and published his *Poems* in 1930. This was in fact his first published collection, although some of the verses contained in it had been produced in a privately printed edition two years earlier. *Poems* was well received, and, when it was followed in 1932 by *The Orators*, it was clear that a major poet had arrived, the outstanding talent of the period. His third selection, *Look Stranger!*, appeared in 1936. Prior to that, having spent some time in travelling and a short period as a teacher, Auden had become involved in the theatre, and his play, *The Dance of Death*, was produced in 1933. With his close friend Isherwood, he wrote three other plays, *The Dog Beneath the Skin*, which appeared in 1935, *The Ascent of F6* in the following year, and *On the Frontier* in 1938. Further collaboration produced two travel books, the first being *Letters from Iceland*, written with MacNeice after a journey to that country in 1936, and the second, *Journey to a War*, with Isherwood, following their visit to China in 1938. In 1937 he had gone to Spain to support the Republicans, and his poem 'Spain' was published in that year. In 1935 he married Erika Mann, but it was purely a marriage of convenience, designed to allow her to escape persecution and probable death at the hands of the Nazis, and it was with Isherwood that he left England in 1939 for the United States, a move which was not well-regarded in wartime Britain. Auden became a US citizen seven years later. Before his death he produced many more volumes of poetry, in which he abandoned the overtly political tone of his earlier work, while

Pen and ink sketch of W.H. Auden by Don Bachardy, dated 1967. A gifted poet and playwright he became Professor of Poetry at Oxford in 1962.

the influence of Christianity gradually became more marked. Among his collections, *Another Time* was published in 1940, *The Double Man* (English title: *New Year Letter*) in 1941, *For the Time Being: A Christmas Oratorio* in 1944, *The Age of Anxiety: A Baroque Eclogue*, which won the Pulitzer Prize, in 1948, *Nones* in 1951, *The Shield of Achilles* in 1955, and *Homage to Clio* in 1960. In addition to his poetry, Auden edited several anthologies, published some volumes of criticism, and provided the librettos for a number of operas, including Benjamin Britten's *Paul Bunyan* and Igor Stravinsky's *The Rake's Progress*. He had been forgiven by the British for his wartime 'desertion' and indeed was regarded with the greatest respect and affection, as was evidenced by his appointment in 1962 as Professor of Poetry at Oxford. Sharing his life with his friend Chester Kallman, he spent many of his last years in Oxford, visiting Austria regularly during the summer. His death in Vienna was sudden and unexpected. Gifted with a superb sense of form and structure, W.H. Auden was able to handle themes of great complexity with the utmost ease, and an unfailing ear allowed him to blend contemporary speech into his poetry in a most effective and often beautiful way. He undoubtedly ranks among the major literary figures of the twentieth century, and his influence on later generations of poets has been immense.

A beautifully colourful and flamboyant engraving of Blue Jays produced by Audubon for his book *The Birds of America* in 1831.

Audubon was one of the most successful illustrators of ornithological texts of the nineteenth century. Despite the criticism that he shows no great appreciation of the anatomy of the living bird, he captures the spirit and beauty of the creatures. His paintings are still in great demand and fetch enormous prices. Reproductions of his work are popular world-wide.

Audubon, John James (1785–1851) The celebrated American artist-ornithologist was born of a French father and a Spanish Creole mother. Educated in Paris, he returned to the United States in 1798, living there until 1826, when he went to England, seeking a publisher for his work. *The Birds of North America*, reproducing over a thousand superb life-size paintings of birds in 435 colour plates, was first published in England between 1827 and 1838. Written in collaboration, the accompanying text, *American Ornithological Biography*, was published in five volumes between 1831 and 1839. With the naturalist John Bachman, Audubon also produced *Viviparous Quadrupeds of North America*, which appeared between 1842 and 1854.

Auerbach, Erich (1892–1957) Born in Berlin, Erich Auerbach was an academic who taught in Marburg, Germany, until 1935, when he escaped the Nazi regime and found refuge at the State University of Turkey. In 1947 he went to the United States, and became Professor of French and Romance philology at Yale. His many books on literature include *Mimesis: The Representation of Reality in Western Literature*, first published in English in 1953.

Augustan Age Strictly speaking, the term 'Augustan Age' pertains to the reign of the Roman Emperor Augustus from 27BC to AD14, while in a literary sense it was originally used with specific reference to the fact that the great Roman authors, Virgil, Horace and Ovid, were all writing during that period. However, it has also been applied, in the history of literature, to the first half of the eighteenth century. The principal English authors of that time, including Pope, Swift, Addison and Steele, believed themselves to be following in the footsteps of the Roman poets and claimed to represent a new Augustan Age.

Augustine, St (354–430) Born in Tagaste, North Africa, Augustine grew up as a pagan, but was converted to Christianity by Ambrose, Bishop of Milan, in the year 386. After some years spent in meditation, he became presbyter to a Christian community at Hippo, and in 396 was appointed Bishop. He wrote a number of religious treatises which had great influence in defining various aspects of Christianity, and he is considered to be one of the great fathers of the Roman Church. His best known works are the *Confessions*, an account of his life written shortly after he became a bishop, and *The City of God*, his major vindication of Christianity and the Christian Church, which was produced over a fourteen year period beginning in 413.

Aureng-Zebe A verse tragedy by John Dryden, first presented in 1675, and published the following year.

Aurora Leigh Described by its author, Elizabeth Barrett Browning, as 'a novel in verse', *Aurora Leigh* was first published in 1857.

Austen, Jane (1775–1817) The Reverend George Austen was Rector of Steventon, a village in Hampshire, England, and it was there that his youngest child, Jane, was born. She had five brothers and a sister, Cassandra (named after her mother, who had been a Miss Cassandra Leigh), of whom she was especially fond. Jane was from childhood a voracious reader, and herself began to write at an early age. *Love and Friendship*, *A History of England*, *Lesley Castle* and *Lady Susan* were all produced while she was still in her teens. *Sense and Sensibility*, originally drafted as *Elinor and Marianne*, was rewritten in 1797 and 1798 under the now familiar title, but another thirteen years were to pass before a publisher could be induced to bring it out, and it did not appear until 1811 – published anonymously, as were all Jane Austen's books during her lifetime. It was reasonably successful, and was followed by *Pride and Prejudice* (also a revision, having originally been called *First Impressions*) in 1813. This was to prove her most popular novel (though many critics believe *Mansfield Park* and especially *Emma* to be much finer works), partly, perhaps, because of the comparative simplicity of the plot, which has also allowed the book to be easily adapted for the stage, the screen and television. *Mansfield Park* came out in 1814, and *Emma* in 1816. Both *Northanger Abbey*, which had been written much earlier, and *Persuasion* appeared posthumously in 1818. At the time of her death, Jane Austen was engaged on a novel called *Sanditon*. An

A pencil and watercolour portrait of Jane Austen by her sister Cassandra.

earlier book, *The Watsons*, which she appears to have worked on during the period between 1798 and 1809 when despairing of publication of her work, was also left uncompleted. She did not marry, but lived happily with her family in Steventon and later in Bath, and, after her

A sketch of Steventon Rectory, Hampshire, where Jane Austen was born and lived for the first 25 years of her life.

father's death, in Southampton. In 1809, the Austens moved to Chawton, where Jane joined in the social life of the area, and occasionally visited Bath. She embroidered, she copied out music, she wrote letters, she helped with domestic duties, and above all, with that very acute eye, she observed her family, her friends and acquaintances, and any members of polite society that she happened to meet. Seated at a small table in the parlour of the house at Chawton, writing on postcard-sized paper and concealing her work whenever any strangers entered the room, she composed the last three of the published novels, *Mansfield Park*, *Emma* and *Persuasion*. She died at Winchester, after some months of declining health. All Jane Austen's books were quite well-received on publication, and Coleridge and Scott were among her fervent admirers. She has never, however, been without her critics, among them Charlotte Brontë, whose contempt for her work is perhaps not surprising when the dark, brooding passion of the Brontë novels is compared to the detached and amused attitude which Jane Austen brought to her writing. Moreover, her depiction of her characters and the society in which they moved was, as she herself described it, like painting with a fine brush on a 'little bit (two inches wide) of ivory'; the Brontës, on the other hand, worked with bolder strokes and on a much larger canvas. Jane Austen has also been criticised for the cruelty with which some of the more foolish personages in her novels are portrayed. There was undeniably much acid in her pen, but with it she created some of the most memorable comic characters in English literature, and, indeed, it is for her delicious ironic wit that she is so much admired, as well as for the brilliance of her portrait of contemporary middle-class life. Although the stories she told may appear superficially to be simple, an analysis of the construction of any of the major novels will clearly reveal the ingenuity with which they are plotted. While Jane Austen may not rank among the truly great, she remains one of the brightest jewels in English literature.

Austin, Alfred (1835–1913) Like so many authors, Alfred Austin, who was born at Headingley, England, practised as a barrister for a short while before turning to writing as a career. He wrote prolifically, producing criticism, journalism, dramas, and prose idylls, but his reputation was that of a poet, though it has long been considered that his work was shorter on quality than on quantity. Following the death of Tennyson in 1892, the position of Poet Laureate was left vacant, since no suitable candidate was available. When Alfred Austin was eventually given the title in 1896, the appointment caused much derision in literary circles.

Autocrat of the Breakfast-Table, The Essays and poems by Oliver Wendell Holmes, first published in *The Atlantic Monthly* between 1857 and 1858.

Awkward Age, The A novel of London society by Henry James, first published in book form in 1899.

Ayala's Angel A novel by Anthony Trollope, first published in 1881.

Ayckbourn, Alan (1939–) Born in London, Alan Ayckbourn is currently Britain's most prolific and successful playwright. His comedies, while hilarious, always have an undertone of sharp comment on the fragility of human relationships. His first major success came in 1967, with *Relatively Speaking*. Other plays, many of which exhibit great skill in the ingenuity of their settings and the tricks which the playwright plays with time, include *How the Other Half Loves*, first seen in 1970, the triple bill *The Norman Conquests*, in 1974, and *Woman in Mind*, in 1986.

Aytoun, Sir Robert (1570–1638) A Scottish poet, writing in both Latin and English, Robert Aytoun became a favourite at court, was knighted in 1612, and was appointed private secretary to the queens of both James I and Charles I. Several of his songs and sonnets in English are still regularly included in anthologies.

Aytoun, William (1813–65) A descendant of Sir Robert Aytoun, William Edmondstoune Aytoun was educated at Edinburgh University, where he eventually became Professor of Rhetoric and Belles-Lettres. He wrote many popular ballads, including *Lays of the Scottish Cavaliers*, and a number of humorous works, the latter including his parody, *Firmilian, or The Student of Badajoz: A Spasmodic Tragedy*, which appeared in 1854.

William Aytoun.

B

Babbit A classic American novel by Sinclair Lewis, set in a small mid-Western town, the values of which are questioned by the central character, George Babbitt. It was first published in 1922.

Babel Isaak (1894–c.1941) The son of a Jewish shopkeeper, Isaak Emmanuilovich Babel was born in Odessa. His early experiences as a soldier resulted in a major collection of stories, *Red Cavalry*, published in the early 1920s. He wrote many more stories, but his work was not acceptable in Russia, and he was arrested in 1939 and died in prison not long thereafter, although the mode and the exact date of his death are not known.

Back to Methuselah A play by G. Bernard Shaw, first produced in 1921 and published the following year.

Bacon, Francis (1561–1626) Francis Bacon was the son of Sir Nicholas Bacon, Lord Keeper of the Seal to Queen Elizabeth. He was educated at Trinity College, Cambridge, where he formulated the philosophy which he was later to set down in many writings. He became a barrister, and subsequently a Member of Parliament. Under James I, his career progressed meteorically. He became Attorney-General and a Privy Councillor, and in 1618 was appointed Lord Chancellor. Soon after, he was created Baron Verulam, and three years later he became Viscount St Albans. At this point, he had achieved almost all he wanted: his wisdom and prudence, added to his unfailing ability to secure the friendship of anyone of high rank with the power to advance his career, had brought him to a position of almost unrivalled power as the King's confidant and chief minister, and he had been suitably ennobled. Moreover, he had just published his most important work, *Novum Organum*, setting forth many of his philosophical beliefs. A few months later his world collapsed when he was accused of bribery and corruption. There was enough truth in the charges to make a total defence impossible, and he pleaded guilty. He was sentenced to imprisonment and a crippling fine, but was permitted to escape these punishments, and eventually granted a pardon. Forced to retire from public affairs, for the last five years of his life he devoted himself to writing. He had already published a number of books, including two of his most famous works, the *Essays* and *The Advancement of Learning*, which first appeared in 1597 and 1605 respectively, while *De Sapienta Veterum* was published in 1609 and later translated as *The Wisedome of the Ancients*. *Novum*

Organum, the first of his two major philosophical works, had appeared in 1620; now came the second, in the form of a greatly expanded version, this time in Latin, of *The Advancement of Learning*, published in 1623 as *De Augmentis Scientarium*. He intended to complement these books with others in which his whole theory of philosophy would be expounded, but he did not live to complete the project. He did, however, bring out *The Historie of the Raigne of King Henry*

An engraving by Simon van de Passe for the frontispiece of Bacon's philosophical work *Instauratio Magna*. Bacon, a successful statesman as well as philosopher, was an early advocate of the scientific method.

the Seventh in 1622, a new edition of the *Essays*, expanded to almost six times its original length, in 1625, and *The New Atlantis* in 1626. He died in London of a chill. In one of his Essays Bacon wrote, 'Nothing doth more hurt in a state than that cunning pass for wise.' He seems not to have been a very likeable man, and was probably far from devoid of cunning, but his literary work remains admirable. His philosophy was extremely influential, and his general writings show both wisdom and wit, while the richness and clarity of his style have been acclaimed for more than three and a half centuries.

Baconian Theory, The Since Shakespeare was apparently neither well born nor well educated, some scholars through the ages have poured doubt on his ability to have written such towering masterpieces as his plays. Among a number of possible candidates as their true author, Francis Bacon has been regarded as the most likely, but the evidence for this theory, often derived from supposedly cryptic references buried within the language of the plays, remains scanty. The theory, despite the eminence of some of its supporters, is widely regarded with scepticism.

An oil painting by John Vanderbank of the philosopher and writer Sir Francis Bacon, who was appointed Lord Chancellor in 1618 and later became Baron Verulam and Viscount St Alban. The King's confidant and chief minister, he was extremely influential in Stuart Society.

Badman, The Life and Death of Mr An allegory in dialogue form by John Bunyan, first published in 1680.

Baedeker, Karl (1801–59) The son of a printer and bookseller, Karl Baedeker, who was born in Essen, Germany, became the editor and publisher of the celebrated guide books. They were indispensable to all travellers in the nineteenth and early twentieth centuries, especially because of their time-saving system of indicating the comparative importance of the various tourist attractions by the number of asterisks allocated to them.

Bagehot, Walter (1826–77) The English journalist Walter Bagehot was born in Langport, Somerset. He published some volumes of literary criticism and books on political subjects. His most successful works were *The English Constitution*, published in 1867, and his study of the London money markets, *Lombard Street*, which appeared in 1873.

Bagnold, Enid (1889–1981) Born in the West Indies, Enid Algerine Bagnold wrote a number of novels, including the bestseller, *National Velvet*, first published in 1935, and later to become an extremely popular film. She was also a playwright, and *The Chalk Garden*, produced in 1955, is revived from time to time. She published her *Autobiography* in 1969.

Bainbridge, Beryl (1934–) The work of the Liverpool-born novelist, Beryl Bainbridge, has received considerable critical acclaim and some popular success. Her novels include *The Dressmaker*, first published in 1973, *Injury Time* in 1977, and *Winter Garden* in 1980. A commission to examine for the BBC the divisions between the currently deprived North of England and the prosperous South resulted in her study of six families, *North and South*, published in 1986.

Baldwin, James (1924–) James Arthur Baldwin, the son of a preacher, was born in Harlem, New York, and is one of the most well-known and highly regarded Black novelists and playwrights. His first novel, *Go Tell It On the Mountain*, was published in 1953 to considerable acclaim, and has been followed by several others, including *Giovanni's Room*, which appeared in 1956, *Another Country*, in 1972, and *Just Above My Head*, in 1979. He has also written a number of short stories, collected in 1965 in *Going to Meet the Man*. His fiction, like all his work, is written from the standpoint of a Black homosexual, and contains a strong crusading element. Baldwin's plays include *The Amen Corner* and *Blues for Mr Charlie*, seen in 1955 and 1964 respectively. He is perhaps most respected as a powerful essayist, in which capacity he is one of the leading anti-

The author James Baldwin at London Airport on one of his many visits to England.

racist writers in the world. His first collection of essays, *Notes of a Native Son*, immediately established his reputation on its publication in 1955, a reputation which was enhanced by *Nobody Knows My Name*, *The Fire Next Time*, *The Devil Finds Work*, and other similar books. *The Price of the Ticket*, published in 1986, is a collection of his non-fiction from 1948 to 1985, and *Evidence of Things Not Seen* is a later polemic on racism issued in 1986.

Bale, John (1495–1563) Born in Suffolk, England, John Bale was educated at Cambridge, took holy orders, and eventually became Bishop of Ossory in Ireland. A colourful and versatile author, his vocation did not prevent him from writing in the coarsest of terms, especially in his virulent attacks on the Roman Catholics. His most important work was a catalogue of major British writers, the second edition of which, published between 1557 and 1559, covered fourteen centuries, but he also wrote many plays, mostly moralities, a typical title being *Thre Laws of Nature, Moses and Christ, corrupted by the Sodomytes, Pharisees and Papystes most wicked*. His drama *Kynge Johan*, again a vehicle for anti-Catholic sentiments, is regarded as the first historical play in English.

ballad Originally a song used as accompaniment to dancing, the term 'ballad' has come to mean a popular song, or, in its literary sense, a narrative poem, usually written in short stanzas. For many centuries, ballads were often political and of a highly tendentious character, but this form fell into disuse in the nineteenth century.

ballade A poem of one or more triplets of seven- or eight-lined stanzas, each ending with the same line. An envoy is usually added. Nowadays, the term is frequently loosely used for any poem written in stanzas of equal length.

Ballad of Reading Gaol, The A poem by Oscar Wilde, first published in 1898 under the nom-de-plume 'C.3.3.', Wilde's prison number.

Ballantyne, R.M. (1825–94) Robert Michael Ballantyne as born in Edinburgh. He went to Canada at the age of sixteen, and, soon after his return six years later, published his first book *Hudson's Bay: or, Life in the Wilds of Canada*. He worked for a while for a publisher, and then, in 1856, became a full-time author. He produced over a hundred adventure stories for boys, the most famous of which is *The Coral Island*, first published in 1857.

Balzac, Honoré de (1799–1850) Most critics acknowledge Honoré de Balzac as the greatest of French novelists, and there are some who claim him to be the most important novelist of all time and in any language. He was born in Tours, France. He left school at seventeen, and at his father's insistence began to train as a lawyer.

The famous French novelist Honoré de Balzac, who is best known for his detailed portrayal of French bourgeois society.

After qualifying, however, he refused to continue a legal career, and instead devoted himself to writing. He published his first two works of fiction at the age of twenty-two, nine more novels following in the next two years. In 1827 he started work on 'La comédie humaine', a vast work, intended to comprise well over one hundred and twenty volumes, in which Balzac set out to delineate a complete picture of French society over a hundred-year period, beginning in the mid-eighteenth century and linked by the appearance of many of the characters in more than one book. In the space of some twenty years, he wrote ninety-one novels and stories in the series, but did not complete the project, dying before he had written the additional forty-seven works he had planned. 'La comédie humaine' remains an outstandingly impressive achievement. Though the subject of this huge masterpiece may be confined to eighteenth- and nineteenth-century France, the penetration of Balzac's vision of humanity and the breadth of the canvas which he uses removes any sense of parochialism, making it a work of universal application and interest. The most famous of the novels included in 'La comédie humaine' are *La peau de chagrin* and *La cousine Bette*.

Bancroft, George (c.1800–91) The son of a clergyman, George Bancroft was born in Worcester, Massachusetts, and educated at Harvard and in Germany. He became a politician, rising to cabinet rank, and was later minister first in London and then in Berlin. He contributed to the *North American Review* and to the *American Quarterly*, and in 1834 published the first volume of his monumental *A History of the United States*. Occupying ten volumes in all, the last of which appeared in 1874, it was hugely successful, and was regarded as a standard work for a quarter of a century. He later added to it a *History of the Formation of the Constitution*, first published in 1882.

Barchester Towers A novel by Anthony Trollope, first published in 1857, the second in the 'Barsetshire' series.

Barham, R.H. (1788–1845) The Reverend Richard Harris Barham was born in Canterbury and educated at Brasenose College, Oxford. He contributed light verse and other humorous material to many periodicals, and also wrote a novel, but is celebrated as the author of *The Ingoldsby Legends: or Mirth and Marvels, by Thomas Ingoldsby, Esquire*, which first appeared in *Bentley's Miscellany* and *The New Monthly Magazine*. The verses were collected and published in book form in 1840 and a definitive edition, with a memoir by Barham's son, appeared in 1847.

Barlow Joel (1754–1812) Born in Redding, Connecticut, and educated at Yale, Joel Barlow was a clergyman, a diplomat and the editor of the *American Mercury*, but he is remembered primarily as a poet and as one of the Hartford Wits. His somewhat overblown poem, *The Vision of Columbus*, was published in 1787, bringing him popular esteem. An extended and even more absurd version, under the title *The Columbiad*, appeared in 1787. Barlow also produced some political writings, but probably his only work which is still read today is *Hasty Pudding*, first published in 1796, the amusing mock-heroic tribute to a favourite American dish.

Barnaby Rudge A novel by Charles Dickens, set at the time of the Gordon Riots of 1780, first published in 1841.

Barnfield, Richard (1574–1627) The English poet Richard Barnfield was born at Norbury, Staffordshire, and educated at Oxford. He published *The Affectionate Shepheard*, a romance, in 1594, and *Cynthia, with certaine Sonnets* in the following year. His third book was a long poem in praise of money, *The Encomion of Lady Pecunia*, issued in 1598. A collection of poetry entitled *The Passionate Pilgrim* appeared in 1599, with 'By W. Shakespeare' on the title-page, but it is doubtful that Shakespeare had any part in it. Several of the poems in it, however, have been attributed to Barnfield.

Barrack-Room Ballads Popular verses by Rudyard Kipling, first collected and published in book form in 1892.

Barrie, J.M. (1860-1937) After completing his education at Dumfries Academy and Edinburgh University, James Matthew Barrie began his career as a journalist, writing for a number of different periodicals. His first literary success came with the publication of a series of stories and novels set in 'Thrums' (a fictional name for Kirriemuir, the Scottish town in which he was born). These included *Auld Licht Idylls*, published in 1888, *A Window in Thrums*, which appeared the following year, and *The Little Minister*, which became a bestseller in 1891. He had already tried his hand at writing plays, and before long achieved considerable success in this field, especially with his dramatization of *The Little Minister*, produced in 1897, and the light comedies, *Quality Street* and *The Admirable Crichton*, first seen in 1901 and 1902 respectively. In 1904, *Peter Pan* had its first public production. Its enormous appeal overshadowed all Barrie's other work, and it is still regularly performed today, though recent versions have been updated and have made use of modern theatrical techniques.

Dear Brutus followed in 1917 and *Mary Rose* in 1920. Barrie was created a baronet in 1913, and received many other honours during his lifetime. Today, he is slipping into obscurity – except for *Peter Pan*. The Boy Who Would Not Grow Up appears to be immortal.

Barstow, Stan (1928–) The son of a coalminer, Stanley Barstow was educated at a local school and worked as a draughtsman before becoming a writer. He achieved his first major success in 1960 with his novel, *A Kind of Loving*, which, like most of his work, is set in his native Yorkshire. He has written extensively for the theatre and television, and has produced a dozen books, including *A Raging Calm*, which appeared in 1968, and *Just You Wait and See*, published in 1986.

Barth, John (1930–) The American novelist and short story writer John Simmons Barth was born in Cambridge, Maryland, and educated at John Hopkins University. His work has received much critical acclaim ever since the publication of his first novel, *The Floating Opera*, in 1956. His best-known novels are *The Sot-Weed Factor*, first published in 1962, *Giles Goat Boy: or The Revised New Syllabus*, which appeared in 1966, and *Chimera*, which gained the National Book Award in 1974.

Barthes, Roland (1915–80) The influential French critic Roland Barthes first came to prominence in 1953 with the publication of his *Le degré zero de l'écriture*. Other publications include *Mythologies*, in 1957, *Sur Racine*, in 1963, and *Sade, Fourier, Loyola*, in 1971. He was a leading member of the Structuralist movement.

Bartholomew Fayre A farcical comedy by Ben Jonson, presented in 1614 and first published in 1631.

Bates, H.E. (1905–74) Born in Northamptonshire, England, Herbert Ernest Bates was a prolific novelist and short story writer. He also produced some volumes of autobiography. He became very popular during the Second World War, writing as 'Flying Officer X'. Several collections of short stories were published, and among his longer works of fiction are his first novel, *The Two Sisters*, published in 1926, *Love for Lydia*, which appeared in 1952, and *The Darling Buds of May*, published in 1958.

Battle of the Books, The The full title of this satire by Jonathan Swift, first published in 1704, is *A Full and True Account of the Battel Fought Last Friday, Between the Antient and the Modern Books in St James's Library*. Written in prose, it is concerned, in vigorous and often knockabout style, with disputes raging at the time between the merits of classic and contemporary authors.

The French lyrical poet and critic Charles Baudelaire. His poetry originally outraged public morality but it is now regarded as being of the highest order.

Baudelaire, Charles (1821–67) The French writer Charles Pierre Baudelaire learned English as a child, and in his twenties read the works of Edgar Allan Poe, which had a profound influence on him. Born in Paris, he was the son of a civil servant, from whom he inherited sufficient money, despite his youthful extravagances, to allow him to spend many years in the slow translation of Poe's work into French, a task which he carried out with great skill. In 1857, he published his celebrated collection of lyrical poetry, *Les fleurs du mal*, and immediately achieved notoriety, for the poems outraged public morals of the time by treating subjects which were considered morbid and perverse. Baudelaire was prosecuted, and the offending poems were suppressed. A new edition, in which the banned pieces were replaced by much new material, appeared in 1861, and in 1866 he published in Belgium *Les epaves*, a collection of poems which included the six censored pieces. Baudelaire was also a critic of considerable ability and the essays that he wrote on art, literature and music are highly respected, but for many more years *Les fleurs du mal* retained an aura of indecency (the ban was not lifted in France until 1949), and Baudelaire himself was condemned for his dissipated way of life and his addiction to both opium and alcohol. Nowadays, however, his poetry is increasingly regarded as being of a very high order, in which the eroticism is seen as sensitive and beautiful, and the 'morbidity' of certain of the subjects is entirely justified by the poet's skill and honesty of vision.

Baum, L. Frank (1856–1919) Among the many books for children written by Lyman Frank Baum, one is outstanding: *The Wonderful Wizard of Oz*, published in 1900. It was so successful that Baum wrote thirteen sequels to it. Although previously little known outside the United States, the story became familiar all over the world when it provided Judy Garland with her greatest role as Dorothy, the little girl who travels 'over the rainbow'.

Bay Psalm Book, The The full title of this book is *The Whole Booke of Psalmes Faithfully Translated into English Metre* edited by Richard Mather, John Eliot and Thomas Welde. Published at Cambridge, Massachusetts, by Stephen Daye in 1640, it was the first book to be printed in what were then the American colonies. A revised edition appeared some years later.

Beardsley, Aubrey (1872-98) In his early years,

Cover illustration to *The Yellow Book* by its art editor, Aubrey Beardsley.

The Yellow Book

An Illustrated Quarterly

Volume I April 1894

London: Elkin Mathews & John Lane
Boston: Copeland & Day
SECOND EDITION

Price
5/-
Net

Aubrey Vincent Beardsley gave concerts in the guise of an 'infant musical phenomenom'. In 1891, however, he began a career as an artist, and became the outstanding illustrator of literary work of the 1890s, and art editor of *The Yellow Book* and later of *The Savoy*. His work, in black and white, was almost always erotic in tone, and in recent years many of his pornographic drawings have been made available. Among other works, he provided illustrations for Pope's *The Rape of the Lock*, Wilde's *Salome*, and Jonson's *Volpone*. He wrote and illustrated a novella, *The Story of Venus and Tannhauser*.

Beat Generation, The A self-descriptive term used by a number of American writers in the 1950s – 'beat' because they were world-weary, and because they believed they could release themselves from their stultifying surroundings and reach a beatific condition, achieving this, at least in part, by following those cults which make use of meditation and hallucinogenic drugs. In their writings they wanted to abandon what they saw as restrictive middle-class conventions, and much of their output was experimental and iconoclastic. Prominent in the movements were the novelist, Jack Kerouac, who first used the term, and the poet Allan Ginsberg, and these two can indeed be regarded as its leaders. Other writers of the Beat Generation include William Burroughs, Gregory Corson, Lawrence Ferlinghetti, John Clellon Holmes, Peter Orlovsky and Gary Snyder. The influence of the movement was considerable, affecting other branches of the arts, including popular music.

Beaumarchais, Pierre Augustin Caron de (1732–99) Watchmaker, music teacher, secret agent, and dramatist, Pierre Augustin Caron de Beaumarchais was born in Paris. Many of his plays enjoyed great success at the time, but his two famous comedies, *The Barber of Seville*, first produced in 1775, and *The Marriage of Figaro*, which came nine years later, although familiar to students of French, are now presented on the stages of the English-speaking world only in their operatic versions, by Rossini and Mozart respectively.

Beaumont, Francis (1584–1616) Born at Grace-Dieu, Leicestershire, the youngest son of a justice of the common pleas, Francis Beaumont was educated at Oxford and trained for the legal profession. He became a successful dramatist, almost all of his work being written in collaboration with John Fletcher. As sole author, he is believed to have written *The Woman Hater*, performed about 1607, and *The Knight of the Burning Pestle*, produced about 1610.

Beaumont and Fletcher In an age when collaboration between two or more dramatists was commonplace and attributions are very uncertain, so that we can never be sure that the accepted authorship of many plays is either correct or complete, the work of Beaumont and Fletcher was extraordinary. Both of them wrote plays on their own, and Fletcher, in particular, collaborated with several other dramatists, but their partnership produced work of such quality that the pairing of their names has endured. Introduced to each other, it is said, by Ben Jonson, they became close friends, sharing their bachelor accommodation. It was long believed that they had produced fifty or more plays, but this is unlikely, since they worked together for no more than six years, between 1608 and 1614, and while some present-day scholars would limit the number of their joint works to seven, a total of about a dozen seems to be more probable. The best-known of these are *Philaster or Love Lies a-Bleeding*, *The Maid's Tragedy* and *A King and No King*, all of which were probably first seen between 1609 and 1611, and were printed some ten years later. The plays of Beaumont and Fletcher are rarely performed nowadays, but the authors retain an important place in the history of English Drama, and would perhaps be more highly regarded if they were not, like all their contemporaries, overshadowed by the genius of William Shakespeare.

Beauvoir, Simone de (1908–86) The French writer Simone de Beauvoir, who was born in Paris, has written a number of novels, including *She Came to Stay* and *The Mandarins*, published in English in 1949 and 1956 respectively, and several volumes of autobiography. She is much associated with the Existentialist movement, and was the companion of Jean-Paul Sartre until his death in 1980. *The Second Sex*, one of the earliest statements of the modern feminist movement and perhaps her most influential book, was first published in 1953.

Beaux' Stratagem, The George Farquhar's comic masterpiece, first presented in 1707 and published the same year.

Beckett, Samuel (1906–) Samuel Barclay Beckett was born in Dublin, the son of a quantity surveyor, and educated at Portora Royal School in Enniskillen and Trinity College, Dublin. After leaving university, he took a teaching job, and then moved to Paris, where he became a friend of James Joyce. During an unsettled period of his life in the 1930s, he travelled in Europe, and began to write, publishing poems, stories and a number of novels. Some years before the beginning of World War II, he decided to live

Samuel Beckett, the Irish novelist and playwright.

permanently in France, and during the Occupation he was active in the French Resistance. He writes sometimes in English, sometimes in French, providing his own translations. His novels *Molloy*, *Mallone Dies* and *The Unnameable* were first published in English between 1951 and 1958, and his *Collected Poems in French and English* appeared in 1977. His famous play *Waiting for Godot* was first presented in Paris in 1953, and was seen in the English version two years later. An example of the Theatre of the Absurd, this tragicomedy has proved baffling to many theatre-goers, but it never fails to intrigue, amuse and disturb its audiences. It is, in short, a stunning piece of theatre, written in a highly individual style, and, despite its experimental and apparently uncommercial nature, it was immediately, and immensely, successful internationally. *Endgame* and *Krapp's Last Tape* followed, together with other plays. Some of these, such as *Come and Go*, which is no longer than a brief revue sketch, and *Breath*, a drama lasting for less than a minute, seemed even more obscure than *Godot*. Beckett's recent books have included *Disjecta*, consisting of reviews, letters and fragments of an early play, which appeared in 1983, and *Complete Dramatic Works*, collected and issued in 1986. Future generations will have to judge whether their author is as profound and important a writer as his admirers believe, and whether, indeed, he was worthy of the Nobel Prize awarded to him in 1969. But although some of his output may eventually be seen as highly eccentric and ephemeral, his influence in the theatre, and his major works, in which are included his novels and *Waiting for Godot*, will undoubtedly retain their value.

Beckford, William (1759–1844) At the age of eleven, William Beckford inherited a fortune from his father, a former Lord Mayor of London. He spent most of his life thereafter in travel and in building the folly of Fonthill Abbey in Wiltshire, the county in which he was born. His journeys resulted in two travel books, *Dreams, Waking Thoughts and Incidents* and *Recollections of an Excursion to the Monasteries of Alcobaca and Batalha*, and he also wrote a number of satires. He is remembered chiefly, however, as the author of *Vathek, An Arabian Tale*, which he wrote in French in 1782, and which was published in an English translation in 1786.

Beddoes, Thomas (1803–49) Thomas Lovell Beddoes was born at Clifton, England, into a family with literary connections. His father was a doctor and a writer, and had been the friend of Wordsworth, Coleridge and Southey, and his mother was a sister of the novelist Maria Edgeworth. The young Thomas Beddoes was educated at Charterhouse and Pembroke College, and while still at Oxford he published, in 1821, *The Improvisatore, in Three Fyttes, with Other Poems* and the following year a play, *The Bride's Tragedy*. Soon after, he began work on a fantastic drama entitled *Death's Jest-Book, or The Fool's Tragedy*, which he completed in 1829. However, he laboured for many years over revisions of this play, which was in blank verse and much in the style of the Elizabethan and Jacobean dramatists, in whose work he was deeply interested. In 1825 he went to Germany to study medicine, and some years later settled in Zurich. He made a number of attempts at suicide, before finally succeeding by the use of curare. *Death's Jest-Book*, when it was published posthumously in 1850, was revealed as of little dramatic merit, its construction being weak and haphazard. It did, however, establish Beddoes as a poet of some distinction, and both his lyrics and his blank verse have been highly praised.

Bede (673–735) St Bede (or Baeda), often known as 'The Venerable Bede', spent his life from the age of seven in the monasteries of Wearmouth and Jarrow, near to where he was born in County Durham, England. An historian and theologian, he wrote many books, mostly of a religious nature, though natural science was also covered. His *Historia Ecclesiastica Gentis Anglorum*, a history of the English Church and its people, was completed in 731, and for the beauty of its style, the skill with which the narrative has been constructed, and the depth of research that it demonstrates, is a masterpiece of the highest order.

Scene from a twelfth-century edition of Bede's *Life of St Cuthbert*, showing Cuthbert curing a thane's servant with a dose of holy water.

Beerbohm, Max (1872–1956) The satirist and caricaturist Henry Maximilian Beerbohm was born in London and educated at Charterhouse and Oxford. His first published writings appeared in the 1890s in the *Yellow Book*. At twenty-four, he published a collection of these witty essays under the title, *The Works of Max Beerbohm*. In 1897 came *The Happy Hypocrite: A Fairy Tale for Tired Men*, which was still in print fifty years later. More volumes of essays followed, and his period as drama critic of the *Saturday Review*, from 1898 to 1912, later resulted in three collections of his reviews. A short novel of Oxford in the 1890s, *Zuleika Dobson*, first published in 1911, became widely popular. He also wrote many short stories, and his considerable talent as a caricaturist was shown in several books of drawings. In the 1930s he became a popular broadcaster, and a collection of his talks, *Mainly on the Air*, was published in 1946. The keynote of all Max Beerbohm's work is elegance. He was knighted in 1939.

Beggar's Opera, The A musical play by John Gay, first presented in 1798. *The Threepenny Opera*, a later version by Bertolt Brecht, with music by Kurt Weill, was produced in 1928.

Behan, Brendan (1923–64) Born in Dublin, Brendan Behan attracted notice with his first book, *Borstal Boy*, published in 1958, an account of his experiences in a prison for young offenders where he had been sent because he had been working for the IRA. Behan's wild personality and the vigour of the book resulted in considerable publicity, and this brought about the production of several plays, among which *The Hostage* and *The Quare Fellow* both enjoyed a brief success.

The Irish author Brendan Behan, by Sir David Low.

Behn, Aphra (1640–89) Aphra Behn is believed to have been the first woman professional writer. She was born in Kent, the daughter of a barber named Johnson, and while still a child was taken with her parents to Surinam. She spent some time there, and this experience was the inspiration of her later novel, *Oroonoko, or The History of the Royal Slave*, first published about 1668. Having returned to England, she married a London merchant of Dutch descent named Behn, but was widowed shortly after. A clever and attractive woman, she became a member of the court of Charles II, and in 1666, during the Dutch wars, she was sent to Antwerp as a spy

on behalf of the English king. Disgusted when the intelligence she had gathered was ignored, she returned to London, and began to support herself by her writings. She produced more than a dozen plays, among them *The Rover, or the Banished Cavalier*, presented in two parts in 1677 and 1681, the success of which, despite accusations that her wit was too coarse for a woman, crowned her career as a dramatist. She also wrote some verse and a number of novels, but *Oroonoko* is her only work which is still of interest.

Belloc, Hilaire (1870–1953) Joseph Hilary Pierre Belloc, the son of a French barrister, was born near Paris. He attended the Oratory School, Edgbaston, and after serving his compulsory term in the French army completed his education at Balliol College, Oxford. In 1902 he became a naturalized British subject. For the four-year period from 1906 to 1910 he was a Member of Parliament, but most of his life was dedicated to writing, and he produced something in the order of a hundred and fifty books of many different kinds. He wrote poetry, novels, travel books, essays, literary criticism and biographies, and was also a working journalist and editor. His first books, both published in 1896, were *Verses and Sonnets* and *A Bad Child's Book of Beasts*. Perhaps not surprisingly in view of his background, his biographies were often concerned with French historical persons, and included *Danton*, *Marie Antoinette*, *Robespierre* and *Richelieu*, but he also wrote on *Cromwell* and *Charles II*. Among his travel books, the most successful was *The Path to Rome*, first published in 1902. Hilaire Belloc is often associated with G.K. Chesterton, whom he first met in 1900. Their friendship continued for more than thirty years, and they frequently worked closely together. Nowadays, Belloc is mostly remembered for his poetry, and especially for such lyrics as 'Tarantella'.

Bellow, Saul (1915–) Of Russian-Jewish descent, Saul Bellow was born in Quebec, but grew up in Chicago, to which city he moved with his parents in 1924. He was educated at Chicago, Northwestern and Wisconsin universities, and he has divided his life between academic work and writing. His first published novel, *Dangling Man*, appeared in 1944, and was followed three years later by *The Victim*. *The Adventures of Augie March* attracted much favourable critical attention, and some commercial success, when it was published in 1953, and it won the National Book Award. A short novel, *Seize the Day*, came out in 1956, and this book was singled out for special praise as a modern classic when Bellow was awarded the Nobel Prize for Literature in 1976. However, the two major works of fiction, *Henderson the Rain King* and *Herzog*, appearing in 1959 and 1964, had earlier established Bellow as one of the most important novelists of the twentieth century. He won the National Book Award again in 1970, with *Mr Sammler's Planet*, and this was followed in 1975 by *Humboldt's Gift*, in 1976 by *To Jerusalem and Back*, and in 1982 by *The Dean's December*. In 1977 he won the Gold Medal for the Novel awarded every six years by the American Academy and Institute of Arts and Letters. He has also written many short stories as well as three plays, *The Wrecker*, *The Last Analysis* and *The Wen*. His non-fiction works include *Recent American Fiction*, published in 1963, and *Technology and the Frontiers of Knowledge*, which appeared in 1974. As a novelist, Saul Bellow seeks to dissect the soul of

Saul Bellow signing copies of his Pulitzer Prize-winning novel *Humboldt's Gift.*

modern civilized man and examine the moral dilemmas which face him, but the seriousness of his work and its intentions has not resulted in obscure or difficult texts, and his admirers are not confined to highbrow intellectuals.

Belton Estate, The A novel by Anthony Trollope, first published in 1866.

Bely, Andrei (1880–1934) The reputation of the Russian novelist, poet and literary critic Andrei Bely has continued to grow since his death. He was born in Moscow, and after completing his education at Moscow University published his first book, *Second Symphony*, in 1902. He wrote many novels, but *Petersburg*, first published when he was thirty-three but frequently revised thereafter, is regarded as a major work. Its publication brought Bely comparison with Joyce and Kafka, and established him as a powerful and innovative writer.

Benchley, Robert (1889–1945) Robert Charles Benchley, who was educated at Harvard, might be described as a founder member, with Dorothy Parker and Robert Sherwood, of the Round Table group of writers and actors who met regularly at the Algonquin Hotel in New York. Known primarily as a humorist, but also a prominent theatre critic, Benchley published many collections of his articles, from *Of All Things*, in 1921, to *Benchley Beside Himself*, in 1943.

Bend in the River, A Set in a developing Central African country, this novel by V.S. Naipaul is seen through the eyes of a Muslim trader, Salim, and tells of his relationships with friends and lovers and with the State itself. It was first published in 1979.

Benét, Stephen Vincent (1898–1943) Born in Pennsylvania and educated at Yale, Stephen Benét wrote a number of novels, short stories, screenplays, and a folk opera, but his reputation rests on his poetry, including his long poem *John Brown's Body*, with its background of the American Civil War, first published in 1928, and his *Ballads and Poems*, first published in 1931.

Ben-Hur: A Tale of the Christ An historical novel by Lew Wallace, first published in 1880.

Bennett, Alan (1934–) A Yorkshireman who was educated at Exeter College, Oxford, Alan Bennett first attracted attention as one of the four performers in the revue, *Beyond the Fringe*. He has since written a number of successful stage plays, including *Forty Years On*, first produced in 1968, *Habeas Corpus*, produced in 1973, and *Kafka's Dick*, first seen in 1986. He has also been much praised for his television dramas, which were collected and published in 1985 under the title *The Writer in Disguise*.

Bennett, Arnold (1867–1931) Enoch Arnold Bennett grew up in that part of England called 'the Potteries', which later became the background for many of his most successful books. The son of a solicitor, born and educated in Hanley, Staffordshire, it had been intended that he should follow in his father's footsteps, but when he was sent to London at the age of twenty-one, he began a second career in his spare time as a journalist. He was successful enough to abandon the law altogether in 1893, and by 1896 he had become editor of the periodical, *Woman*. In 1898 his first novel, *A Man from the North*, appeared, and it was followed in 1902 by *Anna of the Five Towns*, set in the Potteries. At this time he removed himself to Paris, where he married and lived for ten years. The second of the 'Five Towns' books, *The Old Wive's Tale*, came out in 1908, and established Bennett as a popular best-selling novelist. His status as a literary figure was confirmed with the publication between 1910 and 1915 of the trilogy, *Clayhanger*, *Hilda Lessways* and *These Twain*, which are again set in the Five Towns, and are generally considered to be his most outstanding achievement. He wrote well over thirty other novels, including *The Card*, published in 1911, *Riceyman Steps*, in 1923, and *Imperial Palace*, in 1930, and also produced several volumes of short stories. A stream of non-fiction books flowed from his pen on subjects ranging from *How to Become an Author* to *Those United States* and *Things That Have Interested Me*. Additionally, he pursued an extremely successful, if more ephemeral, career as a dramatist, writing both full-length and one-act plays, and also collaborating on others, sometimes with Edward Knoblock and sometimes with Eden Philpotts. *Milestones*, written with Knoblock and produced in 1912, is the only one of his dramas which is likely to endure. Despite this vast output in so many different genres, he continued to work as a journalist, and became one of the most influential literary critics the world has ever seen. A word of praise from Bennett in his column in London's *Evening Standard* could turn an unknown novelist into a bestselling lion overnight. His autobiographical *Journal*, published after his death, is a fascinating record of the period and of a dedicated author's life. The popularity which Arnold Bennett's own books enjoyed in his life-time has faded in recent years, perhaps unjustly, for in the best of his novels he shows himself able to construct an absorbing plot with an evocatively-described background, many penetrating character studies, and a welcome leavening of humour.

Benson, E.F. (1867–1940) Edward Frederick Benson was the second of three writing brothers (the others were A.C. Benson and R.H. Benson), all of whom were extremely prolific. Of the three, E.F. Benson, who wrote some eighty books, produced the most popular work. His first novel, *Dodo*, was published in 1893, and he wrote a series of novels featuring the same character. Even more successful were the 'Lucia' novels, which date from 1920, when the first of them, *Queen Lucia*, appeared. These amusing books have been revived very successfully in recent years as a result of television adaptations. Benson also wrote a number of entertaining autobiographical works.

Bentham, Jeremy (1748–1832) Born in London and educated at Westminster School and The Queen's College, Oxford, Jeremy Bentham was a philosopher and jurist, whose first work, *Fragment on Government*, was published anonymously in 1776. Under his own name, *Defence of Usury* followed in 1787, and his major work, *Introduction to Principles of Morals and Legislation*, in 1789. Bentham also wrote a number of short works on

The English novelist Arnold Bennett, by Walter Tittle.

Parliamentary reform, on religion, on prison management, on the freedom of the press, and on politics and legal matters. In 1791, he published *Anarchical Fallacies*, in response to the *Declaration of the Rights of Man*, which had been produced in France by the leaders of the Revolution, of which he did not approve. In 1823, at the age of seventy-five, he founded the *Westminster Review*. Jeremy Bentham is also remembered for the quirk of having left instructions that after death his body was to be dissected in the presence of his friends. His wishes were carried out, and his skeleton is still preserved in University College, London.

Bentley, Richard (1662–1742) The classical scholarship of the celebrated academic Richard Bentley, who was born at Oulton, Yorkshire, was widely admired during his lifetime, though a somewhat combative nature made him many enemies. He was appointed Keeper of the Royal Library in 1694, and became Master of Trinity College, Cambridge, in 1700. He published two major works in defence of Christianity, *The Folly and Unreasonableness of Atheism*, in 1693, and *Remarks on a Late Discourse of Freethinking*, in 1713. He also edited the works of Horace, Terence and Manilius, and produced an 'improved' version of Milton's *Paradise Lost*.

Beowulf The most important poem written in Old English and known to us today. *Beowulf* is over three thousand lines long, and exists in the form of a tenth-century manuscript, though it was almost certainly first composed some centuries earlier. The narrative, which has a strong Christian content, concerns Beowulf's fights against two monsters. The importance of *Beowulf* in the history of Western Literature is immense, as it is the earliest known major poem to be written in a European vernacular language.

Beppo: A Venetian Story A mock-heroic poem by Lord Byron, first published in 1818.

Berkeley, George (1685–1753) Although of English descent, George Berkeley was born in Co. Kilkenny, Ireland, and educated at Trinity College, Dublin. He rose to become Bishop of Cloyne. Many years earlier he spent some time in England, and became the friend of Swift, Addison, Steele and Pope. Berkeley's best-known works were first published between 1709 and 1713; they are *An Essay Towards a New Theory of Vision*, *A Treatise concerning the Principles of Human Knowledge* and *Three Dialogues between Hylas and Philonous*. In 1728, he went to the United States, intending to found a missionary college in the Bermudas and extend its benefits to the Americans. After three years spent in Rhode Island, the promised government money

Oil painting of the philosopher George Berkeley, Bishop of Cloyne, by John Simbert.

was not forthcoming, and he returned to Ireland. His plans for the college were later used for King's College, New York, which became Columbia University. The city of Berkeley, California, was named after him.

Berryman, John (1914–72) Born in McAlester, Oklahoma, and educated at Columbia University and Cambridge, John Berryman published his first book, *Poems*, in 1942. *77 Dream Songs*, a series of poems forming a kind of narrative, won the Pulitzer Prize in 1964, and was completed by *His Toy, His Dream, His Rest* in 1968. Berryman also wrote a biography of Stephen Crane and a novel, *Recovery*, which was published after his death.

Bertrams, The A novel by Anthony Trollope, first published in 1859.

Besant, Walter (1836–1901) Once an extremely successful novelist but now little read, Walter Besant was born at Portsmouth, England, and educated at King's College, London, and Christ's College, Cambridge. His stories include *Ready-Money Mortiboy*, written in collaboration with James Rice, *All Sorts and Conditions of Men*, and *Beyond the Dreams of Avarice*. He also wrote several books on London, and some critical and biographical works. He was instrumental in founding the British Society of Authors in 1884, and was knighted in 1895.

bestiaries During the Middle Ages, many books were written about animals, sometimes consisting largely of stories or fables, and often illustrated. Known as bestiaries, these works were usually intended to preach or to underline Christian morals by the use of allegory, and a short homily was often added to drive the message home.

Betjeman, John (1906–84) It was said at one time that John Betjeman was the only poet in England able to live, and live extremely well, on the money his verse earned him. He was born in London, the son of a factory owner, and was educated at Marlborough and Magdalen College, Oxford. His first published book was a collection of verse under the title *Mount Zion*, which appeared in 1931. The poems which Betjeman wished to preserve from this and a number of subsequent selections were brought together in 1958 in his *Collected Poems*, of which several more editions were issued, each containing additional poems written since the publication of its predecessor. In 1960, Betjeman produced *Summoned by Bells*, his autobiography, written in blank verse. He also wrote books on architectural and topographical subjects, and became a practised performer on television. Adored by the middle classes, of whom he wrote with both affection and irony, his work was not always admired by literary critics, but, although it is easy to dismiss much of his work as over-facile, the apparently naive simplicity often hides a careful craftsmanship. Betjeman was knighted in 1969, and became Poet Laureate in 1972.

Betrothed, The An historical novel by Sir Walter Scott, set in the time of Henry II. It was first published in 1825.

Bible, The Regarded by millions as divinely inspired – 'the word of the Lord' – the Bible is the most widely read book in the world, and our daily speech is filled with quotations from and allusions to its texts. In whatever language it is read, whether rich in the vocabulary of a bygone age or prosaic in some uninspired modern version, it is an extraordinary storehouse of history and beliefs, fable and legend, law, and moral and religious instruction, and poetry too. The origins of the Old Testament lie as far back as the ninth or tenth century BC, but although it was written many thousands of years ago by and for the Hebrews and their descendants, who had left Egypt in search of the promised land, it has become relevant to the entire Western world. The New Testament, mostly written in the first century AD is the basis of the most widespread of all Western religions. Apart from its religious significance, the Bible has contributed enormously to the cultural heritage of the Western world, and the various translations of the original Hebrew and Greek texts have had an incalculable influence on our literature.

Bible, English translations of the It can be assumed that from Anglo-Saxon times onwards parts of the Bible were translated into the kind of English then current, simply because of the needs of the ordinary people, who would have been unable to understand Latin or Greek. Certainly, in the eighth century Bede and Caedmon rendered certain sections into the vernacular, and both before and after that time other scholars working in monasteries were engaged on similar tasks. It was not, however, until the fourteenth century that John Wycliffe produced the first complete English translation of the Bible, working from the Vulgate (the Latin version produced by St Jerome in the fifth century). This was completed about 1382. One hundred and fifty years later came the translation by William Tyndale, which, while recognizing the Vulgate and also Martin Luther's German version, was mainly based on Greek and Hebrew texts. The importance of Tyndale's translation cannot be over-emphasized, for it was to be a main source for the versions that would follow. In 1535, Miles Coverdale produced a new edition of the Bible, basing it upon the Vulgate, Luther's Bible, the Zurich Bible, a Latin version by Pagninus, and, inevitably, the Tyndale translation. Coverdale was then commissioned by Archbishop Cranmer to prepare the Great Bible, published in 1539 at the command of Henry VIII. A revision of the Great Bible appeared in 1568, and became known as the Bishops' Bible. The Authorized Version, published in 1611, during the reign of King James I, is largely based on Tyndale's translation. It was produced as a result of a suggestion made during a conference which the king had called in 1604 in order to settle various arguments between the High and Low factions within the Church. Forty-seven scholars were appointed, their main brief being to follow the Bishops' Bible wherever possible, and their work continued for three and a half years before the new version was completed. It is often referred to as the 'King James Bible', and is, of course, the familiar text which has provided so many phrases and sayings for our daily language. It remained the standard translation for more than two centuries, and the first major departure from it was not seen until the Revised Version

'Christ's miracles of healing' from a thirteenth-century French *Bible moralisée*, every page of which looks like an elaborate design for a contemporary stained-glass window.

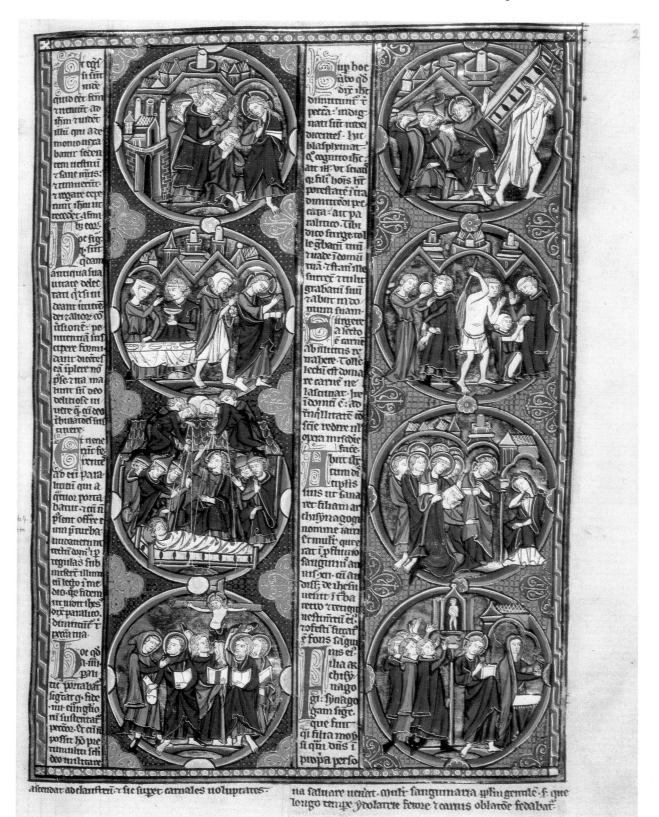

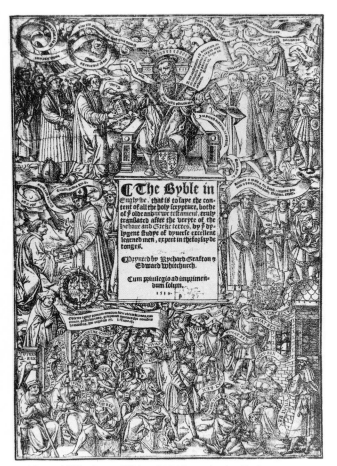

Henry VIII's Great Bible of 1539 made the Scripture officially available in English for the first time. On this title-page he is depicted as handing down copies of the Bible to his Archbishops, who then distribute them to the priests and lay people.

was prepared and published in the 1880s. Several attempts have been made during the twentieth century to produce a Bible, or certain parts of it, in the modern idiom. All such versions are condemned by the traditionalists as soon as they appear, and certainly they cannot equal the beauty, at least in the ears of the older generation, of the language which was contemporary and commonplace to James I, and which has become not only familiar, but literally hallowed, by long usage. Nevertheless, many of the modern translations have much merit, including a greater clarity of meaning and, in some cases, a more faithful rendition of the original texts. Future generations may perhaps treat them with the reverence now accorded to the Authorized Version.

Bible in Spain, The An account of his travels in Spain by George Borrow, first published in 1843.

Bierce, Ambrose (1842–*c*.1914) Ambrose Gwinnet Bierce was the son of a farmer living in Horse Cave Creek, Ohio. He received little formal education, but, after fighting in the American Civil War, he became a well-known journalist and writer of short stories, which were collected in *In the Midst of Life*, first published in the 1890s. *The Devil's Dictionary*, which appeared in 1906, is a collection of ironically humorous definitions, and is much quoted. Bierce went to Mexico in 1913, disappeared, and is presumed to have died in the Mexican Civil War which was in progress at the time.

Biggers, Earl Derr (1884–1933) A journalist who became a prolific novelist, Earl Derr Biggers is chiefly remembered for the novel *Seven Keys to Baldpate*, published in 1913, and as the creator of the Chinese detective Charlie Chan, whose adventures he chronicled in many books, later adapted for the screen.

Big Sleep, The A thriller by Raymond Chandler, his first full-length book, first published in 1939.

Billings, Josh (1818–85) Josh Billings was the pseudonym of Henry Wheeler Shaw, a humorous writer who was born in Massachusetts. His newspaper articles, with their homespun philosophy, their attacks on the pretentious, wherever it was to be found, and their comic spelling, were extremely popular. Beginning with *Josh Billings, His Sayings*, which appeared in 1865, several collections of his pieces were published in book form.

Billy Budd, Foretopman A short novel by Herman Melville, first published posthumously in 1924, since when the power of its allegory has been widely acclaimed. It was the basis of Benjamin Britten's opera, *Billy Budd*.

Binyon, Laurence (1869–1943) Robert Laurence Binyon was born in Lancaster, England. After his education at St. Paul's School and Trinity College, Oxford, he eventually became a keeper of prints and drawings in the British Museum. He published a number of books on paintings, and also wrote plays, but is principally remembered as a poet, and especially for his war poem, 'For the Fallen'. His *Collected Poems* appeared in 1931.

Biographia Literaria A book of autobiography, philosophy and literary criticism by Samuel Taylor Coleridge, first published in 1817.

Birds, The An allegorical comedy by Aristophanes, in which a land peopled by birds is built between heaven and earth in order to separate men from the gods. It was written in 421BC.

Bishop, Elizabeth (1911–79) The poet Elizabeth Bishop was born in Massachusetts and was educated at Vassar. In 1946 she published a volume of verse, *North and South*, which she later revised. When it was published under the new title *North and South — A Cold Spring* it won the Pulitzer Prize. Much of her poetry was inspired by her love of travel, as is indicated by such titles as *Questions of Travel* and *Geography III*. Her *Complete Poems 1927 to 1979* was published in 1983. For the last years of her life she lived in Brazil.

Black Arrow, The A novel for young readers by Robert Louis Stevenson, first published in serial form in 1883, and as a book in 1888.

Black Boy The autobiography of Richard Wright, first published in 1945 and seen as one of the most impressive and important works by a Black writer of the period.

Blackmore, R.D. (1825–1900) Born at Longworth, Berkshire, England, the son of a clergyman, and educated at Exeter College, Oxford, Richard Doddridge Blackmore was trained for the legal profession, but he was forced by ill-health to live in the country, and became a market gardener. He published poetry and translations from the Latin, as well as a large number of popular novels. He is remembered today only for his romantic classic of the English West country *Lorna Doone: A Romance of Exmoor*, first published in 1869.

Blackwood's Magazine First issued in April 1817 as *The Edinburgh Monthly Magazine* and later known as *Blackwood's Edinburgh Magazine*, dropping 'Edinburgh' only in 1905, this literary periodical was noted for its partisan criticism. Coleridge, Keats, Leigh Hunt and Hazlitt were all savaged. Hazlitt sued and received damages; Keats is said to have been brought closer to death by the bitter attacks. On the other hand, *Blackwood's* admired and supported Wordsworth, Scott, Shelley and de Quincey, among others. In later years, the magazine, which was published until 1980, became much more staid.

Blake, William (1757–1827) From an early age, William Blake was a voracious reader, and his talent as a writer was first shown in some very early poetry. His ability as an artist was even more marked, and although he received little formal education, his father, a somewhat impecunious London hosier, sent him at the age of ten to a drawing school, and later apprenticed him to an engraver. At the end of his apprenticeship, in 1778, he went for a short period to the School of the Royal Academy. In 1780 one of his pictures was accepted for the Royal Academy Exhibition, and for nearly three decades he continued to receive a similar accolade for his work year by year. Meanwhile, he had taken employment as an engraver with a bookseller

The visionary poet and painter William Blake, when he was fifty, painted by Thomas Phillips.

and publisher, and his painting and his work brought him into contact with artists and men of literature. The sculptor John Flaxman and another friend, the Reverend Henry Mathew, became Blake's patrons and were instrumental in arranging the publication of his first collection of verse. *Poetical Sketches* appeared in 1783, showing promise of the finer poetry which was to follow in his maturity. By 1784 he had begun his own business as a print seller and engraver, and in 1787 himself published his *Songs of Innocence*, illustrated with his own engravings. Many more works followed, in which Blake not only exercised his twin talents as writer and artist, but also began to give rein to the mysticism to which Flaxman had first introduced him, and with which he became increasingly preoccupied. This obsession was evidenced in *The Book of Thel*, which appeared in 1787, *The Marriage of Heaven and Hell*, his major prose work, and *The Vision of the Daughters of Albion*, which came out in 1790 and 1793. *Songs of Experience* was published in 1794, complementing *Songs of Innocence* and confirming beyond doubt his status as a poet of considerable stature. Blake now embarked on a series of books devoted to the mystical quasi-

religious world he had created, in which Urizen, the law-giver, was opposed by the rebellious Orc, the son of Los and Enitharmon, and in which he attacked the hypocrisy of Puritan Christianity, and showed Jesus as a powerful revolutionary whose teachings were of a free, rather than a restricted, morality. These 'Prophetic books' include *The Book of Urizen, The Song of Los, The Book of Ahania, The Book of Los*, all published in 1794 and 1795, and, published later, *The Four Zoas*. In 1800, Blake and his wife – he had married in 1782 – went to live at Felpham in Sussex, where he began to write two more major works, *Milton* and *Jerusalem: the Emanation of the Giant Albion*, before returning to London in 1803, where he then remained. He continued to produce engravings, and towards the end of his life a commission from the prosperous painter John Linnell resulted in the magnificent illustrations to *The Book of Job*, published in 1826. However, excluding the interest of a few friends like Linnell, his work as an artist was scarcely more appreciated at the time than his writings, and neither brought him popular recognition or pecuniary reward. Today, however, his place in both literature and art is secure. *The Songs of Innocence and Experience* remain familiar – 'Tiger! Tiger! Burning bright' must be one of the most quoted poems in the language – and Sir Hubert Parry's setting of the poem 'Jerusalem', lines which come from Blake's *Milton*, is still sung with patriotic fervour by young, middle-aged and elderly members of England's middle classes. The complexity, which often amounts to impenetrability, of Blake's later writings, the extraordinary vision of his mystical mythological world, and the unmatched individuality of his drawings led many of his contemporaries to accuse Blake of insanity. Perhaps he was indeed mad, but if so it was the madness of a genius, and later generations have recognized him as such.

blank verse A term used for unrhymed verse, but usually referring to the iambic pentameter, or unrhymed heroic, the metre used in most English epic poetry and in which almost the whole of Shakespeare's plays are written

Bleak House A novel by Charles Dickens, concerned with the case of Jarndyce and Jarndyce in the Court of Chancery. It was first published in book form in 1853.

A relief etching from Blake's *America*, painted with gold and watercolours. The poetry, a denunciation of Orc by Albion's Angel, is in direct opposition to the scene of innocence portrayed. Two children and a ram sleep peacefully under a spreading birch tree, next to a budding vine. Birds of paradise adorn both tree and sky.

Blessed Damozel, The Dante Gabriel Rossetti's most famous poem, first published in 1850. The poet later produced revised versions.

Blithedale Romance, The A novel by Nathaniel Hawthorne, based on his own experiences at Brook Farm, the Transcendentalist commune. It was first published in 1852.

Bloomsbury Group, The An avant-garde literary and artistic coterie formed about 1906, and so named because they met in the Bloomsbury area of London at the home of the Stephen sisters, later to marry and to become better known as Vanessa Bell and Virginia Woolf. Its members were much influenced by the views of Professor G.E. Moore, as expressed in his book, *Principia Ethica*, which had been published a few years previously. They wished to escape from the limitations of Victorian attitudes, and believed in the pleasures of human intercourse and the enjoyment of beautiful objects. As the leaders of innovative literary and artistic attitudes, their works were accorded great importance, and their influence on succeeding generations of writers was considerable. Among the members of the group were Clive and Vanessa Bell, E.M. Forster, Roger Fry, David Garnett, Duncan Grant, John Maynard Keynes, Lytton Strachey and Leonard and Virginia Woolf.

Blume, Judy (1938–) The American writer Judy Blume published the first of her books for children, *Iggie's House*, in 1970. Her next book, *Are You There, God? It's Me, Margaret*, became a major bestseller. It was followed by several more, including *Blubber, Then Again, Maybe I Won't* and *Tales of a Fourth Grade Nothing*. In 1975 came the controversial novel *Forever*, described as a book for young adults. Although condemned by many parents for her frank and explicit description of the sexual experiences and traumas of adolescents, the realism with which she deals with their problems has been immensely popular with the children for whom she writes. She has also published an adult novel, *Wifey*.

Blunden, Edmund (1896–1974) Born in London, Edmund Charles Blunden was educated at Christ's Hospital and The Queen's College, Oxford. After military service in World War I, he turned to journalism, but later pursued an academic career, teaching, at various times, at the universities of Tokyo and Hong Kong, and becoming Professor of Poetry at Oxford from 1966 until 1968. He wrote many works of literary criticism, and biographies of Leigh Hunt, Hardy and Shelley, and also edited collections of poetry by Wilfred Owen, Christopher Smart, and especially John Clare, whose work was a lifelong interest. His own poetry appeared first in

1914, and he published many volumes of verse, including *The Waggoner and other poems*, *The Shepherd, and other poems of Peace and War*, and *English Poems*, which all appeared in the 1920s, and *After the Bombing*, which came out in 1950. A collection, *Poems of Many Years*, was published in 1957. Although much of his poetry was of a pastoral nature, his most memorable verses were inspired by his youthful experiences as a junior officer fighting in France, as was his most famous book, *Undertones of War*, first published in 1928, in which prose and poetry were used in combination.

Blunt, Wilfred Scawen (1840–1922) The diplomat and traveller Wilfred Scawen Blunt was born at Petworth House in Sussex, England. He married Byron's granddaughter in 1869. The first of his volumes of poetry, *Sonnets and Songs by Proteus*, was published in 1875. Other publications include *Ideas about India*, which appeared in 1885, and *The Future of Islam*, in 1888, in which he ardently supported the cause of Indian independence and Islamic aspirations. He also extended his anti-Imperialist views to oppose British rule of Ireland.

An illustration from Boccaccio's most famous book *The Decameron*, depicting Galeso falling in love at first sight with the beautiful Ephigenia whom, after much intrigue, he later abducted and married.

Boccaccio, Giovanni (1313–75) Florence, Paris and Certaldo all have claims to be the birthplace of Giovanni Boccaccio, but most authorities appear to agree that Florence is the most likely contender. Boccaccio was illegitimate, but his father saw that he was given a rudimentary education, and then apprenticed him to a merchant. Later he studied law, but at the age of about twenty went to live at the court of Naples, and there he met and fell in love with Maria, the daughter of the King of Naples. She was to inspire much of his work, in which he referred to her as 'Fiammetta'. He had begun to write as a child, and now, about 1341, he produced both *Filocopo*, a romance in prose, and *Teseide*, the first heroic poem to be written in Italian. Returning to Florence, he wrote *Ameto*, in a mixture of prose and verse, *L'amorosa Fiammetta*, in prose, and the extraordinary long poem, *L'amorosa Visione*, which is a kind of giant acrostic of immense complexity. In 1344 he went back to Naples, and during the next six years set down most of the stories which he was to collect in his most famous book, *The Decameron*. The plague which devastated Florence in 1348 gave him a framework for the hundred tales, which are supposedly told by a group of people staying in a villa for a period of ten days in order to escape the epidemic. It was first published in

1353, and was immediately successful. The stories are often ribald and *The Decameron*, used as source material by writers from Chaucer to Tennyson, has frequently suffered, even in recent times, from censorship. Boccaccio wrote a number of other works, in both poetry and prose, and towards the end of his life demonstrated his scholarship in four treatises, written in Latin, which covered ancient mythology, geography and history. It should not be forgotten that, in addition to his work as an author, he was responsible, virtually single-handed, for reviving an interest in western Europe in the language and literature of ancient Greece.

Boethius, Anicius Manlius Severinus (*c*.475–525) The Roman statesman and philosopher Boethius wrote a number of books of logic, but his principal literary achievement was the translation of the works of Aristotle into Latin. He thus made the Greek philosopher known in western Europe, with enormous effect on the growth of civilization and culture during the Dark Ages. His own major work was *De Consolatione Philosophiae*, itself frequently translated into English. Among those who produced versions were King Alfred the Great, Chaucer and Queen Elizabeth I.

Bogan, Louise (1897–1970) Born in Maine, Louise Bogan published several volumes of poetry, mostly metaphysical in tone, including *Body of This Death*, in 1923, *Dark Summer*, in 1929, *The Sleeping Fury*, in 1937, and *Poems and New Poems*, in 1941. Her *Collected Poems* came out in 1954. She also wrote literary criticism.

Boldrewood, Rolf (1826–1915) Rolf Boldrewood was the nom-de-plume of Thomas Alexander Browne, who was born in London but lived almost all his life in Australia, where he wrote a number of popular novels portraying life in the bush and the goldfields. His best-known work is *Robbery Under Arms*, first published in book form in 1888.

Bolingbroke, Henry St John (1678–1751) The statesman Henry St John Bolingbroke spent much of his youth in dissipation before entering Parliament as a Tory in 1701. His eloquence soon marked him out for high office, and he became Secretary for War and later Secretary of State. A staunch supporter of the Stuart cause, he was created Viscount Bolingbroke in 1712, but was stripped of his title and dismissed from office on the accession of George I in 1714. He fled to France, where he spent ten years before being pardoned and allowed to return to England. Unable to resume his political career, he became active and influential as a journalist, writing articles which attacked corruption in government and set forth the principles of republicanism,

A formal portrait of the statesman and writer Henry St John Bolingbroke by Alexis Belle.

and these writings appeared in book form in 1735 and 1743. He also published a number of works on philosophy and religion. His work for parliamentary reform had considerable influence, not least on the American political leaders who were to form the United States after the War of Independence.

Böll, Heinrich (1917–85) Born in Cologne, Germany, Heinrich Böll came to prominence with his fictional portrayal of post World War II Germany. His novels include *And Never Said a Word*, first published in 1953, *The Lost Honour of Katherine Blum*, which appeared in 1974, and *The Safety Net*, published in 1979. *A Soldier's Legacy*, written in 1947, was not published in English until 1985. Böll was awarded the Nobel Prize for Literature in 1972.

Bolt, Robert (1924–) The English playwright Robert Oxton Bolt became widely known in 1957 with *Flowering Cherry*. Other plays include *The Tiger and the Horse, Vivat! Vivat Regina!*, and his best-known work, *A Man for All Seasons*, the dramatic story of Sir Thomas More, which was produced in 1960 and was later a major success as a film. Robert Bolt has also written screenplays, including that for *Lawrence of Arabia*.

Book of Martyrs, The The popular title of *Actes and Monuments of these latter perillous Dayes, touching matters of the Church* by John Foxe, first published in Latin in 1559, and in English in 1563.

Book of Snobs, The First published in 1848, the pieces in this collection, by William Makepeace Thackeray, had previously appeared in *Punch*.

Book of the Duchess, The A long poem by Geoffrey Chaucer, alternatively known as *The Deth of Blaunche*, probably written in 1369 to commemorate Blanche, Duchess of Lancaster and wife to John of Gaunt.

Booker Prize The most prestigious of British awards for works of fiction. Recent winners include Thomas Keneally, Anita Brookner and Kingsley Amis.

Borges, Jorge Luis (1899–1986) The distinguished Argentinian writer, the recipient of many literary prizes, Jorge Luis Borges was born in Buenos Aires, and educated in Geneva. After spending some years in Spain, he returned to Argentina, where he began his literary career by publishing in 1923 a volume of verse, *Fervor de Buenos Aires*. Other selections of poetry and some volumes of essays were to follow in the next decade, but it was as a writer of short stories that he became celebrated. The first of his many collections, published in 1935, was *A Universal History of Infamy*, and, although the book attracted comparatively little notice at the time, it has since been seen as a seminal work of Latin-American literature. A later volume, *Labyrinths*, first published in 1953, brought him great acclaim, and, when it was published in English in 1962, a truly international reputation. A further volume of stories, *Doctor Brodie's Report*, appeared in 1971. Borges worked in libraries in Argentina, and after the overthrow of Peron in 1955 became Director of the National Library of Buenos Aires, a post which increasing blindness eventually forced him to relinquish. He was a prime exponent of Magic Realism, in which fantastic, dream-like incidents and references are introduced into a straightforward, realistic narrative.

Argentine poet, essayist and short-story writer, Luis Borges, just before his eighty-second birthday in Mexico. The blind poet traditionally went into seclusion on his birthday. In later life, as his health and sight failed, Borges turned to the creation of the short fictional narratives for which he is best known. These fantastic and esoteric stories reflect the author's irony and scepticism.

Borough, The A long narrative poem by George Crabbe, first published in 1810, some sections of which provided the inspiration for Benjamin Britten's opera, *Peter Grimes*.

Borrow, George (1803–81) Born in East Dereham, Norfolk, England, and educated in Norwich, George Henry Borrow was intended for a career in the law, but soon abandoned it for literature, publishing in 1826 a translation of a selection of Danish *Romantic Ballads*. His lack of success as a writer prompted him to take to the road, and this resulted in his enduring interest in the Romany world. He later travelled widely in Europe, for some time as an agent of the British and Foreign Bible Society, and wrote a number of books based on his experiences, though embroidered with a certain amount of fictional material. The first of these, published in 1841, was *The Zincali, or an account of the Gypsies in Spain*. *The Bible in Spain*, published two years later, was extremely successful, and Borrow was encouraged by the Victorian fascination for Gypsy life to write *Lavengro*, which appeared in 1851. Although far from a failure, it was not as well received as *The Bible in Spain* had been and its sequel, *The Romany Rye*, was not published until 1857. A tour of Wales which Borrow later made with his step-daughter resulted in *Wild Wales*, published in 1862, and in 1874 he brought out his last book, a dictionary of the Gypsy language.

Bostonians, The A novel by Henry James, first published in 1886.

Boswell, James (1740-95) The son of a judge, Lord Auchinleck, and originally himself intended for the law, James Boswell was determined from an early age on a literary career, though he did eventually qualify and practise as a lawyer. In 1762 he left his native Edinburgh for London, where he met Samuel Johnson, and his association with the good Doctor was to bring him lasting fame. Johnson, not impressed at their first meeting, subsequently took a liking to Boswell, and encouraged him to keep a diary, which was suppressed for many years, but finally published in the 1950s as *Boswell's London Journal*, *Boswell in Holland 1763–1764* and *Boswell on the Grand Tour*. It is a lively account of a man with great curiosity, a gift for observation, an insatiable sexual drive, and a love of travel and of literary lion-hunting. During 1765 Boswell spent some time in Corsica and met Pasquale di Paoli, the Corsican freedom fighter. The result

James Boswell, diarist and writer, who devoted many years to his definitive biography of his famous friend Dr Samuel Johnson. Boswell was well known for his books on travel which highlighted his gift for observation.

was his first important work to be published during his lifetime, *An Account of Corsica, Journal of a Tour to that Island, and Memoirs of Pascal Paoli*, which appeared in 1768. In the following year he married his cousin, Margaret Montgomery, by whom he had five children, but in the years to come he frequently left his family in Scotland while he visited the fleshpots of London. In 1773, he was invited by Johnson to accompany him to Scotland, and Boswell's account of their travels, *Journal of a Tour to the Hebrides*, although largely written during the journey, eventually came out in 1785. By this date, Johnson was dead, and Boswell now devoted himself for many years to his magnificent biography of the Doctor, though he also found time to contribute essays to the *London Magazine*. *The Life of Samuel Johnson*, first published in 1791, established him as a major author in his own right.

Boucicault, Dion (1820–90) At the age of twenty-one, Dionysius Lardner Boucicault (originally Boursiquot) launched himself on an extremely successful career as a playwright with his comedy, *London Assurance*. He was born in Dublin, the son of a French father and an Irish mother, but thought of himself as Irish, and used an Irish background for many of his plays. He was an extremely prolific dramatist, popular on both sides of the Atlantic, and he had a considerable success in the United States with, among other plays, *The Colleen Bawn*, produced in 1860, and his adaptation of *Rip Van Winkle*, first seen in 1865.

Bowdler, Thomas (1754–1825) Born near Bath, England, Thomas Bowdler is celebrated as the author of *The Family Shakespeare*, from which he excised all those parts 'which cannot with propriety be read aloud in a family'. His motives were undoubtedly sincere, and his work was much appreciated in the nineteenth century. Bowdler's name is now celebrated in the verb 'to bowdlerize', usually used contemptuously of the expurgation in a literary work of passages which the prudish may consider indelicate or offensive.

Bowen, Elizabeth (1899–1973) Dublin-born Elizabeth Dorothea Cole Bowen was a highly-regarded novelist, short story writer and critic. In 1923 she published a volume of short stories, *Encounters*, and her first novel, *The Hotel*, came out in 1927. Altogether, she published some twenty books, including her *Collected Stories* in 1980. The most celebrated of her novels are *The Death of the Heart*, which appeared in 1938, and *The Heat of the Day*, first published in 1949. All her work is noted for the excellence and sensitivity of her prose, and her skill in portraying human relationships.

Bowles, Paul (1910–) Paul Bowles, who was born in New York and educated at the University of Virginia, began his career as a musician and composer before deciding to dedicate himself to writing. He had published some poetry many years earlier, but his first important work, a novel called *The Sheltering Sky*, appeared in 1949. Other novels followed, including *Let It Come Down* and *The Spider's House*, published in 1984 and 1985 respectively. He has also edited and translated a number of accounts of their lives by residents of Morocco, where he lives, and has published poetry and short stories. *Their Heads Are Green*, a travel book, appeared in 1985.

Bradbury, Malcolm (1932–) The respected English academic Malcolm Stanley Bradbury was born in Sheffield and educated at Leicester, London and Manchester universities. He has written a number of works of literary criticism, and has had considerable success as a novelist, particularly in books such as *Eating People is Wrong*, *Stepping Westward* and *The History Man*, with their satirical portraits of university life. A novella, *Cuts*, was published in 1987.

Bradbury, Ray (1920–) Born in Waukegan, Illinois, Ray Douglas Bradbury is one of the foremost practitioners of science fiction, or, more properly, fantasy. His stories, included in such collections as *The Martian Chronicles*, *The Illustrated Man* and *The Golden Apples of the Sun*, all published in the 1950s, are marked not only by the brilliance of his imagination, but by a rich and yet delicate prose style. His novel *Fahrenheit 451*, appearing in 1953, is a powerful indictment of censorship. *Death is a Lonely Business*, his first novel for twenty-three years, was published in 1985.

Braddon, Mary Elizabeth (1837–1915) As recently as the 1920s Mary Elizabeth Braddon was considered a novelist of some importance. She began her career in 1861 with *The Trail of the Serpent*, and many lushly melodramatic novels followed. She is now remembered solely for *Lady Audley's Secret*, thought to be shocking at the time of its publication in 1862, although it was dignified by a favourable review in *The Times*.

Bradford, William (1590–1657) In 1620, William Bradford, a Puritan from Austerfield in Yorkshire, England, sailed to the New World on the *Mayflower*. In the following year he was elected governor of Plymouth Colony in New England, and served in that capacity for some thirty years. He wrote a *History of Plimouth Plantation* covering the years up to 1646, which has been regarded as of enormous historical value. It remained available only in manuscript form until 1856, when the Massachusetts Historical Society published it in their journal.

Bradstreet, Anne (*c*.1612–72) Regarded as America's first woman poet, Anne Bradstreet was born in England, but emigrated in 1630 with her father and her husband and settled in Massachusetts. A collection of her work, published in England without her knowledge and entitled *The Tenth Muse Lately Sprung Up in America*, appeared in 1650. She corrected and added to this edition, and the revised version was issued posthumously in Boston in 1678.

Braine, John (1922–86) The English novelist John Gerard Braine was born in Bradford, England, and his Yorkshire origins were frequently reflected in his work. He achieved instant fame with his first novel, *Room at the Top*, published in 1957, although it is said to have been rejected by no fewer than thirty-eight publishers before its final acceptance. He produced many novels thereafter, his last, published in 1985, being *These Golden Days*.

Bran, The Voyage of Consisting of both prose and verse, *The Voyage of Bran* is an epic of Irish origin and was written in the seventh or eighth century. It tells of a journey to the world below.

Brathwaite, E.K. (1930–) The West Indian poet Edward Kamau Brathwaite was born in Barbados and completed his education at Cambridge, after which he spent some time as a teacher in Ghana. He has published several volumes of poetry, three of which were collected as *The Arrivants, a New World Trilogy*, which first appeared in 1973. A more recent collection, *X-Self*, was published in 1986. Brathwaite is seen as a major exponent of Caribbean culture.

Brave New World A novel by Aldous Huxley, in which he examines the situation of the individual in a future world where everything is scientifically controlled. It was first published in 1932.

Brecht, Bertolt (1898–1956) The leftwing poet and dramatist Bertolt Brecht was born in Bavaria. His plays, experimental in their time and later much imitated, were first seen in Germany in the 1920s. His dramatic effects were achieved with a minimum of traditional theatrical techniques, often with little or no scenery, and using a number of short scenes without any striving for dramatic curtain-lines. He also exploited the dramatic effect of music, and frequently incorporated songs into his plays. His early plays, such as *Baal*, produced in 1922, were quite well received, but it was *The Threepenny Opera*, his version of Gay's *The Beggar's Opera*, with music by Kurt Weill, which brought him real success when it was produced in 1928. *St Joan of the Stockyards* followed in 1929. In the period between 1937 and 1948 Brecht wrote a number of major plays, including *The Life of Galileo*, *The*

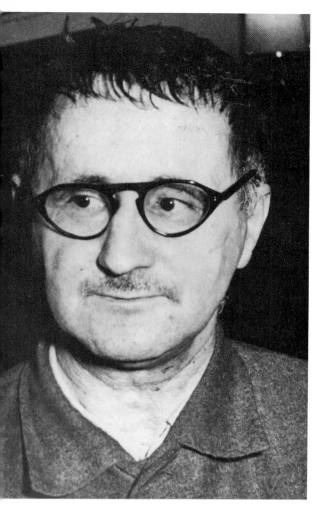

Photograph of the notorious left wing poet and playwright Bertolt Brecht.

Good Woman of Setzuan, Mother Courage, The Caucasian Chalk Circle and *The Resistible Rise of Arturo Ui*, and it was these works which confirmed his reputation as one of the leading dramatists of the twentieth century. Having spent several years in the United States, he returned to East Berlin in 1949, where he set up his own theatrical company, the Berliner Ensemble. In that year he published an essay, *Little Treatise on the Theatre*, in which he set forth his theories. Their influence on contemporary dramatists has been very considerable indeed.

Breton, Nicholas (*c*.1555–1626) Born in London and educated at Oxford, Nicholas Breton wrote a number of books in many genres, including *Fantastickes*, a collection of short pieces on the Christian festivals, the months and the hours. He is chiefly remembered, however, as the poet-author of *The Passionate Shepheard*, which appeared

in 1604. A number of his lyrics appeared in *Englands Helicon*, an anthology of Elizabethan verse published in 1600.

Bride of Lammermoor, The A novel by Sir Walter Scott, first published in 1819. The story was used by Verdi for his opera *Lucia di Lammermoor*.

Brideshead Revisited A novel by Evelyn Waugh in which the narrator, Charles Ryder, is involved with a decadent Roman Catholic family, the Marchmains, who live in the stately home called Brideshead. It was first published in 1945.

Bridge of San Luis Rey, The The novel which made Thornton Wilder famous when it was published in 1927. It concerns a group of people who die in a disaster in Peru.

Bridges, Robert (1844–1930) The English poet Robert Bridges was born at Walmer, Kent. While at Oxford, he met Gerard Manley Hopkins, and their friendship had a lasting influence on him. He published his first book, *Poems*, in 1873, and for the next thirty years continued to produce volumes of poetry. He also wrote a number of verse dramas and masques on classical themes, and some works of literary criticism. The publication of his *Poetical Works* in 1913 made him widely known, and the following year he was appointed Poet Laureate. During World War I, he edited an anthology, *The Spirit of Man*, published in 1916 and aimed at a war-conscious public. He included some poems by Hopkins, whose executor he was, and in 1918 he published Hopkins' *Poems*, the first complete collection of his friend's work. Bridges brought out more collections of his own verse in 1920 and 1925, and *The Testament of Beauty*, a long philosophical poem, finally brought him major popular acclaim in 1929.

Bridie, James (1888–1951) James Bridie was the pseudonym of Osborne Henry Mavor, a doctor born in Glasgow who became a popular playwright, although his work was sometimes experimental in approach. His first success was with *The Anatomist* in 1930, and over the next twenty years or so he produced many plays in varying styles. Among them are *Tobias and the Angel*, *A Sleeping Clergyman* and *Daphne Laureola*.

Brighton Rock A novel by Graham Greene, probably his best-known work, in the genre which the author classifies as 'entertainments'. It was first published in 1938.

Brink, André (1935–) A South African novelist, André Philippus Brink was educated in Potschefstroom and at the Sorbonne. He is much admired for the anti-apartheid content of his novels, including *Looking on Darkness*, published in 1974, *A Chain of Voices*, in 1982, *The Wall of the Plague*, in 1984, and, in 1985, *The Ambassador*.

Brittain, Vera (1893–1970) Vera Mary Brittain became well-known as the result of the publications in 1933 of *Testament of Youth*, in which she related her struggles to achieve a university education and her experiences in France during World War I. A later book, *Testament of Friendship*, recorded her association with the novelist Winifred Holtby. In more recent times, interest in her writings has been greatly increased because of her feminist views.

broadside A large sheet of paper printed on one side only, used from the earliest days of printing for many official documents, and, particularly in the sixteenth and seventeenth centuries, for ballads, poems and other literary work, and also for political propaganda. The term 'broadsheet' has the same meaning.

Bromfield, Louis (1896–1956) Born in Ohio, Louis Bromfield published his first novel, *The Green Bay Tree*, in 1924. It was the first volume of a trilogy, completed by *Possession*, which appeared in 1925, and *Early Autumn*, which won the Pulitzer Prize in 1926. Among his other very successful novels were *The Rains Came*, in 1937, *Wild is the River*, in 1941, and *Bitter Lotus*, in 1945. He also published several collections of short stories.

Brontë, Anne (1820–49) The youngest of the Brontë children, Anne was born some three months before the family moved to Haworth, at Thornton, near Bradford, England, where the Revd. Patrick Brontë held a curacy. Her four older sisters were sent to the Clergy Daughters' School at Cowan Bridge, but after the deaths of Maria and Elizabeth in 1824, the remaining three girls were mainly educated at home. They were encouraged in their attempts to write and soon began to produce tiny booklets of stories, poetry and essays, inventing imaginary countries as the background to much of this work. Perhaps because Emily was closest to Anne in age, their relationship was particularly warm, and together they developed the country called Gondal. In 1835, Anne went as a pupil to Miss Wooler's school at Roe Head, where Charlotte was a governess. She herself became a family governess in 1839, not returning to live at Haworth until 1845. At this time, following a suggestion from Charlotte, the three sisters collected together their poetry and paid some fifty pounds for it to be published under the title *Poems, by Currer, Ellis and Acton Bell*. Anne contributed twenty-one verses to the collection. Only two copies of the poems were sold, but this did not discourage the sisters. Each of them had also written a novel, and they began to submit their work to London publishers. Anne's novel, *Agnes Grey*, was eventually accepted by T.C. Newby, and was published in December, 1847, again with the use of the pseudonym Acton Bell. She had by then completed a second novel, *The Tenant of Wildfell Hall*, and this was published six months later in June, 1848. Meanwhile, Charlotte Brontë's *Jane Eyre* had been wildly successful, and Newby attempted to delude the reading public into believing that Anne's two novels and Emily Brontë's *Wuthering Heights* were all by Charlotte. In the summer of 1848, Charlotte and Anne travelled to London in order to establish their separate identities. The death of Branwell Brontë in September of that year was followed, shortly before Christmas, by that of Emily. Soon afterwards, the gentle, reserved Anne also became seriously ill. In May, 1849, Charlotte accompanied her to Scarborough, where the sea air was supposed to be particularly efficacious, but four days after their arrival Anne died. Anne Brontë's position in English literature is a somewhat curious one: her work cannot be considered as great as that of her sisters, and she is overshadowed by them. Her eminence as a novelist is in part due to the fact that she is the third member of an astonishing family of literary genius, but the quality of her writing is such that, even without that qualification, she would undoubtedly still be remembered and read as an author of genuine and individual talent, whose portrayals of characters and social backgrounds of the period have considerable vitality.

Brontë, Charlotte (1816-55) Charlotte Brontë was born in Thornton, near Bradford, England, but lived at Haworth from the age of four. In 1824 she went with her sisters, Maria, Elizabeth and Emily, to the Clergy Daughters' School at Cowan Bridge, but returned in the following year to Haworth, and completed most of her education at home. When the young Brontës wrote their juvenile stories, essays and poems – all in minute writing in miniature books – Charlotte joined with Branwell to create the imaginary country, Angria. At the age of sixteen she attended Miss Margaret Wooler's school at Roe Head, Dewsbury, and there met her lifelong friends, Mary Taylor and Ellen Nussey, with whom she corresponded until her death. Leaving the school after a year, she went back to Haworth to help her aunt, Elizabeth Branwell, in the education of the younger children, but in 1835 became a governess, or teacher, at Miss Wooler's school, staying there for three years. Returning to Haworth, she received two offers of marriage, from her friend Ellen Nussey's brother, Henry, and from a curate called Bryce. She rejected both, and became a nursery

Oil painting by Patrick Brontë of his famous literary sisters Anne, Emily and Charlotte (*left to right*), c.1834. Painted when he was only seventeen, it is the only known portrait of the three sisters together. Unlike his sisters, Patrick never fulfilled his artistic promise, but found his escape in drug- and alcohol-induced delirium.

governess, but this did not satisfy her ambitions, and, in the hope eventually of opening a school of her own, she went with Emily to Belgium in 1842 with the object of increasing her proficiency in languages, studying at the Pensionnat Héger in Brussels. Later that year the two girls had to return to Haworth because of the death of their aunt, but Charlotte then resumed her stay at the Pensionnat Héger, partly because she wanted to continue her studies, but also, perhaps, because she had fallen in love with M. Héger. She spent the following year there as a governess, returning home in 1844. Elizabeth Branwell had left sufficient money for the sisters to remain at their father's vicarage without needing to earn a living, but they discussed the possibility of opening a school in their home. This did not materialize, and in 1845 their joint literary aspirations began

to play a more prominent part in their lives. All three sisters had written poetry, and Charlotte, particularly recognizing the undoubted quality of Emily's work, persuaded Emily and Anne to join her in paying for the publication of *Poems, by Currer, Ellis and Acton Bell*, to which Charlotte contributed nineteen verses. The book appeared in 1846. It was a failure, but the three sisters were soon seeking publishers for their novels. Both Emily and Anne received acceptances, while Charlotte's work, *The Professor*, was rejected. One of the publishers, Smith, Elder & Company, was, however, sufficiently impressed by *The Professor* to ask to see a longer work. Charlotte had already written *Jane Eyre*, which was quickly accepted, and published with great success in October, 1847. In the following year, Charlotte went with Anne to London (*see* entry for Anne

Brontë), and this visit was followed shortly by the deaths of Branwell, Emily and Anne. After returning from Scarborough, where Anne had been buried, Charlotte completed her new novel, *Shirley*, which was published in 1849. Although still using the pseudonym of Currer Bell, Miss Charlotte Brontë became much sought after, and met many of the literary lions of the day, including Mrs Gaskell, who was later to write her biography. A third novel, *Villette*, appeared in 1853. The following year she married her father's curate, the Revd. Arthur Bell Nicholls, but died after less than a year of marriage, from an illness believed to have been connected with pregnancy. Charlotte Brontë's work is marked by its intensity and its individuality. *Jane Eyre*, although the prototype for the modern so-called Gothic romance, is written with passionate realism. It has remained popular for close on a hundred and fifty years, and its author, Charlotte Brontë, must certainly be ranked among the greatest novelists writing in the English language.

A delicate chalk drawing by George Richmond of the renowned English novelist Charlotte Brontë, whose novel *Jane Eyre* set the genre for modern Gothic romance.

A portrait of Emily Brontë by her brother Patrick.

Brontë, Emily (1818–48) Born, as were her sisters Charlotte and Anne, at Thornton, near Bradford, England, Emily Jane Brontë moved with the rest of the family to Haworth, of which parish her father was the perpetual incumbent, in 1820. After a brief period at the School for Clergy Daughters at Cowan Bridge, she was largely educated at home by her aunt, Elizabeth Branwell, later assisted by Charlotte. In the sisters' early writing, Emily collaborated with Anne in the creation of the imaginary country Gondal, which later featured in some of her finest poetry. At the age of seventeen, she spent a few months at Miss Wooler's school at Roe Head, Dewsbury, where Charlotte was teaching, and in 1842 accompanied her sister to Belgium to study languages at the Pensionnat Héger, but because of the death of her aunt was there for a few months only. She also worked briefly as a governess, but almost all her life was passed at Haworth, and she loved her home and the surrounding countryside with great intensity. In 1845, Charlotte, rightly impressed by Emily's poetry, proposed the publication of *Poems, by Currer, Ellis and Acton Bell*, which included twenty-one of Emily's verses. The failure of the book fortunately did not discourage any of the sisters from seeking publishers for their novels. They did not immediately place the books, though Charlotte found more difficulty in this respect than either Emily or Anne, both of whom eventually received acceptances from T.C. Newby. However, Newby proved to be slow-moving, and Charlotte's book, *Jane Eyre* by Currer Bell, was actually published two months before Anne's *Agnes Grey* by Acton Bell, and Emily's *Wuthering Heights* by Ellis Bell. *Wuthering Heights* was not very well received, though the soaring reputation of Currer Bell helped to avoid a complete disaster. Indeed, Newby tried at one time to pretend that both *Wuthering Heights* and *Agens Grey* were by Currer Bell, and Charlotte and Anne were forced to go to London in the summer of 1848 to establish the sisters' separate identities. Emily did not accompany them, perhaps because she was looking after her brother, Branwell, who died in September of that year, or perhaps because she was too ill with the tuberculosis which caused her own death in December 1848. However much *Wuthering Heights* may have been misunderstood and underrated at the time of its publication, it is now seen as one of the greatest masterpieces in the English language. It is a work of great passion, powerful and grim in the atmosphere of tragedy which pervades it, yet both truthful and tender in its romance. Emily Brontë must be regarded as the pre-eminent member of her remarkable literary family, both for this superb novel, and also for the quality of her verse, which is much finer than that of Charlotte or Anne, and which indeed ranks her among the most inspired of poets.

Brontës, The The three illustrious Brontë sisters, Charlotte, Emily and Anne (*see* separate entries), were the daughters of the Revd. Patrick Brontë

Thornton Vicarage, Bradford, the birthplace of the Brontë sisters, Emily, Charlotte and Anne, who are among the most famous English nineteenth-century novelists.

and his wife Maria, née Branwell. Patrick Brontë came of peasant stock, and although his wife was of a higher social class, there was little to suggest that they would produce children of such extraordinary ability. They were married at Hartshead, in Yorkshire, and their first two children, Maria and Elizabeth, were born there. Patrick Brontë then removed to Thornton, where the other four children of the family were born. In 1820, he accepted the living of Haworth, near Keighley in Yorkshire, where he and his children lived for the rest of their lives. His wife Maria Brontë died in 1821, and her unmarried sister, Elizabeth Branwell, came to Haworth to look after the six Brontë offspring. Maria and Elizabeth died in childhood, possibly as the result of poor food and harsh treatment at their school, although a constitutional weakness in the family may have been at fault. Charlotte and Emily were withdrawn from the same school, and from 1825 the remaining Brontë children were largely educated at home by their aunt, who encouraged them in their literary aspirations. The only son, Branwell, had some artistic talent, and was sent in 1835 to study at the Royal Academy. After a month he returned home, continued his studies for a short time in Leeds, and, with brief interludes as a tutor and a railway booking clerk, spent the rest of his life in dissipation. A wastrel and a drunkard, he died in 1848 at the age of thirty-one. The Revd. Patrick Brontë outlived all his children, surviving until 1861.

Brooke, Rupert (1887–1915) Rupert Chawner Brooke was born at Rugby, England, and educated at Cambridge. He started writing poetry while still at school, and his first collection of poems, published in 1911, immediately established his reputation. That same year, he made his home at The Old Vicarage, Grantchester, but the much quoted poem of that name was in fact written in Berlin in 1912. On the outbreak of World War I, he joined the Royal Navy as an officer. In December 1914 he completed his five 'War Sonnets', which include the celebrated 'The Soldier'

If I should die, think only this of me:
That there's some corner of a foreign field
That is forever England …

In April 1915, he was sent to the Dardanelles. Falling ill with acute blood poisoning while on the island of Scyros, he was transferred to a French hospital ship, but died two days later. A few volumes of his work, including *1914 and other poems*, were published after his death.

Brook Kerith, The A novel by George Moore, first published in 1916.

Brookner, Anita (1938–) Professor Anita Brookner is an international authority on eighteenth- and nineteenth-century painting. She has written a number of novels, including *A Start in Life*, published in 1981, *Hotel du Lac*, which won the Booker Prize in 1984, and *Family and Friends*, which appeared in 1985.

Brophy, Brigid (1929-) Brigid Antonia Brophy, daughter of the novelist John Brophy, is primarily known as a novelist, although she has also written non-fiction books, including biographies of Aubrey Beardsley and Ronald Firbank. Among her novels are *Hackenfeller's Ape*, first published in 1953, and *The Snow Ball*, 1962.

Brothers Karamazov, The A novel by Fyodor Dostoevsky, first published in 1880, and concerned with the hatred of the brothers Ivan, Dmitri and Alyosha for their father, and the latter's murder by their half-brother Smerdyakov.

Brown, Charles Brockden (1771–1810) Born in Philadelphia, Charles Brockden Brown is considered to have been the first professional American author, and the first to set his novels in America. In 1797 he published *The Dialogue of Alcuin*, an essay on the subject of women's rights. He wrote six novels, of which the first four, *Wieland; or the Transformation*, *Arthur Mervyn; or Memoirs of the Year*, *Ormond* and *Edgar Huntly*, are the best known. These books, which came out between 1798 and 1801, are all Gothic in character.

Browne, Charles Farrar (1834–67) Charles Farrar Browne, who was born in Maine, was a humorist who wrote under the pen name Artemus Ward. His books, such as *Artemus Ward: His Travels*, first published in 1865, were very popular on both sides of the Atlantic. In 1866, he went to live in London, where he became editor of *Punch*. He died in England of consumption the following year.

Browne, Hablôt Knight (1815–82) The English artist Hablôt Knight Browne was born in London. He made his reputation with his illustrations for *The Pickwick Papers*. Using the pseudonym 'Phiz', he produced drawings for many other books by Dickens, and for the work of other authors, including Robert Surtees and William Ainsworth.

Browne, Thomas (1605–82) Born in London, the philosopher and moralist Thomas Browne was educated at Winchester and Oxford, and received his Doctorate of Medicine at Leiden University. He married in 1641 and fathered a large family. His first book, *Religio Medici*, was published in 1642, and this was followed in 1646 by *Pseudodoxia Epidemica*. His other works include *Urn Burial*, published in 1658. A committed Royalist, he was knighted in 1671 by King Charles II.

Browning, Elizabeth Barrett (1806–61) Elizabeth Barrett was the eldest daughter in a large family. The picture of her father, Edward Moulton Barrett, given in the well-known play *The Barretts of Wimpole Street*, is far from accurate. He was in fact a kindly man, and held Elizabeth in great affection, an instance of which is the fact that he had fifty copies printed of her childhood work, *The Battle of Marathon*, written when she was no more than eleven or twelve. *Essay on Mind and other poems*, dating from her teens, did not appear in print until 1826, and her first adult book, a translation of *Prometheus Bound* by Aeschylus, was published together with some poems in 1833. Her poetry began to appear regularly in various periodicals, and *The Seraphim and other poems* followed in 1838, by which time Elizabeth Barrett had become involved in English literary life, meeting and corresponding with many authors of the day, including Miss Mitford, Wordsworth and Harriet Martineau. Her *Poems*, published in 1844, brought her considerable acclaim, both in England and in America, and in the following year she received her first letter from Robert Browning. The Barretts were now living in London, in Wimpole Street, and although Elizabeth had become an invalid, she

The poetess Elizabeth Browning by Michele Gordigiani.

was able to receive visitors, and Browning began to call upon her regularly. Their mutual admiration rapidly changed to love, and she eventually accepted his proposal of marriage. Despite her father's kindly attitude, he was strangely opposed, sometimes violently, to the idea that his children should marry, and Elizabeth's wedding to Robert Browning, possible in September 1846 since her health had by then improved, had therefore to be a secret one. Mr Barrett never forgave her. One week after the marriage, the Brownings left for Italy, where they spent the whole of their married life, apart from a few brief visits to England and France. While in Pisa that winter, Robert discovered his wife's *Sonnets from the Portuguese*, and insisted that they should be published. They appeared in 1847, and were later included in a new collection of *Poems*. The Brownings' son, Robert Wiedemann Barrett, was born in 1849. In 1853, Elizabeth began to write her major work, *Aurora Leigh*, which was completed in 1855 and published in 1857. This poem had an immediate popular success, and was reprinted several times. Mrs Browning had espoused a number of causes, chief among them the unification of Italy, and in 1860 she attacked the United States on the subject of slavery in her *Poems Before Congress*, which was less successful than her other work. Elizabeth Barrett Browning died in her husband's arms in 1861. Her *Last Poems* appeared in 1862. The high regard in which she was held during her lifetime is exemplified in the fact that her name was canvassed as the successor to Wordsworth as Poet Laureate. She did not receive that honour, and later generations have judged her work with less enthusiasm than did her contemporaries. Nevertheless, much of her poetry, especially the *Sonnets from the Portuguese*, is admirable in its ardour.

A bronze cast by Harriet Homer of the right hand of Elizabeth Browning clasping that of her husband, Robert.

Robert Browning by Michele Gordigiani. A series of dramatic dialogues, *The Ring and the Book*, re-established him in the literary world and is considered to be his masterpiece.

Browning, Robert (1812–89) Although he was born into a fairly well-to-do London family, Robert Browning received little formal education, leaving school at the age of fourteen. However, his father, an employee of the Bank of England, was a man of literary and artistic leanings who owned an extensive library, and he encouraged the boy to read widely. From a very early age, Robert had dabbled with verse, and by the age of twelve had put together a volume of poems under the title *Incondita*. His admiring parents tried, although without success, to get it published, and were clearly not surprised, and indeed were ready with their support, when the young man later announced that he did not wish to become a clerk in the Bank, but intended instead to make a career as a poet. It was not until 1833 that Browning succeeded in appearing in print with a poem called *Pauline*, but two years later, after he had spent some time in travel in Europe, *Paracelsus* brought him critical acclaim and he was accepted into the literary circles of the time. The actor Macready persuaded him to write for the theatre, and over the next few years he brought out a number of dramas, the first of which, *Strafford*, was produced in 1837. The plays were not particularly successful, and Browning's reputation was further, and quite substantially, diminished by the publication in 1840 of *Sordello*, the obscurity of which was much criticized. Between 1841 and 1846 a series of pamphlets followed (almost the equivalent of first publication in softcover form today) under the general title, *Bells and Pomegranates*. In these were included some of the dramas and also many of the poems which came to be regarded as among his most popular works, such as 'Pippa Passes', 'The Pied Piper of Hamelin' and 'Home Thoughts from Abroad'. In 1845 Browning met Elizabeth Barrett, having previously corresponded with her, and fell deeply in love. The fifteen years which they spent together, living in Italy, did not result in great literary productivity on Browning's part, but the marriage was an extremely happy one, and he apparently accepted without rancour the fact that Elizabeth's work was more greatly admired than his own. He published *Christmas Eve and Easter Day* in 1850, and the two volumes

An imaginative Kate Greenaway illustration of Robert Browning's famous dramatic poem 'The Pied Piper of Hamelin'. This poem has become one of his most popular works and dramatic adaptations are often enacted.

And the muttering grew to a grumbling ;
And the grumbling grew to a mighty rumbling ;
And out of the houses the rats came tumbling.
Great rats, small rats, lean rats, brawny rats,
Brown rats, black rats, grey rats, tawny rats,
Grave old plodders, gay young friskers,

of *Men and Women*, which included 'Fra Lippo Lippi', 'Childe Roland to the Dark Tower Came' and 'Andrea del Sarto', in 1855, and these books clearly demonstrated the gradual maturing of his talents, although his genius was by no means recognized and his work was still not truly popular. After Elizabeth's death in 1861, Browning returned to England, and in 1864 published *Dramatis Personae*. This met with some success, but it was the publication of the four volumes of *The Ring and The Book*, in 1868 and 1869, which regained for him to the full the public favour he had lost as the result of *Sordello*. Between this time and his death twenty years later, he brought out sixteen other books, mostly volumes of poetry, but also including his celebrated version of the *Agamemnon* of Aeschylus. Several collections of his earlier work also appeared. Overshadowed during her lifetime by his wife, he was now greatly admired by his literary contemporaries, many of whom became his personal friends, and by an enthusiastic readership. He was granted honorary degrees by Oxford, Cambridge and Edinburgh universities. Having refused to visit Italy for seventeen years after Elizabeth's death, he was at last persuaded to return when his son, the only child of the marriage, settled in Venice. It was there, during his visit, that Robert Browning died. His poetry is unique. In whatever style he wrote – whether in the highly dramatic narratives, or in the fanciful or didactic poems, or in the gentler lyrics – Browning was concerned to present the human condition in all its manifestations. He did so with great strength and insight, and much of his poetry is of the very highest order.

Brownjohn, Alan (1931–) The poet Alan Charles Brownjohn was born in London and educated at Oxford. He published his first poetry in 1954, a small collection under the title *Travellers Alone*. Many other volumes have been published since, and he eventually became sufficiently successful to abandon his career as a teacher and devote himself to writing. His *Collected Poems 1952–83* appeared in 1983.

Brunanburh This verse account of the Battle of Brunanburh, written in Old English, is the most important of the poems included in the *Anglo-Saxon Chronicle*. It consists of a little over a hundred and twenty lines. The battle took place in the year 937, when the English defeated a combined force of Danes, Scots and Welsh.

Bryant, William Cullen (1794–1878) The American poet William Cullen Bryant was born at Cummington, Massachusetts. He overcame the handicap of a sketchy education to qualify as an attorney, but in 1825 he abandoned the law for journalism, becoming editor and owner of the *Evening Post*, New York, from 1829 until just before his death. His poem *Thanatopsis*, written while he was still in his teens, was first published in 1817 and immediately attracted notice. He published several volumes of verse, including two selections of *Poems*, in 1821 and 1832, and his *Poetical Works* in 1876. He also made verse translations of Homer's *Iliad* and *Odyssey*.

Buchan, John (1875–1940) The future Baron Tweedsmuir, Governor General of Canada, was born in Perth, Scotland, the son of a clergyman. While at Brasenose College, Oxford, John Buchan won the Newdigate Prize for a poem on 'The Pilgrim Fathers', and by the time he was twenty he had published his first novel, *Sir Quixote of the Moors*. Despite a busy and impressive diplomatic career, he wrote poems, essays, biographies and other works of non-fiction, but as an author he is chiefly remembered for a large number of bestselling adventure novels, including *Prester John*, first published in 1910, and the stories featuring Richard Hannay, of which the most famous is *The Thirty-Nine Steps*, published in 1915.

Buchanan, George (1506–82) Born in Killearn, Scotland, George Buchanan was educated at the universities of St Andrews and Paris. Returning to Scotland, he was engaged by James V of Scotland as a tutor to one of his bastard sons, and later was tutor both to Mary, Queen of Scots, whose bitter enemy he became following the murder of Darnley, and to James VI. Considered one of the great Scottish scholars, Buchanan wrote much verse, two tragedies, and a number of imaginative translations from Latin and Greek. His two major works were a libertarian treatise on the relationship between a monarch and his subjects, *De Jure Regni apud Scotos*, published in 1579, and *Rerum Scoticarum Historia*, his huge history of Scotland, which appeared in the year of his death.

Büchner, Georg (1813–37) The German dramatist Georg Büchner, who was born near Darmstadt, was the son of a doctor, and himself successfully pursued a medical career. However, he became much involved in political struggles, which inspired him to write plays. The first of these was *Danton's Death*, produced in 1835. His most famous play, *Woyzeck* was not published until 1879, and received its first performance in 1913. It was the basis of Alban Berg's opera *Wozzeck*.

Buck, Pearl (1892–1973) Pearl Sydenstricker Buck, who came from Hillsboro, West Virginia, wrote many very successful novels set in China, where she lived and worked as a missionary. Her first novel, *East Wind, West Wind*, appeared in 1930.

Nobel Prize-winning authoress Pearl Buck at a Senate Committee hearing on the future use of Ellis Island.

The Good Earth, first published in 1931, was awarded the Pulitzer Prize, and was the first volume in the trilogy, 'The House of Earth', the others being *Sons* and *A House Divided*, published in 1932 and 1935 respectively. Pearl Buck won the Nobel Prize for Literature in 1938.

Bulwer-Lytton, Edward (1803–73) Born in London and educated at Cambridge, Edward George Earle Bulwer-Lytton was the youngest son of General William Bulwer and his wife Elizabeth, née Lytton. While still at school, he published a volume of verse, *Ishmael and other poems*, and followed it with other collections, which he later disowned as juvenilia. In 1827 he published a novel, *Falkland*. It was not a great success, but it was the first in a long list of books, and before long, adding his mother's surname to his own, Bulwer-Lytton had become a very well established novelist and playwright, and had also launched himself into journalism. He combined his busy literary career with that of a politician, and rose to become Secretary for the Colonies. He was created first Baron Lytton of Knebworth in 1866. Bulwer-Lytton's best-known works were his novels *Eugene Aram*, first published in 1832, *The Last Days of Pompeii*, in 1834, and *The Last of the Barons*, in 1843. Greatly differing literary views were held about him during his lifetime: Thackeray and Tennyson were among his harshest critics, while Dickens was the most eminent of his admirers. He is no longer taken seriously, and few of his books are still read, but he is perhaps still remembered for the opening line ('It was a dark and stormy night') of his novel, *Paul Clifford*.

Ivan Bunin, the Nobel Prize-winning poet and novelist, with his wife in Paris, his home after leaving Russia.

Bunin, Ivan Alekseevich (1870–1953) The Russian novelist and poet Ivan Alekseevich Bunin was born of a well-to-do family in Voronezh. He published a number of works of various kinds in the 1890s, and increased his reputation in the years up to the Russian Revolution, especially with such books as *The Gentleman from San Francisco*. Appalled at the new regime in Russia, he sought exile in France, where he lived until his death. *The Life of Arsenev*, which he published in 1927, is perhaps his most important novel. He was the first Russian to be awarded the Nobel Prize for Literature, which he won in 1933.

Bunyan, John (1628–88) The son of a tinker, John Bunyan was born near Bedford, England. A Puritan by inclination rather than upbringing, he enlisted and fought in the Parliamentary army during the Civil War. He returned home in 1646, and married his first wife two years later. As a result of reading the pious books which she brought with her as her dowry, he became so deeply interested in religion as to bring himself to the verge of insanity. After his wife's death in 1656, he joined St John's, a Baptist church in Bedford, where he began to preach. Following the Restoration in 1660, he was arrested for preaching without a licence, and spent the next twelve years in Bedford jail. While there, he wrote the autobiographical *Grace Abounding to the*

Chief of Sinners, first published in 1666, as well as a number of other books and tracts. He may also have begun, during this incarceration, the work for which he has been renowned for three hundred years and more, *The Pilgrim's Progress*. It was certainly partly written during a second, much shorter, period of imprisonment in 1676 – again punishment for a religious misdemeanour – and the first part of the book appeared in 1678. It was immediately hugely successful, in America as well as in Britain, and Bunyan became famous, enormous crowds gathering whenever he preached. He clearly had to write more equally moral works, and in 1680 brought out *The Life and Death of Mr Badman*, followed in 1682 by *The Holy War*, while *The Pilgrim's Progress* was completed in 1684 with the second part of the book.

Bunyan's Dream, depicting John Bunyan dreaming of his famous religious epic about man's battle against temptation.

Anthony Burgess, whose talent for writing in many styles has made him one of the most widely-read modern authors.

Burgess, Anthony (1917–) John Anthony Burgess Wilson was born in Manchester, England, and educated at the University of Manchester. He served as an education officer in Malaya and Borneo for a period beginning in 1954, and during that time wrote three novels, which together form 'The Malayan Trilogy'. These are *Time for a Tiger*, first published in 1956, *The Enemy in the Blanket*, 1958, and *Beds in the East*, 1959. *A Clockwork Orange* appeared in 1962, and later became a disturbing film. Burgess has written many other novels, including *The Piano Players*, published in 1986, and those which he brings out under the pseudonym of Joseph Kell (he once caused considerable controversy by favourably reviewing, as Anthony Burgess, one of the Kell novels). The long novel *Earthly Powers* brought him a major success in 1980. He has also written scripts for radio and television, and a number of books in other genres, among them *The Kingdom of the Wicked*, an epic account of the martyrdoms and triumphs of the early Christians contrasted with the depravities of Ancient Rome, and *Flame Into Being: the Life and Work of D.H. Lawrence*, both published in 1985. The first volume of his autobiography, *Little Wilson and Big God*, was published in 1987. He is also a highly respected literary reviewer.

Burke, Edmund (1729–97) Born in Dublin, the son of a Catholic mother and a Protestant father, Edmund Burke was educated at Trinity College, Dublin, and then went to London to follow his father's calling as a lawyer. However, he was more interested in writing and in politics, and in 1756 he published a satire, *A Vindication of Natural Society*, and an essay, *Philosophical Inquiry into the Origin of our Ideas on the Sublime and Beautiful*. In 1759, with the support of the footman-turned-publisher, Robert Dodsley, he set up *The Annual Register*, a review of the main trends of each year, and contributed to it for close on half a century. His involvement in the literary and artistic life of London brought him the friendship of Dr Johnson, Oliver Goldsmith and Sir Joshua Reynolds, among others. In 1765 Burke became a Member of Parliament, and from the start of his political career he was both prominent and influential. He supported the aspirations of the American colonies for freedom from British rule, and similarly believed in independence for Ireland; he campaigned vigorously on behalf of William Wilberforce in his efforts to end the slave trade; he fought to free India from the control of the East India Company and was the chief prosecutor in the impeachment of Warren Hastings, the first Governor-General of British India; and he

Sir Joshua Reynold's portrait of Edmund Burke.

worked to reduce the power of the throne over Parliament. He wrote and published a considerable body of work, much of it in the form of pamphlets and transcriptions of his speeches. The pamphlet *Thoughts on the Cause of the Present Discontents*, appearing in 1770, expounds the arguments against a dictatorial monarchy with great eloquence, and is a fine example of Burke's mastery of his subject and the powerful effect of his style. His most celebrated work, *Reflections on the Revolution in France*, appeared in 1790, and caused a sensation with its condemnation of the French Revolution. That a man of strong anti-monarchical views should have taken such an attitude is explained mainly by his fear of the possible excesses of the Revolution's radical and atheist leaders. Many critics attacked him, notably Thomas Paine with his *The Rights of Man*, but Burke did not waver in his beliefs, even when they cost him the lifelong friendship of his fellow Whig Charles Fox. Of Edmund Burke Dr Johnson said, 'Burke, Sir, is such a man that if you met him for the first time in the street, where you were stopped by a drove of oxen, and you and he stepped aside to take shelter but for five minutes, he'd talk to you in such a manner that when you parted you would say "This is an extraordinary man". To Dr Johnson's judgment can be added the fact that Burke is widely regarded as one of the greatest names in the history of political literature.

Burnet, Gilbert (1643–1715) The historian Gilbert Burnet, who was born in Edinburgh, was a brilliant and precocious scholar. He entered the Church in 1661, and after a period in exile in Holland eventually became Bishop of Salisbury. He wrote a number of devotional works, and spent much time on his *History of the Reformation in England*, the three parts of which were published in 1679, 1681 and 1715. His *History of His Own Time*, his most important work, consists of two volumes of memoirs, which, in accordance with instructions in his will, were not published until some years after his death.

Burnett, Frances Hodgson (1849–1924) Frances Eliza Hodgson Burnett was born in Manchester, England, but went to the United States with her parents in 1865 and settled in Knoxville, Tennessee. Beginning with stories for magazines, she progressed to novels, her first major success being *That Lass o' Lowries*, published in 1877. Her best-known work is probably *Little Lord Fauntleroy*, which appeared in 1886 and was immensely successful. Most present-day readers find that book absurd, but Mrs Burnett still has many admirers for her children's book, *The Secret Garden*, published in 1910.

The diarist and novelist Fanny Burney, Madame d'Arblay, painted by her cousin Edward Burney.

Burney, Fanny (1752-1840) Frances Burney was born in London, the daughter of the musical historian, Dr Charles Burney, and was brought up in literary and artistic circles. She published her first novel, *Evelina, or the History of a Young Lady's Entrance into the World*, in 1778. It was immediately successful, as was her next book, *Cecilia, or Memoirs of an Heiress*, in 1782. In 1786 Fanny Burney was appointed Second Keeper of the Robes to Queen Charlotte, the wife of George III. This honour proved uncongenial, and she retired from the post in 1791. Two years later she married General D'Arblay, a Frenchman who had sought refuge in England following the Revolution. Her next novel, *Camilla, or a Picture of Youth*, appeared in 1796. She also wrote two unsuccessful plays and a disastrous novel called *The Wanderer; or Female Difficulties*. She spent the last years of her life in editing her father's papers. She is remembered for *Evelina*, and also for her *Diary*, which she began in 1768 and continued for seventy-two years. First published in seven volumes posthumously, the *Diary and Letters of Madame D'Arblay* is a vivid, revealing and fascinating book.

Burns, Robert (1759–96) Scotland's greatest literary figure, Robert Burns, was born at Alloway, Ayrshire, the eldest son of a small farmer. Despite his father's poverty, the boy was given a good education, and it was while he was at school that he began to write poetry. His first book, published in 1786, *Poems, chiefly in the Scottish Dialect*, contained among other verses some of his best-loved work, such as 'To a Mouse', 'To a Daisy', 'The Cotter's Saturday Night' and 'The Twa Dogs'. Until this time Robert's circumstances had continued to be those of poverty, shared with his brother Gilbert. Failing in his desire to marry Jean Armour, he had decided to emigrate, but the success of the book changed his mind. His financial reward from the first edition was slight, but Burns enjoyed his new status as a literary lion, and the second edition, brought out in 1787, provided him with enough money to marry his Jean in the following year and to lease

A romantic portrait of Burns by Alexander Nasmyth, commissioned by William Creech as the basis for an engraving in the Edinburgh edition of *Poems, chiefly in the Scottish dialect*. Proud son of 'a very poor man', Burns became a legend in his own brief lifetime. Revered by the Scots nation as their national poet, his lyrical poetry is largely based on a native ballad tradition.

a farm near Dumfries. His difficulties were not, however, at an end, for the farm turned out to be a poor one, and in 1789 he was glad to abandon farming and accept a post as an excise officer, which brought him first an income of fifty pounds, and later, when he secured a similar but more responsible position, seventy pounds a year. Meanwhile, he had been enrolled as a contributor to a collection of folksongs called *The Scots Musical Museum*, for which he wrote or adapted some two hundred songs, including 'Auld Lang Syne', 'A Red, Red Rose', 'The Banks o' Doon' and 'Scots Wha Hae'. Similarly, in 1792 he contributed about one hundred songs to George Thomson's *Select Collection of Original Scottish Airs with Symphonies and Accompaniments for the Pianoforte and Violin: the poetry by Robert Burns*. For *The Scots Musical Museum* he received, by an arrangement against which he did not argue, no payment, but he was disappointed when his rewards for George Thomson's *Collection* amounted to no more than a painting, a shawl for his wife, and five pounds. The last of his major works, the long poem *Tam O'Shanter*, was published in 1791. Little more literary work was to come from him, and the poems which were published posthumously had mostly been written very much earlier. Burns had always been a philanderer and a carouser, and any money he had ever had, usually disappeared faster than it came. The acclaim he had received in literary circles had largely vanished because he was loud in his championing of the French Revolution, which most of Britain looked at with horror, and he was forced to seek his companionship among the coarse and ill-educated, which in any case he may have preferred. By 1796, the hardships of his childhood, the struggles, both physical and mental, which farming had demanded, and principally perhaps his lifelong dissipations, had together taken their toll, and he died in July of that year. He is remembered still all over the world, and especially on his birthday, January 25th, which the majority of Scots celebrate as 'Burns Night'.

Burnt-Out Case, A A novel by Graham Greene, first published in 1961.

Burroughs, Edgar Rice (1875–1950) Although he was a writer of little literary merit, the American author Edgar Rice Burroughs was undoubtedly inspired in his invention of the eponymous hero of *Tarzan of the Apes*, first published in 1914, a character who, if not immortal, will certainly be a long time dying. Burroughs wrote many books featuring Tarzan, and was also an early practitioner in the field of pulp science fiction.

The Beat Generation novelist William Burroughs seated at his typewriter in his study.

Burroughs, William (1914–) Born in St Louis, William Seward Burroughs, a writer of the Beat Generation, has written a number of novels, some of which are experimental, and almost all of which are concerned with the worlds of homosexuals and drug addicts. Among them are *Junkie*, first published in 1953, *The Naked Lunch*, 1959, and *The Wild Boys*, 1971. His collected essays, *Mind Wars*, appeared in 1985.

Burton, Sir Richard (1821–90) The son of an Irish Army officer, Richard Francis Burton was educated somewhat haphazardly as a child, but later went to Oxford. He left without completing his studies to become an officer in the Indian army. He possessed quite remarkable gifts as a linguist, and during his seven years in India began his serious studies of Oriental tongues. Four books on the province of Sind, where he had been stationed, were published on his return to England. In 1853 he became famous as a result of his journey to Mecca, disguised as a Pathan. He gave an account of this experience in *The Pilgrimage to Al-Medinah and Meccah*, published in 1855. He went next to East Africa as leader of an expedition which, seeking the source of the Nile, discovered Lakes Victoria and Tanganyika. In 1861 he began service with the Foreign Office as Consul in Fernando Po, and subsequently served in that capacity in Santos, Damascus and Trieste. He was knighted in 1885. He wrote over twenty books about his travels, but his fame as a writer rests principally on his translations of the *Arabian Nights Entertainments* and the *Kama Sutra*. Burton made no attempt to expurgate these books, and in deference to the anti-obscenity laws of the period they could be printed only privately. At the time of his death he had been working for many years on a new translation from the Arabic of *The Perfumed Garden*. His wife destroyed the translation together with his other papers.

Burton, Robert (1577–1640) Robert Burton was born at Lindley, Leicestershire, England, the son of a country gentleman, and educated at Oxford. He took holy orders, but appears to have remained an academic rather than a parish priest. His claim to fame is his authorship of *The Anatomy of Melancholy*, first published in 1621.

Title-page to Burton's *The Anatomy of Melancholy*, depicting various states of man, 'Zelotypia', 'Inamorato', 'Superstiosus', 'Solitudo', 'Hypocondriacus', and 'Maniacus' with 'Democritus Abderites' at the top and 'Democritus junior', the author, at the bottom.

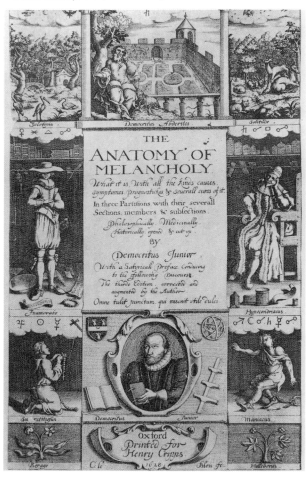

Bussy d'Ambois A tragedy by George Chapman, first published in 1607.

Butler, Samuel (1613–80) Born at Strensham, Worcestershire, England, Samuel Butler was educated at the King's School in Worcester. Having gained some knowledge of the law, he was employed as a secretary by a number of aristocratic families, including that of Sir Samuel Luke, a prominent Puritan and Parliament man. Following the Restoration he was appointed in 1661 as steward of Ludlow Castle, and he married soon after. In 1662, he published *Hudibras: The First Part: written in the Time of the Late Wars*, a verse satire on the Roundheads, no doubt at least partially inspired by his years with Sir Samuel Luke. It was immensely successful, as was indicated by the swift publication of a spurious second part, written by an imitator. Butler produced the genuine second part in 1664. Charles II is said to have showed his approval by gifts of substantial sums of money, and the Duke of Buckingham is believed to have become Butler's patron, but some doubt has always existed on these scores, largely because the poet complained bitterly of his ill-treatment. The third part of *Hudibras* appeared in 1678. Butler's other works, mostly of a minor character, did not appear until 1759, when they were collected in the charmingly titled *The Genuine Remains in Verse and Prose of Mr Samuel Butler*.

Butler, Samuel (1835–1902) Following his education at Shrewsbury and St John's College, Cambridge, Samuel Butler, who was born at Langar, Nottinghamshire, England, intended to follow in his father's footsteps and enter the Church, but a loss of faith prevented him from taking holy orders, and he emigrated to New Zealand in 1859, where he became a sheep farmer. After five reasonably successful years, he returned to England, settled in London, and studied painting. His work was hung with some regularity in Royal Academy exhibitions between 1868 and 1876. In 1872, he published anonymously *Erewhon, or Over the Range*, a romance which satirized both the conventions of religion and the theories of Charles Darwin. He followed it in 1873 with *The Fair Haven*, in which he mocked many Christian beliefs. *Erewhon* had caused a sensation on its publication, and after the appearance in 1877 of *Life and Habit*, the first of his works to appear under his own name, Butler decided to devote himself henceforth to a literary life. He next brought out two books attacking Darwinism, the first, with the resounding title *Evolution Old and New, or the Theories of Buffon, Dr Erasmus Darwin and Lamarck as compared with that of Mr C. Darwin*, being published in

Charles Gogin's grave portrait of satirist Samuel Butler.

1879, while the second, *Unconscious Memory*, appeared in 1880. A third book on the same theme, *Luck or Cunning*, was published in 1886. Butler also produced a number of books on subjects such as art, travel and literature, wrote the words for two oratorios, translated both the *Iliad* and the *Odyssey* into colloquial prose, prepared *The Life and Letters of Dr Samuel Butler*, his grandfather, and suggested, in *Authoress of the Odyssey*, published in 1897, that the Greek epic had been written by a woman, and emanated not from Greece but from Trapani in Sicily. In 1901 *Erewhon Revisited* appeared, again a satire on conventional religion. Butler's most famous book is *The Way of All Flesh*, on which he was still working at the time of his death, having begun it many years previously. The novel, in part based on his own life, was edited by R.A. Streatfield and published posthumously in 1903. *The Notebooks of Samuel Butler* were edited by Henry Festing Jones from a large quantity of material left in rough form and published in 1912. Samuel Butler's reputation has diminished in recent years, his books are not widely read, and his satire is considered heavy-handed. During his lifetime, however, he was seen as an author of startling originality and versatility, who dared to blow a draught of fresh air through the stuffy, smug drawing-rooms of Victorian England, and thereby exercised a major influence on future generations of writers.

Byatt, A.S. (1936–) Antonia Susan Byatt (née Drabble) was born in Sheffield and educated at Newnham College, Cambridge. She published her first novel, *Shadow of a Sun* in 1964. A number of other novels have followed, including *The Virgin in the Garden*, which appeared in 1978 as the first part of a planned trilogy. The second volume in the sequence, *Still Life*, was published in 1985. A.S. Byatt is also a much respected critic.

Byron, Lord (1788–1824) George Gordon Byron was the only child of his father's second marriage. In 1798, on the death of his great-uncle (his father having died some years previously), the boy inherited the family title and estates and became sixth Baron Byron. Born in London, he was educated at Harrow School, and went on from there to Trinity College, Cambridge. While still at university he put together his first volume of poetry, which appeared in 1807 under the title *Hours of Idleness* and was generally well received. In March of 1809 he took his seat in the House of Lords, and set out soon after on a tour through Portugal and Spain, and then on to Albania, Greece and Turkey. Byron was a handsome young man and extremely attractive to women. He seems never to have been much handicapped by his celebrated lameness, although during his childhood he suffered painful attempts to cure it. During his travels he spent a month in Malta making love to a Mrs Spencer Smith, swam the Hellespont, and began to write *Childe Harold's Pilgrimage*, which contains an account of his journeyings. He returned to London in 1811, and early the following year made a brilliant maiden speech in the House of Lords in defence of certain oppressed factory workers. This was followed in March by the publication of the first two cantos of *Childe Harold's Pilgrimage*, which was immediately sensationally successful. Byron embarked on a new series of love affairs – in turn with Lady Caroline Lamb, Lady Oxford and Lady Frances Wedderburn Webster – and also wrote prolifically, *The Curse of Minerva*, *The Giaour*, *The Bride of Abydos*, *The Corsair*, *Lara*, *Jacqueline*, *Hebrew Melodies*, *The Siege of Corinth* and *Parisina* all being published in the space of four years. His work became immensely popular, in America and in Europe as well as in Britain. In January 1915 Byron married Anna Isabella Milbanke, but the marriage lasted barely a year before breaking down, shortly after the birth of his daughter Augusta Ada. In the meantime he had met his half-sister Augusta, who had given birth in 1814 to a child which was widely supposed to be his, and this scandal, added to the failure of his marriage, forced him to leave England in April 1916. He was not to return. He went first to Lake Geneva, where he joined Claire Claremont, who had recently become his mistress and who bore his daughter, Allegra, the following January, and Shelley and his wife. In Switzerland he wrote *The Prisoner of Chillon* and the third canto of *Childe Harold* and began his play, *Manfred*. Moving to Italy, he completed *Manfred* and wrote *Beppo*, the fourth canto of *Childe Harold* and the beginning of *Don Juan*, which was to become his greatest work. All these were successfully published, though he experienced some difficulties with *Don Juan*, which many critics and even some of his friends, found, as Byron himself ruefully said, 'too free for these modest days'. In 1821 he met the Countess Guiccioli, who became his mistress and later left her husband for his sake; the liaison lasted nearly four years, an indication of Byron's devotion to her. He now produced a number of plays, including *The Two Foscari* and *Sardanapalus*, and also wrote additional cantos of *Don Juan*. He had become increasingly interested in the politics of Europe, and at the end of 1823

Thomas Phillip's romantic portrait of the poet Lord Byron. His sensational love affairs caused his exile from England, but it is his poetry for which he is remembered.

he decided to go to Greece to join the struggle against the Turks. Although he provided large sums of money for the cause, he did not, as he had hoped, engage in fighting, and after a few weeks died of fever at Missolonghi in April, 1824. The Greeks still revere Lord Byron as a hero, but his reputation as a rake prevented his burial in Westminster Abbey, and there is no bust of him in Poet's Corner. His memorial is of course his poetry, which is filled with zest for life, humour, and an earthy realism, and clearly reflects the character of its author.

C

Cabell, James Branch (1879–1958) Following his education at William and Mary College, James Branch Cabell, who was born in Richmond, Virginia, became a journalist. He wrote a number of short stories, and published his first novel, *The Eagle's Shadow*, in 1904. This was followed by a great many amusing, mannered and slightly bawdy novels, many of which were set in Poictesme, a medieval country of his own imagining. The most celebrated of these was *Jurgen*, first published in 1919, and considered at the time to be obscene.

Cable, George Washington (1844–1925) A native of New Orleans, George Washington Cable fought for the Confederates in the American Civil War, after which he worked in civil engineering and as a journalist. He published his first book, *Old Creole Days*, a collection of his articles, in 1879. He produced a number of novels with Creole backgrounds, and then in 1884 and 1885 brought out his history, *The Creoles of Louisiana*, and a collection of essays, *The Silent South*, the critical anti-slavery content of which forced him to leave the South and to settle for the rest of his life in New England.

Caesar and Cleopatra A play by G. Bernard Shaw, which he saw as a companion piece to Shakespeare's *Antony and Cleopatra*. It was first published in 1901.

Cain: A Mystery A verse tragedy by Lord Byron, based on the story in *Genesis*. It was considered blasphemous when it was first published in 1821.

Cakes and Ale A novel of literary life in England by W. Somerset Maugham, first published in 1930.

Calderón de la Barca, Pedro (1600–81) Born in Madrid, Pedro Calderón de la Barca studied for the Church and then the law, became a soldier, and ended as a priest. But he was also a major Spanish dramatist, who wrote well over a hundred plays, the last of them at the age of eighty-one. They are of varying quality, and

include both religious and secular works. Among the best known of them are *El Alcalde de Zalamea* and *El Magico prodigioso*.

Caldwell, Erskine (1903–) The American writer Erskine Caldwell, who was born in Georgia and educated at the University of Virginia, achieved fame in 1932 with the publication of his novel *Tobacco Road*, which went on to become an extremely long-running theatrical success. In 1933 he brought out *God's Little Acre*, and followed this with many more novels. He is particularly acclaimed as a writer of short stories, of which he has published many collections, and he has also written travel books and documentaries.

Erskine Caldwell standing in front of a screen of book jackets from a selection of his successful novels.

Caldwell, Taylor (1900–) Janet Taylor Caldwell was born in England, but lived most of her life in the United States. Her first novel, *Dynasty of Death*, was published in 1938. Among her other books are the bestselling novels, *The Earth is the Lord's*, which came out in 1941, *Dear and Glorious Physician*, in 1959, and *A Prologue to Love*, in 1961.

Callaghan, Morley (1903–) Toronto-born Morley Edward Callaghan studied law, but turned to journalism, and published his first novel, *Strange Fugitive*, in 1928, having been encouraged to do so by Ernest Hemingway. He has published a large number of novels since then, and some collections of short stories.

Call It Sleep A novel of Jewish-American boyhood by Henry Roth, first published in 1934. It was greatly influenced by Joyce's *A Portrait of the Artist as a Young Man*.

Call of the Wild, The A novel of the Klondike by Jack London, first published in 1903. Its hero is the dog Buck, loyal to his master John Thornton until the call of the wild leads him to join a wolf pack. London's masterly treatment of canine psychology made this one of his most successful books.

Calvin, Johannes (1509–64) Born at Noyon in Picardy, France, Johannes Calvin was trained for the Roman Catholic Church and marked for early preferment, but after some years he became an adherent of Protestantism. In 1536 he published his major work, *Institutes of the Christian Religion*, and then moved to Geneva, where he published a number of tracts, commentaries and other religious works, and established himself as one of the most influential leaders of the Reformation.

Calvino, Italo (1923–85) Novelist and short story writer Italo Calvino, who was born in Cuba, was a leading member of the Italian neo-realist movement, which was particularly concerned with portraying the poor and under-privileged in a naturalistic style, yet with a tendency to blur slightly the harshness of the subject. He also produced fantasies, such as *Invisible Cities*, published in 1972, perhaps placing him additionally among the Magic Realists. Three of his most successful novels, later collected under the title *Our Ancestors*, were *The Cloven Viscount*, *Baron in the Trees* and *The Non-Existent Knight*, which appeared in 1951, 1957 and 1959. A more recent novel was *Mr Palomar*, published in 1983.

Camden, William (1551–1623) The historian William Camden was born in London and educated at Oxford. His book *Britannia*, of which he produced a number of editions, first appeared in 1586, and his major work, *Annales Rerum Anglicarum et Hibernicarum Regnante Elizabetha*, a history of England and Ireland during the reign of Queen Elizabeth I, was published in two parts, the first in 1615 and the second, posthumously, in 1627.

Camoës, Luis de (1524–80) Probably born in Lisbon, Luis Vaz de Camoës came from a noble family and was given a classical education. Despite an adventurous and somewhat perilous life, he became Portugal's greatest poet. He worked in several genres. His masterpiece is the poem known as the *Lusiads*, an epic version of Portugal's history, first published in 1572.

Campbell, Roy (1901–57) Ignatius Royston Dunnachie Campbell, the South African poet, received immediate acclaim on the publication in 1924 of his long narrative poem, *The Flaming Terrapin*. The volumes of poetry published thereafter mostly added to his reputation, although *Flowering Rifle*, published in 1939, was condemned for its Fascist approach. His *Collected Poems* appeared in 1949, and he also wrote two volumes of autobiography.

Campbell, Thomas (1777–1814) Thomas Campbell, a Scot from Glasgow, supported himself by teaching until he became sufficiently well known as a poet to live and travel on the proceeds of his writing. He enjoyed a considerable following in his day, but is now remembered only as the author of such ballads as 'Lord Ullin's Daughter' and 'Ye Mariners of England', and as the originator of the line 'distance lends enchantment to the view'.

Campion, Thomas (1567–1620) Thomas Campion was born in London and educated at Cambridge. He was a poet, the author of a number of masques, and a musician. He published some anyonymous poems in 1591, and his first work under his own name, *Poemata*, a collection of Latin panegyrics, epigrams and elegies, appeared in 1595. He published several groups of songs under the title *A Book of Ayres*, and his *New Way of making Foure Parts in Counter-point* became a standard musical text book. In 1602 he brought out *Observations in the Art of English Poesie*, a defence of rhymeless verse.

Camus, Albert (1913–60) The eminent French writer Albert Camus was the son of a labourer.

Albert Camus with Laurence Payne, Mary Morris and Michael Yannis, reading over the script of 'Caligula'.

From 1935 he was active in the theatre, and during World War II took part in the Resistance. In 1942 he attracted attention with his novel, *L'Etranger* (published in English as *The Outsider* in 1946) and with a book of essays, *Le mythe de Sisyphe*. Among his later novels, many of which were set in Algeria, the country of his birth, are *The Plague* and *The Rebel*, first published in English in 1948 and 1953 respectively. He also produced short stories, essays and many plays, but in translation these works have been less successful than the novels. A member of the Existentialist movement, he had a considerable influence, through his work, on the dramatists of the Theatre of the Absurd, and all his writings reflected his belief in the essential individuality of human beings, their responsibility for their own development, and the ridiculous nature of the human condition. He was awarded the Nobel Prize for Literature in 1957.

Candida One of G. Bernard Shaw's "Plays Pleasant", first published in 1895.

Candide A satirical tale by Voltaire, featuring Dr Pangloss, first published in 1759. It i s similar in style to Dr Johnson's *Rasselas*.

Canetti, Elias (1905–) Born in Bulgaria, Elias Canetti was educated in Germany, Switzerland and Austria. In 1939 he went to live in London. He has published essays, plays, autobiographical works, and sociological studies. His most widely-read work is his novel, *Die Blendung*, which was first published in 1935, although the English translation, *Auto da Fé*, did not appear until 1946. More recent books include *The Conscience of Words* and *Earwitness*, both published in 1986. Canetti was awarded the Nobel Prize for Literature in 1981.

Canopus in Argus Archives A group of five novels by Doris Lessing, published between 1979 and 1983. Set in a fictional universe, the books are: *Re: Colonised Planet 5, Shikasta*, first published in 1979, *The Marriages Between Zones Three, Four and Five*, 1980, *The Sirian Experiments*, 1981, *The Making of the Representative for Planet 8*, 1982, and *Documents Relating to the Sentimental Agents in the Volyen Empire*, 1983.

Canterbury Tales, The More than sixty fifteenth-century manuscripts are still extant of *The Canterbury Tales*, Geoffrey Chaucer's most famous and popular work, which was probably written between 1386 and 1400. It consists of some seventeen thousand lines, using both prose and verse. The Prologue tells of the meeting at the Tabard Inn in Southwark of a group of almost thirty pilgrims making for the shrine of St Thomas à Becket at Canterbury. It describes them in some detail, and it is clear that all strata

The Friar from Chaucer's *The Canterbury Tales*.

of fourteenth century society, except the very highest and humblest, are represented. The upper ranks are present in the person of the Knight and his Squire, and perhaps to them may be added the Franklin and the sophisticated Wife of Bath; the Church provides the Prioress, Monk, Oxford Clerk, Parson and Friar, not to mention the less reputable Summoner and Pardoner; and there are professional men and tradespeople in the persons of the Doctor of Physic, the Serjeant-at-Law, and a number of others. The Prologue also contains the suggestion of the Host of the Tabard Inn, one Harry Bailly (possibly based on a real-life person), that, to pass the time as they travel, the pilgrims should tell each other stories. The Host will accompany them, and award a free supper on their return to

The Knight from *The Canterbury Tales*.

the person whose tale he considers the best. Chaucer's original conception was that each pilgrim should tell four stories, which would have meant well over a hundred tales, but the work was not finished, and of the twenty-four stories that were written only twenty are complete, and certain of the pilgrims do not entertain their fellows at all, while two of the tales are told by Chaucer himself. The narratives are linked by conversation (sometimes itself almost in the nature of a tale) between the pilgrims, and by the Host's part as master of ceremonies. By his choice of who is to tell the next tale, the work is given some structure, but this aspect cannot be said to be its strongest point. The stories, with prologues and epilogues, vary in content from the bawdy to the romantic to the moral, and include homilies and parodies. Although clearly incomplete, the book ends with the 'Retractiouns', in which the poet apologises for the light-heartedness of its contents, suggesting that Chaucer had abandoned his original plan and was content to leave *The Canterbury Tales* in the form in which we know it today. Certainly it was published in this unfinished state, though there are variations in the different manuscripts, but it seems curious that Chaucer should not have attempted a more polished version. It is possible, of course, that he intended to do so, but did not have the opportunity before his death. He used numerous sources for the stories, among them Boccaccio's *Decameron* and works by Livy and Petrarch (though some scholars have argued that he would not in fact have read Boccaccio), and the majority of the tales were not original, having been popular in Europe for a very long time. However, *The Canterbury Tales*, even in its somewhat confused and incomplete state, has its own originality in the setting of the work, the brilliant evocation of contemporary personages, and the splendour of its language. It is undoubtedly the major work in English of its period, and one of the glories of English literature.

Can You Forgive Her? The first of the 'Palliser' novels by Anthony Trollope, originally published in parts between 1864 and 1865.

Čapek, Karel (1890–1938) The best-known play by the Bohemian dramatist Karel Čapek is the futuristic *R.U.R. (Rossum's Universal Robots)*, first performed in English in 1923. With his brother, Josef Čapek, he also wrote *The Insect Play*, first seen in 1921, in which many human foibles are satirized. The science fantasy element was also strongly marked in several of his novels, such as *War with the Newts*, published in 1936. In addition he published short stories and essays.

Truman Capote, the American fiction and travel writer, who founded the 'faction' genre of novels.

Capote, Truman (1924–84) A native of New Orleans, Truman Capote achieved considerable success in 1958 with the publication of his novel, *Breakfast at Tiffany's*. He produced many more books, ranging from fiction to travel and collections of articles and including *In Cold Blood*, published in 1966, in which he presented a thinly fictionalized account of a true-life murder story, and with it began a trend for 'faction', the term coined to describe the genre.

Captains Courageous A novel by Rudyard Kipling about a spoilt rich boy who learns the meaning of life when he sails with rough fishermen from Massachusetts. It was first published in 1897.

Carew, Thomas (c.1595–1640) Born at West Wickham, Kent, England, and educated at Oxford, Thomas Carew rose to a position in the royal household of Charles I, for whom he wrote a masque, *Coelum Britannicum*, performed in 1634. He is best known as a lyrical Cavalier poet. His collection, *Poems*, appeared in 1640, which is generally supposed to have been the year of his death. However, revised editions appeared up to 1651, and may have been prepared by the poet himself.

Carlyle, Thomas (1795–1881) The eldest son of a stonemason from Ecclefechan, Dumfriesshire, Scotland, Thomas Carlyle was educated at Annan Grammar School and Edinburgh University. He as a subject, he and his wife returned to London in 1834, and he began his major work. Volume One of *The French Revolution* was completed within five months, but was accidentally burnt. Carlyle had to start again, but had finished the whole book by mid-January 1837, and it was published later that year. Despite its mannered and often ponderous style, it was immediately successful, and Carlyle became a highly respected figure in literary circles. In 1840 he gave a very successful series of lectures, *On Heroes, Hero-Worship and the Heroic in History*, which appeared in book form the following year. Many of the works which followed *The French Revolution*, such as the treatises *Chartism* and *Past and Present*, published in 1839 and 1843 respectively, were political in nature, and expressed his belief that a benevolent dictatorship was preferable to democracy. He admired such autocrats as Cromwell and Frederick the Great of Prussia, and published in 1845 an edition of *Oliver Cromwell's Letters and Speeches, with Elucidations*, while he worked for years on *The History of Friedrich II of Prussia, called Frederick the Great*, which was published in six volumes between 1858 and 1865. Although Carlyle's marriage is believed to have been sexually unsatisfactory, he and Jane lived together for forty years, during which time she had become one of the foremost literary hostesses in England and had developed a reputation as a brilliant correspondent. Her death in 1866 devastated Carlyle, and no more major works were to come from him. He did, however, prepare his *Reminiscences* and *Letters and Memorials*, consisting of his wife's correspondence. Both books were published after his death, without the editing that Carlyle had expected, and were regarded as tasteless in their frankness.

The study in Thomas Carlyle's house in Cheyne Row, Chelsea. His home is now open to the public.

studied for the ministry, but soon abandoned that intention, thereafter devoting himself to teaching and writing. He came to London, worked on a biography of Schiller and a version of Goethe's *Wilhelm Meister*, and wrote a number of articles for the *Edinburgh Encyclopaedia* and an essay on Goethe's *Faust* for the *Edinburgh Review*. *The Life of Schiller* began to appear in serial form in 1823, and Carlyle was much encouraged when Goethe wrote to him in complimentary terms on the publication of his translation of *Wilhelm Meister*. In 1826 he married Jane Welsh, and the couple lived in Scotland until 1831, when Carlyle returned to London in search of employment. In the meantime he had written *Sartor Resartus*, a mixture of philosophy and autobiography, which eventually appeared somewhat unsuccessfully in *Fraser's Magazine*, and was published first in book form in the United States in 1836. After another period in Edinburgh, during which Carlyle began to consider the French Revolution

A caricature of Carlyle by Charles Bell Birch.

Carmina Burana A collection of love poems, drinking songs, and quasi-religious verses dating from the twelfth and thirteenth centuries, written in German, Latin and French. The manuscript was discovered in 1803 at the monastery of Benediktbeuren in Bavaria. Several of the poems were used by the composer Carl Orff for his well-known cantata.

carol Originally a ring-dance accompanied by song, the term came to be applied to a song of celebration, and is now used almost exclusively for songs and hymns celebrating the birth of Christ. Carols have been sung since the early days of the Church, and were often included in the Mystery Plays. Major poets and song-writers through the centuries have added to the Christmas carols which are familiar today.

Caroline literature The literature of the period of King Charles I, who reigned from 1625 to 1649. The term is applied particularly to the drama of the period, the leading playwrights being Philip Massinger, John Ford and James Shirley. The Caroline era is also notable for some excellent lyric poetry, the leading voice being that of Robert Herrick, and for the work of the metaphysical poets such as John Donne.

Carroll, Lewis (1832–98) Charles Lutwidge Dodgson, the son of a clergyman, was born in Daresbury, Cheshire, England, and educated at Rugby and Christ Church, Oxford, where he was later appointed lecturer in mathematics. In 1861 he was ordained deacon, but did not continue to become a priest. His first published works, *A Syllabus of Plane Algebraic Geometry* and *The Formulae of Plane Trigonometry*, appeared in 1860 and 1861. He wrote many other mathematical

The celebrated author, mathematician and photographer Lewis Carroll. Best known for his children's stories and whimsical poems, he was also a talented photographer, innovating self-portraits.

works, the best known of which is *Euclid and his Modern Rivals*, which appeared in 1879. But it is of course under the pseudonym Lewis Carroll, which he adopted for his children's books, that he is chiefly remembered. Originating as a story told aloud during a boat-trip to Alice Liddell and her two sisters, *Alice's Adventures in Wonderland* was published in 1865, with illustrations by Sir John Tenniel, who also provided the drawings for *Through the Looking Glass*, which came out in 1871. It is worth noting that the Alice of *Through the Looking-Glass* was not Alice Liddell, but a cousin of Dodgson, Alice Raikes. Both books were immediately and immensely successful, and are still popular today. Innumerable editions, particularly of *Alice in Wonderland*, illustrated by innumerable artists, have appeared, and the most eminent actors have queued to play the well-loved and wildly eccentric characters in stage and screen versions. A number of other books appeared under the Carroll nom-de-plume, including *Phantasmagoria*, *Rhyme and Reason* and *Sylvie and Bruno*, but only *The Hunting of the Snark*, published in 1876, has endured with anything remotely approaching the tenacity of the 'Alice' books.

One of the illustrations by Sir John Tenniel to Lewis Carroll's poem 'You are old, Father William' from *Alice's Adventures in Wonderland*.

Carson, Rachel (1907–64) Educated at John Hopkins University, Rachel Carson was a zoologist who achieved bestseller status with her book *The Sea Around Us*, published in 1951. She had previously published *Under the Sea Wind* in 1941, and in 1955 came *The Edge of the Sea*. She was also successful in 1963 with another popular polemic, *Silent Spring*.

Cartland, Barbara (1901–) English writer Barbara Cartland is one of the most prolific and successful authors of romantic novels in the world. She has written a staggering number of books, some of them produced at the steady rate of one every two weeks, and her total is currently well over four hundred and thirty volumes. This figure is not made up exclusively of romances, but also includes biographies, a number of books on health and health foods, and other works of non-fiction.

Cary, Alice and Phoebe The sisters Alice Cary (1820–71) and Phoebe Cary (1824–71) were born near Cincinatti. Their poetry was first collected in a joint volume in 1850. Their work was highly regarded by their contemporaries, and they went to New York and were active in literary circles there. Alice became the first president of Sorosis, the first club for women in New York. Although they published separate volumes, they always worked closely together, and have been regarded almost as collaborators. The collected *Poetical Works of Alice and Phoebe Cary* was published posthumously in 1886.

Cary, Joyce (1888–1957) Arthur Joyce Lunel Cary was born in Londonderry, Ireland, and educated at Clifton College and Trinity College, Oxford. He became a soldier and a colonial administrator, and eventually settled to the life of a writer. Although he published poetry and some non-fiction, he was primarily a novelist. Among more than a dozen novels, the most successful were the trilogy featuring the artist, Gulley Jimson, consisting of *Herself Surprised*, *To be a Pilgrim* and *The Horse's Mouth*, first published in 1941, 1942 and 1944 respectively.

Casanova, Giovanni (1725–98) Born in Venice, Giovanni Jacopo Casanova di Seingalt was by turns journalist, preacher, diplomat, spy, historian, and friend of kings, cardinals and princes. He was an inveterate traveller, a begetter of scandal, and a philanderer on a grand scale. His *Memoires*, first published in Germany between 1826 and 1838, were written in French and record his volatile career and, with enthusiasm, his innumerable sexual adventures.

Castle, The A novel by Franz Kafka, first published in 1926, which presents a nightmare world dominated by bureaucracy to the point of absurdity.

Castle of Otranto, The A novel by Horace Walpole, sub-titled 'A Gothic Story', first published in 1765. It was immediately successful, and, having originally announced it as a translation from the medieval Italian, Walpole was encouraged by its success to reveal himself as the author. He intended 'Gothic' to refer to the fact that the novel is set in the Middle Ages, but the term was adopted to describe a genre of macabre fiction, of which *The Castle of Otranto* is the first example in English.

Castle Rackrent A novel by Maria Edgeworth, first published in 1800, and often considered to be the first historical and regional novel to be written in English.

Castle Richmond A novel by Anthony Trollope, first published in 1860.

Catch-22 A satirical novel by Joseph Heller about Yossarian, an American pilot in World War II, trying to avoid the inevitable death he sees ahead. It was first published in 1961, since when its title has entered the language.

Catcher in the Rye, The A novel by J.D. Salinger, first published in 1951. Narrated by teenager Holden Caulfield, it is still immensely popular for its comic and frank portrayal of post-war youth.

Cather, Willa (1876–1947) Although the American author Willa Sibert Cather was born in Virginia, she was brought up and educated in Nebraska,

The American authoress Willa Cather in the McClure Magazine days.

where she attended the university. She published her first poetry, *April Twilights*, in 1903, and a book of short stories, *The Troll Garden*, in 1905. Her first novel, *Alexander's Bridge*, was published in 1912. A number of other novels followed, often set in Nebraska and dealing with the frontier life of pioneers. *My Antonia* appeared in 1918, and in 1922 she won the Pulitzer Prize with *One of Ours*, while *A Lost Lady* came out the next year. Each book enhanced her reputation, the development of her talent showing in the breadth and depth of the material she used. In 1925 she published *The Professor's House*, for which she abandoned the Mid-West and took New Mexico as the setting for the story, and she used this background again for her most celbrated work, the historical novel, *Death Comes for the Archbishop*, which first appeared in 1927. She continued to bring out works of fiction, including novellas and short stories, until 1940, and also published an autobiographical work, *Not Under Forty*, in 1936. Her writing is still highly regarded and seen as of considerable importance in the history of American literature.

Cato A tragedy by Joseph Addison, first presented and published in 1713.

Cat on a Hot Tin Roof A psychological drama by Tennessee Williams, revolving around the family of a wealthy Southern cotton planter. It was first produced in 1955.

Catriona A novel by Robert Louis Stevenson. The sequel to *Kidnapped*, it was first published in 1893.

Catullus, Gaius Valerius (*c*.84–54BC) Thought to have been born in Verona, Gaius Valerius Catullus was the greatest Roman lyric poet. Of his works, one hundred and sixteen have survived, some of them fragmentary, written between 62BC and the poet's death in 54BC. They include both passionate love poems and lampoons, and are particularly interesting for the vivid picture which they provide of social conditions in Italy at the time.

Caucasian Chalk Circle, The A play by Bertolt Brecht, first produced in 1948 in the United States where Brecht lived at this time.

Causley, Charles (1917–) The English poet Charles Causley was born in Launceston, Cornwall. He is a teacher, and much of his work has been inspired by his wartime service in the Royal Navy. His first volume of verse, *Farewell, Aggie Weston*, appeared in 1951, and since then he has published many further selections, including some for children. His *Collected Poems 1951–1975* was published in 1975, and *Secret Destinations* came out in 1985.

Cavalier Lyrics The collective name given to the works of the poets who supported Charles I, many of them belonging to his court. Chief among them are Robert Herrick, Thomas Carew, Richard Lovelace and Sir John Suckling.

Caxton, William (*c*.1422–91) William Caxton, who was born in Kent, is renowned as the first English printer, but he did not engage himself in that career until he was about fifty years old, having previously been a businessman and diplomat. He was also a translator, and the first book which he printed, at Bruges, was his version of the French medieval romance, *The Recuyell of the Historyes of Troye*. By 1476 he had set up as a printer in Westminster, and the first dated book which he printed in England was *The Dictes or Sayinges of the Philosophres*, which appeared in 1477. From then until shortly before his death, he set in type and printed over eighteen thousand pages. Although he is known

A page from *The Game of the Chesse*, printed in 1480 by William Caxton who was the first printer in England to use movable type, combined with woodcut illustrations.

to have trained other printers, including Wynkyn de Worde and Robert Copland, he is believed to have achieved this production virtually single-handed. Included in the output of his press were several more of his own translations, a number of works by Geoffrey Chaucer, including *The Canterbury Tales*, and Malory's *Morte d'Arthur*.

Cecil, Lord David (1902–86) Lord Edward Christian David Gascoyne Cecil was educated at Eton and Christ Church, Oxford. As a biographer, he specialized in the lives of literary figures, including William Cowper, Thomas Hardy, Thomas Gray, Jane Austen and Charles Lamb. He also published in 1939 and 1954 the two volumes of his biography of Lord Melbourne, *The Young Melbourne* and *Lord M*.

Cecilia, or Memoirs of an Heiress A novel by Fanny Burney, first published in 1782.

Celebrated Jumping Frog of Calaveras County, The Mark Twain's first successful story, published in the New York *Saturday Press* in 1865, and reprinted in 1867 as the title piece of his first book.

Céline, Louis-Ferdinand (1894–1961) Louis-Ferdinand Céline was the pseudonym of Louis-Ferdinand Destouches, the French novelist. His first book, *Journey to the End of the Night*, a powerful study of a slum doctor, appeared in 1932, and was published in English in 1934. A number of other novels followed, mostly received with increasing critical acclaim for their striking contents and very individual style.

Cellini, Benvenuto (1500–71) Giovanni Cellini, a Florentine musician and maker of musical instruments, expected his son, Benvenuto, to follow in the family business, but the boy was determined from an early age to become a goldsmith, to which art he later added that of a sculptor. His *Memoirs*, which were not published until 1730, have tremendous vitality, and can justifiably be described as one of the most fascinating books ever written, presenting not only a bizarre account of the artist himself, his adventures and amours, but also providing a brilliantly colourful picture of the period.

Cenci, The A five-act tragedy in verse by Percy Bysshe Shelley, first published in 1819.

Centlivre, Susannah (*c*.1667–1723) Susannah Centlivre was an actress who, having been twice widowed, began writing plays, the first of which was *The Perjured Husband*, a tragedy. Her later comedies enjoyed great success. They included *The Wonder! a Woman keeps a Secret*, first seen in 1714, with David Garrick in the leading male role. Her third husband, Joseph Centlivre, was chief cook to Queen Anne.

Cervantes, Miguel de (1547–1616) Miguel de Cervantes Saavedra was born at Alcala de Henares, the son of an apothecary and surgeon, and was to become Spain's most famous writer, and indeed one of the greatest novelists of all time. The circumstances of his education are vague, but he appears to have been attached to the entourage of Cardinal Giulio Acquaviva, and later served in the Spanish army. After many bizarre adventures, including a period of slavery in North Africa, which resulted when a ship on which he was travelling was captured by corsairs, Cervantes returned to Spain and settled to his life's work as an author. Six of his poems had appeared in print as early as 1569, and now, between 1582 and 1587, he produced a large number of plays, few of which are now extant. In 1585 he published his first novel, *Primera parte de la Galatea*. It helped to establish his reputation, but although it was reprinted twice during his lifetime, at the time of publication it was considered a failure, which is perhaps why, despite the fact that the *Galatea* was his own favourite among his works, Cervantes never produced the second part of the novel. Although his surviving dramatic work is not now highly regarded, some of his plays were very successful at the time, and he also produced much acclaimed poetry, but the living that he made from his writing was

Engraved title-page from a 1612 edition of *Don Quixote*.

a very precarious one, and his own improvidence increased his financial problems. For most of the next decade he virtually abandoned literature, writing only a few poems, and earning his living by helping in the provisioning of the Spanish Armada. He continued to be plagued by a desperate shortage of money, and, indeed, there is some reason to believe that his great masterpiece, *Don Quixote*, was originally conceived while its author was languishing in jail for debt, at some time between 1597 and 1602. The first part of the novel was published in 1605 and was immediately triumphantly successful, though again Cervantes appears to have derived little financial benefit from it, partly because of the appearance of pirated editions originating in Lisbon. During the next years he produced a volume of stories, *Novelas exemplares*, and more verse, but was chiefly engaged on the second half of *Don Quixote*. In 1614 a spurious sequel by another hand appeared, and this may have spurred Cervantes to complete his own version. The genuine second part was published in 1615, only a few months before his death. *Don Quixote* began in Cervantes' mind as a parody of the romances of chivalry, but it developed into a superb portrayal of the whole of sixteenth century Spanish society. The novel is filled with a great variety of adventure, with comedy, with satire, with pathos, and above all with a remarkable insight into the human condition. Some of his other stories have very considerable merit, and his poetry is far from negligible, but *Don Quixote* towers above all his other work as a masterpiece of undeniable greatness.

Chance A novel by Joseph Conrad, the story of the heiress Flora de Barral. It was Conrad's first major success when published in 1913.

Chandler, Raymond (1888–1959) Although the American writer Raymond Thornton Chandler was born in Chicago, he was educated in England, at Dulwich College, and did not return to the United States until 1912. He began to write and publish crime stories in 1933. His first novel, *The Big Sleep*, featuring his urbane and resilient 'private eye' Philip Marlowe, was published in 1939, and was acclaimed as a brilliant example of its genre. The standard was maintained in the books which followed, *Farewell, my Lovely*, first published in 1940, *The High Window*, 1942, *The Lady in the Lake*, 1943, *The Little Sister*, 1949, *The Long Goodbye*, 1953, and *Playback*, 1958. Three collections of his short stories were published, two of them posthumously, and Chandler also wrote about his craft in *The Simple Art of Murder*, published in 1950. *Raymond Chandler Speaking*, a collection of

letters, articles, and the first pages of an uncompleted novel, *The Poodle Springs Story*, came out in 1962.

chansons de gestes The name given to the French epic verse chronicles dating from the twelfth to the fifteenth century. Sung by itinerant *jongleurs*, these poems provided a means of handing on legends and stories, and sometimes historical information, to their largely illiterate audiences. The most famous of the poems is the *Chanson de Roland*, which celebrates the deeds of one of Charlemagne's knights.

chapbooks A term given in comparatively recent times to the small tracts and booklets sold by chapmen, or pedlars. They began to appear as soon as printing became commonplace, and reached their peak in the eighteenth century. Designed for purchase by the ill-educated, and often vulgar in style and appeal, the contents of chapbooks varied from popular stories to religious instruction to collections of jokes.

Chapman, George (*c.*1559–1634) The English playwright George Chapman was born near Hitchin, Hertfordshire. He came to London after leaving university and began a career as a dramatist, poet and translator. Over the next forty years he wrote prolifically for the stage, his best-known drama being the tragedy *Bussy d'Ambois*, first presented in 1604. Its success resulted some six or seven years later in a sequel, *The Revenge of Bussy d'Ambois*. Prior to that, in 1605, *Eastward Hoe*, a play in which Chapman had collaborated with Ben Jonson and John Marston, gave offence and resulted in a short prison sentence for the authors. Chapman was again in jail more than once thereafter for similar reasons. This, however, was not regarded as untoward, since political censorship was rife. Chapman's major work was a translation, *The Whole Works of Homer: Prince of Poets*, published in 1616 and for centuries a standard text. It was the inspiration for the well-known sonnet by John Keats, 'On First Looking into Chapman's Homer'.

Chatterton, Thomas (1752–70) Born in Bristol, England, Thomas Chatterton was the son of a schoolmaster. His father had died before his birth and the boy received little formal education, but he was an avid reader and began writing at an early age – a poem was published when he was only eleven. He was also fascinated by the tombs, the monuments, the ancient treasures of the Church of St Mary Redcliffe, where his uncle was sexton. Leaving school at fourteen, he was apprenticed as a clerk to an attorney, but he continued to write, and many of his articles and open letters were published in various periodicals. His interest in

A dramatic and imaginative portrayal by Henry Wallis of the highly original poet Thomas Chatterton's suicide by taking poison at the untimely age of only seventeen. He is chiefly remembered for his unusual medieval collection of 'Rowley' poems.

medieval matters, which had begun in St Mary Redcliffe, then led him to write poems which he claimed to be the work of a fifteenth-century monk named Thomas Rowley, forging 'antique' manuscripts to give verisimilitude to his story. Chatterton also wrote much poetry in contemporary vein, but it is primarily for the 'Rowley' poems that he is remembered. The pseudo-archaic language has a beauty of its own, and the verses show great originality and a surprising maturity from so young an author. In April 1770 Chatterton travelled to London, determined to become successful, but only one of the 'Rowley' poems was taken for publication, and he received minimal payment for the astonishingly large output of political articles, lyrics and other poems, satires and other writings which he produced over a period of four months. His poverty and lack of success reduced him to despair, and on August 24th, 1770, he committed suicide, by taking poison, at the age of seventeen years and nine months.

Chaucer, Geoffrey (*c*.1340–1400) Born in London, the son of a vintner, Geoffrey Chaucer appears to have been attached as a boy to the household of Lionel, the Duke of Clarence. There are many uncertainties concerning his early life, but it is known that he was at the wars in France in 1359, was taken prisoner, and was ransomed by King Edward III. By 1368 he had become one of the king's esquires, and before long he was spending much of his time abroad on official business for the king, who in 1374 granted him an annuity of twenty marks. Later that same year he was appointed Comptroller of the Custom and Subsidy of Wools, Hides and Woodfells and of the Petty Customs of Wine for the port of London. More expeditions abroad and further promotions in the excise department were to follow. His wife, Philippa, had been an attendant to the Queen, and was connected, through her sister, to John of Gaunt, who became, and remained, Chaucer's patron. The family was prosperous. Meanwhile, a steady flow of poetry had been coming from Chaucer's pen, including translations from the French and the Latin. In 1369 or thereabouts he had produced the first of the surviving works that can with certainty be attributed to him, a long poem written to honour the memory of John of Gaunt's wife and entitled *The Book of the Duchess*. The doubt surrounding the events of Chaucer's youth extends to much of his later life, and also to the dates of many of his works, but his official duties appear to have left him a certain amount of time for writing, and the fragmentary *Quene Anelida and Fals Arcyte* and *Troilus and Criseyde* were probably written in the 1370s. *The Parlement of Foules* may have been produced to celebrate the marriage of Richard II and Anne of Bohemia in 1383, while *The Hous of Fame* and *The Legende of Good Women*, though neither was completed, were probably composed before 1385. Chaucer continued to rise in the Customs service and was granted additional comptrollerships, and in 1385 he was made a Justice of the Peace in Kent, to which county he then moved. Soon after, he was elected a knight of the shire for Kent, and represented the county in Parliament for a brief time. In 1387 his wife died. Between 1388 and his death twelve years later, his fortunes fluctuated, apparently dependent on whether his protector, John of Gaunt, was in England or abroad. He was in the king's favour — or he was out of it; he was rewarded with a handsome salary and a yearly butt of wine — or he was on the borders of poverty, wholly dependent on a tiny pension from John of Gaunt; he was appointed the king's clerk of the works, in charge of various royal palaces, he became a commissioner responsible for the maintenance of the banks of the Thames, he was given the sinecure position of sub-forester at North Petherton in Devon — or he was ignominiously dismissed from this or that post. It is probable that, despite various official duties, he spent much time in Kent, working on his masterpiece, *The Canterbury Tales*, a task which is believed to have occupied him for many years. The works mentioned above do not by any means represent all his output. In addition there were lyrics and other poetry, such as roundels and ballades and the *A.B.C.*, a poem in honour of the Virgin, each verse of which begins with a different letter of the alphabet. And there were various prose writings, including *A Treatise on the Astrolabe*, written for 'Litel Lowis, my son'. It seems highly possible that Chaucer regarded himself primarily as a civil servant, seeing his writing as more of a pastime than a profession, and this may explain why many of his works were never completed or did not follow his original plans for them. Nevertheless, his technical mastery of many forms of poetry, allied to the brilliance of his narratives, makes Geoffrey Chaucer without any doubt the first truly great writer in the history of English literature.

Chayevsky, Paddy (1923–81) Much of the work of the New York playwright Paddy Chayevsky was originally seen on television. His plays, first appearing between 1953 and 1968, include *Marty*, *The Bachelor Party*, *The Tenth Man*, *Gideon*, *The Passion of Josef D.* and *The Latent Heterosexual*. In 1978 he published a science fiction novel, *Altered States*.

Cheever, John (1912–82) Born in Quincy, Massachusetts, John Cheever was expelled from school at the age of seventeen, but soon established himself as a writer of short stories, many of which appeared first in the *New Yorker* and were later published in volume form in a number of collections. In 1957 he won the National Book Award with his first novel, *The Wapshot Chronicle*. This was followed in 1964 by *The Wapshot Scandal*. His other novels include *Bullet Park*, *Falconer* and *Oh What a Paradise It Seems*.

Chekhov, Anton (1860–1904) Anton Pavlovich Chekhov was born in Taganrog, Russia, the son of illiterate liberated serfs. The boy was given a good education, however, and studied medicine

An original portrayal of Geoffrey Chaucer on horseback, taken from an early manuscript which is owned by the Marquis of Stafford.

Anton Chekhov, the Russian playwright, with the cast of his play *The Seagulls*, at the Moscow Art Theatre. A failure at first, the play is now a popular classic.

at the University of Moscow before turning to a literary career. Many of the short sketches and stories which he contributed to various periodicals were slight, but the merits of his more serious work in this genre were quickly recognized. Two of the stories, 'My Life' and 'In the Ravine', have been regarded as masterpieces in the genre. Before long, Chekhov had also achieved success in the theatre, with the production of *Ivanov* in 1887. The first of his four major plays, *The Seagull*, was a failure when it first appeared in 1895, but this was largely the fault of a poor production, and in 1898 it was revived happily at the Moscow Art Theatre, under the direction of Stanislavsky, where *The Seagull* was followed by *Uncle Vanya* in 1900 and *The Three Sisters* in 1901. In that year Chekhov married the actress Olga Knipper. *The Cherry Orchard* was presented in 1904, shortly before his death. Chekhov also wrote a number of one-act plays, such as *The Bear*, *The Proposal* and *A Jubilee*. Innovative, atmospheric, ironic and allusive, his plays are often lacking in highly dramatic content, but the characters are superbly drawn and the interaction between them presents us with human beings who are funny or sad or tragic, or sometimes all of those at once. Chekhov's influence on the dramatists who came after him has been immense, and the four principal plays have become part of the standard classic repertoire.

Cherry Orchard, The A comedy by Anton Chekhov, first performed in Moscow in 1904. The destruction of the cherry orchard to make way for modern development symbolizes the changes that Chekhov foresaw in Russia.

Chesterfield, Lord (1694–1773) Philip Dormer Stanhope, fourth Earl of Chesterfield, was born in London and educated at Cambridge. After a somewhat wild youth he entered politics and rose to become a diplomat of very considerable standing. He also has two claims to fame in the annals of literature. The first is Dr Johnson's quarrel with him over his *Dictionary*. Johnson had expected to receive substantial patronage from Chesterfield, but instead he was given only a subscription of ten pounds. The second and more important claim is in respect of his *Letters*, the first series of which was addressed to his natural son, Philip Stanhope, who, as his father had done at a similar age, was leading a life of dissipation. The second series was addressed to his godson, also called Philip Stanhope. The letters, which were not published until after Chesterfield's death, consist of a fascinating compendium of advice and instruction on all matters, such as deportment, behaviour towards

Chesterton, G.K.

women and the nature of vice, that a well-to-do young man of the period should understand. Johnson condemned them as teaching the morals of a whore and the manners of a dancing master. To twentieth-century eyes they are witty and wise, foolish and even appalling, but above all entertaining.

Chesterton, G.K. (1874–1936) The English writer Gilbert Keith Chesterton, who was born in London and educated at St Paul's School and the Slade School of Art, worked for a publisher before adopting literature as his profession. He soon established himself as a successful journalist, and was to continue as such for the rest of his life, many of his articles and essays being published later in book form. He achieved more lasting fame, however, with his fiction and verse. In 1900 he published a volume of poems, *The Wild Knight*. This was followed three years later by his first novel *The Napoleon of Notting Hill*. In 1908 came *The Man Who Was Thursday*, both books being remarkable for their imaginative fantasy, the piquancy of their style and the vigour with which they present some of Chesterton's unconventional ideas. He wrote other novels and also produced a considerable amount of literary criticism, including several books on writers of the Victorian period. But while his much-anthologised poems, such as 'The Donkey' and 'The Rolling English Road', must not be forgotten, his present-day fame

A chalk sketch of G.K. Chesterton by Sir James Gunn. Chesterton is perhaps best known for his stories about a priest detective, Father Brown.

rests largely on the Father Brown stories, in which a small, humble, roly-poly Roman Catholic priest contrives to solve crimes which have baffled all the experts involved. The first collection of these was *The Innocence of Father Brown*, published in 1911.

Childe Harold's Pilgrimage A long, semi-autobiographical narrative poem by Lord Byron. The various cantos were published between 1812 and 1818.

Childers, Erskine (1870–1922) Robert Erskine Childers was educated at Haileybury and Trinity College, Cambridge. He worked ardently for Irish Home Rule and eventually settled in Ireland, becoming a prominent member of the Dail. He joined the Republican movement in 1922, and in November of that year was arrested by the British, tried for treason and executed by firing squad. He wrote one or two political books, but is remembered as an author for his novel *The Riddle of the Sands*, which was very successfully published in 1903.

Children of Violence The general title given to a sequence of five novels by Doris Lessing. These are: *Martha Quest*, first published in 1952, *A Proper Marriage*, in 1954, *A Ripple from the Storm*, in 1958, *Landlocked*, in 1965, and *The Four-Gated City*, in 1969.

Chimes, The One of the 'Christmas Books' by Charles Dickens, first published in 1845.

Chopin, Kate (1850–1904) Born in St Louis, Missouri, Kate O'Flaherty moved to New Orleans after her marriage to Oscar Chopin. In 1882 her husband died, leaving her with a large family to support, and it was then that she turned to writing. Her collections of stories about people of the Bayou were well received, but her second novel, *The Awakening*, published in 1899, aroused a storm of protest for its frank presentation of a woman's innermost feelings, and, upset by the strength of the attacks on her, she wrote little thereafter. In recent years she has been seen as a forerunner of the feminist movement in literature.

Chrétien de Troyes (c.1150–c.1200) So-called because he was born at Troyes in the Champagne district of France, Chrétien de Troyes is the most famous of French medieval poets. Little is known of his life, but he appears to have been attached to royal courts of the time, and his work was very popular. His poems, of which only five remain, consist of romantic narratives in rhyming couplets. Almost all of them deal with the Arthurian legend, in the development of which he played a major part.

Christie, Agatha (1890–1976) Agatha Miller was born in Torquay, England, and became Agatha Christie on her marriage to Archibald Christie in

1914. She was later divorced, and married Max Mallowan in 1930. *The Mysterious Affair at Styles*, published in 1920, was the first of a very large number of her crime novels which were hugely popular. She also wrote plays, many of them adapted from the novels. The most successful of these is *The Mousetrap*, which ran continuously in London for more than three decades. The creator of both Hercule Poirot and Miss Marples, she became Dame Agatha Christie in 1971.

Christmas Books The title of the collection of novellas by Charles Dickens, first published separately between 1843 and 1848. They comprise *A Christmas Carol*, *The Chimes*, *The Cricket on the Hearth*, *The Battle of Life* and *The Haunted Man*. They are not to be confused with the 'Christmas Stories', which appeared in some collected editions of Dickens and which are much shorter tales taken from the magazines *Household Words* and *All the Year Round*.

Christmas Carol, A The most popular of the 'Christmas Books' by Charles Dickens, telling the story of the conversion of the miser Ebenezer Scrooge. It was first published in 1843.

Chrysostom, St John (*c*.347-407) Born at Antioch in Syria, the son of a Roman military commander, St John Chrysostom became a priest, and was eventually appointed Archbishop of Constantinople. His zeal and strongly held views made him an extremely influential figure in the Christian church, and his eloquence earned him the name 'Chrysostom', which means 'golden-mouthed'. He was the author of many religious works, including commentaries on some books of the New Testament, *On Priesthood* and *On the Statues*. His writings also contain much information, of great historical interest, about the society in which he lived.

Churchill, Winston (1871–1947) The American writer Winston Churchill was born in St Louis, Missouri. He entered the Navy, and during his service began a career as a journalist. He later became editor of *The Cosmopolitan Magazine*, and in 1899 achieved fame with his second novel, *Richard Carvel*. He went on to write a substantial number of historical and contemporary romances, including *The Crisis*, *The Crossing*, *Coniston* and *The Inside of the Cup*. His last novel, *The Dwelling Place of Light*, was published in 1917, and after that he wrote very little. His books all enjoyed considerable success when first published, though they are little read nowadays.

Churchill, Winston (1874–1965) The Right Honourable Sir Winston Leonard Spencer Churchill was born in Blenheim Palace, England, and educated at Harrow School. He will always be remembered as Britain's leader during World War II, but he

Sir Winston Churchill by Walter Sickert.

was also a writer of outstanding ability. After training at Sandhurst, he served with the Army in many countries, and then became a war correspondent, his experiences resulting in a number of books on the Boer War. His somewhat

A colourful picture by the illustrator John Leech of Fezziwig's Ball from Charles Dicken's *A Christmas Carol*.

chequered political career began when he entered Parliament in 1900, and he served in various ministerial capacities before eventually becoming Prime Minister in 1940. Despite the pressures of public life, he found time to produce a long list of books, consisting of political commentaries, histories, autobiographical works, and major biographies of his ancestor, Marlborough, and of his father, Lord Randolph Churchill. His *History of the Second World War*, published in six volumes between 1948 and 1954, is a masterly and detailed account. The four volumes of *A History of the English-speaking Peoples* were published between 1956 and 1958 and were immensely successful and much admired for the elegance of their prose. Sir Winston was awarded the Nobel Prize for Literature in 1953.

Cibber, Colley (1671–1757) The actor Cibber Colley was born in London. His first play, *Love's Last Shift, or the Fool in Fashion*, was produced in 1603, and over the next forty years a score of other plays followed. Some of his contemporaries believed that his dramas and comedies would withstand the test of time. Others, notably Pope and Fielding, thought less highly of him, and greeted his appointment as Poet Laureate in 1730 with much derision. Their verdict proved correct, and Cibber's plays are now virtually forgotten. His autobiography, *An Apology for the Life of Mr Colley Cibber, Comedian*, published in 1740, is perhaps more enduring.

Cicero (106–43BC) Marcus Tullius Cicero was born at Arpinum in southern Italy, and was given the best education available to the son of a wealthy father. He became renowned as an orator, improving his skills in Greece, where he first met his close friend, Titus Pomponius Atticus, and in Rhodes. His speeches, whether defending a parricide or castigating a tyrant, were not only impressive but effective too, and he soon received important political appointments, eventually rising to become a Consul in 63BC. In this capacity he was responsible for the defeat of the rebellion led by Catiline, and was hailed as the saviour of the State. During the next twenty years, however, his career as a politician declined, and his support of Julius Caesar and then of Octavian earned him the enmity of Marc Antony, which finally resulted in his murder at the hands of a small military detachment. He left a number of works, many of them transcripts of his speeches, including his attacks on Antony, known as the *Philippics*. He also wrote philosophical, moral and rhetorical treatises, and his numerous letters, especially those to Atticus, give us a remarkable picture of Roman life at the time. As

Cicero, sometimes referred to as Tully, was Rome's greatest orator and most articulate philosopher.

the greatest Roman writer of prose, Cicero had a major effect on the literature of western Europe, the clarity of his style being a model for all authors. His ethical and political thinking was also extremely influential as the Roman concept of civilization grew and spread.

Citizen of the World, The A collection of satirical letters by Oliver Goldsmith, first appearing in the periodical *Public Ledger* and published in book form in 1762.

City of God, The The most important of St Augustine's works, *The City of God (De Civitate Dei)*, a defence of Christianity, was begun in the year 413 and was issued in a number of sections between then and 427.

Clare, John (1793–1864) The poet John Clare was born in Helpstone, Northamptonshire, England. He had little formal education, but read widely and soon began to write verse. While working as a farm labourer, he published in 1820 a first volume, *Poems Descriptive of Rural Life and Scenery*. It met with some success, and in the following year he brought out *The Village Minstrel and other poems*. The quality of his work was recognized to some extent, but it was really as a

A sixteenth century illustration to *The Shepherd's Calendar*, on which John Clare based his collection of poems two hundred years later.

curiosity that he was celebrated — 'the Northamptonshire peasant poet'. His admirers subscribed to provide him with an annuity, but the money was soon dissipated, and Clare's fortunes were not revived by his later collections, *The Shepherd's Calendar* and *The Rural Muse*, which appeared in 1827 and 1835, and which were less well received. Although he married in 1820, an earlier unhappy love affair appears to have preyed on his mind, and his mental stability was always open to question. In 1837 he became insane, and, apart from a brief period in 1841, was confined in an asylum until his death. The poems that he wrote in moments of lucidity during these years were not widely known until almost a century after they were written, when Edmund Blunden and others began to promote his work as more than that of a primitive 'peasant poet'. He is now recognised as gifted with a truly poetic vision, which he expressed in verses whose deceptive simplicity gives them great beauty and strength.

Clarendon, The Earl of (1609–74) Edward Hyde, the historian, was born in Cheshire, England, and educated at Oxford. He rose to high political office under Charles I. He spent the period of the Commonwealth in France, and on the Restoration was created Earl of Clarendon. The most notable of his many books is *The True Historical Narrative of the Rebellion and Civil Wars in England*, published between 1702 and 1704.

Clarissa, or The History of a Young Lady The second of Samuel Richardson's novels, in which he again used the epistolary style. It was first published between 1747 and 1748.

Clark, Arthur C. (1917–) Educated at Kings College, London, Arthur Charles Clarke, the distinguished science fiction writer, published his first books, *Prelude to Space* and *The Sands of Mars*, in 1951. Among his other books are *2001: A Space Odyssey*, which appeared in 1968 and of which he wrote the screenplay in collaboration with Stanley Kubrick, and *The Fountains of Paradise*, published in 1979. He has also written many non-fiction works on the subject of space travel.

Clarke, Austin (1896–1974) An Irishman, born and educated in Dublin, Austin Clarke published his first poetry, *The Vengeance of Fionn*, in 1917, and continued to produce volumes of verse until his death. His *Collected Poems* appeared in 1974. He was also a dramatist of note, the first of his many verse plays, *The Son of Learning*, appearing in 1927. His founding of the Dublin Verse-Speaking Society resulted in the establishment of the Lyric Theatre, Dublin, where several of his plays and those of other poet playwrights were first performed. Clarke also wrote three novels, a small number of autobiographical works and some studies in Irish literature.

Classicism A term used in antithesis to 'Romanticism'. However, it usually refers to the literature of ancient Greece and Rome. It is especially applied to the works of Virgil, Horace and Ovid, the three great poets of the Augustan Age, who were writing at the beginning of the first century AD. 'Classicism', or 'Neo-classicism', is also used to describe the works of those authors such as Pope, Swift, Addison and Steele, who saw themselves as having inherited the mantle of the Roman poets.

Claudel, Paul (1868–1955) The early plays of Paul Louis Charles Marie Claudel, diplomat, poet and dramatist, were of a Symbolist character, while his later work was much influenced by his conversion to Roman Catholicism. The best known of the early plays is *Partage de midi*, which was successfully revived in 1948, but his most important dramatic works are *L'Otage* and *L'Annonce faite à Marie*, which were seen in 1911 and 1912. Outstanding in his published poetry are *Cinq Grandes Odes suivies d'un Processional pour saluer le siècle nouveau*, published in 1910, and *Corona benignitatis Dei*, in 1914.

Claverings, The A novel by Anthony Trollope, first published in 1867.

Clayhanger A novel by Arnold Bennett, the first of the four books in the 'Clayhanger' series, published in 1910.

Cleland, John (1709–89) Born and educated in London, John Cleland is famous as the author of *Memoirs of a Woman of Pleasure*, popularly known as *Fanny Hill*. First published between 1748 and 1749, its sexual frankness resulted in immense sales, which increased to phenomenal proportions when the book became freely available in the 1960s. Its initial success did not make Cleland rich, for, as was usual at the time, he had sold the rights in the book for a comparatively small sum. In addition to some plays and three books on philology, he also wrote two other novels, *Memoirs of a Coxcomb* and *The Surprises of Love*.

clerihew An amusing form of four-lined verse invented by Edmund Clerihew Bentley, usually taking a well-known person as its subject, as, for instance:

George the Third
Ought never to have occurred.
One can only wonder
At so grotesque a blunder.

Cleveland, John (1613–58) The Cavalier poet John Cleveland was born in Loughborough, England, and educated at Cambridge and later at Oxford. A noted satirist, he wrote a number of works for the Royalist cause, including elegies for Charles I. His work has both quality and charm, despite the fact that it contains much fanciful obscurity in the manner of the metaphysical poets. During his lifetime Cleveland's poetry enjoyed huge popularity, and many of his contemporaries considered him to be greater than Milton, a verdict that posterity has not confirmed.

Clockwork Orange, The A novel by Anthony Burgess, first published in 1962. A disturbing screen version appeared in 1971.

Cloister and the Hearth, The An historical novel, set in the fifteenth century, by Charles Reade, first published in 1861.

Clough, Arthur Hugh (1819–61) Educated at Rugby School and Balliol College, Oxford, Arthur Hugh Clough, who was born in Liverpool, published in 1848 a long poem entitled *The Bothie of Toper-na-Fuosich*. This was followed in 1849 by *Ambarvalia*, a collection of shorter earlier poems. His novel in verse, *Amours de Voyage*, and the satire, *Dipsychus*, were not published until after his death. *Plutarch's Lives*, a revision of Dryden's translation, appeared in 1859.

Cobbett, William (1763–1835) The English politician and writer William Cobbett was born at Farnham, Surrey, England, and was almost entirely self-educated. After a period as a soldier, he went in 1792 to the United States, where he spent eight years, supporting himself by teaching and writing. In 1794 he caused a sensation with a pamphlet entitled *Observations on the Emigration of a Martyr to the Cause of Liberty*, an attack on the chemist, Joseph Priestley, who had just arrived in America complaining of his treatment in England. Cobbett did not like the United States, and *The Life and Adventures of Peter Porcupine*, published in 1796, was virulently anti-American. Returning home, he decided to involve himself in politics, and founded the *Weekly Political Register*. His radical views earned him a large fine and a period in prison, but this did not seriously hamper his journalistic activities. By 1817, however, he was seriously in debt, and fled to America, where he wrote his successful *English Grammar*. After two years he returned to England, bearing with him the bones of Thomas Paine, which he vainly hoped to sell for a substantial sum (the bones were later re-interred). He then continued his career as a political journalist, and published a number of books on a variety of political subjects. In 1832 he at last achieved his long-held ambition of entering Parliament, of which he was a member until shortly before his death. His most famous and enduring work, the *Rural Rides*, a fascinating account of his journeys through the English countryside on horseback, first appeared in the *Political Register*, and was published in book form in 1830.

Cocteau, Jean (1889–1963) Born in Maisons-Lafitte, Jean Cocteau was a French poet, dramatist, novelist, screenwriter and film director. He was widely regarded, during the period between the two World Wars, as the most innovative writer in France. As well as fiction, he wrote essays and screenplays, but his most notable works were his poetry, collected in *Poèmes 1916-55*, and his plays, such as *Orphée*, presented in 1934, *The Infernal Machine*, in 1934, and *The Eagle Has Two Heads*, in 1946.

Coleridge, Hartley (1796–1849) The eldest son of Samuel Taylor Coleridge, Hartley Coleridge was born at Clevedon, Somerset, and educated at Oxford. He wrote many essays and the biographies *Worthies of Yorkshire and Lancashire,* and edited the works of the dramatists Massinger and Ford, but is mainly regarded as a poet. His *Poems, Songs and Sonnets* was published in 1833.

Coleridge, Mary (1861–1907) Mary Elizabeth Coleridge, who was born in London, was a great-great-niece of Samuel Taylor Coleridge. Her first work of fiction, *The Seven Sleepers of Ephesus*, appeared in 1893, and was followed in 1897 by *The King With Two Faces*. She also published two volumes of poetry, *Fancy's Following* and *Fancy's Guerdon*, and a collection of essays. Her work was highly praised at the time of publication, but is now little read.

Coleridge, Samuel Taylor (1772–1834) Born in the vicarage of Ottery St Mary, Devonshire, England, Samuel Taylor Coleridge was originally expected to follow in his father's footsteps and enter the Church. Having begun his education at Christ's Hospital, he went on to Jesus College, Cambridge, but in 1793, pressed by his debts, impulsively enlisted in the 15th Dragoons. After a short period he was bought out by his brother, and returned to Cambridge, but he left the university in 1794 without taking a degree, and settled with his close friend, the poet Robert Southey, in Bristol. In 1795 he and Southey married the sisters Sara and Edith Fricker. Three years later, following a quarrel with Southey, he moved to Nether Stowey in Somerset. In the same year he published his first volume of poetry, *Poems on Various Subjects*. His verses had previously appeared in the *Morning Chronicle*, and with Southey he had collaborated on a drama in verse, *The Fall of Robespierre*. In June 1797, Coleridge met William Wordsworth and his sister Dorothy, and their deep friendship began. For more than a year, living near each other in Somerset, Coleridge and Wordsworth worked closely together. In 1798 they published *Lyrical Ballads*, in which was included 'The Rime of the Ancient Mariner', written at least partly at Wordsworth's instigation, and certainly with his active encouragement. 'Kubla Khan', the poem which came to Coleridge in a dream, was also composed at this time. A journey to Germany followed, during which he studied at the University of Göttingen. On his return, desperately in need of money, he took employment on *The Morning Post*. Soon after, he published his translation of Schiller's *Wallenstein*. In 1800 he went to live near Southey and the Wordsworths in the Lake District. His marriage was failing, and he had become an opium-addict, but he continued to write, and, in addition to a certain amount of journalism, he completed the second part of 'Christabel' and wrote his 'Hymn to Sunrise'. In 1804, in the hope of restoring his health, Coleridge travelled to the Mediterranean, a journey financed by Wordsworth. He spent ten months in Malta, working as secretary to the Governor, and went on to Naples and Rome. His travels did not repair his physical condition, nor did they heal the breach with his wife Sara, from whom he separated in 1807. He returned to the Lake District, and shortly thereafter founded and edited a short-lived literary magazine, *The Friend*. He also gave the first of the literary lectures which, over the next ten years, were to bring him a considerable reputation as a critic. In 1810, quarrelling with Wordsworth, he went to London, where his play, *Remorse*, was produced

A romantic oil painting of the lyrical poet Samuel Taylor Coleridge, painted by Peter Vandyke in 1795 when the poet was only twenty-three. His literary output was mainly criticism, political journalism and philosophy especially in his later years. However, he is mainly remembered for his powerful poems 'The Rime of the Ancient Mariner', 'Kubla Khan' and 'Christabel', which are especially popular with school children. In 1798 he and his celebrated friend Wordsworth published *Lyrical Ballads*, a principal composition of the English Romantic movement.

in 1813. Hoping to conquer his addiction to opium, he took residence with his friend James Gillman in Highgate, and spent the rest of his life there, succeeding at least in keeping the opium habit under control. Although he published some poetry, and his collected poems appeared in 1817 in *Sybilline Leaves*, most of the work which he produced in the last years of his life consisted of essays and literary studies. Among them are *Lay Sermons*, published in 1816 and 1817, *Aids to Reflection*, in 1825, and the major work, *Biographia Literaria*, which mixes autobiography with philosophy and criticism and appeared in 1817. Highly respected in his final years, and at last financially secure, he held weekly *conversazioni* at which he entertained his friends and young disciples with the brilliance of his talk, and expounded such influential concepts as the need for poets to return in their work to the expression of imagination and the emotions. Coleridge has a dual place in English literature, as a poet and as a critic, and in both capacities remains a major figure.

Coleridge, Sara (1802–52) Samuel Taylor Coleridge's fourth child and only daughter, Sara Coleridge was born in Keswick in the Lake District. In 1834 she published *Pretty Lessons in Verse for Good Children; with some Lessons in Latin in Easy Rhyme*, which was very popular. She also wrote a long poetical work, *Phantasmion, a Fairy Tale*, and a number of essays, and her *Memoirs and Letters* is interesting for the portraits it includes of the Lake Poets. After her husband's death in 1843, she took over the task that he had begun of editing her father's works.

Colette (1873–1954) Born in Saint-Sauveur-en-Puisaye, France, Sidonie-Gabrielle Colette was married at the age of twenty to the publisher Henri Gauthier-Villars, who was always known as 'Willy'. At his instigation she wrote her first books, the *Claudine* series, which Willy published under his own name. After divorcing him, she became a music hall artiste, remarried in 1913, and then achieved success as a writer with her novel *Chéri*, published in 1920. Many more novels were to follow, including *La Fin de Chéri*, which appeared in 1926, and *Gigi*, in 1943. She married her third husband, Maurice Goudeket, in 1935. After World War II she received many literary honours, and became President of the Académie Goncourt and a Grand Officier de la Légion d'Honneur. Essentially French, she was renowned for her wit, the elegance of her style and her brilliant, sensuous re-creation of *la belle époque*, the period of her youth. More importantly, perhaps, she fought for her independence as a woman, and won triumphantly.

Colin Clouts Come Home Againe An allegorical poem by Edmund Spenser, first published in 1595.

Collins, Wilkie (1824–89) The son of a successful artist, William Wilkie Collins, who was born in London, became a barrister, but did not practise as a lawyer, preferring a literary career. Having written a biography of his father, he published his first novel, an historical romance, *Antonina: or the Fall of Rome*, in 1850. He then began to write novels of suspense and, after bringing out three books in this genre, achieved a major success with *The Woman in White*, published in 1860. More novels followed, although after the appearance of his other most popular work, *The Moonstone*, which came out in 1868, his powers of invention began to wane. Nevertheless, his works continued to be much admired at the time for their narrative strength. His output also included many short stories, articles and plays. He was a close friend of Charles Dickens, and the two men worked together, travelled abroad together, and acted in amateur productions

A poster from *c*.1910 advertising Collette's *Claudine à Paris*. She used her husband's pseudonym Willy.

A watercolour cartoon by the illustrator Adriano Cecioni of the suspense writer Wilkie Collins. It was published in *Vanity Fair* in 1872.

together. Wilkie Collins suffered from ill-health for most of his life; like Coleridge, he became an opium-addict, and this blighted his last years. Although all his books but *The Woman in White* and *The Moonstone* are largely forgotten, Wilkie Collins must still be accorded the honour of having been the first writer of full-length crime stories in English, and his meticulous attention to detail set the standard in this field.

Collins, William (1721–59) A precocious poet, who was born in Chichester and educated at Winchester and Magdalen College, Oxford, William Collins published his first verses at the age of thirteen. In 1742 his *Persian Eclogues* appeared, followed four years later by *Odes on Several Descriptive and Allegorical Subjects*. Although his output was small and his work was not highly regarded in his lifetime, some critics now grant him a standing equal to that of Thomas Gray as the finest lyric poet of the eighteenth century.

Colonel Jack, The History and Remarkable Life of Colonel Jacque, commonly called, A novel of adventure by Daniel Defoe, published in 1722.

Color Purple, The The remarkable novel by the Black writer Alice Walker. First published in 1983, it has recently been made into a highly successful film.

Colum, Padraic (1881–1972) The Irish poet and playwright Patrick Colm, who later always used the Irish version of his name, was born in Co. Longford and educated at Trinity College, Dublin. He began his literary career as a tragic dramatist, and his early plays, the first of which was *Broken Soil*, presented in 1903, were seen at the Abbey Theatre, Dublin. He published much poetry, his first volume, *Wild Earth*, appearing in 1907 and his *Collected Poems* in 1953. Although from 1939 he lived in the United States, almost all his work reflects his strong attachment to his native land.

Comédie Humaine, La The epic series of novels and stories by Honoré de Balzac in which he portrayed French society over a period of a hundred years. The works were first collected and published under this title between 1856 and 1859.

comedy A light and amusing work, usually a play, although the term 'comedy' is frequently applied to novels, particularly those with a satiric or ironic content. Originally descriptive of dramas which were concerned with unimportant characters (as opposed to the kings and princes of tragedy), and with their absurdities, the term has come to embrace a wide variety of theatrical work, ranging from out-and-out farce to more serious explorations of the human condition as exemplified in such a play as Chekhov's *The Cherry Orchard*. A comedy, however, almost invariably presents characters at whom an audience can smile or laugh, and avoids any sense of the tragic in its conclusion.

Comedy of Errors, The A comedy by William Shakespeare, set in Ephesus and involving the twin brothers Antipholus and their twin servants Dromio. It was first produced about 1592, and published in 1623.

comedy of manners The term sometimes given to comedies dating from the late seventeenth and eighteenth century by such playwrights as Congreve, Wycherley and Sheridan, in which the humour derives largely from the foibles of the characters rather than from the plot.

Common Prayer, The Book of The familiar version of the services of the Anglican Church, together with the Psalms and passages from the Bible allocated for reading on Sundays and other Holy Days throughout the year. It was produced in 1662. The establishment of the Church of England under Henry VIII had underlined the need for services in the vernacular, and the first Prayer Book in English had grown from this demand, though it was not in fact completed and pub-

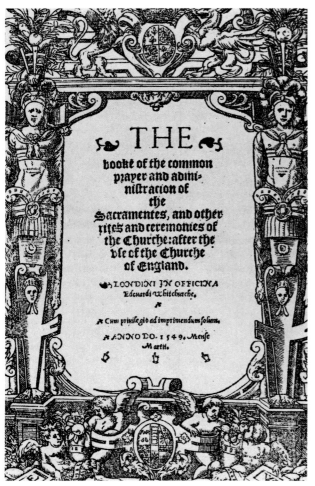

The title-page to Cranmer's *Book of Common Prayer*, 1549.

lished until 1549, during the reign of Edward VI. The book was prepared under the direction of Thomas Cranmer, Archbishop of Canterbury. He is believed to have written most of it, although his protégé Nicholas Ridley undoubtedly made some contributions, and others may have been involved. Revisions, mostly of a minor nature, were made in 1552, and other small changes were also made under Elizabeth I and James I, with the addition, for instance, of Collects written by Archbishops Whitgift and Laud. However, the 1662 version still consists chiefly of Cranmer's text. A further revision was produced in 1928, and the *Alternative Service Book*, which appeared in 1980, is now widely used, though many Anglicans, and others who are not churchgoers, greatly prefer the language of the 1662 edition, which undoubtedly possesses both beauty and power, and also enjoys the veneration that centuries of use have attached to it.

Compleat Angler, or the Contemplative Man's Recreation, The The celebrated discourse on fishing, in dialogue form, by Izaak Walton.

Compton-Burnett, Ivy (1884–1969) Born in London and educated at London University, Ivy Compton-Burnett published her first novel, *Dolores*, in 1911. After a gap of fourteen years, *Pastors and Masters* appeared, and she continued to write and publish novels, almost entirely in dialogue, for the rest of her life. They include *A House and its Head*, published in 1935, *Manservant and Maidservant*, in 1947, and *Mother and Son*, in 1955. Never a truly popular writer, she was nevertheless highly regarded among a wide coterie of intellectuals, and the quality of her work was recognized when she was made a Dame in 1947.

Comus A masque by John Milton, first performed at Ludlow Castle in Shropshire in 1634, and published in 1637.

Confessio Amantis A long poem by John Gower, dating from the end of the fourteenth century and containing many classical and medieval stories.

Confessions An autobiographical work by St Augustine, covering his early life. It was written about AD400.

Confessions of an English Opium Eater The auto-biographical account by Thomas de Quincey, first published in 1822.

Confessions of Nat Türner, The A novel by William Styron, first published in 1967.

Congreve, William (1670–1729) The playwright William Congreve was born at Bardsey, near Leeds, England, but educated in Ireland. He studied law, published a novel, and at the age of twenty-three achieved instant success and fame with his first comedy, *The Old Bachelor*, produced, with Dryden's encouragement, in 1693. *The Double Dealer* appeared the following year and *Love for Love* was presented in 1695. Congreve's sole tragedy, *The Mourning Bride*, came in 1697, and *The Way of the World* in 1700. Apart from these five plays, Congreve wrote comparatively little, producing only one or two masques and various poems celebrating contemporary events. It is uncertain whether he gave up writing for the stage as a result of the comparative failure, on its first appearance, of *The Way of the World*, or because the sinecure government posts which he had obtained had given him too much financial security, or for some other reasons. His theatrical works had, however, brought him great renown and the friendship of Swift — with whom he had been at college — and of Pope and Steele, and the admiration of Voltaire. Despite the poor reception that it received initially, *The Way of the World* has since come to be regarded as a superb example of Restoration comedy, and, together with his other masterpiece, *Love for Love*, has established Congreve as one of the greatest writers of comedy in the English language.

Coningsby A novel by Benjamin Disraeli, first published in 1844.

Conquest of Granada: or Almanzor and Almahide, The A two-part tragedy by John Dryden, first performed in 1670 and 1671, and published in 1672.

Conrad, Joseph (1857–1924) Of Polish origin, though born in the Ukraine, Teodor Josef Konrad Korzeniowski adopted the name Joseph Conrad when his first book, *Almayer's Folly*, which was written in English, was published in 1895. His father, Apollo Korzeniowski, was a writer and translator but also a political dissident, and his involvement in the Polish insurrection of 1863 resulted in the exile of the family to the town of Vologda in the north of Russia, where Condrad's mother died. In 1869 he and his father were able to go to Cracow, but his father died very soon after, and the boy was cared for by an uncle. At the age of nineteen, Conrad went to Marseilles and became a sailor, a career which he was to follow for the next twenty years. In 1878 he came to Lowestoft on the east coast of England, and from then on sailed in British ships, eventually rising to qualify as a master mariner in 1886. His sailing experiences provided the background for much of his fiction, though he also used political themes. Principally because of ill-health, he left the sea in 1894 and thereafter lived in England, devoting himself to writing. He had been granted British nationality in 1886. He married in 1896, and in due course fathered two children. His second book, *The Outcast of the Island*, appeared in 1896, and from that time until his death Conrad produced a steady stream of novels, novellas and short stories, writing so prolifically that hardly a year passed without the appearance of at least one new work. 1902, for instance, saw the publication of *Typhoon*, *Heart of Darkness* and *Youth*, despite the fact that he was also working at that period on the two novels which he wrote in collaboration with Ford Madox Ford, *The Inheritors* and *Romance*. Although he is so highly regarded nowadays, and books such as *The Nigger of the Narcissus*, published in 1897, *Lord Jim*, in 1900, *Nostromo*, in 1904, and *The Secret Agent*, in 1907, are accorded the status of

Conrad wrote this note in his first novel *Almayer's Folly*.

Characteristic oil study by Walter Tittle, dated 1923-4, of the classical novelist Joseph Conrad in reflective mood. His early years as ship's officer in Asian, African and Latin American seas evoked the exotic settings of many of his novels. His mastery of the English language, which he only acquired as an adult, is widely acclaimed.

classics, Conrad, while receiving some critical acclaim for his work, failed for many years to appeal to the reading public at large, and his pecuniary rewards were minimal. It was not until 1913, with the publication of *Chance*, that his work became popular and brought him both world-wide celebrity and financial security. *Chance* was followed by *Victory*, published in 1915, *The Arrow of Gold*, in 1919, *The Rescue*, in 1920, and *The Rover*, in 1923. In addition to fiction, he also wrote numerous essays, adapted three of his stories for the stage, and published his autobiography, *A Personal Record*, in 1912. Perhaps the most astonishing thing about Joseph Conrad is his total mastery in his writing of a language which was not his native tongue, of which he did not know a word until he was a grown man, and which he was never able to speak with total fluency. Indeed, some critics have attributed the excellence of his style to the fact that he had always to write with a precision and care that an English-speaking author would not have needed. It is not, however, solely as a stylist that he is renowned. A moralist, frequently preaching the responsibility that we each bear for our actions, Conrad was also one of the world's great story-tellers. Despite the claims of such writers as Henry James, he may be considered as the most important novelist writing in English in the first years of the twentieth century.

Conscious Lovers, The A comedy by Richard Steele, first presented in 1722.

Contarini Fleming A novel by Benjamin Disraeli, first published in 1832, and the third in the trilogy of which the other books are *Vivian Grey* and *Alroy*.

Contrast, The A play by Royall Tyler, first produced in 1787 and published in 1790, *The Contrast* is claimed to be the first comedy to be written by an American playwright.

Cook, Eliza (1818–89) London-born Eliza Cook was self-taught, and began to write poetry while still very young. Her first collection, *Lays of a Wild Harp*, appeared in 1835. *Melaia and other poems* was published in 1838, and other volumes followed in later years. Her sentimental poem 'The Old Armchair', which was first seen in the *Weekly Dispatch* in 1837, made her famous, both in Britain and in the United States.

Cooke, John Esten (*c.*1830–86) The American writer John Esten Cooke achieved great popularity with his historical romances and novels of his native Virginia, such as *Leather Stocking and Silk* and *The Virginia Comedians*, both first published in 1854. Cooke fought for the Confederacy during the American Civil War, and the biographies that he wrote of Stonewall Jackson and Robert E. Lee were naturally sympathetic in tone.

Cookson, Catherine (1906–) Currently Britain's most popular author, Catherine Cookson was born in South Shields. Immensely prolific and a gifted story-teller, her novels sell in huge quantities and are borrowed from public libraries more frequently than those of any other author. She published her first novel, *Kate Hannigan*, in 1947, and close on a hundred books, using both contemporary and carefully-researched historical settings, have followed. *Our Kate*, which appeared in 1969, is ostensibly her mother's story, but is in fact a volume of autobiography.

Cooper, James Fenimore (1789–1851) Born at Burlington, New Jersey, to a well-to-do family, James Fenimore Cooper became a seaman after being expelled from Yale, and later joined the American Navy as a midshipman. His first novel, *Precaution*, was published anonymously in 1820. The following year, this time using his own name, he brought out *The Spy*, which was immediately successful, and in 1823 came *The*

James Fenimore Cooper's celebration of the American landscape and his romantic creation of Leatherstocking constitute the foundation of American literature.

J. Fenimore Cooper

Pioneers, the first of his 'Leatherstocking Tales'. These novels not only presented exciting stories, with the scout Natty Bumppo (Hawkeye) as their daring and sympathetic hero, but also provided exceptionally fine pictures of the conflict between the white man and the American Indians. They made their author famous on both sides of the Atlantic. The second in the series, *The Last of the Mohicans*, his most enduring and celebrated novel, appeared in 1826, and the remainder of the 'Leatherstocking Tales', *The Prairie*, *The Pathfinder* and *The Deerslayer*, came out in 1827, 1840 and 1841 respectively. Cooper wrote many other novels, of varying quality, and also produced a number of works of non-fiction, several on political subjects, including criticism of the workings of society both in Europe, where he travelled extensively, and in the United States. The years he had spent at sea as a young man provided him with the background for much of his fiction, and also, no doubt, inspired him to write *The History of the Navy of the United States*, which was published in 1839.

Cooper, William (1910–) William Cooper is the pseudonym of the English writer Harry Summerfield Hoff. Educated at Cambridge, he has had a distinguished career in the Civil Service. His first novels, published under the name of H.S. Hoff, were *Trina*, *Rhea*, *Lisa* and *Three Marriages*. His best-known books are *Scenes from Provincial Life*, first published in 1950, *Scenes from Married Life*, in 1961, *Scenes from Metropolitan Life*, in 1982, and *Scenes from Later Life*, in 1983.

Coppard, A.E. (1878–1957) Alfred Edgar Coppard was a prolific writer of poetry and short stories. He first attracted attention in England in 1921 with his collection of stories, *Adam and Eve and Pinch Me*, and this was followed by over thirty books, including his *Collected Poems*, which appeared in 1928, many other volumes of verse, and his *Collected Tales*, published in 1948.

Corelli, Marie (1855–1924) Marie Corelli was the daughter of an Italian father and a Scottish mother, but was adopted and brought up as Mary Mackay. Her first novel, *A Romance of Two Worlds*, was published in 1886, and was an immediate popular success. She wrote many more extremely popular novels, including *The Sorrows of Satan*, which appeared in 1895. Her work was romantically melodramatic, always conveyed a strong moral message, and was remarkably poorly written. She is said to have been Queen Victoria's favourite novelist.

Coriolanus A tragedy by William Shakespeare, probably first presented in 1608, and printed in 1623. It concerns a Roman general, who joins the enemies of Rome, and is finally killed by them.

Corneille, Pierre (1606–84) Born at Rouen, France, Pierre Corneille qualified as a lawyer, and later became the first of the great French classical tragedians. His first play, *Mélite*, was presented in 1629. He attracted the attention of Cardinal Richelieu, and under his protection wrote many dramas. These were not always well received, and Corneille's reputation and financial status rose or fell accordingly. For some time the Académie Française had rejected him as a member, but he was admitted in 1647, as was the right of the author of such undoubted masterpieces as *Le Cid*, *Horace*, *Cinna* and *Polyceeute*.

Corsair, The A narrative poem by Lord Byron about a pirate chief taken prisoner by the Turkish Pacha. It was first published in 1814.

Cortazar, Julio (1914–) The reputation of this noted Argentinian writer is mainly based on his many collections of short stories, especially *Bestiario*, published in 1951. His novels include *Rayuela*, which appeared in 1963, and *Libro de Manuel*, in 1973.

Coryate, Thomas (*c*.1577–1617) The English traveller and writer Thomas Coryate was born at Odcombe, Somersetshire, and educated at Oxford. In 1611 he published an account of a long walking tour under the curious title *Coryate's Crudities hastily gobbled up in Five Months Travels in France, Italy, etc.* A second journey to Greece, Palestine, Persia and India resulted in a number of letters, some of which were published in 1616 under the title of *Letters from Asmere, the Court of the Great Mogul, to several Persons of Quality in England*.

Count of Monte Cristo, The The popular novel by Alexandre Dumas the elder, first published between 1844 and 1845. The wrongfully imprisoned Edmond Dantès escapes, finds a fortune, and takes revenge on his enemies.

Country Wife, The A satirical comedy and the best-known play by William Wycherley, first presented in 1675 and published the same year.

Courtship of Miles Standish, The A long poem by Henry Wadsworth Longfellow, first published in 1858.

Cousin Phyllis A novella by Mrs Gaskell, first published in 1864.

Coverdale, Miles (1488–1569) Born in Yorkshire, England, and educated at Cambridge, Miles Coverdale became Bishop of Exeter in 1551. Before then he had produced translations of the Bible and of the Apocrypha, and he was employed first by Thomas Cromwell and later by Thomas Cranmer in the production of the Great Bible of 1539. He published some twenty-six works, mostly translations from the German, and was active in the reform of the Church.

Coward, Sir Noel (1899–1973) Noel Pierce Coward, actor and entertainer, was born in Teddington, Middlesex, England, and trained for the stage. He began writing plays while still in his teens. His first full-length play, *'I'll Leave it to You'*, was presented in 1920, and in 1924 the somewhat melodramatic *The Vortex* gave him his first big success. A series of brilliant comedies followed, equally popular in Britain and the United States, including *Hay Fever*, first produced in 1925, *Private Lives*, in 1933, *Blithe Spirit*, in 1941, and *Present Laughter*, in 1942. *Cavalcade*, first seen in 1931, has been dismissed as patriotic sentimentality, but a recent revival at the Festival Theatre, Chichester, proved that it retains its entertainment value. Coward also wrote one-act plays, several of which were presented in *Tonight at 8.30* in 1935 and 1936, and he wrote and contributed to many revues. A popular composer and lyricist, he wrote a number of musical comedies, and his witty songs, such as 'The Stately Homes of England' and 'Mad Dogs and Englishmen', continue to amuse, while ballads such as 'I'll See You Again', from his operetta *Bitter Sweet* have become 'standards'. His versatility was additionally demonstrated in the screenplays for *Brief Encounter* (based on his play, *Still Life*) and *This Happy Breed*, in several collections of short stories, and in his two volumes of autobiography, *Present Indicative*, published in 1937, and *Future Indicative*, which appeared in 1954. He was knighted in 1969.

Cowley, Abraham (1618–67) The metaphysical poet Abraham Cowley was born in London and educated at Trinity College, Cambridge, and St John's College, Oxford. He published his first book of poetry, *Poetical Blossoms*, in 1833. Included in the volume were his *Tragicall History of Piramus and Thisbe* and another long poem, *Constantia and Philetus*, the former written when he was no more than ten years old and the latter when he was twelve, probably the most mature writing ever produced by a child of that age. *The Mistress*, consisting of love poems, appeared in 1647, and in 1656 he published his collected *Poems*. Cowley also wrote plays, and a number of essays and pamphlets on political and philosophical subjects, notably *The Advancement of Experimental Philosophy*, published in 1661. A supporter of Charles I, he spent some years during the Commonwealth in Paris at the court of the exiled Queen Henrietta Maria, later returning to England as a spy, an escapade which landed him in prison for a short spell. Many of his writings were fervently Royalist in content, but his loyalty to the cause was not rewarded as munificently as he had hoped at the time of the Restoration. However, certain of his contemporaries ranked him as the finest poet of his age, believing him to be greater than Milton, and this assessment resulted in burial in Westminster Abbey, an honour not granted to Milton.

Cowper, William (1731–1800) Born in Great Berkhampstead, Hertfordshire, England, and educated at Westminster School, William Cowper trained as a lawyer and became a barrister, but did not practise. His first publication did not appear until he was in his forties, when he collaborated with a curate on a book of hymns, his contributions including 'God moves in a mysterious way His wonders to perform'. In 1782 a volume of secular verse appeared, *Poems of William Cowper of the Inner Temple, Esq.*, which included a number of satirical works. It was not a success, but in 1785 his second book brought him great acclaim. It contained not only his major work, a long poem entitled 'The Task', but also 'Tirocinium, or a Review of Schools', a strong attack on the British public school system, and the still popular 'The Diverting History of John Gilpin'. For most of his life Cowper was subject to fits of melancholy, which at times degenerated into outright insanity, and his autobiography, the *Memoir*, written when he was in his thirties and published posthumously in 1816, reveals the anguish that his deep religious convictions caused him. Despite his mental illness, he continued to write poetry, and in 1791 published a translation of Homer. The simplicity, naturalness and humour of Cowper's verse exercised a considerable influence on many poets of succeeding generations.

Cozzens, James Gould (1903–78) The American writer James Gould Cozzens was born in Chicago and educated at Harvard, where he wrote his first novel, *Confusion*, published in 1924. Among his other novels, distinguished for their portraits of somewhat Olympian characters, are *Men and Brethren*, published in 1936, *Guard of Honour*, which won the Pulitzer Prize in 1948, and the very successful *By Love Possessed*, which appeared in 1957.

Crabbe, George (1754–1832) A native of Aldeburgh, Suffolk, England, George Crabbe was for a time a doctor, and in 1781 entered the Church. He published a poem, *Inebriety*, in 1775, but his first success was *The Village*, in 1783. Two years later *The Newspaper*, a satirical work, was published, to be followed by more than twenty years of silence. Between 1807 and 1817, he brought out four more books, including *The Borough*, a long verse portrait of Aldeburgh, which tells the story of Peter Grimes. Benjamin Britten's opera of that name brought Crabbe back into public interest.

Crane, Hart (1899–1932) Harold Hart Crane, who was born in Garretsville, Ohio, published two books only, a collection of poetry, *White Buildings*, which came out in 1926, and a long poem, *The Bridge*, in 1930, though additional verses and some prose writings appeared in a collected edition in 1960. Crane's childhood was unhappy, and he never overcame the damage that it did to his psyche. He became an alcoholic, and committed suicide when returning by sea from a visit to Mexico. His output of verse, though small, is much admired for the power and careful construction of his writing.

Crane, Stephen (1871–1900) The American novelist Stephen Crane was born in Newark, New Jersey. After a somewhat scanty education, he became a New York journalist and wrote his first novel, *Maggie: A Girl of the Streets*, which he published himself in 1893, since the publisher to whom he submitted it believed that its realism was too sordid for popular taste. It was a failure, but his major work, *The Red Badge of Courage*, achieved immediate success when it appeared in 1895, and it remains the classic novel of the American Civil War. Crane's health was poor,

Two pages from *The Red Badge of Courage*, showing the rail fence at Hagerstown pike during the battle of Antietam.

but volumes of verse and several other novels followed in the few years that were left to him, and he also produced some collections of short stories, the latter including one of the best examples of his writing, 'The Open Boat'. *The Red Badge of Courage* is all the more remarkable since Crane did not fight in the war, and it is therefore almost entirely a work of imagination. Much of the rest of his writing was, however, based on his own experiences, especially as the accuracy of his picture of the Civil War had led to a number of assignments as a war correspondent in Mexico, Greece and Cuba. After a period in England, where his work was much admired, Crane went to Baden-Baden in search of a cure for his tuberculosis. He died there, too young to fulfil his promise or to repeat the brilliance of *The Red Badge of Courage*.

Cranford The best-known novel by Mrs Gaskell, presenting a series of portraits of the ladies of the village of Cranford. It was first published in book form in 1853.

Cranmer, Thomas (1489–1556) Archbishop Thomas Cranmer was born at Aslacton, Nottinghamshire, England, and educated at Jesus College, Cambridge. He gained the friendship of Henry VIII by helping to resolve the king's marital problems, and was appointed Archbishop

Chapter 5

THERE WERE MOMENTS OF WAITING. THE YOUTH thought of the village street at home before the arrival of the circus parade on a day in the spring. He remembered how he had stood, a small, thrillful boy, prepared to follow the dingy lady upon the white horse, or the band in its faded chariot. He saw the yellow road, the lines of expectant people, and the sober houses. He particularly remembered an old fellow who used to sit upon a cracker-box in front of the store and feign to despise such exhibitions. A thousand details of colour and form surged in his mind. The old fellow upon the cracker-box appeared in middle prominence.

Someone cried, 'Here they come!'

There was rustling and muttering among the men. They displayed a feverish desire to have every possible cartridge ready to their hands. The boxes were pulled around into various positions, and adjusted with great care. It was as if seven hundred new bonnets were being tried on.

The tall soldier, having prepared his rifle, produced a red handkerchief of some kind. He was engaged in knitting it about his throat with exquisite attention to its position, when the cry was repeated up and down the line in a muffled roar of sound.

'Here they come! Here they come!' Gun-locks clicked.

Across the smoke-infested fields came a brown swarm of running men who were giving shrill yells. They came on, stooping and swinging their rifles at all angles. A flag tilted forward, sped near the front.

As he caught sight of them, the youth was momentarily startled by a thought that perhaps his gun was not loaded. He stood trying to rally his faltering intellect so that he might recollect the moment when he had loaded, but he could not.

A hatless general pulled his dripping horse to a stand near the colonel of the 304th. He shook his fist in the other's face. 'You've got to hold 'em back!' he shouted savagely; 'you've got to hold 'em back!'

In his agitation the colonel began to stammer. 'A-all r-right, general, all right, by Gawd! We-we'll do our—we-we'll d d-do—do our best, general.' The general made a passionate gesture and galloped away. The

57

'Bits of dark debris' [p 61]

Crashaw, Richard

of Canterbury in 1533. He played an important part in the Reformation, and continued in office until the accession of Mary I. Imprisoned in the Tower in 1553, he was burnt at the stake as a Protestant in 1556. His principal literary work was concerned with the *Book of Common Prayer* of the Anglican Church, and the version prepared in 1662 consists largely of his text.

Crashaw, Richard (*c*.1613–50) English academic, cleric and poet, Richard Crashaw was born in London and educated at the Charterhouse and at Cambridge. He published his first book, a collection of verses in Latin, in 1634, and in 1646 brought out *Steps to the Temple*, a selection of his religious verse, and, in the same volume, *The Delights of the Muses*, which consists of secular poems.

Crèvecoeur, J. Hector St John de (1735–1813) Born at Caen, France, Michel-Guillaume Crèvecoeur later adopted the name under which his work was published. He emigrated to Canada and then moved to Orange County, New York, where he became a farmer and took American citizenship. He wrote a travel book and some essays, but is now known solely for his *Letters from An American Farmer*, the romantic charm of which brought the book an enormous success when it was published in 1782.

Cricket on the Hearth, The A Christmas book by Charles Dickens, first published in 1846.

Crime and Punishment Fyodor Dostoevsky's most famous novel, in which the student Raskolnikov commits a murder and thereafter suffers great agonies of the soul. It was first published in 1866.

Critic, The A burlesque comedy by Richard Brinsley Sheridan, first presented in 1779.

Croker, John Wilson (1780–1857) Although born in Galway, Ireland, and educated at Trinity College, Dublin, John Wilson Croker became a British politician. He wrote a number of books in various genres, including French history, and contributed regularly to the *Quarterly Review*. His literary criticism was noted for its rancorous approach, and his attack on Keats in his review of *Endymion* is supposed to have contributed to the poet's early death.

Crome Yellow A satirical novel by Aldous Huxley, first published in 1921.

Cronin, A.J. (1896–1981) Dr. Archibald Joseph Cronin was born in Dumbartonshire, Scotland, and received his medical training in Glasgow. After some years of practice he turned, very profitably, from medicine to writing. His novel *Hatter's Castle* became an immediate bestseller when it was published in 1931, and he followed it with a string of equally successful books, including, *The Stars Look Down*, in 1935, *The Keys*

of the Kingdom, in 1942, and *The Citadel*, perhaps his most popular work, which appeared in 1937.

Crotchet Castle A satirical novel by Thomas Love Peacock, first published in 1831.

Crucible, The A play by Arthur Miller, based on the Salem witch trials, first presented in 1953.

Cruikshank, George (1792–1878) Born in London, George Cruikshank was a satirical cartoonist who became also the most successful book illustrator of his age. His vast output included drawings for Grimm's *Fairy Tales*, Cowper's *John Gilpin*, Defoe's *Robinson Crusoe*, Scott's *Waverley* and Harriet Beecher Stowe's *Uncle Tom's Cabin*. He is probably most remembered today for the illustrations to many works by Dickens, an association which began with *Sketches by Boz* and was especially successful in *Oliver Twist*.

'A pickpocket in custody' from *Sketches by Boz*.

Cummings, e.e. (1894–1962) Edward Estlin Cummings was born in Cambridge, Massachusetts, and educated at Harvard. His first book, *The Enormous Room*, appeared in 1922, and was a narrative of his experiences in France in 1917. It was very successful, but Cummings was soon to establish himself as a poet. A volume of verse, *Tulips and Chimneys*, appeared in 1923. A number of other collections followed, in which his unconventional approach to the typographical appearance of his work and the freedom of his language undoubtedly disturbed many readers. Nowadays his work no longer appears eccentric, but it is still admired. Cummings also published some plays and essays and a travel book.

Cymbeline A play by William Shakespeare, first presented about 1610 and printed in 1623. It is concerned with Imogen, daughter of Cymbeline, King of Britain. She undergoes many unhappy experiences before being reunited with her husband and her father.

Cynewulf Believed to have lived in the northern part of England at the end of the eighth or beginning of the ninth century, Cynewulf is the only Old English poet, writing in the vernacular, of whom any undisputed works still exist. These are the four religious poems, *The Ascension*, *St Juliana*, *Elene* and *The Fate of the Apostles*, which are preserved in two eleventh century manuscripts, the Cercelli Book and the Exeter Book.

Cyrano de Bergerac A romantic play by Edmond Rostand about the gallant Cyrano, whose life is blighted by the extraordinary size of his nose. It was first presented in 1897.

D

Daisy Miller A novel by Henry James, first published in 1879. An American girl travels to Europe and innocently offends local conventions.

Dana, Richard Henry (1815–82) The son of a poet of the same name, Richard Henry Dana was born in Cambridge, Massachusetts, and educated at Harvard. He went to sea in 1834, and the notes which he kept of his experiences were later turned into his classic account, *Two Years Before the Mast*, first published in 1840. After leaving the sea, Dana qualified as a lawyer and later wrote *The Seaman's Friend*, which for many years was the standard work on the legal rights and duties of seamen.

Dance to the Music of Time, A A sequence of twelve connected novels by Anthony Powell providing a picture of England in the years immediately before and after World War II. The novels were first published between 1951 and 1975.

Daniel, Samuel (1563–1619) Born near Taunton, Somersetshire, England, Samuel Daniel published his first volume of sonnets, *Delia*, in 1592. The book was frequently reprinted, and an edition which appeared in 1594 also contained his tragedy, *Cleopatra*. His other works included a long poem, *The Civil Wars*, a *Panegyric Congratulatorie* on the accession of James I, and a series of plays and masques. In 1602 he published *A Defence of Rime* in answer to Thomas Campion's plea for free verse. His last book, published in 1612, was a *History of England*, written in prose.

Daniel Deronda George Eliot's last novel, first published in 1876.

D'Annunzio, Gabriele (1863–1938) An Italian nationalist from the Abruzzi, Gabriele D'Annunzio was a novelist, poet and playwright, and also a politician and soldier. His writings and speeches were partly responsible for Italy's entry in the First World War, during which he fought for the Allies with great gallantry. After the war, in protest at the treatment meted out to Italy in President Wilson's peace plans for Europe, he led a force to occupy the town of Fiume (now Rijeka), and for two years Fiume was an independent state under his dictatorship. His political writings, although influential at the time, now seem hysterical in tone. His first publication was a volume of verse, *Primo Vere*, which appeared in 1879. More poetry followed, and in 1889 his first novel, *Il Piacere* (*The Child of Pleasure*), brought him an international reputation. The many other novels which he wrote were well received, as were his plays, including the tragedy *Francesca da Rimini*, produced in 1901, but nowadays it is particularly for his lyric poetry that he is admired.

Gabriele D'Annunzio the Italian novelist, poet and playwright, whose writings stirred his fellow countrymen into entering the First World War.

Domenico di Michelino's beautifully intricate depiction of Dante holding a book of his poems. He is set against a backdrop of heaven, hell and his native Florence.

Dante (1265–1321) The greatest of all Florentines, Dante Alighieri was the son of a lawyer, whose family belonged to the lower ranks of the nobility. The details of his early life are obscure, but it can be assumed that he received the best education then available. Like others of a similar background, he wrote poetry as a youth, and familiarized himself with painting and music. The painter Giotto was an intimate friend. In 1274, when they were both nine years old, Dante met Bice, or Beatrice, Portinari, and fell in love with her. They had few meetings, and Beatrice was later married to Simone de' Bardi, but Dante continued to idealize and idolize her until her death in 1290. Dante himself married in 1292, his wife, Gemma Donati, eventually bearing him seven children, but Beatrice was the subject of most of the poems in his collection, *Vita Nuova* (*New* or *Young Life*), probably completed about 1300. By this time Dante had become prominent in the political life of Florence, and had been appointed one of the six *priori* who

governed the city. In 1301 a major dispute broke out between the Neri (Black) and Bianchi (White) factions within the Guelph party in Florence. Pope Boniface was invited to mediate, and Dante was one of the three councillors sent to Rome to meet him. During his absence the Neri gained dominance, and Dante, whose sympathies were with the Bianchi group, was fined and banished, and a subsequent sentence condemned him to be burnt alive. As an exile, he was henceforth to lead a wandering life, visiting many cities of Italy and also venturing into France. Although he was able to stay with certain of his friends, his inability to return to Florence meant that the twenty years that elapsed before his death in Ravenna were for the poet a period of unhappiness and suffering. During this time, however, he wrote his greatest works, and one may wonder whether, had he remained in Florence, his involvement in politics would have allowed him the time and the inclination to write. The dates of composition of Dante's works are uncertain, but it is probable that the *Convito* (*The Banquet*) and *De Monarchia* were both written between 1304 and 1313. The former was intended as a kind of handbook of universal knowledge, but was not completed; the latter is a long political treatise on the subject of the Holy Roman Empire. He also produced *De Vulgari Eloquio*, a treatise on the Italian language and the writing of poetry, and *Il Canzoniere*, a collection of lyrics, ballads and sonnets. Dante's great masterpiece, the *Divina Commedia* (*The Divine Comedy*), which had probably been many years in the writing, was completed just before his death. Written in *terza rima*, rhyming lines of eleven syllables, grouped in triplets, it consists of the *Inferno*, the *Purgatorio* and the *Paradiso*, and is a magnificent compound of many elements, including theology and morality and history, a vision of life after death which is also a commentary of the human condition. The poet is conducted by Virgil through Hell and Purgatory, and it is Beatrice who leads him to Paradise, where he ascends through the various spheres until he eventually attains the tenth, where the Deity is veiled in light. In subtlety, depth of characterization and intensity, and in the sense of personal passion with which it is written, the range of this great work can be compared only to that of Shakespeare's plays. Its power and beauty have been recognized ever since it first appeared, many of Dante's contemporaries considering it to be divinely inspired. Italy's finest poet, and one of the greatest writers the world has ever known, Dante can be regarded as the first major author in the modern tradition, and his influence on Western writers, from Chaucer onwards, has been immense.

Darkness at Noon A novel by Arthur Koestler presenting a powerful attack on the Stalinist régime in Russia. It was first published in 1940.

Darley, George (1795–1846) The Irish poet George Darley was born in Dublin and educated at Trinity College, Dublin. He published his first poem, *Errors of Ecstasie*, in 1822. He followed this in 1826 with a book of prose stories, *Labour in Idleness*, and in 1827 produced *Sylvia, or the May Queen*, a lyrical drama. He wrote two other plays, a great deal of dramatic and art criticism, and many lyrics of considerable quality, as well as mathematics text books. Some of his finest work was seen in the poem *Nepenthe*, first published in 1835.

Darwin, Charles (1809–82) Charles Robert Darwin was born at Shrewsbury, England, and educated at Edinburgh University and Christ's College, Cambridge. He published in 1839 his *Journal of Researches into the Geology and Natural History of the various countries visited by H.M.S. Beagle*.

Observations made during that voyage resulted in the publication in 1859 of his great work, *On the Origin of Species by Means of Natural Selection, or the Preservation of Favoured Races in the Struggle for Life*, followed in 1871 and 1872 by two further books on the same subject, *The Descent of Man, and Selection in Relation to Sex* and *Expression of the Emotions*. Darwin's other works, many of them on botanical subjects, were less contentious, and enhanced his reputation as a naturalist.

Darwin, Erasmus (1731–1802) The grandfather of Charles Darwin, Erasmus Darwin was born at Elton, Nottinghamshire, England, and educated at Cambridge. He published in 1791 a long poem entitled *The Botanic Garden*, the first part of which was *The Economy of Vegetation*, and the second *The Loves of the Plants*. The verses set out a great deal of botanical information, and, interestingly enough in view of his grandson's major work, hinted at the idea of evolution.

Daudet, Alphonse (1840–97) A native of Nimes in France, Alphonse Daudet was a prolific novelist and short story writer, noted for the charm and humour of his work. He first attracted attention in 1866 with *Lettres de mon moulin*, and in 1872 he brought out both the first of his four very popular novels about the comic character Tartarin de Tarascon and his play *L'Arlésienne*, for which Bizet wrote the incidental music. *Fromont jeune et Risler aîné*, published in 1874, achieved an enormous success, and Daudet was compared for his humour and the depth of his characterizations to Dickens. For the rest of his life he continued to produce works in various genres, including books for children.

D'Avenant, Sir William (1606–68) William D'Avenant, who was born and educated in Oxford, was for some time supposed to be a bastard son of Shakespeare, a theory now discounted. In 1629 his first play, *The Tragedy of Albovine*, appeared, and he subsequently wrote many masques and plays. His best known comedy, *The Wits*, was first seen in 1636. In 1637 he was made Poet Laureate. A dedicated Royalist, he was knighted by Charles I for his bravery during the siege of Gloucester in 1643. Captured by the Parliamentarians, he was condemned to death, but was eventually pardoned, possibly as a result of Milton's intervention. D'Avenant avoided the embargo on plays during the Commonwealth by producing a series of 'operas', the first seen in England. In the earliest, *The Siege of Rhodes*, a woman appeared on the stage for the first time. More innovation followed with the Restoration, when D'Avenant opened a new theatre, used movable scenery, and brought the flamboyance of French theatrical style to England.

David Copperfield A partly autobiographical novel by Charles Dickens, first published between 1849 and 1850. Among its memorable characters are Aunt Betsey Trotwood, Mr Micawber and Peggoty.

Davidson, John (1857–1909) The Scottish poet John Davidson was born at Barrhead, Renfrewshire, Scotland, and educated at Edinburgh University. He published a great many books in a variety of genres, but made his name with a volume of poetry, *Fleet Street Eclogues*, first published in 1893. His other verse, often much grimmer than that of most of his contemporaries, included a series of works in which he set out his down-to-earth theories of life.

Davies, John, of Hereford (*c*.1565–1618) John Davies was a poet, epigrammist and calligrapher. His publications include *Microcosmos*, in 1603, and *The Muse's Sacrifice*, in 1612. His collection of epigrams, *The Source of Folly*, which includes tributes to many eminent men of letters, appeared about 1610, and he also published, in 1633, *An Anatomy of Fair Writing*.

Davies, Sir John (1569–1626) Born in Wiltshire and educated at Winchester and Oxford, Sir John Davies published some volumes of poetry, including *Orchestra, or a Poeme of Dauncing*, in 1596, and *Hymns to Astraea*, a homage to Elizabeth I, in 1599. A politician and lawyer, he also wrote a prose work with the now ironic-sounding title, *Discoverie of the true causes why Ireland was never entirely subdued untill the beginning of his Majestie's happie raigne*, first published in 1612.

Davies, Robertson (1913–) Following his education at Queen's University, Kingston, Ontario, and Balliol College, Oxford, Robertson Davies, who was born in Thamesville, Ontario, worked as an actor and then as a journalist. From 1960 he pursued a distinguished academic life. His first book was *Shakespeare's Boy Actors*, published in 1939. Since then he has written many books in different genres, including essays, plays and text books. A book of literary criticism, *A Voice from the Attic*, came out in 1960, and a study of *Stephen Leacock* appeared in 1970. His novels include *Tempest Tost*, in 1951, *The Rebel Angels*, in 1970, and *What's Bred in the Bone*, in 1985.

Davies, W.H. (1871–1940) A native of Newport, Wales, William Henry Davies spent much of his early manhood in America, including a period seeking for gold in the Klondike. Returning to England, he made determined efforts to publish his poetry, and three collections of verse appeared before the publication in 1908 of *The Autobiography of a Super-Tramp*, in which he recorded his experiences, and which brought him considerable fame. Although he wrote further books of autobiography and some novels, he is best known as a poet. A prolific versifier, his *Complete Poems* appeared in 1963.

Day, John (*c*.1574–*c*1640) The English dramatist John Day was born at Cawston, Norfolk, England, and educated at Cambridge. He not only produced work of his own but, in the fashion of the period, collaborated with other playwrights, the best known of whom was Thomas Dekker. Day's own plays included *The Isle of Gulls* and *Humour out of Breath*, and his most successful work was a masque, *The Parliament of Bees*. The dates of performance of these works is uncertain, but all are believed to have been presented from about 1606 to 1608.

Day-Lewis, C. (1904–72) Born in Ballintogher, Sligo, Ireland, and educated at Oxford, Cecil Day-Lewis published his first volume of poetry, *Beechen Vigil*, in 1925. Further collections of verse followed, those published in the 1930s reflecting his left-wing views, while his later work became less overtly political. In 1940 he published the first of his translations of Virgil, *The Georgics*, and he also wrote novels, children's books, plays, literary criticism, and an autobiography. He also produced, under the pseudonym Nicholas Blake, a large number of detective stories. In 1951 he became Professor of Poetry at Oxford, and in 1968 was appointed Poet Laureate in succession to John Masefield. His *Collected Poems* appeared in 1954.

Day of the Locust, The A satirical novel about Hollywood by Nathanael West, first published in 1939.

Death Comes for the Archbishop An historical novel by Willa Cather, first published in 1927. Set in nineteenth-century New Mexico, it tells of the struggles and eventual deaths of two French missionaries.

Death in the Afternoon Ernest Hemingway's account of bull-fighting, first published in 1932.

Death in Venice A novella by Thomas Mann, first published in 1912.

Death of a Salesman A play by Arthur Miller, presenting the tragedy of Willie Loman, betrayed by the society in which he lives. It was first produced in 1949.

Death of the Heart A novel by Elizabeth Bowen, first published in 1938.

Decameron, The A collection of one hundred tales by Giovanni Boccaccio, first published in 1353, but almost certainly written much earlier over a period of years. The stories are supposedly told by ten young people seeking refuge for ten days from the plague which struck Florence in 1348. The prologue, an account of the plague, is a brilliant piece of descriptive writing. Many of the stories are ribald, and most of them are versions of legends and folk-tales which had been current for centuries. *The Decameron* itself provided source material for a great many writers in English, including Chaucer.

Decline and Fall A satirical novel of England in the 1920s by Evelyn Waugh, first published in 1928.

Decline and Fall of the Roman Empire, The History of the The history by Edward Gibbon, published in six volumes between 1776 and 1788.

Deerslayer, The A novel of the American frontier, one of the 'Leatherstocking Tales' by James Fenimore Cooper, first published in 1841.

Defoe, Daniel (1660–1731) The son of James Foe, a London butcher, Daniel Defoe was educated at the Stoke Newington Academy. He travelled widely in Europe before marrying and establishing himself in Cornhill, London, as a hosier. It was at about this time that he changed his surname from Foe to Defoe. As a Dissenter he was opposed to the Catholic king, James II, and in 1685 he took part in the unsuccessful insurrection led by the Duke of Monmouth. In 1688 he joined the invading army of William of Orange, soon to become William III of England. Defoe tried to establish himself in a variety of trades, but lack of success in his business ventures turned his attention to writing. His first major work was a study of economics, *An Essay upon Projects*, published in 1697. *The True Born Englishman*, a verse satire defending William III against those who objected to him as a foreigner, was extremely well received when it appeared in 1701, but as a man of strongly-held religious and political convictions – as well as being a Dissenter he was a fervent Whig – Defoe was often prosecuted for expressing his opinions too freely in his writings. He could not remain silent while the Dissenters were so often subject to vicious persecution, and as a result of the publication in 1702 of *The Shortest Way with the Dissenters* he was put in the pillory and then imprisoned in Newgate. It was not his only spell in jail, but he was fortunate in having friends in high places who were able to secure his release and to intervene on his behalf when he was in serious trouble. Imprisonment did not prevent him from continuing to campaign vigorously for a number of causes, nor did it stop him from founding, while actually in Newgate, a political and literary periodical, *The Review*, which he continued to produce for nine years. As he grew older, his political stance appears to have been softened by expediency, and he was frequently employed as an agent and pamphleteer by the

Daniel Defoe in the pillory. He was prosecuted and imprisoned for his seditious writings.

Tory politicians Robert Harley and Sidney Godolphin. On behalf of the government, he also played a major part in the negotiation for the union of England and Scotland, a subject which he covered in 1708 in his *History of the Union*. His career as a journalist continued with great vigour, and he also wrote histories, biographies, and other non-fiction books, all produced with the unflagging industry which resulted in a lifetime's total of well over four hundred works. It was not until 1719, at the age of sixty, that Defoe published *The Life and Strange Surprizing Adventures of Robinson Crusoe*. It was at once immensely successful, and launched him on a new career as a novelist. In 1720 *The Life and Adventures of Mr Duncan Campbell* and *Captain Singleton* both appeared, and in 1722 Defoe brought out no fewer than three major works, *The Fortunes and Misfortunes of Moll Flanders*, *The Journal of the Plague Year* and *The History of Colonel Jack*. 1724 was even busier, with the publication of two novels, *Roxana* and *Memoirs of a Cavalier*, and two travel books, *A New Voyage round the World* — which was apparently written largely from research rather than from personal experience — and the first book of the three-volume *A Tour through the whole Island of Great Britain*, which, in contrast, was based on his journeys. At the same time he was writing his stories of famous criminals, such as Jack Sheppard, Jonathan Wild and Rob Roy. 1726 saw the curiosities *Everybody's Business is Nobody's Business, or Private Abuses Public Grievances, exemplified in the Pride, Insolence, and Exorbitant Wages of our Women-Servants, Footmen &c*, *The Political History of the Devil* and *A System of Magic*, as well as one of the last major books he produced, *The Complete English Tradesman*. *A Plan of English Commerce*, concerned with the export trade, appeared in 1728. The innovative quality of Daniel Defoe's writing has brought him general recognition as the first English novelist, and he is also widely regarded as the father of English journalism. His fiction is marked not only by the imaginative scope of his narratives, but in particular by his ability to identify with, and therefore bring to life, his principal characters. *Robinson Crusoe* is one of the world's great classics.

Deighton, Len (1929–) London-born Len Deighton first came to prominence with his thriller, *The Ipcress File*, published in 1962. A number of other novels followed, nearly all spy stories, including *Funeral in Berlin*, which appeared in 1964. In 1977 he brought out *Fighter: The True Story of the Battle of Britain*. The trilogy, *Berlin Game*, *Mexican Set* and *London Match*, was completed in 1985.

Dekker, Thomas (*c*.1570–1632) A very successful playwright of his period, Thomas Dekker often worked in collaboration with others. The best known of his own plays is *The Shoemaker's Holiday*, written about 1599. He wrote *The Honest Whore* in collaboration with Thomas Middleton, *Westward Hoe* and *Northward Hoe* with John Webster, *The Virgin Martyr* with Philip Massinger, and *The Witch of Edmonton* with John Ford and William Rowley. Dekker also produced a great many tracts and pamphlets and some autobiographical accounts. *The Guls Hornebooke*, published in 1609, is a mock etiquette book for the gallants of the time.

De la Mare, Walter (1873–1956) Walter John De la Mare, who was of Huguenot descent, was born at Charlton, Kent, England, and educated at St Paul's School, London. He began his career by working for an oil company. After contributing to various literary magazines, he published his first volume of poetry, *Songs of Childhood*, in 1902, under the pseudonym Walter Ramal. *Poems* appeared under his own name in 1906, and some years later he was awarded a Civil List grant which enabled him to become a full-time writer. By 1912, with the publication of *The Listeners*, he was firmly established as a poet with a distinctive and appealing voice, and the many volumes of his verses which subsequently appeared found a ready audience. The final edition of his *Collected Poems* was published in 1979. His poetry was marked by its lyricism and spiritual qualities, and almost all his work reveals his own fascination with the strange, the fantastic and the mysterious. He also wrote essays, literary criticism, novels and many short stories. Among his novels are *Henry Brocken*, published in 1904, and *Memoirs of a Midget*, which appeared in 1921. He was particularly successful in his work for children, which included both prose works and the poetry collections, *Peacock Pie*, *Tom Tiddler's Ground* and *Bells and Grass*. As an anthologist he was much in demand, placing his own stamp on the selection of work in each volume, as exemplified in the splendid *Love*, published in 1943.

Delaney, Shelagh (1939–) Born in Salford, England, Shelagh Delaney is the author of *A Taste of Honey*, a play presented in 1958 and subsequently filmed. It is in the realistic vein first seen in John Osborne's *Look Back in Anger* and very much in the post-war spirit of disillusionment with traditional values.

De la Roche, Mazo (1885–1961) The Canadian writer Mazo De la Roche published her first book, *Explorers of the Dawn*, in 1922. She wrote some plays and a volume of autobiography, but became famous as the author of the 'Jalna' books, an extremely successful series of family sagas. The first of these, *Jalna*, appeared in 1927, and the last, *Morning at Jalna*, in 1960.

Deloney, Thomas (*c*.1560–1600) Thomas Deloney was a silk-weaver who became famous as a writer of ballads and short prose pieces which formed extremely popular penny chapbooks. The best known of his works are the broadsides published to celebrate the defeat of the Armada in 1588, his booklet in praise of shoemakers, *The Gentle Craft*, and the story of *Thomas of Reading or the Six Worthie Yeomen of the West*.

Democracy in America The controversial report by the French laywer, Comte Alexis de Tocqueville, first published in 1835.

Denham, Sir John (1615–69) Born in Dublin and educated at Trinity College, Oxford, John Denham was a lawyer and a Royalist. He was knighted in 1660. In his early twenties he published a free translation of part of Virgil's *Aeneid* and *The Anatomy of Play*, a tract against gambling, to which he was nevertheless addicted. He then wrote a five-act tragedy, *The Sophy*, which was presented in 1641, and in 1642 produced his major work, *Cooper's Hill*, a long poem, much praised by such writers as Dryden, Pope and Johnson, describing the Thames scenery around his home at Egham, Surrey.

Denis Duval A novel by W.M. Thackeray, unfinished at his death, first published in 1864.

Dennis, John (1657–1734) John Dennis was born in London and educated at Harrow and Cambridge. He was more successful as a self-important critic than as a playwright, though several of his tragedies were produced, and a virulently anti-French play, *Liberty Asserted*, was very popular. His most important work was perhaps *The Grounds of Criticism in Poetry*, first published in 1704. Much of his work seems to have consisted of scurrilous attacks on Addison and Pope, neither of whom hesitated to reply in kind.

De Profundis A work by Oscar Wilde, in the form of a letter written while in Reading gaol, which examines his relationship with Lord Alfred Douglas and his own failings. It was first published in an abridged version in 1905 by Wilde's friend, Robert Ross, who gave it its title. The full text was not seen in print until 1962.

De Quincey, Thomas (1785–1859) Celebrated as the author of *Confessions of an English Opium Eater*, Thomas De Quincey was born in Manchester and educated at schools in Bath and Manchester, where he was known as a distinguished Greek scholar, and at Worcester College, Oxford. He began taking opium while at Oxford, and within a few years had become an addict. He was a

Thomas De Quincey by Sir John Watson-Gordon

friend of Coleridge, Southey and the Words-worths, and lived for a time in the Lake District in the North of England, where he married and started his family of eight children. He had inherited a family fortune, but by 1820 nothing of it was left. Having quarrelled with Words-worth, he left Grasmere for London, determined to earn his living by writing. Through Charles Lamb, he was introduced to the proprietors of the *London Magazine*, to which he began to contribute, and *Confessions of an English Opium Eater* first appeared in 1821 in that magazine. It was published in book form the following year and made De Quincey famous, not merely because of its sensational content, but because of the power of its writing. He published a novel, *Klosterheim*, in 1832, and in 1844 produced *The Logic of Political Economy*, but from the time of his first success, contriving to keep his addiction more or less under control, he lived almost entirely by his journalism, contributing to a number of periodicals, including *Blackwood's Magazine* and the *Edinburgh Literary Gazette*. His writing was often remarkable for its style and wit, and he built a large following for such essays as 'On Murder Considered as One of the Fine Arts' and 'On the Knocking at the Gate in Macbeth'. A collection of his work, edited by himself under the title *Selections Grave and Gay*, was completed in the year of his death.

An engraving of Descartes from the painting by Franz Hals.

Descartes, René (1596–1650) A native of the Touraine, France, René Descartes was educated at a Jesuit college and later joined the army. After extensive travels in Europe, both as a serving soldier and afterwards as a civilian, he settled in Holland in 1629, and spent the rest of his life there. Celebrated for his doctrine 'cogito ergo sum (I think, therefore I am)', he is often regarded as the father of modern philosophy, and his influence has lasted for more than three centuries. His three great works are *Discourse of Method*, *Meditations on the First Philosophy* and *Principles of Philosophy*, which appeared in 1637, 1641 and 1644 respectively.

Deserted Village, The A long pastoral poem by Oliver Goldsmith, evoking the idyllic past of the village of Auburn. It was first published in 1770.

Desperate Remedies Thomas Hardy's first published novel, which appeared in 1871.

Deus ex machina A term literally translated as 'god out of the machine'. It is derived from the Greek classical drama, in which plays often ended with the arrival on the stage, by means of some mechanical device, of an actor playing a god, who would thereupon solve the characters' problems and bring everything to a satisfactory conclusion. Nowadays the term is used to mean a contrived ending to a play, resulting from an occurrence for which the audience has not previously been prepared.

De Vere, Aubrey (1814–1902) Born at Curragh Chase, County Limerick, Ireland, and educated at Trinity College, Dublin, Aubrey Thomas de Vere was the son of a poet. He published his first poetry, *The Waldenses*, in 1842. He brought out many volumes of verse and some collections of essays, and also wrote two verse dramas. He is remembered chiefly for his championship of Celtic legends and early Irish poetry.

Devil's Disciple, The A play by G. Bernard Shaw, set in New England in 1777. It was first performed in New York in 1897 and published in 1901.

De Vries, Peter (1910–) A supreme practitioner in the field of witty, humorous novels, Peter de Vries was born in Chicago and educated at Calvin College, Michigan and Northwestern University. On the staff of the *New Yorker* for many years, he has been a freelance writer since 1931. His first novel, published in 1940, was *But Who Wakes the Bugler? The Tunnel of Love*, perhaps his best-known book, appeared in 1954, and others have included *Comfort Me with Apples* and *Consenting Adults, or the Duchess will be Furious*.

Dewey, Melvil (1851–1931) Born at Adams Center, New York, Melvil Dewey was a librarian and the inventor of the 'Dewey Decimal System of Classification', which is used for cataloguing purposes in libraries throughout the world.

Diary of a Nobody, The A comic novel by George and Weedon Grossmith, both of whom were men of the theatre. George Grossmith created many of the 'little men' parts in the Gilbert and Sullivan operas. *The Diary of a Nobody*, first published in 1894, is still much enjoyed for its satire on middle-class values as seen in the absurd pretensions of its fictional diarist, Mr Pooter.

Dickens, Charles (1812–70) Charles John Huffham Dickens was born in Portsmouth, England, where his father, John Dickens, worked for the Navy Pay Department. The family soon moved to Chatham, where young Charles attended a school for two years, learned to read, and devoured his father's small library. In 1824 the family transferred itself to London, and was soon in such dire financial trouble that John Dickens, an improvident man, was imprisoned for debt in the Marchelsea Prison. Meanwhile, twelve-year-old Charles had unhappily taken employment in a blacking factory, an experience which was to colour much of his life and work. When his father was released from prison, he was able again to pay for Charles to be given a limited education, but by 1827 the boy had been articled as a clerk in a lawyer's office. Soon after, having taught himself shorthand, he became a parliamentary reporter for *The Morning Chronicle*, and also began to contribute to various

A fine chalk sketch of Dickens by Samuel Laurence.

was received, his *American Notes*, published in the same year, was highly critical of the American way of life and caused much anger in the States. On his return he wrote *Martin Chuzzlewit*, which appeared in 1844, and also *A Christmas Carol*, the first of the Christmas Books. A visit to Italy in 1845 resulted in *Pictures from Italy*, and the next novels were *Dombey and Son* and the largely autobiographical *David Copperfield*. In 1850 Dickens became editor of *Household Words*, in which *Bleak House*, the now largely forgotten *A Child's History of England*, *Hard Times* and *Little Dorrit* all received their first publication in serial form. The periodical *All the Year Round* replaced *Household Words* in 1859, and for this he wrote *A Tale of Two Cities*, *Great Expectations*, *Our Mutual Friend*, and the first chapters of *Edwin Drood*, the novel which was unfinished at the time of his sudden death. Charles Dickens was an actor *manqué*, and this was undoubtedly why he was not only addicted to amateur theatricals but in the last years of his life, devoted himself to public readings of his work, given both in England and in the United States, where his previous deprecatory comments had been forgiven. He had always driven himself hard, but the strain of these lectures, allied perhaps to the problems he had in his personal relationships — his wife left him after twenty-two years of marriage — probably contributed to his death at a

One of George Cruikshank's illustrations to Dicken's *Oliver Twist*. He also illustrated several other works by Dickens.

periodicals. His first book, *Sketches by Boz*, a collection of some of his magazine writings, was published in 1836, just after his twenty-fourth birthday, and a few weeks before his marriage to Catherine Hogarth. At the instigation of the publishers, Chapman and Hall, he had by then already started work on *The Posthumous Papers of the Pickwick Club*, which first appeared in twenty monthly parts between 1836 and 1837. By the time it came out in book form at the end of 1837, Dickens' reputation was made. Over the next twenty-eight years he produced a whole series of long novels, each eagerly awaited and, although not all his books were received with the same enthusiasm — *Martin Chuzzlewit*, for instance, was considered disappointing — most of them increased his popularity. In 1837 he became editor of *Bentley's Miscellany*, a periodical for which he wrote *Oliver Twist*, and *Nicholas Nickleby*. Dickens then started a new magazine, *Master Humphrey's Clock*, to which he contributed articles and sketches and in which both *The Old Curiosity Shop* and *Barnaby Rudge* appeared. His success had been repeated across the Atlantic, and in 1842 he and his wife visited the United States. Despite the great acclaim with which he

This half-finished painting by R.W. Buss depicts Dickens dozing in his study at Gad's Hill Place in Kent. It is thronged with visionary characters from his many books. A sickly child, Dickens found happiness in reading and this, in conjunction with his own experiences of poverty and deprivation, gave rise to the compassionate insight which marks his reformist writings and actions.

comparatively early age. It is not difficult to be critical of Dickens' work – his construction is often undisciplined, ends are left untied, and he can be repetitive and long-winded – but these faults are largely the result of the pressure under which he worked, needing to complete each instalment of the novels to a prescribed length and in a minimal amount of time for the next issue of the magazine. His heroines are often considered insipid, but they exhibit the feminine qualities which were admired at the time. As for the charge that he could produce scenes of turgid sentimentality, again it must be remem-

bered that he was attuned to the attitudes of the period – the whole of Britain and the United States wept at the death of Little Nell! No criticism, however valid, can detract from Dickens' genius. From Sam Weller onwards, he created a gallery of enduringly comic characters; he presented a powerful and detailed picture of the age, especially, perhaps, in his satirical, crusading depiction of various social ills, including the suffering of children; and the humour, the vitality and the imagination of his story-telling are unsurpassed.

Dickey James (1923–) James Lafayette Dickey, who was born in Atlanta, Georgia, and educated at Vanderbilt University, Tennessee, has published a number of volumes of poetry since his first *Into the Stone and other poems*, appeared in 1960. A collection of his verse, *Poems 1957–1967*, came out in 1968. He has also translated the Russian poet, Yevgeny Yevtushenko.

Dickinson, Emily (1830–86) Born in Amherst, Massachusetts, and educated in Amherst and at Mount Holyoake, Emily Elizabeth Dickinson is known as one of America's finest poets. The daughter of a lawyer, she did not marry, and lived all her life in Amherst, becoming more and more of a recluse from the early 1860s onwards. It is uncertain whether or not this withdrawal from society was the result, as has often been suggested, of an unrequited love for the Revd. Charles Wadsworth. Although cutting herself off from physical contact with others, she did conduct a regular correspondence with many friends. She had been writing poetry since childhood and produced a vast amount of highly individual verse, almost all of which was discovered only after her death, when many hundreds of poems, often in different stages of composition, came to light. Only a small handful of her verses had been published during her lifetime, partly because of her reluctance to seek publication, but also because her work was considered too idiosyncratic for the public taste. More than thirty years were to pass before selections of her poems were prepared for publication by her friend Mabel L. Todd and one of her regular correspondents, T.W. Higginson, a Unitarian minister. The verses were substantially edited, and only in 1955, with the appearance of *The Poems of Emily Dickinson*, edited by Thomas H. Johnson, was her full output seen and in its original form. It then became clear, as some critics had always claimed, that Emily Dickinson

The only known portrait of Emily Dickinson, which is in Amherst College, Mass.

was a poet of major stature. Her work is always short, extremely individual, and often disturbing. Writing of love and death, of mysticism and the poet as creator, she has a passionate intensity and a strength of imagery which make it not unreasonable, however different their styles may have been, to compare her with her namesake, Emily Brontë.

dictionary A book which contains the words of a language, in alphabetical order, with definitions and often with derivations. Samuel Johnson's authoritative but sometimes idiosyncratic *Dictionary*, published in 1755, was the first great dictionary of the English language.

Didion, Joan (1934–) The Californian novelist Joan Didion had her first big success with *Run, River*, published in 1963. Subsequent novels include *Play It As It Lays*, in 1970, and *A Book of Common Prayer*, in 1977. She has also written three non-fiction books, *Slouching Towards Bethlehem*, which appeared in 1968, *White Album*, in 1979, and the more recent *Salvador*, an account of a visit to El Salvador.

Digby, Sir Kenelm (1603–65) Educated at Oxford, Kenelm Digby was a man of many parts. A diplomat, a naval commander, and a scientist, he was also the author of a number of works on religious and botanical subjects. The splendidly titled *The Closet of the Eminently Learned Sir Digby Kenelm Knt. Opened*, published posthumously in 1677, contained his medical prescriptions. His *Private Memoirs*, mainly concerned with his courtship of his wife, a famous beauty, did not appear in print until 1827. He was knighted in 1623.

Disraeli, Benjamin (1804–81) The Son of Isaac D'Israeli, a well-known author, Benjamin Disraeli was brought up with a love of literature. He entered Parliament in 1837 as a Tory, and began a glittering career in politics which culminated in two terms of office as British Prime Minister. He became the first Earl of Beaconsfield in 1876. Intended for a career in the law, he soon became involved in literary pursuits. His first published novel, *Vivian Grey*, appeared in 1826 and was immediately successful. In the next twenty years he wrote and published a number of political works, various short stories and several more novels, including *Alroy* and *Contarini Fleming*, which completed the trilogy begun with *Vivian Grey*. In 1837 *Henrietta Temple* and *Venetia* added to his reputation, and they were followed, in 1844, 1845, and 1847 respectively, by *Coningsby*, *Sybil* and *Tancred*, the trilogy which has remained his most celebrated work. Although in 1852 he produced a *Life of Lord George Bentinck*, politics now took precedence over writing. In 1868 Disraeli became Prime Minister for the first time, and began his friendship with Queen Victoria. As a mark of her approbation, she presented him with a copy of her *Leaves from the Journal of Our Life in the Highlands* in exchange for a complete set of his works, and he delighted her thereafter by speaking of 'We authors, Ma'am'. *Lothair*, Disraeli's first new novel for twenty-three years, appeared in 1870. He was to complete one more book, *Endymion*, which was published in 1880, but he did not finish *Falconet*. Although immensely popular at the time of publication, his novels are now little read.

Divina Commedia Dante's masterpiece, *The Divine Comedy*, consisting of the *Inferno*, the *Purgatorio* and the *Paradiso*, was completed just before the poet's death in 1321, and was first printed in 1472. Dante did not himself attach the adjective 'divina' to the work, and it was not so-called until the sixteenth century. Although *The Divine Comedy* was known to English writers from its earliest days – Chaucer translated some fragments – the first complete English translation did not appear until 1805.

Dobell, Sydney (1824–74) Born in Cranbrook, Kent, and educated privately, Sydney Thomson Dobell published his two long poems, *The Roman* and *Balder*, in 1850 and 1854. He and his friend Alexander Smith brought out a volume of sonnets on the Crimean War in 1855, and the following year Dobell's *England in Time of War* appeared. His work possessed a certain lyric charm, but was also often marked by a wild extravagance of language.

Dobson, Austin (1840–1921) The English poet Henry Austin Dobson was born in Plymouth and became a civil servant. He published *Vignettes in Rhyme* in 1873, and several other volumes of verse followed. From 1885 on he wrote more prose than poetry, producing several volumes of essays and a number of biographies of eighteenth-century literary and artistic figures, including Fielding, Goldsmith, Walpole, Bewick and Hogarth.

Doctor Faustus, The Tragical History of A drama by Christopher Marlowe, published in 1604, but first presented some years earlier.

Dr Jekyll and Mr Hyde, The Strange Case of The celebrated horror novel by Robert Louis Stevenson, first published in 1886.

Doctor Thorne A novel by Anthony Trollope, the third in the 'Barsetshire' series, first published in 1858.

Doctor Wortle's School A novel by Anthony Trollope, first published in 1881.

Doctor Zhivago The great novel by Boris Pasternak, first published in Italy in 1957. Publication in the author's native Russia is promised in 1988.

Doctor's Dilemma, The A satirical play by G. Bernard Shaw, first presented in 1906, and published in 1908.

Dodgson, Charles Lutwidge *See* Lewis Carroll.

Dodsley, Robert (1703–64) Although he has some claim to recognition as a poet and dramatist, Robert Dudsley, who was born near Mansfield in Nottinghamshire, England, is known chiefly as the publisher of works by many writers of the time, including Goldsmith, Pope, Gray and Dr Johnson, whose *Dictionary* he suggested and partly financed.

Doll's House, A A play by Henrik Ibsen in which he struck a blow for the independence of married women. It was first presented in English in 1879.

Dombey and Son A novel by Charles Dickens chronicling the downfall of rich Mr Dombey, who loses everything, including his son. It was first published between 1847 and 1848.

Domesday Book The name given to the record of the Great Inquisition or Survey of the lands of England, their extent, value, ownership, and liabilities, made by order of William the Conqueror and completed in 1086. The original manuscript, in two volumes, still exists.

Don Juan A long narrative poem by Lord Byron, first published between 1819 and 1824. It consists of sixteen cantos, and, with the dedication to Robert Southey, runs to well over fifteen thousand lines of verse. It was Byron's intention, had he lived, to add further cantos.

Donleavy, J.P. (1926–) James Patrick Donleavy was born in Brooklyn, New York, but educated at Trinity College, Dublin. He is the author of the bestselling *The Ginger Man*, first published in 1955. His other novels include *The Beastly Beatitudes of Balthazar B*, which appeared in 1968, and *The Destinies of Darcy Dancer, Gentleman* and its sequel, *Leila*, published in 1977 and 1983 respectively. He has also written a number of plays, the best known of which is *Fairy Tales of New York*, first presented in 1960.

Donne, John (1572–1631) A Catholic, born in London and educated privately and at both Oxford and Cambridge, John Donne turned Anglican at about the time that he attained his majority. He originally intended to become a lawyer, but abandoned this project to sail with Essex to the siege of Cadiz and later with Raleigh to the Azores. His first writings also appeared in these early years. He produced a number of *Satires*, which were not printed but were circulated from hand to hand. Both the voyages resulted in a number of poems, including 'The Calm' and 'The Storm'. On his return to England, he became Secretary to Sir Thomas Egerton, Lord Keeper of the Great Seal, and while in his employ wrote his longest poem, the satirical *The Progress of the Soul*, though this was not published until 1633. In 1602 his secret marriage to Egerton's niece, which eventually produced twelve children, angered Sir Thomas and caused his dismissal and a brief period of imprisonment. Donne spent the next decade trying to support his growing family, writing anti-Papist pamphlets and other minor works, and seeking a patron. He gained the friendship at various times of Thomas Norton, later to become a bishop, of Lucy, Countess of Bradford, to whom he addressed a number of verse epistles, of the wealthy Sir Robert Drury, on the death of whose daughter he wrote two poems, and of Robert Ker, Viscount Rochester. Norton suggested that he should enter the church, but Donne, though a man of deep religious feelings, did not feel himself ready for such a commitment. He later changed his mind, and sought Rochester's help in taking holy orders, but was dissuaded by the Viscount. In 1610 Donne had published a major treatise in prose entitled *Pseudo-Martyr*, which attempted to persuade Roman Catholics to take the oath of allegiance to King James I. This had naturally engaged the sympathies of the king, and it was through James's encouragement, and his insistence that the University of Cambridge should grant Donne a degree in divinity, that Donne finally entered the ministry in 1615. He received a number of minor appointments, including the livings of Keyston in Huntingdonshire and Sevenoaks in Kent, and a preachership in Lincoln's Inn. He also served as a royal chaplain and, in 1619, as chaplain to Lord Doncaster during the latter's official visit to Germany. In 1621, his favour with the king having been further advanced by the Duke of Buckingham, who had recently become his patron, he was appointed Dean of St Paul's, a position which he held until his death. Donne was an eloquent speaker, and his sermons were greatly admired – his first, given in the presence of the king, is said to have transported his congregation 'to heaven, in holy raptures'. Several collections of the sermons were subsequently published, as was a book of *Devotions*, while among his prose works are a bitter attack on the Jesuits, *Ignatius his Conclave*, which appeared in 1611, and two posthumous publications, his *Essays in Divinity* and *Biathanatos*, in which he set out to demonstrate that suicide (to which he himself confessed to having a 'sickly inclination') was not necessarily sinful. But it is as a poet that Donne is primarily remembered. Two sets of religious verse, *Holy Sonnets* and *La Corona*, date from 1618, but there is little certainty as to when

The poet and divine John Donne, after Isaac Oliver (1616). Donne's love poems, satires and religious sonnets are noted for their wit, flamboyant imagery and passion. An eloquent orator, his popular sermons as Dean of St Paul's drew large congregations. However, his poems are his main commemoration.

much of the other poetry was written. While it is thought that the secular poems were probably mostly composed when Donne was in his early twenties, some may belong to a period shortly after his marriage. The language of his poetry is often fantastic, the themes can be obscure, and the style complex, and it was with these criticisms in mind that Dr Johnson invented the term 'metaphysical school' and applied it to the work of Donne, as leader of the movement, and to that of those poets influenced by him, among them George Herbert and Henry Vaughan. The criticisms may be valid, but the love poems, such as 'The Sun Rising', 'The Triple Fool', 'The Flea', and the 'Song', which begins 'Go, and catch a falling star', are much remembered and loved.

Don Quixote de la Mancha The great novel, in which the elements of satire, romance and adventure are fused, by the Spanish writer Miguel de Cervantes. The first part of the book was published in 1605 and the second in 1615, shortly before the author's death. The first part was translated into English in 1612, but it was not until the beginning of the eighteenth century that a complete version was seen.

Don Sebastian A play by John Dryden, first performed in 1689 and published in 1691.

Doolittle, Hilda (1886–1961) The American writer Hilda Doolittle was born in Bethlehem, Pennsylvania, and educated at Bryn Mawr. From 1911 she lived in Europe, and was much influenced by another expatriate, Ezra Pound. She published several novels, wrote plays and brought out a translation of Euripides' *Ion*, but is better known for her poetry, the first volume of which, *Sea Garden*, appeared in 1916. All her work was signed 'H.D.' She was married to Richard Aldington, the British novelist and biographer, but the marriage was a failure.

Doors of Perception, The An account of his experiments with LSD and mescalin by Aldous Huxley, first published in 1954 and followed two years later by a second book, *Heaven and Hell*, on the same subject.

Dos Passos, John (1896–1970) Born in Chicago and educated at Harvard, John Roderigo Dos Passos based his early fiction on his experiences in World War I. His first major success as a novelist came in 1925 with *Manhattan Transfer*, which largely succeeded in capturing the essence of New York. His subsequent trilogy 'U.S.A.', made up of *The 42nd Parallel*, *1919* and *The Big Money*, published between 1930 and 1936, attempted, again quite effectively, to do the same for the nation as a whole. He wrote many other novels and some non-fiction.

Dostoevsky, Fyodor (1821–81) The son of a Moscow surgeon, whose family lay on the fringes of nobility, Fyodor Mikhailovich Dostoevsky was educated in Moscow and at the academy for military engineering in St Petersburg. In 1843, on the death of his father, he resigned from the army, with the intention of devoting himself to a

An original, heavily annotated and illustrated, manuscript page, from Dostoevsky's *The Possessed*.

A serious study by V.G. Perov of Fyodor Dostoevsky.

career as an author. He was to become one of the giants of nineteenth-century Russian literature. He first made a name for himself with a short story, 'Poor People', published in 1846. For the next few years he regularly contributed stories to the magazine *Annals of the Country*, but his financial rewards were minimal, and the bitterness with which he viewed his situation led him to join a revolutionary movement. In 1849 he was arrested as a dangerous socialist and condemned to death, but the sentence was commuted into exile in Siberia, to be followed by military service for the rest of his life. In Siberia he spent four years of horror. These experiences, which not suprisingly affected him for the rest of his life and contributed to his sombre view of the human condition, form the basis for his book, *Notes from the House of the Dead*, which came out in 1860. (It was later turned into an opera by Janacek.) His sufferings continued in the army, but he was finally released in 1859 when Czar Alexander II came to the throne. His next novel, *The Insulted and the Injured*, followed in 1861, and was published, as *Notes from the House of the Dead* had been, in *Time*, a magazine which he launched jointly with his brother Mikhail. From 1862 he frequently travelled in western Europe, and although by the time he was released from Siberia he had largely discarded his socialist beliefs, turning instead to the Russian Orthodox religion, he was nevertheless appalled at the excesses of the capitalist countries he visited, and at the contrast he saw between the rich and the poor. The first of his journeys was recorded in *Winter Notes on Summer Impressions*, published in 1863 in *Time*. He was about to embark on the series of great works

which would immortalize him. *Notes from Underground* appeared in 1865, and in the following year came *Crime and Punishment*. This long novel, which probes deeply into the soul of a murderer, and does so with enormous understanding, compassion and power, caused a sensation in Paris in 1867. By modern standards, like so many of the great classics of that period, it may be considered slow-moving, but the writing has tremendous strength and the narrative maintains its grip on the reader's attention. Four more great novels were to come. *The Idiot* appeared in 1868, and was followed by *The Devils* in 1872. The previous years had not been easy. Dostoevsky's wife had died in 1867, he had suffered chronic ill-health, including epileptic fits, and moreover he had frequently been in debt. During the last eight years of his life, however, at least his financial difficulties disappeared, and he was able to live in comparative comfort in St Petersburg. A new novel, *A Raw Youth*, came out in 1875, and the last great book, *The Brothers Karamazov*, was published in 1880. By the time of his death he was enjoying great popularity in Russia, and his fame was rapidly spreading through the western world. Not all critics were enthusiastic – some found him dull and morbid, and those who recognized the influence of Dickens in his work had to admit that his novels were rarely leavened by the humour which the English writer used to such good effect. Nevertheless, Dostoevsky's reputation has survived all attacks, and, with the possible exception of Tolstoy's *War and Peace*, his books are the best known of all the Russian classics.

Double Dealer, The A comedy by William Congreve, first presented in 1693 and published the following year.

Doughty, C. (1843–1926) Charles Montagu Doughty was born in Suffolk, England, and educated at Caius College, Cambridge. He thought of himself primarily as a poet and published several books of extremely individual verse, including the six volumes of *The Dawn in Britain*. However, he is remembered nowadays solely for his *Travels in Arabia Deserta*, first published in 1888.

Douglas, Lord Alfred (1870–1945) A son of the eighth Marquess of Queensbury, Lord Alfred Bruce Douglas was born near Worcester, England, and educated at Winchester School and Magdalen College, Oxford. He is famed as 'Bosie', the young man whose friendship with Oscar Wilde resulted in the latter's trial and imprisonment for homosexual practices. Douglas published much mediocre verse, translated Wilde's *Salome* from the French, and wrote an autobiography and some highly biased books about Wilde.

Douglas, Gavin (*c*.1475–1522) Born in Scotland, Gavin Douglas was the son of the Earl of Angus. He entered the Church, and eventually became Bishop of Dunkeld. A poet, his allegories *The Palice of Honour* and *King Hart* were much admired, but his major work was the translation into English (or, rather, into the Scottish dialect) of Virgil's *Aeneid*. This translation and *The Palice of Honour* appeared in print about 1553, but *King Hart* was not formally published until 1786.

Douglas, Lloyd C. (1877–1951) The American writer Lloyd Cassel Douglas was a Lutheran minister, and many of his works had a religious background. He had his first major success with *Magnificent Obsession*, published in 1929. Among his other novels are *The Robe*, which appeared in 1942, and *The Big Fisherman*, which was published in 1949.

Douglas, Norman (1868–1952) George Norman Douglas was born in Falkenhorst in Austria and educated at Uppingham School England, and in Karlsruhe. He worked for a short time for the British Foreign Office and then settled in Italy, where he spent most of his life. After publishing a volume of short stories, he produced a series of loosely-structured but enjoyable travel books, but achieved real success only with his first novel, *South Wind*, published in 1917.

Dowden, Edward (1843–1913) An academic who was born in Cork, Ireland, and educated at Queen's College, Cork, and Trinity College, Dublin, Edward Dowden wrote a number of works of literary criticism, some verse, and several biographies of poets and other literary figures. He first came to attention in 1875 with *Shakspere, A Critical Study of His Mind and Art*, and his reputation was always that of a Shakespearian scholar, but his most successful book was a biography of Shelley, published in 1886.

Dowson, Ernest (1867–1900) The poet Ernest Christopher Dowson was born in Kent, England, and educated at Oxford. He made his name as a contributor to the fashionable magazines of the 1890s, such as *The Yellow Book* and *The Savoy*. His output of poetry was small, and his verses, while often charming, are those of no more than a minor poet, but some of his lines have become very familiar (though the Latin titles of the poems may be less so!): 'I have been faithful to thee, Cynara! in my fashion' comes from the poem 'Non sum qualis eram bonae sub regno Cynarae', while 'Vitae summa brevis spem nos vetat incohare longam' gives us 'the days of wine and roses'.

Doyle, A. Conan (1859–1930) Arthur Conan Doyle studied medicine in his native Edinburgh and practised as a doctor until the age of thirty-one,

Sir Arthur Conan Doyle, the creator of the famous fictional detective Sherlock Holmes. The portrait is by Henry Gates.

by which time he had become a successful writer. His first novel, *A Study in Scarlet*, was published in 1887, and introduced the most celebrated detective in fiction, Sherlock Holmes. Next, in 1888, came an historical romance, *Micah Clarke*. The success of the first Sherlock Holmes story demanded a second, and *The Sign of Four* came out in 1889. Doyle always preferred to write historical novels, and the next years saw the publication of *The White Company*, *Rodney Stone* and *The Exploits of Colonel Gerard*. Meanwhile, however, he had published a number of Sherlock Holmes short stories in *The Strand Magazine*. These were collected in 1891 as *The Adventures of Sherlock Holmes*, and were immensely popular. A further volume of stories followed, and then in 1893, having tired of his famous detective, Doyle tried to kill him off in the desperate struggle with his arch-enemy, Professor Moriarty, at the Reichenbach Falls, chronicled in *The Final Problem*. But he was forced by the outcry of his readers to resurrect Holmes for *The Hound of the Baskervilles*, pub-

. lished in 1902, and thereafter invented a number of other cases for him to solve. He continued to write historical novels, and in 1906 produced one of the most successful of them, *Sir Nigel*, a sequel to *The White Company*. *The Lost World*, published in 1912, introduced as its hero Professor Challenger, another enduring character who featured in a number of stories. A prolific writer, Doyle also published several plays and a great many non-fiction books on a variety of subjects, including spiritualism, in which he was deeply interested. He was knighted in 1902.

Drabble, Margaret (1939–) Margaret Drabble was born in Sheffield and educated at York and Cambridge. She published her first novel, *A Summer Birdcage*, in 1963, and has written many other novels, among them *The Waterfall*, published in 1969, and *The Middle Ground*, in 1980, which have placed her among the most respected English writers today. Her non-fiction includes biographies of Wordsworth and Arnold Bennett and *A Writer's Britain*. She edited the most recent edition of *The Oxford Companion to English Literature*, published in 1984.

Dracula Bram Stoker's famous novel of vampirism, set in Transylvania, first published in 1897.

drama A drama is simply a play, but the term was often used, although it is no longer fashionable to do so, to denote a serious play with a strong emotional content. 'The drama' usually signifies all literature written for or presented in the theatre, whether it is comedy, tragedy, or of any other genre.

Drapier's Letters, The A number of political pamphlets by Jonathan Swift, published in 1724.

Drayton, Michael (1563–1631) The poet Michael Drayton was born at Hartshill, Worcestershire, England. In 1591 he published his first book, *The Harmonie of the Church*, consisting of verse renderings of certain parts of the Bible, including 'The Song of Solomon'. In the next forty years he produced much poetry, on many different themes. *Idea: The Shepheards Garland*, which appeared in 1593, was a collection of pastoral poems, and in the same year he published the first of a number of historical poems. These included the *Ballad of Agincourt*, first printed in 1627, which begins with the celebrated line 'Fayre stood the winde for France'. He also published sonnets, much lyric poetry, satires, and an extraordinary and huge poem on the topography of England, *Poly-Olbion*, the first twelve books of which appeared in 1612 and the remaining eighteen in 1622.

Dreiser, Theodore (1871–1945) Born in Terre Haute, Indiana, and briefly educated at Indiana University, Theodore Herman Albert Dreiser

Theodore Dreiser, the American novelist and playwright.

worked as a journalist in Chicago and St Louis, and in 1895 became editor of *Every Month*, a magazine devoted to literature and music. His first novel, *Sister Carrie*, was printed and, technically speaking, published in 1900, but the book was in fact suppressed at the last minute by the publishers, who feared that its realism was too outspoken. It did, however, appear in England in 1901, attracting considerable attention, and Dreiser eventually managed to find an American publisher for it, the new edition being published in 1907. Meanwhile, he had continued his career in journalism as the editor of various magazines, and was editor-in-chief of the Butterick publications from 1907 to 1910. A second novel, *Jennie Gerhardt*, came out in 1911, but was not a great success. However, *The Financier* and its sequel, *The Titan*, which appeared in 1912 and 1914, at last established Dreiser as a novelist of considerable power. These two books were part of a trilogy, the third volume of which, *The Stoic*, was published posthumously in 1947. Dreiser continued to produce both novels and plays, and in 1925 scored a major success with *An American Tragedy*, which is widely regarded as his best book. He also wrote short stories and verse and a substantial number of non-fiction books, including collections of essays, autobiographical material, and works in which he set forth his socialist views. His writing is somewhat lacking in grace, but his realism and the strength of his viewpoint give Dreiser, who was something of a pioneer in his day, a permanent place in American literature.

Drinkwater, John (1882–1937) The English poet and dramatist John Drinkwater was born at Leytonstone, Essex. He published the first of many volumes of verse in 1906, and also wrote a number of books of literary criticism, including works on Swinburne, William Morris and Byron. He is, however, best known as a playwright. His first play, in verse, was *Cophetua*, but he scored his greatest successes in the early 1920s with a series of chronicle plays, among which were *Abraham Lincoln*, *Oliver Cromwell*, *Mary Stuart* and *Robert E. Lee*.

drolls During the period of the Commonwealth, from 1649 to 1660, when theatres in England were closed and the presentation of stage plays was forbidden, the law could be circumvented by the presentation of short scenes, sometimes taken from existing plays, sometimes improvised, and performed wherever an audience could be gathered together. These comic or farcical interludes were known as drolls. Many drolls were published after the Restoration, and the term 'droll-house', for a place where such pieces were performed, survived into the eighteenth century.

Drummond of Hawthornden, William (1585–1649) Known by his birthplace of Hawthornden, near Edinburgh, William Drummond was one of the first graduates, in 1605, from the recently founded Edinburgh University. He published a considerable amount of poetry, much of his best work appearing in 1616 in a volume with the comprehensive title *Poems: Amorous, Funerall, Divine, Pastorall: in Sonnets, Songs, Sextains, Madrigals*. He wrote several prose works, including some volumes of history, and is noted for *The Cypresses Grove*, his essay on the folly of the fear of death, published in 1623.

Dryden, John (1631–1700) Born at Aldwincle, Northamptonshire, England, John Dryden was educated at Westminster School and Trinity College, Cambridge. He began writing poetry while still at school and university, but it was not until 1659 that his reputation was established with the publication of his *Heroic Stanzas*. Although he had inherited a private income, it was a very small one, and it is perhaps because of his need to supplement it by his writings that Dryden appears always to have had an eye to the main chance. The *Heroic Stanzas* were in memory and in honour of Oliver Cromwell, but a year after he was hailing Charles II with *Astrea Redux* and *To His Sacred Majesty, A Panegyrick on his Coronation*. Twenty-five years later, when James II acceded to the throne, Dryden became a Catholic, and in 1687 he published *The Hind and the Panther transversed to the story of the Country Mouse and the City Mouse*, an allegory in defence

A dramatic formal portrait by Sir Godfrey Kneller of the Poet Laureate John Dryden. He was a prolific writer of popular Restoration comedies, as well as serious poetry.

of Roman Catholicism. Long before that, however, he had begun to write for the theatre. His first effort, a comedy called *The Wild Gallant*, was a failure when it was presented in 1663, the year of his marriage to Lady Elizabeth Howard, but in 1664 a verse tragedy, *The Indian Queen*, on which he had collaborated with his brother-in-law, Sir Robert Howard, was hugely successful, as was its successor, *The Indian Emperor, or the Conquest of Mexico by the Spanish*, which Dryden wrote alone and which appeared the following year. These triumphs may have come about partly because he had greater confidence in himself as a tragedian, believing that his temperament was more suited to the serious vein, but in subsequent years he proved himself perfectly capable of producing popular Restoration comedies, and of outdoing many of his contemporaries in vulgarity – a later play, *The Kind Keeper, or Mr Limberham*, was banned in 1680 for its indecency. By 1667, however, he was so highly regarded as a playwright that he was retained by the King's Theatre to write plays for performance there, a post which he held until 1678. For a period of more than thirty years in all, large numbers of tragedies, comedies and tragi-comedies flowed from his pen, some in prose and others in verse. They include *The Conquest of Granada*, first seen in 1670, *Aureng-Zebe*, in 1675, and the two tragedies which are probably his finest writing for the theatre, *All for Love*, a version of the Antony and Cleopatra story, in 1678, and *Don Sebastian* in 1690. Many of the plays were meretricious, clearly written to keep the ever-present wolf from Dryden's door, and even those of some quality have rarely been performed in modern times. However, his poetry is a different matter. He was appointed Poet Laureate in 1668, but, apart from plays in verse, wrote little poetry between 1666, when he produced *Annus Mirabilis*, a long poem which deals with the Great Fire of London and the war against the Dutch, and 1681, when *Absalom and Achitophel*, the first of a number of political satires, appeared and swiftly ran through nine editions.

The title-page of Dryden's political satire in verse.

ABSALOM

AND

ACHITOPHEL.

A POEM.

N pious times, e'r Prieft-craft did begin,
Before *Polygamy* was made a fin ;
When man, on many, multiply'd his kind,
E'r one to one was, curfedly, confind ·
When Nature prompted, and no law deny'd
Promifcuous ufe of Concubine and Bride ;

Its success resulted from its topical interest rather than from its literary merits, but in the last twenty years of his life Dryden produced much fine poetry, including, in 1687, 'A Song for Saint Cecilia's Day' and, a decade later, the second of his great poems, the Ode on 'Alexander's Feast'. Equally notable were the large number of translations in verse of works by many classic authors, including Ovid, Horace, Theocritus, Juvenal and Lucretius, and his version of *The Works of Virgil*, which appeared in 1697. Shortly before his death he brought out *Fables, Ancient and Modern*, which consisted of verse renditions of stories by Chaucer and Boccaccio and the *Metamorphoses* of Ovid. Like the plays, the historical and satirical verses may now be largely forgotten, but Dryden still demands and deserves classification as a major poet.

Du Bois, William E.B. (1868–1963) The Black leader William Edward Burghardt Du Bois was born in Great Barrington, Massachusetts, and educated at Fisk University and Harvard. During his lifelong campaign for the rights of his people, he wrote a number of books on the subject, including *The Souls of Black Folk*, published in 1903. Towards the end of his long life he became increasingly militant, and at the age of ninety-four went to live in Ghana, of which state he became a citizen.

Duchess of Malfi, The A tragedy by John Webster, published in 1623, but first presented some years earlier.

Duenna, The A comedy by Richard Brinsley Sheridan, with music, first presented in 1775.

Duffy, Maureen (1933–) English writer Maureen Patricia Duffy was educated at King's College, London. She published her first novel, *That's How It Was*, in 1962. Other novels, mostly conveying a serious and well-presented radical message, have followed, including *I Want to Go to Moscow*, which appeared in 1986, and *Change*, published in 1987. She has also written some non-fiction, a play, and several volumes of poetry. Her *Collected Poems 1949–84* came out in 1985.

Dugdale, Sir William (1605–86) William Dugdale was a Herald at the courts of Charles I and Charles II and was knighted in 1677, when he was created Garter Principal King-at-Arms. He wrote a number of books on antiquarian subjects, including *The Antiquities of Warwickshire*, published in 1656, a *History of St Paul's Cathedral*, in 1658, and *Baronage of England*, between 1675 and 1676.

Duke's Children, The A novel by Anthony Trollope, the sixth and last of the 'Palliser' series, first published in 1880.

Dumas, Alexandre (1802–70) Born in Villers-Cotterets in the department of Aisne, France, Alexandre Dumas the elder, known as 'Dumas père', was the son of a General in the French army. His father died when he was four, and the boy received little education. He entered a solicitor's office, became a clerk in Paris, and then began to write for the theatre. His romantic drama, *Henri III et sa cour*, was a huge success, and several other plays followed. He then met Auguste Maquet, and with him produced the long series of historical novels of adventure and romance which made him famous. The extent of Maquet's contribution is not clear, but it is certain that Dumas was very much the senior partner in their collaboration, as he was when he worked subsequently with others. The first two novels, which proved his most celebrated and popular stories, both appeared in 1844. One was *The Three Musketeers*, which introduced Gascon D'Artagnan (loosely based on a real-life gentleman of that name) and his friends, the inseparable trio, Athos, Porthos and Aramis, while the second book was Dumas' masterpiece, *The Count of Monte Christo*. A huge number of

Alexandre Dumas, père, prince of romantic storytellers and creator of the Three Musketeers. He owes his dramatic looks and possibly his romantic outlook to his father, a General in the French army and to his mother, Marie-Cessette, a Haitian negress.

novels followed, in the majority of which Dumas used factual historical events as the background for the romances, covering periods from the late-sixteenth up to the mid-nineteenth centuries. He also wrote many non-fiction books, including histories and his autobiography. He worked at prodigious speed and with incredible industry, and apparently once told Napoleon that he had written twelve hundred volumes. That figure may have been exaggerated, or at least inflated by the contemporary fashion of issuing a novel in several volumes, but we do know that, when his *Complete Works* were issued between 1860 and 1884, it took two hundred and seventy-seven volumes to accommodate the novels, the plays and the other writings.

Dumas, Alexandre (1824–95) Alexandre Dumas the younger, known as 'Dumas fils', was the natural son of the famous novelist and a Parisian dress-maker. He began writing in order to pay off substantial debts, and eventually became a highly successful dramatist. He was sufficiently respected to be elected to the Académie Française, an honour which was not granted to his father. Before beginning to write for the theatre, he produced a volume of verse and three novels, the first of which, *The Lady of the Camelias*, published in 1848, became world-famous. He adapted it himself for the stage, and Verdi later used the story for his opera *La Traviata*.

Du Maurier, Daphne (1907–) Born in London, and educated privately and in Paris, Daphne du Maurier published a number of plays, including the popular *September Tide*, biographies of her father, the actor Gerald du Maurier, and of Branwell Brontë, and a charming study, *Vanishing Cornwall*, published in 1967. But she is best known as a novelist. Her first book, *The Loving Spirit*, appeared in 1931, and she is the author of such romantic adventure stories as *Jamaica Inn*, *Frenchman's Creek*, and her most famous and successful novel, *Rebecca*, which appeared in 1938. She was created a Dame in 1969. She is the grand-daughter of George du Maurier.

Du Maurier, George (1834–96) George Louis Palmella Busson du Maurier was born in Paris, the son of a Frenchman who had become a naturalized Briton. He was an artist and humorous writer who worked for *Punch* for thirty-six years, and was also much in demand as a book illustrator. In the last years of his life he produced three novels, two of which, *Peter Ibbetson* and *The Martian*, were largely autobiographical. The third, first published in 1894, was the immensely successful *Trilby*, and it is for this book, and its portrayal of the villainous hypnotist Svengali, that du Maurier is remembered.

Dunbar, Paul Laurence (1872–1906) A native of Dayton, Ohio, Paul Laurence Dunbar was at various times an elevator boy, a mechanic, a journalist, and on the staff of the Library of Congress, but for the last eight years of his short life he devoted himself to writing and lecturing. He was for some time regarded as the foremost Black poet, following the publication in 1896 of his *Lyrics of Lowly Life*. He published eleven other volumes of verse, much of his poetry being in dialect, and also produced three novels and five collections of short stories, but his work is little read nowadays, especially because of the 'Uncle Tom' elements it contains.

Dunbar, William (c.1460–c.1513) East Lothian, Scotland, is believed to have been the birthplace of William Dunbar. He was educated at St Andrew's University and was later attached to the household of James IV of Scotland and his English wife, Margaret Tudor. He is generally regarded as the most important Scottish poet of his period. Noteworthy among an output of close on a hundred works are two allegorical poems, *The Thrissil and the Rois*, written in 1503, and *The Golden Targe*, which probably dates from five years later.

Dunciad, The The verse satire by Alexander Pope, the first three books of which were published anonymously in 1728. The fourth and final part appeared in 1742, by which time Pope had acknowledged his authorship of the work.

Dunne, Finley Peter (1867–1936) Born in Chicago, of Irish descent, and educated in public schools, Finley Peter Dunne became a successful journalist, first in Chicago and later in New York. He created for the *Chicago Journal* the honest and shrewd Irish barman, Mr Dooley, whose wry comments on current events were collected in a number of books, the first of which, *Mr Dooley in Peace and War*, was published in 1898. This, and the subsequent volumes, were widely popular in Britain as well as in the United States.

Dunsany, Lord (1878–1957) Edward John Moreton Drax Plunkett, eighteenth Baron Dunsany, was born in London and educated at Eton and Sandhurst. He published several collections of stories, essays, verse and autobiographical works, but is best known for his involvement as a playwright with the Abbey Theatre, Dublin. Encouraged by Yeats, he wrote a number of plays with a strong vein of fantasy, the first of which, *The Glittering Gate*, was produced in 1909. Successful at the time, his work has since been little seen.

Duns Scotus (c.1270–1308) It is uncertain where John Duns Scotus was born, but it is known that he became a Franciscan monk quite early in life and studied at Merton College, Oxford. Later he went to Paris and received his doctorate there. Noted for his oratory, he was awarded the title *Doctor Subtilis* for his defence of the doctrine of the Immaculate Conception. One of the foremost theological philosophers and teachers of the day, his principal works consisted of commentaries on the writings of Aristotle and Lombard.

Durrell, Lawrence (1912–) The English writer Lawrence George Durrell was born in India. He began writing poetry at an early age, and his first short collection of verse appeared in 1931. Four years later his first novel, *Pied Piper of Lovers*, was published. Many more selections of poetry were to follow, and Durrell became well-known in that genre. His *Collected Poems 1931–1974* was published in 1980. In 1957, however, he published *Justine*, the first of the tetralogy known as the 'Alexandria Quartet', of which the remaining titles were *Balthazar*, *Mountolive* and *Clea*, and this brought him a much wider public. He has published many other successful novels since then, including the 'Avignon Quincunx', made up of *Monsieur*, *Livia*, *Constance*, *Sebastian* and *Quinx*, which came out between 1974 and 1985. He has also written short stories, and his books on Cyprus, Corfu and Rhodes, *Bitter Lemons*, *Prospero's Cell* and *Reflections on a Marine Venus*, have been widely read.

Dürrenmatt, Friedrich (1921–) A dramatist whose powerful, ironic plays have a bitter humour, Friedrich Dürrenmatt was born in Konolfingen, Switzerland, and educated at the universities of Berne and Zurich. He has written novels, detective stories, essays and radio plays, but is best known for his dramas *The Visit*, first seen in 1956, and *The Physicists*, produced in 1962.

Dyer, John (1699–1757) Born at Aberglasney, Carmarthenshire, Wales, and educated at Westminster School, John Dyer was an artist, poet and priest. His first poem, the Pindaric ode *Grongar Hill*, appeared in a miscellany in 1726. Dyer reprinted it on its own in a revised version the following year, when it was hugely successful. His other main works were a descriptive piece, *The Ruins of Rome*, published in 1740, and his longest poem, *The Fleece*, which appeared in 1757 and dealt with all aspects of the wool trade, from rearing sheep to selling woollen goods.

Dynasts, The Described by its author, Thomas Hardy, as 'an epic-drama of the War with Napoleon, in three Parts, nineteen Acts and one hundred and thirty scenes', the publication of this long work began in 1904 and was completed in 1908.

E

Eastman, Max (1883–1969) Max Forrester Eastman was an American social critic and poet. His first book, *Enjoyment of Poetry*, published in 1913, was hugely successful. He followed it with numerous books of literary criticism and works on the politics of the left, which included *Marx, Lenin and the Science of Revolution*, published in 1926, and *Reflections on the Failure of Socialism*, in 1955. He also wrote two volumes of essays and sketches concerning eminent people whom he had known and an autobiography, *Love and Revolution*. His poetry was collected in 1954 in *Poems of Five Decades*.

Eberhart, Richard (1904–) An academic who was born in Austin, Minnesota, Richard Eberhart was educated at the University of Minnesota, St John's College, Cambridge, and Harvard. He has published some thirty volumes of poetry, including *A Bravery of Earth*, in 1930, and *Collected Verse Plays*, in 1962. He was awarded a Pulitzer Prize in 1966 for his *Collected Poems 1930–65*, and an updated selection, *Collected Poems 1930–76*, won the National Book Award in 1977.

eclogue A short poem, especially one of a pastoral nature.

Edda The name given to two collections of ancient Icelandic literature. The *Poetic* or *Elder Edda* contains a number of narrative poems, many of them fragmentary, recounting various Norse legends. Possibly written in the tenth and eleventh centuries, they are thought to have been assembled in about 1240. The *Prose* or *Younger Edda* consists of a short history of the world, a summary of Scandinavian mythology, and a treatise on poetry. These pieces probably date from the middle of the twelfth century, but it is believed that they were put together in their present form in 1222 by the Icelandic historian, Snorri Sturlason.

Edgeworth, Maria (1767–1849) Born in Black Bourton, Oxfordshire, Maria Edgeworth was of Irish descent, the daughter of the writer Richard Lovell Edgeworth. Her first publication, *Letters to Literary Ladies*, which appeared in 1795, was a plea for the education of females. In the following year *The Parent's Assistant*, a collection of moral tales for children, was published, and in 1801 she brought out her first novel, *Castle Rackrent*, with the daunting subtitle, *An Hibernian Tale taken from the Facts, and from the Manners of the Irish Squires before the year 1782*. The book was innovative, both in the author's realistic portrayal of the Irish peasantry and in her use of an historical background, and she exercised a

Maria Edgeworth, the innovative writer, whose realistic treatment of Irish life influenced many historical novelists.

profound influence on Scott and other regional and historical novelists. *Castle Rackrent* was followed by a number of other novels. She also continued to write for children and produced some collections of shorter adult works, among which are the two series of Tales of Fashionable Life, the second of which contained *The Absentee*. Although her books are currently little read, in her day she had many devoted admirers, including Scott, Jane Austen and Thackeray.

Edinburgh Review, The Founded by Francis Jeffrey, Sydney Smith and Henry Brougham, *The Edinburgh Review* was a quarterly magazine which ran from 1802 to 1929. Particularly in its early days it had a remarkably high circulation and was extremely influential, and the contributors to its literary section included all the foremost critics of its period.

Edmonds, Walter D. (1903–) A native of New York State, in which many of his books were set, Walter Dumaux Edmonds was an historical novelist, whose best-known works include *Rome Haul*, published in 1929, *Drums Along the Mohawk*, which appeared in 1936, and *The Boyds of Black River*, in 1953. He also wrote many short stories and some books for children.

Education of Henry Adams, The The autobiography of Henry Brooks Adams, first published in 1918.

Edward II A tragedy by Christopher Marlowe, first published in 1594, but probably originally performed some two years earlier.

Edwards, Jonathan (1703–58) Born in Connecticut and educated at Yale, Jonathan Edwards became, like his father, a minister of religion. A philosopher and a powerful orator, he led the 'Great Awakening', a religious revival which had its origins in Northampton, Massachusetts. He published several religious books, and in 1754 brought out a group of philosophical treatises, including his major work, *An Inquiry into the Modern Prevailing Notions Respecting that Freedom of the Will which is supposed to be Essential to Moral Agency.*

Edwin Drood, The Mystery of A novel by Charles Dickens, uncompleted at his death and published in its unfinished form in 1870. Several attempts to provide a conclusion to the story have been made since, one of the most successful being a version by Leon Garfield.

Eggleston, Edward (1837–1902) Born in Indiana, Edward Eggleston became a Methodist minister, but from 1879 onwards devoted himself entirely to writing. He produced many novels, biographies for young people and history texts. His best known book is *The Hoosier Schoolmaster*, published in 1871.

Egoist, The A novel by George Meredith, first published in 1879.

Eisler, Loren (1907–77) Loren Corey Eisler was Professor of Anthropology at Pennsylvania University. His books include *The Immense Journey*, published in 1957, *Darwin's Century*, in 1960, and *The Man Who Saw Through Mirrors*, in 1973. He also published two volumes of poetry, *Notes of an Alchemist*, which appeared in 1972, and *Another Kind of Autumn*, in 1977. His Autobiography, *All the Strange Hours*, came out in 1975.

Electra A drama by Sophocles. Electra was the daughter of Agamemnon and Clytemnestra and sister to Orestes and Iphigenia.

elegy A song of lamentation, especially a poem written in mourning on the occasion of someone's death, such as Milton's *Lycidas* or Tennyson's *In Memoriam*. The term is also used for a contemplative poem such as Gray's *Elegy Written in a Country Church-Yard*.

Elegy Written in a Country Church-Yard The much-quoted poem by Thomas Gray, first published in 1751.

Eliot, George (1819–80) George Eliot was the pseudonym used by Mary Ann Evans. She was born at Arbury, Warwickshire, England. Her schooling ended at seventeen, when her mother died and she had to keep house for her father. For some years she lived a very narrow life, but in 1841 her father moved to Coventry, where for the first time she began to move in literary circles. Her first published work was a translation of Strauss's *Life of Jesus*, published in 1846. In 1849 her father died, and after spending some time in travel she became assistant editor of the *Westminster Review* in 1851, an appointment which brought her into contact with many writers of the time, including George Henry Lewes. She was to share her life with Lewes for twenty-five years until his death, though she was unable to marry him since his wife was still living; and while their union brought her great happiness, it also troubled her conscience. In 1854 and 1855 she brought out translations of Feuerbach's *The Essence of Christianity* and Spinoza's *Ethics* and also wrote a number of articles for various periodicals. In 1858 the novelist at last emerged with the appearance of *Scenes from Clerical Life*, published first in *Blackwood's Magazine* and then in volume form.

A beautiful sketch in chalk by Sir Frederick William Burton of George Eliot, the famous English novelist. Her work was influenced by her liaison with George Lewes.

Her deep religious feelings always showed through in her writings, and this combined with the verisimilitude and sincerity of the three stories led to the widely-held belief that 'George Eliot' was a clergyman. *Scenes from Clerical Life* was not notably well received, though Charles Dickens gave some encouragement, but in 1859 *Adam Bede* appeared and met with a success which its author said was 'triumphantly beyond' anything she had dreamed of. Encouraged to continue writing, during the next seventeen years she produced an outstanding series of important novels. 1860 saw the publication of *The Mill on the Floss*, and then came *Silas Marner* in 1861. A visit to Florence inspired her historical novel, *Romola*, which was published between 1862 and 1863, and her next book, *Felix Holt, The Radical*, came out in 1866. A verse drama, *The Spanish Gypsy*, was greeted warmly on its appearance in 1868, perhaps at least in part because its author's reputation was now firmly established as the leading novelist of the day. She had been somewhat disappointed, however, that, although accorded that status and widely praised by the most respected of critics and fellow-authors, none of her books since *Adam Bede* had met with the same unstinted enthusiasm. And then, in 1872, *Middlemarch*, often considered to be her masterpiece, was published, and welcomed in deservedly extravagant terms. Here was a writer, clearly influenced by Jane Austen, Mrs Gaskell, Charlotte Brontë and Maria Edgeworth, who yet had her own voice, an approach unlike any of theirs, and an unequalled depth of understanding of the often strange characters, rebels against conventional society, of whom she wrote. Two years after *Middlemarch* she brought out a book of verse, *The Legend of Jubal and other poems*, and in 1876 her last major novel, *Daniel Deronda*, appeared. The death of George Henry Lewes in 1878 was a catastrophic emotional blow, and it appears to have dried up the well of her inspiration. A collection of essays, *Theophrastus Such*, was published in 1879, but no more was to follow. In the following year she married John Walter Cross, a man twenty years her junior. The marriage was apparently happy, but in a few short months George Eliot was dead. Her following during her lifetime was huge, and she was fêted and almost universally admired. For the first half of the twentieth century she was less highly regarded, but nowadays her genius is again recognized, and her novels are justly praised for their deep and compassionate psychological insights.

Eliot, T.S. (1888–1965) Thomas Stearns Eliot was born in St Louis, Missouri, of American parents, and was educated at Harvard, the Sorbonne and Merton College, Oxford. He settled in England while in his twenties, married an Englishwoman in 1915, and eventually became a British subject and a practising member of the Church of England. His first wife died in 1947, and ten years later he married for the second time. When he came to England at the time of the World War I he worked, after a brief spell as a teacher, in a bank, in which employment he remained until 1925. Encouraged by Ezra Pound and Conrad Aiken among others, he published his first volume of poetry, *Prufrock and other Observations*, in 1917. The poem 'The Love Song of J. Alfred Prufrock' had appeared earlier in *Poetry* magazine. In 1919 Leonard and Virginia Woolf brought out a hand-printed volume of his *Poems* as one of the first publications of their recently-founded Hogarth Press. Any doubts that remained concerning Eliot's stature as a major poet were dispelled with the publication in 1922 of *The Waste Land*, a long poem in five sections, to which are added the author's Notes. This work was seen as encapsulating the mood of disillusion which characterized the years immediately following World War I; it fitted perfectly into the period in which it was written, yet the individuality and strength of Eliot's poetry allowed it to transcend such ephemeral considerations. Several volumes of his verse

George Eliot's house in Foleshill Road, Coventry, where she first began to meet literary personalities and started her career as a writer.

A modern representation by Patrick Heron of the famous poet and playwright T.S. Eliot. He was awarded both the Order of Merit and the Nobel Prize for Literature.

appeared at intervals during the next two decades, and included such well-known poems as 'The Hollow Men', 'Ash Wednesday' and 'The Journey of the Magi'. His poetry culminated in *Four Quartets*, published in 1943, in which his religious convictions, increasingly seen in his earlier works, received their strongest expression. *Old Possum's Book of Practical Cats*, published in 1939, was intended for children, but the verses delighted adults too, and found a new audience in the 1980s when Andrew Lloyd-Webber used them for his musical, *Cats*. This was not, of course, Eliot's first success on the stage. He had begun writing verse drama in the 1920s; *Sweeney Agonistes* was published in 1932 and a pageant, *The Rock*, was presented in 1934. Then came the very successful *Murder in the Cathedral*, which was first seen in 1935 and is still widely regarded as the finest poetic drama of the twentieth century. More plays followed: *The*

Family Reunion in 1939 and the three comedies, *The Cocktail Party*, in 1950, *The Confidential Clerk*, in 1954, and *The Elder Statesman*, in 1959. Eliot was also a distinguished writer of prose, and in 1920 published a collection of pieces, originally written for various periodicals, under the title *The Sacred Wood: Essays on Poetry and Criticism*. Several other books of literary criticism appeared, including *The Use of Poetry and the Use of Criticism*, in 1933, *Notes Towards a Definition of Culture*, in 1948, and *On Poets and Poetry*, in 1957. On leaving the bank in 1925, Eliot joined the publishing house of Faber & Faber, of which he became a director. He brought many distinguished poets to the list, and indeed founded and maintained the firm's reputation as Britain's foremost publishers of poetry, a title which it can still claim today. Through this practical encouragement of other poets he undoubtedly affected the course of modern poetry, but his own writings were influential to a much greater extent. As a poet, Eliot had a very individual voice; he used or discarded metre and rhyme innovatively; he could leaven a serious poem with satiric humour; he expressed everyday matters in haunting imagery, and described wonders in simple, ordinary language; and his work was sinewy, powerful and beautiful. With advancing years, his stature grew, and his position in literature was acknowledged in 1948 when he was awarded both the Order of Merit and the Nobel Prize for Literature.

Elizabeth I (1533–1603) The great English queen has a place in English literature primarily as the inspiration for works by a great many contemporary poets, including Spenser and Shakespeare. She was a fine scholar and had some pretensions as a versifier, but the small body of work attributed to her, among which are translations of writings by Boethius, Plutarch and Horace, is not now as effusively praised as it undoubtedly was by her courtiers.

Ellison, Ralph (1914–) Ralph Waldo Ellison, who was born in Oklahoma City, is a Black academic and writer whose first writings, in the form of stories and articles, were published in various magazines before World War II. In 1952 he published his novel, *The Invisible Man*, which was immediately acclaimed as of outstanding quality, and with which he won the National Book Award. In 1964 he brought out a volume of essays, *Shadow and Act*.

Elmer Gantry A satirical novel by Sinclair Lewis about a corrupt evangelist in America's Mid-West, first published in 1927.

Elsie Venner A novel, set in New England, by Oliver Wendell Holmes, first published in 1861.

Elyot, Sir Thomas (*c.*1490–1546) An English diplomat and scholar, Sir Thomas Elyot published in 1531 a philosophical work called *Boke named the Governour*, which he dedicated to Henry VIII. As a reward he was sent as the king's ambassador to the Emperor Charles V. In 1534 he brought out *The Castell of Helth*, a popular treatise on medicine, and in 1538 he produced the first comprehensive Latin *Dictionary*. All his books were extremely successful in their day.

Elytis, Odysseus (1911–) The Greek poet, much of whose work is Surrealist in character, was born in Heraclion, Crete. He has received many literary honours, including the award of the Nobel Prize for Literature in 1979. Several books of verse appeared between the publication of *Clepsydras of the Unknown* in 1937 and that of *Six Plus One Remorses for the Sky* in 1960. A long gap then ensued before the appearance in 1972 of *The Light Tree and the Fourteenth Beauty*, which was followed by a number of other volumes, including *Signalbook*, published in 1977.

Emerson, Ralph Waldo (1803–82) The son of a minister, Ralph Waldo Emerson, who was born in Boston, was educated at Harvard. After three years as a teacher in a school for young ladies run by his brother, William, he entered the Unitarian Church and by 1829 had become a minister in his native city. In the same year he married, but only three years later his wife died, and about this time he became disenchanted

RIGHT: **Emerson with his literary peers (see page 184). He died a month before he was seventy, and is buried beside Thoreau and Hawthorne in Sleepy Hollow Cemetery.**
BELOW: **Emerson's home in Concord, Massachusetts.**

with the forms of worship to which he was committed, and resigned from the ministry. At the end of 1832 he visited Europe, and after travelling in Italy and France spent some months in Britain, where he established friendships with Wordsworth, Landor, Coleridge and Carlyle. His talks with them appear to have led him farther towards the philosophy which would henceforth direct the course of his life. On his return to the United States he settled in Concord, Massachusetts, where he was to live for the rest of his life, marrying for the second time in 1835. Meanwhile, he had launched into a new and successful career as a lecturer. At first his subjects were largely literary, but gradually he extended their range, and he became the leading exponent of the Transcendental doctrine, which may be very briefly summed up in his own words, 'The purpose of life seems to be to acquaint man with himself ... The highest revelation is that God is in every man.' His first book, an essay entitled *Nature*, was published in 1836, and was followed the next year by *The American Scholar*. This was the text of a lecture given at Harvard on the need for America to develop its own intellectual life. In 1838, at the Divinity School in Cambridge, Massachusetts,

THE LATE R. W. EMERSON'S HOME.

he gave an equally controversial talk, this time on the subject of Christianity, and these two addresses brought him a considerable reputation as an original and influential thinker. In 1840 he founded a periodical, *The Dial*, of which he was, for a short period, the editor. Two volumes of *Essays* appeared in 1841 and 1844, and collections of his lectures, under such titles as *Representative Men*, *The Conduct of Life* and *Society and Solitude*, were published regularly. *English Traits*, an admiring study of the English national character, although it did not appear until 1856, was the direct result of a second visit to England in 1847, during which he undertook a successful series of lectures. Before that journey he had published in 1846 his first volume of verse, *Poems*. A second collection, *May Day and other Pieces*, was to appear in 1867. Although a man of strongly held views, Emerson's attitude to life was essentially sensible and balanced, and he had no hesitation in abandoning experiments in vegetarianism and equality between masters and servants when he found that, at least in his household, the ideas did not work effectively. He deplored the excesses of many proponents of causes such as temperance, women's rights, and the abolition of slavery, and himself campaigned actively only for the last of these. In his old age, the Sage of Concord, as he became known, was highly respected and regarded with much affection, as was evidenced in 1872 when his house was rebuilt by popular subscription after being destroyed by fire. He lived for another ten years, but wrote little of importance, as his mind gradually failed. Emerson had a considerable effect on American thought and on many writers, notably Walt Whitman. His own style was greatly admired in its time, but nowadays his prose is seen to be of uneven quality, sometimes brilliant and rich with epigrams, at other times convoluted and obscure. His poetry is similarly uneven, but there is much in all his writing which remains powerful enough to maintain his reputation as a writer of considerable importance.

Emma A novel by Jane Austen, which many consider to be her best work. Emma Woodhouse, a somewhat overbearing young lady, is finally humbled, but wins the love of Mr Knightley. It was first published in 1816.

encyclopaedia A book which sets out to cover all branches of knowledge. From ancient times, many men have devoted much of their lives to the compilation of such works. The oldest book in existence which can properly be called an encyclopaedia is the *Natural History* by Pliny. Other authors of important encyclopaedias include Vincent of Beauvais (*c.*1190–*c.*1264),

Diderot edited his massive *Encyclopédie* as a voice for the *philosophe* party. The sale of the book was banned again and again.

Johann Heinrich Alsted (1588–1638), Louis Moreri (1643–80), and Pierre Bayle (1647–1706). The first English encyclopaedia was compiled by John Harris and published in 1704. In 1728 Ephraim Chambers brought out his *Cyclopaedia*, which became the basis of the French *Encyclopédie*, published towards the end of the eighteenth century, at much the same time as the *Encyclopaedia Britannica* was making its first appearance in Edinburgh. A number of different British publishers brought out new editions of the *Britannica* at various periods in history, but it is now constantly revised and published both in the United States and in Britain.

End of the Affair, The A novel of a wartime love affair by Graham Greene, first published in 1951.

Endymion A novel by Benjamin Disraeli, first published in 1880.

Endymion An allegorical poem by John Keats in which he retells several Greek myths. It was first published in four books in 1818.

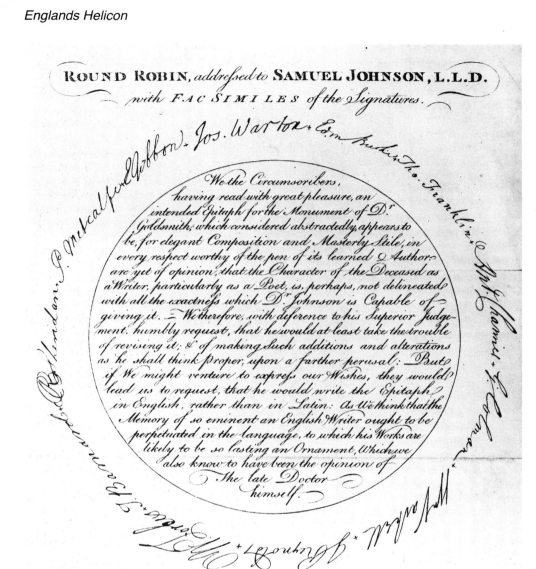

ROUND ROBIN, *addressed to* SAMUEL JOHNSON, L.L.D. *with* FAC SIMILES *of the Signatures.*

We the Circumscribers, having read with great pleasure, an intended Epitaph for the Monument of Dr. Goldsmith; which considered abstractedly, appears to be, for elegant Composition and Masterly Stile, in every respect worthy of the pen of its learned Author: are yet of opinion, that the Character of the Deceased as a Writer, particularly as a Poet, is, perhaps, not delineated with all the exactness which Dr. Johnson is Capable of giving it. — We therefore, with deference to his Superior Judgement, humbly request, that he would at least take the trouble of revising it; & of making Such additions and alterations as he shall think proper, upon a farther perusal: — But if We might venture to express our Wishes, they would lead us to request, that he would write the Epitaph in English, rather than in Latin: As We think that the Memory of so eminent an English Writer ought to be perpetuated in the language, to which his Works are likely to be so lasting an Ornament, Which we also know to have been the opinion of The late Doctor himself.

A 'round robin' addressed to the writer and journalist Samuel Johnson in contemporary English, requesting that his epitaph to the poet and writer Oliver Goldsmith be rewritten in English rather than Latin.

Englands Helicon An anthology of Elizabethan pastoral and lyric poetry, first published in 1600. Among the contributors are Richard Barnfield, Nicholas Breton, Michael Drayton, Robert Greene, Thomas Lodge, Christopher Marlowe, Anthony Munday, Sir Walter Raleigh, Sir Philip Sidney and Edmund Spenser.

English The English language was originally brought to Britain by the invading Angles, Saxons and Jutes of the fifth and sixth centuries. Although the long occupation of the country by the Romans had made Latin familiar, and it was the language of the literate, the ordinary people still spoke the Celtic tongue of the early Britons. The Danish invasion swiftly resulted in a radical change and in the emergence of Old English, which was very similar to Anglo-Saxon. This form of the language, largely Teutonic in character, was in use until the Norman Conquest in the eleventh century. Thereafter, Norman French was used by all educated people, and Middle English soon evolved as an amalgam made up of words and constructions originating in either Teutonic or Romance languages. Over the next four hundred years or so other changes came about, principally in the simplification of plurals and of inflexive endings to verbs, and Modern English, which can be dated from approximately 1500, had come into being. It has, of course, changed quite considerably since then, in pronunciation as well as in spelling and grammar, and it continues to change, especially as new areas of knowledge demand new vocabularies. On the other hand, the invention of printing has tended to slow the process by standardization. In France every effort has been made, although not entirely successfully, to keep the language 'pure', by the exclusion of words of foreign origin. It has been of the greatest benefit that no such attempt has been made on behalf of English, which has shown itself always ready to absorb and adapt any useful words and phrases from other cultures, sucking them in like a philological vacuum cleaner. Throughout the centuries the language has been enriched by the new usages brought back by English explorers, traders, soldiers and sailors. Especially in the twentieth century, with its rapid communications, the process has become easier. The English spoken in the United States often differs from that known as the Queen's English, but the one is readily absorbed into the other. The final result is that English, already in the sixteenth century the richest language in the world, has become even more marvellous a tool, unsurpassed in the variety and flexibility of its vocabulary. This fact explains not only why it is currently the most widely used language internationally but also why, over so many centuries, it has produced a literature of such splendour.

Enoch Arden A narrative poem by Alfred, Lord Tennyson, telling of the sacrifice made by Enoch Arden when he is rescued from shipwreck. It was first published in 1864.

envoy The last stanza of a poem or the concluding part of a book, often containing words specifically addressed to the reader. The French spelling, 'envoi', is sometimes preferred.

epic A narrative poem recounting the story of an historic or legendary hero or event. Two of the most famous examples are the *Illiad* and the *Odyssey*. The term is often loosely applied nowadays to almost any long work of fiction, but should be restricted at least to those which have a theme in the heroic mould.

epigram A term used to describe a verse inscription on a tomb in ancient Greece, although for this meaning the alternative 'epigraph' is often substituted. 'Epigram' then came to mean any short poem ending with an ingenious or witty thought, and as a development was applied to any pithy, witty, and often faintly malicious saying. 'Epigraph' can also indicate a quotation placed at the beginning of a book or a chapter.

epitaph Strictly an inscription on a tomb, but the term is often used for a more elaborate commemoration of a dead person, in prose or verse, but without necessarily including the biographical details which would be included in an obituary notice.

Epithalamion A poem by Edmund Spenser, thought to be in celebration of his marriage, and first published in 1555.

Erasmus (1466–1536) A Dutch scholar and theologian, Desiderius Erasmus became a monk and was ordained priest in 1492. He was allowed to travel and visited England, where he made a number of influential friends, including Sir Thomas More and Archbishop Warham. He spent most of his life from 1621 onwards in Basel, where he wrote and edited works published by the printer Froben. He produced a large number of pious works, including translations of the Greek Testament and other versions of the Scriptures and of religious commentaries and texts, and was, in his writings, a forerunner of those who brought about the Reformation. His *Adagia*, a collection of Greek and Latin proverbs, published in 1500, his *Colloquia*, which appeared in 1524, and his other secular works, including letters, were much used as source material, and provide a fascinating picture of his age.

This edition of Erasmus' work was printed in Germany in 1522. Printers of the day used highly decorative title-borders.

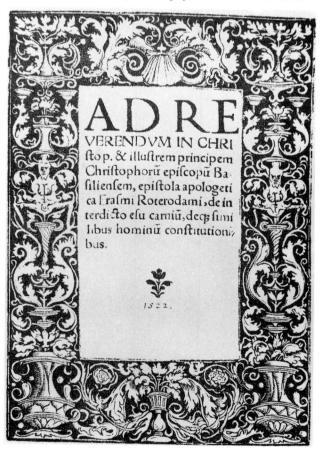

Erewhon A satirical novel by Samuel Butler, first published in 1872.

Erewhon Revisited A novel by Samuel Butler, the sequel to *Erewhon*, first published in 1901.

Ervine, St John (1883–1971) Born in Belfast, St John Greer Ervine was a playwright, novelist and biographer. He was associated with the Abbey Theatre, Dublin, in its early days, and many of his plays were presented there. He later moved to London and became a theatre critic. In 1929 his play *The First Mrs Fraser* was very successful, and it was followed by many other popular but now forgotten comedies. He published a number of novels and biographies of Parnell, General Booth, and Bernard Shaw.

Esenin, Sergei (1895–1925) Sergei Alexandrovich Esenin, who was born to a peasant family in Constantinovo, Russia, moved to Moscow in 1912 and published his first volume of poetry, *Memorial Service*, in 1915. He was immediately recognized as an outstanding lyric poet, with a particular talent for interpreting the folklore and the innate religious feelings of the Russian peasantry in verses which use simplicity to great effect. His later work attacked the evils of city life. He was married for a short while to Isadora Duncan and later to a grand-daughter of Tolstoy. Out of favour and feeling that his life was useless, he committed suicide at the age of thirty.

Esperanto An international language invented by a Russian physician, Dr Zamenhof. Based on the principal European languages, it had a modest success for some years, although its devotees were never numerous. It has now largely vanished with the increasing use of English for international communication.

essay Originally used in the sense of a draft, this term has come to mean, strictly, a written composition devoted to a single subject, and of a shorter length than a treatise (which might be expected to cover its theme more exhaustively).

Essay Concerning Human Understanding A philosophical work by John Locke, first published in 1690.

Essay on Criticism, An An early poem by Alexander Pope, first published anonymously in 1711.

Essay on Man A poem in which Alexander Pope examined human nature and society. It was first published between 1732 and 1734.

Essays, or Counsels, Civill and Morall, The The essays of Francis Bacon, first published in 1597. A new edition containing additional material appeared in 1612, and the fullest edition, in which fifty-eight essays were included, came out in 1625.

Essays of Elia, The Essays by Charles Lamb, first published between 1820 and 1823 and in 1833.

Esther Waters A novel by George Moore, first published in 1894.

Ethan Frome A novel by Edith Wharton, set in Massachusetts and telling of a poor farmer, his wife and the cousin he loves. It was first published in 1911.

Euclid The Greek mathematician lived during the third century BC. Little is known of his life, but he spent much of it in Alexandria, where he is believed to have founded a school in mathematics. His best-known work is the *Elements*, which was used for centuries as an introduction to geometry. In addition to this and other mathematical treatises, he wrote two books on music, an *Introduction to Harmony* and the *Section of the Scale*, and works on astronomy and logic.

Eugene Aram A novel by Bulwer-Lytton, first published in 1832.

Eumenides A tragedy by Aeschylus, the third part of *The Oresteia*, in which the Furies pursue Orestes for the murder of his mother and her lover.

Euripides (480–406 BC) Born at Salamis, Euripides was the third of the three great Greek dramatists. During his lifetime he was very much in the shadow of Aeschylus and Sophocles. He wrote his first play, *The Peliades*, at the age of twenty-five, and is reputed to have produced over ninety plays in the course of his long career as a dramatist. His work was extremely popular with Athenian theatregoers, but was strongly criticized by the literary cognoscenti, including the comic poet Aristophanes, and he did not win the annual contest for tragic plays until he was

Sarah Siddons as Medea. The theme of the Greek tragedy *Medea* by Euripedes has been adapted throughout European literature.

thirty-nine, and indeed won it only five times in all. The reason for this criticism was that Euripides was moving away from the dramatic traditions of the past: he greatly reduced the importance of the chorus and increased the number of actors in a play to as many as eleven (whereas Aeschylus had been considered daringly innovative to introduce a single actor in addition to the chorus), and he gave them far more scope for acting, as opposed simply to declaiming, than his predecessors. Moreover, Euripides was prepared to question the truth of the ancient myths and religious practices, and this attitude was reflected in his plays and their themes. Although some modern critics still see his work as inferior to the more austere purity of the tragedies of Sophocles and Aeschylus, others believe that his less formal approach, and his understanding portrayal of ordinary people, brought new life to the theatre of ancient Greece. In this light, Euripides can indeed be considered as the first practitioner of what might be termed the romantic drama. Nineteen of his plays are still extant; these are: *Alcestis, Medea, Hippolytus, Hecuba, Andromache, Ion, Suppliants, The Heracleidae, Heracles, Iphigenia among the Tauri, The Trojan Women, Helena, Phoenissae, Electra, Orestes, Iphigenia at Aulis, Bacchae, Cyclops* and *Rhesus.*

Europeans, The A novel by Henry James, first published in 1878. An English brother and sister visit relatives in the United States.

Eusden, Laurence (1688–1730) The academic, cleric and poet Laurence Eusden was born in Yorkshire and educated at Trinity College, Cambridge. He was appointed Poet Laureate in 1718 by the Duke of Newcastle, on whose marriage Eusden had written a fulsome poem. He was apparently more noted for his addiction to the bottle than for the quality of his verse, and he was a frequent target for Pope's wit.

Eustace Diamonds, The A novel by Anthony Trollope, the third in the 'Palliser' series, first published in 1873.

Evangeline A narrative poem of unrequited love by Henry Wadsworth Longfellow, first published in 1847.

Evelina, or the History of a Young Lady's Entrance into the World An amusing epistolary novel by Fanny Burney, first published in 1778.

Evelyn, John (1620–1706) The English diarist John Evelyn was educated at Oxford, but left without taking his degree. He became a minor member of the court of Charles II and was a founder member of the Royal Society. He published a number of books on a variety of subjects, but is remembered chiefly for his *Diary*, which covers the years from 1641 until 1706, a much longer period than that recorded by Pepys. Though far less detailed than Pepys's work, Evelyn's *Diary*, which was not published until 1818, supplies much fascinating detail of a period which was filled with dramatic events.

Eve of St Agnes, The A narrative poem by John Keats, first published in 1820.

Everyman The best known of all morality plays, *Everyman* was first performed at the end of the fifteenth or the beginning of the sixteenth century, and is still occasionally presented in modern times. It was almost certainly based on an earlier Dutch play, *Elckerlijc*.

Every Man in his Humour A comedy by Ben Jonson, first presented in 1598, a performance in which William Shakespeare took part as an actor. The play was published in 1601.

Every Man out of his Humour A comedy by Ben Jonson, first presented in 1599, and published in 1600.

Ewart, Gavin (1916–) Gavin Buchanan Ewart was educated at Wellington College and Christ's College, Cambridge. His first volume of verse, *Poems and Songs*, was published in 1939. A long silence followed before *Londoners* appeared in 1964, since when a dozen more volumes have been published, including *The Collected Ewart 1933–1980*, and, in 1987, a selection of his shorter pieces, *The Complete Little Ones*.

Excursion, The A long poem in nine books by William Wordsworth, first published in 1814.

Exeter Book, The A collection of Anglo-Saxon poetry, of considerable antiquity, preserved in a manuscript which dates from the tenth century. The manuscript was given to Exeter Cathedral – where it is still preserved – by Leofric, Bishop of Exeter from 1050 to 1071. In addition to the many poems, which are of varying lengths and both secular and religious in subject, it contains some legal documents and a celebrated collection of riddles. It is considered to be among the most important documents of the period still extant.

Existentialism A somewhat loosely-formulated philosophy based on the importance and individuality of each human being. Since, it argues, there is no set of rules, either in-built genetically or imposed by society, to which the whole of humanity must conform, each person is free to make all those choices and decisions which will form his or her character and chart the progress of his or her life. The individual, and the individual alone, is therefore responsible for what he or she becomes, and must be accepted as such by others. The emphasis placed in Existentialism on the value of the individual results sometimes in too easy an acceptance of the idea that sincerity of belief is a justification for all actions, but it also demands rigorous self-examination. The basic doctrine has been accepted both by rationalists and by those with deep religious convictions, including Christians. Its principal literary exponents have been Jean-Paul Sartre, Simone de Beauvoir, Albert Camus and the philosopher Gabriel Marcel, but the movement has also had adherents outside France, and its theories have been expressed both in philosophical essays and through the medium of novels and plays.

F

fables The most famous collections of stories and legends known as fables are probably those of Aesop, who lived in the sixth century BC, and La Fontaine, whose work was published at the end of the seventeenth century. The term is often used with the special meaning of a story which points a moral, and La Fontaine's tales adhere to this convention, as do, with their ironic humour, the *Fables for Our Time* of James Thurber.

An illustration by Fragonard to one of La Fontaine's fables.

Fables, Ancient and Modern A collection of tales in verse, both taken from the classics and original to the author, written by John Dryden and first published in 1700.

Faerie Queen, The Edmund Spenser's allegorical masterpiece. The first three volumes of the poem were published in 1590 and the second three in 1596.

Fair Maid of Perth, The A novel, set in fourteenth-century Scotland, by Sir Walter Scott, first published in 1828.

Fanny Hill The popular title for *Memoirs of a Woman of Pleasure* by John Cleland, first published between 1748 and 1749.

Far Away and Long Ago Sub-titled 'A History of my Early Life', this is a volume of autobiography by W.H. Hudson, first published in 1918.

farce A form of comedy in which the audience is asked to accept as the basis of the plot a situation which is patently absurd, and which usually continues to develop even more nonsensically, although always adhering, in the best examples of the genre, to its own internal logic. Since the situation in a farce is all-important, the characters are often shallowly drawn, and may often be outright caricatures.

Farewell to Arms, A A novel by Ernest Hemingway, telling of the love of an American soldier and an English nurse during World War I. It was first published in 1929.

Far From the Madding Crowd A novel by Thomas Hardy, first published in 1874. It tells how the shepherd Gabriel Oak finally wins the love of Bathsheba Everdene.

Farquhar, George (1678–1707) The playwright George Farquhar was born in Londonderry, Ireland. He left Trinity College, Dublin without completing his education. He began a career on the stage, but was the cause of a near-fatal accident during a performance in Ireland of Dryden's *The Indian Emperor*, and abandoned acting as a result. Encouraged by the comedian Robert Wilks, he turned to writing plays, and his first comedy, *Love and a Bottle*, was performed at Drury Lane in 1698. In the following year he was very successful with *The Constant Couple: or a Trip to the Jubilee*, and in 1701 a sequel, *Sir Harry Wildair*, was produced, Wilks taking the leading role in both plays. By now Farquhar was well-enough established to publish a short book, *Love and Business; in a Collection of Occasionary Verse and Epistolary Prose*, which appeared in 1702 and contained, among other pieces, an attack on the Aristotelian doctrine of the dramatic unities, entitled 'A Discourse on Comedy in reference to the English Stage', in which he said that the reaction of the audience was more important than arbitrary rules. Three more plays followed, *The Inconstant, or the Way to win Him*, the one-act farce *The Stage Coach* and *The Twin Rivals*, and then in 1706 came *The Recruiting Officer*, the first of the two plays for which he is remembered. His masterpiece, *The Beaux' Stratagem*, was presented in 1707, only a few weeks before his tragically early death. As fine a comedy of manners as those of Congreve, it has been regularly performed since.

Farrar, F.W. (1831–1903) Frederick William Farrar was a clergyman who taught at Harrow and eventually became Dean of Canterbury. He published a large number of books on religious and philological subjects, but is remembered nowadays as the author of the best known of his three stories for young people, *Eric, or Little by Little*, the excessively moral story of a pious schoolboy.

Farrell, James T. (1904–79) The American writer James Thomas Farrell was born in Chicago. He published a large number of novels and collections of short stories and some volumes of literary criticism. His best-known works are the three novels, written in some bitterness, which mirror his own background and in which he features as the hero, Studs Lonigan. These are *Young Lonigan*, *The Young Manhood of Studs Lonigan* and *Judgment Day*, which appeared in 1932, 1934 and 1935 respectively. He was also successful with the five stories about Danny O'Neill, *A World I Never Made*, *No Star is Lost*, *Father and Son*, *My Days of Anger* and *The Face of Time*, published between 1936 and 1953.

Fast, Howard (1914–) The New York author Howard Melvin Fast has published many novels, almost all with an historical background and concerned with man's struggle for freedom. Among them are *The Children*, which appeared in 1935, *The Last Frontier*, in 1941, *Freedom Road* in 1944, *Spartacus*, in 1952, and *The Immigrants*, in 1972. He has also published several volumes of short stories, and a number of mysteries under the pseudonym E.V. Cunningham.

Faulkner, William (1897–1962) William Harrison Faulkner (the name was originally spelt 'Falkner') was a native of New Albany, Mississippi. He worked at a number of jobs before publishing *The Marble Faun*, a volume of verse, in 1924. While employed as a journalist in New Orleans, he was encouraged to write by Sherwood Anderson, and brought out his first novel, *Soldier's Pay*, in 1926. The next book was *Mosquitos*, and then in 1929 came *Sartoris*, the first of the novels which were to feature the Compson, Sartoris and Snopes families. They were set in and around 'Jefferson', the chief

William Faulkner, one of America's outstanding novelists. He was awarded the Nobel Prize for Literature in 1949 and his reputation as one of the twentieth-century's great novelists has grown since his death.

town of the fictional Yoknapatawpha County in Mississippi. Also in 1929 he published the novel which established him as one of the most important writers in America, *The Sound and the Fury*, confirming his promise a year later with a second major work, *As I Lay Dying*. In this work he demonstrated that he could use a lighter touch as well as the sombre tones that had previously coloured his writings. Then in 1931 he dismayed the critics, who expected from him only work of the highest literary standards, by publishing a pot-boiler, *Sanctuary*. However, it brought him financial success and made his name familiar to a wide reading public. Many years later, in 1951, he produced a sequel, *Requiem for a Nun*. But with *Light in August*, published in 1932, and *Absalom, Absalom!*, which came out in 1936, he returned to his serious portrayal of the American South, and continued to mine this rewarding vein in *The Hamlet*, 1940, *Intruder in the Dust*, 1948, *The Town*, 1957, *The Mansion*, 1959, and his last book, *The Reivers*, 1962. He published a number of other novels, including *A Fable*, a religious allegory, which won the Pulitzer Prize in 1954. He was also a distinguished and fairly prolific author of short stories, which were collected and published in several volumes. William Faulkner was acclaimed during his lifetime as one of the twentieth century's outstanding novelists, and his reputation has increased since his death. To the breadth of his canvas, and the detail in his portrayal of the American South, must be added the complex and very individual power of his writing. He was awarded the Nobel Prize for Literature in 1949.

Faust A drama by Johann Wolfgang von Goethe, based on the legends which surrounded a real-life sixteenth-century magician. Goethe worked on this masterpiece over a period of fifty years. The first part was published in 1808 and the second in 1832.

Felix Holt, the Radical A novel with a political background by George Eliot, first published in 1866.

Ferber, Edna (1887–1968) Novelist and short story writer, Edna Ferber was born in Michigan. She published her first novel, *Dawn O'Hara*, in 1911, and among her later books are *Fanny Herself*, which appeared in 1917, *The Girls*, in 1921, *Saratoga Trunk*, in 1941, *Giant*, in 1950, and *Ice Palace*, in 1958. She is probably best remembered for *Show Boat*, which she brought out in 1926, and which shortly afterwards became an extremely popular musical. Edna Ferber also collaborated on a number of plays with George S. Kaufman.

Ferdinand Count Fathom, The Adventures of A novel by Tobias Smollett, first published in 1753. It was a forerunner of the Gothic genre.

Fergusson, Robert (1750–74) Born in Edinburgh and educated at St Andrews, Robert Fergusson spent his life as a clerk in a lawyer's office. He published his first verses in a weekly magazine, and when his poem 'The Daft Days', written in the Scottish vernacular, appeared in 1772, it became clear that an original talent was at work. He continued to produce poetry in this style, and his work was an important influence on Robert Burns. A collection of his poetry was published in 1773, the year before he died in a lunatic asylum.

Feuchtwanger, Lion (1884–1958) The novelist Lion Feuchtwanger was born in Germany but lived for much of his life in France. He was interned there during the World War II, but escaped to the United States and made his home in Hollywood. He is remembered as the author of the novels *The Ugly Duchess*, published in 1923, and his major bestseller *Jew Süss*, which came out in 1925.

Feydeau, Georges (1862–1921) A disciple of Eugène Labiche, and like him a great exponent of French farce, with its inevitable marital complications, Georges Feydeau wrote a large number of plays, many of which have been very successful in English adaptations. Among these are *Look After Lulu*, *A Flea in Her Ear*, and the very well-known farce written in collaboration with Maurice Desvallières, *Hotel Paradiso*.

Field, Nathan (1587–1633) Nathan Field, the son of a clergyman, became one of the children of Queen Elizabeth's chapel, and in so doing launched himself on an extremely successful theatrical career. He acted in plays by Ben Jonson, George Chapman and William Shakespeare, among other dramatists, creating many leading parts. Later he took to writing plays himself. He worked with a number of other playwrights of the period, including Philip Massenger and John Fletcher, but was the sole author of two comedies, *A Woman is a Weathercock* and *Amends for Ladies*, published in 1612 and 1618 respectively.

Fielding, Henry (1707–54) Born near Glastonbury, England, the son of a well-to-do army officer, Henry Fielding was educated at Eton and later at Leiden University. His plan to elope with a young heiress having been frustrated, he moved to London and began his career as a playwright, his first comedy, *Love in Several Masques*, being produced at Drury Lane in 1728. It was not particularly successful, and it was after this that he went to Leiden. Returning to London after eighteen months, he embarked during the next six years on the writing of a series of comedies, burlesques and farces which, although they are no longer performed, were well received, and he was additionally successful with some translations of works by Molière. In 1734 he married the beautiful Miss Charlotte Craddock, and two years later he was successfully managing the Haymarket theatre. Everything in his life seemed to be highly satisfactory. However, in 1737 the government, provoked by the bitter satire of much of Fielding's work, introduced the licensing of plays by the Lord Chamberlain, a form of censorship which endured in Britain until 1968. Fielding was forced to abandon the theatre, and decided to study law. He was called to the bar in 1740, but ill health prevented him from pursuing this career as energetically as he would have wished. Meanwhile, he had been writing again – first satirical articles and then, in 1741, under a nom-de-plume, a skit on Samuel Richardson's recently published *Pamela*, entitled *An Apology for the Life of Mrs Shamela Andrews*. This appears to have given him a taste for fiction and in the following year, using his own name, he produced *The History of the Adventures of Joseph Andrews and his Friend, Mr Abraham Adams*,

An etching after Hogarth, of the innovative playwright and novelist Henry Fielding, whose original approach pioneered the style of the modern novel. A social reformer, magistrate and philanthropist, he campaigned against crime, corruption and the unbridled sale of alcohol.

which was again intended as a parody of *Pamela*, but which developed into an original novel with its own validity. The success of *Joseph Andrews* was followed in 1743 by the publication of three volumes of *Miscellanies*. These included a play called *The Wedding Day*, a number of poems and essays, the fragmentary fantasy, *Journey from this World to the Next*, and his bitterly ironic novel, *History of the Life of the late Mr Jonathan Wild the Great*. To his great sorrow, his wife died in 1744. In the next few years he was largely occupied by the production of two newspapers and published little of importance, but he had been working on the book which was to prove his masterpiece. *Tom Jones, or, the History of a Foundling* was published in 1749 and was immediately successful. In the meantime Fielding, who in 1747 had married again, had been appointed a Principal Justice of the Peace, and he devoted much of his time to his duties, working tirelessly to end corruption in the magistracy and leading a campaign against crime, in which causes he wrote a number of influential pamphlets. *Amelia*, published in 1752, was his last major work, the third of his great novels. In that same year he started another newspaper, *The Covent Garden Journal*, and two years later, in search of the improvement in his health which a warmer climate might bring, visited Portugal with his second wife and one of his children, a journey which resulted in the posthumously published *The Journal of a Voyage to Lisbon*. Fielding's position in literature is one of immense importance. Although fiction had been developing, particularly with the work of his predecessors Defoe and Richardson, Fielding set out consciously to alter its form and also to widen its scope to present a much more profound portrayal of characters and the contemporary scene. In these innovative aims he was supremely successful, and, as he himself believed, was therefore 'the founder of a new province of writing'. He can truly be called the father of the modern novel.

Fielding, Sarah (1710–68) Sarah Fielding was a younger sister of Henry Fielding. She shared his interest in exploring the characters of a novel in some depth, as she demonstrated when she published in 1744 *The Adventures of David Simple*, to which her brother, by now celebrated as a playwright and novelist, contributed a preface. The story was continued in *Familiar Letters Between the Principal Characters in David Simple* and *David Simple, Volume the Last*, which appeared in 1747 and 1753 respectively. She wrote a number of other works of fiction, including *The History of the Countess of Dellwyn*, published in 1759, and *The History of Ophelia*, in 1760, and also translated works of Xenophon from the Greek.

Fiennes, Celia (1662–1741) Born near Salisbury, the daughter of a Roundhead colonel, Celia Fiennes wrote an account, for the interest and edification of her family, of her lengthy travels in England, which she undertook for the sake of her health, and during which she visited every county. Filled with detailed observations, the book is comprehensive and fascinating. A shortened version was eventually published in 1888 by a descendant of her family, under the title *Through England on a Side Saddle in the time of William and Mary*, and a complete edition, prepared by Christopher Morris, appeared in 1947.

Finnegans Wake A long and complex novel by James Joyce, relating the dreams during one night of Humphrey Chimpden Earwicker, a Dublin innkeeper. It was first published in 1939.

133

Firbank, Ronald (1886–1926) Arthur Annesley Ronald Firbank was born in London. He was the author of a large number of mannered novels which are more highly regarded nowadays than they were in his lifetime. Coming from a wealthy family, he was able himself to pay for the publication of most of his books, which included the novels, *Vainglory*, in 1915, *Caprice*, in 1917, and *Valmouth*, in 1919. The first of his novels to be brought out by a commercial publisher was *Prancing Nigger*, which appeared in the United States in 1924, and in England (under the title *Sorrow in Sunlight*) in 1925. His last book, *Concerning the Eccentricities of Cardinal Pirelli*, was published posthumously, as were a number of fragmentary works.

FitzGerald, Edward (1809–83) For the first nine years of his life, Edward FitzGerald, who was born near Woodbridge, Suffolk, England, was known as Edward Purcell. In 1818 his father changed the family name to that of his wife, who had been a Miss FitzGerald. Educated at Trinity College, Cambridge, where he became a friend of Thackeray, Edward FitzGerald had no financial need to take up any profession other than that of occasional author, although in later life he developed an interest in the sea and became part-owner of a herring-lugger. In 1849 he married the daughter of Bernard Barton, the Quaker writer, and helped her to prepare a book about her father. The marriage was short-lived, however, and they soon separated. A few of

FitzGerald's beautiful translation from the Persian of the *Rubaiyat of Omar Khayyam* is a masterpiece of English poetry in its own right.

FitzGerald's verses had appeared some years previously, but his first book, *Euphranor, a Dialogue on Youth*, was published in 1851 and followed in 1852 by *Polonius*, a collection of 'wise saws and modern instances'. Translations of *Six Dramas of Calderon* and *Salaman and Absal*, by the Persian poet Jami, led him towards the work for which he is famous, and in 1859 he brought out, anonymously, his verse translation of *The Rubaiyat of Omar Khayyam*, a collection of quatrains by the twelfth-century Persian poet. He later published other translations from the Spanish and the Persian, in addition to versions of plays by Aeschylus and Sophocles. His lively *Letters to Fanny Kemble* appeared posthumously in 1895. *The Rubaiyat* was not immediately successful, but with the support of such poets as Dante Gabriel Rossetti and Algernon Swinburne it eventually achieved widespread recognition, and its popularity was greatly increased in 1885, when his friend Tennyson dedicated his *Tiresias* to FitzGerald's memory, thus making his name and his work known to a much larger public. FitzGerald brought out new and substantially revised editions of *The Rubaiyat* in 1868, 1872 and 1879, but the original translation remains the most familiar and widely quoted version.

Fitzgerald, F. Scott (1896–1940) Francis Scott Key Fitzgerald was born in St Paul, Minnesota, and educated at Princeton. After leaving college he served briefly in the army during World War I. From his youth on, he had believed that he was destined for fame and fortune, and his faith was justified when he published his first novel, *This Side of Paradise*, in 1920. The book was immediately and rightly successful, and he was hailed as a major novelist. In the same year he married the beautiful and highly-strung Zelda Sayre, with whom he lived – partly in the States and partly in Europe – a life of indulgence, extravagance and instability. He had been writing short stories for many of the major magazines, and a volume of these, *Flappers and Philosophers*, was also published in 1920. A further collection, *Tales of the Jazz Age*, appeared in 1922, the year in which his second novel, *The Beautiful and the Damned*, was also published. It was less successful than *This Side of Paradise*, largely because of its satirical content, but this did not seriously damage his reputation. Meanwhile, he was living in Paris, where he met Ernest Hemingway,

Scott Fitzgerald with his wife Zelda and daughter 'Scottie' on holiday in 1941 during one of the periods when Zelda was suffering a breakdown and spending most of her time in a mental institution.

A scene from the film version of the novel *The Great Gatsby*, considered Fitzgerald's greatest literary achievement and one which exemplified the spirit of the era.

whose encouragement was of immense value to him. There he produced *The Great Gatsby*, published in 1925, the novel which is undoubtedly his finest achievement and which can be claimed to represent more effectively than any other work of fiction the frenetic spirit of the period. He published another collection of short stories, *All the Sad Young Men*, in 1926, and then went to Hollywood, which was not congenial to him and where he spent some unhappy months before returning to Europe in 1928. Zelda's mental balance had always been precarious, and it was not long before her condition deteriorated into complete breakdown. The strain that this imposed on him, coupled with his own increasing dependence on alcohol and the continual struggle to find money to pay for his extravagant lifestyle – all this prevented Fitzgerald from ever again reaching the heights of *The Great Gatsby*. A new novel, *Tender is the Night*, which appeared in 1934, showed, however, that his powers had not yet completely deserted him, although, as his later attempts at revision proved, even Fitzgerald was aware of its imperfections. More short stories, *Taps at Reveille*, came the following year, and in 1936 he contributed a number of autobiographical pieces to the magazine *Esquire*. In an effort to achieve financial security, he returned to Hollywood in 1937 as a scriptwriter, and there he worked on a new novel, *The Last Tycoon*. This was unfinished at the time of his death, and the version which appeared in 1941 was edited by his lifelong friend and supporter, the literary critic Edmund Wilson, who also published in 1945 a collection of Fitzgerald's last pieces, *The Crack-Up*. It was a tragedy that Fitzgerald's own flawed character should have brought about an early death and a failing of his talent before he could produce more work with the brilliance of *The Great Gatsby*, but he himself was a product of the brittle unease which gripped much of the world between the two wars, and especially in the 1920s, when hedonism was seen as the cure for underlying insecurity – at least for those who could afford it. He remains the foremost literary representative of America's Jazz Age, outstanding for his ability to capture its very essence on paper.

Flaubert, Gustave (1821–80) Born and educated in Rouen, France, Gustave Flaubert was the son of a surgeon. In 1840 he went to Paris to study law, but, inheriting a reasonable income on the death of his father, abandoned any pretence at a legal career and indulged his pleasure in travel. In 1850 he began to write his first novel, *Madame Bovary*, one of the world's great classics. He wrote slowly and took infinite pains – his

Gustave Flaubert. His contempt for bourgeois society is revealed in his novel *Madame Bovary*.

constant search for *le mot juste* is legendary, and the careful quality of his research should be a model to all authors. *Madame Bovary* took him six years to complete and did not appear until 1857, when it was published in serial form in the *Revue de Paris*. It caused an outcry, and both Flaubert and the publisher were taken to court. They were eventually acquitted of the charge of immorality, and the novel was very successful when published in book form. For the background of his next story, *Salammbo*, which appeared in 1862, Flaubert moved from contemporary provincial France to historical Carthage. On the other hand, *L'Education sentimentale*, which appeared in 1869, was set in Paris in the 1840s. The less realistic *La tentation de Saint-Antoine* was published in 1874, in which year Flaubert's play, *Le candidat*, was unsuccessfully presented. Only one more book was published before his death. This was *Trois Contes*, which includes the long stories 'Un Coeur Simple', 'La Légende de Saint-Julien-l'Hospitalier' and 'Hérodias'. In the last years of his life he was working on a vast and complex novel, *Bouvard et Pécuchet*, which he believed to be his masterpiece. The fragment which was published posthumously does not compare in any way with the perfections of his other books. Flaubert's particular genius lay in the detailed truthfulness of his writings. He was the prophet of realism, and *Madame Bovary* is a superb example of his craft.

Flecker, James Elroy (1884–1915) After attending both Oxford and Cambridge the poet and playwright James Elroy Flecker was employed as a British consul, first in Constantinople and later in Beirut. He published his first volume of poetry in 1910, and one of his best-known works, *The Golden Journey to Samarkand*, appeared in 1913. He wrote other verses, a novel and two plays, *Don Juan* and his famous Oriental drama *Hassan*, neither of which was performed or published until several years after his early death from tuberculosis.

Fleming, Ian (1909–64) Ian Lancaster Fleming was educated at Eton and Sandhurst. He became a journalist, and worked for ten years as Foreign Manager of Kemsley Newspapers. He published *Casino Royale*, his first thriller, in 1953. It introduced James Bond, the undercover agent who featured in a series of adventures, including *Diamonds Are Forever*, *Dr No*, *From Russia With Love* and *Goldfinger*. The stories were all transferred to the screen, and Bond, 007, proved so popular that more novels and screenplays about him were written after Fleming's death.

Fletcher, John (1579–1625) The son of a bishop, John Fletcher was born in Rye, Sussex, England, and educated at Corpus Christi College, Cambridge. When his father died, having lost the favour of Queen Elizabeth, his family was left penniless, and John entered the theatre and became a dramatist. The authorship and the dates of first performance of plays of the period is often in doubt, especially since it appears to have been common practice for playwrights at that time to collaborate with each other, or to make various amendments to each other's plays, though the degree of their contribution, and indeed the fact of the joint authorship, is not always fully acknowledged. We know that Fletcher worked on many plays with Philip Massinger, and that he also collaborated with William Rowley, George Chapman, Thomas Middleton and Ben Jonson. It is widely believed that he was responsible for a large part of Shakespeare's *Henry VIII*, and he certainly shared more or less equally with Shakespeare the authorship of *The Two Noble Kinsmen*, first published in 1634. There are several plays, however, of which John Fletcher was the sole author. Most of them are comedies, and indeed this seems to have been his forte. They include *The Faithful Shepherdess*, first printed about 1609, *The Woman's Prize, or the Tamer Tam'd*, which was an attempt at a sequel to *The Taming of the Shrew*, and *A Wife for a Month*, both the latter being printed in 1647. But it is primarily for his collaboration with Sir Francis Beaumont that Fletcher is remembered. They worked together for a short period only — some seven or eight years, beginning in 1606 — and produced comparatively few plays, but their names are inseparably linked as the distinguished authors of, among other works, *A King and No King*, *Philaster* and their best-known play, *The Maid's Tragedy*.

Flowers of Evil The English title of *Les fleurs du mal*, a collection of lyrics by Charles Baudelaire, first published in 1857, often the subject of censorship, but nowadays seen as representing some of the finest French poetry ever written.

Folios, Shakespearian The Folio editions of Shakespeare's works, which are so-called in a reference to the size of the books (and to distinguish them from the Quartos), are the main basis for our present-day texts of the plays. The First Folio was printed in 1623, and second, third and fourth versions appeared in 1632, 1663, 1664 and 1685. Although the Folios were published after Shakespeare's death, whereas most of the Quarto versions were published during his lifetime, the plays are printed in the Quartos as they were remembered, often faultily, by the actors, and the Folios are known to be generally more accurate.

Ford, Ford Madox (1873–1939) Born in Surrey, England, Ford Madox Ford changed his name from Ford Hermann Hueffer at the end of World War I. He published *The Brown Owl: A Fairy Story* in 1892, and this was followed by a stream of books, fiction, non-fiction and verse, on a variety of subjects. He worked in close collaboration with Joseph Conrad for a period, and their partnership resulted notably in the publication of *The Inheritors* and *Romance*, in 1901 and 1903 respectively. Between 1907 and 1908 he brought out a trilogy of novels concerning King Henry VIII and Katherine Howard, and in 1915 published the work by which he is chiefly remembered, a novel entitled *The Good Soldier*. He founded both *The English Review* and *The Transatlantic Review*.

Ford, John (1586–*c*.1640) John Ford was born in Devon, England, and educated at Oxford. He began to study law but soon embarked on a literary career, and in 1606 published his first work, an elegy on the death of the Earl of Devonshire. He wrote other poetry, but is primarily remembered as a playwright. His dramatic work appears to have been written at first in collaboration with others, and the most notable of the plays of which he was a joint author was *The Witch of Edmonton*, written with Thomas Dekker and William Rowley and first presented about 1621. From 1628 he worked alone, producing a large number of plays, beginning with *The Lover's Melancholy* and including his *Perkin Warbeck*, seen in 1634, an unsuccessful attempt to rival Shakespeare. His best-known drama, *'Tis Pity She's a Whore*, was first produced in 1633.

Forester, C.S. (1899–1966) The English writer Cecil Scott Forester was educated at Dulwich College. He published his first books in the 1920s, and later became the author of a number of highly popular historical sea adventure stories featuring the naval office Horatio Hornblower. These included *Captain Hornblower, R.N.*, published in 1939, *Mr Midshipman Hornblower*, in 1950, and *Hornblower and the Hotspur*, in 1962. Of his earlier novels, *Brown on Resolution* was very successful, and *The African Queen*, published in 1935, became a classic of the screen.

Forster, E.M. (1879–1970) Edward Morgan Forster, a Londoner by birth, was educated at Tonbridge School and King's College, Cambridge. After spending some time in travel, he began to write, and his first novel, *Where Angels Fear to Tread*, appeared in 1905. It was followed in 1907 by *The Longest Journey* and in 1908 by *A Room With a View*. His reputation as one of the outstanding novelists of the early twentieth century had not yet been established, but with the publication in 1910 of *Howards End* his talent was fully recognized. Two works of non-fiction came next, inspired by wartime service for the Red Cross in Egypt. His most celebrated book, *A Passage to India*, was published in 1924. He had spent a considerable time in India, and was able to bring an authentic quality to a story which, at the time of publication, was more controversial than it might appear today. A recent adaptation for the screen has resulted in a revival of interest in the book, demonstrating that it can still speak tellingly to later generations. After the completion of *A Passage to India*, Forster wrote no more novels, but mention should be made of the collections of short stories, which include *The Celestial Omnibus*, published in 1911, and *The Eternal Moment*, in 1928. His other main work of fiction, *Maurice*, was written many years before *A Passage to India*, but remained unpublished, because of its homosexual theme, until after his death. He also published a number of books of essays, among them *Aspects of the Novel*, which consisted of transcripts of a successful series of lectures which he gave in 1927, and he produced biographies of his friend, *Goldsworthy Lowes*

Dickson, and his great-aunt, *Marianne Thornton*. Perhaps partly because some of his own work had to be suppressed during his lifetime, he was always a vigorous campaigner against the censorship of books. E.M. Forster's reputation rests on a small output, but one of very considerable quality.

Forster, John (1812–76) Born at Newcastle, England, and educated at London University, John Forster was a journalist and also a biographer. He contributed to many periodicals, and was editor successively of *The Foreign Quarterly Review*, *Daily News* and *The Examiner*. His books included a number of histories and books on British statesmen, as well as studies of Goldsmith and Landor. His *Life of Charles Dickens*, published between 1872 and 1874, was long considered to be the standard biography of the novelist.

Forsyte Saga, The John Galsworthy's previous published novels, *The Man of Property*, *In Chancery* and *To Let*, together with two short 'interludes', were brought together and published in 1922 as *The Forsyte Saga*.

Forsyth, Frederick (1938–) Frederick Forsyth was a successful foreign correspondent until his first novel, *The Day of the Jackal*, was published in 1971 and became an immediate international bestseller. A number of other novels, including *The Odessa File* and *The Dogs of War*, have followed. *The Fourth Protocol* was published in 1984.

Fortescue, Sir John (*c*.1394–*c*.1476) The lawyer Sir John Fortescue, who was born in Somersetshire, became Chief Justice of the King's Bench under Henry VI. His principal work of literature was *De Laudibus legum Angliae*, in praise of the laws of England. He also wrote a second major treatise on *The Difference between an Absolute and Limited Monarchy*.

For Whom the Bell Tolls Ernest Hemingway's novel of the Spanish Civil War, first published in 1940.

Four Horsemen of the Apocalypse, The A novel by Vicente Blasco Ibanez, first published in English in 1916.

Four Quartets The last major work of T.S. Eliot, a sequence of four poems, 'Burnt Norton', 'East Coker', 'The Dry Salvages' and 'Little Gidding', first published between 1935 and 1942 and collected in one volume in 1943.

Fowler, H.W. (1858–1933) Henry Watson Fowler's *A Dictionary of Modern English Usage* was first published in 1926. Recent editions have been updated by Sir Ernest Gowers. With his younger brother Frank, Fowler also compiled dictionaries for the Oxford University Press and wrote *The King's English*, which, according to *The Times*, 'took the world by storm' when it appeared in 1906.

Fowles, John (1926–) John Robert Fowles was born in Essex, England, and educated at Bedford School and New College, Oxford. After a period as a teacher, he became a full time writer. He published his first novel, *The Collector*, in 1963, and was immediately recognized as a major literary talent. His subsequent novels include *The Magus, Mantissa* and *A Maggot*, which first appeared in 1966, 1982 and 1985 respectively. *The French Lieutenant's Woman*, which was published in 1969, was later made into an outstanding motion picture. Despite the somewhat sensational elements which frequently appear in his novels, John Fowles is a highly serious novelist and his work is invariably treated with respect by the critics. Nevertheless, his idiosyncratic style and choice of subjects, and his often experimental approach to the form of the novel, have resulted in a mixed reception for the later books.

Foxe, John (1516–87) The English martyrologist John Foxe was born at Boston, Lincolnshire, and educated at Oxford. His strongly held Puritan views frequently brought him into conflict with the authorities, and eventually he went into exile in Europe. In Basel he wrote his great work, known familiarly as *The Book of Martyrs*, which was published there in Latin in 1559. He returned to England, became a priest, and brought out an English edition in 1563. It was immensely popular. Three revised editions appeared during Foxe's lifetime, and yet more revisions were made in subsequent posthumous printings.

Framley Parsonage A novel by Anthony Trollope, the fourth in the 'Barsetshire' series, first published in 1861.

France, Anatole (1844–1922) Anatole France was the pseudonym of Jacques-Anatole-François Thibault, born in Paris. He was awarded the Nobel Prize for Literature in 1921. An extremely prolific writer, he produced a large number of novels, including *The Crime of Sylvestre Bonnard*, which established his reputation, the satirical *Penguin Island*, and his story of the French Revolution, *The Gods Are Athirst*. He also published many short stories, volumes of verse, and several books of imaginative autobiography. For much of his lifetime he was the dominant figure in French literature.

Frankenstein, or the Modern Prometheus The famous horror novel by Mary Wollstonecraft Shelley, in which the scientist Frankenstein creates a monster and gives it life. It was first published in 1818.

Franklin, Benjamin (1706–90) Benjamin Franklin, who was born in Boston, Massachusetts, was apprenticed at the age of twelve to his brother James, a printer, who in 1721 started the *New England Courant*, one of the earliest American newspapers, to which Benjamin frequently contributed articles. After a journey to England, where he stayed for two years, he returned to Philadelphia, became the owner of *The Philadelphia Gazette*, and established one of the earliest circulating libraries. In 1732 he published the first of his *Poor Richard's Almanacks*, which appeared regularly for twenty-five years. His industry was immense: in addition to achieving fame as a scientist and inventor, he became Postmaster in Philadelphia, organized the first police and fire forces in America, was instrumental in the founding of an Academy, which later developed into the University of Philadelphia, and of the American Philosophical Society. He became a member of the General Assembly of Pennsylvania, eventually being given responsibility for the military defence of the north-western frontier of the province. He

'The wisest American', Benjamin Franklin, painted in 1783, at the time of his peace negotiations with Great Britain.

was sent to England in 1757 to negotiate greater independence for the American colonies, and there met many members of the British literary world. Returning to America in 1774, after a second visit to England, he was one of those who drafted the Declaration of Independence. He was later sent on a diplomatic mission to France, and on his return in 1785 was elected a delegate to the Convention which drew up the Constitution of the United States. Throughout his life he wrote assiduously, producing many influential pamphlets on such matters as slavery and protectionism and paper currency. He published his *Autobiography* in England in 1793.

Fraser, Antonia (1932–) Lady Antonia Fraser, who was educated at Lady Margaret Hall, Oxford, is a member of the distinguished Pakenham family and is married to Harold Pinter, the playwright. Noted as a biographer, her subjects have included *Mary Queen of Scots* and *Cromwell*, and in 1984 she published *The Weaker Vessel – Woman's Lot in 17th Century England*. She has also written novels and a number of stories featuring the female detective Jemima Shore, including *Oxford Blood*, published in 1985.

Frazer, Sir James George (1854–1941) Born in Glasgow, Scotland, James George Frazer was educated at Glasgow University and Cambridge. An academic, he wrote a number of books on religion and anthropology, and is celebrated as the author of *The Golden Bough*, a vast study of ancient religious beliefs throughout the world, first published in 1890, and completed with a final volume in 1936. He was knighted in 1914.

Freeman, Mary E. Wilkins (1852–1930) The American writer Mary Eleanor Wilkins Freeman was born in Randolph, Massachusetts. She wrote a large number of short stories and novels with New England settings. *A Humble Romance and Other Stories*, published in 1887, and *A New England Nun and Other Stories*, which appeared in 1891, were her most successful books, demonstrating the careful characterization and the realism of her approach.

French Lieutenant's Woman, The A novel by John Fowles, first published in 1969.

French Revolution, The Thomas Carlyle's major history, first published in three volumes in 1837.

Freneau, Philip (1752–1832) Often called the poet of the American Revolution, Philip Morin Freneau was born in New York of Huguenot parentage and educated at the College of New Jersey, which later became Princeton. He wrote a number of satirical works in verse in support of the American cause; *The British Prison Ship*, published in 1781, was the best known and most influential of these. Collections of his poems

appeared in 1786 and 1795, and he was also well known as a journalist. A volume of essays, under the title *Letters on Various Interesting and Important Subjects*, appeared in 1799.

Freud, Sigmund (1856–1939) The father of psychoanalysis, Sigmund Freud was born in Freiburg, Germany. He practised in Vienna, but left that city for London after the Nazi invasion of Austria. He published a large number of books – the *Complete Psychological Works* occupied twenty-four volumes. The majority of his publications were academic works, but some, such as *Totem and Tabu*, had a wider appeal.

Frisch, Max (1911–) Max Rudolf Frisch, who was born and educated in Zurich, Switzerland, trained as an architect and worked in that profession until 1955, when he became a full-time writer. His first play was published in 1945, and he has gone on to write more than two dozen novels and plays, for which he has received many awards. The best known of his works are *Stiller*, which appeared in 1954, *Homo Faber* in 1957, and *Andorra*, in 1961.

Frogs, The A comedy by Aristophanes, first presented in 405BC. It has a literary subject, being concerned with the rivalry between Aeschylus and Euripides.

Frost, Robert (1874–1963) Robert Lee Frost was born in San Francisco but returned as a boy to Massachusetts, where his family had its origins.

The American lyrical poet Robert Frost relaxing in his home. He celebrated his eighty-eighth birthday by publishing his last collection of poems *In the Clearing*.

He was educated at Dartmouth College and Harvard. By 1913 he was married and living with his family in England, and it was there that his first collection of poetry, *A Boy's Will*, was published. It was followed in 1914 by *North of Boston*. These books brought him the entrée into English literary circles and the friendship of a number of poets, especially that of Edward Thomas. In 1915 he returned to the United States, where his verse had already made him known. He lived in New Hampshire for the rest of his life. Supplementing his income by teaching and lecturing, he continued regularly to bring out volumes of poetry, the last of which, *In the Clearing*, appeared in 1962, the year before his death. His work, traditional in style, but at the same time unmistakably contemporary in the use of colloquial language, has been admired both by critics and by the public at large. Because his verse is easy to understand and enjoy, Frost has often been thought of as a simple soul, given to extolling the beauties of nature. But he has far more power and complexity than that would imply, and the fact that he won no fewer than four Pulitzer Prizes for his poetry may be seen as some proof of his outstanding talents. His prize-winning collections were *New Hampshire*, published in 1923, *Collected Poems*, 1930, *A Further Range*, 1936, and *A Witness Tree*, 1942.

Froude, J.A. (1818–94) Born in Dartington, Devonshire, England, and educated at Westminster School and Oriel College, Oxford, James Anthony Froude intended to enter the Church, but grew disillusioned. After publishing two volumes of fiction with a religious background in 1847 and 1849, he turned to journalism and to the writing of history. His major work, the *History of England from the Fall of Wolsey to the Defeat of the Spanish Armada*, was published in twelve volumes between 1856 and 1870. It was extremely successful, and is still regarded as an important source book, though Froude's work, in this and other books, has often been considered tainted by his one-sided and strongly anti-clerical approach to his subjects. Following the *History*, he wrote the controversial *The English in Ireland*, published between 1872 and 1874, and a number of other works, including historical studies, biographies and essays. He was a close friend of Thomas Carlyle, and was appointed his literary executor. This resulted in a number of books about Carlyle and his wife, among them Carlyle's *Reminiscences* and *Letters and Memorials of Jane Walsh Carlyle*, published in 1881 and 1883 respectively. They scandalized the literary world by their outspokenness on matters which, at

that time, were thought better left unrevealed. Froude's last book, *The Two Chiefs of Dunboy*, was an historical novel, set in Ireland, of remarkable dullness.

Fry, Christopher (1907–) Christopher Harris, who later adopted the family name Fry as his surname, was born in Bristol, England. He has been connected with the theatre for most of his life. He had his first major success in 1949 with his play, *The Lady's Not For Burning*, which delighted audiences with its clever, witty verse. His other works include *Venus Observed*, *A Sleep of Prisoners*, *The Dark is Light Enough* and *Curtmantle* and the one-act plays, *The Boy with a Cart* and *A Phoenix Too Frequent*. He successfully translated and adapted a number of plays by the French playwrights Giraudoux and Anouilh, and has also received much praise for his versions of *Peer Gynt* and *Cyrano de Bergerac*.

The dramatist Christopher Fry, by Angus McBean.

Frye, Northrop (1912–) Herman Northrop Frye was born in Sherbrooke, Quebec, and educated in Toronto and at Oxford. An academic, he has published a number of works of literary criticism, including *Fearful Symmetry: A Study of William Blake*, which appeared in 1947, *Anatomy of Criticism*, in 1957, *T.S. Eliot*, in 1963, *The Critical Path*, in 1971, and *Creation and Recreation*, in 1980.

Fuentes, Carlos (1928–) The Mexican diplomat and academic Carlos Fuentes was born in Mexico City and educated at the University of Mexico and in Geneva. In 1954 he published *Los dias enmascarados*, and among his other works are *Don Quixote, or the Critique of Reading*, which appeared in 1974, and the books by which he is best known to English-speaking readers, the prize-winning volumes *Cambio de piel* (*A Change of Skin*) and *Terra nostra*, which came out in 1967 and 1975 respectively.

Fugard, Athol (1932–) The South African play-wright Athol Fugard, who was educated at Cape Town University, has written a number of plays almost all of which are deeply concerned with the racial problems of his native country. Among them are *The Blood Knot*, first performed in 1961, *A Lesson from Aloes*, 1980 and *'Master Harold' … and the boys*, 1982.

Fuller, Henry Blake (1857–1929) A native of Chicago, where much of his fiction was set, Henry Blake Fuller was a novelist, short story writer and poet. His early work, mostly in the form of historical romances, was published under the pseudonym Stanton Page. Many more works of fiction followed, including the posthumous publications, *Gardens of This World*, which was a sequel to his first book, and *Not on the Screen*. *The Cliff Dwellers*, published in 1893, was his most successful novel.

Fuller, Margaret (1810–50) Born at Cambridgeport, Massachusetts, Sarah Margaret Fuller was educated by her father, a politician, and by her own efforts. She knew Latin at the age of six, and later studied French, German, Spanish and Italian. She was a member of the Transcendentalist movement and a campaigner for women's rights. After publishing some translations and engaging in journalism – she started *The Dial*, a magazine which spoke for the Transcendentalists, in 1840 – she wrote a book called *Women in the Nineteenth Century*, which appeared in 1845, and in 1846 she published a volume of her literary criticisms, *Papers on Literature and Art*. Later that year she visited England and France and settled in Italy, where she eventually married the Marquis Ossoli. Returning to the United States in 1850, she was drowned, as were her husband and small son, when their ship was wrecked off Fire Island.

Fuller, Roy (1912–) Roy Broadbent Fuller was born in Lancashire, England, and educated at Blackpool High School. He became a solicitor and has been prominent in the world of British Building Societies, but is also a highly respected poet and novelist. His first book of verse, *Poems*, was published in 1940, since when several volumes of his poetry have appeared, including *Collected Poems 1936–1961* and, in 1980, *The Reign of Sparrows*. His novels include *Image of Society*, published in 1956, and he has also written some autobiographical works. His lectures, given while he was Professor of Poetry at Oxford University, from 1963 to 1968, were collected and published in two volumes in 1971 and 1973.

Fuller, Thomas (1608–61) Born at Aldwincle St Peter's, Northamptonshire, and educated at Cambridge, Thomas Fuller was a cleric who, in 1631, published a poem dealing with David and Bathsheba entitled *David's Hainous Sinne, Heartie Repentance, Heavie Punishment*. He produced a number of histories and some religious works, including his *Church-History of Britain*, published in 1655. Noted for its quirky humour, his best-known book is *The History of the Worthies of England*, which appeared posthumously in 1662.

G

Gaddis, William (1922–) William Gaddis, the American writer, was born in New York City and educated at Harvard. His first novel, *The Recognitions*, was published in 1955. A long gap then ensued before *J.R.*, which won the National Book Award on its appearance in 1976. *Carpenter's Gothic* was published in 1986.

Galsworthy, John (1867–1933) The English novelist and playwright John Galsworthy was born at Coombe, Surrey, England, and educated at Harrow and New College, Oxford. Like so many authors, he began his career as a lawyer, but a lifelong friendship with Joseph Conrad, and the encouragement of his wife and of Edward Garnett, the celebrated publisher's reader, led him to devote himself to writing. He published a book of short stories in 1897 and his first novel, *Jocelyn*, appeared in the following year. In 1906 came both the first of the novels about the Forsyte family, *The Man of Property*, and his first play, *The Silver Box*. From this time on he pursued with great success a double career, as novelist and playwright. His dramas, which include *Strife*, *Justice* and *The Skin Game*, first produced in 1909, 1910 and 1920 respectively, were usually concerned with serious social issues, and are still effective today as 'period pieces'. His fame rests principally, however, on *The Forsyte Saga*, which was first published as such in 1922. In addition to *The Man of Property*, it contained the novels *In Chancery* and *To Let*, which had previously appeared in 1920 and 1921, and the two linking 'interludes', *The Indian Summer of a Forsyte* and *Awakening*. Galsworthy continued the

A bronze effigy of John Galsworthy. His satires on English upper middle-class life were based on his own experiences.

story of the Forsyte family in a trilogy consisting of *The White Monkey*, *The Silver Spoon* and *Swan Song*, published together, again with two 'interludes', in 1929, under the general title *A Modern Comedy*. The final instalments of the family story were contained in *Maid in Waiting*, *The Flowering Wilderness* and *Over the River*, three novels which appeared together in 1935 under the title *The End of the Chapter*. His *Collected Poems* were published posthumously in 1934. He was awarded the Nobel Prize for Literature in 1932.

Galt, John (1779–1839) Born in Ayrshire, Scotland, John Galt was trained as a lawyer, but, perhaps influenced by an early association with Byron, turned to writing and became the extremely prolific author of a large number of novels, biographies, histories and essays. He spent part of his life in Canada, where he founded the city of Guelph. The town of Galt (now Cambridge), also in Ontario, was named after him. His best-known novels, all set in Scotland and published between 1820 and 1823, are *The Ayrshire Legatees*, *The Annals of the Parish*, *The Provost* and *The Entail*.

Gammer Gurton's Needle One of the earliest of English comedies, written in doggerel verse and first published in 1575. Its authorship is uncertain, and for some time it was attributed to John Still, later Bishop of Bath and Wells. It is much more likely to have been the work of William Stevenson, who was at Christ's College, Cambridge, at the time of a performance of the play there in

1566, and is known to have been interested in the drama. Further evidence is provided by the fact that the first printed edition of the play stated that it was 'made by Mr S. Mr of Art'.

García Lorca, Federico (1898–1936) Federico García Lorca, who was born in Andalusia, Spain, and educated at Granada and Madrid universities, was one of the so-called '1927 Generation', the name given to the Spanish poets who emerged during the 1920s. His first book, *Impresiones y paisajes (Impressions and Landscapes)*, an account in prose of journeys through Spain, came out in 1918. Then came a play, *The Butterfly's Evil Spell*, which was a failure, and in 1921 a first volume of poetry, *Libro de poemas*. Some subsequent collections of verse, especially the *Romancero gitano (Gypsy Ballads)*, made him known as 'the poet of the gypsies'. This nickname was not entirely to his liking, and he began to write poetry in more complex and literary forms. After a visit to New York in 1929, he became deeply involved in the theatre, touring provincial Spain, under official sponsorship, with a company which presented both classic and modern drama. It was during this period that he wrote the plays, both tragedies and comedies, for which he is famous, and which express more clearly, perhaps, than any other literary works of the twentieth century the spirit of traditional Spanish life. It is the tragedies which are best known; these include *Blood Wedding*, first per-

The Spanish poet and dramatist Federico Garcia Lorca.

143

formed in 1933, *Yerma*, in 1934, *Dona Rosita the Spinster*, in 1935, and *The House of Bernarda Alba*, which was neither performed nor published until 1945, almost ten years after his tragically early death. In 1935 he also produced his very fine elegy, *Llanto por Ignacio Sanchez Mejias*, written in memory of his bullfighter friend. Lorca was killed by Nationalists during the Spanish Civil War.

García Márquez, Gabriel (1928–) The eminent Colombian writer Gabriel García Márquez was born in Aracataca and educated at universities in Bogota and Cartagena. He became a journalist and worked in many countries, including a long spell in Europe. While in Caracas, Venezuela, he published his first novel, and this was followed by several others before the appearance in 1967 of his most important work, *A Hundred Years of Solitude*. The English translation was seen in 1970. This extraordinary novel tells the story, over seven generations, of the people of a small Colombian village, and is a fine example of Magic Realism, in which flights of fancy and bizarre happenings are mingled in a matter-of-fact way with commonplace events, all described with careful attention to detail. Márquez has published several other novels, including *Autumn of the Patriarch*, which came out in 1977, and a number of volumes of short stories such as *Innocent Erendira and other stories*, published in 1978. He was awarded the Nobel Prize for Literature in 1982.

Gardiner, Samuel Rawson (1829–1902) The academic and historian Samuel Rawson Gardiner was born near Alresford, Hampshire, England, and educated at Winchester and Christ Church, Oxford. The fact that he was a descendant of Oliver Cromwell may have been the reason why he concentrated in his major works on the history of England under the first Stuart kings and especially on the period of the Commonwealth, from 1649 to 1660.

Gargantua The first of a series of exuberant and often bawdy works by François Rabelais telling the comic and satirical stories of the giants Gargantua and Pantagruel. It was first published in 1534 under the pseudonym Alcofribas Nasier, and was translated into English by Sir Thomas Urquhart in 1653.

Garland, Hamlin (1860–1940) Hamlin Hannibal Garland was born in West Salem, Wisconsin, and brought up on a farm. He published his first collection of short stories, *Main-Travelled Roads*, in 1891. A prolific writer, he brought out several volumes of short stories, a biography of Ulysses S. Grant, and a selection of essays, but is best known for his novels of the American Midwest and the autobiographical works – *A Son of the Middle Border*, first published in 1917, *A Daughter of the Middle Border*, which won the Pulitzer Prize in 1921, and *Trail-Makers of the Middle Border* and *Back-Trailers of the Middle Border*, published in 1926 and 1928 respectively.

Garnett, Constance (1862–1946) Constance Garnett, who was educated at Newnham College, Cambridge and was the wife of the eminent publisher's reader, Edward Garnett, was for many years considered to be the foremost translator of the Russian classics by such authors as Chekhov, Dostoevsky, Gogol, Tolstoy and Turgenev. Although less highly regarded nowadays, her work undoubtedly helped considerably in familiarizing English-speaking readers with the great works of nineteenth-century Russian literature.

Garnett, David (1892–1981) The son of Edward Garnett, the celebrated publisher's reader, and Constance Garnett, the translator, David Garnett studied botany, but later turned to literature. He published many books in different genres, including autobiography, but is best known for his fiction, and especially the novella, *Lady Into Fox*, first published in 1922.

Garrick, David (1717–79) David Garrick, a Huguenot by descent, was born at Hereford, England. A pupil of Dr Johnson, he went with him to London, and there began his theatrical career by writing *Lethe, or Aesop on the Shades*, performed at Drury Lane in 1740. By 1747 he was the most successful actor of his period and had become joint owner and manager of Drury Lane, where he introduced a great classic repertoire, including the plays of Shakespeare, whose works, in Garrick's adaptations, found a new popularity. Garrick also wrote operas and a number of farces, which included *Miss in her Teens, Bon Ton, or High Life Above Stairs* and, in collaboration with George Colman, *The Clandestine Marriage*.

Gascoigne, George (*c.*1535–77) Born at Cardington in Bedfordshire, England and educated at Cambridge, George Gascoigne was a politician, soldier, poet, playwright, and something of a wastrel. While fighting as a mercenary in Holland, his poems, plays and other pieces were published in England under the imposing inscription *A hundreth Sundrie Floures bound up in one small Posie. Gathered partely (by translation) in the fyne outlandish Gardens of Euripides, Ovid, Petrarke, Ariosto and others; and partely by Invention out of our owne fruitfull Orchardes in England, Yelding Sundrie Savours of tragical, comical and moral discourse, bothe pleasaunt and profitable, to the well-smelling noses of learned Readers*. A revised edition, *The Posies of George Gascoigne, Esquire,* appeared in 1575. An innovative writer, Gascoigne also published a considerable number of other works on a variety of subjects, including *The Noble Art of Venerie or Hunting*, the verse satire, *The Steele Glas*, a novella called *A Discourse of the Adventures of Master F.J.* and *The Pleasant Tale of Hemetes the Heremite*, written for performance before Queen Elizabeth I but not published until after his death.

Gaskell, Mrs (1810–65) Elizabeth Cleghorn Gaskell, née Stevenson, was born in London. Her mother died shortly after her birth, and she was brought up by an aunt in Knutsford, Cheshire. When she was twenty-one she married William Gaskell, a Unitarian minister, and it was with him that she first began to write. Their joint efforts had little success, but Mrs Gaskell persevered on her own, and her first novel, *Mary Barton: A Tale of Manchester Life*, was published anonymously in 1848. It was well received, and as a result Charles Dickens invited the author to contribute

A chalk sketch by George Redmond of the novelist and biographer Elizabeth Gaskell.

to his magazine *Household Words*. *Cranford* appeared in it in serial form between 1851 and 1853. This idyll of village life, based on Knutsford, her childhood home, was to prove to be Mrs Gaskell's masterpiece. She wrote four other novels, *Ruth, North and South, Sylvia's Lovers* and *Wives and Daughters*, the last of which was not completed at her death, and published several collections of short stories, including *Cousin Phyllis and other Tales*, but these works have never achieved the fame of *Cranford*. At the time, however, all her books were much admired, and Elizabeth Gaskell soon became famous. She moved in the literary circles of the day, and in 1850 she met Charlotte Brontë, with whom she developed a close friendship, expressed not only in meetings but in regular correspondence. Two years after Charlotte's death, Mrs Gaskell brought out her *Life of Charlotte Brontë*. The first two editions contained material, both about the school that the Brontë sisters had attended and about Branwell Brontë, which was thought to be libellous, and this was removed for the third printing. The picture of the Brontës which emerges from the book is so vivid and engaging that it has been rated as one of the best biographies in the English language, and stands beside *Cranford* as Mrs Gaskell's finest work.

Gauthier, Théophile (1811–72) A native of Tarbes, France, Théophile Gautier was a prominent member of the French Romantic movement. As a journalist he produced a vast number of essays and articles covering all kinds of subjects, including travel and theatrical, literary and art criticisms, and this was in addition to poetry, stories and a number of novels. The most famous of his works of fiction is the novel, *Mademoiselle de Maupin*, first published in 1835, and for long considered to be indecent.

Gay, John (1685–1732) John Gay was born and educated in Barnstaple, England. He published his first poem, *Wine*, in 1708. He became the friend of Pope and Swift, both of whom encouraged his literary efforts. *Poems on Several Occasions*, published by subscription in 1720, brought him a thousand pounds, but soon afterwards he lost all his money in a rash investment. Influential friends saved him from ruin, and his *Fifty-one Fables in Verse* appeared successfully in 1727, but it was not until the production of *The Beggar's Opera* in 1728 that he achieved fame and fortune. Presented by John Rich, the play was said to have made 'Rich gay and Gay rich'. Performance of a sequel, *Polly*, was banned, but it was profitably published in 1729. Among his other works, Gay wrote an opera, *Achilles*, and the libretto for Handel's *Acis and Galatea*.

Genet, Jean (1910–86) Jean Genet was a French novelist and playwright who began life as a petty criminal and spent much of his time in prison. His books include the autobiography, *The Thief's Journal*, and the novel, *Our Lady of the Flowers*. The best known of his works are probably the plays, *The Maids* and *The Balcony*, first seen in English in 1964 and 1967.

Gentleman Dancing-Master, The A comedy by William Wycherley, first presented about 1671 and published in 1673.

Gentleman's Magazine, The A periodical founded by Edward Cave in 1731, the date which dictionaries give as the first for the use of the word 'magazine' to describe a periodical written by various hands and intended for the general reader. Published for almost two centuries, *The Gentleman's Magazine* contained essays, literary criticism and political reports. It has been much consulted by historical novelists looking for period material.

Geoffrey of Monmouth (*c*.1100–54) In 1151 Geoffrey of Monmouth was appointed Bishop of St Asaph, a preferment which appears to have owed much to his celebrity as the author of *Historia Regum Britanniae*, written about fifteen years earlier. This history of Britain appears to have been a mixture of fact, legend and the author's imagination, but, however inaccurate it may have been, it can claim not only to have been the origin of most of the stories about Arthur but to have provided Shakespeare with the plot of *King Lear*.

George, Henry (1839–97) Born in Philadelphia, Henry George began his career as a printer, but became a political economist. He wrote a number of books on the subject, but his most important work, a revised edition of his earlier *Our Land Policy*, was *Progress and Poverty*, published in 1879 and widely read both in the United States and in Europe. In it he proposed that all taxes should be supplanted by a single levy on land, the revenue from which would be used for the benefit of the whole community.

Georgian Poetry Five volumes of verse appeared under this title, the first in 1912 and the last in 1922. The project was originated by Rupert Brooke, Sir Edward Marsh, who edited the books, and H.E. Monro, who published them. The contributors included Edmund Blunden, Brooke himself, W.H. Davies, Walter de la Mare, John Drinkwater, Robert Graves, D.H. Lawrence, John Masefield and Siegfried Sassoon.

Gerard, John (1545–1612) John Gerard was for many years superintendent of gardens belonging to Lord Burghley, and he later became an eminent surgeon. He is remembered as a herbalist, the author of the *Herball or Generall Historie*

The engraved title-page to an early edition of Gerard's *The Herball*. Ceres and Pomona, the Roman goddesses, adorn the top, with portraits of the first botanists Theophrastus (*right*) and Dioscorides (*left*) and the author at the foot.

of Plantes, first published in 1597. Although Gerard claimed it as 'the first fruits of these mine own labours' it was in fact largely an adaptation of a work by one Rembert Dodoens, *Stirpium historiae pemptades*, which had appeared some fourteen years earlier.

Ghosts A drama by Henrik Ibsen, originally produced in 1881 and first seen in an English translation ten years later. Both productions were greeted with outrage as a result of Ibsen's defiance of conventional morality of the period.

Gibbon, Edward (1737–94) The English historian Edward Gibbon was born in Putney, Surrey, England, and educated at Westminster and Magdalen College, Oxford. He spent five years in Lausanne, met Voltaire, fell unsuitably in love, and continued his education by extensive reading. Having returned to England in 1758, he became a soldier the following year, and while serving in the militia published his first book in

1761. Written in French, it was an essay on the study of literature. When the militia was disbanded in 1762, he travelled extensively in Europe. In 1774 he was elected a member of Parliament, but before that date, finding his inspiration during a visit to Rome, he had already begun his monumental *The History of the Decline and Fall of the Roman Empire*, the first volume of which was published in 1776. It was immediately successful, although Gibbon was not without his critics, especially in regard to his attack on Christianity. Some of the comments were strident enough for him to reply in *A Vindication of Some Passages in the XVth and XVIth Chapters*, published in 1779. Presumably, however, he took less notice of such comments as that of the Duke of Gloucester, when he presented him with a copy of the second volume: 'Another damned, thick, square book! Always scribble, scribble, scribble! Eh! Mr Gibbon?' In 1783 when he was a famous and successful author, having published the second and third volumes of his history and retired from politics, he went to live in Lausanne, where the remaining

A stylish cartoon of the historian Edward Gibbon, noted for *The History of the Decline and Fall of the Roman Empire*.

three volumes of the *Decline and Fall* were written. They were published in 1788. After his death, his friend the Earl of Sheffield edited and published Gibbons' *Memoirs* and *Miscellaneous Works*.

Gide, André (1860–1951) A Parisian by birth, André Gide was educated at the Ecole Alsacienne and the Lycée Henri IV. He wrote in a number of different genres, including essays and plays, but is best known for his autobiographical works, including *Si le grain ne meurt...*, his celebrated *Journals*, and his novels, which include *The Counterfeiters*, first published in English in 1927. He was awarded the Nobel Prize for Literature in 1947.

Gilbert, William (1544–1603) Born at Colchester, England, and educated at Cambridge, William Gilbert is considered to be the most eminent of Elizabethan scientists. Also a doctor, he was appointed physician to Elizabeth I in 1599, and continued in that office under James I. In 1600 he published *De magnete, magneticisque corporibus, et de magno magnete tellure*. This work, which records his examplary experiments in magnetism, is the first major work on a scientific subject ever to appear in England.

Gilbert, W.S. (1836–1911) A Londoner and the son of a novelist, William Schwenk Gilbert was educated at King's College, London. After a brief period as a civil servant, he became a lawyer, but was not very successful. So in order to occupy his time and earn a little money, he began to write. His first book, *Bab Ballads*, consisting of comic verses which had previously appeared in the magazine *Fun*, was published in 1869. He then wrote a number of plays, mostly burlesques and parodies, and in 1871 began his famous collaboration with the composer, Arthur Sullivan. Their first joint work, *Thespis*, appeared in 1871, followed four years later by *Trial by Jury*. By this time the two men were working under the aegis of Richard D'Oyly Carte, the theatrical producer, and their collaboration lasted for some twenty years, producing success after success, including *H.M.S. Pinafore*, *The Pirates of Penzance*, *Patience*, *Iolanthe* and *The Mikado*. The partnership was not always a happy one. Both were prominent in their respective fields – Sullivan was among the most respected composers of serious music, while Gilbert was an extremely popular playwright (and his work with Sullivan did not prevent him from continuing to write a string of successful comedies and more serious dramas). They disagreed over whether it was Sullivan's tunes or Gilbert's witty, satiric libretti which were the most important, and Sullivan grew to dislike Gilbert's 'topsy-turvy' plots. This resulted in Gilbert's most poetic and serious work, *The Yeoman of the Guard*, produced in 1888. More comic operas followed, including *The Gondoliers*, but Gilbert and Sullivan finally quarrelled and parted. Gilbert continued to write plays, light verse and operas. He was knighted in 1907, an honour which he considered much overdue, since Sullivan had become Sir Arthur more than twenty years previously.

Gil Blas A picaresque novel, the masterpiece of Alain-René Le Sage, first published between 1715 and 1735.

Gilpin, The Diverting History of John An amusing ballad by William Cowper, first published in *The Public Advertiser* in 1782, and included with 'The Task' in the volume published in 1785.

Ginsberg, Allen (1926–) The American poet Allen Ginsberg was born in Paterson, New Jersey. He published his first volume of poetry, *Howl and Other Poems*, in 1956, and established himself as one of the leaders of the movement known as the Beat Generation. Many more collections of verse have followed, and in 1974 he won the National Book Award for *Allen Verbatim: Lectures on Poetry, Politics, Consciousness*. His *Collected Poems 1947–1980* appeared in 1985.

Giraldus Cambrensis (c.1146–c.1220) The author known as Giraldus Cambrensis, or Gerald of Wales, is sometimes also referred to as Gerald de Parri. He was born in Pembrokeshire, Wales. He became a priest and a historian. His best-known work is *Itinerarium Cambrense*, a study of Wales resulting from his journeys in that country in 1188. Among his other works are the *Topographia Hibernica*, written during an expedition to Ireland, and *Expugnatic Hibernica*, an extremely biased account of Henry I's invasion of Ireland in 1172.

Giraudoux, Jean (1882–1944) The French diplomat and playwright began his literary career as a novelist, with such books as *Provinciales*, published in 1909, *Simon le pathétique*, in 1918, and *Suzanne et le Pacifique*, in 1921. From 1928 onwards, although he published a few more novels and some essays, he wrote almost exclusively for the stage, often adapting stories from classical mythology or the Bible. *Siegfried*, which was presented in 1928, was adapted from one of his earlier novels. Among his best-known plays are *Amphitryon 38*, *Judith*, *Tiger at the Gates* and *The Mad Woman of Chaillot*, which were first seen in 1929, 1931, 1935 and 1945 respectively.

Gissing, George (1857–1903) George Robert Gissing was born at Wakefield and educated at Owens College, Manchester. He spent his early life in poverty, attempting to support himself in London and briefly in the United States by private teaching. His first novel, *Workers in the Dawn*, came out in 1880. After the publication in 1886 of his fourth book, *Demos*, he found a ready audience for his fiction, most of which was concerned with the poor and oppressed lower classes. Among many novels, the two best known, *New Grub Street* and *Born in Exile*, were published in 1891 and 1892. *The Private Papers of Henry Ryecroft*, a quasi-autobiographical book, appeared in 1903. He also wrote a travel book about Italy, two books on Dickens, some political works and many short stories.

Glasgow, Ellen (1874–1945) Ellen Anderson Gholson Glasgow was born in Richmond, Virginia, and educated privately. She published her first novel, *The Descendant*, in 1897. beginning a long career as a writer. Her socialism and her belief in women's rights were reflected in her novels and stories, which portrayed Virginia society in a realistic fashion. Her first major success came in 1913 with *Virginia*. The best known of her other books are *Barren Ground*, published in 1925, *Vein of Iron*, in 1935, and *In This Our Life*, which won the Pulitzer Prize in 1941.

Glass Menagerie, The A family drama, set in St Louis, by Tennessee Williams. It was first presented in 1944.

God's Little Acre Erskine Caldwell's famous novel, first published in 1933.

Godwin, William The son of a Nonconformist minister, William Godwin was born at Wisbech in Cambridgeshire. Trained as a Calvinist minister himself, he went to London in 1782, and soon abandoned his clerical calling. He published a *Life of Lord Chatham* in 1783, and ten years later brought out his major work, *The Inquiry concerning Political Justice, and its Influence on General Virtue and Happiness*. He wrote a number of other books, including novels, the best known of which is *Caleb Williams, or Things as they are*, which appeared in 1794. In 1798 he published a biography of his first wife, Mary Wollstonecraft. Their daughter Mary was later to marry Percy Bysshe Shelley. Godwin's second wife, Mary Jane Clairmont, was the mother of two girls, one of whom, Clara, became a mistress of Lord Byron.

Goethe, Johann Wolfgang von (1749–1832) Germany's greatest writer was born in Frankfurt am Main, the son of a prosperous gentleman who had been granted the prestigious title of Imperial Councillor. He was at first educated privately, and then went to Leipzig University and later to Strasbourg, where he studied law. Meanwhile, he had begun to write, and his love for Friederike Brion inspired some fine lyric poetry. He became friendly with the critic Johann Gottfried Herder, who encouraged him

This flamboyant picture *Goethe in the Roman Campagna* was painted by Goethe's friend Johann Heinrich Tischbein in 1786. As well as writing, Goethe held a prominent cabinet post at the court in Weimer, directed the court theatre and undertook scientific research.

to write for the theatre, and the result was not only Goethe's first drama, *Götz von Berlichingen*, but the beginning of the revolutionary Romantic literary movement known as 'Sturm und Drang' ('Storm and Stress'), of which he became the prophet. Returning to Frankfurt, he wrote prolifically, producing a number of minor dramatic works, a volume of literary criticism, and his novel, *The Sorrows of Young Werther*, published in 1774. At this time he also wrote the larger part of his play, *Egmont*, and began the first draft of his masterpiece, *Faust*. In 1775, the Duke of Weimar invited Goethe to his court. The invitation was accepted, and before long Goethe was playing a part in the State government. His literary activity diminished for the time being, although some excellent poetry dates from this period. Then in 1786 he set out to visit Italy, and there he began to move away from 'Sturm und Drang' towards

classicism, and was inspired to rewrite in verse an earlier play, *Iphigenie au Tauris*, to compose the drama *Torquato Tasso*, to complete *Egmont*, and to work further on *Faust*. In 1790, now back in Weimar, Goethe, a man of many parts, produced an important work on the morphology of plants, and followed it with the first of his books on optics and light, and at this time also he became director of the court theatre, a post which he held for twenty-two years. In 1794 Goethe began a friendship with the poet and playwright Friedrich von Schiller which was to last until Schiller's death in 1805. This friendship had a profound effect on Goethe, since Schiller encouraged him to continue to produce works of literature, and it was under this stimulus that he finally completed a novel which he had started many years earlier, and which was published between 1795 and 1796 as *Wilhelm Meisters Lehrjahre* (*Wilhelm Meister's Apprenticeship*). An epic poem of great beauty, *Hermand and Dorothea*, appeared in 1798, and a number of new plays were written in this period, as well as some of his finest ballads and lyrics. Goethe did not marry until 1806, and only then because he felt it sensible to regularize his situation in view of a possible invasion of Weimar by the French. He had always been much attracted to women, and Christiane Vulpius, who became his wife, had been his mistress for many years and bore him his only child, a son, in 1789. His feelings for her had been largely expressed in the *Roman Elegies*, published in 1795. In 1808 the first part of *Faust* was at last published, and acclaimed as a great masterpiece of Romantic writing (though in fact the influence of Goethe's classicism is also plainly visible). Several volumes of his entertaining and informative autobiography, *Dichtung und Wahrheit* (*Poetry and Truth*), were published between 1811 and 1832, and two other important works which must be mentioned are *Wilhelm Meisters Wanderjahre* (*Wilhelm Meister's Travels*), the sequel to the earlier novel, which came out between 1821 and 1829, and the second part of *Faust*, published in 1832, shortly before the poet's death. Goethe's greatness does not depend simply upon the breadth of his achievements — he wrote many more books in additon to those already mentioned, including other scientific works, and plays and poetry, which cannot be listed in a brief summary. His towering stature results also from the fact that in almost every field he succeeded in producing work of the very highest standard.

Gogol, Nikolai Vasilievich (1809–52) A native of the Ukraine, Nikolai Vasilievich Gogol began writing while still at the Niezhin Gymnasium, where he produced, among other works, a tragedy, *The Brigands*. Having settled in St Petersburg in 1829, he tried various occupations, but, despite an unkind review of an idyll he had written (which caused him to buy all available copies and burn them), eventually he devoted himself to literature. From 1830 onwards he published a number of short stories and essays, the first collection of tales, *Evenings in a Farm near Dikanka*, appearing in 1831. Having begun by setting his fiction in the provincial Russia where he had grown up, his later stories used the background of St Petersburg, and with them his growing reputation was enhanced. His plans for two major histories, although never fulfilled, resulted in his appointment as a professor of history at the University of St Petersburg. In 1836 his celebrated play, *The Government Inspector*, was produced, and his satirical portrait of officialdom and the corruption of a small country town was warmly received. The targets of his wit still exist today, and the comedy remains popular. Also in 1936 he left St Petersburg, travelling widely and living for most of the rest of his life in Italy. Here

Nikolai Gogol's work marks the transition from Romanticism to Realism. Dismayed by public criticism, he increasingly turned to religion and mysticism for spiritual support.

he worked on his major novel, *Dead Souls*, the first part of which was published in 1842. Increasingly a prey to introspection and mysticism, he laboured over several drafts of the second part of the novel, but destroyed them all. His last published works, *Confession* and *Correspondence with Friends*, were failures. After a pilgrimage to Jerusalem, he returned to Russia and died in Moscow.

Gold, Herbert (1924–) Born in Cleveland, Ohio, and educated at Columbia University, Herbert Gold is a novelist whose works include *Birth of a Hero*, published in 1951, *The Man Who Was Not With It*, in 1956, and *Salt*, in 1963. His short stories have also appeared, and in 1962 he published a volume of essays on the contemporary American scene, *The Age of Happy Problems*.

Golden Ass, The The better-known title of the *Metamorphoses* by Apuleius, a collection of linked stories, often bawdy, written during the second century and much used as source material by many later writers, including Boccaccio.

Golden Bough, The Sir James George Frazer's summary of ancient religious beliefs throughout the world. The original edition consisted of twelve volumes and a supplement, first published between 1890 and 1936.

Golden Bowl, The A story of the relationship between American Maggie Verver, her father, her husband and her friend Charlotte Stant. Henry James's last completed novel, it was published in 1904.

Golden Notebook, The A major novel on feminist themes by Doris Lessing, first published in 1962.

Golden Treasury of English Songs and Lyrics, The Palgrave's *Golden Treasury*, one of the best known of all anthologies, was first published in 1861. Its compiler, Francis Turner Palgrave, subsequently revised his selection to make it more comprehensive, and a number of amended and extended versions have appeared, edited by, among others, the poet Laurence Binyon. In particular, attention has been paid to the fifth and final volume in order to include the work of more recent poets.

Golding, William (1911–) William Golding's first novel, *Lord of the Flies*, was published in 1954 and made him instantly famous. He was born in Cornwall and educated at Marlborough Grammar School and Brasenose College, Oxford. A volume of poetry had appeared in 1935, and he has also written plays and essays, but it is as a novelist that he is renowned. Among his best-known books are *Pincher Martin* (US title: *The Two Deaths of Christopher Martin*), published in 1956, *The Spire*, in 1964, and *Rites of Passage*, which won the Booker Prize in 1980. He was awarded the Nobel Prize for Literature in 1983.

Goldoni, Carlo (1707–93) Although he studied law, Carlo Goldoni was much more interested, from a very early age, in the theatre. After some unsuccessful attempts at tragedies, he decided to mould himself into an Italian Molière and wrote a series of successful comedies, the most effective of which were in his native Venetian dialect. Although he continued in this vein, he also later returned more rewardingly to the tragic muse, and by the time of his death had produced well over two hundred plays. Among his best works are the early comedy *The Servant of Two Masters*, presented in 1749 and, at the other end of his career, *The Soft-Hearted Despot*, produced in Paris in 1771.

Goldsmith, Oliver (1728–74) The son of a Protestant clergyman, Oliver Goldsmith was of Irish descent and grew up in West Meath, where his father had a living. After attending various schools, he completed his education at Trinity College, Dublin. He then spent some years in failing to become a lawyer or a doctor or a successful musician, and finally settled to a literary career, less out of conviction than because there was no other way in which to earn money. Although he was undoubtedly something of a spendthrift, and has also been called foolish and vain, he appears to have been possessed of great charm, and this perhaps was a factor in his eventual success. Beginning at the age of thirty, he was engaged, with considerable industry, in writing articles, essays, children's books, biographies, and any other work that he could find, including translations. For many years all this work was anonymous, including the series of satirical letters written for the periodical *The Public Ledger*, which appeared in book form in 1762 as *The Citizen of the World*. Then in 1764 he published both a long poem, *The Traveller*, and, with Dr Johnson's help, his novel, *The Vicar of Wakefield*, and at last began to have some real success. He now tried his hand in the theatre, and his comedy, *The Good Natur'd Man*, although it was not particularly well received, at least brought its author a considerable sum of money. It was followed in 1773 by the triumph of *She Stoops to Conquer*. He continued to produce various hack works, including several school text-books which depended more on their author's imagination than on facts, as instanced by his highly inaccurate *History of England*. Particularly in the last years of his life, he also wrote and published a number of poems. Among them was the celebrated *The Deserted Village*, which appeared in 1770.

Goncourt, Edmond and Jules de Edmond Louis Antoine Huot de Goncourt (1822–96) and Jules Alfred Huot de Goncourt (1830–70) collaborated on the production of several histories of eighteenth-century France and its art, and worked together on many novels, which were intended to form a social history of their age. After the death of Jules, Edmond continued to write fiction, and also published nine volumes of the celebrated *Journal*, which covers the years 1851 to 1896. Under Edmond de Goncourt's will an Académie was set up which each year awards France's most prestigious literary prize, the Prix Goncourt.

Gone With the Wind Margaret Mitchell's bestselling novel of the American Civil War, first published in 1936.

Goodbye to All That A volume of autobiography by Robert Graves, first published in 1929.

Goodbye to Berlin A semi-autobiographical and loosely constructed novel by Christopher Isherwood, first published in 1939. It introduced Sally Bowles, the central character of the musical *Cabaret*.

Good Companions, The J.B. Priestley's first successful novel, about a travelling theatrical group, first published in 1929.

Good Natur'd Man, The A comedy by Oliver Goldsmith, first presented in 1768.

Good Soldier, The Sub-titled 'A Tale of Passion', this book was Ford Madox Ford's most successful novel, and was published in 1915.

Gorboduc The earliest English tragedy, performed in 1561 in the presence of Elizabeth I. It was written jointly by Thomas Sackville and Thomas Norton. Gorboduc was a legendary king of Britain, and the tragedy is concerned with him, his wife, and their two sons, Ferrex and Porrex. An inaccurate edition of the play was published in 1565 and was later corrected, appearing in 1570 under the title *The Tragedy of Ferrex and Porrex*.

Gordimer, Nadine (1923–) A highly regarded writer of fiction, except perhaps in the eyes of the rulers of her native South Africa, Nadine Gordimer, who was born near Johannesburg, has produced several novels and volumes of short stories containing a strong element of protest against apartheid. Her books include *A Guest of Honour*, published in 1970, and *The Conservationist*, which was joint winner of the Booker Prize in 1974.

Gordon, Adam Lindsay (1833–70) Sent to Australia in disgrace in 1853, Adam Lindsay Gordon, who was born in the Azores and educated at Oxford, was a noted horseman and a politician in his adopted country. In 1867 he published two volumes of poetry, and followed them in 1870 with *Bush Ballads and Galloping Rhymes*, which after his death was to make him enormously popular in Australia. At the time, however, the book did not do very well, and this compounded the depression which caused him to take his own life at the age of thirty-seven.

Gore, Catherine (1799–1861) Catherine Grace Frances Moody was born at East Retford, Nottinghamshire, England. In 1823 she married Captain Charles Gore, and in the following year her first novel, *Theresa Marchmont, or the Maid of Honour*, was published. Mrs Gore produced a large number of novels, and also wrote short stories and plays. Her work, which was mercilessly parodied by Thackeray, was always concerned with the high society of the time, and was extremely popular with her contemporaries.

Gorky, Maxim (1868–1936) A fervent supporter of the Russian revolution, Alexei Maximovich Pyeshkov, who became famous under the pseudonym Maxim Gorky, was orphaned at the age of eight, and worked in all kinds of capacities from that time until he became secretary to a barrister. He began to write, and several of his stories were published in various periodicals. He became well known with the publication in 1895 of the story 'Chelkash', and thereafter found a ready audience for his work. After some years in Italy, he returned to Russia in 1928, and was elected President of the Union of Soviet Writers. He wrote many novels, including *Foma Gordeyev*, *Konovalov* and *The Mother*, and was also a successful playwright. His autobiographical works were very highly regarded.

Gosse, Edmund (1849–1928) Poet, literary critic, biographer and translator, Edmund Gosse, a Londoner, was educated privately. He began publishing verse during his twenties, and soon became the friend of all the major British poets of the time. His biographies and literary studies include a *Life of William Congreve*, *A History of Eighteenth Century Literature* and a *History of Modern English Literature*, published, along with other similar books, between 1888 and 1897. In 1891 he translated *Hedda Gabler* by Henrik Ibsen. His best-known work, the autobiographical *Father and Son*, appeared in 1907. He was knighted in 1925.

Gothic novels *The Castle of Otranto* by Horace Walpole is generally accepted as the first Gothic novel, the essential ingredients of which are terror, the supernatural and the fantastic, and a background in which gloom and decay are

Horace Walpole wrote the first Gothic novel. This lithograph shows in the background Strawberry Hill where Horace Walpole established his printing press.

important elements. The many practitioners of the genre include Mary Shelley, Sheridan Le Fanu and, in more recent times, William Faulkner. Jane Austen's *Northanger Abbey* was intended to mock the absurdities of the Gothic novel. During the 1960s a vogue for Gothic novels, or more properly 'Gothic romances', flourished, but this was really a debasement of the term. The Gothic romance was usually concerned with a frightened young woman, an imposing and sinister house, and a hero of forbidding aspect and behaviour.

Götz von Berlichingen Johann Wolfgang von Goethe's first play, presented in 1773, *Götz von Berlichingen* heralded a Romantic revolution in German literature.

Gould, Nat (1857–1919) Born in Manchester, England, Nathaniel Gould wrote a very large number of novels, almost all of which were about horse-racing. His first publication, *The Double Event*, was published during the period which he spent in Australia, and his experiences there formed the background to many of his books.

Government Inspector, The A satirical comedy, set in a Russian provincial town, by Nicolai Gogol, first presented in 1836.

Gower, John (c.1330–1408) Little is known of the origins of the poet John Gower, except that he belonged to a Kentish land-owning family, and himself owned property in East Anglia. A man of considerable learning, he was a contemporary and friend of Chaucer. Although from about 1377 he lived in the priory of St Mary Overy in Southwark, when Chaucer went to Italy in 1378, he appointed Gower as one of his representatives during his absence. He was much involved in the politics of the time, and was an ardent supporter of the young King Richard II, of whom he wrote in glowing terms in the first edition of his major work, the *Confessio amantis*, which was written in English in about 1383. In a later edition, dismayed at Richard's failings, he removed his praises and dedicated the work to Henry of Lancaster, who was to become Henry IV. This work, which is about twice as long as *The Canterbury Tales*, is a collection of stories, linked by the device of a lover confessing himself to a priest of Venus. Before that, Gower had written a long allegorical poem in French entitled *Speculum meditantis*. It was thought to have been lost, but a version under the title *Mirour de l'omme* was discovered in 1895. His third important work, *Vox Clamantis*, written in Latin, was inspired by the Peasant's Revolt in 1381, and is concerned with that event and with the political situation in England at the time. Gower also produced two collections of ballades

in French and some minor verses in English, the latter including *In Praise of Peace*. After Henry IV had come to the throne he wrote *Cronica tripartita*, which was an account in Latin verse of the last years of Richard's reign. The *Confessio amantis* allows Gower to stand beside Chaucer, even if much in his shadow, as one of the fathers of English literature.

Goytisolo, Juan (1931–) The Spanish novelist Juan Goytisolo was born in Barcelona. He studied law in Barcelona and Paris, but has lived in France for many years, where he works as a publisher. His first novel was *The Young Assassins*, very successfully published in 1954. Next came *The Children of Chaos*, in 1955. This was followed by a trilogy, 'El mañana efimero', which began in 1958 with *Fiestas*. Other novels include *Island of Women*, in 1961, and *Marks of Identity*, in 1969. His work is distinguished for its realistic portrayal of Spanish life.

Grahame, Kenneth (1859–1932) A native of Edinburgh, Kenneth Grahame went into banking, and became Secretary of the Bank of England. After contributing essays to the *Yellow Book*, he published *The Golden Age* and its sequel, *Dream Days*, in 1895 and 1898 respectively. These evocations of childhood were extremely successful on both sides of the Atlantic. His masterpiece, *The Wind in the Willows*, appeared in 1908, and gradually became recognized as a classic of children's literature. It was dramatized by A.A. Milne under the title *Toad of Toad Hall*.

Grapes of Wrath, The The most famous of John Steinbeck's novels, it tells of a family of poor farmers and their journey from Oklahoma to California. It was first published in 1939.

Grass, Günter (1927–) The German novelist Günter Wilhelm Grass was born and educated in Danzig, and was partly of Polish descent. He studied art, and his first publication was a collection of nonsense rhymes with his own illustrations. He then began to write somewhat experimental plays; among them were *Hochwasser* (*High Water*) first seen in 1956, *Onkel-Onkel* (*Uncle-Uncle*) and *Noch zehn Minuten bis Buffalo* (*Still Ten Minutes to Buffalo*). The last two appeared in 1957. The translations in 1959 of his novel *Die Blechtrommel*, under the title *The Tin Drum*, brought him fame in English-speaking countries. Later books include *Dog Years*, published in 1963, and *The Meeting at Telgte*, in 1979. A volume of essays, *On Writing and Politics*, appeared in 1985, and a novel, *The Rat*, in 1987.

Grass Is Singing, The Doris Lessing's first novel, published in 1950. It is the story of a white woman and her relationship with her black servant.

The English poet and novelist Robert Graves, painted at the age of seventy-three by John Aldridge.

Graves, Robert (1895–1985) Robert von Ranke Graves was born in London and educated at Charterhouse and Oxford. Although primarily regarded as a poet – he was Professor of Poetry at Oxford from 1961 to 1966 – he wrote in many genres, and his novels *I, Claudius* and *Claudius the God*, which were published in 1934, were already extremely successful when a television series propelled them again into the bestseller class. Other novels include *Count Belisarius, Sergeant Lamb, Wife to Mr. Milton, King Jesus* and *Homer's Daughter*. He also wrote a number of works of literary criticism, among them *A Survey of Modernist Poetry*, written in collaboration with Laura Riding and published in 1927, *The White Goddess: A Historical Grammar of Poetic Myth*, which appeared in 1948, and *The Crane Bag and Other Disputed Subjects*, in 1969. His autobiography, *Goodbye to All That*, which deals with his youth and his experiences in the trenches of World War I, was published in 1929, and remains a classic account of war. He also wrote biographies and books for children. Another facet of his work was shown in *The Greek Myths*, which came out in 1955. His first collection of poetry,

Over the Brazier, was published in 1916, and was followed by many other volumes, in which he demonstrated the wide range of his poetic vision. In 1938 he published his *Collected Poems*, of which several substantially revised versions appeared subsequently, the last of them in 1975. In all these collections Graves was ruthless in editing his own work and in expunging those verses which he considered to be below standard.

Gray, Thomas (1716–71) The only one of twelve children to survive, Thomas Gray was born in London and educated at Eton and Cambridge. He began seriously to write poetry at the age of twenty-five or thereabouts, and it was then that he produced his first major poem, the 'Ode on the Spring'. In 1742 he composed, among other pieces, the 'Ode on a Distant Prospect of Eton College', the 'Hymn to Adversity' and an incomplete tragedy, *Agrippina*, written in the style of Racine. His interest in the French dramatist had been kindled while he was in Paris during the two-and-a-half-year continental tour he had earlier undertaken in company with Horace Walpole. Until 1748, none of his work had been published, but in that year the odes on Eton and

Thomas Gray, classical scholar and poet, strikes a romantic pose in this portrait by John Giles Eccardt.

on spring and an 'Ode on the Death of a Favourite Cat' all appeared, anonymously, in *Dodsley's Miscellany*. In 1750 he sent to Walpole from Stoke Poges, where his mother and aunt were living, 'a thing to which I have at last put an end'. This was his celebrated masterpiece, the 'Elegy Written in a Country Church-Yard'. It was published in the following year, and Gray became famous. A slim volume representing almost all the poetry he had written was published in 1753, and in 1757 he was offered, and declined, the Poet Laureateship. In that year Walpole published two of Gray's Pindaric odes, 'The Progress of Poesy' and 'The Bard'. He wrote a few other poems of lesser importance, but he was never a prolific writer, preferring to revise and polish his work over a long period of time. His output may have been small, but Gray ranks as a major poet.

Great Expectations A novel by Charles Dickens, telling of Pip and his love for the tantalizing Estella. It was first published in book form in 1861.

Great Gatsby, The F. Scott Fitzgerald's most important novel provides a brilliant picture of New York and Long Island society in the 1920s. It was first published in 1925.

Greek Anthology, The An extraordinary collection of some six thousand short poems by more than three hundred Greek writers, ranging in date from the seventh century BC to the tenth century AD. The *Anthology* was begun by the poet Meleager of Gadara in the first century BC and subsequently extended several times, the most notable edition, prepared a millennium later, being by Constantine Cephalas.

Greeley, Horace (1811–72) After a somewhat turbulent childhood, Horace Greeley, who was born in Amherst, New Hampshire, began a career in journalism, and rose to become one of the most influential of American newspaper proprietors. At the age of twenty-three he founded a magazine called *The New Yorker*. It appeared for seven years, and at the end of that time Greeley started the *New York Tribune*. Later he entered politics, and was one of the founders of the Republican party. He was the originator of the famous exhortation, 'Go west, young man!' His publications include *The American Conflict*, published in two volumes in 1864 and 1866, and *Recollections of a Busy Life* which appeared in 1868.

Green, Henry (1905–73) Henry Green was the pseudonym of Henry Vincent Yorke, who was born in Tewkesbury, Gloucestershire, England, and educated at Eton and Oxford. His first novel, *Blindness*, was published in 1926. While working

in the family engineering business, he published a volume of autobiography and another eight novels, almost all with titles consisting of single words, such as *Caught*, *Nothing*, *Doting*, and — his best-known book — *Loving*, which appeared in 1945.

Greenaway, Kate (1846–1901) Kate Greenaway, who was born in London, first established herself as an artist. She then began to specialize in illustrating work written for children, and in 1879 published a collection of rhymes and drawings entitled *Under the Window*. It was immensely successful, and she followed it with several more books of a similar nature, preferring to write her own texts, although she also illustrated many children's classics. Her simple, pretty, if sentimental, drawings had a great influence on other illustrators of books for children.

Greene, Graham (1904–) The first book published by Henry Graham Greene was a volume of verse, *Babbling April*, which appeared in 1925 while he was still at university. A descendant of Robert Louis Stevenson and the son of a headmaster, Greene was born in Berkhamsted, Hertfordshire, England, and educated at his father's school in that town before going to Balliol College, Oxford. For a short period he worked as a journalist, but then determined to earn his living as an author, though there were subsequent periods when he contributed regularly to various periodicals. His novel *The Man Within*, which first established his name, was published in 1929 and was followed by *The Name of Action*, in 1930, and *Rumour at Nightfall*, in 1931. He later preferred to regard these three books as juvenilia. The next novel was *Stamboul Train* (retitled *Orient Express* in the United States): this brought him considerable success when it came out in 1932. It was the first of his novels to be labelled 'An Entertainment'. That designation is presumably intended to indicate a less serious approach than in the fiction which he calls 'A Novel', but it is sometimes not altogether easy to distinguish between the two, since even those of his books which bear the greatest resemblance to a conventional 'thriller' have a depth and a concern for the spiritual issues which few other writers in the genre ever attempt. *Brighton Rock*, perhaps his most famous book, and typical in the seediness of its characters and setting, was published in England in 1938 as 'A Novel', but appeared in the United States as 'An Entertainment'. Before the appearance of *Brighton Rock* he had published *It's a Battlefield*, *England Made Me* and *A Gun for Sale* (retitled *This Gun for Hire* in America), in 1934, 1935 and 1936 respectively. In 1940 *The Power and the Glory* appeared. During World War

II he was working in the British Foreign Office, and it was not until 1948 that the next book, *The Heart of the Matter*, was published. With it his reputation as a major novelist of outstanding quality was even more firmly established. Subsequent novels include *The End of the Affair*, in 1951, *The Quiet American*, in 1955, *A Burnt-Out Case*, in 1961, *The Comedians*, in 1966, *The Honorary Consul*, in 1973, *The Human Factor*, in 1978, and *The Tenth Man* , in 1985. Among the 'entertainments' are *The Confidential Agent*, in 1939, *The Third Man* (originally a screenplay), in 1950, *Loser Takes All*, in 1955, and *Our Man in Havana*, in 1958. Greene's conversion to Roman Catholicism, which took place in 1926 at the time of his marriage, has had a profound effect on his writing and is reflected in his preoccupation with moral issues and the choice between good and evil, right and wrong, which his characters have to face. He has also chosen to visit and to use as backgrounds many areas of the world where political activities have brought those moral issues sharply to the fore; the books in this category include *The Quiet American*, *A Burnt-Out Case*, *The Honorary Consul*, *Our Man in Havana* and *The Comedians*. Several collections of stories have appeared, including some for children, and he has published two volumes of autobiography, *A Sort of Life*, which appeared in

1971, and *Ways of Escape*, in 1980. Many of the novels have been made into films, and Greene has also had a successful career as a dramatist with his plays *The Living Room*, *The Potting Shed*, *The Complaisant Lover* and *Carving a Statue*, which were first seen in 1953, 1957, 1959 and 1964 respectively. Graham Greene has long been regarded as the most distinguished of living British novelists, and it is perhaps remarkable that his work has not only been accorded the highest critical acclaim but has also enjoyed immense popular success.

Greene, Robert (*c.*1558–92) A graduate of both Cambridge and Oxford, Robert Greene was born at Norwich, England. He published thirty-seven works in various genres, including plays, pamphlets and prose works. His accounts of low life in London, which included *The Art of Connycatching*, were drawn from his own experiences, for he spent his last years in wild dissipation. His best-known work is perhaps the comedy *Frier Bacon and Frier Bungay*, published in 1594.

Green Mansions A novel set in Venezuela by W.H. Hudson, first published in 1904.

Gregory, Lady (1852–1932) Isabella Augusta Persse was born in Galway, Ireland. She married the Irish Member of Parliament, Sir Henry Gregory, in 1881, and after his death in 1892 devoted herself to literary interests. She was one of the founders of the Abbey Theatre in Dublin, and worked closely with Yeats, collaborating with him on some of his plays. She published a number of works of Irish folklore, and translated or adapted a number of dramatic works as well as writing her own original plays. She was particularly successful with the one-act form, as in *The Rising of the Moon*, published in 1906, and *The Travelling Man*, in 1910.

Grenfell, Julian (1888–1915) The Hon. Julian Henry Francis Grenfell, the son of the first Baron Desborough, was educated at Eton and Balliol College, Oxford. A regular soldier, he was killed in France at the battle of Ypres during World War I. His best-known work is the poem 'Into Battle', which was published in *The Times* on the day of his death.

Greville, Fulke (1554–1628) Knighted in 1597 and created first Baron Brooke in 1621, Fulke Greville was a friend of Sir Philip Sidney, with whom he was educated at Shrewsbury School before going on to Cambridge. He wrote poetry and plays, but his major work is his biography of his friend, *The Life of the Renowned Sir Philip Sidney*, which was published posthumously in 1652.

Grey, Zane (1872–1939) Pearl Zane Grey was born in Zanesville, Ohio, and qualified as a dentist at the University of Pennsylvania. He practised in

New York from 1898 to 1904, but then abandoned dentistry for writing. His first book, *Betty Zane*, was published privately in 1903, but he went on to produce more than sixty Western novels, which sold a total of over fifteen million copies. His most famous book, *Riders of the Purple Sage*, appeared in 1912.

Grimm, The brothers Jacob Ludwig Carl Grimm (1785–1863) and Wilhelm Grimm (1786–1859) were born in Hesse-Kassel, Germany. They were philologists and published a number of works on the German language, including the first part of the most authoritative German dictionary, the *Deutsches Wörterbuch*. They are best known in the English-speaking world for their collection of folk tales, *Kinder-und Haus Märchen*, which first appeared in an English translation in 1823 under the title *German Popular Stories*.

Gryll Grange A satirical novel by Thomas Love Peacock which appeared in serial form in 1860 and as a book in 1861.

Gulag Archipelago, The The long and detailed account of Soviet labour camps by Alexander Isayevich Solzhenitsyn, first published between 1973 and 1975.

Gulliver's Travels The celebrated satirical novel by Jonathan Swift, in which Lemuel Gulliver visits Lilliput, Brobdingnag, Laputa and the country of the Houyhnhnms and the Yahoos. It was first published in 1726.

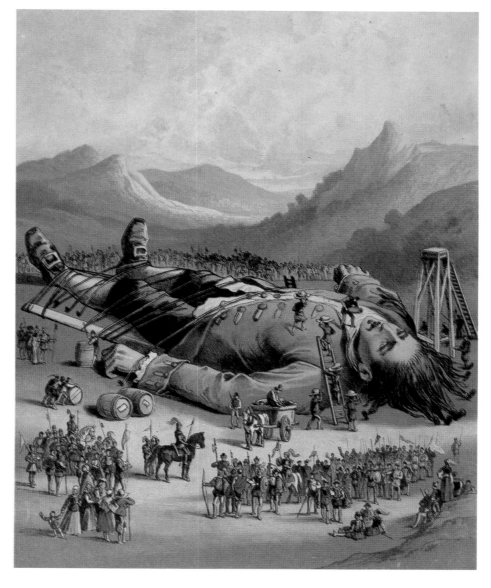

A detailed and picturesque illustration 'Gulliver held captive by the Lilliputians' in a *c.*1860 edition of Jonathan Swift's *Gulliver's Travels*.

Gunn, Thom (1929–) The poet Thomson William Gunn was born in Gravesend, England, and educated at Cambridge. He published his first volume of verse, *Poetry from Cambridge*, in 1953, and followed it with *Fighting Terms* in 1954. At this time he moved to California, where he is now resident. Several other collections of verse, much of it influenced by the metaphysical poets, have been published, including *Molly*, in 1971, *Selected Poems*, in 1979, and *The Passages of Joy*, in 1982.

Gunther, John (1901–70) Educated at the University of Chicago, John Gunther wrote a number of novels, including *The Lost City*, published in 1964, and some political works, but was best known for his popular if somewhat superficial surveys of continents and countries. These were *Inside Europe*, which appeared in 1936, *Inside Asia*, in 1939, *Inside Latin America*, in 1941, *Inside U.S.A.*, in 1947, *Inside Africa*, in 1955, and *Inside Russia*, in 1957.

Gutenberg, Johann (c.1398–1468) The German printer Johann Gutenberg was born in Mainz. Little if any of his work has been preserved, but various fragments have been attributed to him. On the other hand, the so-called *Gutenberg Bible*, in Latin, consisting of 1282 pages printed in two columns each of forty-two lines, may not in fact have been produced by him. Nevertheless, Gutenberg is commonly credited with the invention of printing by the use of movable type.

H

Haggard, H. Rider (1856–1925) Born in Norfolk, England, Henry Rider Haggard went to South Africa as a young man. Returning to England, he published his first book, *Cetywayo and his White Neighbours*, in 1882, and then turned to fiction. His third book, published in 1886, was *King Solomon's Mines*. It was enormously successful, and he followed it in 1887 with *She*. He published a great many novels of adventure, not all of which were set in Africa, and also a number of books on agriculture. He was knighted in 1912.

Hailey, Arthur (1920–) The Canadian writer Arthur Hailey was born in England and educated in elementary schools. He was a pilot in the Royal Air Force from 1939 to 1947. He then emigrated to Canada, where he has been resident ever since. In 1956 he became a full-time writer. His first novel, *Flight Into Danger*, was written in collaboration with John Castle, and was published in 1958. His other novels include *The Final Diagnosis*, which appeared in 1959, *Hotel*, in 1965, *Airport*, in 1968, *Wheels*, in 1971 and *Strong Medicine* in 1984.

THE PRINCIPALL NAVIGATIONS, VOIAGES AND DISCOVERIES OF THE English nation, made by Sea or ouer Land,

to the most remote and farthest distant Quarters of the earth at any time within the compasse of these 1500. yeeres: Deuided into three seuerall parts, according to the positions of the Regions whereunto they were directed.

The first, conteining the personall trauels of the English vnto *Iudæa, Syria, Arabia*, the riuer *Euphrates, Babylon, Balsara*, the *Persian* Gulfe, *Ormuz, Chaul, Goa, India*, and many Ilands adioyning to the South parts of *Asia*: together with the like vnto *Egypt*, the chiefest ports and places of *Africa* within and without the Streight of *Gibraltar*, and about the famous Promontorie of *Buona Esperança*.

The second, comprehending the worthy discoueries of the English towards the North and Northeast by Sea, as of *Lapland, Scrikfinia, Corelia*, the Baie of *S. Nicholas*, the Isles of *Colgoieue, Vaigats*, and *Noua Zembla* toward the great riuer *Ob*, with the mightie Empire of *Russia*, the *Caspian* Sea, *Georgia, Armenia, Media, Persia, Boghar* in *Bactria*, & diuers kingdoms of *Tartaria*.

The third and last, including the English valiant attempts in searching almost all the corners of the vaste and new world of *America*, from 73. degrees of Northerly latitude Southward, to *Meta Incognita, Newfoundland*, the maine of *Virginia*, the point of *Florida*, the Baie of *Mexico*, all the Inland of *Noua Hispania*, the coast of *Terra firma, Brasill*, the riuer of *Plate*, to the Streight of *Magellan*: and through it, and from it in the South Sea to *Chili, Peru, Xalisco*, the Gulfe of *California, Noua Albion* vpon the backside of *Canada*, further then euer any Christian hitherto hath pierced.

Whereunto is added the last most renowmed English Nauigation, round about the whole Globe of the Earth.

By Richard Hakluyt Master of Artes, and Student sometime of Christ-church in Oxford.

Imprinted at London by GEORGE BISHOP and RALPH NEWBERIE, Deputies to CHRISTOPHER BARKER, Printer to the Queenes most excellent Maiestie.

1589.

The title-page of Hakluyt's *Voyages*, 1589. His work glorified the adventures of Elizabethan voyagers.

Hakluyt, Richard (c.1553–1616) The British geographer Richard Hakluyt was born in London and educated at Westminster and Oxford. In 1582 he published *Divers Voyages touching the Discoverie of America*. Other similar works followed, including *A notable historie containing foure voyages made by certayne French captaynes into Florida*. The revised version of his major book, *The Principall Navigations, Voiages, Traffiques and Discoveries of the English Nation*, appeared in three volumes between 1598 and 1600.

Hale, Edward Everett (1822–1909) A Boston Unitarian clergyman, Edward Everett Hale published a great many stories and novels, including *The Man Without a Country*, which appeared in 1865. As a result of *Ten Times One is Ten*, published in 1870, a large number of 'Lend a hand' clubs were formed. He also wrote a comprehensive study, *Franklin in France*, published in two volumes in 1887 and 1888, and two autobiographical works, *A New England Boyhood*, in 1893, and *Memories of a Hundred Years*, in 1902.

Haliburton, Thomas Chandler (1796–1865) The Canadian judge and writer Thomas Chandler Haliburton was born and educated in Nova Scotia. He published some serious works, including *An Historical and Statistical Account of Nova Scotia*, but is primarily remembered for a series of humorous satirical sketches featuring the Yankee Sam Slick. The first of these collections was *The Clockmaker, or Sayings and Doings of Samuel Slickville*, published in 1837.

Hallam, Henry (1777–1859) Born at Windsor, the historian Henry Hallam was educated at Eton and Oxford. Three of his works were outstanding; in 1818 he published *The View of the State of Europe during the Middle Ages*; the authoritative *Constitutional History of England* appeared in 1827; and his *Introduction to the Literature of Europe in the 15th, 16th and 17th Centuries* was published between 1838 and 1839.

Hamilton, Patrick (1904–62) The English playwright and novelist Anthony Walter Patrick Hamilton is best known for his play *Gaslight*, the Victorian thriller which was first seen in 1939. Another play, *Rope*, had been almost equally successful ten years earlier. His many novels include the trilogy 'Twenty Thousand Streets Under the Sky', published in 1935, and the thriller *Hanover Square*, which appeared in 1941.

Hamlet A tragedy by William Shakespeare, probably first presented in 1601 or 1602. Hamlet, Prince of Denmark, seeks vengeance on his uncle, Claudius, who murdered Hamlet's father and married his mother, Gertrude. The Folio edition of the play appeared in 1623, but a much earlier Quarto version, published in 1603, contains some additional material.

Hammett, Dashiel (1894–1961) The American writer Samuel Dashiell Hammett was born in Maryland. He worked for a time for the Pinkerton Agency, and later used his background knowledge to become one of the foremost practitioners of the 'tough guy' school of detective fiction. He also wrote screenplays, and several of his books were filmed, including his best-known works, *The Maltese Falcon* and *The Thin Man*, published in 1930 and 1932.

Hammon, Jupiter (*c.*1720–1800) The first Black poet in America, Jupiter Hammon was a slave, owned by a family living in Long Island. In 1760 he published *An Evening Thought*. He continued to produce verse on religious themes and some prose, but of greater interest is his *Address to the Negroes of the State of New York*, published in 1787, at a time when the anti-slavery movement was beginning to gain ground.

Hamsun, Knut (1859–1952) Born of poor parents in the Gudbrandsdal, Norway, Knut Hamsun became a shoemaker's apprentice, a coal trimmer and, after he had emigrated to the United States, a tram conductor and farm labourer. In 1888 he published part of a novel, *Sult*, which was later completed and translated into English as *Hunger*. It was immediately successful, and launched him on a long career as a novelist, playwright and poet. Apart from *Hunger*, his best-known work is probably *Growth of the Soil*, which was published in 1917. Hamsun was awarded the Nobel Prize for Literature in 1920.

Handke, Peter (1942–) The Austrian author Peter Handke was born at Griffen in Carinthia and studied law at the University of Graz. An influential and innovative writer, he published his first novel, *Die Hornissen* (*The Hornets*), in 1966, and his first full-length play, *Kaspar*, was produced in 1968. His first major success in fiction came with the publication in 1970 of *Die Angst des Tormanns beim Elfmeter* (*The Goalie's Anxiety at the Penalty Kick*). Other novels include a trilogy published in English in 1984 under the title 'Slow Homecoming', which 'builds into an unfinished autobiography', and *Across*, which appeared in 1986. He has also brought out collections of verse and essays.

Hand of Ethelberta, The A light novel by Thomas Hardy, first published in 1876.

Hard Times A novel by Charles Dickens, first published in 1854. It tells the story of Thomas Gradgrind and his family against a background of the industrial North of England.

Hard Times is Dickens' harshest indictment of mid-nineteenth century industrialism in England.

Hardy, Thomas (1840–1928) The great English novelist and poet Thomas Hardy was the son of a mason. He was educated at local schools in Dorsetshire, where he was born, and at the age of sixteen was articled to an ecclesiastical architect. At one time he considered entering the Church, but abandoned this idea and went in 1862 to London, where he became assistant to an eminent architect of that period. Some years previously he had begun writing essays and verse – he was perhaps always first and foremost a poet – and in 1865 his first short story was published in *Chamber's Journal*. Returning to Dorset in 1867, he wrote a novel which, although it was not published, brought him considerable encouragement from George Meredith. He tried again, and this time his novel, *Desperate Remedies*, was accepted and appeared in 1871. It was followed by *Under the Greenwood Tree* and *A Pair of Blue Eyes*, in 1872 and 1873. The next year saw the publication of *Far From the Madding Crowd*,

Thomas Hardy was born in this idyllic thatched cottage in Higher Brockhampton, which had been in the family since his grandfather built it in 1800. He later recalled how, in his childhood, he did not want to grow up or to possess things but to remain as he was 'in the same spot'. Later on his novels were to celebrate and immortalize the environment of the rural Dorset that he loved.

which proved to be his first major popular success. It came out first anonymously in the *Cornhill* magazine, and many readers believed it to be the work of George Eliot. His future as a writer was assured, and he now married a Miss Emma Lavinia Gifford. His next work was a lightweight novel, *The Hand of Ethelberta*, but the sombre strength of his pen was seen in *The Return of the Native*, published in 1878. *The Trumpet-Major* came in 1880, *A Laodicean* in 1881, *Two on a Tower* in 1882, *The Mayor of Casterbridge* in 1886, and *The Woodlanders* in 1887. Hardy now produced two volumes of stories, *Wessex Tales* and *A Group of Noble Dames*, before bringing out in 1891 the most famous of all his novels, *Tess of the d'Urbervilles*. It seems extraordinary in today's climate of opinion that this book should have been the subject of bitter critical attacks. Hardy's writing was often too realistic for late Victorian tastes, and when his books were serialized he was often forced to make concessions and cuts, but in book form *Tess of the d'Urbervilles* was uncensored. In 1892 he published *The Well-Beloved* in the *Illustrated London News*, but it did not appear in book form until 1897. Then came another volume of stories, *Life's Little Ironies*. In 1895 his last major novel, *Jude the Obscure*, appeared and met with an even more hostile reception than *Tess of the d'Urbervilles*. From this time on, disillusioned by this reaction to his fiction, Hardy concentrated on poetry. In 1898 he brought out *Wessex Poems*, a collection of verses which had been written over the previous thirty years, and several more volumes followed. *Time's Laughing-stocks*, published in 1909, marked the beginning of the last period in his writing, during which his poetry consisted solely of lyrical work. The last collection, *Winter Words*, appeared in the

This portrait of Thomas Hardy, painted by R.G. Eves in 1923, captures the character of the subject when he was eighty-three years old. Thomas Hardy was a native of Dorset and wrote with affection and insight about his environment. His frank treatment of sexual attraction initially shocked his Victorian readers.

year of his death. He was in fact a prolific poet, and the posthumous *Collected Poems* contained a very substantial body of work. He was engaged for a long period on his enormous verse drama *The Dynasts*, the three volumes of which were published in 1904, 1906 and 1908. In 1912 his wife died, and two years later he married Florence Dugdale. By this time his reputation had grown, his books were no longer considered outrageous and he had gained a great following among the members of the reading public. He was the recipient of many honours, including the Order of Merit. An essentially English writer, Hardy always had a great sense of his environment, and especially of the Wessex which he loved so much and where his books were set. His major characters fight against the sufferings that Fate imposes on them; the minor ones, especially the peasants, give him the opportunity for humour. For many years Hardy was seen as a great novelist and little more, but increasingly it has been realized that he is equally important as a poet – and that would please him.

Harland, Henry (1861–1905) The American novelist Henry Harland was born in New York and educated at Harvard. He published a number of novels under the pseudonym of Sidney Luska, without much success, and then, in London, became editor of the *Yellow Book*. In that capacity, and as a contributor to the magazine, he began to establish a reputation, but it was only with the publication in 1900 of *The Cardinal's Snuff-box* that he achieved real popularity. He wrote a number of other novels and stories before his early death.

Harmonium A collection of poems by Wallace Stevens, first published in 1932.

Harpur, Charles (1813–68) The son of parents sentenced to transportation to Australia, Charles Harpur could claim to be the first Australian-born poet. His *Thoughts: A Series of Sonnets* appeared in 1845. Later he turned for inspiration to the bush and produced a series of narrative and descriptive verses which are considered to be his best work.

Harris, Frank (1856–1931) James Thomas Harris, who preferred to call himself 'Frank', was born in Galway, Ireland. After travels in America and Europe, he made his home in London, and became an extremely successful newspaper and magazine editor. He published short stories, novels and plays, but is probably best remembered for his four-volume autobiography, *My Life and Loves*, in which fanciful accounts of his business life and relationships are interposed with even more imaginative stories of his love affairs. The book was banned as obscene for many years because of its explicit sexual content.

Harris, Joel Chandler (1848–1908) The American author Joel Chandler Harris was born in Georgia. He started work as an apprentice printer, studied law, and then turned to journalism, eventually becoming editor of the *Atlanta Constitution*. He had always been interested in Black folklore, and in 1880 published his first collection of tales featuring Uncle Remus, *Uncle Remus: his Songs and his Sayings*. More than a dozen similar books followed, including a number aimed specifically at children.

Harte, Bret (1839–1902) Francis Bret Harte was born at Albany, New York. He moved to California in 1856 and worked in many occupations before settling to journalism. *The Overland Monthly*, the first literary magazine to be published on the West Coast of America, was launched in 1868, with Harte as editor. He contributed to its pages, and soon established a reputation as an innovative short story writer with a gift for capturing the atmosphere of early days in the Old West. *The Luck of Roaring Camp and Other Sketches*, which appeared in 1870, was just one of the forty-four books which he brought out between 1867 and 1898. In addition to the stories for which he is famous he produced much verse, in which sentiment and humour were adroitly mixed. From 1878 to 1885 he was a United States consul, first at Crefeld in Germany and then at Glasgow in Scotland. He lived the last seven years of his life in England.

Hartford Wits, The The name given to a group of writers from Hartford and New Haven who came together in the late eighteenth century with the aim of fostering American literature. The most prominent members were Timothy Dwight and John Trumbull, both of whom were engaged at Yale in a campaign to increase the study of contemporary literature, and it is possible that the Wits were originally formed as part of this literary battle. Another well-known member was Joel Barlow. The group is also sometimes called 'The Connecticut Wits'.

Hartley, L.P. (1895–1972) Leslie Poles Hartley was born in Cambridgeshire, England, and educated at Harrow and Balliol College, Oxford. After service in the army during World War I he began writing seriously and published his first book, a volume of short stories called *Night Fears*, in 1924. This was followed in 1925 by a short novel, *Simonetta Perkins*, and it was not until 1944 that he brought out his first full-length novel, *The Shrimp and the Anemone*. It was the first part of the 'Eustace and Hilda' trilogy, the other volumes in which were *The Sixth Heaven* and *Eustace and Hilda*, published in 1946 and 1947. These three books established Hartley as an important novelist. He wrote over a dozen novels in all, and also published several collections of short stories. His most successful book was probably *The Go-Between*; his evocation in it of the early years of the century undoubtedly appealed to readers who looked back to that period with nostalgia, and to the charm of the story and its background were added its author's excellent style and craftsmanship. Among his other novels *The Hireling*, published in 1957, and *The Brickfield*, in 1964, are particularly worthy of mention.

Harvey, Gabriel (c.1545–1630) The English scholar Gabriel Harvey was born in Saffron Walden, Essex, England. He was educated at Cambridge, where he later spent some years as an academic. Although he published a few books, mostly in Latin, his main claim to literary fame is as a friend and tutor to Edmund Spenser, although he was less than enthusiastic when shown a manuscript of *The Faerie Queene*.

Hauptmann, Gerhart (1862–1946) The German dramatist Gerhart Hauptmann was born at Obersalzbrunn in Silesia. Originally intending to be a sculptor, he eventually decided on a literary career. His first play, *Vor Sonnenaufgang*, (*Before Sunrise*) which was produced in 1889, heralded a new, essentially realistic approach to the theatre, which he again demonstrated in the powerful drama *Die Weber*, (*The Weavers*), which was based on the uprising of weavers in Silesia in 1844. Many more plays were written – comedies, tragedies and what he called 'dramatic fairy-tales', with both contemporary and historical backgrounds, and in styles ranging from meticulous realism to symbolism. He was awarded the Nobel Prize for Literature in 1912.

Havelok the Dane*, *The Lay of This romantic story of a Danish prince, an English princess and the prince's wicked guardian is considered to be an important example of Middle English literature. Two versions exist, both written in Anglo-Norman. The earlier and very much shorter work dates from the twelfth century, while the later, more important, poem consists of some three thousand lines and was probably written in about the middle of the thirteenth century.

Hawes, Stephen (c.1474–1511) Believed to be a native of Suffolk, the English poet Stephen Hawes was educated at Oxford and became a court attendant to Henry VII and later to Henry VIII. His most important work was *The Passetyme of Pleasure, or the History of Graunde Amour and la Bel Pucel, conteining the knowledge of the Seven Sciences and the Course of Man's Life in this Worlde*. This long allegorical poem was printed by Wynkyn de Worde in 1509.

Hawthorne, Nathaniel (1804–64) Salem, Massachusetts, was the birthplace of the American writer Nathaniel Hawthorne, a descendant of the Puritan emigrant William Hathorne and of the Justice Hathorne who conducted the witch trials in Salem at the end of the seventeenth century. By the time he entered college in Brunswick, Maine, at the age of seventeen, Nathaniel Hawthorne had already made up his mind to be an author, and after his graduation he returned to Salem to write. At first he was far from successful. His earliest published book, *Fanshawe,* was printed at his own expense and

Nathaniel Hawthorne, an American writer in the age of 'transcendentalism', was a pioneer in the development of the American short story.

came out anonymously. It created little interest, and he made no impact either with the pieces that he published in a periodical called *The Token*, although they received some small recognition in England, where his *Twice-Told Tales* appeared in 1837. He married in 1842 and moved to Concord, where he lived in the old manse for four years before returning to Salem. For much of this period, in order to earn a living, he was employed as a customs officer, and he also spent a year at a farm at West Roxbury, Massachusetts, which was run as a co-operative by a group of Transcendalist thinkers. Nevertheless, he did succeed in publishing more of his short pieces in *Mosses from an Old Manse* and in a further selection of *Twice-Told Tales*, as well as some stories for children, *Grandfather's Chair*. In 1850 came *The Scarlet Letter*, the first of his major works. It made him famous and brought him the admiration of, among others, Herman Melville. It was followed in 1851 by *The House of the Seven Gables* and in 1852 by *The Blithedale Romance*, the two books which set the seal on his reputation. In 1851 he also brought out another work for children, *A Wonder Book*, and in 1852 *The Snow Image and other Twice-Told Tales* also appeared. He moved back to Concord, and there wrote a biography of his friend Franklin Pierce, who was the Democratic candidate for the Presidency of the United States. The *Life of Franklin Pierce* was published in 1852. In the following year he brought out a further collection of stories from Ancient Greece under the title *Tanglewood Tales*, and this proved to be the most enduring of his children's books. Pierce was now the President, and he rewarded Hawthorne for his support by appointing him to be United States consul in Liverpool. He held the position until the administration changed in 1857, but he remained in Europe for a further three years, passing his time in England, France and Italy. His stay in the last country inspired *The Marble Faun*, which he wrote on his return to England, despatching the manuscript to the United States, where it was published in 1860. In that year he went back to Concord and remained there for the rest of his life. He was to produce only one more completed book, *Our Old Home*, a collection of pieces on England. It suffered the misfortune of being dedicated to ex-president Pierce, who at that time was very much out of favour because of his support for the pro-slavery States. Hawthorne began two more stories, *Septimius Felton* and *The Dolliver Romance*, but both were unfinished at his death. His work, small in quantity, is large in quality, and some critics believe that few writers in either Britain or the United States have ever equalled him in the excellence of his prose. It is not, however, solely as a stylist that he is so highly regarded, but also for the imaginative content of his stories, his sensitive exploration of moral issues and the pressures which they exert upon his characters, and the power of his allegories. Not least, he was a splendid story-teller.

Hay, John (1838–1905) A native of Salem, Indiana, John Milton Hay was educated at Brown University, and while still in his twenties was selected to be President Lincoln's assistant private secretary. He became an international statesman and diplomat of high repute. He published two books in 1871 – *Pike County Ballads* and *Castilian Days*, an account of a period he had spent in Spain. A novel, *The Breadwinners*, was published anonymously in 1883, and *Poems* followed in 1890. In that same year he and John George Nicolay completed and published their ten-volume *Abraham Lincoln: A History*. Hay also prepared an edition of *Lincoln's Complete Works*, which appeared in 1894.

Hayward, Sir John (c.1560–1627) Born in Suffolk and educated at Cambridge, John Hayward published *The First Part of the Life and Raigne of King Henrie IV* in 1599 and spent two years in prison because Queen Elizabeth did not like what he had written. In greater favour with James I, he brought out *Lives of the Three Norman Kings of England* in 1613, and was knighted in 1619. His *The Life and Raigne of King Edward VI* and *Certain Yeres of Queen Elizabeth's Raigne* were published posthumously.

Hazlitt, William (1778–1830) The son of a Unitarian minister, William Hazlitt was born at Maidstone, Kent, England. He was sent to a theological college, but had no vocation for the Church and decided to become a portrait painter. However, his true talent lay in literature, and in 1805 he published his first book, *An Essay on the Principles of Human Action: being an argument in favour of the Natural Disinterestedness of the Human Mind*. A number of other books, on a variety of subjects, soon followed. In 1812 he began a series of lectures on 'The Rise and Progress of Modern Philosophy' after which he concentrated on a journalistic career, contributing to many periodicals, and especially to *The Examiner*, as essayist, parliamentary reporter and dramatic critic. Between 1818 and 1822 he produced much of his best literary criticism, including *Characters of Shakespeare's Plays*, *Lectures on the English Poets*, *Lectures on English Comic Writers* and *Lectures on the Dramatic Literature of the Age of Elizabeth*. His *Table Talk; or Original Essays on Men and Manners* and *Political Essays* also belong to this period. *Liber Amoris; or the New Pygmalion*, published in 1823, was an account of his desperate love for a certain Sarah Walker, his divorce from his first wife and his falling out of love with Miss Walker. He was married again soon after, to a widow. In 1825 he produced *The Spirit of the Age; or Contemporary Portraits*, and more essays appeared in 1826 in *The Plain Speaker; opinions on*

A sensitive portrait of William Hazlitt, the English essayist, journalist and critic, by William Bewick.

Books, Men and Things. He wrote a four-volume *Life of Napoleon Buonaparte*, which appeared between 1828 and 1830. Hazlitt is particularly notable as the first literary critic to deal at all adequately with the literature of the past.

Hearn, Lafcadio (1850–1904) The son of an Irish father and a Greek mother, Lafcadio Hearn adopted his first name as a tribute to the Greek island where he was born. At the age of nineteen he travelled to America, where he worked as a journalist. A period in Martinique resulted in his first book, *Two Years in the French West Indies*. In 1891 he went to Japan, and lived there for the rest of his life, teaching at the University of Tokyo. He married a Japanese wife, became a Buddhist and changed his name to Yakumo Koizumi. He wrote a number of books on Japan and Japanese subjects, including

Glimpses of Unfamiliar Japan, published in 1894, *In Ghostly Japan*, in 1899, and *Japan, an Attempt at Interpretation*, in 1904.

Hearne, Thomas (1678–1735) The English antiquary Thomas Hearne was born in Berkshire. He was educated at Oxford, where he became the second keeper of the Bodleian Library. He was dismissed from this post for refusing to take the oath of allegiance to George I, but not before he had performed an invaluable service to later historians by his scrupulous editing of a large number of ancient texts, especially those of the English chroniclers.

Heartbreak House A play by G. Bernard Shaw to which he gave the subtitle 'A fantasia in the Russian manner on English themes'. It was first published in New York in 1919, and given its first production there in the following year.

Heart of Darkness A novel set in Africa by Joseph Conrad, in which he explores with deep psychological insight the character and motives of the strange ivory agent Kurtz. It was first published in 1902.

Heart of Midlothian, The A novel by Sir Walter Scott, set in the eighteenth century. It was first published in 1818.

Heart of the Matter, The A novel of corruption in West Africa by Graham Greene, first published in 1948.

Hecht, Ben (1894–1964) The American novelist and playwright Ben Hecht was born in New York, but reared in Wisconsin. He was an acrobat, a violinist and a reporter before embarking on a literary career. He published his first novel, *Erik Dorn*, in 1921, and *Gargoyles* in 1922. He was also successful with a number of volumes of short stories, but it is perhaps for his plays that he is best remembered, particulary *20th Century*, which was produced in 1932, and two works written in collaboration: *The Front Page*, with Charles Macarthur, seen in 1928, and *The Great Magoo*, with Gene Fowler, in 1933.

Hedda Gabler A drama by Henrik Ibsen, exploring the character of a deeply frustrated woman. It was first produced in 1890.

Hegel, Georg Wilhelm Friedrich (1770–1831) Most of the books of the German philosopher Georg Wilhelm Friedrich Hegel, a native of Stuttgart, were based on the lectures he gave at universities in Heidelberg and Berlin. The most important of his works were *Phänomenologie des Geistes* (*Phenomenology of Spirit*), which appeared in 1807, *Wissenschaft der Logik* (*Science of Logic*), the first two volumes of which came out in 1812 and the third in 1816, and *Grundlinien der Philosophi des Rechts* (*Philosophy of Rights*), published in 1820.

Heine, Heinrich (1797–1856) Born of Jewish parents in Düsseldorf, Heinrich Heine (usually called 'Harry') graduated in law from the university at Göttingen. He did not, however, practise, but became a journalist and editor. In 1826 he published the first volume in a series of books called *Reisebilder* (*Travel Pictures*), and many more collections of essays were to follow. Of more lasting importance was his poetry. *Buch der Lieder* (*Book of Songs*), which appeared in 1827, immediately established him as a lyric poet whose work was both strongly romantic and self-mocking, and his reputation was enhanced by the publication in much later years of further volumes, including his last collection, *Neueste Gedichte* (*Latest Poems*), which came out in 1851.

He Knew He Was Right A novel by Anthony Trollope, first published in 1869.

Heller, Joseph (1923–) The American writer Joseph Heller was born in New York. He served during Word War II in the US Army Air Corps, and only after that was he able to resume his education at New York, Columbia and Oxford universities and in due course to embark on an academic career. His wartime experiences provided the material for his first book, *Catch-22*, a funny and bitter satire on war and the army and its administrators. It fitted the public mood of its time to perfection, and became an immediate bestseller when it was published in 1961. A second novel was eagerly

Joseph Heller, author of the satirical novel *Catch-22*.

awaited, but the only work that Heller published during the next thirteen years was a play, *We Bombed in New Haven*, which was seen in 1968. Then in 1974 he produced another play, *Clevinger's Trial*, and in the same year a new novel at last appeared. *Something Happened* was inevitably considered as a disappointment – it is very difficult to follow successfully an extra-ordinary, indeed unique, book such as *Catch-22*. Two more novels, *Good as Gold* and *God Knows*, were published in 1979 and 1984 respectively, but the somewhat mixed reception which they received may again have been due more to a failure to measure up to *Catch-22* than to an intrinsic lack of quality. *No Laughing Matter*, written in collaboration with Speed Vogel, which came out in 1986, is an account of Heller's sucessful struggle against a disease which could have left him totally paralysed.

Hellman, Lillian (1905–84) The playwright Lillian Hellman was born in New Orleans. Her first play, *The Children's Hour*, was acclaimed when it was produced in 1934, and she went on to produce a number of other dramas which combined popular appeal with a considerable quality of writing. Her biggest success was *The Little Foxes*, presented in 1939, but the wartime play *Watch on the Rhine*, seen in 1941, and *Toys in the Attic*, in 1960, were also well-received. Lillian Hellman also wrote three volumes of autobiography.

Hemans, Mrs Felicia Dorothea (1793–1835) Felicia Dorothea Browne was born in Liverpool, England, and was married at the age of nineteen to a soldier, Captain Alfred Hemans. She had published her first volume of poems as early as 1808, and she continued to write and publish verse for the rest of her life. Sir Walter Scott greatly admired her work, and their friendship was a lasting one. The best known of the poems by Mrs Hemans is 'Casabianca' ('The boy stood on the burning deck …').

Hemingway, Ernest (1899–1961) The son of a doctor, Ernest Miller Hemingway was born in Oak Park, Illinois. He became a newspaper reporter, first for a Kansas City paper and later, after serving in World War I with an ambulance unit, in Toronto. He then went to Paris, where he lived for many years, a friend of such writers as Ezra Pound, Gertrude Stein and Ford Madox Ford, who encouraged him in his ambitions as an author. His first book, *Three Stories and Ten Poems*, was published in 1923. Two years later a collection of short stories, *In Our Time*, appeared; many of the tales and fragments in the book were centred around the semi-autobiographical figure of Nick Adams. A full-length novel, *The Torrents of Spring*, came in

War II, and the former conflict provided the background for the very successful novel, *For Whom the Bell Tolls*, published in 1940, and memorably translated to the screen as a vehicle for Humphrey Bogart and Ingrid Bergman. A gap of ten years ensued before the publication of *Across the River and Into the Trees*, which was considered one of the weakest of his books, but he overcame any damage to his reputation with another novel, *The Old Man and the Sea*, set in Cuba, where he was then living, which appeared in 1952. In 1954 he was awarded the Nobel Prize for Literature. He worked on other books, but did not complete any of them before failing health and unhappy personal relationships drove him to shoot himself in July 1961. Three years after his death, a volume of autobiography, *A Moveable Feast*, was published, and since then a considerable quantity of his previously unpublished writing has appeared, including the novel *Islands in the Stream* and the memoir of Spain and bullfighting, *Dangerous Summer*. The latest such venture has been the publication of *The Garden of Eden*, a novel which Hemingway left at his death as a disorganised manuscript of 1,500 pages; an American publisher cut it and gave it a shape which the author had been unable to achieve, despite having worked on it for fifteen years. This 'Hemingway industry' can only be regarded as regrettable, since it damages the reputation of a major and very individual writer. On the other hand, it must be said that Hemingway himself bears some responsibility for having so assiduously fostered his 'macho' image and built himself into a public personality, whose every word must therefore be preserved and read. In fact, at his best, he was an innovative and influential writer of considerable power. He invented for himself a style which was terse, spare and immensely powerful, which many writers have attempted to copy. Few, however, have observed with so sharp an eye, and even fewer have been able to achieve the depth of characterization and feeling which lie beneath those tough, sinewy short sentences; nor have his imitators managed to find the poetry that he could sometimes strangely produce in the midst of the often repetitve rhythms of his prose. Discussion continues as to whether he was a finer short story writer than a novelist, and in any such argument stories such as 'The Undefeated', 'The Snows of Kilimanjaro' and 'The Short Happy Life of Francis Macomber' must be considered, along with the novels, as outstanding contributions to the literature of the twentieth century.

Ernest Hemingway and his cats taking breakfast in the bedroom of his farmhouse home, Finca Vegia. Above him is Juan Gris' painting *The Guitar Players*.

1926, and in the same year he established his reputation with the success of *The Sun Also Rises*; the bullfighting at Pamplona in Spain which plays an important part in the book, gave it the title by which it was known in England, *Fiesta*. The next book was another volume of short stories, *Men Without Women*, published in 1927, and in 1929 he brought out *A Farewell to Arms*, the novel which for many people represents his finest work. After more short stories, collected in 1933 in *Winner Take Nothing*, Hemingway turned to non-fiction, producing *Death in the Afternoon*, his hymn to bullfighting, in 1935, and *The Green Hills of Africa*, on big-game hunting, in 1935. Hemingway was a war correspondent during both the Spanish Civil War and World

Henley, W.E. (1849–1903) Born at Gloucester, England, the poet William Ernest Henley was also a journalist and literary critic, and collaborated with his friend Robert Louis Stevenson on four plays. As an editor, he encouraged and published the work of many rising authors, including Hardy, Kipling and Wells. He wrote a number of non-fiction books, and his own verse was published in several volumes. He is particularly remembered for his poem 'Invictus'.

Henrietta Temple A novel by Benjamin Disraeli, first published in 1837.

Henry IV, Parts 1 and 2 Chronicle plays by William Shakespeare, probably first presented about 1597, and printed in 1598 and 1600. The plays both deal with rebellions against Henry Bolingbroke, who succeeded Richard II, and introduce the great comic character of Falstaff.

Henry V, King The historical play by William Shakespeare, almost certainly first performed in 1599, printed in 1623. The play is principally concerned with Henry's campaign in France, the Battle of Agincourt, and his courtship of the French princess Katherine.

Henry VI, Parts 1, 2 and 3 Among the earliest of William Shakespeare's works, these chronicle plays were probably first presented in the early 1590s. They appeared in print at dates varying between 1594 and 1623. The plays deal with the King's troubled reign, involving war with France, court intrigue and civil war.

Henry VIII An historical play by William Shakespeare. However, John Fletcher almost certainly also had an important hand in writing it. It was first performed in 1613. The principal events of the play include Henry's divorce from Katherine of Aragon, and the downfall of Cardinal Wolsey.

Henry Esmond, Esq., The History of A novel by William Makepeace Thackeray, first published in 1852.

Henry, O. (1862–1910) William Sydney Porter, who used the pseudonym O. Henry, was born in Greensboro, North Carolina. He began to write at about the time of his first marriage in 1887. After working for a short while on the Houston *Post*, he was accused of embezzlement (a crime of which he may have been innocent). He fled to Honduras, but returned in 1897 because his wife was dying. He was tried in 1898 and sent to prison for five years, and while there capitalized on the small success he had already had with some short stories by starting to write seriously. Released in 1901, because of good behaviour, he went to New York in the following year and secured a contract to write a short story every

O. Henry, the pseudonym of William Sydney Porter, working as a teller behind the counter at the First National Bank of Austin, Texas, c.1892. A short time later he was accused of embezzlement and imprisoned for five years.

week for the *New York World*. His first book, *Cabbages and Kings*, was published in 1904. Over the last six years of his life he wrote prolifically and very successfully, and twelve more collections of his stories were published, the last three appearing posthumously. He married again in 1907. His stories, often set in New York but sometimes given southern or western backgrounds, were marked by his humour and noted for their ingenuity of plot. O. Henry was the supreme exponent of the 'twist ending' genre, in which the last words of the story provided a neat and surprising conclusion.

Henryson, Robert (c.1425–c.1500) Comparatively little is known of the Scottish poet Robert Henryson, though he is believed to have been a teacher. In addition to a small number of short poems, he produced three substantial works: *Morall Fabillis of Esope*, *Orpheus and Eurydice* and *Testament of Cresseid*, a sequel to Chaucer's *Troilus and Criseyde*.

Henry the Minstrel (c.1440–c.1492) Also known as Blind Harry, Henry the Minstrel is thought to be the Scottish author of *The Wallace*, a long poem written in heroic couplets on the exploits of the Scottish hero. The earliest manuscript dates from 1488.

Henty, G.A. (1832–1902) George Alfred Henty, who wrote adventure stories for boys, was born near Cambridge and educated at Westminster and Cambridge. After long experience as a war correspondent, he became the editor of a boys' magazine called *Union Jack* and wrote for it a very large number of serials, later published in book form, mostly with a military background. Seen now as old-fashioned in their jingoistic attitudes, the exciting narratives of such stories as *Under Drake's Flag* and *With Clive in India* made them extremely popular in their day.

Heptameron, The A collection of seventy-two romantic tales supposedly told by a group of travellers staying together in an inn over a period of seven days. The book was written by Marguerite d'Angoulême, Queen of Navarre, although it is possible that she was assisted by others of her household. It was first printed in 1558 under the title *Les amants fortunés*, and only later became known as *The Heptameron* in direct reference to Boccaccio's *Decameron*, which it resembles in construction.

Herbert, A.P. (1890–1971) Alan Patrick Herbert, the English humorist and novelist, was educated at Winchester and New College, Oxford. A member of Parliament for many years, he had an abiding desire to change many of the absurdities in British law, and much of his writing was aimed at doing so, largely by means of riducule, as in *Holy Deadlock*, a novel published in 1934, which pointed to reform of the divorce laws, and his popular one-act Shakespearian skit, *Two Gentlemen of Soho*, which poked fun at licensing restriction in private clubs. His best-known novel was *The Water Gypsies*, which appeared in 1930. He contributed regularly to *Punch*, and also wrote revues and several musicals, including *Bless the Bride*. He was knighted in 1945.

Herbert, Edward (1583–1648) Born in Shropshire, England, the elder brother of George Herbert the poet, Edward Herbert was educated at Oxford. A soldier and diplomat, he was created Baron Herbert of Cherbury in 1629. He wrote poetry, satires, a number of treatises and *The Life and Raigne of King Henry VIII*, published in 1649. However, his literary fame rests on his major work of religious philosophy, *De Veritate*, which appeared in 1624 and which he supplemented with later writings. He also wrote an entertaining *Autobiography*, first published in 1764.

Herbert, Frank (1920–1986) The American science fiction writer Frank Patrick Herbert was born in Washington and educated at the University of Washington. His first novel, *The Dragon in the Sea*, was published in 1956. He is renowned as the author of the 'Dune' series, which began in 1965 with *Dune*, a book which won both the Hugo and the Nebula awards. The series continued with *Dune Messiah*, in 1969, and *Children of Dune* in 1976. A second trilogy, consisting of *God Emperor of Dune*, *Heretics of Dune* and *Chapter House Dune*, was completed in 1985. Other writings include a collection of short pieces, *Eye*, and *Man of Two Worlds* (written in collaboration with his son Brian Herbert), both of which appeared in 1986.

Herbert, George (1593–1633) The metaphysical poet George Herbert was born in Montgomery Castle, Wales. Educated at Westminster and Cambridge, he was a distinguished scholar. He became the friend of John Donne, Izaak Walton and Francis Bacon, and for some time he divided his life between academic studies, politics and attendance on King James I. He then took Holy Orders and was appointed prebendary of Leighton Bromswold in Huntingdonshire, where he rebuilt the church. He passed the last three years of his short life as a dedicated priest in the parish of Fugglestone with Bemerton, near Salisbury. Apart from some poems in Latin which appeared in 1612, none of his poetry was published during his lifetime, but when he was dying he gave his manuscripts to his friend Nicholas Ferrar, and these, *The Temple: Sacred Poems and Private Ejaculations*, were published almost immediately after his death. They were extremely popular and greatly admired for the simple faith which they expressed, although their language and Herbert's use of images lend them a rewarding depth. Other writings, including some in prose, appeared in 1652 under the title *Herbert's Remains; or, Sundry Pieces of that Sweet Singer of the Temple, Mr George Herbert*.

Hereward the Wake A novel by Charles Kingsley based on the legends of the celebrated British outlaw, who led a resistance movement against William the Conqueror. The book was first published in 1866.

Herodotus (*c*.484–425BC) The Greek historian Herodotus was born at Helicarnassus in Asia Minor, the son of a well-to-do family. He travelled widely, gathering material for his *History*, in the writing of which he subsequently spent many years. Concerned principally with the wars of the Greeks against the barbarians and the Persians, it is the first historical account which attempted to present a well-organized and detailed story, the facts of which had been verified as far as the author was able (although Herodotus has been accused of too readily accepting hearsay). Herodotus is known as the Father of History.

heroic couplet Two rhyming lines of verse in iambic pentameters. The heroic couplet is the form in which Chaucer, who was the first to use it, wrote much of *The Canterbury Tales*. It has been frequently used by subsequent authors.

heroic drama This term is usually applied to the tragedies of such Restoration playwrights as Dryden and Otway. Written in heroic couplets and extravagant language, the plays dealt with royal or noble personages, and their plots were usually concerned with valour, especially in war, and love. Although described as tragedies, the dramas often ended happily as far as the hero and heroine were concerned.

heroic verse In the poetry of Ancient Greece heroic verse is written in dactylic hexameters, while in French the term applies to the alexandrine, a line of twelve syllables. In English the term is used for epic poetry in rhyming iambic pentameters — in other words, in heroic couplets.

Herrick, Robert (1591–1674) The son of a goldsmith, the poet Robert Herrick was born in London, and after a period of apprenticeship to his uncle, who was also a goldsmith, went to Cambridge. After graduating as a Master of Arts he became a priest, and in 1629 was presented with the living of Dean Prior in Devonshire. In 1648 he was dismissed from the parish by the Puritans, and went to live in London. Although a strong supporter of the monarchy, he did not move in court circles, but is nevertheless numbered among the Cavalier poets. In 1662 he was able to return to Dean Prior, where he spent the remainder of his life. From an early age he had been acquainted with other writers of the day and had established a reputation as a poet, but his work was not published until 1635, when he made some contributions to the collection *A Description of the King and Queen of Fairies*. In 1648, immediately after his ejection from Dean Prior, he published his major work, *Hesperides; or the Works both Human and Divine of Robert Herrick*, the religious verses being given the additional title of *Noble Numbers*. He appears to have written no more poetry thereafter, but his total output amounts to some thirteen hundred poems. They are all, without exception, short lyrics, and a remarkably high proportion are of such quality that Herrick must rank among the finest of all English poets.

Herrick, Robert (1868–1938) The American novelist Robert Herrick was born in Cambridge, Massachusetts, and educated at Harvard. As an academic working at the University of Chicago, he published his first book, a collection of short stories, *The Man Who Wins*, in 1897. A novel, *Gospel of Freedom*, appeared in 1898, and was followed by many others, including *His Great Adventure*, in 1913, *Chimes*, in 1926, and *Sometime*, in 1933. He also published several additional volumes of short stories.

Herriott, James (1916–) James Herriott is the pseudonym of James Alfred Wight. A veterinary surgeon since 1939, he began to write comparatively late in life and in 1972 published *If Only They Could Talk*. He has written several semi-fictional books about a vet's life, including *All Creatures Great and Small*, which appeared in 1972, and *All Things Bright and Beautiful*, in 1973.

Hersey, John (1914–) John Richard Hersey was born in Tientsin, China, of American missionary parents. After completing his education at Yale, he became secretary to Sinclair Lewis. His first book, *Men on Bataan*, was published in 1942, and was followed in 1943 by *Into the Valley*. His novel *A Bell for Adano* won the Pulitzer Prize in 1944. Other writings include the novels *The Wall*, in 1950, *A Single Pebble*, in 1956, *The War Lover*, in 1959, and *The Conspiracy*, in 1972. The non-fiction *Aspects of the Presidency* appeared in 1980.

Hesiod (Eighth century BC) Most of the information about Hesiod, the Greek epic poet, is speculative. Of the three major poems attributed to him, *Works and Days*, *The Theogony* and *The Shield of Heracles*, only the first seems likely to have been truly his, and even that, an account in verse of his life as a farmer, embellished by the addition of fables and allegories, may have been written in part by others. Whether Hesiod is one person or a school of writers, the work to which his name is given is regarded as the first Greek poetry in the didactic vein.

Hesse, Hermann (1877–1962) The German author Hermann Hesse was born in Calw in Wurttemberg. Abandoning his education at a comparatively early age, he worked for some years in the book trade. His first volume of poetry, *Romantische Lieder* (*Romantic Songs*) was published in 1899. Five years later he produced his first novel, *Peter Camenzind*, and followed it with other works of fiction, including *Gertrud*, in 1910, *Rosshalde*, in 1914, and *Demian*, in 1919. In the 1960s his work attracted renewed interest, and he became a much-admired cult writer, particularly in the United States, when his novel *Siddharta*, based on the life of Buddha and originally published in 1922, was widely read and recognized as a major work of mysticism. Similar qualities were to be found in his other works, which also became popular at that time. These included *Der Steppenwolf* (*Steppenwolf*), which had first appeared in 1927, the experimental *Narziss und Goldmund* (*Narcissus and Goldmund*), dating from 1930, and his last long

A scene from a 1973 film version of Hesse's mystical novel on the life of Buddha, *Siddharta*. It was directed by Conrad Rooks and starred Shashi Kappor as the hero.

novel, *Das Glasperlenspiel* (*The Glass Bead Game*), which came out in 1943. Among his other books were fairy stories and essays, and in 1960 he published *Letzte Gedichte* (*Last Poems*). He was awarded the Nobel prize for Literature in 1946.

Hewlett, Maurice (1861–1923) The English historical novelist Maurice Henry Hewlett was born at Weybridge, Surrey. He was working as a lawyer when he published his first novel, *The Forest Lovers*, in 1898. Its success allowed him to devote himself thereafter to writing, and he produced a large number of romances, including *Richard Yea-and-Nay*, which appeared in 1900, and *The Queen's Quair*, in 1904. In 1916 he brought out a long poem, *The Song of the Plow*, and his work from then on was confined to poetry and essays.

Heyer, Georgette (1902–74) Although she also wrote a number of successful detective novels, Georgette Heyer found her greatest popularity with her Regency romances. Her first novel was *The Black Moth*, and her bestsellers include *Regency Buck*, *Arabella*, *Devil's Cub* and *Lady of Quality*.

Heyerdahl, Thor (1914–) The distinguished Norwegian anthropologist was educated at the University of Oslo. His great bestseller, *The Kon-Tiki Expedition*, was published in 1948. He has written a number of learned works, but his other popular books include *Aku-Aku: The Secrets of Easter Island*, which appeared in 1957, and *The Ra Expeditions*, in 1970.

Heywood, John (*c*.1497–*c*.1580) The birthplace of the English dramatist John Heywood is uncertain, but he is known to have been a chorister of the Chapel Royal and a player of the virginals at the court of King Henry VIII. He wrote a number of plays, or interludes, which form a link in style between the mediaeval morality plays and later drama in which characters became persons rather than types. He is known to have written *The Playe called the foure PP; a newe and a very mery interlude of a palmer, a pardoner, a potcary, a pedlar* and *The Play of the Wether, a new and very mery interlude of all maner of Wethers*. The more briefly, but perhaps less exotically, titled *The Play of Love* is also attributed to him.

Heywood, Thomas (*c*.1574–1641) A native of Lincolnshire, educated at Cambridge, Thomas Heywood was an actor and the author, according to his own account, of some two hundred and fifty plays. These included farces, comedies, tragedies, historical plays, dramatization of classic fables and pageants. Most of these no longer exist. His best-known work is *A Woman kilde with kindnesse*, which was probably first performed about 1600. The prolific Mr Heywood also wrote a number of long poems, some histories, *The Life of Merlin surnamed Ambrosius*, and *An Apology for Actors*.

Hiawatha, The Song of A long narrative poem by Henry Wadsworth Longfellow in which he recounts the life story of the Ojibway Indian chieftain. It was first published in 1855.

Highsmith, Patricia (1921–) The distinguished American crime writer was educated at Barnard College and Columbia. Her first novel, *Strangers on a Train*, was published in 1950, and achieved great success. Among many other books, the series featuring Tom Ripley, which began in 1956 with *The Talented Mr Ripley*, have proved extremely popular, not merely because of their entertainment value, but because of the quality and wit of their writing. A straight novel, *Found in the Street*, appeared in 1986.

Hilda Lessways A novel by Arnold Bennett, the second in the Clayhanger series, first published in 1911.

Hilton, James (1900–54) The English novelist and screenplay writer James Hilton was born at Leigh, Lancashire, England, and educated at Cambridge. He published his first novel, *Catherine Herself*, in 1920. The most famous of his books are *Lost Horizon*, published in 1933, and *Goodbye, Mr Chips*, which came out in the following year.

Historia Ecclesiastica Gentis Anglorum A history of the English from the Roman invasion to the year 731, written in Latin by the Venerable Bede.

History of Mr Polly, The A novel by H.G. Wells, first published in 1910.

History of the English-Speaking Peoples, A A history by Winston S. Churchill. The first two volumes, *The Birth of Britain* and *The New World*, were published in 1956, the third, *The Age of Revolution*, in 1957, and the fourth, *The Great Democracies*, in 1958.

Hobbes, Thomas (1588–1679) Born in Wiltshire, England, and educated at Malmesbury School and Magdalen Hall, Oxford, Thomas Hobbes became a tutor to the powerful Cavendish family. He made several journeys to Europe and

The very distinctive title-page of Thomas Hobbes' major work, *Leviathan*, printed in 1651 for Andrew Crooke. It is uncertain who is the designer of this symbolic and highly decorative title-page.

met Galileo and Descartes among other prominent scientists and philosophers, and in England was a friend of Francis Bacon. In 1640 he went with other Royalist supporters to France, and spent the next eleven years there, becoming tutor to the future Charles II in 1647. Hobbes had already aroused controversy with a treatise on political philosophy which had been circulated privately. He now published it in 1650 in two short volumes, *Human Nature, or the Fundamental Elements of Policy* and *De Corpore Politico, or the Elements of Law, Moral and Politic*, and this was followed in 1651 by the publication of his major work, *Leviathan, or the Matter, Form and Power of a Commonwealth, Ecclesiastical and Civil*. The doctrines which it set forth were widely disliked, and lost him the patronage of his royal pupil. He returned to London, submitted to the Commonwealth government and retired into private life in the Cavendish household, where he remained for the rest of his life. He published a number of other philosophical works, and in his old age brought out translations of *The Iliad* and *The Odyssey*.

Hobbit, The A novel, originally intended for children, by J.R.R. Tolkien, first published in 1937. From this story of Middle Earth, Tolkien later developed his fantasy *The Lord of the Rings*.

Hoccleve, Thomas (*c.*1368–*c.*1426) The first known poem by Thomas Hoccleve, whose surname is often rendered as Occleve, 'The Letter of Cupid', appeared in 1402, and was a translation from the French. His principal work, *The Regement of Princes*, was composed about 1411, and is preceded by an autobiographical account of life in London, where he was a clerk in the office of the Privy Seal. Towards the end of his life he suffered a long physical and mental collapse, and some of his later poems give an account of his experiences.

Hoffmann, E.T.A. (1776–1822) The German writer Ernst Theodor Wilhelm Hoffmann changed his third name to Amadeus in homage to Mozart. He was born in Königsberg, where he attended the university. At first a composer and musician, he turned to literature, and in 1814 published his *Phantasiestücke*. His novel, *The Devil's Elixir*, appeared in 1816, and added to his reputation as a writer with a bizarre imagination. Several more volumes of fantastic stories followed. The ballet *Coppélia* was based on one of his tales, and Offenbach used not only some of his stories but incidents from the author's life in his *Tales of Hoffmann*.

Hoffmann, Heinrich (1809–74) The German physician Heinrich Hoffmann was the author of the moral, and faintly terrifying, tale of

Struwwelpeter (*Shockheaded Peter*), which he wrote for his own children. Published in 1847, it became a classic in nurseries of the period.

Hofmannsthal, Hugo von (1874–1929) Born and educated in Vienna, Hugo von Hofmannsthal began writing poetry while still at school. His work attracted considerable attention, and indeed he was a forerunner in the Romantic School in Austria. A collection of his poems appeared in 1911. Long before then he had made a name for himself as a dramatist with such plays as *Gestern* (*Yesterday*), produced in 1892, and a number of dramas which were new versions of plays by classic dramatists, ranging from Sophocles to Calderón, Molière and Otway. He wrote the libretti for several of the Richard Strauss operas, including *Der Rosenkavalier* and *Ariadne auf Naxos*.

Hogg, James (1770–1835) The 'Ettrick Shepherd', as James Hogg was called, was in fact a shepherd, born at Ettrick in Scotland. In 1801 he published a volume of poetry, *Scottish Pastorals*, and a further collection, *The Mountain Bard*, appeared in 1807. *The Queen's Wake*, which appeared in 1813, made his name, and he became the friend of many literary lions of the day and a member of the editorial board of *Blackwood's Edinburgh Magazine*. He published a great many other works, including a novel, *The Private Memoirs and Confessions of a Justified Sinner*, which came out in 1824. In tribute to an early benefactor, he brought out *The Domestic Manners and Private Life of Sir Walter Scott* in 1834.

Holcroft Thomas (1745–1809) After working as a stable-boy and shoemaker, Thomas Holcroft, who was born in London, became an actor. His first play, *The Crisis; or, Love and Famine* was produced at Drury Lane in 1778. Other plays followed, including *The Follies of the Day*, an English version of *Le mariage de Figaro*, which he wrote after watching Beaumarchais' original often enough in Paris to be able to reproduce it accurately. His most successful play was *The Road to Ruin*, presented in 1792. He also wrote several novels, poetry and some accounts of his travels, and made translations of works from French and German.

Holinshed, Raphael The date of birth and early circumstances of Raphael Holinshed are not known, and there is also uncertainty about the date of his death, which took place possibly in 1580. His great work was the history, *Chronicles of England, Scotland and Ireland*, which appeared in two illustrated volumes in 1578 and became a source book for many authors, including Shakespeare. A revised version, with additional material, came out in 1587, but parts of it gave offence to Queen Elizabeth, and several of its pages had to be deleted.

Holmes, Oliver Wendell (1809–94) The son of a clergyman, Oliver Wendell Holmes was born in Cambridge, Massachusetts. He was educated at Harvard, and then went to Paris, where he studied medicine before returning to the United States in 1835. In 1847 he became Professor of Anatomy and Physiology in the Medical School of Harvard University, an appointment which he held until 1882. In 1836 he had published his first volume of poetry, *Poems*. He continued to write verse throughout his life – his collected poems fill three volumes – but it was not until 1858 that he made his name as a writer. In 1857 he was asked to join James Russell Lowell in editing a new magazine, which Holmes himself named *The Atlantic Monthly*, and to this he contributed regularly the papers of *The Autocrat of the Breakfast-Table*. It is said that the magazine would not have survived without them, and they certainly made Dr Holmes famous. *The Professor at the Breakfast-Table*, *The Poet at the Breakfast-Table* and *Over the Tea-Cups* followed in 1860, 1872 and 1891. He also wrote three novels, *Elsie Venner*, which appeared in 1861, *The Guardian Angel*, in 1867, and *A Mortal Antipathy*, in 1884. A trip to Europe in 1886, which included a triumphant reception in Britain, where his work was almost as popular as in the United States, resulted in *Our Hundred Days in Europe*, published the following year.

A handwritten poem by Oliver Wendell Holmes.

This title-page to Homer's *Batrachomyomachia* depicts Homer, seated, reciting to Apollo, Mercury and Athene. The translator, George Chapman, is pictured below surrounded by the 'Battle of Frogs'.

Homer According to the Greek historian Herodotus, Homer, the greatest of all epic poets of Greece, was a contemporary of Hesiod, and both were alive during the eighth century BC. In this respect Herodotus cannot be relied on, and in fact nothing at all is known of Homer, except that for many centuries *The Iliad* and *The Odyssey* were attributed to him, together with thirty-three *Hymns*, a mock-epic called *The Battle of the Frogs and Mice*, and a few *Epigrams*. *The Iliad* is the story of the Trojan War and the exploits of Achilles while *The Odyssey* tells of the wanderings of Odysseus on his way home to Ithaca after that war — two slightly related stories that one man might well have told, but many modern scholars are doubtful as to whether the two epics were written by the same person, since they differ considerably in structure and style. The provenance of the *Hymns*, the *Epigrams* and the mock-epic is equally uncertain. It is probable that an author, or perhaps a story-teller, named

Homer did exist at some period, and he may well have been sufficiently celebrated to be remembered; it has been suggested, however, that whoever he was and whether or not he was blind (as tradition maintains he was), the works which are commonly called his were probably in existence long before he was born, that he then edited them, as it were, and passed them on to future generations, who added their own alterations before the final versions were written down and copied in a standard form. On the other hand, other authorities incline to the view that, despite the stylistic differences, *The Iliad* and *The Odyssey* were in fact written by the same person and have been preserved in much the form in which their author left them. Whatever the experts may say, the two great narrative poems will no doubt continue to be described, if only for the sake of convenience, as 'by Homer', and they will be translated and studied as assiduously as they have been for centuries. Not that Homer has always been accorded the same degree of reverence — he was in some decline, for instance before interest was revived during the eighteenth century — and nowadays, when Greek is not a required part of all education, far fewer people can read him in the original than was true a hundred years ago. However, it is not difficult to find one of the many existing translations, and although these may never be able to capture the full beauty and majesty of the Greek poetry, at least they make available the two greatest legends of the Ancient world (which may, incidentally, although they are in epic verse form, be regarded in some ways as the first novels in Western literature). In any case, some of the translations, notably those by E.V. Rieu, possess a high literary quality of their own.

Hood, Thomas (1799–1845) The son of a London bookseller, Thomas Hood was fortunate enough to be taught by an enlightened schoolmaster who encouraged his interest in reading and writing. After spending some time in Dundee, during which he began to submit his work to various magazines, he returned to London and studied engraving. He was later to use that skill to illustrate some of his work. In 1821, thanks to the good offices of his friends, he was appointed sub-editor of the *London Magazine*, and in this position he came to know a great many of the literary luminaries of the time, including Clare, de Quincey, Hazlitt and Lamb. His first book, *Odes and Addresses*, published in 1825, was written in collaboration with his brother-in-law, J.H. Reynolds. In 1827 he published *The Plea of the Midsummer Fairies*, a collection of poetry showing the influence of Keats, while *The Dream* *of Eugene Aram* appeared in 1829. However, his real talent was for humorous verse, of which he wrote a great deal and in which he indulged his predilection for puns. He edited several magazines for short periods between 1829 and 1843, including the *Comic Annual* and his own *Hood's Magazine*. His health was always precarious, and he never recovered sufficiently to leave the sick-bed to which he had taken in 1843, but he continued to work, and it was at this time that he wrote that very popular work 'The Song of the Shirt', a savage attack on sweated labour which was published anonymously in *Punch*.

Hooker, Richard (*c*.1553–1600) A native of Exeter, Devonshire, England, Richard Hooker was a distinguished Hebrew scholar at Corpus Christi College, Oxford. He became a priest, and wrote a major work defending the Anglican Church. This was his *Laws of Ecclesiastical Politie*, of which five volumes came out between 1593 and 1597. The remaining three were published posthumously. His marriage was curious — he apparently asked his landlady to choose him a wife; she selected her daughter, Joan, who was neither comely nor equipped with a good dowry; he had agreed to abide by her choice, and did so.

Hope, Anthony (1863–1933) The son of a London clergyman, Sir Anthony Hope Hawkins became a lawyer after completing his education at Balliol College, Oxford. He wrote some pieces for the *Westminster Gazette*, and then in 1894, using the pseudonym Anthony Hope, published *The Prisoner of Zenda* (for which he invented the country Ruritania). Its enormous success allowed him to give up his practice and devote himself to writing. He produced a number of other novels, including *Rupert of Hentzau*, published in 1898, a sequel to *The Prisoner of Zenda*.

Hopkins, Gerard Manley (1844–89) The English poet Gerard Manley Hopkins was born at Stratford, Essex, England, and educated at Highgate School and Balliol College, Oxford. He was an outstanding scholar, and as a boy had shown a propensity for verse. At Oxford, where he met his life-long friend, the poet Robert Bridges, he wrote a great deal of poetry. The Oxford Movement (a High Church sect within the Church of England) was flourishing, and Cardinal Newman, who had become a Roman Catholic in 1845, published his *Apologia pro Vita Sua* in 1864; under these influences, Hopkins himself joined the Roman Catholic Church in 1866, and two years later became a Jesuit. For a period of eight years he taught, and also studied theology, writing little, but in 1876, much moved by the loss of the *Deutschland* in the December of the previous year, he wrote 'The

Wreck of the Deutschland'. He attempted to have it published in the Jesuit periodical *The Month*, but it was rejected as being too obscure. In fact, hardly any of Hopkins' work appeared in print during his lifetime. This was partly because he was reluctant to publish without the approval of his religious superiors, and partly because his poems were little understood at the time. Nevertheless, despite this rejection, he was not totally discouraged, and continued to produce poems. 'Pied Beauty', which is probably his most frequently quoted work ('Glory be to God for dappled things ...'), was written while he was preparing for ordination in 1877. After becoming a priest he worked in a number of parishes before returning to an academic life. In 1884 he was appointed Professor of Greek at University College, Dublin, where he stayed until his death of typhoid fever five years later. Although his poetry had been admired by many of his friends, it was almost totally unknown to the public at large. He left many of his papers to his

The English poet Gerard Manley Hopkins at the age of fourteen. This watercolour portrait was painted by his aunt, Anne Eleanor Hopkins.

old friend Robert Bridges, but it was not until 1918 that Bridges published a volume of his *Poems*. At first the poetry was little appreciated, and those who believed Hopkins to be a major poet were in a tiny minority. Gradually, however, his reputation grew, and his work came to be seen as of very considerable quality. In certain quarters it has been regarded with little short of veneration. Hopkins is undoubtedly a great and innovative poet, but the reason for this excessive adulation lies perhaps in the individuality of his style. He devoted a great deal of thought to his theories of poetry, encapsulated, as it were, in the words he invented or applied to his work − 'inscape', 'instress' and 'sprung rhythm'. The first two of these refer to the essential quality of a thing and the way in which an observer becomes aware of it; 'sprung rhythm' is a system of scansion based on the stresses on words rather than on syllables, and is a throw-back, to some extent, to the rules which governed poetry in the Middle Ages. To the general public, the hallmarks of Hopkins' poetry are the alliterations and the coupled words ('Fresh-firecoal chestnut-falls').

Horace (65–8BC) The Roman poet Quintus Horatius Flaccus, known as Horace, was born at Venusia, an ancient town in southern Italy. After some years spent in travelling and as a soldier, he settled in Rome, where under the patronage of the benevolent politician Maecenas, to whom he was introduced by Virgil, he began to produce the *Satires*, *Odes*, *Epodes* and *Epistles*, which made him famous. The *Ars Poetica*, his most important critical piece of writing, was a seminal work which had great influence for many centuries.

Horgan, Paul (1903–) The American writer Paul Horgan was born in Buffalo, New York. He is both a novelist and a historian. His novels include *The Fault of Angels*, published in 1933, *A Distant Trumpet*, in 1960, and the trilogy *Things As They Are*, *Everything to Live For* and *The Thin Mountain Air*, which came out between 1964 and 1977. He wrote many histories, and won the Pulitzer Prize in 1954 for *Great River: The Rio Grande in North American History*, and again in 1975 for *Lamy of Santa Fe*. A great devotee and friend of the composer Stravinsky, he published *Encounters with Stravinsky* in 1972.

hornbook A hornbook consisted of a sheet of paper which was mounted on wood and protected by a layer of transparent horn. It was used as a child's primer, and printed on the paper were the letters of the alphabet. Frequently a large cross was placed at the top of the page, and the alphabet was followed by the Lord's Prayer and the Roman numerals. The term was first used in the latter half of the sixteenth century.

Horne, Richard Henry (1803–84) After training at Sandhurst, Richard Henry Horne, who was born in London, joined the Mexican Navy and fought in the war against Spain. Returning to England he worked as a journalist, wrote a number of verse tragedies, and published his most famous work, the epic poem *Orion*. During this period he changed his second name from Henry to Hengist (which no doubt sounded more romantic). He corresponded with Elizabeth Barrett, giving her considerable literary encouragement, and she later helped him with his book of essays, *A New Spirit of the Age*, published in 1844. He went to Australia in 1852, staying there for fifteen years, and brought out *Australian Facts and Prospects* in 1859.

Hound of the Baskervilles, The A Sherlock Holmes novel by Sir Arthur Conan Doyle, first published in 1902.

House for Mr Biswas, A V.S. Naipaul's novel, set in Trinidad and first published in 1961, tells of an unsuccessful trader's continual search for independence and status.

Household Words The popular weekly magazine which Charles Dickens started in 1850 and edited until 1859, when it was replaced by *All the Year Round*. As well as publishing in serial form many of Dickens' own novels, the magazine was a vehicle for many other major writers of the period.

House of Mirth, The A novel by Edith Wharton in which Lily Bart brings disaster upon herself by her schemes to become rich, marry well and take a prominent position in society. It was first published in 1905.

House of the Seven Gables, The First published in 1851, this novel by Nathaniel Hawthorne relates the story of the hypocritical Judge Pyncheon of Salem, Massachusetts, and his persecution of his cousins.

House of Fame, The An uncompleted poem by Geoffrey Chaucer, in which he recounts a number of classical legends. It was probably written before 1385.

Housman, A.E. (1859–1936) The English poet Alfred Edward Housman was educated at Bromsgrove School and St John's College, Oxford. Surprisingly, he failed to pass his final exams, and for ten years worked as a clerk in the London Patent Office. However, he proved his scholarship in a number of essays on classical subjects which he wrote for learned journals, and in 1892 he was appointed Professor of Latin at University College, London. In 1896 he

Alfred Edward Housman, British poet and classical scholar, portrayed at the age of sixty-seven by Francis Dodd. His verses are marked by their melancholy and youthful dissillusionment, ascribed to his academic failure and unrequited love.

published privately his lyric sequence *A Shropshire Lad*, and then continued to work on his editions of Manilius, the five volumes of which appeared between 1903 and 1920, and of Juvenal, published in 1905. In 1911 he became the Kennedy Professor of Latin at Cambridge. The charm of *A Shropshire Lad* had slowly begun to gather admirers, and during World War I its nostalgic, pastoral mood made it very popular. A volume of *Last Poems*, which came out in 1922, was extremely successful. Fortunately, they were not in fact the last of Housman's verses, for although he appears to have written little if any poetry after 1923, he still had a number of unpublished lyrics which had been written earlier, and in the year of his death some of these appeared in *More Poems*. A further group was included in a *Memoir* written by his brother Laurence, and in 1939 his *Collected Poems* was published. In 1933 Housman gave a lecture, 'The Name and Nature of Poetry', in which he revealed his own methods of writing. His carefully constructed poems, always meticulously honed and polished, retain their popularity.

Housman, Laurence (1865–1959) Laurence Housman, the younger brother of A.E. Housman, was a very successful book illustrator but became better known as a poet, novelist and dramatist. His light and often amusing episodic plays about Queen Victoria, *Victoria Regina* and *Happy and Glorious*, were very popular when first produced in 1937 and 1945 respectively.

Howards End A novel by E.M. Forster, contrasting two families in Edwardian England. It was first published in 1910.

Howe, Julia Ward (1819–1910) The American poet Mrs Julia Ward Howe, a native of New York, was also a crusading essayist on behalf of civic liberties, including suffrage for women. She made her reputation as a poet with *Passion Flowers*, published in 1954, but is remembered now only as the author of 'The Battle Hymn of the Republic', written during the Civil War, and first published in the *Atlantic Monthly* in 1862.

Howells, William Dean (1837–1920) Born at Martin's Ferry, Ohio, William Dean Howells was the son of a printer-journalist, and at first followed his father's trade. Having helped Lincoln in his Presidential campaign, in 1861 he was appointed American consul in Venice. After five years, he returned to the United States and joined the *Atlantic Monthly*, becoming its editor in 1872, a position which he occupied for nine years, before beginning an association with *Harper's Magazine*. By the time he was thirty he had published some poetry, a book on Abraham Lincoln and accounts of travels in Italy. He now turned to fiction, and in 1872 published his first novel, *Their Wedding Journey*. Other novels followed in rapid succession, including his best-known work, *The Rise of Silas Lapham*, which appeared in 1885, *Indian Summer*, in 1886, and *A Hazard of New Fortunes* in 1890. Immensely prolific, he continued to produce novels at regular intervals until he was nearly eighty, and he also wrote a large number of plays, short stories, verse, volumes of travel and autobiography and literary criticism. His work was widely admired, and he came to be regarded as one of the foremost literary figures in the United States, and in particular as the leader of the realistic movement in fiction. He is little read nowadays, but deserves to be remembered not only for the popularity which he enjoyed in his day and for his vast industry, but because his encouragement of such writers as Henry James, Stephen Crane and many others was of crucial importance in their development.

Hoyle Edmond (1672–1769) Little is known about Edmond Hoyle except that he lived in London and was an expert in the game of whist. He gave lessons, and eventually produced a *Short Treatise on Whist*, which he later expanded to include other card-games. For many years he was regarded as the great authority – hence the saying 'according to Hoyle' – and versions of his book continue to appear, although these have been so totally revised and expanded that nothing of the original is left except his name.

Huchoun One of the minor mysteries of literature, Huchoun 'of the Awle Ryale', as he is usually known, was a fourteenth-century Scottish poet. All that is known of him is a reference in a history of Scotland written about 1420 by Andrew of Wyntoun, which suggests that Huchoun composed a number of works on the subject of King Arthur. He has been identified as Sir Hew of Eglyntoun, a prominent public figure of the time, but there is little evidence for this. Even the meaning of 'the Awle Ryale' appears to be doubtful, but it has been interpreted as 'the Royal Palace'.

Huckleberry Finn, The Adventures of A novel by Mark Twain, a sequel to *The Adventures of Tom Sawyer*, and considered to be his finest work. It was first published in 1884.

Hudibras A verse satire by Samuel Butler, the three parts of which were first published in 1662, 1663 and 1680.

Hudson, W.H. (1841–1922) William Henry Hudson was born near Buenos Aires, Argentina. His father, a farmer, was English by birth, but came from Massachusetts. Hudson stayed with his family until he was twenty-nine, and then went to London. He had already published a number of nature articles, and he now devoted his life to writing. He published his first book of stories, *The Purple Land*, in 1885, and followed it with a fantasy, *A Crystal Age*, which appeared in 1887. He had always been especially interested in birds, and wrote a number of books on ornithology, some of which became standard works. The first of these, *Argentine Ornithology*, published in 1888, was written in collaboration with P.L. Schlater, but Hudson was the sole author of *British Birds*, which appeared in 1895, and of *Birds of La Plata*, in 1920. He produced several other works with a background of natural history. Among them were *The Naturalist in La Plata*, which came out in 1892, *Idle Days in Patagonia*, in 1893, and *Nature in Downland*, in 1900. His three best-known books are the novel *Green Mansions*, published in 1904, the biographical work *A Shepherd's Life*, in 1910, and the story of his own boyhood, *Far Away and Long Ago*, in 1918.

Hughes, Richard (1900–76) Born in Surrey and educated at Charterhouse and Oxford, Richard Arthur Warren Hughes published his first book, a volume of poems entitled *Gipsy Night*, in 1922. A second collection, *Confessio Juvenis*, appeared in 1926. He achieved a minor success as a playwright, but the publication in 1929 of *A High Wind in Jamaica*, with its realistic portrayal of children, established him as a bestselling novelist. The next novel, *In Hazard*, did not appear until 1938, and there was an even longer gap before *The Fox in the Attic* came out in 1961. This was the first volume in 'The Human Predicament', his proposed sequence of novels which would chronicle the inter-war years in a mixture of fact and fiction. Only one other volume was published – *The Wooden Shepherdess*, in 1973. Hughes also brought out a collection of short stories, *A Moment of Time*, and two books for children.

Hughes, Ted (1930–) Edward James Hughes was born in Mytholmroyd, Yorkshire, England and educated at Cambridge. His first volume of poetry, *The Hawk in the Rain*, was published in 1957 and was well received. Subsequent volumes confirmed his status as a leading poet. Much of his poetry reflects his intense interest and joy in the natural world, but in a number of volumes, beginning with *Crow*, which appeared in 1970, he has chosen to make the crow the central figure in a more sombre vision of life. His prolific output includes short stories, plays, several books for children and translations. Many of his books have been illustrated by the artist Leonard Baskin, including *Flowers and Insects*, published in 1986, and he has also collaborated with photographers, notably in *Remains of Elmet* and *River*, published in 1979 and 1983 respectively. Two new collections, *Flowers and Insects* and *Moonbells and other poems*, both appeared in 1986. Ted Hughes was married to the American poet Sylvia Plath. In 1984 he became Poet Laureate.

Hughes, Thomas (1822–96) The English author Thomas Hughes was born in Berkshire, England, and educated at Rugby School and Oxford. He became a judge and a Member of Parliament. He wrote half-a-dozen books, only one of which is still remembered – *Tom Brown's School-Days*, the classic account of Rugby School and its great headmaster, Dr Arnold, which was published in 1857. In its time it was an influential work, setting an example of 'manly' behaviour for generations of schoolboys.

Hugo, Victor (1802–85) The French poet, dramatist and novelist Victor Marie Hugo was born at Besançon and educated in Spain and France. He published his first volume of poetry in 1822, and it was followed by a number of other collections which established him as a lyric poet of the highest quality. His dramatic poem, *Cromwell*, was published in 1827, and in a Preface to it he set forth the principles of the Romantic movement. His revolutionary approach to drama was demonstrated in the first of his major works, the play *Hernani*, which was greeted, when it was produced in 1830, with a storm of protest from diehard critics who disapproved of the flouting of all the rules of French classical theatre. He wrote many more plays, including the verse drama *Ruy Blas*, which was first seen in 1838. In 1841 his literary status was confirmed with his election, at the comparatively early age of thirty-eight, to the *Académie Française*. The two great novels, *Notre Dame de Paris* (*The Hunchback of Notre Dame*) and *Les misérables*, appeared in 1831 and 1862 respectively, but there were numerous other major works of fiction, including *Les travailleurs de la mer* (*Toilers of the Sea*), published in 1866, and *Quatre-vingt-treize* (*Ninety-three*), a story of the French Revolution, in 1873. *La légende des siècles*, (*The Legend of the*

Victor Hugo's political convictions sent him into exile to the Channel Islands for twenty years. He is pictured here on the balcony of his house in Guernsey.

Centuries) published in three volumes between 1859 and 1883, and completed posthumously with a further two volumes, was a kind of history of mankind, a philosophical epic in verse comparable in some respects to Dante's *Divine Comedy*. Hugo was also a politician. He campaigned vigorously on behalf of many causes, and his distaste for the venality of the Second Republic under Charles Louis Napoleon Bonaparte caused him, in 1851, to go into a twenty-year exile in Guernsey. He returned to France in 1870, to engage in politics again and to be increasingly admired as one of the greatest writers that France has produced.

Hulme, T.E. (1883–1917) Thomas Ernest Hulme was born in Staffordshire, England, and was educated at Cambridge. His literary criticism, in which he preached against the Romantic influence, was important in the Imagist movement. His own output of poetry was extremely small: *The Complete Poetical Works of T.E. Hulme*, which appeared in *The New Age*, in 1912, consisted of five poems only, although a few other poems were published after his death. He was killed in action during Word War I.

Humanists, The A term used to cover the writers who, from the fifteenth century onwards, revived in Europe the study of the classical writings of ancient Greece and Rome. In England, the movement reached its height in the early sixteenth century, when such men as Erasmus, Sir Thomas More, William Grocyn and John Colet became the leaders of the English Reformation.

Hume, David (1711–76) The philosopher, economist and historian David Hume was born in Edinburgh. After leaving Edinburgh University, he spent three years in France, and while there wrote his *Treatise of Human Nature*, published in two volumes in 1739, with a third volume in 1740. This may be considered his most important work, since, although later works expanded and refined his beliefs, it contained the essence of his philosophical views concerning the relationship between reason, experience and instinct in their influence on human behaviour. His *Essays*, appearing in 1741 and 1742, met with some success, and these were followed in 1748 and 1751 by the *Enquiry concerning Human Understanding* and the *Enquiry concerning the Principals of Morals*. He also published in 1751 his *Political Discourses*, which established his reputation in Europe, where he was more admired than in Britain. The first of the nine volumes of the *History of Great Britain*, from the Roman invasion to the end of the reign of James II, appeared in 1754, subsequent volumes coming out until

1762. Another major work, published in 1757, was *Four Dissertations: The Natural History of Religion, Of the Passions, Of Tragedy, Of the Standard of Taste.*

Humphry Clinker, The Expedition of A novel in epistolary form, telling the story of an adventurous journey to Scotland and back. Published in 1771, it is generally considered to be Tobias Smollett's finest work.

Hunt, Leigh (1784–1859) James Henry Leigh Hunt was born in Middlesex, England, and educated at Christ's Hospital. The verses he wrote while at school were published in 1801 as *Juvenilia*. He became a journalist, and as the editor of a number of periodicals, many of them started in collaboration with his brother John Hunt, published poetry and essays by, among others, Shelley, Keats, Byron, Lamb and Hazlitt, as well as his own work. His long poem, *The Story of Rimini*, appeared in 1816, and was followed by other volumes of poetry, including *Foliage*, in 1818. Although the poems 'Abou Ben Adhem' and 'Jenny kiss'd me' remain popular, Leigh Hunt was perhaps more successful as an essayist than as a poet. His several collections of articles on a variety of subjects, ranging from Edmund Spenser to the village of Kensington, where he lived for many years, were very successful. He also wrote plays, edited the works of some of the Restoration dramatists, and produced in 1850 an exuberant *Autobiography*.

Hunting of the Snark, The A long nonsense poem by Lewis Carroll, first published in 1876.

Hutchinson, Lucy Mrs Lucy Hutchinson was born in 1620. After her husband's death in 1664 she wrote her *Memoirs of the Life of Colonel Hutchinson*. It provides a fascinating account of England at the time of the Civil War. It was not published until 1806, when it also included some autobiographical material.

Huxley, Aldous (1894-1963) A grandson of the biologist T.H. Huxley, Aldous Leonard Huxley was born at Godalming, Surrey, England, and educated at Eton and Oxford. He had planned to study medicine, but a serious eye complaint left him nearly blind, and he was forced to abandon the idea. Instead, he became a journalist, and published his first book of poems, *The Burning Wheel*, in 1916. More poetry followed, and then, after *Limbo*, a collection of short stories, had appeared, his first novel, *Crome Yellow*, made his reputation as a witty and cynical writer when it came out in 1921. His next book *Mortal Coils*, published in 1922, was another volume of short stories, and included one of his best-known short works, 'The Giaconda Smile'. It was followed by the novels *Antic Hay*, in 1923,

A cartoon of Aldous Huxley by Sir David Low.

Those Barren Leaves, in 1925, and *Point Counter Point*, in 1928. He achieved a major success in 1932 with his prophetic story of the future, *Brave New World*. He published several more novels, including *Eyeless in Gaza*, in 1936, *Ape and Essence*, in 1948, and *The Genius and the Goddess*, in 1955, and some collections of short stories, but after emigrating to the United States in 1938 and settling in California, he also produced a number of non-fiction works. Among these were *The Perennial Philosophy*, which appeared in 1946 and was the first of a series of books in which he wrote of art and reality; *The Devils of Loudun*, examining a case of mass sexual hysteria; and the two books, *The Doors of Perception* and *Heaven and Hell*, which, when published in 1954 and 1956, caused considerable controversy because they described Huxley's experiences under the influence of LSD and mescalin.

Huxley, T.H. (1825–95) The biologist Thomas Henry Huxley was born at Ealing, on the outskirts of London. He was educated in medicine at the University of London and began his career as a surgeon in the Royal Navy. He wrote a number of papers on the marine biology of the Australian waters, which he had surveyed during service on HMS *Rattlesnake*. His work challenged many previously held zoological views, and was much admired. He was appointed Professor of Natural History at the Royal School of Mines in 1854, and his public lectures were popular. The definitive editions of his *Collected Essays* and his *Scientific Memoirs* were published posthumously.

Huysmans, Joris Karl (1848–1907) The French writer Joris Karl Juysmans (born Charles Marie Georges Huysmans) was a Parisian. His first volume of poetry, *Le drageoir aux épices*, was published in 1874. His novels portrayed the lives of the poor and depressed, in the so called 'decadent' style, notably *Là-bas*, which was concerned with black magic and satanism in Paris. His later novels included *En route*, which appeared in 1895, and *La cathédrale*, in 1898.

Hyde, Douglas (1860–1949) Born in Roscommon, Ireland, and educated at Trinity College, Dublin, Douglas Hyde was an academic, a politician, and a writer. A fervent patriot, he founded the Gaelic League in 1893, and many of his writings were concerned with native Irish traditions and literature. The most notable of his books were *The Love Songs of Connacht* and *A Literary History of Ireland*. He was one of the founders of the Abbey Theatre, and his play *Casadh an tSúgáin*, was the first in Erse to be given a professional performance. In 1938 he became the first President of Eire.

I

I, Claudius The remarkable novel by Robert Graves, published in 1934, in which he recreated the life of the Emperor Claudius, who reigned in Rome from AD41 to AD54. The sequel, *Claudius the God*, appeared in the same year.

Ibánez Vicente Blasco (1867–1928) The Spanish novelist Vicente Blasco Ibánez was born in Valencia. He was imprisoned several times for his activities as a republican agitator, and eventually chose exile in Paris. He published several novels, the best known of which are *Sangre y arena* (*Blood and Sand*), which appeared in 1908, and *Los cuatros jinetes del apocalipsis* (*The Four Horsemen of the Apocalypse*), published in 1916.

Ibsen, Henrik (1828-1906) Born in Skien, Norway, Henrik Ibsen spent the early years of his life in considerable poverty. He received little formal

education, and was apprenticed at the age of fifteen to an apothecary, by whom he was employed for seven unhappy years. In 1850 he went to Christiana (Oslo), attempted to earn his living as a journalist, and published a play in verse, *Catalina*, using the pseudonym Brynjolf Bjarme. In the following year he became playwright-in-residence at a small theatre in Bergen, and there he wrote a number of plays,

An imaginative illustration by Arthur Rackham to Ibsen's mock-heroic fantasy *Peer Gynt*. Ibsen, the father of modern drama, abandoned the Scribean formula of nineteenth-century plays. The twin themes, that the individual, not the group, is of paramount importance and that the denial of love is the one unforgivable sin, run through all his plays.

A typical nineteenth-century portrayal of the once controversial Norwegian playwright Henrik Ibsen. His plays, which originally shocked society by their outspoken denial of current bourgeois morality, are now classics.

without, however, achieving great success. Back in Christiana in 1857, he again struggled to make a living, but it was not until 1866 that he gained recognition with his satirical drama, *Brand*. Its success was supplemented by the award of a pension by the Norwegian parliament. *Brand* was followed in 1867 by *Peer Gynt*, the great verse allegory which can be regarded as his masterpiece. During the next years he wrote more plays, revised earlier work, and in 1871 published a collection of his lyric poetry. He then decided to abandon verse and to work for the theatre. The first of his prose plays was *The Pillars of Society*, and this was also the first of his dramas to be seen in English translation, when it was performed in William Archer's translation in 1880. *A Doll's House*, which appeared in Norway in 1879, was widely translated – the English version was produced in 1889 – and was greeted everywhere with outrage because of Ibsen's unfashionable plea for the emancipation of women. Even more violent reactions came with

Ghosts in 1881. The next plays were, however, less controversial, although they were equally concerned with social problems. These were the comedy *An Enemy of the People*, in 1882, the dramas *The Wild Duck*, in 1884, and *Rosmersholm*, in 1886, and the mystical play *The Lady from the Sea*, in 1888. Then in 1890 Ibsen was again at the centre of controversy when *Hedda Gabler* appeared, although some critics, such as Bernard Shaw, were enthusiastic when *Ghosts* and *Hedda Gabler* were produced in England in 1891. *The Master Builder*, regarded by many critics as the finest of his prose plays, followed in 1892, and three more plays were to come: *Little Eyolf*, in 1894, *John Gabriel Borkman*, in 1896, and *When We Dead Awaken*, in 1900. Although critical acclaim was sparing outside Norway, at least in his own country, where Ibsen was recognised as the greatest of all Norwegian writers, this prophet was far from being without honour. Before long, however, the rest of the world came to realize not only that he was a major playwright but also that he had single-handedly revolutionized the drama. No dramatist previously had written about ordinary people with such power and realism, ignoring traditional dramatic extravagances, nor had any dared to tackle subjects of social and political significance so directly. His influence on drama throughout the world was immeasurable. His outstanding achievement was perhaps to have written crusading works in which his preaching never lost sight of the human qualities of his characters, and because his plays, although classics, are alive and entertaining, they are still frequently performed and enjoyed today.

Idiot, The A major novel by Fyodor Dostoevsky, first published in 1868.

idyll A short poem, usually with a pastoral theme, an alternative term to 'eclogue'. However, an idyll can also be a narrative poem, and in this sense it is used, for instance, in Tennyson's *The Idylls of the King*.

Idylls of the King, The A group of poems by Tennyson in which he retold the legends of King Arthur and the Knights of the Round Table. The poems were written and published over a period of thirty years, and were not gathered together until 1891.

Iliad, The The great epic by the Greek poet Homer (if such a person in fact existed and was its author – *see* under Homer). It tells of the Trojan War, which began when Paris, Prince of Troy, abducted Helen, the wife of Menelaus, and is particularly concerned with the feud between Achilles and Agamemnon and the former's final conflict with Hector.

Il Penseroso A poem by John Milton, first published in 1645. In praise of contemplation, it is complemented by the joyful 'L'Allegro'.

imagism A poetic movement during the second decade of the twentieth century. Strongly influenced by the artistic philosophy of T.E. Hulme, the Imagist poets reacted against Romanticism and sought to avoid symbolism and abstraction and to use images for their own direct value. Leading exponents included Ezra Pound, Hilda Doolittle, Richard Aldington and Amy Lowell.

Imlay, Gilbert (c.1754–c.1828) The American writer Gilbert Imlay was born in New Jersey. He left America in 1783 and lived for some years in London, where he formed an attachment for Mary Wollstonecraft. In 1792 he published *A Topographical Description of the Western Territory of North America*, and in 1793 brought out a novel, *The Emigrants*, written in the form of letters and set in Pennsylvania.

Immortals, The A name given to the members of the *Académie Française*, partly because their work is assumed to have lasting fame and also, perhaps, because any vacancies among the forty members are immediately filled.

Importance of Being Earnest, The The most popular of all Oscar Wilde's comedies, which approaches farce in its absurdities. Sub-titled 'A Trivial Comedy for Serious People', it was first presented in 1895.

imprimatur A Latin word meaning 'let it be printed', imprimatur is in effect a licence to print a book or other work. It is generally used by an authority, such as the Roman Catholic Church, to signify its approval (or, at least, its lack of disapproval) of the work in question.

Inchbald, Mrs Elizabeth (1753–1821) An English novelist and playwright, Mrs Elizabeth Inchbald was born Elizabeth Simpson in Suffolk. She left home in 1772 to become an actress on the London stage, and was married shortly after to an actor by the name of Joseph Inchbald. She wrote a number of plays, including *Wives as They Were and Maids as They Are*, *Lover's Vows* (which features in Jane Austen's *Mansfield Park*) and *I'll Tell You What*. Her best-known works are the two novels *A Simple Story*, published in 1791, and *Nature and Art*, which appeared in 1796.

incunabula The term given to books printed before 1501, when the art of printing was 'in its cradle' – the literal meaning of the Latin from which the word is derived.

Index Expurgatorius A list of passages which must be expurgated before the works containing them can be permitted reading for Roman Catholics. The term is wrongly used to refer to a list of banned books, which should properly be called the 'Index Librorum Prohibitorum'.

Inferno, The The first part of Dante's *Divine Comedy*. It is a description of hell, through which the poet is guided by Virgil, and which is depicted as a huge hollow cone reaching to the centre of the earth. The souls suffering there are placed at various levels according to the nature of their sins, which are divided into the three main categories of incontinence, brutishness and – worst of all – malice, these being based on Aristotle's classification of vices.

Inge, William (1913–73) The American playwright William Inge was born in Independence, Kansas, and educated at Kansas University. His first play, *Farther Off From Heaven*, was produced in 1947, and he achieved a major success with *Come Back, Little Sheba* in 1950. He won the Pulitzer Prize in 1953 for *Picnic*. Several more plays followed, including *Bus Stop*, in 1955, and *A Loss of Roses*, in 1959. He was also a novelist, and *Good Luck, Miss Wyckoff* proved popular when it was published in 1971.

In Memoriam, A.H.H. A long poem by Tennyson, written in memory of his friend Arthur Henry Hallam, who died in 1833 at the tragically early age of twenty-two. The poem, written over a long period of time, was first published in 1850.

Innocents Abroad, The A comic account of travels in Europe by Mark Twain, first published in book form in 1869.

interludes A term used to describe short plays, usually of a broadly comic nature and often in doggerel verse, which were performed by small companies of professional or amateur actors for the entertainment of royal, noble or otherwise well-to-do audiences. Interludes might be given at a banquet or in the interval during a performance of a long play. They were popular during the fifteenth and sixteenth centuries.

Invisible Man, The A powerful novel by Ralph Waldo Ellison, first published in 1952.

Invisible Man, The A novel by H.G. Wells, first published in 1897. Claude Rains played the title role in the classic screen version.

Ionesco, Eugène (1912–) The Romanian-born French playwright Eugène Ionesco was educated in Bucharest and Paris. He is one of the leading exponents of the Theatre of the Absurd. His plays include *The Bald Prima Donna*, first seen in 1950, *The Lesson*, in 1951, and *Rhinoceros*, in 1959. He has written much more for the theatre, but comparatively few of his other plays have been translated into English. He has also produced many works in other genres, including fiction, autobiography, articles and essays, screenplays and ballets.

Irving, John (1942–) The American novelist John Winslow Irving was born in New Hampshire. He published his first novel, *Setting Free the Bears*, in 1968, *The Water-Method Man* followed in 1972 and *The 158-Pound Marriage* in 1974. Already noted as a writer with a highly individual voice, he achieved a major success in 1978 with *The World According to Garp*. *The Hotel New Hampshire* appeared in 1981.

Irving, Washington (1783–1859) The son of an English merchant, Washington Irving was born in New York. He qualified as a lawyer, but did not practise, and embarked on a career as a writer. In 1808 he published *Salmagundi, or the Whim-Whams and Opinions of Launcelot Langstaff and others*, a collection of humorous pieces which he had written in collaboration with his brother and with a friend by the name of J.K. Paulding. In the following year came his two-volume *History of New York from the Beginning of the World to the End of the Dutch Dynasty* by 'Diedrich Knickerbocker', a work which firmly established his reputation as a humorist. Troubles with his family business forced him to abandon writing for the next decade, but in 1819 and 1820, while he was living in England, *The Sketch Book of*

Christian Schussele's 'Washington Irving and his literary friends at Sunnyside' (1864). *Left to right:* Tuckerman, Holmes, Simms (*foreground*), Halleck, Hawthorne, Longfellow, Willis, Prescott, Irving, Paulding, Emerson, Bryant, Kennedy, Cooper and Bancroft.

Geoffrey Crayon, Gent was serialized in New York, and in 1820 was published in book form in London. This work contained not only amusing sketches of English life, but also those enduring tales 'Rip Van Winkle' and 'The Legend of Sleepy Hollow'. *Bracebridge Hall* and *Tales of a Traveller* followed in 1822 and 1824. A journey to Spain then inspired Irving to more serious work, and in 1828 and 1829 he brought out his *History of the Life and Voyages of Christopher Columbus* and *The Voyages and Discoveries of the Companions of Columbus*. Two other, less serious works also resulted from his long residence in Spain. In 1832 he returned to the United States, and four years later published *Astoria*, a history of a fur-trading settlement in Oregon. Next came *The Adventures of Captain Bonneville*, in 1837, an account of an explorer. In 1842 he was appointed American ambassador to Spain, and occupied the post for four years. His next works were a *Life of Oliver Goldsmith, with Selections from his Writings*, which appeared in 1849, and *The Lives of Mahomet and his Successors*, in 1849 and 1850. He then began work on his exhaustive *Life of George Washington*, completing it just before his death. It was published in five volumes between 1855 and 1859. One of the most successful of American authors in his day, Irving may now be largely forgotten as a biographer, but is still warmly remembered as a humorist and teller of tales.

Isherwood, Christoher (1904–86) Christopher William Bradshaw Isherwood was born in Cheshire, England, and educated at Repton and Cambridge. He began to write while at university, and published his first novel, *All the Conspirators*, in 1928. A second novel, *The Memorial*, appeared in 1932, and then in 1935 and 1939 came the two books, *Mr Norris Changes Trains* and *Goodbye to Berlin*, which resulted from a four year residence in Berlin, and which established his reputation more firmly than before. His account in *Goodbye to Berlin* of the cabaret entertainer, Sally Bowles, became the basis of John Van Druten's play, *I am a Camera*, and of the musical, *Cabaret*. In the period between the publication of these two books he had collaborated with W.H. Auden on the plays *The Dog Beneath the Skin, The Ascent of F6* and *On the Frontier*, produced in 1935, 1936 and 1938, and on the account of their travels in China, *Journey to a War*, which appeared in 1939. In 1938 he had also published *Lions and Shadows*. He and Auden left England for the United States in January 1939, an emigration which was not admired in Britain, since it seemed clear that they had gone to avoid the threat of war. Isherwood settled in California, and became an American citizen in 1946. He wrote screenplays, a number of novels, including *Prater Violet*, which appeared in 1945, and *A Single Man*, in 1962, and translated and wrote books which set out to make the philosophy of Hinduism accessible to the English-speaking world. His translation of the *Bhagavad-gítá* appeared in 1944. Among his last works was *Christopher and His Kind*, in which he wrote freely of his early homosexual experiences.

Ivanhoe An historical novel by Sir Walter Scott, set in England at the time of Richard Coeur de Lion and Robin Hood. It was first published in 1819.

J

Jacobs, W.W. (1863–1943) Willian Wymark Jacobs was born in Wapping, London, where his father was manager of a wharf. He wrote short stories for various magazines, and published a collection, *Many Cargoes*, in 1896. He wrote several novels, and other volumes of short stories appeared, including *Light Freights*, which came out in 1901. His best-known work is probably the story 'The Monkey's Paw', a grisly tale of the supernatural which became very popular when he turned it into a one-act play.

James I (1566-1625) King James I of England, who was also James VI of Scotland, was the only son of Mary, Queen of Scots. He reigned from 1603 to 1625. As well as the famous *A Counterblaste to Tobacco*, which appeared in 1604, he wrote many poems, a treatise on Scottish poetry, and works of both a political and religious nature. A conference, which he called in 1604 to settle differences within various religious factions of the time, resulted in the preparation, under his authority as head of the Church of England, of a new English version of the Bible. This, the Authorized Version, is often referred to as the 'King James Bible'.

James, Henry (1843–1916) The most distinguished member of a literary family, Henry James was born in New York. His father, also Henry James, was a well-known author of theological works, and his brother William built a reputation in the field of psychology. The young Henry James was brought up in Europe, where he was educated, and returned to the United States in

A fine portrait of Henry James by John Sargent, painted in 1913, three years before the writer's death.

1860 with the intention of studying law at Harvard. But he soon turned to literature, and his first short piece of fiction, 'The Story of a Year', was published in the *Atlantic Monthly* in 1865. Many more stories and articles appeared in American magazines during the ensuing years, and William Dean Howells, sub-editor and later editor of the *Atlantic Monthly*, gave him considerable encouragement. In 1869 James returned to Europe, eventually settling in England, which he came to love and to regard as a spiritual as well as a physical home. He became a British subject in 1915. His first short novel, *Watch and Ward*, was published in 1871. Next came *Transatlantic Sketches* and *A Passionate Pilgrim*, both appearing in 1875. A more important novel, *Roderick Hudson*, was serialized in the *Atlantic Monthly* in 1875, and was followed by *The American* in 1877. Another short novel, *Daisy Miller*, brought him acclaim on both sides of the Atlantic when it was published in 1878, and numerous major works of fiction, as well as a long list of short stories, were produced from this time on. The novels include *Washington Square* and *Portrait of a Lady*, which both appeared in 1881, *The Bostonians*, in 1886, *The*

Aspern Papers, in 1888, *What Maisie Knew*, in 1897, and *The Awkward Age*, in 1898. 1898 also saw the publication of the novella, *The Turn of the Screw*, one of the most chilling stories ever written, which was later to be used as the basis of an opera by Benjamin Britten. By this time James had removed from London to Lamb House in Rye, a small town on the Sussex coast, and it was there that he spent the rest of his life and wrote the last novels, *The Wings of the Dove*, published in 1902, *The Ambassadors*, in 1903, and *The Golden Bowl*, in 1903. At his death he left two unfinished novels, *The Ivory Tower* and *The Sense of the Past*. Although he is always thought of as a novelist, Henry James wrote a large number of non-fiction books, including *A Life of Hawthorne*, which appeared in 1879, collections of essays, travel books, and works of literary criticism, such as *French Poets and Novelists*, published in 1878. In one area only he was unsuccessful, for none of the plays that he wrote ever survived for long on the stage, and it is perhaps ironic that one of his novels, *Washington Square*, should have been so successful when dramatized by Ruth and Augustus Goetz under the title *The Heiress*. Finally, among his works, mention must

Lamb House in Rye, where the novelist Henry James lived from 1898 until his death in 1916.

be made of the three volumes of autobiography which he wrote in his later days. These were *A Small Boy and Others* and *Notes of a Son and a Brother*, published in 1913 and 1914 respectively, and *The Middle Years*, which he did not complete and which was published posthumously in 1917. Henry James and Joseph Conrad were, without question, the two most important novelists working at the turn of the century. There are some readers who find James less approachable than Conrad, largely because of his predilection for long, complex sentences, hung about with strings of subordinate clauses. In fact, his writing is careful, highly polished and, although it may be regarded as often impressionistic rather than direct, it is very far from impenetrable and has considerable rewards to offer to those who persevere. James was a magnificent chronicler of his times, and had an immense psychological insight into his characters, whom he depicted always with great subtlety.

James, M.R. (1862–1936) Montague Rhodes James, who was born near Bury St Edmunds, Suffolk, England, was a scholar of considerable distinction. In 1904 he published his *Ghost Stories of an Antiquary*, followed in 1911 with *More Ghost Stories of an Antiquary*. Additional volumes appeared in 1919 and 1925, and in 1931 came *The Collected Ghost Stories of M.R. James*. He is widely regarded, especially for such tales as 'Oh, Whistle and I'll Come to You, My Lad', as one of the foremost practitioners of this genre, which his fine prose raised to a high literary level.

James, P.D. (1920–) Phyllis Dorothy James was educated in Cambridge. She became a senior civil servant. Her first detective story, *Cover Her Face*, was published in 1962, and it was immediately recognized that a new mistress of the genre had appeared – a novelist, rather than a mere concoctor of crime puzzles. Among her subsequent books are *A Mind to Murder*, in 1963, *An Unsuitable Job for a Woman*, in 1972, *The Skull Beneath the Skin*, in 1982, and the long and ambitious *A Taste for Death*, in 1986.

James, William (1842–1910) Born in New York, William James was the elder brother of Henry James. Two years after completing his education at Harvard he was appointed a lecturer there in anatomy and physiology but before long he developed an interest in psychology and philosophy and eventually held professorships in those subjects. He is credited with the origination of the phrase 'stream of consciousness'. He attracted wide attention in 1890 with the publication of *Principles of Psychology*, and was seen as the principal spokesman for the empirical theories of psychology. He published a number

of other books, including *The Varieties of Religious Experience*, in 1902, *A Pluralistic Universe*, in 1909, and *Essays in Radical Empiricism*, in 1912. One of his most important works, and the one which most clearly established his philosophical position, was *Pragmatism – a New Name for Some Old Ways of Thinking*, which appeared in 1907.

Jane Eyre A novel by Charlotte Brontë, first published in 1847 under the pseudonym Currer Bell. It is the classic romantic story of the poor governess Jane Eyre, the forbidding Mr Rochester and the terrible secret of Thornfield Hall. It has been widely imitated, and was the prototype for the spate of so-called Gothic romances popular in recent years.

Jefferies, Richard (1848–87) The English naturalist Richard Jefferies was born in Wiltshire. He developed early a deep, instinctive sympathy for the countryside, and seemed to many of his eventual readers to see it with fresh and interesting eyes. In 1873 he began to write articles on farming for *Fraser's Magazine*, and became well-known in 1878 with the publication of *The Gamekeeper at Home*, a collection of his essays which had originally appeared in the *Pall Mall Gazette*. A number of books on similarly rural subjects were to follow, including *Wild Life in a Southern County* and *The Amateur Poacher*, both published in 1879, and *Bevis: The Story of a Boy*, which appeared in 1882 and was one of his most attractive books, with a particular appeal to young people. Also worthy of mention are *Life of the Fields*, which appeared in 1884, *The Open Air*, in 1885, and *Amaryllis at the Fair*, in 1887. He wrote a number of other works, including fiction. The autobiographical *The Story of My Heart* made a considerable impression when it came out in 1883.

Jeffers, Robinson (1887–1962) John Robinson Jeffers was born in Pittsburgh, Ohio, the son of an academic, and educated in Europe and at Occidental College in California. He published his first volume of poetry, *Flagons and Apples*, in 1912, and followed it in 1916 with *Californians*, but it was his third book, *Tamar and other poems*, which established him as a poet of importance and gave him a considerable following. The insignificance of man when compared to the grandeur of nature was the theme which he constantly explored in his work. *Tamar and other poems* also set the pattern for many of the collections that he brought out regularly thereafter, in which a long narrative poem, giving its title to the book, would be followed by shorter pieces. He published more than a dozen books, including *The Woman at Point Sur*, in 1927, *Descent to the Dead*, in 1931, *Give Your Heart* *to the Hawks*, in 1933, and *Hungerfield*, in 1954. He also translated the *Medea* and the *Hippolytus* of Euripides.

Jerome, Jerome K. (1859–1927) Born in London, Jerome Klapka Jerome, the son of a shopkeeper, became a clerk, a teacher, and an actor, and eventually settled to a career as a journalist. In 1885 he published *On the Stage and Off*, and then became widely known as a humorist with *Idle Thoughts of an Idle Fellow*, which appeared in 1886. *Three Men in a Boat*, his enduringly popular comic account of a few fairly disastrous days spent on the River Thames, came out in 1889. *Three Men on the Bummel*, about a vacation in Germany, was also successful when it was published in 1900, even if it did not reach the hilarious heights of the earlier book. Jerome published several other light-hearted works, and also became well-known as a playwright, especially in 1907 with *The Passing of the Third Floor Back*, a gentle morality about a Christ-like figure and his effect on the other residents in a small London hotel.

This delightful dedication appears in Jerome K. Jerome's *Three Men on a Bummel* which appeared a year after his magnificently ridiculous *Three Men in a Boat*.

TO THE GENTLE

GUIDE,

WHO LETS ME EVER GO MY OWN WAY, YET BRINGS ME RIGHT——

TO THE LAUGHTER-LOVING

PHILOSOPHER,

WHO, IF HE HAS NOT RECONCILED ME TO BEARING THE TOOTHACHE PATIENTLY, AT LEAST HAS TAUGHT ME THE COMFORT THAT THIS EVEN WILL ALSO PASS——

TO THE GOOD

FRIEND,

WHO SMILES WHEN I TELL HIM OF MY TROUBLES, AND WHO, WHEN I ASK FOR HELP, ANSWERS ONLY "WAIT!"——

TO THE GRAVE-FACED

JESTER,

TO WHOM ALL LIFE IS BUT A VOLUME OF OLD HUMOUR——

TO GOOD MASTER

Time

THIS LITTLE WORK OF A POOR

PUPIL

IS DEDICATED.

Jerrold, Douglas William (1803–57) The son of an actor, Douglas William Jerrold became a sailor during the Napoleonic Wars, but left the sea to become a printer, a journalist and a playwright. In 1829 his melodrama, *Black-eyed Susan; or, All in the Downs*, was wildly successful, and for some years he continued to write plays, the majority of which were comedies. In the meantime he had continued his activities as a journalist, and later as the editor of various magazines. From 1841 onwards he contributed regularly to *Punch*, where the articles published as *Mrs Caudle's Curtain Lectures* first appeared.

Jewett, Sarah Orne (1849–1909) The American short story writer and novelist Sarah Orne Hewett was born in South Berwick, Maine. She published her first story in the *Atlantic Monthly* in 1869, and a collection of her work, *Deephaven*, came out in 1877. She wrote three novels, some poetry and books for children, but was always happiest in the short stories and sketches in which she drew such memorable pictures of Maine and its people. Her collection, *The Country of the Pointed Firs*, was published in 1896 and was her most successful book.

Jew of Malta, The A drama by Christopher Marlowe, first performed towards the end of the sixteenth century, but not published until 1633.

Jhabvala, Ruth Prawer (1927–) Born in Cologne of Polish parentage, the novelist Ruth Prawer Jhabvala was educated at London University. She married an Indian architect and lived for some years in India, where many of her novels are set. Her first book, *To Whom She Will*, was published in 1955. Among her other novels are *Heat and Dust*, which won the Booker Prize in 1975, and *In Search of Love and Beauty*, which appeared in 1983. A selection of her best short stories, *Out of India* was published in 1987.

Jiménez, Juan Ramón (1881–1958) The major Spanish poet of his generation, Juan Ramón Jiménez was born in Andalusia and educated at the University of Seville. He published two volumes of verses, *Almas de violeta* and *Ninfeas*, in 1900. *Rimas* appeared in 1902, *Arias tristes*, in 1903, and *Elegias puras*, in 1908. His best-known work, a series of prose poems, *Platero y yo* (*Platero and I*) came out between 1914 and 1917. His last collection, *Animal de fondo*, was published in 1949. He was awarded the Nobel Prize for Literature in 1956.

John Bull's Other Island G. Bernard Shaw's play about Ireland, first presented in 1904.

John Gilpin, The Diverting History of An amusing ballad by William Cowper, first published in *The Public Advertiser* in 1782, and included with 'The Task' in the volume published in 1785.

John Halifax, Gentleman A novel by Mrs Craik (Dinah Maria Mulock), first published in 1856.

Johnson, Edward (*c*.1598–1672) Emigrating from England in 1636, Edward Johnson, who was born in Canterbury, settled in Massachusetts. Several years later he wrote *A History of New England*, which was published anonymously in London in 1653. It provides a striking account of life and attitudes at the time, but cannot be considered to be of importance as a strictly historical document.

Johnson, Lionel Pigot (1867–1902) Born in Broadstairs, Kent, England, Lionel Pigot Johnson was educated at Winchester and Oxford. He contributed to the *Yellow Book* and was a member of the Rhymers' Club, to which Richard Le Gallienne, Ernest Dowson and his friend Samuel Butler Yeats also belonged. He published *The Art of Thomas Hardy* in 1894, and a volume of *Poems* appeared in the following year. *Ireland and other poems* came out in 1897, and a collection of essays, *Post liminium*, was published posthumously after his death from alcoholism.

Johnson, Samuel (1709–84) The son of a bookseller and magistrate, Samuel Johnson was born in Lichfield, Staffordshire, England. As a child he suffered from scrofula, and at the age of three was taken to London in the hope that he would be cured if Queen Anne could be prevailed upon to touch him. She did so, without effect. He was educated at Lichfield College and Pembroke College, Oxford, but, because of his poverty, left without taking his degree. For some years he was a teacher, and during this time he married a widow, Mrs Elizabeth Porter. He opened a school, but it was a failure, and in 1737, accompanied by his pupil David Garrick, he went to London with the hope of pursuing a literary career. He spent his first months there on the edge of destitution, and then succeeded at last in obtaining employment as a parliamentary reporter for *The Gentleman's Magazine*. The anonymous publication of his poem, *London*, in 1738, was extremely successful, but brought him little financial reward. Next came a biography of a poet who had become his friend, *Life of Mr Richard Savage*, published in 1744. Although this work too came out anonymously, Johnson was known to be the author, and it enhanced his reputation to such an extent that in 1747 he was commissioned by a group of bookseller/publishers to produce a *Dictionary of the English Language*. They were prepared to pay him fifteen hundred guineas, but it took him nine years to write, and he also had to pay for his assistants. No wonder that he described a lexicographer as 'A writer of

dictionaries; a harmless drudge...'! While he was engaged on this work he also brought out, in 1749, a poem, *The Vanity of Human Wishes*, and saw his tragedy, *Irene*, produced by Garrick at Drury Lane. He continued to contribute to *The Gentleman's Magazine* and other periodicals, and from 1750 edited and largely wrote his own paper, *The Rambler*, which lasted until 1752, the year in which his wife died. The *Dictionary* was published in 1755, and immediately won the greatest acclaim. While etymologically weak, and although Johnson made no attempt to exclude his own quirky predilections and prejudices, it was written with immense gusto and wit, and it was not only instructive, but entertaining too. He was rewarded by the conferring of an honorary degree from Oxford, which no doubt gave him great pleasure, but he

This portrait of Samuel Johnson was painted by his friend and contemporary Joshua Reynolds about 1756. It was about this time that Johnson won great acclaim for his authoritative but sometimes idiosyncratic *Dictionary*.

would also have liked a greater pecuniary benefit, and the failure of Lord Chesterfield to provide him with the expected substantial patronage caused him great bitterness. He supported himself by additional journalism until 1762, when he was awarded a state pension of £300 a year, and was at last released from penury. Meanwhile he had earned further praise for his novel, *Rasselas, Prince of Abyssinia*, published in 1759, which he had written in great haste after the death of his aged mother in order to pay off the debts she had left. In 1762 James Boswell entered his life as the result of a chance meeting in a bookseller's (Johnson at first disliked him); two years later he became a member of 'The Club', along with Edmund Burke, Oliver Goldsmith and Sir Joshua Reynolds; and in 1765 he met the Thrales, who were to become his close friends. In the same year his long-awaited new edition of Shakespeare's plays was published; it was not his best work, although some of the notes and comments are valuable. Also in 1765 he was able, for the first time, to style himself 'Doctor Johnson', following the grant of an honorary doctorate at Trinity College, Dublin. His celebrated expedition to Scotland in the company of Boswell took place in 1773, and his account of it, *A Journey to the Western Islands of Scotland*, was published in 1775. His reputation was at its highest, and now Oxford followed Dublin in making him an honorary Doctor. The first four volumes of his last major work, *Lives of the English Poets*, which he was asked to undertake by forty leading London booksellers, appeared in 1779, and six more in 1781. He died in his seventy-sixth year and was buried in Westminster Abbey. One of the most extraordinary characters in the history of literature, Samuel Johnson was a boorish, ill-tempered eccentric. He was also witty, brilliant and great. He became truly, in the cliché phrase, a legend in his lifetime, and he remains one today.

Johnson's Dictionary Samuel Johnson's great work was published in 1755. It contains definitions of over forty thousand words, supported by immense numbers of literary quotations. It remained the ultimate authority on the English language for well over a hundred years, until supplanted by the *Oxford English Dictionary*.

Jolly Beggars, The A poem by Robert Burns, written in 1786, but at first published posthumously.

Jonathan Wild the Great, The Life of A satirical novel by Henry Fielding, first published in 1743 as one of his *Miscellanies*.

Jones, Henry Arthur (1851–1929) The English dramatist Henry Arthur Jones was born in Buckinghamshire. He left school early, worked for a draper, and wrote in his spare time. His first play, *Only Round the Corner*, was produced in 1878 in a provincial theatre, and in 1882 he achieved success with *The Silver King*, a melodrama written in collaboration with Henry Herman and presented in London. Immensely popular in the 1890s, he wrote a very large number of plays, the best known of which is probably *Mrs Dane's Defence*, first seen in 1900.

Jones, James (1921–) James Jones was born in Robinson, Illinois. He served with the US Army in the Pacific during World War II, and *From Here to Eternity*, his first novel, was based on his experiences. When it was published in 1951 it became an instant bestseller and won the National Book Award. It was followed by several novels, including *Some Came Running*, which appeared in 1957, *Go to the Widow-Maker*, in 1967, and *A Touch of Danger*, in 1973. Collections of short stories have also been published.

Jones, LeRoi (1934–) Everett LeRoi Jones was born in New Jersey and educated at Rutgers, Howard and Columbia universities. A militant campaigner for Black power, he has written a great many plays, beginning with *A Good Girl is Hard to Find*, presented in 1958, and has published several volumes of poetry since his first collection, *Preface to a Twenty-Volume Suicide Note*, appeared in 1961. He has now changed his name to Amiri Bakara.

Jonson, Ben (1572–1637) The son of a Scottish minister, Benjamin Jonson was born in London and educated at Westminster School. His father had died before his birth, and his mother had married again, her second husband being a master bricklayer. After leaving school, Ben Jonson worked for his stepfather, then became a soldier, and eventually joined a troupe of actors. By 1597 he was in London as a regular member of the company known as the Admiral's Men, under the management of Philip Henslowe, and was imprisoned with his fellow actors for taking part in a play called *The Isle of Dogs*, which had offended the authorities. However, it was not Henslowe's company but the Lord Chamberlain's Men who in 1598 performed his first play, the very successful *Every Man in his Humour*, in which Shakespeare played a part. In that year he was in trouble with the law again, having killed a fellow actor in a duel, but escaped being hanged by invoking an ancient law under which he claimed 'benefit of clergy'. He was fined, imprisoned and branded on his thumb as a felon, but in 1599 he was back with Henslowe and writing again. The success of *Every Man in his Humour* had revealed his true métier, and from now on he was a prolific dramatist. *Every*

ABOVE: Ben Jonson, poet, dramatist and carouser. His fierce disputes with Shakespeare at The Mermaid Tavern, a meeting place for actors and dramatists, were renowned.

RIGHT: The engraved title-page of his *Workes*.

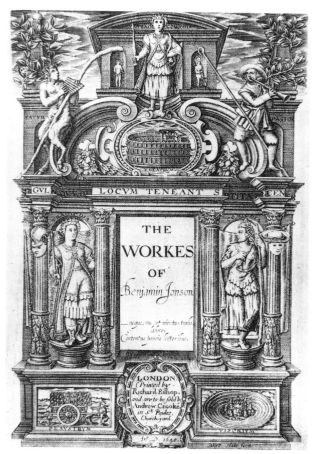

Man out of his Humour came in 1599, and *Cynthia's Revels* and *Poetaster* were performed by the Children of the Queen's Chapel in 1600 and 1601. More plays and masques followed, including the tragedy *Sejanus*, presented in 1603. A third spell in prison resulted from the play *Eastward Hoe*, a comedy written in collaboration with George Chapman and John Marston, which gave offence to the Scots. His four most important plays were written between 1605 and 1614; these are *Volpone, or the Fox, Epicene, or the Silent Woman, The Alchemist* and *Bartholomew Fair*. He was by now the most successful writer of his day, and was king of his own court at the Mermaid Tavern, where his courtiers included all the best-known poets and playwrights from Shakespeare to John Donne, and from Beaumont and Fletcher to Sir John Suckling. He journeyed to France as tutor to Sir Walter Raleigh's son, and to Scotland, where he was fêted in Edinburgh and spent some time with the Scottish poet Drummond of Hawthornden. In 1616 he published a collected edition of his works, and his pre-eminent position (and ability to turn out an unending stream of masques for performance at Court) received recognition in the form of a small pension granted to him by King James I. Because of this he is regarded as the first Poet Laureate, although the title was not in fact used. He also received an honorary degree from Oxford. In 1626 he began to write for the stage again, but his later plays, such as *The Magnetic Lady*, produced in 1631, and *The Tale of a Tub*, in 1633, were not written with the same degree of skill as those which came earlier. He was not exclusively a playwright, but also wrote an *English Grammar*, and much verse, including the *Epigrams*, published in 1616, and, of course, the lyric 'To Celia' ('Drink to me only with thine eyes …'). He was buried in Westminster Abbey under a tombstone inscribed with the words 'O rare Ben Jonson'.

Jorrocks Jaunts and Jollities A collection of comic sporting sketches by Robert Surtees, first published in 1838.

Joseph Tetralogy, The A quartet of novels by Thomas Mann. The titles were *Die Geschichten Jaakobs, Der Junge Joseph, Joseph in Ägypten* and *Joseph der Ernährer*. They were first published between 1933 and 1942.

Joseph Andrews A novel by Henry Fielding, the full title being *The History of the Adventures of Mr Joseph Andrews, and of his Friend, Mr Abraham Adams*. Originally intended as a parody of Samuel Richardson's *Pamela*, it developed into a major work. It was first published in 1742.

Josephus, Flavius (*c*.37–*c*.98) The Jewish historian and military commander Flavius Josephus gave early signs of a studious nature, but later became a determined fighter against the Romans in Palestine. Eventually captured, his life was spared by Vespasian, who became his patron. After the year AD70 he devoted himself to writing, and produced, among other works, *The Jewish War* and a history of the Jews from the Creation to AD66, *The Jewish Antiquities*.

Journal of a Tour to the Hebrides, The James Boswell's account of his travels in Scotland with Dr Johnson in 1773. It was first published in 1785.

Journal of the Plague Year, A A fictional account by Daniel Defoe of London in 1664 and 1665, first published in 1722.

Journey to the Western Islands of Scotland, A Samuel Johnson's account of his travels in Scotland with James Boswell in 1773. It was first published in 1775.

Joyce, James (1882–1941) James Augustine Aloysius Joyce was born in Dublin and educated at Jesuit schools and at University College, Dublin. After graduating, he went to Paris in 1902, ostensibly to study medicine, and spent a year there, living on the brink of starvation and writing poetry. When he returned home he met Nora Barnacle, his life-long companion, and with her left Ireland and settled for several years in Trieste, where he taught English. While he was there, his first two books were published in London. These were a volume of poetry, *Chamber Music*, which appeared in 1907, and *Dubliners*, his collection of short stories, which came out in 1914. The latter attracted the attention of the American poet Ezra Pound, who gave Joyce considerable encouragement and was instrumental in arranging publication of *A Portrait of the Artist as a Young Man* in serial form in the magazine *The Egoist* in 1914 and 1915. This autobiographical novel appeared as a book in 1916. By that time Joyce had moved to Zurich, where he and his family – Nora bore him a son and a daughter – remained until the end of World War I, after which they made their permanent home in Paris until the outbreak of World War II forced them to return to Switzerland. In 1915 Joyce had received a grant from the Royal Literary Fund, and in 1916 he was given a grant from the Civil List. These monies helped the Joyces to survive while he

James Joyce, one of this century's most influential writers, died almost blind. This portrait was painted in 1935.

was working on the next book, which was to be *Ulysses*. In the following year he was afflicted by glaucoma, and suffered from problems with his eyes for the rest of his life. A play, *Exiles*, was presented in Munich in 1918. It did not achieve popular success either then or in a later production in England. *Ulysses* was published in Paris in 1922 and immediately became famous, partly because it was banned as obscene in both Britain and the United States. Many leading literary figures of the day, including Arnold Bennett, T.S. Eliot and Ernest Hemingway, acclaimed it as a major work of literary art and one of the finest novels of the twentieth century. Virginia Woolf, on the other hand, was not alone in dismissing it with contempt. Modern authorities agree that she was wildly wrong to describe it as 'the work of a queasy undergraduate scratching his pimples', and call it, instead, a major work of literature. It is not an 'easy' book

—Joyce used all manner of experimental devices, playing exuberantly with language, abandoning many of the traditional forms of straightforward narrative, and using the 'stream of consciousness' technique—but even now, so long after it was written, it remains extraordinary, and exciting, for those who meet it for the first time. *Ulysses* remained proscribed in the United States until 1933, and was not published in England until 1936. The text that was available for the next fifty years was corrupt in many respects—words had been wrongly printed, proof corrections not made, Joyce's intended alterations not carried out—and in 1986 a new version appeared, edited by Hans Walter Gabler with Wolfhard Steppe and Claus Melchior, which was the result of years of painstaking work in an attempt to produce a definitive text. Joyce published another collection of verse, *Pomes Penyeach*, in 1927, but meanwhile was working on *Finnegans Wake*. Parts of this second major novel appeared between 1928 and 1937 under the title 'Work in Progress', and the complete novel, like *Ulysses* a very long book, was published in 1939. In it Joyce continued his experimental approach to a point approaching, or perhaps even reaching, obscurity. James Joyce's output was small—no more than five books and a play—but no writer has had greater influence in the development of the modern novel, and he may justly be acclaimed as a genius.

Jude the Obscure Thomas Hardy's last novel, first published in 1895. The tragic story of Jude Fawley and his cousin Sue Bridehead was greeted on publication by widespread condemnation.

Julius Caesar A tragedy by William Shakespeare, in which Caesar is murdered by a group of conspirators, opposed by Marc Antony. It is believed to have been written and presented in 1599, and was published in 1623.

Jung, Carl (1875-1961) The Swiss psychiatrist Carl Gustav Jung was born in Kasswyl, and obtained his degree in medicine at the University of Basle. He worked with Sigmund Freud, and was his chief disciple, from 1907 to 1913, but then left to lead a different school of psychology. He published *Psychology of Dementia Praecox*, in 1906, and followed it with many other studies in psychology.

Jungle, The The best-known novel of Upton Sinclair, which attacked the meat-packing industry of Chicago. It was first published in 1906.

Jungle Books, The *The Jungle Book* and *The Second Jungle Book*, published in 1894 and 1895, are collections of stories for children by Rudyard Kipling.

Juno and the Paycock A tragedy by Sean O'Casey set in Dublin in 1922, first presented in 1924 and published in 1925.

Just So Stories Tales 'for Little Children' by Rudyard Kipling, first published in 1902.

Juvenal (*c*.60–*c*.136) The Roman poet and satirist Decimus Junius Juvenalis was born at Aquinum in southern Italy. Comparatively little is known of his life, except what can be gleaned from the sixteen *Satires* which he left. These, which were probably written between the years 100 and 130 and are presented in five books, show him as a well-to-do country gentleman, a misogynist, and the vituperative scourge of the corrupt in government and public life.

K

Kafka, Franz (1883–1924) The Czech novelist and short story writer Franz Kafka was born in Prague. He studied law at the University of Prague, gaining his doctorate, and worked in an office dealing with workers' welfare until 1922, when tuberculosis, which had been diagnosed in 1917, forced his retirement. He wrote in German, and from 1910 kept a diary in which he analysed the workings of his mind and the depression and self-doubts from which he suffered throughout his life, and which were compounded by the feeling of isolation engendered by the fact that he was a German-speaking Jew. He became engaged to Felice

The perplexing Czech novelist Franz Kafka.

Braun, but did not marry her, and spent his last year in the company of Dora Dymant, who was with him at the time of his death in Kierling, near Vienna. The most dominant person in his life was his father, a merchant of coarse and overbearing temperament, who disapproved of his sensitive son and his literary bent. Their unhappy relationship was reflected in all Kafka's writing, and especially in the autobiographical *Letter to His Father*, which he composed in 1919. The comparatively few works which appeared during his lifetime include the long short stories, *Der Heizer* (*The Stoker*), *Das Urteil* (*The Judgement*), *Die Verwandlung* (*The Metamorphosis*) and *In Der Strafkolonie* (*In the Penal Colony*), and three books, *Betrachtung* (*Reflection*), which appeared in 1913, *Ein Landarzt* (*A Country Doctor*), in 1919, and *Ein Hungerkünstler* (*A Hunger-Artist*), in 1924. The three major novels, *Der Prozess* (*The Trial*), *Das Schloss* (*The Castle*) and *Amerika*, were not published until 1925, 1926 and 1927 respectively, when they were brought out by his friend Max Brod, who had disobeyed Kafka's wish to see them, and other miscellaneous works, destroyed after his death. Their publication brought immediate recognition of their author's extraordinary talents, especially in Germany and France, where the Existentialist writers were particularly influenced by his work, and later in the English-speaking countries. The mysterious, brooding nightmare quality of the books has given rise to the word 'kafkaesque' to describe similar works concerned with the conflict between good and evil in which the central character is surrounded by inimical authoritarian forces. They are not, perhaps, immediately accessible novels, but have received the highest critical acclaim.

Kalavela The Finnish epic poem, *Kalavela* (*Land of Heroes*), containing many ancient legends and folk stories. Handed down orally, it did not appear in print until 1822, and the first edition in English was published in 1887. It provided inspiration for the composer Sibelius in such works as 'The Swan of Tuonela'.

Kangeroo A partly autobiographical novel by D.H. Lawrence, written after he and his wife had visited Australia in 1922. It was published in 1925.

Kant, Immanuel (1724–1804) The German philosopher Immanuel Kant was born at Königsberg in East Prussia, the son of a saddler. After completing his university education he was employed for a time as a tutor. His early published writings were in the form of essays, and his first book, *A General Natural History of the Heavens*, appeared in 1755. In 1770 he at last obtained his desired position as Professor of Logic and Metaphysics at Königsberg University. In 1781 he published his major work, *Critique of Pure Reason*, in which he expressed his view that knowledge is derived from the senses and from understanding. He wrote a great many more books, a large number of which are devoted to developing the theories put forward in the *Critique of Pure Reason*.

Kantor, Mackinlay (1904–77) The American novelist Mackinlay Kantor was born in Iowa. His novels include *Long Remember*, first published in 1934, *Arouse and Beware*, in 1936, *Andersonville*, which won the Pulitzer Prize in 1955, and *Valley Forge*, in 1975. He also wrote short stories and some non-fiction.

Kaufman, George S. (1889–1961) The playwright George S. Kaufman was born in Pittsburg, Ohio. He began his career as a journalist, writing a humorous column for the *Washington Times*. He then became drama critic for the *New York Times*, and a member of the Round Table group of writers who met regularly at the Algonquin Hotel in New York. His success as a dramatist was achieved by writing in collaboration. With Marc Connelly he produced a comedy, *Dulcy*, in 1921, and a number of other light plays. He also worked with Edna Ferber, and then found his best partnership with Moss Hart. Among the plays which they wrote together are *Merrily We Roll Along*, in 1934, *You Can't Take It With You*, which won the Pulitzer Prize, *The Man Who Came to Dinner*, produced in 1939, and *George Washington Slept Here* (George Washington being translated into Queen Elizabeth for British audiences), in 1940.

Kavanagh, Patrick (1905–67) Born in County Monaghan, Ireland, Patrick Kavanagh began life as a farmer, but later became a writer. Although he published a novel and other works in prose, he is best known as a poet. His first book of verse was *Ploughman and other poems*, published in 1936. It was followed by the long poem, *The Great Hunger* which appeared in 1942. His *Collected Poems* came out in 1964.

Kazantzakis, Nikos (1883-1957) The Greek writer Nikos Kazantzakis was born in Heraklion, Crete, and educated at Athens University and in Paris. An active politician, he travelled widely after World War II, and became President of the Greek Union of Socialist Workers. His writings were extremely diverse, covering fiction, both for adults and for children, literary criticism, film scenarios, essays, and translations into modern Greek of the *Odyssey*, the *Iliad*, Dante's *Divine Comedy* and Goethe's *Faust*. His major work was the epic poem *The Odyssey: A Modern Sequel*, published in 1938, but he is best known for his novels, which include, as well as the famous *Zorba the Greek*, which appeared in 1943, *The Last Temptation of Christ*, in 1951. He published a volume of autobiography, *Report to Greco*, in 1956.

Keats, John (1795–1821) The son of the manager of a livery stable, John Keats was born at the sign of the Swan and Hoop in Moorfields, London. He was educated at a private school, and was then apprenticed to a surgeon. In 1814 he began to study medicine at Guy's and St Thomas's Hospitals, but abandoned this career in 1816, choosing instead to write poetry. He had already written some verses, and he was now befriended by Leigh Hunt and Shelley, and encouraged to publish a first volume, *Poems by John Keats*, which appeared in 1817, and which included the sonnet 'On First Looking into Chapman's Homer'. The book attracted some praise, but was harshly criticized in both *Blackwood's Magazine* and the *Quarterly Review*, at least in part on account of the author's lowly birth – the writing of poetry being apparently an occupation fit only for gentlemen. By November of that year he had completed *Endymion: A Poetic Romance*, and it was published in the late spring of 1818. It was hardly more successful than the first book. In the summer, he set off on a long walking tour of Scotland with his friend Charles Armitage Brown, but became ill and was forced to return to London by boat. Shortly afterwards *Blackwoods Magazine* and the *Quarterly Review* carried notices of *Endymion* which were even more virulent than their earlier attacks. Keats was greatly distressed by them, and more anguish followed when his youngest brother Tom fell grievously ill. He spent the last months of 1818 with Tom, who died in December. Keats went to live with his friend Armitage Brown, and it was then that he met Fanny Brawne, and fell passionately in love with her. Later they became engaged, but were unable to marry because of Keats' inability to provide for a wife. A period of great creativity ensued, in which he wrote many of his finest poems, including 'The Eve of St Agnes', 'The Eve of St Mark', 'La Belle Dame Sans Merci', 'Ode to a Nightingale', 'Ode on a Grecian Urn', 'Ode to Psyche', 'Ode on Melancholy' and 'To Autumn'. He also completed the two parts of 'Lamia', wrote and revised 'Hyperion', finished 'Otho the Great', which he had begun in collaboration with Armitage Brown, and began a tragedy, *King Stephen*. His third book, *Lamia, The Eve of St Agnes and other poems*, appeared in July, 1820. Not surprisingly, it was his most successful publication. It received much praise, and even the sternest of his critics treated it with less

cruelty. Earlier that year Keats had been taken ill with a consumptive attack, and when he recovered he went to live with the Leigh Hunts. In August he left their house and went to the Brawnes. He refused an invitation from Shelley to go to Pisa for the winter, but in September set off for Italy with his friend, the artist Joseph Severn. They established themselves in Rome, where Keats succumbed again to tuberculosis. He died in February 1821. Shelley believed that his death had been hastened by the attacks on his poetry, but, however painful he may have found them at the time, his later works show no signs of a writer forced into despair by critics. Keats is increasingly regarded as the greatest poet of his era, unsurpassed in the music of his words and in his ability to re-create the beauty of his subjects. In a short life his output was

Joseph Severn's ivory miniature of John Keats when he was twenty-four. He died two years later from consumption.

necessarily limited, although in addition to his poetry he left a number of lively, witty and profound letters. What might he have achieved had he lived longer?

Keble, John (1792–1866) Educated by his father, a clergyman, and later at Oxford, John Keble, who was born in Gloucestershire, England, himself entered the Church, and later led the High Church movement which became known as the 'Oxford Group'. He was also a poet, and was Professor of Poetry at Oxford for the ten years beginning in 1831. He published a number of books, including collections of sermons and various other religious writings, but nothing approached the success of his volume of verse, *The Christian Year*, which was published in 1827 and achieved enormous popularity, being reprinted well over a hundred and fifty times.

Kells, Book of An eighth-century copy of the Gospels in Latin, together with various tables and local records. The manuscript is particularly remarkable for the beauty of its elaborate illuminations, probably the finest Christian art of its period still in existence. It is believed to have originated at a monastery in the town of Kells, in County Meath, Ireland, but is now kept at Trinity College, Dublin.

Kelly, Hugh (1739–77) The Irish poet and dramatist Hugh Kelly was born in Killarney. He went to London in 1760, and seven years later successfully published a novel, *Memoirs of a Magdalen, or the History of Louisa Mildmay*. In 1768 his first comedy, *False Delicacy*, was produced at Drury Lane, and he followed it with a number of other plays, but then, in a reversal of the more usual sequence of events in the lives of authors, gave up literature for the law. He was less successful as a barrister than he had been as a playwright, and by the time of his death was penniless.

Kemp, William No record exists of the dates of birth and death of William Kemp, but he is known to have been an actor in 1593, and he certainly played some of the comic parts in Shakespeare's plays. His chief fame was as a dancer, and he became celebrated for dancing all the way from London to Norwich, a feat which he described in *Kemps Nine Daies Wonder, Performed in a Daunce from London to Norwich*, which was published in 1600.

Kendall, Henry C. (1839–82) Born in New South Wales, Henry Clarence Kendall was the son of a missionary. He found work in a lawyer's office, and later became a civil servant. One of the first Australian poets, he published an early collection, *Poems and Songs*, in 1862. Later volumes included *Leaves from an Australian Forest*, which appeared in 1869, and *Songs from the Mountains*, in 1880.

Kenilworth A novel, set in Elizabethan times, by Sir Walter Scott, first published in 1821.

Kennedy, John Pendleton (1795–1870) The American politician John Pendleton Kennedy was born and educated in Baltimore. He published *The Red Book*, a collection of miscellaneous writings, in 1818, and *Swallow Barn* in 1832. His best-known work, the novel *Horse-Shoe Robinson*, came out in 1835. From 1838 onwards he devoted all his time to his political activities.

Kennedy, Margaret (1896–1967) Margaret Moore Kennedy was born in London and educated at Oxford. Her first book was a history, *A Century of Revolution*, published in 1922, but she soon took to fiction, and her second novel, *The Constant Nymph*, was a bestseller. She later dramatized it in collaboration with Basil Dean. She wrote many more novels, a biography of Jane Austen, and a number of plays, of which the best known was *Escape Me Never*, produced in 1933.

Kerouac, Jack (1922–69) A native of Lowell, Massachusetts, Jack Kerouac was educated at Columbia. After a period at sea, he published his first novel, *The Town and the City*, in 1950. *On the Road*, a second, semi-autobiographical novel, appeared in 1957, and established him as one of the leaders of the Beat Generation, a term which he himself coined. He published several more books in a similar vein, including *The Subterraneans* and *The Dharma Bums*, both in 1958, *Big Sur*, in 1962, and *Desolation Angels*, in 1965. He also brought out volumes of verse, travel and autobiography.

Kesey, Ken (1935–) Born in Colorado and educated at the universities of Oregon and Stanford, Ken Elton Kesey became famous with his first novel, *One Flew Over the Cuckoo's Nest*, written after he had worked as a ward attendant in a mental hospital. It was published in 1962, and later transferred with great success to the screen. A second novel, *Sometimes a Great Notion*, appeared in 1964. *Demon Box*, published in 1986, is a collection of short pieces, some of which are plainly autobiographical, written over a period of several years.

Key, Francis Scott (1779–1843) The lawyer and poet Francis Scott Key is best known for having written the words of 'The Star-Spangled Banner'. He did so in 1814, during the war between the United States and Great Britain, on the occasion of a British attack on Fort McHenry. In 1834 he published *The Power of Literature and its Connection with Religion*, and his *Poems* appeared posthumously in 1857.

Keyes, Sidney (1922–43) The English poet Sidney Arthur Kilworth Keyes was born in Dartford and educated at Oxford. His poetry was first published as part of a collection, *Eight Oxford Poets*, which appeared in 1941, and his own first volume, *The Iron Laurel*, came out in 1942. He fought and was killed in North Africa during World War II. A second volume of verse, *The Cruel Solstice*, was published posthumously in 1943, and some other pieces were included in his *Collected Poems*, in 1945.

Keynes, John Maynard (1883–1946) The British economist John Maynard Keynes was born in Cambridge and educated at Eton and Cambridge. In 1919, having played an important part in the Paris Peace Conference following World War I, he published a controversial book, *The Economic Consequences of the Peace*. He wrote a number of other books, but the most famous of them was *A General Theory of Employment, Interest, and Money*, which appeared in 1936 and had a profound influence on economists and politicians.

Kidnapped A novel by Robert Louis Stevenson, first published in 1886. The sequel *Catriona*, appeared in 1893.

Kierkegaard, Søren Aaby (1813–55) The Danish philosopher Søren Aaby Kierkegaard was born in Copenhagen and educated at the university there, studying Theology. After graduating he spent two years in travel and then returned to Copenhagen. In 1843 he published his first major work, *Euten − Eller* (*Either − Or*), which was concerned with the ethical and aesthetic qualities of life. He published a great number of books subsequently, many of them expounding his belief in the equal importance of faith and knowledge.

Killigrew, Thomas (1612–83) In 1633 London-born Thomas Killigrew became a page to Charles I, and he remained in royal service throughout his life. In 1635 he visited France, and was present when the nuns of Loudun were exorcized of an evil spirit (a subject which later was to be the subject of works by John Whiting and Aldous Huxley, among others). Always a devotee of the theatre, he was granted a patent at the time of the Restoration to erect a new playhouse, and in 1663 he built the first Theatre Royal, Drury Lane. He was made Master of the Revels in 1673. He wrote a number of plays, the most successful of which was *The Parson's Wedding*, a witty, if salacious, comedy, first performed about 1640 and published in 1664.

Kim A novel by Rudyard Kipling, remarkable for its portrayal of life in India at the period. It was first published in 1901.

King Arthur While it is possible to identify King Arthur with a British chieftain who lived in the sixth century, the legend has become so embroidered that it no longer has any significant relationship to historical fact. The stories of Arthur, the Once and Future King (so called because he will return one day to lead Britain to a new greatness), of Guinevere, his queen, of Sir Launcelot and the other knights of the Round Table, of Sir Galahad, Sir Bors and Sir Perceval and their quest for the Holy Grail, of Merlin and Vivien, of Mordred and Morgan-le Fay — all these have come to us by a long route and through the hands of many writers. They originated in the work of the twelfth-century monk, Geoffrey of Monmouth, were elaborated by the French *jongleurs*, as exemplified by Chrétien de Troyes, and reappeared in Middle English in the fourteenth century. An almost definitive version of the Arthur legends came with *Le Morte D'Arthur*, which is attributed to Sir Thomas Malory and was first printed by Caxton in 1485. They have since provided material for countless works; particularly notable among these are Tennyson's *Idylls of the King* and T.H. White's *The Once and Future King*.

King, Francis (1923–) The English novelist and short story writer Francis Henry King was born in Switzerland and educated at Oxford. He published his first three novels while still an undergraduate, and these were followed by a number of other works of fiction in both full-length and short genres, including *To the Dark Tower*, which appeared in 1946, *The Brighton Belle and other stories*, in 1968, *Act of Darkness*, in 1983, *Voices in an Empty Room*, in 1984, *One is a Wanderer*, in 1985, and *Frozen Music*, in 1987.

King Horn A Middle English romance consisting of some fifteen hundred lines of verse, and telling of the adventures of a prince from the Isle of Man, his exploits in Ireland and his final conquest of his villainous foes. Dating from the early thirteenth century, it is the first surviving work of this nature.

King John, The Life and Death of An historical play by William Shakespeare, originally presented during the 1590s and first published in 1623.

King Lear The tragedy by William Shakespeare in which Lear, King of Britain, divides his land between his treacherous daughters Goneril and Regan, and suffers degradation, the death of his third daughter Cordelia, and final madness, from which death releases him. The play was first performed in 1606 and published in 1623.

King, William (1663–1712) Educated at Westminster School and Christ Church, Oxford, William King established a reputation for himself as a humorous writer. His work included a number of political pieces, and a great many burlesques such as his satire on Richard Bentley, *Dialogues of the Dead*, published in 1699, and his *Useful Transactions in Philosophy*, which appeared in 1709.

Kingsley, Charles (1819–75) After completing his education at Magdalene College, Cambridge, Charles Kingsley, who was born in Devon, England, became a clergyman, and Rector of the parish of Eversley in Hampshire. He remained in that position for the rest of his life, although he was later appointed a Canon of Chester, and eventually a Canon of Westminster. He published *The Saint's Tragedy*, a drama in blank verse about St Elizabeth of Hungary, in 1848. His first novels, *Yeast* and *Alton Locke*, were both published in 1850, and *Hypatia, or New Foes with Old Faces*, followed in 1853. Next, in 1855, came *Westward Ho!*, a novel with a background of the fight against the Spanish Armada, which was probably his most successful book (it also contained the memorable statement that there are 'more ways of killing a cat than choking her with cream'), and in the same year he published

The Water Babies is a fantasy by Charles Kingsley about the adventures of little Tom the chimney sweep who falls into a river and is transformed into a tiny water baby.

Glaucus: or the Wonders of the Shore, a book which reflected his continued delight in the natural world. He brought out *The Heroes*, a retelling for young readers of Greek legends, in 1856. In 1859 he became chaplain to Queen Victoria, and in 1860 was made Professor of Modern History at Cambridge, an appointment which he held until 1869. Two other books for which he is still remembered came out during that period, the highly moral tale for small children, *The Water Babies*, published in 1863, and his romance of the anti-Norman freedom fighter, *Hereward the Wake*, which appeared in 1866. Kingsley was not only popular but highly respected, despite the fact that he was sometimes accused of un-Victorian sensationalism. His public dispute with Cardinal Newman, which took place in 1864 and spurred Newman to write his *Apologia pro Vita Sua*, did not greatly damage his reputation. Among his other published works were essays and poetry, and some of the lines from his verses have remained very familiar – for example, 'For men must work and women must weep' and 'Be good, sweet maid, and let who can be clever'.

Kingsley, Henry (1830–76) The younger brother of Charles Kingsley appears to have been in some kind of disgrace when he left Oxford and emigrated to Australia in 1853. He returned to England five years later and then brought out *Recollections of Geoffrey Hamlyn*, a novel which was set in Australia, and which achieved considerable popularity. He published other fiction, and repeated his earlier success with *Ravenshoe*, which appeared in 1861.

Kipling, Rudyard (1865–1936) The son of an artist who later became curator of the Lahore Museum, Rudyard Kipling ws born in India. He was educated at the United Services College at Westward Ho, Devonshire, England, and in 1882 returned to India and became sub-editor of the *Lahore Civil and Military Gazette*. In 1886 he published *Departmental Ditties*, and 1887 saw *Plain Tales from the Hills*, a collection of remarkably mature stories which had originally been printed in the *Civil and Military Gazette*. During the next few years many more tales appeared in such books as *Soldiers Three, Under the Deodras, The Phantom Rickshaw, Wee Willie Winkie*, and *Life's Handicap*. His first full-length work, *The Light That Failed*, appeared in 1891, by which time he had come to England, where he was already famous. His reputation was rapidly enhanced by the publication in the *National Observer* of a number of the verses, including 'Mandalay', which were to appear in 1892 as *Barrack Room Ballads*. In that year he married Caroline Balestier, the sister of the American

publisher and literary agent Wolcott Balestier, with whom he collaborated on a novel, *The Naulahka*, also published in 1892. Kipling and his wife lived in Vermont until 1896, when he purchased 'Batemans', the house in Burwash, Sussex, which was his home for the remainder of his life. Meanwhile, he had published *The Jungle Book* and *The Second Jungle Book*, in 1894 and 1895 respectively, and with them had established himself as a popular writer for children. The following year he brought out a book of poetry, *The Seven Seas*, and in 1897 his poem 'Recessional', written on the occasion of Queen Victoria's Diamond Jubilee, was printed in *The Times*, enjoyed an immediate success, and increased the ranks of those who felt that he would have made a far better Poet Laureate than the incumbent of the time, Alfred Austin. 1897 was also the year in which *Captains Courageous* appeared, and in 1899 came *Stalky & Co.*, which was based on his own schooldays. The next novel, *Kim*, published in 1901, is probably the most read of all his works, apart from the books for children. A somewhat episodic adventure story, it caught brilliantly the atmosphere of the

LEFT: Rudyard Kipling's own illustration '... the Animal that came out of the sea and ate up all the food ...' to 'The Butterfly that Stamped', one of the *Just So Stories*.

BELOW: Bateman's in Sussex, Kipling's home from 1902 to 1936.

India in which it is set. The whimsical, amusing *Just So Stories*, which he himself illustrated with drawings that have yet to be bettered, came out in 1902, and in 1906 he published *Puck of Pook's Hill*, a collection of stories telling the history of England. In 1907 he became the first British writer to be awarded the Nobel Prize for Literature, an honour which he was happy to accept, although he steadfastly refused other recognitions of his position as England's leading author. He continued to write and publish books for the rest of his life. The autobiographical *Something of Myself* appeared posthumously in 1937, but with the exception of *Rewards and Fairies*, a sequel to *Puck of Pook's Hill*, which came out in 1910, few of the works which he produced in later life are remembered today. Kipling's brand of patriotic and imperialist writing became unfashionable for a period, and his portrayal of the British soldier and his ungrammatical and unaspirated speech was seen as condescending. Now, perhaps, his work can be more easily regarded as simply reflecting the beliefs and prejudices of his period, and the vigorous quality of his writing, and the ease and clarity with which he paints a scene and captures an atmosphere may lead to the appreciation of other of his works besides the perennially popular *Jungle Books*, *Just So Stories* and *Kim*. Whether or not Kipling is read, he is constantly quoted. 'East is East, and West is West, and never the twain shall meet', 'The female of the species is more deadly than the male', 'You're a better man than I am, Gunga Din', 'the White Man's burden' – these and a hundred other familiar lines were created by him, while the words of his poem 'Gentleman Rankers' became well known as the 'Whippenpoof Song'.

Kipps A novel by H.G. Wells, first published in 1905. Kipps, a draper's apprentice, rises in society, but finally returns to his childhood sweetheart.

Kit-Cat Club A group of writers, artists and politicians, all with Whig sympathies, which was formed in about 1703. The name derived from the products of the pie-house where the club first met. Subsequently it moved to other locations, including a purpose-built room in Barn Elms, the home of the publisher Jacob Tonson. Among the members were the Duke of Marlborough, Sir Robert Walpole, Addison, Congreve, Steele and Vanbrugh. The portrait painter Sir Godfrey Kneller, who was also a member, painted many of his fellows; the room in Barn Elms was not lofty, and the paintings, designed to be hung there, had to be restricted in length. So the canvases, measuring 36 by 28 inches, are said to be of 'Kit-cat' size.

Kleist, Heinrich von (1777–1811) The German dramatist Bernd Heinrich Wilhelm von Kleist was born at Frankfurt-am-Oder. After a period as a soldier, he studied philosophy and law, and became a civil servant. His first play, the tragedy *Die Familie Schroffenstein*, was written in 1803. It was followed by a number of others, including the comedy, *Der zerbrochene Krug*, in 1911, and his best-known work, *Prinz Friedrich von Homburg*, which was first published posthumously in 1821. His collected short stories appeared in 1810 and 1811, and included the highly regarded tale of 'Michael Kohlhaas'. Kleist fell desperately in love with a married woman, and at her behest first shot her and then himself.

Knickerbocker Group The name of this group of New York authors was taken from Diedrich Knickerbocker, the pseudonym used by Washington Irving for his comic *History of New York*. Irving himself was the most distinguished member of the group, which also included William Cullen Bryant and James Kirke Paulding.

Knickerbocker Magazine, The A periodical founded in New York in 1883. It continued for more than thirty years, and its impressive list of contributors included Washington Irving, William Cullen Bryant, James Fenimore Cooper, Horace Greeley, Nathaniel Hawthorne, Oliver Wendell Holmes, Henry Wadsworth Longfellow and John Greenleaf Whittier.

Knowles, John Sheridan (1784-1862) Born in Cork, Ireland, John Sheridan Knowles became in turn a soldier, a doctor, an actor, a playwright, a teacher and a Baptist preacher. His first two plays, *Leo* and *Brian Boroihme*, presented in 1810 and 1811, were well received, but it was not until 1815, with *Caius Gracchus*, that he achieved real success. *Virginius*, *William Tell*, *The Hunchback*, *The Wife*, *The Love Chase*, were performed between 1820 and 1837. With actors of the calibre of Kean and Macready in the leading parts, they were very popular.

Knox, John (c.1505–72) The militant Scottish Protestant John Knox was educated at Glasgow and St Andrew's universities. He became chaplain to Edward VI, and fled abroad when the Roman Catholic Queen Mary I came to the throne. In 1558 he published the celebrated *First Blast of the Trumpet against the Monstrous Regiment of Women*, less an anti-feminist tract than an attack on the women rulers of England and Scotland. Returning to Edinburgh, he became the leader in Scotland of the Reformation. He published other works, including a *Treatise on Predestination*, in 1560. His *Historie of the Reformation of Religioun within the Realme of Scotland* appeared posthumously in 1587.

Knox, Monsignor Ronald (1888–1957) The Rt Reverend Monsignor Ronald Arbuthnott Knox was educated at Eton and Oxford. In 1918 he published *A Spiritual Aeneid*, an account of his conversion to Roman Catholicism. He prepared a new translation of the Bible, published between 1945 and 1949, and wrote a number of theological works and detective stories.

Koestler, Arthur (1905–83) Born in Budapest and educated at the University of Vienna, Arthur Koestler worked as an international correspondent in Russia, Germany and France. While reporting on the Spanish Civil War, he was captured and imprisoned by the Fascist forces. In 1939, by which time he had given up his membership of the Communist party, he published his first novel *The Gladiators*, and the following year saw the appearance of his best-known work of fiction, *Darkness at Noon*. When the Germans invaded France in 1940, he was living in Paris. He was interned, but managed to escape to England, where he settled for the rest of his life, writing thereafter in English. His first book in that language, an account of his experiences which he called *Scum of the Earth*, was published in 1941. He produced a large number of books, almost all reflecting his deep political interests. These included collections of essays, autobiographical works, a history of the Jews in Palestine, and the novels *Arrival and Departure*, which appeared in 1943, *Thieves in the Night*, in 1946, and *The Age of Longing*, in 1951. *The Roots of Coincidence*, published in 1972, affirmed his belief in psychic phenomena. As a firm believer in euthanasia, he committed suicide, leaving his money for psychical research.

Kraus, Karl (1874–1936) The Austrian writer Karl Kraus was born in Bohemia and educated at the University of Vienna. In 1899 he founded a journal of literary and social criticism, *Die Fackel* (*The Torch*), which he continued until his death. He published a considerable amount of poetry, and became especially known for his aphorisms, which appeared in the collections *Sprüche und Widersprüche*, in 1909, *Pro Domo et Mondo*, in 1912, and *Nachts*, in 1919. His masterpiece was the anti-war drama *Die Letzten Tage der Menschheit* (*The Last Days of Mankind*), which was written during World War I.

Kubla Khan A poem by Samuel Taylor Coleridge, which came to him in a dream. On wakening he hastened to set it down, but was interrupted by 'a person from Porlock', after whose visit he was unable to remember the rest of the poem. It was first published in 1816.

Kundera, Milan (1929–) The Czech novelist Milan Kundera was born in Brno and educated at the film faculty of the Academy of Music and Dramatic Arts in Prague. After the Russian invasion of Czechoslovakia he moved to Paris, and became a professor at the universities of Paris and Rennes. He published his first novel, *The Joke*, in 1967, the English translation appearing in 1969. Other books include *The Farewell Party, The Book of Laughter and Forgetting, The Unbearable Lightness of Being, Life is Elsewhere* and *Jacques and His Master*. As well as novels, he has also published poetry and plays, and has received many awards for his literary work.

Kyd, Thomas (1558-94) The dramatist Thomas Kyd was born in London and educated at Merchant Taylors' School. His play *The Spanish Tragedy* was first performed between 1584 and 1589, and published in 1592. At the time it was frequently referred to as *Hieronimo*, its full title being *The Spanish Tragedie containing the Lamentable End of Don Horatio and Bel-imperia; with the Pitiful Death of Old Hieronimo*. It was enormously popular, and for many years remained in the repertoire. To this one play Kyd owes his place as a major Elizabethan dramatist, but considerable doubt exists as to his other writings for the theatre. He may have written *Soliman and Persida*, and there is some evidence to suggest that Shakespeare based *Hamlet* on an earlier version by Kyd, but the only play other than *The Spanish Tragedy* which can definitely be attributed to him is *Cornelia*, which he translated from the French of Robert Garnier, and which appeared in 1594. Apart from plays, he was responsible for a translation from the Italian of a work on domestic economy, *The Householder's Philosophy*, published in 1588, and he also wrote a pamphlet entitled *The Most Wicked and Secret Murdering of John Brewer, Goldsmith*, printed in 1592.

L

La Belle Dame Sans Merci A ballad by John Keats, telling of the love of a knight for a faery woman. It was first published in 1820.

La Bruyère, Jean de (1645–96) Born in Paris and educated at the University of Orléans, Jean de La Bruyère became a tutor in the household of the Prince of Condé. In 1688 he published his famous work *Les caractères ou les moeurs de ce siècle*, a series of pen portraits of typical characters of the period, in which he castigated the follies and venalities of mankind.

La Farge, Oliver (1901–63) The American ethnologist Oliver Hazard Perry La Farge was educated at Harvard. Following archeological expeditions in Arizona, Mexico and Guatemala, he published, in collaboration with Frans Blom, *Tribes and Temples*, the two volumes of which appeared in 1925 and 1927. His novels included *Laughing Boy*, which won the Pulitzer Prize in 1929, *Sparks Fly Upward*, in 1931, and *The Copper Pot*, in 1942. He also wrote short stories, and the non-fiction books *Behind the Mountains*, published in 1956, and *Santa Fe: The Autobiography of a Southwestern Town*, in 1959.

La Fontaine, Jean de (1621–95) The friend of Boileau, Racine and Molière, Jean de La Fontaine was born in Château Thierry, France. He wrote a considerable amount of poetry and several volumes of *Contes*, which caused some scandal because of their bawdiness. But he is famous for his *Fables*, written in verse and published in twelve volumes, the first six of which appeared in 1668 and the remainder between 1671 and 1694.

Lady Chatterley's Lover A novel by D.H. Lawrence, concerning the relationship between Constance Chatterley and the gamekeeper Mellors. First published in 1928, it was not available in England in an unexpurgated version until 1960, when the book was the subject of a major trial for obscenity. Its acquittal heralded a new age of freedom of expression.

Lady of Shalott, The A poem by Tennyson, first published in 1832 and later revised.

Lady of the Lake, The A long romantic poem by Sir Walter Scott, which established his reputation when it was published in 1810.

Lady Susan An early novel in letter form by Jane Austen. Probably written in 1793 and 1794, it was not published until 1871.

Lady Windermere's Fan Oscar Wilde's first successful play, presented in 1892.

Lake Poets A term used to refer to William Wordsworth, Samuel Taylor Coleridge and Robert Southey, all of whom lived and wrote for a considerable period in the Lake District in northwest England.

L'Allegro A poem by John Milton, first published in 1645. In praise of mirth, it is complemented by the contemplative 'Il Penseroso'.

Lamartine, Alphonse de (1790–1869) Alphonse Marie Louis de Prat de Lamartine was born at Mâcon, France. He became a soldier, later entered the diplomatic service, and was then for some years active as a politician, becoming briefly Minister of Foreign Affairs in the government of 1848. In 1820 he published a volume of poetry, *Méditations, poétiques et religieuses*, which established him among the leaders of the Romantic movement in France. Several other collections of verse appeared, and he also wrote autobiographical works and a number of histories, the most important of the latter being *Histoire des Girondins*, published in 1847, and *Histoire de la Révolution de 1848*, which appeared in 1849.

Lamb, Charles (1775–1834) The English essayist Charles Lamb was born in London and educated at Christ's Hospital. He was employed for most of his life in the accountant's office of East India House. He suffered a brief period of insanity in 1795, and was confined in an asylum for some months. In 1796 his sister Mary also became deranged and, during her brainstorm, killed their mother. For the remainder of his life Lamb acted as her guardian, repaid by her affection but constantly in fear that her mental illness would return, as indeed it did from time to time. His first published work consisted of four sonnets which appeared in *Poems on Various Subjects*, published by Samuel Taylor Coleridge. More poetry followed, together with a romantic story, *Rosamund Gray*, and two plays, *John Woodvil* and *Mr H–*, both of which were failures. In 1807 he and his sister published, with rather more success, *Tales founded on the Plays of Shakespeare*. He collaborated with her on other books for children, but his reputation was really

A sombre portrait by Francis Stephen Cary of the essayist Charles Lamb and his sister Mary, for whom he had to care after she murdered their mother.

established in 1808 with the publication of his *Specimens of English Dramatic Poets who lived about the time of Shakespeare*. In 1818 he brought out his collected *Works*, which included a number of essays originally published in a periodical called *The Reflector*. The celebrated *Essays of Elia*, which had first appeared in the *London Magazine* were published in 1823, followed by *The Last Essays of Elia* in 1833.

Lamming, George (1927–) The novelist George Eric Lamming was born in Barbados. After working in Trinidad and Venezuela as a teacher, he went to England and worked in a factory. His first novel, *In the Castle of My Skin*, was published in 1953, and *The Emigrants* came out the following year. Several other novels have followed, almost all with some autobiographical content. He has also published a straightforward autobiography, *The Pleasures of Exile*, which came out in 1960.

L'Amour, Louis (1908–) The American writer Louis L'Amour first appeared in print with a book of verse, *Smoke from the Altar*. In 1953 he published a Western, *Hondo*, and has since become the most successful writer in this genre since Zane Grey. Among his books are *Sackett*, which appeared in 1961, and which he has followed with other stories of the Sackett family, *How the West Was Won*, in 1962, and *The Comstock Lode*, in 1981.

Lampman, Archibald (1861–99) The Canadian poet Archibald Lampman was born at Morpeth, Ontario, the son of a clergyman, and educated at Trinity College, Toronto. His first volume of verse, *Among the Millet*, was published in 1888, and was followed in 1896 by a second collection, *Lyrics of Earth*. A final selection, *At the Long Sault*, appeared posthumously in 1943.

lampoon A satire, written in either prose or verse, usually particularly venemous in the ridicule which it heaps on its subject. Since a lampoon is often grossly libellous, it is frequently published anonymously. Although lampoons are still written today, the form was especially rife during the early eighteenth century.

Landor, Walter Savage (1775–1864) Born at Warwick, England, and educated privately and for a brief period at Cambridge, Walter Savage Landor published his first book, *The Poems of Walter Savage Landor*, in 1795. It was succeeded by a long epic poem, *Gebir*, in 1798, and by other volumes of poetry, one of which included his verse tragedy *Count Julian*. He also wrote a number of prose works, among them *The Imaginary Conversations of literary men and statesmen*, which appeared in 1824, with additional volumes appearing over a four-year period, and *The Citation and Examination of William Shakespeare touching Deer-Stealing*, in 1834.

Lang, Andrew (1844–1912) The Scottish writer Andrew Lang was born at Selkirk and educated at St Andrew's and Oxford. He was a poet, a Greek scholar, a historian, a literary critic and essayist, and published work in all these fields, as well as books on religion, myths and psychic phenomena. He is best known, however, for his collection of fairy tales, the first of which, *The Blue Fairy Book*, was published in 1899, and was followed by many others, each with a different colour in the title.

Langland, William (c.1332–c.1400) The fourteenth-century poem *Piers Plowman* has long been attributed to William Langland, although it is not certain whether he wrote it, and it may in fact have been the work of several hands. Little is known on Langland's life, but he was probably born in Shropshire and spent most of his years in London.

Lanier, Sidney (1842–81) The American poet Sidney Lanier was born in Georgia. He served in the Confederate army, was a noted flute-player, and later became a lecturer in English literature at Johns Hopkins University. He published a novel, *Tiger Lilies*, in 1867, and his *Science of English Verse* was well received in 1880, but he is now remembered chiefly for his poetry, which although small in quantity, has been much admired for its musical qualities. A small volume of *Poems* was published in 1877, with an enlarged edition appearing posthumously in 1884.

Laodicean, A A novel by Thomas Hardy, first published in 1881. The title describes the main character, Paula Power, a young woman of irresolute character.

Lardner, Ring (1885–1933) The American author Ringold Wilmer Lardner was born in Michigan. He became a sports writer, and his first book was a collection of his pieces on baseball, *You Know Me: A Busher's Letters*, published in 1916. He later brought out many collections of racy short stories, including *Gullible's Travels*, which appeared in 1917, *The Love Nest*, in 1926, and *First and Last*, in 1934. He also wrote a novel, *The Big Town*, which came out in 1921, and a humorous volume of autobiography, *The Story of a Wonder Man*, in 1927.

Larkin, Philip (1922–85) A native of Coventry, England, the poet Philip Larkin was educated in Coventry and at Oxford, and after graduating became a librarian. His first volume of poetry, *The North Ship*, appeared in 1945. He then turned to fiction, producing the novels *Jill*, in 1946, and *A Girl in Winter*, in 1947. He returned to verse in 1955 with *The Less Deceived*, and this collection was followed in 1964 by *The Whitsun Weddings*, *The Explosion*, in 1970, and *High*

Windows, in 1974. By this time his reputation had been firmly established as one of Britain's leading poets. His work was notable for the facility with which he blended simple contemporary language with formality of construction, and although his poems frequently reflected recurring thoughts of mortality, his lyrical gift could in no way be described as morbid. A lifelong interest in jazz resulted in the publication in 1970 of a volume of essays, *All What Jazz*, and in 1983 he brought out further essays, this time more literary in subject, in *Required Writings*.

La Rochefoucauld, François de (1613–80) François de Marsillac, who, on the death of his father, became Duc de la Rochefoucauld, was born in Paris. A soldier and a politician, he published in 1665, anonymously, and subsequently extended, his famous book of maxims, *Réflexions ou sentences et maximes morales*, an examination of the virtues and vices of mankind.

Last Chronicle of Barset, The A novel by Anthony Trollope, the sixth and final volume in the Barsetshire series, first published in 1867.

Last Days of Pompeii, The An historical novel by Edward Bulwer Lytton, first published in 1867.

Last of the Mohicans, The James Fenimore Cooper's famous novel of the American frontier, featuring Hawkeye, Chingachgook, and the villainous Magua. The second of the 'Leatherstocking Tales', it was published in 1826.

Last Tycoon, The A novel by F. Scott Fitzgerald, unfinished at his death and completed by his friend Edmund Wilson. It was first published in 1941.

Laurence, Margaret (1926–87) The Canadian novelist Jean Margaret Laurence was born in Neepawa and educated in Winnipeg. She began her career as a journalist and published her first book, a collection of poems and stories called *A Tree for Poverty*, in 1954. Her first novel, *This Side of Jordan*, appeared in 1960. Her principal work was a tetralogy set in a Manitoba town similar to Neepawa, and published between 1964 and 1974. The four volumes were *The Stone Angel*, *A Jest of God* (also known as *Rachel, Rachel* and *Now I Lay Me Down*), *The Fire-Dwellers* and *The Diviners*.

Lavengro – The Scholar – The Gypsy – The Priest A story of gypsy life by George Borrow. Part autobiography, part novel, it was published in 1851.

Law, William (1686–1761) A native of Northamptonshire, England, William Law was educated at Cambridge. He entered the Church, but, since he refused to take the oath of allegiance to George I, was unable to pursue his clerical duties, and became tutor to the future father of the historian Edward Gibbon. He also exercised considerable influence on the Evangelical leaders John and Charles Wesley. He published many books and tracts on religious and moral subjects including *The Absolute Unlawfulness of Stage Entertainments*, published in 1726, and the two complementary volumes, *A Treatise of Christian Perfection* and *A Serious Call to a Devout and Holy Life*, which appeared in 1726 and 1728.

Lawrence, D.H. (1885–1930) David Herbert Lawrence, the son of a miner, was born at Eastwood, in Nottinghamshire, England. With his mother's encouragement he won a scholarship to Nottingham High School, but left at fifteen and became a clerk. He later trained as a teacher, but ill health forced him to abandon that career, and henceforth he was a writer. Some poems had already appeared, and he published his first novel, *The White Peacock*, in 1911, following it with *The Trespasser* in 1912. It was in this year that he met and fell in love with Frieda Weekley. She left her husband and eloped with Lawrence to Germany, and they were married in 1914, after her divorce. Meanwhile the autobiographical novel, *Sons and Lovers*, had appeared in 1913, as had his *Love Poems*,

D.H. Lawrence's burning idealism glows through all his work. His views on sex and the dehumanizing effects of industralized Western culture made him a controversial figure of his period.

while a collection of short stories, *The Prussian Officer*, came out in 1914. During World War I Lawrence, who was unfit for military service, was in England. His next work, *The Rainbow*, was published in 1915, but was condemned as offending against the obscenity laws. However, he managed to bring out two collections of poetry, *Amores*, in 1916, and *Look! We Have Come Through!*, in 1917. After the war he and Frieda went to Italy, but they never stayed in the same place for very long, and in the course of their stormy and impecunious marriage lived in many different countries. By 1920 he was beginning to have a little more success with his novels, although he was never in his lifetime to achieve the substantial sales which would have allowed him to escape from serious financial difficulties. In that year *The Lost Girl* was published, and *Women in Love*, which had been waiting for a publisher since 1916, finally appeared in the United States, with publication in Britain following in 1921. *Aaron's Rod* and a collection of stories, *England, My England*, both came out in 1922, and 1923 saw three new books, the novel *Kangaroo*, written while he was in Australia, a further volume of poetry, *Birds, Beasts and Flowers*, and the non-fiction work, *Studies in Classic American Literature*. A period spent in Mexico resulted in another novel, *The Plumed Serpent*, published in 1926, and then he began to write *Lady Chatterley's Lover*. It was printed privately in 1928, but did not become generally available until 1959 in the United States, and 1960 in Britain, where it was the subject of a remarkable trial for obscenity, of which it was cleared. By 1929, when *Pansies*, a volume of poems, appeared, Lawrence was seriously ill with the tuberculosis from which he had suffered for most of his life, and he died in the South of France in the following year. Although always thought of as primarily a novelist, short story writer and poet, he also worked in other fields, and produced a number of plays (none of which was particularly successful), books on psycho-analysis, and the four very personal travel books, *Twilight in Italy*, *Sea and Sardinia*, *Mornings in Mexico* and *Etruscan Places*, the last of these being published posthumously, as were a number of other minor works. Since his death, Lawrence's reputation has grown, and indeed continues to grow, as one of the most important writers of the twentieth century. Few critics would contend that either his fiction or his poetry is without flaws, admitting that his own work often suffers from unevenness, but the passion which infuses almost every line he wrote, the depth of feeling in his exploration of the human condition, the sheer liveliness of his style – these are the qualities of a genius, who can be forgiven the occasional lapse.

lay A poetic and somewhat archaic term to describe a short poem which is either intended to be sung or has the manner of a song.

Lay of the Last Minstrel, The A long narrative poem by Sir Walter Scott. Its success in 1805 launched him on his literary career.

Lays of Ancient Rome A book by Thomas Babington Macaulay consisting of four poems 'Horatius', 'Battle of the Lake Regillus', 'Virginia' and 'The Prophecy of Capys', each preceded by a Preface. It was first published in 1842.

Lazarus, Emma (1849–87) Born in New York, Emma Lazarus published her first book of poetry, *Admetus and other poems*, in 1871. *Alide*, a prose romance based on the life of Goethe, appeared in 1874, and was followed by a tragedy, *The Spagnoletto*, and translations of Heine's poetry. From 1881 onwards she found her voice as a Jewish poet, and her major work, *Songs of a Semite*, which was published in 1882, included her drama, *Dance to Death*. *By the Waters of Babylon*, appearing in 1887, was a collection of prose poems. Her sonnet to the Statue of Liberty, 'The New Colossus', is carved on its pedestal.

Leacock, Stephen (1869–1944) British-born Stephen Butler Leacock grew up and was educated in Canada. He eventually became Professor of Economics and Political Science at McGill University, Montreal, and wrote a number of books on these subjects, but he is best known for his many humorous collections, which began with *Literary Lapses*, published in 1910, and included *Nonsense Novels*, *Frenzied Fiction*, *Short Circuits*, *Moonbeams from the Larger Lunacy* and *Winnowed Wisdom*.

Lear, Edward (1812–88) A Londoner by birth, Edward Lear was a successful artist who wrote and illustrated a number of travel books, mostly

An illustration from Lear's *A Book of Nonsense*.

concerned with his journeys in Mediterranean countries. He is chiefly remembered, however, for his verses for children, including his limericks, a form which he did not invent but which he used a great deal. *A Book of Nonsense* appeared in 1845, and a number of collections of a similar nature followed.

Leaves of Grass The principal collection of poems by Walt Whitman. It was first published in 1855, and subsequently revised and greatly enlarged in the many new editions which appeared during the poet's lifetime.

Leavis, F.R. (1895–1978) Frank Raymond Leavis was born and educated in Cambridge, England. An academic, he became one of the most influential literary critics of the twentieth century. Among his many books the most important are his two major reviews of English verse, *New Bearings in English Poetry*, published in 1932, and *Revaluation*, in 1936, and his reassessment of major English novelists, *The Great Tradition*, which appeared in 1948.

Le Carré, John (1931–) John Le Carré is the pseudonym of David John Moore Cornwell, who was educated at Eton and Oxford and worked in the British Foreign Office before becoming a full-time writer. In 1963 his book *The Spy Who Came in from the Cold* became a bestseller, and he followed it with a number of other intelligent, convoluted thrillers such as *Tinker, Tailor, Soldier, Spy*, which appeared in 1974, *The Honourable Schoolboy*, in 1977, and *Smiley's People*, in 1980.

Lee, Harper (1926–) Nelle Harper Lee was born in Monroeville, Alabama and at Oxford. Her bestseller, *To Kill A Mocking Bird*, was published in 1960 and awarded the Pulitzer Prize.

Lee, Laurie (1914–) The English writer Laurie Lee was born in Gloucestershire. He has published a number of volumes of poetry, the first of which, *The Sun my Monument*, appeared in 1944, but he is best known for his two charming and evocative volumes of autobiography, *Cider with Rosie*, published in 1959, and *As I Walked Out One Midsummer Morning*, which came out in 1969.

Le Fanu, Sheridan (1814–73) The Irish journalist and author Joseph Sheridan Le Fanu was born in Dublin of Huguenot extraction, and educated at Trinity College, Dublin. He became the proprietor and editor of a number of Dublin newspapers, and also wrote a number of very popular books, specializing in tales of mystery and crime and the supernatural. His best-known works are *The House by the Churchyard*, published in 1863, *Uncle Silas, a Tale of Bartram Haugh*, in 1864, and the short stories, *In a Glass Darkly*, which appeared in 1872.

Le Guin, Ursula K. The science fiction writer Ursula Kroeber Le Guin was born in Berkeley, California, and educated at Columbia University and in France. She published her first book, *Rocannon's World*, in 1966, and followed it with *Planet of Exile*, also in 1966, and *City of Illusions*, in 1967. She has written many more novels and won several awards. The 'Earthsea Trilogy', which consists of *A Wizard of Earthsea*, *The Tombs of Atuan*, and *The Farthest Shore*, was published between 1968 and 1972, and among her other books are *The Word for World is Forest*, which appeared in 1977, and *Always Coming Home*, in 1986.

L'Engle, Madeleine (1918–) The New York author Madeleine L'Engle published her first book, *The Small Rain*, in 1945. Since then she has brought out some thirty works in a variety of genres, including novels, short stories, science fiction, plays, poetry, autobiography and books for children. Among them are *A Winter's Love*, which appeared in 1957, *The Moon by Night*, in 1963, *A Circle of Quiet*, in 1972, *A Ring of Endless Light*, in 1980, and *A House Like a Lotus*, in 1984.

Lennox, Charlotte (1720–1804) The daughter of the British Governor of New York, where she was born, Charlotte Ramsay Lennox wrote a number of novels and plays. Her best-known novel, *The Female Quixote; or the Adventures of Arabella*, was published in 1752. Although Dr Johnson admired her inordinately, she became unpopular with many of her contemporaries when she criticized Shakespeare for spoiling his plays by grafting unnecessary material on to the stories he had used as sources.

Leopardi, Giacomo (1798–1837) Count Giacomo Leopardi was born at Recanati, Italy, the deformed and delicate son of an impoverished noble family. He became Italy's outstanding poet of the romantic period. He was not a prolific writer and his fame rests on some forty poems, composed over a period of twenty years and known as the *Canti*. His principal prose work, *Operette Morali (Moral Tales)*, appeared in 1827.

Leroux, Gaston (1868–1927) Born in Paris, Gaston Leroux wrote a number of popular novels, including one of the first 'locked-room' murder stories, *The Mystery of the Yellow Room*, published in 1907. His best-known work is *The Phantom of the Opera*, which appeared in 1911.

Lessing, Doris (1919–) Doris May Taylor, who took the name Lessing from her first husband, was born in Persia and brought up in Southern Rhodesia, now Zimbabwe. Her first novel, *The Grass is Singing*, published in 1950, made an immediate impact. In 1952, with *Martha Quest*, she began the began the sequence of five novels known as 'Children of Violence', the other books being *A Proper Marriage*, *A Ripple from the Storm*, *Landlocked* and *The Four-Gated City*, which appeared in 1954, 1958, 1965 and 1969 respectively. As well as some non-fiction, and a large number of short stories, she has written many more novels. Especially notable among them is the group of five books known as the *Canopus in Argus Archives*, published between 1979 and 1983. Her most popular work to date remains *The Golden Notebook*, a novel which appeared in 1962. *The Good Terrorist* was published in 1985.

Leviathan, The, or the Matter, Form, and Power of a Commonwealth, Ecclesiastical and Civil The famous philosophical work by Thomas Hobbes, first published in 1651.

Levin, Meyer (1905–81) The American writer Meyer Levin was born and educated in Chicago. His first novel, *Reporter*, was published in 1929, and his others include *Citizens*, which appeared in 1940, *Compulsion*, in 1956, *The Fanatic*, in 1964, and *The Settlers* and its sequel *The Harvest*, in 1972 and 1978.

Lewes, G.H. (1817–78) The companion of George Eliot from 1854 until his death, George Henry Lewes was himself a writer. Born in London, he became a journalist and produced a large number of books on a wide variety of subjects, including biology, philosophy and psychology, as well as several plays and some novels. His most successful book was *The Life and Works of Goethe*, published in 1855.

Lewis, Alun (1915–44) The poet Alun Lewis was born in Aberdare, South Wales, and educated at Aberystwyth University. He joined the army shortly after the outbreak of World War II. His first volume of poetry, *Raiders' Dawn*, was published in 1942, and he followed it the next year with a collection of short stories. A second book of war poems, *Ha! Ha! Among the Trumpets*, was published posthumously in 1944.

Lewis, C.S. (1898–1963) Born in Belfast, Clive Staples Lewis was educated at Cambridge, where he later became a Professor of Medieval and Renaissance English at Cambridge. As well as a number of works of literary criticism, he produced a series of books for children about the land of Narnia, the first of which was *The Lion, The Witch, and The Wardrobe*, published in 1950, and among his fiction was a trilogy of science fiction novels. His greatest success came with *The Screwtape Letters*, a work of popular theology, which appeared in 1940 and sold in enormous quantities.

Lewis, Sinclair (1885–1951) The American novelist Harry Sinclair Lewis was born at Sauk Center, Minnesota, and educated at Yale. He began his career as a journalist, and also worked as a publisher's editor. Meanwhile, he was writing short stories and longer fiction, and his first novel, *Our Mr Wrenn*, appeared in 1914. More novels followed, without attracting much attention, and then in 1920 he produced his first major work, *Main Street*, a picture of Gopher Prairie, a typical town of the American mid-west. This highly acclaimed novel was followed in 1922 by *Babbitt*, in which, with his portrayal of George Babbitt, he continued his satirical attack on the smug, self-important inhabitants of small mid-western towns. These two books established him firmly, both in America and abroad, as a highly successful and widely read novelist, who was not only an important literary figure, but whose unashamedly crusading novels could be extremely controversial. He continued to maintain his standard of writing and his popularity with *Arrowsmith*, which won the Pulitzer Prize in 1924, and with *Elmer Gantry* (eventually to become an important screen vehicle for Orson Welles), which appeared in 1927. *Dodsworth*, published in 1929 and later adapted into a very successful play, was his last major work, for, although he continued to write and brought out

Sinclair Lewis ridiculed the conformity and hypocrisy in American middle-class life. He was the first American author to be awarded the Nobel Prize for Literature which he received in 1930.

a considerable number of other novels, he never again achieved the immediacy and power of those five books by which he is remembered. He was awarded the Nobel Prize for Literature in 1930.

Light in August A novel by William Faulkner, first published in 1932. It presents the tragic story of Joe Christmas, supposedly a mulatto, killed by a mob after he has murdered his white lover, Joanna Burden.

limerick A five-line doggerel verse, intended to be amusing, and sometimes obscene. The rhyming scheme is *a, a, b, b, a*, lines three and four being much shorter than the remainder. The form became popular in the Victorian period, especially in the limericks written by Edward Lear.

Lindsay, Vachel (1879–1931) Nicholas Vachel Lindsay was born in Springfield, Illinois. He abandoned his college education to study art, but eventually earned a small living by lecturing and by reading his own poetry. His first published collection was *General William Booth Enters Into Heaven, and other poems*, which appeared in 1913. This was followed by *The Congo, and other poems*, in 1914, *The Chinese Nightingale, and other poems*, in 1917, and some additional volumes of verse, as well as various prose writings. His early success was not maintained and he committed suicide.

Lingard, John (1771–1851) The Roman Catholic historian John Lingard was born at Winchester and educated at Douai. After his ordination in 1795 he spent some years as an academic before devoting himself to writing. His main works are *The Antiquities of the Anglo-Saxon Church*, first published in 1806, and *A History of England, from the first invasion by the Romans to the commencement of the reign of William III*, which was published between 1819 and 1830 and later appeared in substantially revised editions.

Linklater, Eric (1899–1974) The English novelist Eric Linklater was born in Orkney and educated at the University of Aberdeen. His first book was *White Man's Saga*, published in 1928, followed in 1929 by *Poet's Pub*, and in 1930 by *Juan in America*, his first big success. Other books included *Juan in China*, which appeared in 1937, *Private Angelo*, in 1946, and various works of non-fiction and autobiography.

Little Dorrit A novel by Charles Dickens, set largely in the Marchelsea prison for debtors, where the father of Little Amy Dorrit is incarcerated. It was first published in *All the Year Round* between 1855 and 1857.

Little Lord Fauntleroy A novel by Frances Hodgson Burnett, about a child of saccharine goodness. It was first published in 1886.

Little Women Louisa M. Alcott's celebrated book for young readers about the March sisters, Meg, Jo, Beth and Amy. It was first published in two volumes in 1868 and 1869.

Lives Properly called *Parallel Lives*, these forty-six biographical studies were written, probably early in the second century, by the Greek author Plutarch. After their translation into English in 1579, they were used by Shakespeare and other later writers as both inspiration and source material.

Lives of the English Poets, The A critical work by Samuel Johnson, covering fifty-two poets. It was first published in a number of volumes between 1779 and 1781.

Livy (59BC–AD17) Titus Livius, the Roman historian, was born at Padua. His major work was a history of Rome, beginning with the legendary arrival of Aeneas in Italy, and closing in the year 9BC. It consisted originally of one hundred and forty-two books, but only thirty-five are still in existence, and two of those are incomplete.

This highly decorative title-page of Livy's history of Rome is from an edition printed in 1568.

The philosopher John Locke, painted by Verelst in 1689.

Locke, John (1632–1704) The English philosopher John Locke was born in Somersetshire and educated at Westminster School and Oxford. He pursued an academic career until 1683, when, in trouble with the authorities of the time, he fled to Holland in search of a life free of censorship. He returned to England in 1689, after the accession of William and Mary, to whom he had become known, and shortly afterwards he was appointed to a minor office as Commissioner of Appeals. While in the Netherlands he had completed his major philosophical work, the *Essay concerning Human Understanding*, and when it was published in 1690 he became instantly famous. An ardent believer in civil and religious liberty, he also propounded the idea that judgments should be made on the basis of personal experience and with probability in mind, and his work was both acclaimed and sharply criticized. The *Essay* became widely known throughout Europe. He published a number of other writings, including *Thoughts on Education*, which appeared in 1693, *The Reasonableness of Christianity as delivered in the Scriptures*, an attempt to return to the simplicity of the Gospel message, which came out in 1695, and many minor tracts and treatises. In 1700 he retired from public life, and lived quietly in Essex until his death.

Lockhart, John Gibson (1794–1854) A native of Lanarkshire, Scotland, John Gibson Lockhart was educated in Glasgow and at Oxford. After qualifying as a barrister, he joined the staff of *Blackwood's Magazine*, and his reviews of poetry became notorious for the strength of his criticism. Leigh Hunt, Keats and Hazlitt were savaged, but he smiled on Wordsworth and Coleridge. He also published a number of novels, and biographies of Cervantes, Napoleon, Burns and Scott. His *Life of Sir Walter Scott* was at one time considered to be the finest biography in the English language after Boswell's *The Life of Samuel Johnson*.

Lodge, Thomas (*c.*1558–1625) Educated at Merchant Taylor's School and at Oxford, Thomas Lodge, who was born near London, published his *Defence of Poetry, Music and Stage Plays* in 1579 or 1580. *An Alarum Against Usurers* came in 1584, and in the same year he brought out a romantic tale in prose and verse, *The Delectable History of Forbonius and Prisceria*. While on an expedition to the Canary Islands he wrote his best-known work, *Rosalynde, Euphues Golden Legacie*, printed in 1590, the basis of Shakespeare's *As You Like It*. He wrote other romances, as well as poetry, a handbook of popular medicine, and a variety of other works, including the plays *The Wounds of Civill War*, and, in collaboration with Robert Greene, *A Looking Glasse for London and England*, both printed in 1594.

Lofting, Hugh (1886–1947) Although he wrote other books for children, Hugh Lofting is remembered as the creator of Dr Doolittle. He was born in Maidenhead, England, and educated at the Massachusetts Institute of Technology and at the London Polytechnic. He settled in the United States in 1912. *The Story of Dr Doolittle* was published in 1920, the first of a long series of stories featuring the doctor and his animal friends.

Lolita A novel by Vladimir Nabokov, concerned with the sexual obsession of a middle-aged man, Humbert Humbert, with the twelve-year-old nymphet, Lolita. This theme brought the book a *succès de scandale* when it was published in 1955.

London, Jack (1876–1916) John Griffith London was born in San Francisco. An illegitimate child, he adopted the surname of his stepfather. His education was scanty, although he was addicted to reading, and he spent much of his youth trying to scratch a living in a variety of occupations, some of which were outside the law. At the age of seventeen he went to sea, sailing before the mast. Having returned from this voyage, he joined a fruitless protest march to Washington on behalf of those in want, and

Although only forty years old when he died, Jack London had led a full and adventurous life. His writing was based on first-hand experience, which is apparent from the vigour of his style. Although the success of his novels made him wealthy, he never lost his deep socialist convictions.

about this time became a committed socialist. He enrolled at the University of California in 1896, but soon afterwards joined the gold rush to the Klondike, and then tramped his way across Canada and the United States, spending more than one period in prison for vagrancy. Returning to California, he began to write, and in 1900 published *The Son of the Wolf*, a collection of realistic stories based on his own experiences in the north, which made an immediate impact. From this time on, he was a dedicated and successful writer, using to the full the knowledge gained from his own adventurous life. Although he became wealthy and lived extravagantly, he retained his socialist beliefs, and in much of his writing attacked the capitalist system under which he lived. A second novel, *The Cruise of the Dazzler*, taking as its subject the illegal oyster fishing he had joined in as a boy, appeared in 1902. In that year he visited England, where *The Son of the Wolf* had already made him well-known, and then in 1903 he brought out both *The Call of the Wild* and *The*

People of the Abyss, an account of the slums in the East End of London. *The Call of the Wild*, the story of a dog, set in the frozen north, was hugely successful, and established him on both sides of the Atlantic as a bestselling novelist. In 1904 he went to Japan to report on the war between Japan and Russia, and in that year published his next novel, *The Sea-Wolf*, based on his earlier experiences at sea. After two more books, *White Fang*, again with a dog as its hero, was published in 1906 and repeated the success of *The Call of the Wild*. He then set out on a round-the-world voyage on a small yacht, and was not heard of for two years, although *The Iron Heel*, a novel in which he gave full rein to his political beliefs, appeared in 1907. When he returned he published *Martin Eden*, a semi-autobiographical novel concerned with its hero's struggles to become a writer. A later book, *John Barleycorn*, which came out in 1913, reflected his own problems as an alcoholic. *South Sea Tales* appeared in 1911, and *Smoke Bellew* in 1912. In 1914 he was commissioned to go to Mexico, again as a war correspondent. The last novel before his death was *The Little Lady of the Big House*, published in 1916. He wrote a great many other books, including an autobiography, *Sailor on Horseback*, and although almost all his novels were realistic adventure stories, he also experimented with fantasies set in the distant past or the future. He was in addition a prolific journalist and a popular lecturer, and he produced many political tracts. Although there are elements in his novels which seem old-fashioned and even unacceptable today, the vigour of his writing, especially to be seen in his two most popular works, *The Call of the Wild* and *White Fang*, has given him a continuing popularity.

London Magazine, The The first magazine with this title was founded in 1731 and continued until 1785. A second incarnation ran from 1820 to 1829, and its first editor, John Scott, encouraged and published the work of Keats, Leigh Hunt and Hazlitt, the writers who were particularly the target of criticism from the rival publication, *Blackwood's Magazine*. Other notable authors published in this second series of *The London Magazine* include John Clare, William Wordsworth, and Thomas Carlyle. Thomas de Quincey's *Confessions of an English Opium Eater* made its first appearance in the periodical, as did Charles Lamb's celebrated 'Dissertation upon Roast Pig.'

Long Day's Journey Into Night Commonly held to be Eugene O'Neill's masterpiece, this partly autobiographical play, presenting the tragedy of the Tyrone family, was first presented posthumously in 1956.

Longfellow, Henry Wadsworth (1807–82) The American poet Henry Wadsworth Longfellow was born in Portland, Maine, the son of a lawyer and descendant of a Yorkshire-born immigrant who had arrived in America in 1676. He was educated at Bowdoin College, Brunswick, and while there contributed a number of poems to the *United States Literary Gazette*. After graduating he joined his father's firm, but, having been offered a chair in modern languages at Bowdoin, went to Europe and spent more than three years in France, Italy, Spain, Germany, Holland and England perfecting his fluency. He returned to the United States in 1829, and was at Bowdoin for six years. During that time he married, and in addition to a number of text books published his *Outre-mer: a Pilgrimage beyond the Sea*, which included some translations from the Spanish. In 1835 he received an appointment as Professor of Modern Languages and Belles-Lettres at Harvard, in preparation for which he again visited Europe, this time particularly spending time in Scandinavia. His wife accompanied him, but died in Rotterdam soon after their arrival. Returning to take up his Harvard post in 1836, he embarked on his long career as a lecturer and writer. In 1839 he published *Hyperion: a Romance*, and also his first volume of poetry, *Voices of the Night*. In 1842 came *Ballads and other poems*, which included such popular favourites as 'The Wreck of the Hesperus', 'The Village Blacksmith' and 'Excelsior'. *Poems on Slavery*, which followed in the same year, were undoubtedly influential. He married again in 1843, and then produced *The Spanish Student, a Play in Three Acts*, which enjoyed considerable popular success, although it is now largely forgotten. *The Belfry of Bruges* came out in 1846 and one of the finest of his works, *Evangeline, a Tale of Acadie*, appeared in 1847. A novel and more poetry followed before the publication in 1851 of his long poetic drama, *The Golden Legend*. In 1855, after he had resigned his professorship at Harvard, he published the celebrated *The Song of Hiawatha*. Yet another of his best-known works, *The Courtship of Miles Standish* came out in 1858. In 1861 his second wife was burnt to death in a tragic accident, but his private grief did not, happily, dry up his inspiration, and many more important works were still to come. *Tales of a Wayside Inn*, a collection of stories told by a group of travellers, including 'Paul Revere's Ride', was published in 1863, and in 1867 he produced his translation of Dante's *Divine Comedy*, on which he had worked for many years. It was highly acclaimed at the time, but is now considered to be somewhat pedestrian. In 1868 he made another journey to Europe, where he was welcomed as the greatest poet of his country, and received honorary degrees at both Cambridge and Oxford to add to those granted him earlier by Bowdoin and Harvard. Later he was similarly honoured in both Russia and Spain. In 1872 he published *Christus*, a dramatic trilogy consisting of the earlier *The Golden Legend*, *New England Tragedies* and *The Divine Tragedy*. *Three Books of Song*, which appeared in 1872, and *Aftermath*, in 1873, both contained more 'Tales of a Wayside Inn', and further collections, *The Mask of Pandora, and other poems*, *Keramos, and other poems* and *Ultima Thule*, were published in 1875, 1878 and 1880. The last of these was intended to be his final offering, but shortly after his death in 1882 *In the Harbor* was published. The poetry of Henry Wadsworth Longfellow is still widely known and is regarded both with affection and with some mockery. He cannot be considered as one of the greatest poets, and it might be fair to say that his work was more often manufactured than deeply felt, which is perhaps why it so frequently lends itself to parody. Nevertheless, he had great gifts and remains an important figure in the history of literature.

Henry Longfellow. He had a gift of simple romantic story-telling in verse, but his work is not of any great depth.

Longinus (*c*.213–273) Cassius Longinus was a Greek philosopher and critic who taught for many years in Athens. To him has been ascribed a work known as *On the Sublime*, which deals with the importance of deep-felt emotions in poetry, and which had a considerable effect on many eighteenth-century writers. It is almost certain, however, that this work was written at a much earlier period.

Look Homeward, Angel The long novel which made Thomas Wolfe famous when it was published in 1929. It tells of the early life and education of Eugene Gant. Gant is Wolfe himself, and the whole novel is strongly autobiographical.

Loos, Anita (1893–1981) The American writer Anita Loos was born in California. She became an actress and began to write for papers and for the screen. She published her bestseller, *Gentlemen Prefer Blondes*, in 1925, and followed it in 1928 with *But Gentlemen Marry Brunettes*. She wrote other novels, volumes of autobiography and several plays, including her adaptation of Colette's *Gigi*.

Lord Jim A novel by Joseph Conrad, first published in 1900. Jim, a former seaman, becomes successful in Patusan, but is haunted by the memory of an act of early moral cowardice, and finally regains his honour in death.

Lord of the Flies William Golding's powerful first novel, which tells of a group of boys stranded on a desert island where one of them becomes a tyrannical dictator. It was first published in 1954.

Lord of the Rings, The The title generally given to the trilogy by J.R.R. Tolkien, of which it is the final volume. The first two books, *The Return of the King* and *The Two Towers*, were originally published in 1954, and *The Lord of the Rings* appeared in 1955.

Lorna Doone: A Romance of Exmoor A novel by R.D. Blackmore, first published in 1869. Set in the seventeenth century, it tells of John Ridd's struggle against the evil Doone family.

Lotus-Eaters, The A poem by Alfred, Lord Tennyson, inspired by a part of the story of *The Odyssey*. It was first published in 1832, and subsequently revised.

Love for Love One of the finest of Restoration comedies, this play was written by William Congreve and first presented and published in 1695.

Lovelace, Richard (1618–58) The Cavalier poet Richard Lovelace was born at Woolwich, England, and educated at Charterhouse and Oxford. He followed his family tradition and became a soldier, but saw little active service. A Royalist, he was imprisoned in 1642 for offences against Parliament, and while in the Gatehouse wrote his famous lyric 'To Althea from Prison'. A second prison term in 1648 allowed him to gather together his poems, which were published the following year under the title *Lucasta; Epodes, Odes, Sonnets, Songs, etc*. A final volume, *Lucasta; Posthume Poems*, appeared after his death.

Love's Labours Lost A comedy by William Shakespeare, first presented about 1595 and printed in 1598. The King of Navarre and his friends are forced to interrupt a period of abstention from the company of women by the arrival of the Princess of France and her retinue.

Lowell, Amy (1874–1925) Born in Brookline, Massachusetts, Amy Lawrence Lowell was privately educated. She published her first volume of poetry, *A Dome of Many-Coloured Glass* in 1912. A number of other collections followed, including *Sword Blades and Poppy Seeds*, in 1914, *Men, Women, Ghosts*, in 1916, *Can Grande's Castle*, in 1918, and *What's O'Clock*, in 1925. She was a friend of Ezra Pound and D.H. Lawrence, and became one of the leaders of the Imagist movement. She also published some books of literary criticism, wrote many articles, and lectured widely.

Lowell, James Russell (1819–91) The American writer James Russell Lowell was born in Cambridge, Massachusetts, and educated at Harvard. He was appointed United States Minister in Spain in 1877, and Minister in England in 1880, where he served until 1885. He published a volume of poems, *A Year's Life*, in 1841, and followed it with other collections of verse, and in 1848 with *The Biglow Papers*, a collection of witty satires which had a considerable success. He became the first editor of *The Atlantic Monthly* in 1857, and from 1862 to 1872 worked for *The North American Review*. He published several collections of essays, speeches and sketches, and a second series of *The Biglow Papers* appeared in 1867.

Lowell, Robert (1917–77) Robert Traill Spence Lowell, the great-grandson of James Russell Lowell, was born in Boston and educated at Kenyon College. He published his first volume of poetry, *Land of Unlikeness*, in 1944, and was awarded the Pulitzer Prize for his second collection, *Lord Weary's Castle*, which appeared in 1946. Several more volumes appeared subsequently. Something of a rebel, he was imprisoned briefly during World War II for his refusal to fight, and he later opposed the Vietnam war and was a supporter of Senator McCarthy.

Lowry, Malcolm (1905–57) The English novelist Clarence Malcolm Lowry was born in Cheshire and educated at Cambridge. His first novel, *Ultramarine*, was published in 1933. He did not produce another until 1947, when *Under the Volcano* appeared. He lived in many countries, including Mexico and Canada, and complicated a disorganized existence still further by his addiction to drink. A number of works, including poetry and short stories, have been published posthumously.

Luck of Barry Lyndon, The A novel by William Makepeace Thackeray, first published in *Fraser's Magazine* in 1844, and later issued in book form as *The Memoirs of Barry Lyndon, Esq.*

Lucky Jim A comic novel set in a provincial university, which established the reputation of Kingsley Amis when it was published in 1954.

Lucretius (*c*.98–55BC) The birthplace of Titus Lucretius Carus, the Latin poet, is uncertain, but he was probably a Roman. He is believed to have lost his reason, and after some years of madness to have committed suicide. He left a major work, the long didactic poem *De Rerum Natura*.

Luther, Martin (1483–1546) The religious reformer Martin Luther was born at Eisleben, Germany.

The title-page from Luther's *Auslegung der Euangelien*, with a wood-cut border. It was published in 1528.

After attending various schools he went to the University of Erfurt and eventually entered an Augustinian monastery. He visited Rome, and then, in 1517, attacked the practice of Papal Indulgences by nailing his ninety-five 'Theses' to the church door at Wittenberg. As a result, he was banned, and henceforth became the leader of the Reformation in Germany. He produced a number of tracts, but his major literary work was the translation of the Bible into German, his version being known as the Lutheran Bible. It was published in 1534.

Lycidas An elegy on the death of Edward King written by John Milton and published in 1638.

Lydgate, John (*c*.1370–*c*.1451) The Benedictine monk John Lydgate was born in Suffolk, England. He wrote an enormous quantity of verse, much of it in the style of Chaucer. His major works were *The Falls of Princes*, *The Troy Book*, *The Complaint of the Black Knight* and *The Temple of Glas*.

Lyly, John (1553–1606) The writer John Lyly was born in Kent, England, and educated at both Oxford and Cambridge. In 1578 he published *Euphues, or the Anatomy of Wit*, and followed it in 1580 with a sequel, *Euphues and his England*. The affected style of these books gave us the term 'euphuism' for high-flown speech or writing. Lyly also wrote a number of plays, including *The Woman in the Moone*, *Endymion*, *Alexander and Campaspe* and *Love's Metamorphosis*, all written and first performed between 1580, or thereabouts, and 1600.

Lyndsay, Sir David (*c*.1490–*c*.1555) Few details are available of the early years of the Scottish poet David Lyndsay. In 1529 he was knighted and created Lyon King of Arms, and much of his life was spent in diplomatic activities. He wrote a number of long poems, the first of which was *The Dreme*. This was followed by, among other works, *The Testament and Complaynt of the Papyngo*, in which a parrot becomes the mouthpiece for warnings and satirical comments on court behaviour, *Ane Pleasant Satyre of the Thrie Estaitis*, and the charmingly titled *The Complaynt and Publict Confessions of the Kingis Auld Hound, callit Bagsche, directit to Bawtie, the Kingis best belovit Dog*.

lyric A term derived from the musical instrument the lyre, and hence originally applied in ancient Greece to poems designed to be sung (a usage which has been revived in recent times in its application to the words of popular songs). In verse a lyric has come to mean a short poem which may have no direct musical relationship but which is particularly concerned with the expression of the poet's personal feelings and emotions.

Lyrical Ballads, with a few other poems A collection of poems by William Wordsworth and Samuel Taylor Coleridge, including the former's 'Lucy' verses and the latter's 'The Rime of the Ancient Mariner'. The book, which was one of the seminal publications of the Romantic movement in England, was first published in 1798, and enlarged, with Prefaces, in 1801 and again in 1802.

Lysistrata, The A comedy by Aristophanes in which, during time of war, women bring peace by imposing their own sanctions. It was written and performed in 411BC.

M

Mabinogion, The A collection of Welsh stories, published in 1838 by Lady Charlotte Guest, taken from two fourteenth- and fifteenth-century manuscripts, *The White Book of Rhydderch* and *The Red Book of Hergest*. The term 'The Mabinogion', which is derived from the Welsh for 'Bard's apprentice', is strictly applied to only four of the tales, but is widely used for all eleven in Lady Guest's selection.

Macaulay, Rose (1881–1958) Emilie Rose Macaulay, the English novelist, was born in Cambridge and educated at Oxford. She published her first book, *Abbots Verney*, in 1906, and attracted considerable attention with *Potterism*, which

appeared in 1920. The best known of her many novels are *Told by an Idiot*, which came out in 1923, and *The Towers of Trebizond*, in 1956. She also published verse, essays and several travel books. She was made a Dame in 1958.

Macaulay, Thomas Babington (1800–59) An extremely precocious boy, Thomas Babington Macaulay wrote *A Compendium of Universal History* and a long poem *The Battle of Cheviot*, before he was eight years old. Born in Leicestershire, England, he was educated at Cambridge. In 1825 he became famous when his essay on Milton was published in the *Edinburgh Review*, to which he continued to contribute regularly, despite an active career as a politician. After a brief period as a lawyer, he entered Parliament, and from 1834 to 1838 was in India as a member of the Supreme Council of India. On his return to England he became Secretary of State for War, and, in a later administration, Paymaster-General. Meanwhile, he published books on Clive and Warren Hastings, and in 1842 brought out his *Lays of Ancient Rome*, and in 1843 the *Essays Critical and Historical* appeared. These two books were enormously successful, and continued to be popular well into the twentieth century. In 1847 he lost his seat in Parliament, and from that time devoted himself to his massive *History of England*, which he had already begun and on which he was to spend many years. The first

The historian, poet and statesman, Thomas Babington Macaulay in his study, painted by Edward Ward in 1853.

two volumes came out in 1848, and the third and fourth volumes in 1855. The *History* was a bestseller in Britain and the United States and in the eleven European countries where it appeared in translation. Macaulay became a wealthy man, and in 1857 was elevated to the peerage. He did not complete the *History*, but a fifth volume was published posthumously. Although some sections of it are now discredited, other parts have not been superseded, and the author's narrative power makes it one of the most attractive and readable works ever written in this genre.

Macbeth A tragedy by William Shakespeare in which the Scottish Lord Macbeth, spurred on by his wife, murders the King of Scotland, and brings doom upon himself. It was first performed about 1606 and printed in 1623.

MacCaig, Norman (1910–) The Scottish poet Norman Alexander MacCaig was born and educated in Edinburgh. His first collection of poems, *Far Cry*, was published in 1943, and several volumes have followed, including *Riding Lights*, in 1955, *A Common Grace*, in 1960, and *The White Bird*, in 1973. His *Selected Poems* came out in 1971, and the *Collected Poems* appeared in 1985.

McCarthy, Mary (1912–) Born in Seattle, Mary McCarthy published her first novel, *The Company She Keeps*, in 1942. She followed it with several others, including *A Charmed Life*, which appeared in 1955, *The Group*, in 1963, and *Cannibals and Missionaries*, in 1980. She has also produced short stories, essays and two books on Vietnam, *Vietnam* and *Hanoi*, which came out in 1967 and 1968, while a collection of essays, *Occasional Prose*, appeared in 1985.

McCullers, Carson (1917–67) Carson Smith McCullers was born in Georgia. In 1940 she published her first novel, *The Heart is a Lonely Hunter*, and in the following year brought out *Reflections in a Golden Eye*. *The Member of the Wedding* appeared in 1946, and *Clock Without Hands* in 1961. *The Ballad of the Sad Café*, which came out in 1951, was a collection of short stories. A further volume of short stories, *The Mortgaged Heart*, was published posthumously.

McCullough, Colleen (1938–) The Australian novelist Colleen McCullough was born in Wellington, New South Wales, but has lived in America for many years. Her first novel, *Tim*, made little impression when it appeared in 1974, but in 1977 she published *The Thorn Birds*, which became an overnight international bestseller. Subsequent books include *An Indecent Obsession*, in 1981, and the novella, *The Ladies of Missalonghi*, in 1987.

McDiarmid, Hugh (1892–1978) Hugh McDiarmid was the pseudonym used by Christopher Murray Grieve, who was born in Langholm, Scotland. A militant nationalist of the left wing, some of his poetry was political in content, but most of his work was written in Scottish dialect, including his best-known work, *A Drunk Man Looks at the Thistle*, published in 1926. His *Complete Poems 1920–1976* appeared posthumously in 1978.

Macdonald, George (1824–1905) The Scottish novelist George Macdonald was born in Aberdeenshire and educated at Aberdeen University. After a brief period as a minister of the Church, he turned to writing, and in 1856 published the first of three books of poems. In 1862 he achieved popular success with his novel *David Elginbrod*. A number of other novels followed, and he also wrote books for children, the best known of which are *At the Back of the North Wind* and *The Princess and the Goblin*, which appeared in 1871 and 1872 respectively.

Macdonald, John D. (1916–86) The American mystery writer John Dann Macdonald was born in Pennsylvania. After completing his education at the Harvard Graduate School of Business Administration he joined the army, and then, at the end of World War II, turned to writing. His first book was *The Brass Cupcake*, published in 1950. Since then he has produced over sixty novels, many of them featuring the private eye Travis McGee, of which millions of copies have been sold.

Macdonald, Ross (1915–) Ross Macdonald is the pseudonym of Kenneth Millar, who was born in California and educated at the universities of Ontario and Michigan. His first book, published under his own name, was *The Dark Tunnel*, which appeared in 1944. A few years later he embarked on a long series of literate mysteries featuring the private eye Lew Archer. Among them are *The Galton Case*, which appeared in 1959, *The Wycherly Woman*, in 1961, *The Goodbye Look*, in 1969, and *The Blue Hammer*, in 1971.

McGonagall, William (c.1830–1902) Known as the worst poet in the world, William McGonagall wrote prolifically in appalling doggerel, characterised not only by tortured scansion and feeble rhymes, but by the unconscious humour of his wording. His poem on the Tay Bridge disaster, for instance, a railway accident in which many lost their lives, was intended to be deeply moving, but succeeds only in being hilarious.

Machiavelli, Niccolò (1469–1527) The Italian statesman Niccolò Machiavelli was born in Florence. He wrote a great deal of poetry, some plays, including *Mandragola*, first printed in 1524, a history of Florence, and his *Arte della guerra (The Art of War)*, but his best-known work is *Il Principe (The Prince)*, his influential study of political power, which was written in 1513.

McKay, Claude (1890–1948) The Black writer Claude McKay was born in Jamaica, but lived most of his life in the United States. He published his first poetry, *Songs of Jamaica*, in 1912, and his first novel, *Home to Harlem*, the result of his experiences after serving in World War I, appeared in 1928. He published an autobiography in 1937, and a study of *Harlem* came out in 1940.

Mackenzie, Compton (1883–1972) Edward Montague Compton Mackenzie was educated at Oxford. His first published work was *Poems*, which appeared in 1907. The novels *The Passionate Elopement* and *Carnival* followed in 1911 and 1912, but it was the publication of the two volumes of *Sinister Street*, in 1913 and 1914, which first brought him real success. He published a great many other novels, including the light-hearted *Whisky Galore*, which appeared in 1947, and also wrote a number of volumes of autobiography. He was knighted in 1952.

Mackenzie, Henry (1745–1831) The Scottish novelist Henry Mackenzie was born and educated in Edinburgh. His first novel, *The Man of Feeling*, was instantly successful when it was published anonymously in 1771. He followed it with *The Man of the World*, in 1773, and *Julia de Roubigné*, in 1777. He was also a dramatist, the most notable of his plays being *The Prince of Tunis*, presented in 1773, and, as an adherent of the Tory party, he produced many political tracts. He became Comptroller of the Taxes for Scotland.

Maclean, Alistair (1922–87) The Scottish novelist Alistair Maclean was born near Inverness and, after World War II, completed his education at Glasgow University. His first novel, *HMS Ulysses*, became an instant bestseller when it was published in 1955, and he went on to write *The Guns of Navarone*, which appeared in 1957, and a large number of popular adventure stories, including *Where Eagles Dare*, published in 1967.

MacLeish, Archibald (1892–1982) Born in Glencoe, Illinois, and educated at Yale and Harvard, Archibald MacLeish published his first book of poetry, *Tower of Ivory*, in 1917. Much more poetry followed, including *The Pot of Earth*, published in 1924, *New Found Land*, in 1930, and *Conquistador* and his *Collected Poems*, which both won Pulitzer Prizes, in 1933 and 1952 respectively. He also wrote a number of verse plays, some specifically for radio. Particularly notable among these were *The Fall of the City*, in 1937, and *J.B.*, the latter bringing him his third Pulitzer Prize in 1958. MacLeish was Librarian of Congress from 1939 to 1944 and Assistant Secretary of State

Archibald MacLeish at Queen's College, Cambridge.

from 1944 to 1945. He became a professor at Harvard in 1949 and held the post until 1962.

MacNeice, Louis (1907–63) Frederick Louis MacNeice was born in Belfast, Northern Ireland, and educated at Marlborough and Oxford. While at university he published his first book of poetry, *Blind Fireworks*, and many more collections were to follow. A prolific writer, he produced a number of books of literary criticism, a novel and an autobiography, translated the *Agamemnon* of Aeschylus and Goethe's *Faust*, collaborated with his friend W.H. Auden on *Letters from Iceland*, which appeared in 1937, and later added to his considerable reputation as a poet with the plays he wrote for radio, which included *Christopher Columbus*, in 1944, and *The Dark Tower*, in 1947.

Macpherson, James (1736–96) The Scottish poet James Macpherson was born near Kingussie and educated in Aberdeen and Edinburgh. He wrote a *History of Great Britain* and also translated *The Illiad*, but he is remembered as the discoverer of Ossian, a supposed Gaelic poet of the third century. In 1760 he published *Fragments of Ancient Poetry collected in the Highlands of Scotland*, and in the following year produced *Fingal, an Ancient Epic Poem in Six Books, together with Several Other Poems composed by Ossian, the Son of Fingal translated from the Gaelic Language*. *Temora* followed in 1763, and the collected edition of *The Works of Ossian* in 1765. The authenticity of the poems was immediately challenged by Dr Johnson, and it has subsequently become certain that Macpherson provided the larger part of the material himself. The works remained popular, however, and are not entirely without poetic merit.

Madame Bovary Gustave Flaubert's great novel of adultery in a French provincial town, first published in 1857.

Maeterlinck, Maurice (1862–1949) Of Flemish extraction, Maurice Maeterlinck was born and educated in Ghent, Belgium. In 1889 he attracted considerable attention with his play *La Princesse Maleine*, and another play, *Pelléas et Mélisande*, which was later to provide the libretto for Debussy's opera, was a major success in 1892. *L'oiseau bleu (The Blue Bird)* became equally well known after its production in 1908. Maeterlinck also wrote poetry and a number of works on philosophy. He was awarded the Nobel Prize for Literature in 1911.

Magic Mountain, The A novel by Thomas Mann, first published in 1924.

magic realism A term originating in the world of art and adopted to apply to the work of writers such as Borges, Garcia Márquez, Salman Rushdie and Italo Calvino, in which dreamlike elements of the bizarre and fanciful are mixed with realistic sequences in a matter-of-fact way.

Magus, The A novel by John Fowles, first published in 1966 and revised in 1977.

Mailer, Norman (1923–) The American novelist Norman Mailer was born in New Jersey and educated at Harvard. During World War II he served in the Pacific, and his experiences resulted in the war novel *The Naked and the Dead*, which was published in 1948 and made him famous, its enormous success being due, at least in part, to its relentlessly realistic picture of men at war. He followed it with *Barbary Shore* and *The Deer Park*, which appeared in 1951 and 1955. Other novels include *An American Dream*, in 1965, *Why Are We in Vietnam?*, in 1967, and in 1983, the huge story set in the Egypt of three thousand years ago, *Ancient Evenings*, a book which nowhere failed to impress, although press verdicts on it were not universally favourable. *Tough Guys Don't Dance* came out in 1984. In his fiction Mailer is almost always an abrasive social commentator, a crusader, and he has also produced a number of non-fiction works in which this tendency is largely to the fore. In 1959 he brought out *Advertisements for Myself*, an extraordinary mixture of stories, essays, extracts from work in progress and autobiographical material. *The Presidential Papers* came in 1963, and the 1968 publication of *The Armies of the Night: The Novel as History, History as a Novel* brought him both the National Book Award and

The novelist and Pulitzer Prize-winner Norman Mailer.

a Pulitzer Prize. Among his other works are *Cannibals and Christians* and *The Bullfight*, both published in 1967, *Miami and the Siege of Chicago*, in 1969, *The Prisoner of Sex*, in 1971. He collaborated with others in *Marilyn: A Biography*, which appeared in 1973. With *The Executioner's Song*, a long non-fiction account of a murder, he won a second Pulitzer Prize in 1979. *Of Women and their Elegance*, with photographs by Milton H. Greene, came out in 1980. A prolific writer who tackles a variety of genres and delights in surprising his readers with each new book, Mailer has never believed in the idea of the author as a recluse – he is a public figure, much involved in politics, and often the centre of controversy. His writings, like those of most authors, are uneven in quality, and a tendency to self-indulgence is occasionally evident, but at his best the power and directness of his work are outstanding.

Main Street A novel about a small town in the American Mid-West with which Sinclair Lewis scored his first major success in 1920.

Major Barbara A play by G. Bernard Shaw about a major in the Salvation Army and her father, a maker of munitions. It was first presented in 1905 and published in 1907.

Malamud, Bernard (1914–86) Born in Brooklyn and educated at Columbia University, the American fiction-writer Bernard Malamud was a teacher and academic. His first novel, *The Natural*, was published in 1952. He followed it with several novels, and collections of short stories such as *The Magic Barrel*, which appeared in 1960. His writing won him many awards – his novel *The Fixer*, for instance, published in 1967, gained both the National Book Award and the Pulitzer Prize.

malapropism An absurd use of ill-chosen words, often in an effort to impress. As Mrs Malaprop says in Sheridan's comedy *The Rivals*, 'a daughter of mine ... should have a supercilious knowledge in accounts; – and as she grew up, I would have her instructed in geometry, that she might know something of the contagious countries; – but above all ... she should be mistress of orthodoxy ... that she might reprehend the true meaning of what she is saying.' The term derives, of course from Mrs Malaprop herself.

Mallarmé, Stéphane (1842–98) The French poet Stéphane Mallarmé was born in Paris. He spent some time in England, and then returned to Paris where he taught English. His output of poetry was comparatively small, but it was important and influential. In 1887 he published, in a facsimile of his own handwriting, his *Poésies complètes*. It included among other pieces 'L'Après-midi d'un faune', which had been written eleven years earlier and was later to inspire the music by Debussy and the Diaghilev ballet with controversial choreography by Nijinsky. His translations of the poetry of Edgar Allan Poe came out in 1888, and *Pages* and *Vers et prose* appeared in 1891 and 1893 respectively. *Divagations*, a final collection of his prose, was published in 1897, and a revised edition of the *Poésies* was produced posthumously in 1899. Mallarmé was in many ways a forerunner of James Joyce, pushing back the frontiers of language so as to widen its scope. In his later work he often abandoned punctuation, and he was one of the earliest writers to set out his poetry so that the visual effect became an important additional factor in its expression.

Malory, Sir Thomas (*d.*1471) Whether or not Sir Thomas Malory was the author of *Le Morte D'Arthur*, which is generally attributed to him, is uncertain. The work, one of the important sources of the King Arthur legends, was completed in 1469 or 1470. Of the edition which he printed, Caxton wrote that it was 'after a copye unto me delivered which copye Syr Thomas Malorye dyd take oute of certeyn bookes of frensshe and reduced it in to Englysshe'. Malory has been identified as Sir Thomas Malory of Newbold Revel in Warwickshire, who died in 1471.

Malraux, André (1901–76) The French writer André Malraux was born in Paris. He published his first book, a series of prose poems entitled *Lunes en papier (Paper Moons)*, in 1921. His political interests and his education in oriental languages

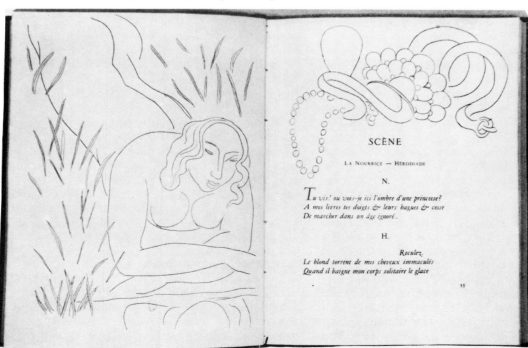

An erotic line illustration in a 1932 publication of Stéphane Mallarmé's poem *Poésies*.

led him to visit China when he was in his early twenties, and later he was to spend time in Spain during the Civil War, both experiences having a powerful influence on his work. His first important novel was *Les conquérants (The Conquerors)*, which appeared in 1928, and in 1933 he won the prix Goncourt for *La condition humaine (Man's Fate)*. As well as writing many novels, he became a much-respected art critic, and his books in this genre include *Les voix du silence (The Voices of Silence)*, published in 1953, and the important *Psychologie de l'art (The Psychology of Art)*, which appeared in three volumes between 1948 and 1950.

Malthus, Thomas Robert (1766–1834) Born in Surrey and educated privately and at Cambridge, Thomas Robert Malthus became a clergyman. In 1798 he published his major work, *An Essay on the Principle of Population as it affects the Future Improvement of Society*. Revised editions appeared in 1803 and 1816.

Man and Superman A play in four acts by G. Bernard Shaw, which he described as 'A Comedy and a Philosophy', and in which he expounded his ideas of the Life Force. It was first published in 1903, and presented, without the long third act, in 1905.

Man Without Qualities, The A long unfinished novel by Robert Musil, first published between 1930 and 1932.

Mandeville, Bernard de (1670–1733) Of English parentage, Bernard de Mandeville was born in Dordrecht, Holland, and educated in Rotterdam and, as a physician, at Leiden University. Apart from various philosophical works he published a number of books and tracts on a variety of subjects, including *A Treatise of the Hypochondriack and Hysterick Passions*, *The Virgin Unmasked*, which might be loosely described as an early feminist piece, *A Modest Defence of Public Stews*, which proposed governmental control of brothels, and his best-known work, *The Fable of the Bees, or Private Vices, Public Benefits*, a satirical poem consisting of two hundred couplets in doggerel.

Mandeville, The Travels of Sir John An extraordinary travel book, written in French and published in about 1357. The authorship is far from certain, and the material probably came from several different sources. Supposedly a guide to the Holy Land, it ranges as far as India and China, and includes information on a wide variety of subjects, from astronomical observations to an account of Prester John and stories of fabulous beasts.

Manfred Byron's verse drama is concerned with Manfred's sufferings as a result of a sin committed in his youth. It was first published in 1817.

Mann, Heinrich (1871–1950) Like his more eminent younger brother Thomas, Heinrich Mann was born in Lübeck, became a novelist, and was later to leave Germany to escape from Nazi rule. His early novels, including *The Little Town*, *The Patriotees*, *The Poor*, *The Chief*, portrayed German society in the days of the Empire. In 1904 he produced *Professor Unrat*, later transferred to the screen as *The Blue Angel*. His most important books were the historical novels, *Young Henry of Navarre* and *Henry, King of France*, published in 1936 and 1938.

Mann, Thomas (1875–1955) The great German novelist Thomas Mann was born in Lübeck. After a brief period as a clerk, he attended lectures at Munich University, went to Italy, and became the editor of the satirical magazine *Simplizissmus*. His first novel, *Buddenbrooks*, which examined the decline of a family, was published in two volumes in 1900. After a slow start, it sold in huge quantities, and made his name, although it was not translated into English until 1924. Subsequently it was banned and burned by the Nazis. In 1903 came *Tonio Kröger*, and this novella was followed in 1906 by a play, *Fiorenza*. In 1912 another short novel, *Der Tod in Venedig (Death in Venice)*, later to be brilliantly translated to the screen, was published, and in 1915 *Königliche Hoheit (Royal Highness)* appeared. He produced a statement of

Thomas Mann became a United States citizen in 1944.

his Conservative political beliefs, *Betrachtungen einer Unpolitischen (Observations of an Unpolitical Man)*, in 1918, and the next major novel, *Der Zauberberg (The Magic Mountain)*, came out in 1925. His stature was acknowledged in 1929 by the award of the Nobel Prize for Literature. The 'Joseph' novels, or 'Joseph and his Brothers', consisted of four books, *Die Geschichten Jaakobs, Der Junge Joseph, Joseph in Ägypten* and *Joseph der Ernährer*, which were published between 1933 and 1942. Meanwhile he had left Germany and was living in Zurich. In 1936 he was deprived of his German citizenship and of his honorary doctorate at the University of Bonn, and in 1937 he brought out *An Exchange of Letters*, an attack on Fascism which was published all over the world. Thereafter he lived mostly in the United States. *Dr Faustus* appeared in 1947, and two years later he produced what might be described as an extended Preface to it in *Die Entstehung des Dr Faustus (The Genesis of Dr Faustus)*. One more major work was to come before his death, and this was *Die Bekenntnisse des Hochstaplers Felix Krull (The Confessions of the Confidence Trickster Felix Krull)*, which was published in 1954. Thomas Mann's work, in which he often presented the relationship of the artist to the society in which he lived, is still greatly admired as literature of the highest quality.

Manning, Olivia (1908–80) The British novelist and short story writer Olivia Manning published her first book, *The Wind Changes*, in 1937. Her most successful publications were 'The Balkan Trilogy', consisting of *The Great Fortune, The Spoilt City* and *Friends and Heroes*, published between 1960 and 1965, and 'The Levant Trilogy', consisting of *The Danger Tree, The Battle Lost and Won* and *The Sum of Things*, which appeared between 1977 and 1980.

Mansfield, Katherine (1888–1923) Katherine Mansfield was the pseudonym adopted by Kathleen Mansfield Beauchamp, who was born in Wellington, New Zealand and educated at Queen's College, London. She published her first collection of short stories, the genre for which she became famous, in 1911. This was *In a German Pension*. It was followed by *Bliss, and other stories* in 1920, and *The Garden Party and other stories* in 1922. Two other collections, *The Dove's Nest* and *Something Childish*, appeared posthumously.

Mansfield Park A novel by Jane Austen, first published in 1814. It tells of Fanny Price and her relationships with the well-to-do Bertrams of Mansfield Park.

Manzoni, Alessandro (1785–1873) The Italian writer Alessandro Francesco Tommaso Antonio Manzoni was born in Milan. His first writings were poetry, and he later wrote two tragedies, but he is remembered chiefly for his novel *I promessi sposi (The Betrothed)*, which was first published in separate volumes between 1825 and 1827. Manzoni subsequently spent many years revising the work, and brought out a final version in 1840.

Marble Faun, The A novel, set in Rome and inspired by Nathaniel Hawthorne's visit to Italy. It was first published in 1860, and appeared in England under the title *The Transformation*.

Marcus Aurelius Antoninus (121–180) The reign of the Roman Emperor Marcus Aurelius Antoninus began in the year 161. Over a long period, and while conducting affairs of state and leading his armies to battle with German tribes, he produced twelve volumes of the *Meditations*, in which he expounds his Stoic philosophy. The first English translation appeared in 1701, and became very popular.

Mardi and a Voyage Thither An allegorical and often satirical romance by Herman Melville, first published in 1849.

Marius the Epicurean A philosophical romance, presented as the biography of a young Roman, by Walter Pater, first published in 1885.

Marlowe, Christopher (1564–93) The son of a Canterbury shoemaker, Christopher Marlowe was educated in Canterbury and at Cambridge. While at University he began a translation of Ovid's *Amores*, which was published posthumously. From Cambridge he went to London, joined the Lord Admiral's Company of Players and began to write plays. It was a period when collaboration was commonplace and dramatic works were not always clearly attributed to their authors, and it is therefore impossible to say with certainty that, as has been alleged, Marlowe was the true author of the most effective scenes in the three parts of Shakespeare's *Henry VI* and also had a major hand in other chronicle plays, such as *King John* and *Richard III*. We do know that Shakespeare knew him, admired his work, and was probably much influenced by it. It is also without question that Marlowe himself wrote four great tragedies, *Tamburlaine the Great*, which was performed in 1587, *Dr Faustus*, in 1588, *The Famous Tragedy of the Rich Jew of Malta*, in 1592, and *Edward II*, which was published in 1594. A fragment of another play, *The Massacre at Paris*, still exists, and *The Tragedie of Dido, Queen of Carthage* was written jointly by Marlowe and Thomas Nashe. There were undoubtedly other collaborations and perhaps other plays by Marlowe alone which are now lost to us. The four major plays are, however, sufficient to testify not only to Marlowe's great talent but also to his innovative importance. He has been

HERO AND
LEANDR:

Begun by *Christopher Marloe*; and
finifhed by George Chapman.

Ut Nectar, Ingenium.

At London
Printed by *Felix Kingfton*, for *Paule Linley*, and
are to be folde in Panles Church-yard, at the
figne of the Blacke-beare.
1598.

LEFT: *Hero and Leander* relates the love story of the legendary Greek youth Leander, who swam the Hellespont nightly to visit Hero and ultimately drowned.
BELOW: Christopher Marlowe at the age of twenty-one.

referred to as the father of tragedy in the English theatre, in whose work the first real flowering of blank verse was seen. In addition to his translation of Ovid he also produced versions of the work of the Roman poet Lucan, and wrote poetry, including the celebrated 'The Passionate Shepherd to His Love' ('Come live with me and be my love …') and two parts of 'Hero and Leander', a long verse narration of their love story which was later completed by George Chapman. Christopher Marlowe led a turbulent life, mixing with unsavoury characters, and was no stranger to violence. Indiscreet and outspoken, he was a professed atheist and probably a homosexual, at a time when it was not acceptable to be either, and was frequently involved in nefarious activities which brought him into conflict with the authorities. He made various journeys to Europe, possibly as a spy, and on one occasion was deported from the Netherlands for issuing forged coins. At the time of his death he was due to appear before the Privy Council to answer serious charges, although there is no record of what these were. He was killed in a fight in a tavern in Deptford by a man called Ingrim Frizer. The quarrel is said to have arisen over the bill, but other versions allege that it was concerned with gambling or resulted from jealousy in a homosexual love affair. It seems quite possible that none of these was the true cause of Marlowe's death, but that he was murdered at the behest of his political enemies. Whatever the truth, the killing cut short the life of a man who, in a few short years, made a major contribution to English literature.

Marquand, John P. (1893–1960) The American novelist John Phillips Marquand was born in Wilmington, Delaware, and educated at Harvard. He began to write short stories and serials for magazines, and won the Pulitzer Prize with his first full-length story, published in book form, *The Late George Apley*, which appeared in 1937. He wrote a number of other novels, including *H.M. Pulham, Esquire*, which appeared in 1941, and several mysteries featuring Mr Moto.

Marquis, Don (1878–1937) Donal Robert Perry Marquis was born in Illinois. He wrote much humorous verse, poetry and many novels, but is remembered for his series of books about *archy and mehitabel*. The first of these dialogues between a literary cockroach and his cat friend appeared in 1927.

Marriage à la Mode One of John Dryden's most successful comedies, first presented in 1672 and published in the following year.

Marryat, Captain Frederick (1792–1848) Entering the Navy at the age of fourteen, Frederick Marryat, who was born in London, had reached the rank of captain by the time he published his first novel, *Frank Mildmay, or the Naval Officer*, in 1829. It was so successful that he left the sea and took to writing, producing several more novels, including *Mr Midshipman Easy* (1836). He also achieved great popularity with his books for children, especially *The Children of the New Forest*, which appeared in 1847.

Marsh, Ngaio (1898–1982) The detective story writer Ngaio Edith Marsh was born in Christchurch, New Zealand. She was an actress before becoming an author. Her first book, *A Man Lay Dead*, was published in 1934. In it she introduced her popular hero, the senior police detective Roderick Alleyn, who was to feature regularly in her later stories. Other books included *Enter a Murderer*, published in 1935, *Final Curtain*, in 1947, and *Grave Mistake*, in 1978. She was made a Dame in 1966.

Marston, John (*c.*1575–1634) The English dramatist John Marston was educated at Oxford and became first a lawyer and later a clergyman. His earliest published work, *The Metamorphosis of Pigmalions Image and certaine Satyres*, appeared in 1598, and in the same year he brought out *Scourge of Villainie*, both books bearing the pseudonym W. Kinsayder. These poems and satires were followed in 1601 and 1602 by his first plays, *The History of Antonio and Mellida, The First Part* and *Antonio's Revenge, The Second Part*. Many more dramatic works were to come, including *The Malcontent*, in 1604, and *The Dutch Courtezan*, in 1605. Sometimes at daggers drawn with Ben Jonson, sometimes his close friend, he collaborated with him and George Chapman on *Eastward Hoe*, the comedy which in 1605 gave offence and caused all three playwrights to be put briefly in prison.

Martial (*c.*AD38–104) Marcus Valerius Martialis, despite his Latin name, appears to have been of Spanish birth, but he spent most of his life in Rome. After publishing some works of lesser importance, he brought out, between the years 86 and 102, twelve volumes of *Epigrammata*. These short verses, of which there are some fifteen hundred, are brilliantly phrased, sometimes bawdy, often malicious, and almost always engagingly witty.

Martin Chuzzlewit A novel by Charles Dickens, first published in parts between 1843 and 1844, and telling of the tribulations caused to Martin Chuzzlewit by the villainous Mr Pecksniff. It was considered at the time to be one of Dickens' less successful novels, and was particularly disliked in America.

Martineau, Harriet (1802–76) Of Huguenot extraction, the English author Harriet Martineau was born in Norwich. Her first published writings were of a religious nature, although she was later to become an atheist. Beginning in 1831 she produced a series of stories, *Illustrations of Political Economy* and *Illustrations of Taxation*, which, despite their titles, achieved a huge and enthusiastic readership. She then, in 1834, visited the United States, angered many Americans with her abolitionist views, and on her return added to their wrath by publishing two critical books, *Society in America* and *A Retrospect of Western Travel*. She also wrote novels, including *Deerbrook*, published in 1839, books for children, travel books, autobiography, works on mesmerism and freethinking, and – from the standpoint of a philosophical Radical – the popular *The History of the Thirty Years' Peace, 1816–1846*, which was published in 1849.

George Richmond's gentle, evocative chalk portrait of Harriet Martineau, *c.*1834. A radical social philosopher and reformer, her books attracted a wide readership.

Martin Marprelate The pseudonym used for a series of Puritan religious pamphlets, issued in 1588 and 1589, which attacked the established Church, using biting satire and personal obloquy to great effect. The authorship of the pamphlets has not been clearly established, but they were printed by one John Penry, a dissident who was hanged in 1593 for his part in the affair.

Marvell, Andrew (1621–78) The son of a clergyman, Andrew Marvell was born in Yorkshire, England, and educated at Hull Grammar School and Cambridge. Although he is regarded primarily as a Puritan poet, vastly overshadowed by Milton but not without considerable merits of his own, he was originally a supporter of Charles I. He then transferred his loyalties to Oliver Cromwell, whom he came to admire greatly, but at the time of the Restoration he became a Royalist again. This vacillation seems to have been due less to expediency than to a fair-mindedness which allowed him to see virtues in both monarchical and republican systems. In 1650, having previously spent some years in Europe, he produced his 'Horatian Ode upon Cromwell's Return from Ireland', and in the same year went to live in Yorkshire as tutor to General Fairfax's daughter. During this period he is believed to have written much of his pastoral poetry, such as 'Thoughts in a Garden' and 'On Appleton House'. In 1653, partly as a result of representations made by his friend John Milton, he became tutor to Cromwell's ward, William Dutton. This appointment brought him into contact with John Oxenbridge, whose experiences in the West Indies are thought to have inspired Marvell to write 'The Bermudas'. In 1659 he became Member of Parliament for Hull, and it may have been partly in this capacity that he helped to save Milton from prison or even execution, when at the Restoration the Royalists took revenge on such political opponents. From about 1667 onwards Marvell's writings became increasingly political and satirical, with attacks on Lord Clarendon and, especially, on Charles II, with whom he had become increasingly disillusioned. The most important of these prose pieces were *The Rehearsal Transposed*, a defence of Dissenters, published in 1672 and 1673, and *Mr Smirke, or the Divine in Mode…* and *An Account of the Growth of Popery and Arbitrary Government in England, more particularly from the Long Prorogation of Parliament*, which appeared in 1676 and 1677. Both preached against the extension of the King's powers and the influence of the Church of Rome. Marvell's *Miscellaneous Poems* came out posthumously in 1781, and the collection known

A somewhat romantic portrait of the Puritan poet and politician Andrew Marvell, painted *c.*1655–60.

as *Poems on Affairs of State* was published in several volumes between 1689 and 1707. If a single short poem can make a poet great then surely Marvell's 'To his coy Mistress' could claim that distinction.

Marx, Karl (1818–83) Heinrich Karl Marx was born in Trèves (now Trier), Germany, and educated at the universities of Bonn and Berlin. He became an editor of a radical paper, which was suppressed early in 1843. He then went to Paris, where he met Friedrich Engels, with whom he was to collaborate as a writer and newspaper editor. He produced a number of works of political philosophy, ranging from articles to books. In 1849, hounded by the authorities, he took refuge in Britain, and it was here that in 1867 he published the first volume – the only one that was completed – of his most famous work, *Das Kapital*.

Masefield, John (1878–1967) The English poet, novelist and dramatist John Edward Masefield was born in Herefordshire. While still in his teens he went to sea, and then spent some years scratching a living in the United States. In 1902 he published his first collection of verses,

Salt-Water Ballads, which contained 'Sea Fever', while the other great favourite, 'Cargoes', was included in *Ballads and Poems*, in 1910. Masefield, who became Poet Laureate in 1930, produced many books of poetry, several of which, such as *Reynard the Fox*, were in narrative form. His *Collected Poems* appeared in 1923. He also wrote several plays and novels.

Mason, A.E.W. (1865–1948) The English novelist Alfred Edward Woodley Mason was born in Dulwich, educated at Oxford, and then began his career as an actor. He published his first novel, *A Romance of Westdale*, in 1895, and followed it with several others before *The Four Feathers*, which was immensely successful when it appeared in 1902. The most notable of his other novels was perhaps *Fire Over England*, published in 1936. Mason also wrote a series of detective stories featuring Inspector Hanaud.

masques Originally a term used to describe a dramatic and musical entertainment performed in mime by masked actors and dancers, the word masque was later applied to such pieces even when dialogue became the main ingredient. Almost invariably performed by aristocratic amateurs, the form was very popular in the sixteenth and seventeenth centuries, and masques were written by many leading dramatists of the period – most notably Ben Jonson.

Massacre at Paris, The A play by Christopher Marlowe, of which we possess only a fragment. It was probably written not long before his death in May, 1593.

Massinger, Philip (1583–1640) Born in Salisbury, England, and educated at Oxford (although he left without taking his degree), Philip Massinger went to London in 1606 with the intention of making a living as a playwright. He is believed to have written over fifty plays, but most of these no longer exist; as was usual in that period, much of his work was done in collaboration with several dramatists, but without clear attribution, so that the exact extent of his contribution is uncertain. His earliest known play, *The Virgin Martyr*, was written jointly with Thomas Dekker, but his major partnership began after 1613 when, Francis Beaumont having retired to the country, he worked for a long period with his friend John Fletcher. Together they wrote a number of plays for the company of actors known as the King's Men, including *Sir John van Olden Barnaveldt*, *The Custom of the Country* and *The False One*. The association with the King's Men was to continue, as far as Massinger was concerned, for the rest of his life, and the larger part of his work was written for them. Fifteen plays of which he was the sole author still exist, others having been lost when a servant of the antiquarian John Warburton contrived to destroy them, along with other early manuscripts from her master's priceless collection, while carrying out her duties as a cook. The majority of those which remain, such as *The Maid of Honour* or *The Roman Actor*, tend to be serious and highly moral in tone, but Massinger also wrote some comedies, including *A New Way to Pay Old Debts*, first seen about 1625, in which he created a classic comic villain, Sir Giles Overreach.

Master of Ballantrae, The: A Winter's Tale A novel by Robert Louis Stevenson, set at the time of the 1745 rebellion and first published in 1889.

Masters, Edgar Lee (1868–1950) The American poet Edgar Lee Masters was born in Kansas but spent most of his life in Illinois, practising as a lawyer in Chicago from 1891 to 1920. He published *A Book of Verses* in 1898, and this was followed in 1902 by a drama in verse, *Maximilian*. For some time he pursued a career as a playwright, and then, after many years without recognition, in 1915 he brought out his masterpiece, the book called *Spoon River Anthology*, and suddenly enjoyed great success. In it he examined in wry, ironic verse the past lives of the inhabitants of a small Illinois town. Once it had established his reputation, he was able to publish a large number of works, which included collections of verse, poetic dramas, and novels such as *Mitch Miller*, which appeared in 1920, and *The Nuptial Flight*, in 1923. Few of these were of lasting merit. He also wrote a sour biography, *Lincoln the Man*, which was published in 1931, and less controversial studies of Vachel Lindsay (1935) and Mark Twain (1938). Earlier, in 1924, he had attempted to repeat his great success by producing *The New Spoon River*, in which he took the opportunity of attacking the falling spiritual values of small-town America in much stronger terms than he had used previously, but the book was not as well received as its predecessor. His autobiography, *Across Spoon River*, came out in 1936.

Masters, John (1914–83) Born in Calcutta, John Masters trained at Sandhurst and served as a British army officer. After Indian independence he settled in the United States, becoming a naturalized citizen in 1954. His first book, *Nightrunners of Bengal*, was immediately successful on publication in 1951. He followed it with a number of other novels, including *Bhowani Junction*, in 1954, and two volumes of autobiography, *Bugles and a Tiger: A Personal Adventure* (1956) and *The Road Past Mandalay* (1961).

Mather, Cotton (1663–1728) Born in Boston, Cotton Mather, the son of Increase Mather, entered

Harvard at the age of twelve, graduated at fifteen, and became a teacher and later a clergyman. He wrote over four hundred works, but that total includes letters, sermons and tracts. An admirer of British advances in immunology, he wrote *An Account of the Method and further Success of Inoculating for the Small Pox in London*, which was published in 1721, but he is chiefly remembered for his involvement in the New England witch trials and for his two books on the subject, *Memorable Providences Relating to Witchcrafts and Possessions*, which appeared in 1689, and *The Wonders of the Invisible World*, in 1693.

Mather, Increase (1639–1723) A native of Dorchester, Massachusetts, Increase Mather went to Harvard when he was only twelve (as his son Cotton was also to do). He later studied at Trinity College, Dublin, and was offered livings in the English Congretional Church, but eventually returned to America as minister of the Second Church of Boston. He became very active in the organization of the church, was President of Harvard College for a period, and led a deputation to England which succeeded in obtaining a new and better Charter for Massachusetts. His many publications included local histories, some of which, such as *A Narrative of the Miseries of New-England*, were plainly political, and works on witchcraft, including *Cases of Conscience Concerning Evil Spirits*, in which he gave his opinion that some of the evidence in the Salem trials had been less than adequate.

Maturin, Charles Robert (1782–1824) The Irish writer Charles Robert Maturin was born and educated in Dublin. He published his first book, *The Fatal Revenge*, a novel in the Gothic style, in 1807. Two more novels followed, and then, with his tragedy *Bertram*, began a brief career as a playwright. In 1820 he published his best-known work, the novel *Melmouth, the Wanderer*.

Maud A long narrative poem by Alfred, Lord Tennyson, first published in 1855.

Maugham, W. Somerset (1874–1965) William Somerset Maugham was born in Paris. Orphaned at the age of ten, he was brought up by an uncle and aunt living in Canterbury, England. After a short spell at Heidelberg University, he trained as a doctor of medicine at St Thomas's, London, but soon decided to devote himself to writing. His first novel, *Liza of Lambeth*, appeared in 1897, but it was not until ten years later that he achieved real success with his comedy *Lady Frederick*, which was rapidly followed by other plays in a variety of genres from farce to melodrama. In 1915 he published *Of Human Bondage*, the autobiographical novel which established his reputation as a writer of

Graham Sutherland's striking portrait of Somerset Maugham was painted when the sitter was seventy-five.

fiction. Meanwhile he had married, but most of his life was to be spent with his secretary and companion, Gerald Haxton. During the next two decades he was one of the most successful playwrights of the period, and long runs were a certainty for such plays as *The Circle*, produced in 1921, *The Constant Wife*, in 1926, *The Sacred Flame*, in 1928, and his anti-war drama, *For Services Rendered*, in 1932. His last play was

Sheppey, seen in 1933. His bestselling novels included *The Moon and Sixpence*, published in 1919, *The Painted Veil*, in 1925, *Cakes and Ale*, in 1930, and *The Razor's Edge*, in 1944. His short stories were also extremely popular – especially 'Rain', which, with its strongly depicted characters and perennially interesting plot, was very successful when adapted for both stage and screen. He also wrote travel books, literary criticism and some volumes of autobiography.

Maupassant, Guy de (1850–93) Henri René Albert Gue de Maupassant was born in northern France. After completing his education he became a clerk in the ministry of marine. He became the friend of many of the major writers of the time, including Alphonse Daudet, Emile Zola and, especially, Gustave Flaubert. In 1880 his story 'Boule de suif' appeared in a collection of short pieces by Zola and others, and it was immediately apparent that he found his métier. Although he was a successful novelist, publishing *Une vie*, in 1883, *Bel-ami* in 1885, and *Pierre et Jean* in 1888, it is primarily for his short

An expressive illustration by René Lelong to the 1903 edition of Guy de Maupassant's collection of realistic short stories *La maison Tellier*, first published in 1881. Maupassant was influenced by the Naturalist movement and many of his stories are graphically realistic portrayals of French life. This led to attempts to censor his work, which only served to increase his popularity.

stories that he is remembered. He published several collections of powerfully realistic tales: among these are *La maison Tellier*, which appeared in 1881, *Clair de lune*, in 1884, *Le Horla*, in 1887, and *Le rosier de Madame Husson*, in 1888. De Maupassant's success at the time was enhanced by the publicity he received from attempts at censorship of his work; his first book, a collection of poems, was threatened with prosecution when it appeared in 1880, and the low-life characters he so often depicted, coupled with his propensity for Rabelaisian humour, led the authorities to regard much of his work as obscene, or at best unnecessarily coarse. Today such attitudes are laughable, and he is acknowledged to have been a truly great master of the short story.

Mauriac, François (1885–1970) Born and educated in Bordeaux, France, François Mauriac published his first books of poems, *Les mains jointes*, in 1909. A novel, *L'enfant chargé de chaînes* (*Young Man in Chains*) appeared in 1913 and was followed by others, including *Le baiser au lépreux* (*The Kiss to the Leper*), which established his reputation on its appearance in 1922. His masterpiece, *Le noeud de vipères* (*Vipers' Tangle*), was published in 1932. He wrote many other novels, several plays and volumes of autobiography. He was awarded the Nobel Prize for Literature in 1952.

Maurois, André (1885–1967) André Maurois was the pseudonym used by Emile Herzog, who was born in Elbeuf, France. Time spent in England resulted in his first book, *Les silences du Colonel Bramble* (*The Silence of Colonel Bramble*), published in 1918. He wrote a number of novels and a history of England, but became celebrated for his literary biographies, *Ariel* (Shelley), *Byron*, *A la recherche de Marcel Proust*, *Victor Hugo*, *Lélia* (George Sand), and *Prométhée* (Balzac), published between 1923 and 1965.

May, Thomas (1595–1650) Born in Sussex and educated at Cambridge, Thomas May produced his first literary work, a comedy called *The Heir*, in 1620, following it with a number of other plays. Having failed to secure the post of Poet Laureate, he deserted his protector, King Charles I, and became a Parliamentarian, an action which resulted in much scathing comment. His most important works were both partisan in approach: *The History of the Long Parliament*, published in 1647, and *A Breviary of the Parliament of England*, which appeared in 1650.

Mayakovsky, Vladimir (1893–1930) The Russian poet Vladimir Vladimirovich Mayakovsky was born in Georgia. His first major work, experimental in nature, was *A Cloud in Trousers*, which appeared in 1915. It was followed by many more similarly long and complex poems, which dealt not only with human emotions but also with political subjects. Although he was a fervent Revolutionary, his work was not well received during his lifetime by the Soviet authorities, and this rejection and the unhappy nature of his love affairs led him to commit suicide. During the Stalin era his reputation was rehabilitated and he was acclaimed as the leading poet of modern Russia.

Mayhew, Henry (1812–87) The London-born journalist Henry Mayhew received comparatively little formal education. He worked for a number of periodicals, including *Punch*, and published several books of an ephemeral character. Beginning in 1849, he wrote a series of articles for the *Morning Chronicle*, which were later published as *London Labour and the London Poor*, and he subsequently produced *The Criminal Prisons of London* and *London Children*. These accurate and vivid pictures of deprivation and the abuses which the poverty-stricken suffered not only secured a wide readership but had a considerable influence on later reforms.

Mayor of Casterbridge, The A novel by Thomas Hardy, first published in 1886. It tells the story of a successful man who is ruined by the essential weakness of his character.

Mazeppa A narrative poem by Lord Byron, set at the time of the war between Sweden and Russia in the early years of the eighteenth century. It was first published in 1819.

Measure for Measure A comedy by William Shakespeare, probably performed about 1604, but not printed until 1623. It is concerned with the efforts to save a young man called Claudio from being executed for a sexual offence.

Medea, The A tragedy by Euripides, first performed in 431BC, and probably the most popular of his plays. The central character is a woman of indomitable character, a 'barbarian' who finds herself surrounded by enemies.

melodrama Derived from two Greek words meaning 'song' and 'play', the term melodrama originally meant a play with songs and music. Nowadays it is used to describe a play in which stock characters – the hero, the heroine, the villain – are placed in highly dramatic situations, ending with the triumph of good over evil. The characters are usually drawn without subtlety, but the audience is nevertheless expected to love and suffer with the heroine and to rejoice the villain's eventual downfall. Victorians were very partial to melodramas, and found them cathartic, but present-day audiences have difficulty in taking them seriously.

Melville, Herman (1819–91) The American writer Herman Melville was born in New York City. His formal education was cut short at the age of eleven, when his father died, and he became a bank clerk and later served in the family store before going to sea. He sailed as a cabin boy to England, and then at the age of twenty-two joined a whaler. Despite the brutality of the captain, he stayed with the ship for eighteen months, before deserting in the Marquesas Islands. After brief experiences on other whalers, and some months spent in Tahiti and later in Hawaii, he joined the US Navy, and eventually returned to his family in 1844. Using his own experiences, he produced the novel *Typee: A Peep at Polynesian Life, or Four Months' Residence in a Valley of the Marquesas*. It was published in 1846 in both England and the United States, and brought him considerable acclaim and the friendship of Nathaniel Hawthorne. *Omoo, a Narrative of Adventures in the South Seas* appeared in the following year and was also generally well received, although Melville was distressed by the doubts expressed in some quarters as to the

Moby-Dick by Herman Melville is a story of whaling, as well as being a profound symbolic study of good and evil. The self-taught scholar opened up a thrilling almost undiscovered South-Sea world for his enthusiastic readers.

authenticity of his stories; he was also attacked by a number of religious groups who disliked his criticism of missionaries and their work. His next book, *Mardi and a Voyage Thither*, an allegorical romance, published in 1849, reinforced the opposition of his detractors, and proved to be the least successful of the books he had produced so far. Meanwhile, Melville had married Elizabeth Shaw, whose father was the Chief Justice of Massachusetts, and was responsible not only for her and for their children, but also for the support of his mother and sisters. He therefore quickly produced two more books, *Redburn: His First Voyage* and *White-Jacket, or The World in a Man-of-War*, which appeared in 1849 and 1850 respectively and achieved some popularity. Then, in 1851, he published *Moby-Dick, or The Whale*, the most ambitious work he had attempted. It was a comparative failure on both sides of the Atlantic, and *Pierre, or the Ambiguities*, which followed in 1852, was seen as obscure and poorly written. For the next few years he wrote short stories, first published in magazines and collected in 1856 as *The Piazza Tales*. His novel of the American Revolution, *Israel Potter: His Fifty Years of Exile*, appeared in 1855, and his last novel, *The Confidence-Man: His*

Moby-Dick by Herman Melville is a story of whaling, as well as being a profound symbolic study of good and evil.

Masquerade, came out in 1857. With the exception of *Billy Budd, Foretopman*, which was uncompleted at the time of his death, from this time on his literary work was confined to poetry, of which three collections appeared: *Battle-Pieces and Aspects of the War*, in 1866, *John Marr and Other Sailors*, in 1888, and *Timoleon*, in 1891. A long poem, *Clarel*, which came out in 1876, was partly inspired by a journey to Europe and the Middle East which he had made in 1856 in an effort to restore his failing health. His lack of success, both as a writer and as a lecturer, had forced him to take employment in 1866 as a customs officer, and he remained in this post until 1885. He died in obscurity, and many years were to pass before his work was to gain recognition. Although his writing is uneven, *Typee* and *Omoo* are now regarded as classics, and Melville has come to be acclaimed as one of America's greatest writers, not only for the brilliance of his evocation of the sea and of the men who sail on it, but also for the depth of mystic vision to be found in his books. In particular, *Moby-Dick* is regarded as a novel in which symbolism is combined with a powerful narrative to produce an undoubted masterpiece.

Memoirs of a Woman of Pleasure A novel by John Cleland, popularly known as *Fanny Hill*, and first published between 1748 and 1749.

Menander (342–291BC) The Greek comic dramatist Menander was born in Athens. He wrote more than a hundred plays, and was the prime exponent of the so-called New Comedy, which was concerned with everyday characters of the period. Although his work was influential and much admired for many centuries, very little of it is now extant, although some fragments have been retrieved from ancient papyri.

Mencken, H.L. (1880–1956) Henry Louis Mencken was born in Baltimore. He became one of the most influential literary critics of his time, especially as co-editor of a magazine called *The Smart Set*, and later as editor of *The American Mercury*. He published many books, including *The American Language*, which appeared in 1919, and championed such writers as Theodore Dreiser, Sinclair Lewis and Sherwood Anderson.

Merchant of Venice, The A comedy by William Shakespeare, first performed about 1596 and printed in 1600. It tells of the attempted vengeance of Shylock, the Jew, on the merchant Antonio, who is defended by Portia.

Meredith, George (1828–1900) Born in Portsmouth, England, George Meredith was educated in Germany. His first published work was the poem 'Cillian Wallah', which appeared in 1849. He was to bring out several volumes of verse,

A classic painting of George Meredith by George Watts.

and he also wrote successful short stories, but it was as a novelist that he made his reputation, with such works as *The Ordeal of Richard Feveral*, published in 1859, *Evan Harrington*, in 1861, *Rhoda Fleming*, in 1865, *The Adventures of Harry Richmond*, in 1865, and *Diana of the Crossways*, in 1885. During the last years of his life he was greatly respected and widely read, but, although some of his work is not without merit, his reputation has greatly declined and he must now be regarded as a minor literary figure.

Merrill, James (1926–) The American poet James Ingram Merrill was born in New York and educated at Amherst College, Massachusetts. His first book, *Jim's Book: A Collection of Poems and Stories*, was printed privately in 1942. *First Poems* appeared in 1951, and several volumes of verse have followed, including a major work, *The Country of a Thousand Years of Peace and other poems*, in 1959. *The Fire Screen*, in 1970, *Mirabell: Books of Number*, in 1978, *Changing Light at Sandover*, in 1982, and *Late Settings*, in 1985. He is regarded as a poet of great technical virtuosity. He has also written two novels and two plays.

Merry Wives of Windsor, The A comedy by William Shakespeare, telling the story of Sir John Falstaff's attempts to seduce Mrs Ford and Mrs Page, first presented about 1597 and printed in 1602.

Metamorphoses A narrative poem written by the Latin poet Ovid in the early years of the first century AD, and consisting of the retelling of ancient legends.

Metamorphosis, The A long short story (*Die Verwandlung*) by Franz Kafka about Gregor Samsa, who turns into an insect and thus faces an extreme, an absurd, alienation. It was first published in 1915.

metaphysical poets A term applied to a group of seventeenth-century poets who included John Donne, George Herbert, Henry Vaughan, Andrew Marvell and others. Their work was distinguished by the use of extravagant imagery and a novel, often obscure, aproach to language.

metre The rhythm of verse, especially when it can be divided on the same syllable in each foot, is known as the metre. The stressed syllables are referred to as 'long' and the unstressed as 'short'. The feet most commonly used are: the iamb – two syllables, one short and one long (˘¯); the trochee – two syllables, one long and one short (¯˘); the dactyl – three syllables, one long and two short (¯˘˘); the anapaest – three syllables, two short and one long (˘˘¯); and the spondee – two syllables, both long (¯¯). Many other combinations are also recognized. The iamb is familiar in the five-footed lines, or iambic pentameters of Shakespearian verse, as in the familiar line from *The Merchant of Venice* 'The quāl/ĭt-y̆/ ŏf mēr/cy̆ ĭs/ nŏt strāin'd'.

Meynell, Alice (1847–1922) The English poet, essayist and anthologist Alice Meynell was born Alice Christina Thompson. Her first volume of poetry, *Preludes*, was published in 1875, and two years later she married Wilfred Meynell. She produced anthologies and several more volumes of her own verse, the complete *Poems* appearing shortly after her death. *Essays*, the best of her work in that genre, was published in 1914.

Michener, James A. (1907–) A foundling discovered in Doylestown, Pennsylvania, James A. Michener was adopted by Mabel Michener. During World War II he was a naval historian, and his *Tales of the South Pacific*, published in 1947, was awarded a Pulitzer Prize. He has since written a large number of lengthy popular novels, including *Hawaii*, in 1959, *Centennial*, in 1974, *The Covenant*, in 1980, *Space*, in 1982 and *Texas*, in 1985.

Middle English Middle English is the term used to describe the English language as it existed from about the middle of the twelfth century to the end of the fifteenth century. By this period, which followed the Norman invasion, the largely Teutonic Anglo-Saxon language had assimilated many words of Romance origin. Middle English found its highest literary expression in Chaucer's *Canterbury Tales*.

Middlemarch, A Study of Provincial Life A novel by George Eliot, often considered her masterpiece, first published between 1871 and 1872.

Middleton, Thomas (*c*.1580–1627) The English dramatist Thomas Middleton was born in London. After publishing some poetry and two prose pamphlets, he began to write for the stage, and collaborated with many other dramatists of the day, including Dekker, Rowley and Webster. His most important work was probably *The Changeling*, a tragedy written with Thomas Dekker and first presented in 1624, but he is also remembered for *A Mad World, My Masters*, seen in 1608, and *Women beware Women*, probably written about the same time as *The Changeling*.

Midsummer Night's Dream, A A comedy by William Shakespeare, largely set near Athens in an enchanted wood, the realm of Oberon and Titania, king and queen of the fairies. It was probably first performed in 1595 or 1596, and published in 1600.

Mill, James (1773–1836) The Scottish historian and philospher James Mill was born in Forfarshire and educated at Edinburgh University. He became a journalist, writing for such periodicals as the *Edinburgh Review* and the *Westminster Review*. His books included a *History of British India*, published in 1817, and *Elements of Political Economy*, which appeared in 1821.

Mill, John Stuart (1806–73) Born in London, the influential philosopher John Stuart Mill received an intensive education from his father, James Mill. He became a clerk in the East India Company, where he remained until 1858, later entering Parliament. He began to write for various periodicals, and in 1843 he published *A System of Logic, etc*, which was followed in 1848 by his most important work, *Principles of Political Economy*. Other major publications included *On Liberty*, which appeared in 1859, *Utilitarianism*, in 1863, *On the Subjection of Women*, in 1869, and the four volumes of *Dissertations and Discussions*, which came out between 1859 and 1876. His *Autobiography* was published in the year of his death.

Millay, Edna St Vincent (1892–1950) The American poet Edna St Vincent Millay was born in Rockland, Maine, and educated at Vassar. Her first book of verse, *Renascence and other poems*, appeared in 1917, and was followed in 1920 by *Figs from Thistles*, a book which established her as a leader of emancipated womanhood. In 1923 she received the Pulitzer Prize for *The Harp-Weaver and other poems*. Her *Collected Sonnets* appeared in 1941 and *Collected Lyrics* in 1943.

Miller, Arthur (1915–) Born in New York and educated at the University of Michigan, Arthur Miller began his career as a playwright by writing scripts for radio. His first play to be produced was *The Man Who Had All the Luck*, which was seen in 1944, and he had his first major success three years later with *All My Sons*. This was the first of four plays in which he demonstrated his considerable talent as a dramatist in the tragic vein. *All My Sons* was

Arthur Miller wrote the filmscript of *The Misfits* for his wife, Marilyn Monroe, who is seen here on the set of the film with him and the director John Huston.

followed in 1949 with the modern classic, *Death of a Salesman*, which was awarded the Pulitzer Prize. His next play, *The Crucible*, produced in 1953, was intended as an attack on the anti-Communist witch-hunts prevalent in the United States at the time, but it has survived because of the intensity and power with which he invested this dramatic account of the witch trials which took place in Salem, Massachusetts, in 1692. *A View from the Bridge* was another success when it was presented in 1955, but his subsequent plays, although none of them can be fairly counted as a failure, have been somewhat less well received. These include *A Memory of Two Mondays*, *After the Fall*, *Incident at Vichy*, *The Price* and *The American Clock*. He has also written a novel, *Focus*, and a number of short stories and essays, and in 1961, during his marriage to Marilyn Monroe, he produced for her the screenplay of *The Misfits*.

Miller, Henry (1891–1980) The American writer Henry Valentine Miller was born in New York. He worked at a number of different occupations before deciding, in his early twenties, to become a writer. In 1930 he went to live in Paris, and it

American author Henry Miller. Many of his novels were originally banned in America and Britain, but were published in Paris where he lived between 1930 and 1939.

was there that his first novel, *Tropic of Cancer*, was published in 1934. The sequel, *Tropic of Capricorn*, came out in 1939. Both books were experimental in construction, autobiographical, and sexually explicit. They were banned until the 1960s, both in the United States and in Britain, as pornographic. After a journey to Greece in 1939, which Miller described in the travel book *The Colossus of Maroussi*, he went back to the States in 1940, eventually settling in California. *The Air-Conditioned Nightmare*, published in 1945, was an assessment of the America he found on his return. The three novels *Sexus*, *Nexus* and *Plexus*, together known as *The Rosy Crucifixion*, appeared in 1949, 1953 and 1960 respectively. Always a rebel and an iconoclast, in his later years he was much respected, especially by the writers of the Beat Generation, and became something of a figurehead for those who campaigned for total freedom of expression.

Mill on the Floss, The A novel by George Eliot telling the tragic story of Maggie Tulliver and her brother Tom, first published in 1860.

Milne, A.A. (1882–1956) Alan Alexander Milne was born in London and educated at Westminster School and Cambridge. He became a prolific author, writing in many genres, but apart from his children's books was most successful as a playwright. His first light play, *Mr Pym Passes By*, appeared in 1919 and was followed by others of a similar nature, including the equally popular *The Dover Road*, first presented in 1921. But it is as the author of the 'Christopher Robin' books that he is remembered. Two of them, *When We Were Very Young* and *Now We Are Six*, published in 1924 and 1927, were collections of verses for children, while *Winnie-the-Pooh* and *The House at Pooh Corner*, which appeared in 1926 and 1928, were stories about Pooh, Piglet, Eeyore and other familiar toy characters, written for Milne's son.

Milosz, Czeslaw (1911–) The novelist, essayist and poet Czeslaw Milosz was born at Sateiniai in Lithuania and educated at the University in Wilno. His first book of verse, *Poem of Frozen Time*, appeared in 1932. During World War II he worked in the Polish resistance and published several clandestine works. His volume of poetry *Ocaleinie* (*Rescue*) was one of the first books published in Communist Poland. In 1951 he sought political asylum in France, and emigrated to the United States in 1960. His best-known work is a collection of essays, *The Captive Mind*, which appeared in 1953. He has also published a novel, more poetry, and a history of Polish literature. He was awarded the Nobel Prize for Literature in 1980.

Milton, John (1608–74) A Londoner by birth, John Milton was educated at St Paul's School and Christ's College, Cambridge. He began to write poetry while still at university, producing works in both Latin and English, and his first major poem, 'On the Morning of Christ's Nativity', belongs to this period. He rejected an earlier idea of entering the Church, and after leaving Cambridge he continued his studies, and also devoted himself to his vocation as a poet. While living at his father's home he wrote the two companion pieces, 'L'Allegro' and 'Il Penseroso', and his masque *Comus*, which was first performed at Ludlow Castle in 1634. The death of Edward King inspired his elegy 'Lycidas', which was published in 1637. From April 1638 until August 1639 he was in Europe, spending most of his time in a leisurely tour of Italy, and he then settled in London, becoming tutor to his two nephews. For the next two decades he wrote very little poetry, dedicating himself instead to the defence of many libertarian principles and producing pamphlets on education, the hierarchy of the Church, and divorce. This last subject was of personal interest to him – he had married in 1642, but soon after the marriage he and his wife separated. In 1644 he published *Areopagitica*, one of the greatest pleas for freedom of the press ever written, which was undoubtedly influential in securing the eventual end of the system of censorship in operation at that time. A small volume of his poems appeared in 1645, and in that year he and his wife were reconciled. After the execution of Charles I in 1649, Milton attacked both tyranny and the Presbyterians in *The Tenure of Kings and Magistrates*, and in the same year he was appointed Latin Secretary to the newly-established Council of State, a post

BELOW: John Milton, master of English epic poetry, painted by Jan der Plaas.

RIGHT: Title-page of Tonson's edition of Milton's masterpiece *Paradise Lost*, printed in 1738.

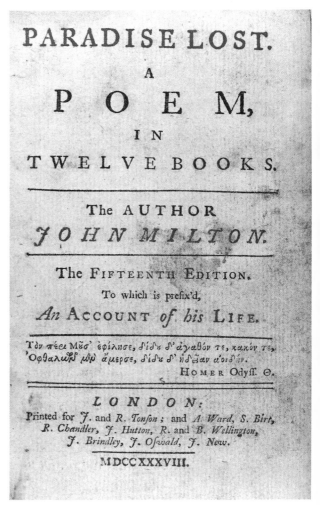

John Milton, one of the greatest figures of English Renaissance literature, became totally blind at the age of forty-three. This picture, painted in 1907 by Francis Walker, shows Milton dictating to his daughter.

which he held throughout the period of the Commonwealth, despite the problems caused by his failing sight, which by 1651 had deteriorated into total blindness. His official replies to Royalist attacks emanating from Europe earned him both an international reputation and much abuse. From September 1657 his assistant secretary was the poet Andrew Marvell. Meanwhile, his wife had died, after bearing him three daughters and a son who died in infancy. He married again in 1656, but fifteen months later this second wife was also dead. When the monarchy was restored in 1660, it seemed more than likely that Milton would be condemned to death, but he was merely dismissed from his post and fined, and it has been suggested that this clemency resulted from pleading on his behalf by William D'Avenant and Andrew Marvell. He now contracted his third marriage, lived quietly, and worked on his great masterpiece, *Paradise Lost*, which he had first begun some twenty years previously. It was completed about 1663, but arrangements for its publication were not finally made until 1667, when he sold the copyright for a mere five pounds, three further instalments of five pounds being payable if and when the first and two subsequent printings of thirteen hundred copies each were sold. He received the first of these instalments eighteen months later. In 1669 a Latin grammar, which he had written earlier, was published, and in the following year he brought out his uncompleted *A History of Britain*,

which ended with the Norman Conquest. *Paradise Regained* and *Samson Agonistes*, his last major works, appeared in one volume in 1671, and in 1673 he brought out a revised collection of his shorter *Poems*. He died in November 1674, and was buried, not, as future generations would have thought his due, in Westminster Abbey, but in the Church of St Giles, Cripplegate. The breadth of vision evident in his work, the excellence of his structure and his mastery of the language are among the qualities which mark John Milton as one of the greatest poets of all time, and to them must be added the undoubted flame of genius.

Minnesingers *Minne* is a German word, now obsolete or poetic, meaning 'love' and the German lyrical poets writing from the twelfth to the fourteenth centuries were called Minnesingers because their works were mainly love poems.

Miracle plays The term miracle plays is strictly applied to medieval dramas specifically concerned with episodes in the life of Christ or in those of the Saints, but is also often used as an alternative to 'mystery plays'.

Miss Lonelyhearts A novel by Nathaniel West, concerned with the tragedy of a male agony columnist, first published in 1933.

Mitchell, Margaret (1900–49) The American novelist Margaret Mitchell was born in Atlanta, Georgia, and educated at the Washington Seminary, Atlanta, and Smith College, Massachusetts. She produced one book only, the bestseller *Gone With* *the Wind*, which won the Pulitzer Prize when it was published in 1936, and was later transferred with enormous success to the screen, Vivien Leigh and Clark Gable playing the leading roles.

Mitford, Mary Russell (1787–1855) The English writer Mary Russell Mitford was born in Hampshire. Her first publications were books of poetry, and she then turned to the theatre and produced a number of plays with some success. She later wrote novels and stories, but is remembered primarily for the five series of sketches which she wrote from 1824 to 1832, when they were collected and published under the title *Our Village*.

Mitford, Nancy (1904–73) The daughter of Lord Redesdale, Nancy Mitford was born in London and educated privately. Her first novel, *Highland Fling*, was published in 1931, but it was with her fourth book, *The Pursuit of Love*, which appeared in 1945, that she achieved success. *Love in a Cold Climate*, in 1949, and *The Blessing*, in 1951, were equally popular. She also wrote biographies, including *The Sun King*, which was a bestseller in 1966.

A beautiful eighteenth-century edition of Molière's first comedy of manners *Les précieuses ridicules*. Illustrated by Boucher and engraved by Laurent Cars, it was one of the most successful typographical products of the period.

Moby-Dick, or, The Whale The classic novel by Herman Melville, first published in 1851. Aboard the *Pequod*, Captain Ahab seeks the great white whale Moby-Dick, and the narrator, Ishmael, tells a story which is both a dramatic narrative and a powerful allegory.

Molière (1622–73) Jean-Baptiste Poquelin, the great French comic dramatist, adopted the name Molière when he decided on a theatrical career. Born in Paris and educated at the Jesuit Collège de Clermont, he studied law, but at the age of twenty-one joined with others to found a company of actors, the Théâtre L'Illustre, with which he toured France for the next fifteen years. In 1658 he returned to Paris, under the patronage of Monsieur, the brother of Louis XIV, and from this time he performed regularly for the court. His first major success as a dramatist (and also as an actor – he played the leading parts in all his plays) came in 1659 with *Les précieuses ridicules*, a satire on the affectations of ladies of the period. Earlier works had been adaptations from the Italian, and Molière's enemies accused him of having no ideas of his own, saying that he had stolen the idea for *Les précieuses* from a novel by the Abbé de Pure. Similar accusations of plagiarism were frequently to be levelled against him, his critics ignoring

LES PRÉCIEUSES RIDICULES

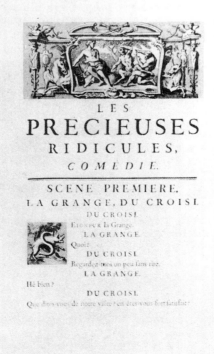

the fact that, even if he had taken ideas from earlier writers, he had added his own originality and thereby created new works of lasting quality. *Sganarelle* was produced in 1660, *L'école des maris* in 1661, and *L'école des femmes* in 1662, in which year Molière married. His popularity was immense, but each new success brought him more enemies; actors in rival companies were jealous, he was hated and feared by those whom he ridiculed in his plays, and the ecclesiastical authorities regarded him as impious. *Tartuffe* of which the first three acts were seen in 1664, and *Don Juan*, in 1665, were both the subject of bitter attacks and attempts at censorship, and even the support of the King, who had become the official patron of his troupe, was not sufficient to prevent performances of the latter play being halted. Nothing, however, could stop Molière from producing new plays, and among them were *Le misanthrope* and *Le médecin malgré lui*, which both appeared in 1666, *L'avare*, in 1669, *Le bourgeois gentilhomme*, in 1770, and *Les femmes savantes*, in 1772. On the 10th February 1773, *Le malade imaginaire* received its first performance. Seven days later, immediately after acting in that play, Molière died, having apparently simulated the imaginary invalid's cough with such vigour that he ruptured a vital organ. A huge crowd attended his burial four days later, but the Archbishop of Paris exacted the Church's revenge for Molière's outspokenness by refusing to allow more than the minimum of ceremony, and his grave is unmarked. The brilliance of his observation, the sharpness of his wit, the natural flow of his dialogue – these are among his outstanding qualities. But it is perhaps to the essential humanity of his characters – even his greatest comic creations are never portrayed, in the absurdity of their foolishness, without understanding – that he owes his position as the greatest playwright France has produced, surpassed in the whole world, many critics believe, only by Shakespeare.

Moll Flanders, The Fortunes and Misfortunes of the Famous A novel by Daniel Defoe, first published in 1722. Set partly in Virginia, it also presents a realistic picture of London's underworld at that time.

Monsarrat, Nicholas (1910–79) The English novelist Nicholas John Turney Monsarrat was born in Liverpool and educated at Winchester and Cambridge. He had published several previous books when, in 1951, *The Cruel Sea* became a major bestseller and established his reputation. He produced a number of other successful novels, including *The Tribe That Lost Its Head*, in 1956, and *The Kapillan of Malta*, in 1973. He died before completing *The Master Mariner*, which he believed would be his most enduring work, but the first volume of this long novel appeared in 1978.

Montagu, Lady Mary Wortley (1689–1762) The daughter of the Duke of Kingston, Lady Mary Pierrepoint eloped in 1712 to marry Edward Wortley Montagu, and with him spent two years in Constantinople. Apart from a quarrel with Alexander Pope and a volume of *Court Poems*, she is remembered chiefly for her celebrated series of *Letters*, which describe her experiences in Turkey.

Montaigne, Michel de (1533–92) The French essayist Michel Eyquem de Montaigne was born at his parents' château at Montaigne, near Bordeaux, and educated at a college in Bordeaux. Later, it is believed, he studied law in Toulouse. During his early life he was a soldier and a court attendant, and he travelled widely, but in 1571, partly for reasons of health, he retired to Montaigne, where he remained until his death, despite a plea from Henry of Navarre to return to the court in Paris. In this retirement, he intended to devote his time to study, contemplation and writing, and in 1580 he published the first two volumes of his *Essais*. He then, apparently somewhat against his inclination, became involved in local politics, and in 1881 was elected Mayor of Bordeaux, in which position he served two terms. The third volume of *Essais* appeared in 1588, together with revised editions of the earlier two books. He wrote no more, but spent the last years of his life in further polishing of the existing works. Montaigne is celebrated not merely as a writer of essays but as having invented and perfected this genre, which had not previously been known. In his writings he looked at life and its vanities with some scepticism, but also with amusement – an attitude which may, perhaps, be considered typically French.

Montale, Eugenio (1896–1981) The Italian poet and translator Eugenio Montale was born in Genoa. In 1922 he was the co-founder of *Primo tempo*, a literary journal. His first volume of poems, *Ossia di seppia* (*Cuttlefish Bones*), appeared in 1925 and was followed by many more collections, including *Finisterre*, in 1943. His work was considered rather obscure, but in later years his poetry became more approachable, especially in *Xenia*, published in 1966. He translated Shakespeare, T.S. Eliot, Gerard Manley Hopkins, Melville, O'Neill and others into Italian. He was awarded the Nobel Prize for Literature in 1971.

Montgomerie, Alexander (*c*.1548–*c*.1610) The poet Alexander Montgomerie was born in Ayrshire, Scotland. In 1578 he received an appointment at the court of King James VI, and in 1583 was granted a pension of five hundred marks. In 1586 he travelled to Europe, where he appears to have been imprisoned, and thereafter little is known of him. He wrote a great many sonnets and other poetry, but his main work was a long poem, *The Cherry and the Slae*, which appeared in 1597.

Montgomery, L.M. (1874–1942) Lucy Maud Montgomery was born and educated on Prince Edward Island, Canada. Her book *Anne of Green Gables* was published in 1908 and immediately achieved great popularity. The sequel, *Anne of Avonlea*, came out in the following year, and she went on to write many similar stories for girls.

Moody, William Vaughn (1869–1910) The American poet and playwright William Vaughn Moody was born at Spence, Indiana, and educated at Harvard. He became an academic, teaching at Harvard and, later, at the University of Chicago. In 1900 he published a verse drama, *The Masque of Judgment*, and this was followed in 1901 by a volume of *Poems*. Other plays were *The Fire-Bringer*, *The Death of Eve*, and *The Faith Healer*, but his greatest success was *The Great Divide*, which was first performed in 1907. He also produced some works of literary criticism.

Moonstone, The One of the earliest mystery novels, written by Wilkie Collins and first published in 1868.

Moorcock, Michael (1939–) The English science fiction writer Michael Moorcock is widely regarded as one of the leaders in the field, producing work of true literary merit. He has published a large number of books, including several sequences such as *The Chronicles of Corum* and the novels concerned with his character Jerry Cornelius.

Moore, Brian (1921–) The Irish novelist Brian Moore was born and educated in Ireland. His first major success came with *Judith Hearne* (published in the United States as *The Lonely Passion of Judith Hearne*), which appeared in 1955. He followed it with *The Feast of Lupercal*, in 1957, *The Luck of Ginger Coffey*, in 1960, *The Emperor of Ice Cream*, in 1965, *The Doctor's Wife*, in 1976, and *Black Robe*, in 1985.

Moore, George (1853–1933) Born in County Mayo, Ireland, George Moore was educated in London and Paris. He published his first volume of poetry, *The Flowers of Passion*, in 1877, following it with a second selection, *Pagan Poems*, in 1881. His first two novels, *A Modern Lover* and *A Mummer's Wife*, which appeared in 1883 and 1885, were both considered unpleasantly frank in their realism, but when *Esther Waters* came out in 1894 it brought him a considerable popular success. Several other novels were to follow, including *Evelyn Innes*, in 1898, and a sequel to it, *Sister Teresa*, in 1901. Meanwhile, he had published a number of other works, including the first of his three autobiographical books, *Confessions of a Young Man*, in 1888, and two volumes of art criticism, *Impressions and Opinions*, in 1891, and *Modern Painting*, in 1893. His interest in the theatre led him to become one of the founders of the Irish Literary Theatre, and he wrote a number of plays, among which were *The Strike at Arlington*, first produced in 1893, *The Bending of the Bough*, a comedy seen in 1900, and *Diarmuid and Grania*, written in collaboration with W.B. Yeats, which was produced in 1901. He wrote many more books in a number of genres, and brought out collections of short stories. The most striking of his later works were the novels *The Brook Kerith* and *Héloïse and Abelard*, which were published in 1916 and 1921 respectively.

Moore, Julia A. (1847–1920) The poet Julia A. Moore, the 'Sweet Singer of Michigan', is the American equivalent of Britain's William McGonagall – a versifier whose work was so poorly written as to be hilarious. She published two volumes of poetry: *The Sweet Singer of Michigan Salutes the Public*, which appeared in 1876, and *A Few Words to the Public with New and Original Poems*, in 1878.

Moore, Marianne (1887–1972) Marianne Craig Moore was born in St Louis, Missouri, and educated at Bryn Mawr. She worked as a teacher and then as a librarian, before becoming editor of *The Dial* in 1925. Her first book, *Poems*, was published in 1921, and was followed by many more collections, including *Observations*, in 1924, *Nevertheless*, in 1944, *O To Be a Dragon*, in 1959, and *Tell Me, Tell Me*, in 1966. Despite the peculiarly American nature of her work, she was much admired in Britain as well as in the United States, and her *Selected Poems*, published in 1935, carried an introduction by T.S. Eliot. Her *Collected Poems* won the Pulitzer Prize in 1951.

Moore, Thomas (1779–1852) The son of a grocer and wine merchant, Thomas Moore was born in Dublin and educated at Trinity College. He wrote a large number of works in a number of genres; these included volumes of poetry, a novel entitled *The Epicurean*, a *History of Ireland*, biographies of Sheridan and Byron, and a series of minor satirical works. He is remembered chiefly, however, for *Lalla Rookh*, a collection of Oriental stories in verse, linked by prose passages, and for the words of *Irish Melodies*, which included 'The Minstrel Boy' and 'The Last Rose of Summer'.

morality plays The term morality plays is used in reference to the early dramas, at their height in the sixteenth century, which were intended not simply to entertain, but more importantly to point a moral and inspire their audiences to virtue. The characters were usually incarnations of human qualities, both good and evil – as, for instance, the Seven Deadly Sins. The best-known of all morality plays in English is *Everyman*.

Moravia, Alberto (1907–) Alberto Moravia is the pseudonym of Alberto Pincherle, who was born in Rome. He became a journalist, and published his first novel, *Gli indifferenti* (*The Time of Indifference*) in 1929, with immediate success. His other novels include *Agostino* (*Two Adolescents*), which appeared in 1944, *Il conformista* (*The Conformist*), in 1952, *La noia* (*The Empty Canvas*) in 1962, and *La ciociara* (*Two Women*), in 1974. He has also published many books of short stories, including *Racconti romani* (*Roman Tales*), in 1954.

More, Hannah (1745–1833) The dramatist, poet and writer on religious subjects Hannah More was born near Bristol, England. She went to London in her twenties, and became the friend of many of the leading literary figures of the day. In 1777 the tragedy *Percy* was successfully presented at Covent Garden, and she followed with more plays, some of which were published as *Sacred Dramas* in 1782. Several poems appeared, including one on 'Slavery'. In later life she devoted herself to philanthropy and wrote, together with her sisters, a vast number of pious works, including the 'Cheap Repository Tracts', which sold in phenomenal quantities.

More, Sir Thomas (1478–1535) Thomas More was born in London and educated there, in the household of the then Archbishop of Canterbury, and at Oxford. He left Oxford without taking a degree, and qualified as a lawyer. He soon

A dignified and serious image of Sir Thomas More, after Holbein, 1527. The gold collar signifies royal service.

A detailed and annotated, preliminary drawing by Holbein of Sir Thomas More and his family.

attracted notice, and became under-sheriff of the City of London in 1502, entering Parliament two years later. During an embassy to the Low Countries he began work on his celebrated *Utopia*, written in Latin and published in 1516. He had gained the favour of Henry VIII, and in 1514 he was knighted and made Master of the Requests and a member of the Privy Council. Further promotions followed, and in 1529 he became Lord Chancellor in succession to Cardinal Wolsey, a position which he held for three years. More had always been a man of the highest principles, speaking out against vice and corruption and refusing to exercise his power for the sake of expediency. He opposed Henry VIII's refusal to admit the Pope's supremacy, and in particular did not accept the validity of the King's divorce from Katherine of Aragon. For this he was indicted, imprisoned in the Tower of London, and beheaded in 1535. During his imprisonment he wrote *A Dyaloge of Comfort against Tribulacion*, and his many other works, among which were a number on religious subjects, included a *History of Richard III*, in which he related the story of the murder of the Little Princes in the Tower. His own last years have been memorably presented in Robert Bolt's play and screenplay, *A Man For All Seasons*, the title being taken from a description of More by his contemporary Robert Whittington.

Morgan, Charles (1894–1958) Charles Langbridge Morgan was born in Bromley, England. He published a number of novels, including *The Fountain*, in 1932, *Sparkenbroke*, in 1941, and *The Judge's Story*, in 1947. He also wrote three successful plays, *The Flashing Stream*, produced in 1938, *The River Line*, in 1952, and *The Burning Glass*, in 1953.

Morris, William (1834–96) The English poet and artist William Morris was born at Walthamstow, and after his education at Marlborough and Oxford trained as an architect. In 1858 he published *The Defence of Guenevere and other poems*, which attracted little attention. He then decided to devote himself for a time to interior decoration, and shortly after his marriage in 1859 set up, with Dante Gabriel Rossetti, Edward Burne-Jones and others, a business which designed furniture, wallpapers, stained glass and other decorative items. His long poem *The Life and Death of Jason* had a considerable success

ABOVE: A photograph of William Morris and Edward Burne-Jones taken in the 1860s, soon after they had set up their famous design business.

BELOW: A lovely illustration 'Friends in need meet in the wild wood' by Edward Burne-Jones to Book III of Morris' *The Well at the World's End* (Kelscott Press, 1896).

when it appeared in 1867, and the four parts of *The Earthly Paradise*, published between 1868 and 1870, achieved wide popularity. He followed it in 1872 with *Love is Enough*, and then produced a verse translation of *The Aeneid*, published in 1875, and his own epic, *Sigurd the Volsung*, which came out in the following year. Although he continued to write poetry, and brought out in 1887 a translation of *The Odyssey*, most of his work from this time on was in prose. It included various writings on Socialist themes and a number of historical tales, among them *The House of the Wolfings*, in 1889, and *The Roots of the Mountains* in 1890. He had become interested in printing and founded the Kelmscott Press, and the last years of his life were devoted to the manufacture of a large number of beautifully designed books written by himself and others, the most notable production being the *Kelmscott Chaucer*.

Morrison, Toni (1931–) The Black writer Chloe Anthony Wofford Morrison was born in Lorain, Ohio, and educated at Howard University, Washington, and Cornell. She published her first novel, *The Bluest Eye*, in 1970, and followed it with *Sula*, in 1974, *Song of Solomon*, in 1978, and *Tar Baby*, in 1981. A major novel, *Beloved*, appeared in 1987.

Morte D'Arthur, Le The celebrated version of the Arthurian legends by Sir Thomas Malory, first printed by Caxton in 1485.

Mortimer, John (1923–) The English writer John Mortimer was educated at Harrow and Oxford. In 1947 he published his first novel, *Charade*, but later became celebrated as a dramatist, writing both short and full-length plays for the theatre and for television. Notable among them are *Two Stars for Comfort*, first seen in 1962, *A Voyage Round My Father*, in 1970, and *Paradise Postponed*, adapted from his novel which was published in 1985. His autobiography, *Clinging to the Wreckage*, was published in 1982. A barrister as well as a writer, he has been particularly active in defence of freedom for literature.

Mother Courage A drama by Bertolt Brecht, first produced in 1941.

Motley, John Lothrop (1814–77) The American historian John Lothrop Motley was born in Boston, Massachusetts, and educated at Harvard. In later life he became United States Ambassador to Austria and later to Great Britain. He published two novels, *Morton's Hope, or the Memoirs of a Provincial* and *Merry Mount, a Romance of Massachusetts Colony*, both of which appeared anonymously, in 1839 and 1849 respectively. He is remembered, however, for his major work, *The Rise of the Dutch Republic*, which was highly acclaimed on its publication in 1856. He con-tinued the history in *The United Netherlands*, which appeared in 1860, and in two further volumes of 1867. His *Life and Death of John Barneveld* was published in 1874.

Mount Olympus The home of the Greek gods, Mount Olympus stands in Thessaly, in northern Greece, but there is some doubt as to whether the ancient Greek poets were referring to this real mountain or to an imaginary, allegorical peak. The father of the gods and of mankind was Zeus, himself the son of Titans. With his wife Hera he ruled over the heavens, while his brothers Poseidon and Dis held sway over the oceans and the underworld. Among the many other deities were Aphrodite, goddess of love and beauty, Ares, god of war, Athene, goddess of wisdom, Dionysus, god of wine, and Hermes, the messenger of the gods. The Greek pantheon was adopted by the ancient Romans, but under different names, the gods and goddesses mentioned above becoming Jove (or Jupiter), Juno, Neptune, Pluto, Venus, Mars, Minerva, Bacchus and Mercury respectively. The legends of the gods and their intervention in human affairs form an important part of the literature of ancient Greece and Rome, and have frequently provided subjects for writers up to the present day.

Mourning Becomes Electra A drama by Eugene O'Neill, first performed in 1931. Set in New England after the Civil War, it is based on *The Oresteia* of Aeschylus.

Mrs Warren's Profession A play by G. Bernard Shaw, published in 1899 and first privately performed in 1902. The subject – Mrs Warren runs a group of brothels – prevented a public performance until 1925.

Much Ado About Nothing A comedy by William Shakespeare, notable for the witty duels of words between Beatrice and Benedick. It was first presented in 1598 or 1599 and published in 1600.

Muir, Edwin (1887–1959) Born in Orkney, Edwin Muir, who came of a poor family, was largely self-educated. He went to London in 1919 and began to contribute articles to various periodicals, and these were republished in book form. He published his first volume of poetry, *First Poems*, in 1925, and several further collections were to appear, including *The Labyrinth*, which appeared in 1949. He also wrote three novels, books of literary criticism and an autobiography, and with his wife Willa translated a number of works from the German, including those of Franz Kafka.

Mulock, Dinah Maria (1826–87) The novelist Dinah Maria Mulock, sometimes also known under her married name of Mrs Craik, was born in Staffordshire, England. She wrote a number of stories for children, poems, short stories and several novels, but is remembered now only for the novel *John Halifax, Gentleman*, which was published in 1857.

Mummers' Play, The Often called the 'St George Play', *The Mummers' Play* is a folk-drama which was widely performed in many versions throughout medieval Britain. Its main action, concerned with the resurrection of characters killed in fighting, is clearly connected with the celebration of spring as the rebirth of the earth.

Münchausen, The Adventures of Baron A collection of fantastic stories by Rudolf Erich Raspe, first published in 1785.

The Adventures of Baron Münchausen, illustrated by Dorè.

Munday, Anthony (*c*.1553–1633) The son of a London draper, Anthony Munday (or Mundy, or Monday) was an actor, a spy, a pamphleteer, a translator, a poet, but was most successful as a writer of pageants and plays. He collaborated with other dramatists of the period, including Thomas Dekker, Michael Drayton and Henry Chettle. Among the small number of his plays still extant are *John a Kent and John a Cumber*, *The Downfall of Robert, Earle of Huntington, Afterward called Robin Hood of Merrie Sherwodde* and *The Death of Robert, Earle of Huntington*.

Munthe, Axel (1857–1949) Axel Martin Fredrik Munthe was born in Oskarshamn, Sweden, and educated at Uppsala, Paris and Montpellier. He became physician-in-ordinary to the Swedish royal family. He is remembered for his book *The Story of San Michele*, a bestseller when it was published in 1929.

Murder in the Cathedral A verse play by T.S. Eliot, concerning the murder of Thomas à Becket in Canterbury Cathedral in 1170. It was first presented in 1935.

Murders in the Rue Morgue, The A story by Edgar Allan Poe, first published in 1841. It is considered to have been the first detective story ever written, the mystery of the murders being solved by Poe's creation, C. Auguste Dupin.

Murdoch, Iris (1919–) Born in Dublin and educated at Oxford, Iris Jean Murdoch published her first novel, *Under the Net*, in 1954. It has been followed by many other distinguished works of fiction, including *The Bell*, which appeared in 1958, *A Severed Head*, in 1961, and *The Sea, The Sea*, which won the Booker Prize in 1978. *The Good Apprentice* was published in 1985, and her study *Sartre* came out in 1987. She has also written plays and books on philosophy. She was made a Dame in 1987.

Murry, John Middleton (1889–1957) A Londoner who was educated at Oxford, John Middleton Murry became editor of the periodical the *Athenaeum*, and later founded *The Adelphi*. He married the New Zealand writer Katherine Mansfield in 1918. He was the author of a large number of works of literary criticism, including studies of Keats and Dostoevsky, and in 1931 he published *Son of Woman, the Story of D.H. Lawrence*.

Muses, The In Greek mythology the nine Muses were the daughters of Zeus and Mnemosyne (Memory), born at the base of Mount Olympus. Each ruled over a particular kind of literature, art or science. Calliope was the muse of epic poetry, Erato of love poetry, Euterpe of lyric poetry, Polyhymnia of sacred poetry, Melpomene of tragedy, Thalia of comedy, Clio of history, Terpsichore of dance and song, and Urania of astronomy.

Musset, Alfred de (1810–57) Louis Charles Alfred de Musset was born in Paris, where he was educated at the Collège Henri IV. From an early age he showed promise as a writer, and after publishing a translation of *Confessions of an English Opium Eater*, in 1828, he produced his own first book, *Contes d'Espagne et d'Italie*, at the age of nineteen in the following year. He wrote a number of plays, the most successful of which was *Les caprices de Marianne*, first presented in 1833. However, it is primarily as a poet that he is esteemed, and especially for such poems as 'Le souvenir', which appeared in 1841, and the earlier series of verses called 'Les nuits'.

Musil, Robert (1880–1942) The novelist Robert von Elder Musil was born in Klagenfurt, Austria. He studied both engineering and philosophy, but turned to writing and published his first novel in 1906. He worked for many years on his masterpiece, *Der Mann ohne Eigenschaften* (*The Man Without Qualities*), which was published in three volumes, beginning in 1930. The last, which was uncompleted, appeared after his death.

Myers, L.H. (1881–1944) Leopold Hamilton Myers was the son of F.W.H. Myers, a poet and essayist, who wrote a number of works of literary criticism and was a founder of the Society for Psychical Research. L.H. Myers, who was born and educated in Cambridge, published his first novel, *The Orissers*, in 1922. His major work was a series of historical novels set in India, which were collected in 1943 under the title *The Near and the Far*.

mysteries The term mysteries is used in the United States for the 'whodunits' which in Britain are usually called detective stories. The first mystery is generally held to be Edgar Allan Poe's 'The Murders in the Rue Morgue', published in 1841. Expanded by Wilkie Collins, whose *The Moonstone* was the first full-length detective story, the genre became and remains extremely popular. Many of the leading practitioners have created detectives who became household names – Conan Doyle's Sherlock Holmes, Agatha Christie's Hercule Poirot, Dorothy L. Sayers' Lord Peter Wimsey. In the United States a further development was the introduction of the tough 'private eye', particularly exemplified in the novels of Raymond Chandler.

mystery plays From the thirteenth to the sixteenth centuries mystery plays were regularly performed in England. Some authorities believe that they were so named because they were performed by members of trade guilds, 'mystery' being used in the sense of 'craft', while others maintain that the term derives from the subject of the plays, which was biblical, ranging from the Creation to the Resurrection of Christ. Usually written in doggerel verse, the plays attempted to relate the stories of both Old and New Testaments in terms of everyday life of the times, and included slapstick comedy and vigorous action as well as religious content. Acted by local townspeople, the performances were often given on Corpus Christi day, June 29th, and took place in market places, where temporary stages, sometimes consisting of farm wagons, were erected. Four complete cycles of mystery plays still exist, known as the York Mysteries, The Wakefield Mysteries, the Chester Mysteries and – since the place of origin of the fourth group is unknown – the N-town Mysteries.

N

Nabokov, Vladimir (1899–1977) Vladimir Vladimirovich Nabokov was born in St Petersburg, Russia, and educated there and at Cambridge. He left Russia in 1919 and lived in Berlin and Paris until he went to the United States in 1940, where he eventually became Professor of Russian Literature at Cornell University. In 1959 he gave up his academic work to devote himself entirely to writing, and from that time on lived in Switzerland. His early novels, the first of which was published in 1926, were written in Russian and only subsequently translated. However, like Conrad, he became so fluent in English that he was able to produce books in that language which were notable for their excellent style and their verbal dexterity and originality. His first novel in English was *The Real Life of Sebastian Knight*, which appeared in 1941, and was followed in 1947 by *Bend Sinister*. Both books attracted some attention, but it was *Lolita* which made him famous and wealthy. First published in Paris in 1955, *Lolita* dealt with the infatuation of

Vladimir Nobokov, arriving in Rome, 1959.

a middle-aged man for a twelve-year old 'nymphet'. Its subject made the book a *succès de scandale*, although it was also recognized as a work of high literary quality. Among his subsequent novels were *Pnin*, which came out in 1957, *Pale Fire*, in 1962, and *Ada*, in 1969. An early novel written in Russian, *The Enchanter*, was translated and published posthumously in 1986. Nabokov also wrote poetry, short stories and a volume of autobiography and translated Pushkin's *Eugene Onegin*.

The West Indian writer Vidiadhur Naipaul was educated in Trinidad and at Oxford. His work clearly reflects these influences.

Naipaul, V.S. (1932–) The novelist Vidiadhur Surajprasad Naipaul was born in Trinidad of Indian parents and educated in Port of Spain and at Oxford. He settled in England, working as a journalist, and published his first novel, *The Mystic Masseur*, in 1957. It was well received, as was his next book, *The Suffrage of Elvira*. A collection of short stories, *Miguel Street*, appeared in 1959, and then came *A House for Mr Biswas*, the novel which established him as a major writer when it appeared in 1961. Subsequent novels include *Mr Stone and the Knights Companion*, published in 1963, *The Mimic Men*, in 1967, *In A Free State*, which won the Booker Prize in 1971, *Guerillas*, in 1975, *A Bend in the River*, in 1979, and the autobiographical *Enigma of Arrival*, which was greeted with the highest praise on its publication in 1987. These novels have placed

Naipaul firmly in the top echelon of writers in the second half of the twentieth century, not only for the brilliance of their narratives, but for the seriousness of their content, in which his political anger and his pessimism are relieved by a mordant humour. He has also written a number of books concerned with travel and politics; among these are *The Middle Passage*, published in 1962, *An Area of Darkness*, his sharply censorious view of India, in 1964, *The Return of Eva Peron; with The Killings in Trinidad*, in 1980, and *Among the Believers: an Islamic Journey*, in 1981.

Nash, Ogden (1902–71) The American writer Frederic Ogden Nash was born in Rye, New York, and educated at Harvard. He became renowned for his comic verse, which often used outrageous rhymes and eccentric line lengths. He published many collections, including *Hard Lines*, in 1931, and *I'm a Stranger Here Myself*, in 1938.

Nashe, Thomas (1567–1601) The English writer Thomas Nashe was born at Lowestoft and educated at Cambridge. His first work, *The Anatomie of Absurditie*, appeared in 1589. A prolific pamphleteer, he was much engaged in a number of literary and religious controversies of the day,

The title-page from the 1589 edition of Thomas Nashe's first work *The Anatomie of Absurditie*.

and his satirical works in this genre, such as *Pierce Peniless, His Supplication to the Divell*, which appeared in 1592, show considerable vigour and wit. In 1592 he wrote a masque, *Summers Last Will and Testament*, but it was not published until 1600, and his next important work to appear was the pious *Christs Teares over Jerusalem*, which came out in 1593. In the following year he produced an extravagant fictional tale, *The Unfortunate Traveller, Or the Life of Jack Wilton*, an early adventure novel. A friend of Christopher Marlowe, he completed the latter's *Dido*, and he worked with Ben Jonson and others on the play *The Isle of Dogs*. This, and subsequent pamphleteering, caused him trouble with the authorities, and in 1599 Archbishop Whitgift suppressed his writing. He removed himself to East Anglia and there wrote his last work, *Lenten Stuffe*, 'in praise of the red herring', a comic which is largely a portrait of the town of Yarmouth.

Nathan, George Jean (1882–1958) The American drama critic George Jean Nathan, who was born in Fort Wayne, Indiana, and educated at Cornell, published a number of collections of reviews and essays on the theatre, including *The Popular Theatre*, which appeared in 1918, *The Critic and the Drama*, in 1922, *Since Ibsen*, in 1933, and many others. He also wrote some books in collaboration with H.L. Mencken, with whom he founded *The American Mercury* in 1924.

Nemerov, Howard (1920–) Born in New York City, Howard Stanley Nemerov was educated at Harvard and has pursued an academic career. He published his first volume of verse, *The Image and the Law*, in 1947. It has been followed by many others, and *The Collected Poems of Howard Nemerov* won the National Book Award in 1977. He has also published novels, including *The Melodramatists*, which appeared in 1949, and several volumes of literary criticism.

Neruda, Pablo (1904–73) The leftwing Chilean poet Ricard Eliecer Neftali Reyes used the pseudonym Neruda Pablo. Born in Parral, Chile, he became a diplomat, serving in Burma, Ceylon, Java, Spain and France. He published his first volume of poetry, *Crepusculario*, in 1923, at his own expense, but *Veinte poemas de amor y una canción desesperada* (*Twenty Love Poems and a Song of Despair*) made him famous in Chile when it appeared in 1924. His *Residencia en la tierra* (*Residence on Earth*), which appeared between 1925 and 1935, was in a new style of his own, which became known as *nerudismo*. His major epic *Canto general* appeared in 1950, and *Cien sonetos de amor* (*A Hundred Love Sonnets*) in 1959. He was awarded the Nobel Prize for Literature in 1971.

Nesbit, E. (1858–1924) Edith Nesbit was born in London. After the failure of her husband's business, she began to write stories for children, and in 1899 published the first of her popular books, *The Story of the Treasure-Seekers*. The family featured in this story were to appear in many subsequent adventures. She wrote prolifically; among her best-known works were *Five Children and It*, which appeared in 1902, *The Phoenix and the Carpet*, in 1904, and *The Railway Children*, in 1906.

Newbolt, Henry (1862–1938) Henry John Newbolt was born in Staffordshire, England, and educated at Oxford, subsequently training as a lawyer. He published a novel, *Taken from the Enemy*, in 1892, and other novels also appeared. It was, however, as a writer of ballads that he achieved fame. *Admirals All and Other Verses* appeared in 1897, and was followed by several more volumes in similar vein, including *Songs of the Sea*, in 1904, and *Songs of the Fleet*, in 1910. He was knighted in 1915.

Newcomes, The A novel by William Makepeace Thackeray, first published between 1853 and 1855.

Newgate Calendar, The First published in about 1773, *The Newgate Calendar* was a catalogue of major crimes committed from 1700 onwards. Several volumes appeared thereafter, including *The New Newgate Calendar*, in 1826. The majority were written by two lawyers, Andrew Knapp and William Baldwin. Apart from supplying their readers with sensational stories, the books provided a number of authors, from Fielding to Hood, with subjects for their work.

Newman, John Henry (1801–90) Born in London and educated at Oxford, John Henry Newman entered the Church in 1824 as an Anglican. A volume of poetry, *Lyra Apostolica*, was published in 1833, following a journey in Europe. He became increasingly unhappy in the Church of England, and in 1845 was received into the Roman Catholic Church. An attack by Charles Kingsley caused him to write his major work, *Apologia pro vita Sua*, an account of his religious development, which was published in 1864. His long mystic poem *The Dream of Gerontius*, later set to music by Elgar, came out in book form in 1866. His other works include two novels, which he brought out anonymously, and *The Grammar of Assent*, a theological work which appeared in 1870. He became a Cardinal in 1879.

newspapers The earliest publications which can be described as newspapers were probably the *Acta Diurna* which were published in ancient Rome, but the first to be printed in modern times appeared in Germany and The Netherlands about 1615. In England the *Weekly Newes* began

THE

NEWES

PUBLISHED FOR THE

SATISFACTION & INFORMATION of the PEOPLE.

WITH PRIVILEGE.

JULY 6, 1665.

BY order from the Right Honourable the *Lord Arlington* principal Secretary of State to His Majestie, I am commanded to publish the following advertisement to satisfy all persons of the great care of the Right Honourable the Lords of His Majesties most Honourable Privy Council, for prevention of spreading of the infection. Who by their order dated the one and thirtieth day of *May* last past did authorise & require the Justices of the Peace for the County of *Middlesex* and City and Libertie of *Westminster*, or any five of them, to treat with *James Angier, Esq.*, upon his offers of certain Remedies and Medicaments for stopping the contagion of the Plague & for disinfecting houses already infected, &c. And whereas *Sir John Rabington*, Knight & Baronet, His Majesties Lieutenant of the Tower, *Sir George Charnocke*, Knight, His Majesties Serjeant at Arms in Ordinary, *Humphrey Weld*, *Thomas Whartin*, *Joseph Ayloffe*, *Robert Jejon*, *James Norfolk*, Serjeant at Arms attending the Honourable House of Commons, and *William Bowle*, Esquires, Justices of the Peace for the said County of *Middlesex*, did at the desire of the said *Angier* & the inhabitants in the house of *Jonas Charles* in *Newton Street*, in the Parish of *St. Giles* in the Fields, in the said County, permit one *Richard Goodall*, servant of the said *Angier*, with his Medicaments, to enter the said house on *Thursday*, the *8th of July*, instant. After four several persons had dyed full of the spots out of the said house and eight more remained therein, whereof two were infected with the Plague. And whereas upon examination of several witnesses upon oath before the said justices, proof was made—that upon application of the said Medicaments there, and in several other houses, no person had dyed in any of the said houses since the same was therein used. And whereas in persuance of the said Order the said Justices upon the *12th* instant did report to the Lords of the Council, to whom the prevention of spreading the infection of the *Pestilence* is referred, their proceedings thereupon. And whereas upon reading the said *Justices* report and the proposals of the said *Angier*: as also of his several Certificates from forcign parts, for proving the happy success of the said *Angiers* Remedies in stopping the Infection in *Lyons, Paris, Stronbourg* and other cities, the said Committee of Lords did

The front page from a 1665 edition of *The Newes*, the first English newspaper, reporting the Great Plague of London.

to appear in 1622, while in the United States (where newspapers have always tended to be local rather than, as in Britain, national) the *Boston News-Letter* made its first appearance in 1704. Most of the other States began to produce papers soon after. In London, *The Times*, under the title 'The Daily Universal Register', began publication in 1785; *The New York Herald*, *The New York Tribune* and *The New York Times* published their first numbers in 1831, 1835 and 1841 respectively. From the start, newspapers began to proliferate all over the world — some two decades after the appearance of the *Weekly Newes* more than a dozen newspapers were on sale in London. Growth was especially rapid during the latter part of the nineteenth century, as printing presses became capable of fast production and the cost of materials fell so that the newspapers could be cheaply priced. A survey in 1886 showed that Britain had over twelve hundred papers and the United States four thousand. By 1900 the world-wide total stood at more than thirty-one thousand newspapers, of which nearly three thousand were British and nearly sixteen thousand were published in the United States.

Newton, Isaac (1642–1727) The great scientist Isaac Newton was born in Lincolnshire and educated at Cambridge, where he remained, at Trinity College, for some thirty-five years. In 1689 he was elected to Parliament, and was appointed Master of the Mint in 1697. He became President of the Royal Society in 1703, and Queen Anne conferred a knighthood on him in 1705. Meanwhile he had already published *Philosophiae Naturalis Principia Mathematica* (*The Mathematical Principles of Natural Philosophy*), which appeared in 1687, and *Optics*, in 1704. His last major work, *Arithmetica Universalis*, came out in 1707.

New Yorker, The In 1925 Harold Ross founded the weekly magazine *The New Yorker*, which he continued to edit for many years. It has had many distinguished contributors, including S.J. Perelman, John O'Hara, John Hersey, Rebecca West, Truman Capote, Dorothy Parker and James Thurber. The best of American humorous cartoons also appear in its pages.

Nibelungenlied A German poem of the thirteenth century, based on earlier traditional legends which are to be found in the Icelandic *Eddas*. The story is loosely based on historical events in the fifth century, to which are added elements of Nordic myth and the trappings of chivalry. It provided Wagner with the inspiration for the sequence of four operas known as *The Ring*.

Nicholas Nickleby A novel by Charles Dickens, which introduces the appalling schoolmaster Wackford Squeers, the theatrical company run by Vincent Crummles, the pathetic orphan Smike, and the benevolent Cheeryble brothers. It was first published between 1838 and 1839.

Nichols, Peter (1927–) The English playwright Peter Richard Nichols was born and educated in Bristol. He became an actor, and then began to write plays for television. His first major success came with the stage play *A Day in the Death of Joe Egg*, first seen in 1967. Other plays include *The National Health*, in 1969, *Forget-me-not Lane*, in 1971, *Passion Play*, in 1980, and *A Piece of My Mind*, in 1987.

Nicholson, Norman (1914–) The Lake District poet, novelist and literary critic Norman Cornthwaite Nicholson was born in Millom, Cumberland. His first book of poems, *Five Rivers*, appeared in 1944, and other collections have appeared since, including *The Pot Geranium*, in 1954, and *Selected Poems 1940–1982*, in 1982. He has published three plays in verse, two novels, a number of works of literary criticism and books on the Lake District.

Nicolson, Harold (1886–1968) Harold George Nicolson was born in Teheran, where his father was a diplomat, and educated at Wellington and Oxford. He himself entered the diplomatic service. He wrote two novels, but was better known as a biographer. *Paul Verlaine* was published in 1921, and was followed by studies of Tennyson, Byron, Swinburne and Sainte-Beuve. He also produced a book on the Congress of Vienna and the official biography of King George V. One of his most attractive books was *Some People*, published in 1927. He was married to the writer Vita Sackville-West.

Nietzsche, Friedrich Wilhelm (1844–1900) The German philosopher Friedrich Wilhelm Nietzsche was born in Leipzig and educated at the universities of Bonn and Leipzig. He became Professor of Philology in the University of Basle. His first published book was an innovative study of Greek literature, *Die Geburt der Tragödie aus dem Geiste der Musik* (*The Birth of Tragedy from the Spirit of Music*), which appeared in 1872. The principal works in which he expounded his philosophy, which presented his concept of a 'superman' in opposition to the Christian virtues, were *Also Sprach Zarathustra* (*Thus Spoke Zarathustra*), first published in 1883 and 1884, and *Jenseits von Gut und Böse* (*Beyond Good and Evil*), in 1886. He left uncompleted his final statement, *Der Wille zur Macht* (*The Will to Power*).

Nigger of the Narcissus, The A novel of the sea by Joseph Conrad, in which the Black sailor James Wait is in conflict with the mutineer Donkin. It was first published in 1897.

Nightmare Abbey A satirical novel by Thomas Love Peacock, first published in 1818.

Night Thoughts A long poem by Edward Young, first published in nine volumes between 1742 and 1745. The full title is *The Complaint, or Night Thoughts on Life, Death, and Immortality*.

Nin, Anaïs (1903–77) Born in Neuilly, France, Anaïs Nin was educated in New York. Her first book, *D.H. Lawrence: An Unprofessional Study*, appeared in 1932. She published a number of other books without much success until she produced *The Diary of Anaïs Nin 1931–34*. Six more volumes of her *Diary* appeared, and she also wrote a sequence of five novels under the general title *Cities of the Interior*.

Nineteen Eighty-Four A prophetic novel by George Orwell, telling of the struggle of Winston Smith to retain his individuality in an authoritarian state and of his final defeat. It was first published in 1949.

Nobel Prize The Nobel Prizes were set up under the will of the Swedish chemist Alfred Bernhard Nobel, who left the bulk of his fortune to provide annual prizes for individuals in the fields of physics, chemistry, medicine, peace and literature. All the prizes are not only valuable but immensely prestigious. The long list of those who have won the literature award since 1901 inevitably includes some whose work is largely unfamiliar to English-speaking readers, and some who may not have withstood the test of time. There are also surprising omissions. Nevertheless, many of the greatest names in twentieth-century literature, such as Shaw, O'Neill, Eliot and Bellow, to single out only a few of those writing in English, have been honoured.

Norris, Frank (1870–1902) Benjamin Franklin Norris, the American novelist, was born in Chicago and educated in Paris, at the University of California and at Harvard. He began his career as a journalist and war correspondent, but published his first novel, *Moran of the Lady Letty*, in 1898. His other novels were *McTeague* and *Blix*, which both appeared in 1899, *A Man's Woman*, in 1900, *The Octopus*, in 1901, and *The Pit*, in 1903, the last two being part of a projected trilogy, 'The Epic of the Wheat'.

Norse mythology The Icelandic *Eddas* contain the stories of Norse mythology, in which the ash tree Ygdrasill supports the whole universe, including Asgard, the home of the gods, of whom the supreme being is Odin. It was Odin who created Man and Woman and gave them Midgard (the Earth) as their dwelling-place, and from Valhalla, the finest palace in Asgard, he watches over all creation. The other gods include Thor, god of war, Frey, god of harvests, Freya, goddess of music and love, and Loki, who is responsible for all mischief. Mention should also be made of the Valkyries, the twelve maidens who conduct fallen warriors to Valhalla, Baldur, the son of Odin, slain through the machinations of Loki, and the Elves, lesser beings than the gods, but nevertheless endowed with many magic powers.

Northanger Abbey A novel by Jane Austen, in which she satirized the popular Gothic horror novels of the period. It was first published posthumously in 1818.

Nostromo A novel of adventure by Joseph Conrad. Set in an imaginary country in South America, it was first published in 1904.

novel, the A novel can be described as a story of considerable length, written in prose, presenting imaginary events and characters, whose actions and emotions nevertheless reflect the real world. The definition is necessarily a loose one, since novels can take so many different forms, and even the most essential element of fiction – that it is not an account of real people and real happenings – can sometimes barely apply, as, for instance, in the unashamedly autobiographical novel in which fact is only lightly disguised as fiction. Using this definition, it is possible to

The fyrſt boke.

¶Here begynneth the fyrſt boke of the mooſt noble and woꝛthy prynce kyng Arthur ſomtyme kyng of grete Bꝛytayne nolw called Englande whiche treateth of his noble actes and feates of armes ⁊ chyualrye / and of his noble knyghtes of the table roūde and this volume is deuyded in to.rrj.bokes.

¶Holw Utherpendꝛagon ſente foꝛ the duke of Coꝛnewayle and Igrayne his wyfe / and of theyꝛ ſodayn departynge agayne. Capſin.j.

¶It befell in the days of y͏ͤ noble Utherpen dꝛagon whā he was kynge of Englande and ſo regned / there was a myghty and a noble duke in Coꝛ newayle that helde longe tyme w∘rre agaynſt hym. And y͏ͤ duke was named the duke of Tyntagyll / ⁊ ſo by meanes kynge Uther ſente foꝛ this duke / char gynge hym to bꝛynge his wyfe w͏ᵗ hym foꝛ ſhe was called a ryght fayꝛe lady / ⁊ a paſſynge wyſe / ⁊ Igrayne was her name. So whan the duke ⁊ his wyfe were comen to y͏ͤ kynge / by the meanes of grete loꝛdes they were bothe accoꝛ ded / ⁊ the kyng lyked ⁊ loued this lady well / and made her grete chere out of

A page from the 1529 edition of Sir Thomas Malory's *Le Morte D'Arthur*. The book was first printed in 1485 and is generally regarded as the first British novel.

consider some very early writing, such as the sixth-century *Daphnis and Chloe*, as novels, but it is generally agreed that the true novel was not seen until the fourteenth century, when the Italian Francesco da Barberino produced his *Documenti d'Amo*, to be followed a hundred years later by the works of Boccaccio. During the sixteenth century the form began to develop in Spain – Cervantes published his *Galatea* in 1585 – while in France and Germany the genre was not seen until the seventeenth century. A claim could be made that Malory's *Morte D'Arthur*, printed in 1485, was the first British novel, and *Euphues* by John Lyly, which appeared in 1578, has also been given that title; but it was not really until the eighteenth century, when Daniel Defoe produced a number of books, including *Colonel Jack*, *Roxana* and, especially, *Robinson Crusoe*, that a major advance was made. However, some literary critics do not ascribe the authorship of the first true novel in English to Defoe, but to Samuel Richardson, whose *Pamela:*

or Virtue Rewarded appeared in 1740. This is what is called an 'epistolary' novel, being told entirely by means of the correspondence which passes between the principal characters. Richardson was soon followed by Henry Fielding, with *Joseph Andrews* in 1742, and Tobias Smollett, who brought out *Roderick Random* in 1748. Of these two writers it was Fielding who substantially developed the genre. His *Tom Jones*, published in 1749, was innovative in being constructed more tightly than any of its predecessors, so that it can truly be said to possess a recognizable and coherent plot. From this time onwards novels and novel-writers proliferated, expanding the scope of their fiction to include, for instance, the historical romance and the Gothic tale of horror, and sometimes taking a form which was not only entertaining but which instructed, brought

A full-length oil portrait of Samuel Richardson by Joseph Highmore. His 'epistolary' novel *Pamela* appeared in 1740 and is regarded as the first true novel in English.

about reform, and held up a mirror to humanity in a way that no other form of writing could do with such effect. These developments occurred especially during the nineteenth century, which was the great classic period for the production of novels, not only in Britain, but also notably in Russia and France. In the United States the genre has generally tended to flower in the twentieth century, rather than earlier, and many critics would agree that the most interesting and original novelists writing today, taken as a whole, are American and Latin American. The popularity of fiction is immense, and although publishers constantly complain of the difficulty of selling novels, unless they are by established bestsellers, many thousands are published every year. Many of these are ephemeral, especially those popular works which fall into such categories as crime novels, romantic novels, science fiction, westerns, war books, and so on, but even within these fields some authors produce work of enduring quality; while some of the more 'serious' novelists continue to produce work which future generations may well consider to be equal in quality to that written by the giants of the past.

Noyes, Alfred (1880–1959) The English poet Alfred Noyes was born in Wolverhampton and educated at Oxford. His first volume of poems, *The Loom of Years*, appeared in 1902. *Drake: an English Epic* was serialized between 1906 and 1908, and led him to write other patriotic verse about the sea. His *Collected Poems* were published in 1950.

nursery rhymes Verses for small children, known as nursery rhymes, have existed for centuries, although some of the more familiar of them, such as 'Twinkle, twinkle, little star', date only from the early nineteenth century. Many are derived from children's games, while others have originated in adult satirical verses ('Lucy Locket', for instance, was a rhyme about notorious prostitutes). The first collection, *Tommy Thumb's Song Book*, appeared in 1744, and included 'Little Tom Tucker', 'Sing a Song of Sixpence' and 'Cock Robin', while *Mother Goose's* Melody, or Sonnets for the Cradle, published in 1781, contained, among others, 'Jack and Jill', 'Ding Dong Bell' and 'Hush-a-bye Baby'.

JACK·AND·JILL·WENT·UP THE·HILL·TO·FETCH·A· PAIL·OF·WATER·

ABOVE: 'Jack and Jill' from an 1897 edition of *The Book of Nursery Rhymes*, by F.D. Berdford.

RIGHT: 'But when she came back, He was feeding the cat' from *c*.1860 edition of 'Old Mother Hubbard'.

O

Oates, Joyce Carol (1938–) The American writer Joyce Carol Oates was born at Lockport, New York, and educated at universities in Syracuse and Wisconsin. A prolific writer, her novels include *With Shuddering Fall*, published in 1964, *Them*, in 1971, *Son of the Morning*, in 1979, *Solstice*, in 1985, and *Marya: A Life*, in 1986. She has also produced many collections of short stories, volumes of verse — including *Women in Love and other poems*, which appeared in 1968 — and books of literary criticism.

O'Brien, Edna (1932–) Born in County Clare, Ireland, Edna O'Brien published her first novel, *The Country Girls*, in 1960. The story of her two main characters, Kate and Baba, was continued in *The Lonely Girl*, which appeared in 1962, and *Girls in Their Married Bliss*, in 1964. Subsequent novels include *August is a Wicked Month*, published in 1964, *Night*, in 1972, and *Johnny I Hardly Knew You*, in 1977. She has also published collections of short stories.

O'Casey, Sean (1880–1964) The Irish playwright Sean O'Casey was born in Dublin. He received little formal education, but read voraciously and taught himself Gaelic. He then came to the attention of Lady Gregory and Lennox Robinson at the Abbey Theatre, where his play, *The Shadow of a Gunman*, was produced with considerable success in 1923. In the following year his best known drama, *Juno and the Paycock*, was given its first performance, and in 1926 came *The Plough and the Stars*, a play about the Irish Easter Rising of 1916. This was greeted at the Abbey Theatre by a riot in the audience, which did not like O'Casey's realistic portrayal of the revolutionaries of the time. His next play, *The Silver Tassie*, was rejected by the Abbey, and O'Casey took it to England, where it was produced in 1928. He wrote several more plays, including *Within the Gates*, seen in 1934, *Red Roses for Me*, in 1943, *Cock-a-Doodle-Dandy*, in 1949, and *The Bishop's Bonfire*, in 1955. He also published six volumes of autobiography.

O'Connor, Edwin (1918–68) The American novelist Edwin O'Connor was born in Rhode Island and educated at Notre Dame. He published his first novel, *The Oracle*, in 1951. *The Last Hurrah* appeared in 1956, and *The Edge of Sadness* was awarded a Pulitzer Prize in 1961. It was followed by *I Was Dancing*, in 1964, and his last novel, *All in the Family*, came out in 1964.

O'Connor, Flannery (1925–64) The American novelist and short story writer Flannery O'Connor was born in Savannah, Georgia, and educated at the Women's College of Georgia. Her first novel, *Wise Blood*, was published in 1952, and a collection of short stories, *A Good Man is Hard to Find*, appeared in 1955. Her second novel, *The Violent Bear It Away*, in 1960, was her last publication during her short lifetime. *Everything That Rises Must Converge*, consisting of more short stories, came out in 1965, and *The Complete Stories* appeared in 1971.

O'Connor, Frank (1903–66) Frank O'Connor was the pseudonym used by Michael Francis O'Donovan, who was born and educated in Cork, Ireland. From 1958 onwards he lived in the United States. He wrote plays for the Abbey Theatre, was an essayist and a translator of Gaelic verse, and also produced two books of autobiography. He is best known, however, for his many collections of short stories, the first of which, *Guests of the Nation*, appeared in 1931. Subsequent volumes included *Three Old Brothers*, in 1937, *Crab Apple Jelly*, in 1944, and *My Oedipus Complex*, in 1963.

ode Originally a song or a poem meant to be set to music, the term ode is now used, without any reference to music, to refer to a comparatively short poem, in which the poet usually speaks directly to his subject. The ancient Greek poet Pindar was the classic writer of odes; his verses, although apparently loosely constructed, do in fact follow a complex and rigid pattern, whereas later poets have felt able to use a very free approach, although in most cases a rhyming scheme has been retained.

Ode on a Grecian Urn A poem by John Keats, first published in 1820.

Ode to a Nightingale A poem by John Keats, first published in 1820.

Ode to the West Wind A poem by Percy Bysshe Shelley, first published in 1820.

Odets, Clifford (1906–63) The American playwright Clifford Odets was born in Philadelphia. He became an actor and worked with the Group Theatre, which produced his first success, *Waiting for Lefty*, in 1935. He followed it with several more plays, almost all of which contained a strong social message. Among them were *Awake and Sing!*, which was also presented in 1935, *Golden Boy*, seen in 1937, *The Big Knife*, in 1948, and *The Country Girl*, in 1950.

Odyssey, The This epic, which is generally said to be by the Greek poet Homer, was probably in existence before the eighth century BC, when Homer is supposed to have lived. Whether Homer was one person or several or did not in fact exist at all and whether, if there was such a person, he was the author or merely the transcriber of verses handed down orally, *The Odyssey* remains attributed to him. It tells the

A dramatic engraving, taken from a grotesque painting by Henry Fuseli, of the blinding of Polyphemus.

story of the wanderings of the hero Odysseus (known in Latin as Ulysses) after the Siege of Troy, and encompasses such familiar stories as his escapes from the one-eyed Cyclops, Polyphemus, and from Circe the enchantress, his avoidance of the twin maritime dangers of Scylla and Charybdis, and his final return to his kingdom of Ithaca and his faithful wife Penelope.

Oedipus The Greek dramatist Sophocles, writing in the second half of the fifth century BC, produced three plays on the subject of Oedipus, the tragic figure who murdered his father and unwittingly married his mother. Two of these plays still exist, *Oedipus the King* and *Oedipus at Colonus*.

O'Faolain, Sean (1900–) Born in Cork, the Irish writer Sean O'Faolain was educated at the National University of Ireland and at Harvard. His first book was *Midsummer Night Madness and other stories*, which was published in 1932. He subsequently produced both novels and further collections of short stories, almost all with an Irish nationalist theme, and wrote biographies of the modern Irish heroes, O'Connell, O'Neill, Countess Markiewicz and De Valera. He also brought out a major study, *The Irish*, in 1947, and published a volume of autobiography in 1964.

Of Human Bondage A partly autobiographical novel by W. Somerset Maugham, first published in 1915.

O'Flaherty, Liam (1897–1984) There are many similarities between the story of Liam O'Flaherty, who was born in the Aran Islands, and that of Sean O'Faolain, including the fact that both were encouraged in their early days as writers by Edward Garnett. Additionally, they were both Irish nationalists and in their literary work excelled at the short story. O'Flaherty published his first book, a novel entitled *The Neighbour's Wife*, in 1923, and followed it the next year with a collection of stories, *Spring Sowing*. Other novels include *The Informer*, which appeared in 1925, and *Famine*, in 1937, and he also published several more volumes of short stories and some autobiographical works.

Of Mice and Men A short novel by John Steinbeck, describing the strange friendship between two farm workers, first published in 1937.

Of Time and the River A long novel by Thomas Wolfe, a sequel to *Look Homeward, Angel*, continuing the story of Eugene Gant. It was first published in 1935.

O'Hara, John (1905–70) A native of Pennsylvania, John O'Hara began his writing career as a journalist, and wrote short stories, which were published regularly in the *New Yorker*, and of which many collections were published. His first novel was *Appointment in Samarra*, which appeared in 1934. Others included *Butterfield 8*, in 1935, *Pal Joey*, in 1940, and *A Rage to Live*, in 1949. *Ten North Frederick*, published in 1955, received the National Book Award.

Old Curiosity Shop, The A novel by Charles Dickens, first published as a weekly serial in 1840 and 1841, and appearing in book form in 1841. The characters include Little Nell and the dwarf Daniel Quilp.

Oldham, John (1653–83) The English satirist John Oldham was born in Gloucestershire and educated at Oxford. He had leanings towards poetry, but his favoured form of expression was the satire, of which he was an undoubted, if coarse, master. He published a broadside, *Garnet's Ghost*, in 1679, and produced a considerable number of translations from Greek, Latin and French, but his best-known works are the *Satire against Virtue* and the *Satires on the Jesuits*, published in 1679 and 1681 respectively.

Old Man and the Sea, The A short novel by Ernest Hemingway, considered to be the best of his later work, first published in 1952. It tells of a Cuban fisherman and his struggle with a marlin.

Old Mortality A novel by Sir Walter Scott, set in Scotland in the late seventeenth century and first published in 1816.

Oliphant, Laurence (1829–88) A member of a Scottish family, Laurence Oliphant was born in

Cape Town, where his father was a lawyer. He travelled extensively, and published two books on his experiences, *A Journey to Katmandu*, in 1852, and *The Russian Shore of the Black Sea*, in 1853. He then began a diplomatic career, later entered Parliament, became embroiled with a spiritualist leader, Thomas Lake Harris, and went to live for three years as a farm labourer in Harris's community at Brocton in New York State. In 1870 he successfully published a novel, *Piccadilly*. By 1884 he and his wife were living in Haifa, and it was there that she dictated to him the extraordinary *Sympneumata: Evolutionary Forces now active in Man*, which was apparently communicated to her by a spirit. After her death, and with the help which, he claimed, she extended to him from beyond the grave, he wrote a book called *Scientific Religion*.

Oliphant, Mrs (1828–97) Margaret Oliphant Wilson was born in Midlothian, Scotland. She published her first novel, *Passages in the Life of Mrs Margaret Maitland*, in 1849. She married her cousin, Frank Oliphant, in 1852, but he died seven years later, and in order to support herself and her children she continued her career as a writer, producing in all more than a hundred and twenty books. These included a number of historical works, the most interesting of which was *A Literary History of England from 1790 to 1825*, published in 1882, and several biographies, among them one of the eccentric Laurence Oliphant, who was not related to her. But her major success was as a novelist, especially with the two series, *The Chronicles of Carlingford* and *Stories of the Seen and Unseen*.

Oliver Twist A novel by Charles Dickens, telling the story of the orphan Oliver Twist, who is forced to join the gang of young thieves working for the villainous Fagin. It was first published between 1837 and 1838.

Omoo A novel of adventure in the South Seas by Herman Melville, a sequel to *Typee* and first published in 1847.

One Flew over the Cuckoo's Nest A novel by Ken Kesey, set in a mental hospital. It was first published in 1962.

One Hundred Years of Solitude A major novel by Gabriel García Márquez, first published in 1967, and in an English translation in 1970. It is the epic story of the founding of the mythical town of Macondo and its eventual destruction over a period covered by six generations.

O'Neill, Eugene (1888–1953) The son of actors, Eugene Gladstone O'Neill was born in New York City. His education was somewhat erratic, although he did attend Princeton for a brief period. He worked in a variety of jobs, including that of journalist, and made some voyages

as a seaman. In 1914, having been through a short-lived marriage and the subsequent divorce, he joined a drama workshop and eventually became part of the Cape Cod theatrical group, the Provincetown Players. His first plays were produced at the theatre in Provincetown; they were *Bound East for Cardiff*, in 1916, *The Long Voyage Home*, in 1917, and *The Moon of the Caribees*, in 1918. All three were one-act plays, and were based on his experiences as a seaman. His first full-length play, *Beyond the Horizon*, was also presented by the Provincetown Players, but this time in New York, and when it appeared in 1920 it was awarded a Pulitzer Prize. *The Emperor Jones* was presented in the same year, confirming that a playwright of outstanding power had arrived. O'Neill became involved in theatrical management, and it was not until several years

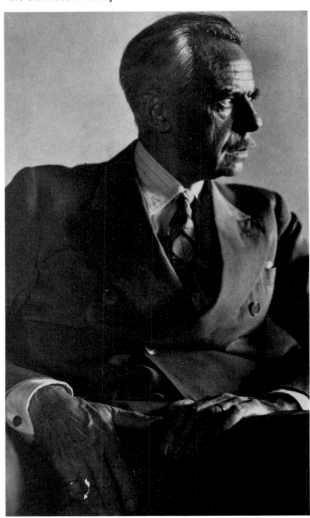

Eugene O'Neill. He said his task was 'to dig at the roots of the sickness of today'.

had passed that he devoted himself entirely to writing. However, his other activities did not seem to hinder his literary output, and in the next few years he produced a whole series of major plays. These included *Anna Christie*, which won him a second Pulitzer Prize in 1921, *The Hairy Ape*, first performed in 1922, *All God's Chillun Got Wings*, in 1924, and in the same year another memorable drama, *Desire Under the Elms*. At least one new play appeared every year until 1928, when his somewhat experimental drama, *Strange Interlude*, won him the Pulitzer Prize for the third time. Then there was a gap of three years before the appearance of *Mourning Becomes Electra*, the first of his trilogy of plays inspired by the Oresteian tragedies of Aeschylus, the second and third in sequence, *Ah! Wilderness* and *Days Without End*, being presented in 1932 and 1934 respectively. Two years later, in 1936, he was awarded the Nobel Prize for Literature. No new play now appeared until 1946, when *The Iceman Cometh* was produced, and only one more play, *A Moon for the Misbegotten*, was to be seen, in 1947, before his death. The finest of all his dramas, the partly-autobiographical *Long Day's Journey Into Night*, was presented posthumously in 1956. Two further dramas, which were part of an uncompleted sequence, *A Touch of the Poet* and *More Stately Mansions*, were staged in 1958 and 1967. Although O'Neill's work has been accused of lapses into melodrama, and it has been suggested that his style is dated, he remains the greatest playwright that America has produced, and a major figure in world drama. His work was firmly based on the traditional drama, even in plays such as *The Great God Brown*, in which he used experimental devices, but he was not restricted by his debt to the past. Few others have matched his ability to show so powerfully and dramatically that tragedy is not the sole prerogative of kings and princes, but can strike at ordinary people with devastating effect. His detractors have said that his plays are full of gloom, but this too is an unfair charge, for, however strong the atmosphere of doom may be, the brooding qualities of his tragedies are always innately dramatic.

Orczy, Baroness (1865–1947) The historical novels of Baroness Orczy, the Hungarian-born wife of Mr Montague Barstow, enjoyed enormous popularity in their day. They were execrably written, but their author was a good enough storyteller to keep her readers interested, especially when writing of her inspirational creation, Sir Percy Blakeney, the gallant rescuer of French aristocrats destined for the guillotine. *The Scarlet Pimpernel*, the first of his adventures, appeared in 1905.

Ordeal of Richard Feverel, The A novel by George Meredith, first published in 1859. It is concerned with the revolt of Richard Feverel against the educational system devised for him by his father, and with Richard's love for Lucy Desborough.

Oresteia, The A trilogy of plays, *Agamemnon*, *Choephoroe* and *Euminides*, by Aeschylus, first presented in Athens in 458BC. The subjects are the murder of Agamemnon by his wife, Clytemnestra; the vengeance taken by Electra, Agamemnon's daughter, and by Orestes, his son, who kills his mother and her lover, Aegisthus; and the hunting of Orestes by the Euminides.

Origin of Species, On the The famous book by Charles Darwin, first published in 1859. The full title is *On the Origin of Species by Means of Natural Selection, or the Preservation of Favoured Races in the Struggle for Life*.

Orlando A novel, spanning four centuries, by Virginia Woolf, first published in 1928.

Oroonoko, or the History of the Royal Slave An anti-slave-trade novel by Aphra Behn, first published about 1688.

Ortega y Gasset, José (1883–1955) The influential Spanish philosopher José Ortega y Gasset was born in Madrid. He studied in Madrid and Germany, and later became Professor of Metaphysics at Madrid University. In 1910 he published *Adán en el paraíso* (*Adam in Paradise*). Other books include *Meditaciones del Quijote* (*Quixote's Meditations*), in 1914, *El tema de nuestro tiempo* (*Modern Theme*), in 1923, *España invertebrada* (*Invertebrate Spain*), in 1922, and *La rebelión de las masas* (*The Revolt of the Masses*), in 1932. He founded the Instituto de Humanidades in Madrid in 1948.

Orwell, George (1903–50) George Orwell was the pseudonym of Eric Arthur Blair, who was born in Bengal and educated at Eton. He served in Burma with the Indian Imperial Police, but resigned in 1927 and returned to Europe, where he embarked on a life of poverty as an unsuccessful writer. His experiences resulted in his first book, *Down and Out in Paris and London*, which was published in 1933. In 1934 he brought out *Burmese Days*, and this novel was followed by *A Clergyman's Daughter* and *Keep the Aspidistra Flying*, in 1935 and 1936. At that stage his fiction attracted little attention, but rather more impact was made in 1937 by *The Road to Wigan Pier*, a book on unemployment in Lancashire. Orwell had fought for the Republicans during the Spanish Civil War, and this experience resulted in his *Homage to Catalonia*, also published in 1937, in which he attacked Stalinist Communism. After publishing another novel, *Coming Up for Air*, in 1939, he confined himself for some time to journalism and political writings, becoming Literary Editor of the Socialist periodical *Tribune*. A collection of essays appeared in 1940, and *The Lion and the Unicorn: socialism and the English genius* in 1941. Worldwide success came suddenly in 1945 with the publication of his satire *Animal Farm*. Another volume of essays followed, and then in 1949 he published the prophetic political novel *Nineteen Eighty-Four*, which became a major bestseller. His last collection of essays, *Shooting an Elephant*, was published in 1950, the year of his death from tuberculosis, from which he had suffered for many years.

Osborne, John (1929–) The English playwright John James Osborne was born in London. He became an actor and achieved a major success in 1956 with his play *Look Back in Anger*, one of the first and certainly the most influential of the 'kitchen sink' genre, which brought a new realism to the theatre. The plays which followed, including *The Entertainer*, first seen in 1957, *Luther*, in 1961, *Inadmissible Evidence*, in 1964, and *A Patriot for Me*, in 1965, were well received, but his later works have been less successful. His autobiography, *A Better Class of Person*, made some stir when it was published in 1981.

Ostrovsky, Alexander Nikolaevich (1823–86) Born in Moscow, Alexander Nikolaevich Ostrovsky trained for the law before beginning to write for the theatre. His first play was *The Poor Bride*, presented in 1853. He continued his highly successful career with a number of other comedies, and then turned to historical dramas, which were equally well received. He wrote both in prose and in verse, and produced close on fifty plays, of which the most important are *The Storm* and *The Forest*, first produced in 1860 and 1871 respectively. Although much favoured by Czar Alexander III, he is still popular in Russia today.

Othello, The Moor of Venice A tragedy by William Shakespeare, first produced in 1604 and printed in 1622. Othello's jealousy, nurtured by Iago, leads him to murder his wife Desdemona.

Otway, Thomas (1652–85) The dramatist Thomas Otway was born in Sussex, England, and educated at Winchester and Oxford. His first play, *Alcibiades*, was produced in 1675. It had little literary merit, but his next play, the tragedy *Don Carlos, Prince of Spain*, written in rhyming verse and presented in 1676, was of much higher quality, and deserved its success. Otway's talent was erratic, and he seemed to alternate between major works and plays of little, if any, value. Next came a bawdy comedy, *Friendship in Fashion*, and then one of his best plays, *The Orphan, or The*

Alan Dobie, Jocelyn Britton and Michael Bryant in a 1950s production of John Osborne's *Look Back in Anger*.

Unhappy Marriage, was seen in 1680. After two more minor works his masterpiece, the tragedy *Venice Preserv'd, or A Plot Discover'd*, appeared in 1680. Despite its success, he died in poverty.

Ouida (1839–1908) Ouida was the pen-name of Marie Louise de la Ramée, who was born of a French father and an English mother in Bury St Edmunds, England. She began to write at an early age, and her most famous novel, *Under Two Flags*, which was published in 1867, was in fact her fourth book. The almost equally well-known *Moths* appeared in 1880. She wrote a large number of novels and some books for children. Her adult work was considered somewhat daring at the time; it is now virtually unreadable, except for the unconscious humour of its melodrama and the absurd nature of its characterization.

Our Mutual Friend A novel by Charles Dickens, first published between 1864 and 1865. It tells of what happens to John Harmon, when, believed to have been murdered, he assumes another identity.

Our Town A play by Thornton Wilder, first presented in 1938. Set in a small New Hampshire town called Grover's Corner, it gently examines the quiet lives of the inhabitants.

Ovid (43BC–AD17) The Roman poet Publius Ovidus Naso was born in Sulmo, a town in the mountains of the Abruzzi. He began to write at a very early age, and was soon successful. His principal works were the love poems known as the *Amores*, the stories and legends collected in the *Heroides*, *The Metamorphoses* and the *Fasti*, and a tragedy, *Medea*. He also wrote *Ars Amatoria* (*The Art of Love*), which provoked a scandal at the time, and which, as recently as the 1920s, could be described as 'perhaps the most immoral work ever written by a man of genius'.

Owen, Wilfred (1893–1918) For many critics the outstanding poet of World War I, Wilfred Edward Salter Owen was born in Shropshire, England. After completing his education he became tutor to a French family in Bordeaux, and then joined the army in 1915. In October 1918 he was awarded the Military Cross for exceptional bravery in the field. In November, a week before the Armistice, he was killed. His poetry did not appear in book form until after his death. *Poems* was published in 1920, and a definitive volume, *The Collected Poems of Wilfred Owen*, came out in 1963.

Owl and the Nightingale, The A poem dating from the early thirteenth century, written in Middle English in rhyming couplets. It consists of more than fifteen hundred lines, and may have been written by Nicholas of Guildford, or by his contemporary, John of Guildford. Two manuscripts of the poem are still extant.

Oxford English Dictionary, The In 1858, with the object of replacing Dr Johnson's still popular *Dictionary* and its rivals as the standard reference works of English philology, work began on *A New English Dictionary on Historical Principles*. The first volume was published in 1884 and the last in 1928, by which time its principal editor, Sir James Murray, had died. A supplement appeared in 1933, when the reprint of the main work used the title *The Oxford English Dictionary* for the first time, and a further supplement was published in four volumes between 1972 and 1986. *The Oxford English Dictionary* can claim to be the most authoritative work of its kind on the English language.

P

Page, Thomas Nelson (1853–1922) The great-grandson of Thomas Nelson and John Page, who had both been Governors of Virginia, Thomas Nelson Page was born in Hanover County, Virginia. He graduated from the University of Virginia and practised for some years as a lawyer. In 1887 he published a collection of stories, *In Ole Virginia*, which was the first in a long list of books covering fiction and non-fiction, poetry, and books for children. An ardent Southerner, he wrote a biography of Robert E. Lee. In 1913 President Wilson appointed him Ambassador in Italy, and thereafter he wrote no more.

Paine, Thomas (1737–1809) The English writer Thomas Paine was born in Thetford, Norfolk. After a somewhat unsuccessful career as an exciseman, he met Benjamin Franklin, and, as a result, sailed for America in 1774. In 1776 he published *Common Sense*, a pamphlet which called for the independence of the American colonies and the setting up of a Republic. A number of pamphlets under the general title of *The Crisis* appeared during the War of Independence and were probably more effective than any other written work in maintaining the impetus of the revolution. In 1787 he returned to Europe, and in England, where his popularity was at its nadir, published *Prospects on the Rubicon*, in which he attacked William Pitt's war policies, at least partly with the object of securing the friendship of France. In 1790 Edmund Burke brought out his highly critical *Reflections on the Revolution in France*, and Paine replied in *The Rights of Man*, of which the first part was published in 1791 and the second part in the following year. It was very widely read, and, not surprisingly, the British government

1234567890

decided that its author should be brought to trial for treason. Paine took refuge in France, where he remained for the next ten years, serving as a deputy in the French Convention from 1792 until 1795 (except for a brief period in prison when he incurred Robespierre's displeasure). *The Age of Reason*, in which he put forward the anti-Christian views of a deist, appeared in 1793, and Paine was immediately vilified, not only in England, where he was already viewed as the Devil incarnate, but also in the United States. An attack on George Washington in 1796 did little to improve his reputation, but he nevertheless returned to America in 1802, and ended his days there. Indignation against Tom Paine and his writings gradually died down, and he began to emerge as one of the most influential of those authors whose works had promulgated the spirit of enlightenment at the turn of the nineteenth century.

Auguste Millière's mild portrait of Thomas Paine, whose radical *The Rights of Man* incited charges of treason.

Painted Veil, The A novel by W. Somerset Maugham, first published in 1925.

Pair of Blue Eyes, A Thomas Hardy's third novel, first published in 1873.

Pale Fire A novel by Vladimir Nabokov, told by means of extensive footnotes to a long poem, first published in 1962.

Paley, Grace (1922–) The short story writer Grace Paley was born in New York City and educated at Hunter College, New York. In 1959 she published a collection, *The Little Disturbances of Man: Stories of Men and Women in Love*, and this has been followed by *Enormous Changes at the Last Minute*, in 1975, and *Later the Same Day*, in 1985.

Palgrave, Francis Turner (1824–97) A native of Great Yarmouth, England, Francis Turner Palgrave was educated at Charterhouse and Oxford and had a distinguished career in education. He published verse and literary criticism, but is remembered now solely for his anthology, *The Golden Treasury of English Songs and Lyrics*, which was published in 1861, and in the compiling of which he received advice from Tennyson. It became immensely popular, as a school textbook as well as for general reading. He revised and expanded it for the edition of 1897, and further emendations and additions have been made since his death.

Pamela, or Virtue Rewarded An epistolary novel by Samuel Richardson, which has some claims to be considered as the first true novel to have appeared in the English language. It was published between 1740 and 1741.

Pantagruel Although published a year earlier than *Gargantua*, this is in fact the second book in the series of comic, bawdy and satirical books by François Rabelais. Published under the pseudonym Alcofribas Nasier, it appeared in 1532 or 1533, and was translated into English by Sir Thomas Urquhart in 1653.

Paracelsus A dramatic poem by Robert Browning, first published in 1835.

Paradise Lost John Milton's great epic poem was first published in 1667. Based on Bible stories and written in blank verse, it tells of the Fall of Man through disobedience and of his eventual Redemption. The first edition comprised ten books, but in a revised version, which appeared in 1674, the material had been rearranged to form twelve books.

Paradise Regained An epic poem by John Milton, first published in 1671, in four books. Much shorter than *Paradise Lost*, to which it is in fact less a sequel than a companion piece, it deals with the temptation of Christ in the wilderness.

Paradiso, The The third part of Dante's *Divine Comedy*. The poet is guided by Beatrice through the various glorious spheres of Heaven, until he reaches the tenth level, where, for one instant, he is permitted to penetrate the light which veils the Godhead, and to gain understanding of all mysteries.

Paris, Matthew (*c.*1199–1259) The monk Matthew Paris was probably English, although he is sometimes called Matthew of Paris (possibly a reference to his having studied in the French capital). Working in the monastery at St Alban's he produced the historical record known as the *Chronica Majora*. He also wrote a shorter version, *Historia Anglorum sive historia minor*, covering the period from 1200 to 1250, and an account of the early Abbots of St Alban's.

A beautiful and subtly coloured illustration of the Madonna and Child from Matthew Paris' *Historia Anglorum*, a chronicle of events in England and Europe between 1067 and 1253.

Parker, Dorothy (1893–1967) Dorothy Rothschild Parker was born in New Jersey. She published some collections of verse, including *Enough Rope*, which appeared in 1926, and she also wrote short stories and collaborated with other writers on plays. But it is as a critic that she is remembered, and above all as a wit. She was one of the founder members of the Round Table group of writers and actors who met at the Algonquin Hotel in New York.

Parkman, Francis (1823–93) The historian Francis Parkman was born in Boston, Massachusetts, and educated at Harvard. Always fascinated by nature and the wilderness, he set out in 1846 with his friend Quincy Shaw on a journey from Boston to Wyoming, during which they lived for some time with the Ogillalah band of Sioux Indians. The result was the classic account, *The Oregon Trail*, which appeared in 1849. Although Parkman suffered from extremely poor health, he succeeded in producing, during the next forty years or so, a series of books of major importance. The first of these, published in 1851, was his *History of the Conspiracy of Pontiac*. It was, in effect, a sequel to the master work which he was yet to write, his great history of *France and England in the New World*, which was published in seven volumes between 1865 and 1892. Parkman is noted for the excellence of his style, the accuracy and depth of his research, and the liveliness which he brings to his portrayal of the past. For these qualities many critics regard him as the outstanding American historian.

American historian Francis Parkman brought first-hand experience to his classic account *The Oregon Trail*.

Parliament of Fowls, The A poem by Geoffrey Chaucer, describing a dream, and probably written about 1382.

Parnell, Thomas (1679–1718) Although of English parentage, the poet Thomas Parnell was born and educated in Dublin, and later became Archdeacon of Clogher, County Louth. A member of the Scriblerus Club, he was a friend of Pope, who in 1721 arranged the publication of *Posthumous Works of Dr Thomas Parnell, containing Poems Moral and Divine, and on various other subjects*.

parody A piece of writing in which the author imitates the style of some other author for comic effect. The more familiar the writing of the parodied author, and the more unsuitable the subject of the parody to him or her, the more ludicrous the result. Parody has existed from the earliest times, and most great writers, from Aristophanes to Cervantes, and from Shakespeare down to modern times, have not only been frequently parodied, but have indulged in the exercise themselves.

Parzifal An epic poem written by Wolfram von Eschenbach in the early part of the thirteenth century.

Pascal, Blaise (1623–62) The French philosopher and mathematician Blaise Pascal was born at Clermont Ferrand. Until he was a little over thirty, he devoted himself to mathematics and science, but in 1654 he entered the Jansenist convent of Port-Royal, and it was there that he began to write the *Provinciales*, a series of eighteen pamphlets defending the Jansenists against the attacks of the Jesuits. After his death, the *Pensées* (*Thoughts*) were published in 1670. They are supposed to have been part of an uncompleted defence of Christianity, but, although firmly attributed to Pascal, some critics have doubted that he wrote them, claiming that he could not have produced so confused a work.

Pasolini, Pier Paolo (1922–75) The Italian film maker, who produced for the screen a succession of innovative and highly regarded films, was also a novelist, essayist and, especially, a poet. A committed socialist, most of his work was concerned with his view of capitalism as an evil force, as expressed in his novels, *The Ragazzi* and *A Violent Life*, and in his poetry, in *Gramsci's Ashes*, *The Heretic Experience* and *Poems in the Shape of a Rose*. In 1975 he was found on a beach, brutally murdered. He left unfinished a new novel, *Petralio*.

Passage to India, A A novel by E.M. Forster, first published in 1924. It describes the circumstances surrounding an unjustified allegation of rape against an Indian, Dr Aziz, by a young British girl.

Pasternak, Boris (1890–1960) Born in Moscow, the son of a painter father and a pianist mother, Boris Leonidovich Pasternak intended to make his career in music, but at an early age decided on literature instead. His first volume of poetry, *A Twin in the Clouds*, appeared in 1914, after he had returned to Russia from a period of study at the University of Marburg. Further collections of verse appeared regularly, including the very highly regarded *My Sister Life* and *Second Birth*, in 1922 and 1932 respectively, and he also brought out some long poems, stories and, in 1931, a volume of autobiography, *A Safe Conduct*. Although his reputation was so high in Russia, he fell foul of the Stalinist régime at this point, and from 1933 until 1943 was prevented from publishing any new work. He turned instead to translation, bringing out Russian versions of Goethe's *Faust*, of poetry by many English writers, and notably of Shakespeare's tragedies. He was permitted to publish two collections of poetry, *On Early Trains* and *The Breadth of the Earth* in 1943 and 1945, but there was no way in which his great novel *Dr Zhivago*, which he had been working on for some years, could be published in Russia, and in 1957 he allowed it to appear in Italy. It rapidly achieved huge sales throughout the free world. It was often referred to as the least read bestseller of all time, but, however unfair that comment may have been, it is certainly true that some who purchased it may have found it rather more solid than they had

The Soviet writer Boris Pasternak.

expected. Its worth, and that of Pasternak's other work, was recognized in 1958 by the award of the Nobel prize for Literature, but a campaign against him forced him to decline the Prize. He has since been, to some extent, rehabilitated in his native land. *Dr Zhivago* is to be published in Russia in 1988.

pastiche The term pastiche is derived from the Italian *pasticchio*, with reference to the pasting together of materials taken from existing works by other creative artists, but it is more often used to apply to writing which deliberately imitates or is in the style of well-known works. Pastiches are not written with the intention of ridiculing the original work, but an essential element of the form is that the reader should recognize the imitation.

pastoral poetry Originally meaning poems, frequently called idylls or eclogues, concerned with shepherds and their life, the term pastoral has been widened to refer to any poetry which takes rural pleasures as its subject. The first major pastoral poet was Theocritus, who lived in the fourth and third centuries BC, and pastorals were much in vogue from the fourteenth to the sixteenth centuries AD. Pastoral works were also written in prose and in dramatic form.

Patchen, Kenneth (1911–72) The American poet Kenneth Patchen was born in Ohio. His first selection of poetry, *Before the Brave*, appeared in 1936, and was followed by many more volumes, including *An Astonished Eye Looks Out of the Air*, in 1945, *Because It Is*, in 1959, and *Collected Poems*, in 1968. He also published several novels as well as prose.

Pater, Walter (1839–94) Born in London, Walter Horatio Pater was educated at Canterbury and Oxford, and after considering the ministry settled to an academic life. His essays appeared in various periodicals and were collected in 1878 in *Studies in the History of the Renaissance*. A friend of the Pre-Raphaelites, he preached the cult of beauty for its own sake, and set forth his doctrine in his best-known work, *Marius the Epicurean*, a novel disguised as biography, which was published in 1885. Other works, in prose which was much admired, included *Imaginary Portraits*, in 1887, *Appreciations, with an Essay on Style*, in 1889, and collections of his lectures and miscellaneous writings.

Pathfinder, The A novel of the American frontier by J. Fenimore Cooper, the fourth of his 'Leatherstocking Tales', first published in 1840.

Patmore, Coventry (1823–96) The English poet Coventry Kersey Dighton Patmore was born in Essex, and educated privately. He published a book of *Poems* in 1844, which was so savaged by the critics that he destroyed the remainder of the edition, but it brought him into contact with the Pre-Raphaelites and he was encouraged to continue writing verse. In 1853 he brought out *Tamerton Church Tower*, which included some of the best pieces from his earlier *Poems*. His best-known work, the sequence known as *The Angel in the House*, appeared in four volumes published between 1854 and 1862. After *The Unknown Eros*, in 1877, and *Amelia*, in 1878, he turned his attention to literary criticism.

Paton, Alan (1903–) The South African writer Alan Stewart Paton was born in Pietermaritzburg and educated at the University of Natal. His anti-apartheid novel *Cry, the Beloved Country* became a bestseller when it was published in 1948. He followed it with *Too Late the Phalarope* in 1953, and *Ah, But Your Land is Beautiful* in 1981. He has also written a number of non-fiction books on South Africa.

Paulding, J.K. (1778–1860) Born in New York State, James Kirke Paulding received his education at a village school. Through his marriage he became connected with Washington Irving, and joined with him and his brother in the writing of *The Salmagundi Papers*, published in 1808. He went on to write a large number of books, many in comic vein, but also including some serious works of non-fiction and volumes of verse. He was the author of the memorable lines: 'Peter Piper picked a peck of pickled peppers; Where is the peck of pickled peppers Peter Piper picked?'.

James Kirke Paulding, American novelist and poet, was also Secretary of the Navy under Van Buren.

Payne, John Howard (1791–1852) The American playwright John Howard Payne was born in New York City. After some early experiments in the theatre, both as dramatist and as actor, he went to England and achieved his first success in 1818 with his play *Brutus: or the Fall of Tarquin*. He went into theatrical management, but lost enormous sums of money, and later collaborated with Henry Irving in a number of plays. He was the author of the lyric of the popular song 'Home, Sweet Home'.

Paz, Octavio (1914–) Born in Mexico City and educated at the University of Mexico, Octavio Paz published his first book of verse, *Bajo tu clara sombra y otoros poemas* (*Beneath Your Clear Shadow and other poems*) in Spain in 1937. Many more collections have followed, including *Piedra de sol* (*The Sun Stone*), in 1957. A selection of his work appeared in 1979. Between 1962 and 1968 he was Mexican Ambassador in India, and for most of the 1970s he was teaching at Cambridge, and for a considerable period, at Harvard.

Peacock, Thomas Love (1785–1866) The satirist and poet Thomas Love Peacock was born in Weymouth, England. He published a number of volumes of poetry before producing in 1816 his novel *Headlong Hall*. This innovative satire was followed by several others, including *Nightmare Abbey*, in 1818, *Maid Marian*, in 1822, *The Misfortunes of Elphin*, in 1829, and *Crotchet Castle*, in 1831. In his old age he published a final satirical novel, *Gryll Grange*, which appeared in 1860. His poetry – some of which is included in his fiction in the form of songs and ballads – was largely unremarkable, except for the long poem *Rhododaphne*, which came out in 1817. He also wrote some notable essays in literary criticism.

Peake, Mervyn (1911–68) Originally trained as an artist, Mervyn Laurence Peake was born in Kuling, China, the son of missionary parents. In 1946 he published *Titus Groan*, the first volume in his 'Gormenghast' trilogy of fantastic novels, the second and third books, *Gormenghast* and *Titus Alone*, appearing in 1950 and 1959 respectively. He also published some volumes of poetry and produced illustrations for his own work and for various literary classics.

Pecock, Reginald (*c.*1395–*c.*1460) Successively Bishop of St Asaph and Bishop of Chichester, Reginald Pecock is believed to have been born in Wales. His works, written in the vernacular, included *Repressor of over much blaming of the Clergie*, published about 1455, which attacked the Lollards. His views were unpopular, and he was forced to resign his bishopric and recant his beliefs.

Peele, George (1558–97) The English dramatist and poet George Peele was born in London and educated at Christ's Hospital and Oxford. He went to London in 1580 and began a career as a writer of pageants and plays. His comedy *The Arraygnement of Paris* was published in 1584, and

his other extant plays include the innovative, if over lengthily-named, *The Famous Chronicle of King Edward the first, surnamed Edward Longshankes, with his return from the holy land. Also the Life of Lleuellen, rebell in Wales. Lastly, the sinking of Queen Elinor, who suncke at Charingcrosse, and rose again at Potters-hith, now named Queenhith*, printed in 1593.

Peer Gynt The great allegorical verse drama by Henrik Ibsen, first performed in 1867.

Pendennis, The History of A novel by William Makepeace Thackeray, first published between 1848 and 1850.

Pepys, Samuel (1633–1703) The most celebrated of all diarists, Samuel Pepys was the son of a London tailor, and was educated at St Paul's School and Cambridge. In 1660 he began to work for the Navy Board, and eventually rose to become Secretary to the Admiralty, a position which he held from 1673 to 1679 and again from 1685 to 1688. His *Memoirs of the Navy* appeared in 1690. He was for some years a Member of Parliament, and in 1684 was elected President of the Royal Society. He began the six volumes of his famous *Diary* on 1 January 1660 and continued until 31 May 1669, when failing eyesight forced him to end it. This fascinating and immensely detailed account of the period,

Samuel Pepys, the great diarist, by John Closterman.

including the uninhibited details of his private life, was written in a form of shorthand, which he complicated by devices of his own, and it was not until 1825 that it was deciphered and a substantial part of it appeared in plain English. Many further editions have been published since, and in recent years a complete and uncensored version, edited by Robert Latham and William Matthews in eleven volumes, has been made available.

Percy, Walker (1916–) The philosophical novelist Walker Percy was born in Birmingham, Alabama, and educated at the universities of North Carolina and Columbia. He became a full-time writer in 1943. His novels include *The Moviegoer*, which appeared in 1961, *The Last Gentleman*, in 1967, *Lancelot*, in 1977, *The Second Coming*, in 1981, and *Lost in the Cosmos*, in 1984.

Percy's Reliques of Ancient English Poetry An anthology edited by Thomas Percy, Bishop of Dromore, and based on a manuscript edition of miscellaneous verse which Percy rescued just in time before a servant lit a fire with it. Some of the poems, principally ballads, were centuries old, while others, especially those added by Percy himself, dated only from the early seventeenth century. The collection was first published in 1765, and was expanded in subsequent editions.

Peregrine Pickle, The Adventures of A satirical novel by Tobias Smollett, first published in 1751.

Perelman, S.J. (1904–86) Sidney Joseph Perelman was born in Brooklyn, New York. He wrote screenplays for the Marx Brothers, and became one of America's most popular humorous writers. His first book, *Dawn Ginsbergh's Revenge*, appeared in 1929. Other books include *Look Who's Talking*, which appeared in 1940, and *The Ill-Tempered Clavichord*, in 1953.

Pericles, Prince of Tyre A play by William Shakespeare, first performed about 1608, and printed in 1609. Despite the succession of misadventures which befall him, Pericles eventually finds his long-lost wife and daughter, and his enemies meet their just deserts.

Perkins, Maxwell (1884–1947) William Maxwell Evarts Perkins was born in New York City and educated at Harvard. He began his career as a journalist and then entered the publishing firm of Charles Scribners' Sons, where he remained for thirty-six years, establishing a reputation as America's greatest editor. He discovered and nurtured dozens of writers, working with them and coaxing them to success. His name will always be associated, in particular, with F. Scott Fitzgerald, Ernest Hemingway and Thomas Wolfe.

French writer Charles Perrault is best known for his popular fairy stories. This 'Puss in Boots' illustration from *Contes du temps passé* is by Marvy.

Perrault, Charles (1628–1703) The French writer Charles Perrault was born in Paris. He trained as a lawyer, but soon turned to literature. He is remembered as the author of *Histoires ou contes du temps passé avec des moralités*, the *Mother Goose Tales*, which included such popular fairy stories as 'Cinderella', 'Puss in Boots', 'The Sleeping Beauty', 'Little Red-Ridinghood' and 'Bluebeard'.

Persians, The An historical play by Aeschylus, first performed in 472BC. It tells of events during the war between the Greeks and the Persians.

Persuasion A novel by Jane Austen, telling of the romance between Anne Elliot and Frederick Wentworth. It was first published posthumously in 1818.

Peter Pan A play for children by J.M. Barrie, first performed in 1904.

Petrarch (1304–74) Francesco Petrarca, the Italian poet, was born in Arezzo, but at the age of eight went with his family to Avignon. He lived in the south of France until 1353, when he returned to Italy. In 1327 he saw for the first time his Laura. Who she was or whether that was in fact her name is not known, but it was to her that he wrote, in Italian, the love lyrics known as the *Rime in vita e morte di Madonna Laura*, or the *Canzoniere*. Most of his works were in Latin, including his epic poem *Africa* and his treatises on philosophical and political subjects, and he was largely responsible for the revival of interest in the literature of the Romans and Greeks. He was highly regarded by his contemporaries, and in 1341 he was given the accolade of Poet Laureate in Rome. His influence was strongly felt for many centuries, particularly among the English poets of the sixteenth century.

Petronius The identity of Petronius is uncertain. He was the author of *The Satyricon*, a somewhat scandalous work of fiction, of which only fragments are still in existence. He may well have been Gaius Petronius Arbiter, a courtier and companion in debauchery of the Emperor Nero, who fell out of his master's favour and committed suicide in AD65.

Phillips, Stephen (1868–1915) After completing his education at Cambridge, Stephen Phillips, who was born in Oxfordshire, became an actor. He established a reputation with some volumes of verse and then turned to drama. His *Paolo and Francesca* was very successfully produced in 1901, and he followed it with a number of other verse plays, including *Herod*, *Ulysses*, *Nero*, and *Faust*.

philosophy, English and American Many works of philosophy were written by English authors in medieval times, but the first comparatively recent work in this genre was by Francis Bacon. He was followed in the seventeenth century by Thomas Hobbes and John Locke, and later by Adam Smith and David Hume. Notable in the nineteenth century were Jeremy Bentham, Herbert Spencer and John Stuart Mill. The most eminent American philosopher is probably Ralph Waldo Emerson, the leading Transcendentalist, but mention should also be made of Henry David Thoreau and William James. In more recent times Bertrand Russell in England and George Santayana in the United States are perhaps the most important names.

Philpotts, Eden (1862–1960) The English novelist and playwright Eden Philpotts was born in India. He published his first book, *Lying Prophets*, in 1896. He is chiefly remembered for two plays, *The Farmer's Wife*, first presented in 1917, and *Yellow Sands*, in 1926.

Phineas Finn A novel by Anthony Trollope, the second in the 'Palliser' series, first published in 1869.

Phineas Redux A novel by Anthony Trollope, the fourth in the 'Palliser' series, first published in 1874.

picaresque A term used to describe novels of adventure in which the central character is a rogue. This type of story was particularly popular in Spain in the sixteenth and seventeenth centuries. The vogue spread, and Thomas Nash produced the first picaresque novel in English, *The Unfortunate Traveller: or the Life of Jack Wilton*, published in 1594. The classic example, *Gil Blas*, came from the French writer Alain-René Lesage, appearing between 1715 and 1735.

Pickwick Papers Charles Dickens' first novel, properly titled *The Posthumous Papers of the Pickwick Club*, first published in book form in 1837. It tells of the adventures of Mr Samuel Pickwick and his friends Tupman, Snodgrass and Winkle.

Picture of Dorian Grey, The A novel by Oscar Wilde, first published in book form in 1891. Dorian Grey's features remain unblemished, while his portrait shows the deterioration brought about by his debaucheries.

Pied Piper of Hamelin, The A poem by Robert Browning, sub-titled 'A Child's Story', first published in 1842.

Pierre, or The Ambiguities A satirical romance by Herman Melville, first published in 1852.

Piers Plowman A fourteenth-century poem, supposedly by William Langland. Its full title is *The Vision of William concerning Piers the Plowman, together with Vita de Do-wel, Do-bet, et Do-best, secundum Wit et Resoun*.

Pilgrim's Progress, The, from this World to that which is to come The allegory by John Bunyan, the first part of which appeared in 1678 and the second in 1684.

Pindar (c.522–443BC) The Greek lyric poet Pindar spent much of his life in Thebes. His work was remarkable for the strength of its imagery and for its complex structure. He wrote numerous religious poems in praise of the gods, but these are now extant only in fragments. Those works which exist in their entirety are *The Epinicia*, the forty-four 'Odes of Victory', written in honour of the winners at various Games. In the seventeenth century there was a vogue for 'Pindaric' odes, written by such poets as Dryden, Cowley and Gray, but these, although attempting to imitate Pindar's works, were written in much looser form.

Pinero, Arthur Wing (1855–1934) At the age of nineteen, Arthur Wing Pinero, who was born in London, became an actor. Three years later his first play, *£200 a Year*, was presented, and from this time on he wrote prolifically for the theatre, and soon became one of the most popular of playwrights. His farces, which included *The Magistrate*, in 1885, and *Dandy Dick*, in 1887, his drama *The Second Mrs Tanqueray*, in 1893, and the comedy *Trelawney of the 'Wells'*, in 1898, were among his greatest successes. He was knighted in 1909. His work went out of favour for some time, but his plays are now occasionally revived.

Pinter, Harold (1930–) The English dramatist Harold Pinter was born in London. He became an actor, and then began to write plays, the first of which, *The Room*, was performed in 1957. It has been followed by many successful dramas, including *The Birthday Party*, seen in 1958, *The Caretaker*, in 1960, *The Homecoming*, in 1965, and *No Man's Land*, in 1975. Often enigmatic in content, his work is noted for the extreme naturalness of the dialogue. He has also written extensively for both the large and the small screens.

Pippa Passes A drama by Robert Browning, written partly in verse and partly in prose, set in Asolo, near Venice. It was first published in 1841.

Pirandello, Luigi (1867–1936) The Italian playwright, novelist and short story writer Luigi Pirandello was born in Sicily and took a degree in philosophy at the University of Bonn. For nearly thirty years he was a teacher at a girls' school in Rome, but he began to publish poetry in 1889 and then went on to write fiction. His first novel, *L'esclusa* (*The Outcast*), appeared in

The Italian playwright and novelist Luigi Pirandello.

1894, and several more novels were to come, including *Il fu Mattia Pascal* (*The Late Mattia Pascal*), in 1904, and *I vecchi e i giovani* (*The Old and the Young*) in 1913. In the meantime, however, he had been building a major reputation with several volumes of short stories, the first collection of which appeared in 1894, and in 1912 he dramatized one of the tales, *La morsa*, as a one-act play. This launched him on a further successful career as a dramatist, and he produced many plays, both dramas and comedies, in which he explored the relationship in human terms between illusion and reality. Among the most celebrated of his theatrical works are *Cosi è se vi pare* (*Right You Are, If You Think You Are*), first seen in 1918, *Sei personaggi in cerca d'autore* (*Six Characters in Search of an Author*), the most famous of them all, which had its first performance in 1921, and *Enrico IV* (*Henry IV*), in 1922. He was awarded the Nobel Prize for Literature in 1934.

Pirate, The A novel by Sir Walter Scott, set in Shetland in the seventeenth century, and first published in 1821.

Plague, The The most important of the novels by Albert Camus. Published in French as *La Peste* in 1947, it appeared in English in the following year.

Plaidy, Jean The English writer Eleanor Hibbert, who is known by many pseudonyms, including Jean Plaidy and Victoria Holt, has published a vast number of romantic historical novels, including the recent *Lady in the Tower*, which appeared in 1986.

Plain Dealer, The A comedy by William Wycherley, published in 1677 and probably first presented in the previous year.

Plain Tales from the Hills A collection of stories, set in India, by Rudyard Kipling, his first prose publication, which appeared in 1887.

Plath, Sylvia (1932–63) The American poet Sylvia Plath was born in Boston and educated at Smith College, Massachusetts, and Cambridge, England. She published her first volume of poetry, *The Colossus*, in 1960. She married the English poet Ted Hughes in 1956, but they separated in 1962. A novel, *The Bell Jar*, appeared under a pseudonym in 1963, and shortly after its appearance Sylvia Plath committed suicide. Several collections of her poetry have been published posthumously, including *Ariel*, in 1965, and *Crossing the Water* and *Winter Trees*, both of which came out in 1971. Her *Collected Poems* appeared in 1981 and *Selected Poems* in 1986, both volumes edited by Ted Hughes.

Plato (427–347BC) The Athenian philosopher Plato was a friend and disciple of Socrates. While in his forties he founded a school of philosophy on the grove known as Academus, and presided over this Academy until his death. He left a considerable body of work, much of it written in dialogue form; these writings include the *Apology*, the *Symposium* (in which the concept of Platonic love is expounded), the *Laws*, and his most important work, *The Republic*, in which an ideal system of government is outlined. His influence on later philosophers, and on writers in many genres, has been profound.

Plautus (*c*.254–184BC) Born in Umbria, Italy, the dramatist Titus Maccius Plautus is believed to have worked in the theatre in Rome from his youth, and his plays appear to date from about 212BC. He wrote a large number of plays, of which twenty are still extant. These are comedies, all based on Greek originals. In translating the Greek, however, he added to the material and adapted it so that the works became original to him.

Playboy of the Western World, The An Irish comedy by J.M. Synge, first produced in 1907.

Plays for Puritans G. Bernard Shaw grouped three of his plays under this title when they were published in one volume in 1901. The plays are *The Devil's Disciple*, *Caesar and Cleopatra* and *Captain Brassbound's Conversion*.

Plays Pleasant and Unpleasant Two volumes of plays by G. Bernard Shaw, both published in 1898. *Plays Pleasant* contained *Arms and the Man*, *Candida*, the one-act play *The Man of Destiny*, and *You Never Can Tell*, while *Plays Unpleasant* consisted of *Widowers' Houses*, *The Philanderer* and *Mrs Warren's Profession*.

Pliny the Elder (*c*.AD23–79) Gaius Plinius Secundus was born in Como in northern Italy and educated in Rome. After a period as a lawyer he went on three punitive expeditions to Germany. He wrote a *History of the German Wars*, and followed it with a *History of his Times*, but these have not survived. His major work was a *Natural History*, of which he published the first ten volumes in the year AD77, while the remaining twenty-seven books appeared posthumously. It covered a wide range of subjects, including geography, anthropology, zoology, agriculture and art. He died during the eruption of Vesuvius which resulted in the destruction of Pompeii and Herculaneum.

Pliny the Younger (*c*.AD61–*c*.133) Publius Caecilius Secundus, who later became known as Gaius Plinius Caecilius Secundus, was the nephew of Pliny the Elder, and like his uncle was born in Como. Educated in Rome, he became a Senator and rose to high office. He is remembered as the author of a great many *Letters*, which cover many aspects of life in Rome at the time and also include a description of the eruption of Vesuvius in AD79.

Plomer, William (1903–73) The novelist, short story writer and poet William Charles Franklyn Plomer was born in South Africa but educated in England. His first novel, *Turbott Wolfe*, was published in 1926. He left South Africa in 1927, spent two years in Japan, and finally settled in England, where he worked in publishing. He produced several other novels and collections of short stories, and his *Collected Poems* appeared in 1973. He also wrote the libretti for four operas by Benjamin Britten.

Plough and the Stars, The A tragedy by Sean O'Casey, set at the time of the Irish rising of 1916. It was first performed in 1926.

Plumed Serpent, The A novel by D.H. Lawrence, first published in 1926. Set in Mexico, it provided Lawrence with a powerful, mystic theme.

Plutarch (*c*.AD46–120) The Greek biographer Plutarch was born in Boeotia and educated in Athens. He spent some years in Rome before returning to Greece, where he wrote his celebrated *Parallel Lives*, in which he paired the

This page from a 1513 edition of Plutarch's work was decorated by Albrecht Dürer and printed in Germany.

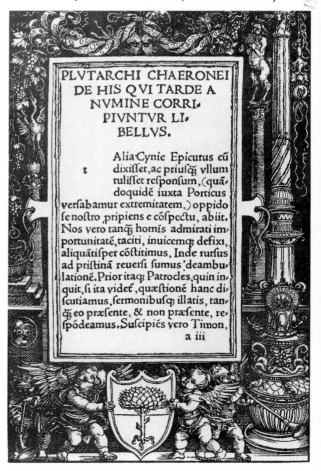

biography of each of his Greek subjects with that of a comparable Roman. These studies, both anecdotal and carefully researched, provided material for many subsequent writers of plays and other works, including Shakespeare. Plutarch also wrote a great many essays, which are particularly valuable for the quotations he included from earlier Greek literature that would otherwise have been lost.

Poe, Edgar Allan (1809–49) The son of an actor, Edgar Poe, who was born in Boston, Massachusetts, was orphaned at the age of nine. He was adopted by a tobacco merchant, John Allan, whose family name Poe later included in his own. He was educated partly in England and partly in Richmond, Virginia, where he entered the university in 1826. His addiction to gambling and liquor forced his guardian to remove him, and he then joined the army, rising to become sergeant-major in 1829. Later that year Mr Allan procured his discharge, and some months afterwards he was sent to West Point, but within a year was court-martialled for neglect of his duties, and expelled. In the meantime, he had published at his own expense a first volume of poetry, *Tamerlane and other poems*, which appeared anonymously in 1827. A second collection, *Al Aaraaf*, was published in 1829, and his *Poems* came out under his own name in 1831. He began to work as a journalist and to publish stories in various periodicals, winning first prize in a competition organized by the Baltimore *Saturday Visitor* in 1833 with the story 'Ms found in a Bottle'. At this period he was living with his paternal aunt, Mrs Clemm, in Baltimore, and in 1836 he married his thirteen-year-old cousin, Virginia, falsifying her age at the time of the wedding. She was to die of consumption eleven years later. In 1840 he published *Tales of the Grotesque and Arabesque*, a collection which included 'The Fall of the House of Usher'. During 1841 and 1842 he worked for *Graham's Magazine*, in which he published, among other stories, 'A Descent into the Maelstrom' and the first modern detective story, 'The Murders in the Rue Morgue', which featured his sleuth C. Auguste Dupin, whom he was to use again in other tales of crime. 'The Gold Bug' won him a prize the following year in a competition organized by a Philadelphia magazine. His perennially popular poem 'The Raven' appeared in 1845, first in a newspaper and then in a collection, *The Raven*

ABOVE: Edgar Allan Poe.

RIGHT: An illustration for 'El Dorado' by Edmund Dulac, whose fantasy-laden style complements Poe's work.

and other poems. 'The Raven' brought him considerable fame but little financial reward, and indeed, having quarrelled with his guardian, who left him nothing in his will, he spent most of his life in a state of acute financial embarrassment, which was exacerbated by his addiction to alcohol. He became for a short period the owner of the *Broadway Journal*, and produced such well-known stories as 'The Pit and the Pendulum', 'The Tell-Tale Heart' and 'The Premature Burial'. He also published some volumes of literary criticism, including *The Philosophy of Composition*, which appeared in 1846, and at one time indulged in an unsuccessful campaign to discredit Longfellow. After the death of Virginia, he became engaged to the wealthy Mrs Sarah Whitman, but the engagement was broken off. In 1849 he went back to Richmond, where he wrote the poem 'Annabel Lee', and there met another well-to-do widow, Mrs Shelton. Before they could marry, Poe was found, while in Baltimore, in an alcoholic coma, and four days later died in hospital there. His stories, usually now called *Tales of Mystery and Imagination*, have remained popular, despite the somewhat heavy, melodramatic style, and their influence extended to many nineteenth-century writers. His poetry, although sometimes marred by monotonous rhythms, was also much admired, especially in France, where many of his works were translated by Baudelaire.

Poetics, The A treatise by Aristotle on the art of poetry, of which only a fragment is still extant. It was written in the fourth century BC.

Poet Laureate The office of Poet Laureate is held by British royal appointment. The first Poet Laureate was, in effect, Ben Jonson, but the title was not used until Dryden assumed the position in 1668. Other notable Poets Laureate have included Southey, Wordsworth, Tennyson, Bridges, Masefield, Day-Lewis and Betjeman. The present incumbent is Ted Hughes. The office is rewarded by a token gift only, and there are no duties, other than the expectation that the Poet Laureate may produce a poem to celebrate such events as a coronation or a royal wedding.

poetry Many people have tried to define the essence of poetry. Samuel Taylor Coleridge, in what he called 'a homely definition', said it consisted of 'the best words in the best order'. Carl Sandburg suggested 'the achievement of the synthesis of hyacinths and biscuits'. In Wordsworth's view it was 'the spontaneous overflow of powerful feelings: it takes its origin from emotion recollected in tranquillity'. To add to these definitions it might be said that poetry is writing which illuminates some aspect of the

IL PLEUT

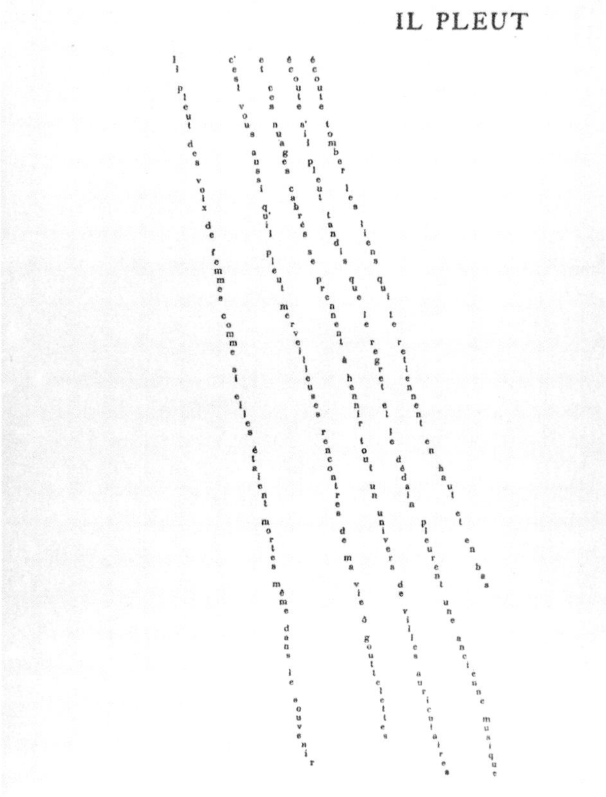

Poetry, like any art form, has evolved with time. Early poetry used alliteration and later regular lines with carefully structured metres, often with rhymes, were the vogue. Modern poetry has a 'freer' style, and experimental typography, as shown above, carries poetry to its limits.

world by selecting words and images, usually with great economy, for their power and value. The words not only have their own meanings and associations, but in combination produce a total effect which is, as it were, greater than the sum of its parts. Above all, a poem should arouse emotions in the reader. For some people, poetry must have rhyme and metre, and they are baffled by modern free verse, which often seems to be no more than a piece of prose arbitrarily split into short lines. But this kind of poetry is less 'free' than might at first appear; it has its rules and it has its rhythm, not necessarily regular or even apparent, but consisting of an essential rightness, flow, and balance in the phrasing, and often in the echoes and contrasts of the actual sounds of the words. 'A good poem,' said Dylan Thomas, 'is a contribution to reality. The world is never the same once a good poem has been added to it. A good poem helps to change the shape and significance of the universe, helps to extend everyone's knowledge of himself and the world around him ...'

Poets' Corner A section of Westminster Abbey in London is known as Poets' Corner, since it is set aside for the tombs or monuments of distinguished British literary persons, including Chaucer, Spenser, Shakespeare, Jonson and Milton. Many, such as Milton, were not buried in the Abbey, and their monuments were erected by later generations who saw their value more clearly than had their contemporaries.

Point Counter Point A witty novel of English society in the 1920s by Aldous Huxley, first published in 1928.

Poor Richard's Almanack An annual and extremely successful publication by Benjamin Franklin, which appeared regularly for twenty-five years, beginning in 1832.

Pope, Alexander (1688–1744) The poet Alexander Pope was born in London, the son of a linen-draper, and was educated privately and by his own efforts. A delicate child, he suffered an illness at the age of twelve which left him with a misshapen spine. By that time he had already determined on a literary career, and his first published work, a group of pastoral poems, which appeared in 1709, had been written when he was sixteen. The playwright William Wycherley befriended him and introduced him into London society, where he was soon welcomed as a new star in the literary firmament. His reputation was made with the publication in 1711 of his *Essay on Criticism*, which was much admired for its youthful author's brilliance of style and originality of content, although later critics realized that Pope had borrowed many of his ideas from the Roman rhetorician Quintilian and from the French writers René Rapin and René le Bossu. The wit and the erudition were, however, Pope's own, and are still remarkable. In the same year he brought out his eclogue 'Messiah', and in 1812 *The Rape of the Lock* was published by Barnaby Lintot in *Miscellaneous Poems and Translations by several hands*. The poem was subsequently revised, and appeared in its finished version in 1714. *Windsor Forest*, which came out in 1713, and which he had begun to write many years previously, was a long pastoral poem with political overtones. Its literary qualities and its blatantly Tory attitudes aroused great controversy, and Pope was attacked by, among others, his former friend Addison. Never averse to engaging in literary warfare, he replied with spirit, and Addison remained an enemy. A new friend was Jonathan Swift, who introduced him to the Scriblerus Club, of which Pope became an enthusiastic member, joining vigorously in the attempt to raise standards by ridiculing less talented writers, particularly if they were Whigs. In 1715 he published the first volume of his verse translation of *The Iliad*, further instalments appearing in 1717, 1718 and 1720, and in 1726 he

Pope's manuscript for his version of Homer. The original is in the British Museum.

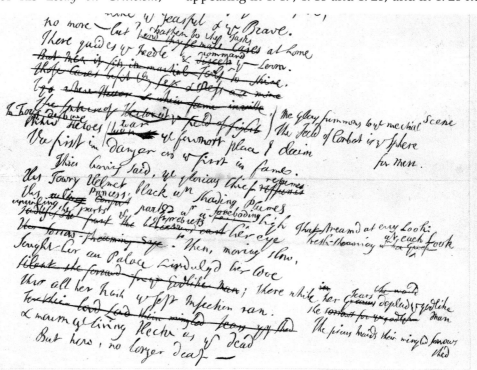

Charles Jervas may have painted this portrait of the vicious satirist Alexander Pope. A great poet of the Augustan Age, he was a master of intrigue and parody.

followed this with a companion version of *The Odyssey*, in which he was assisted by Elijah Fenton and William Broome. The two translations were immensely successful, bringing him more than £8,000, a veritable fortune in those days.

In 1725 he had published an edition of Shakespeare's plays, in which his always suspect scholarship was evident and was criticised in a pamphlet by Lewis Theobald. Theobald, whom he had already ridiculed with others in a prose work, *Peri Bathous, or the Art of Sinking in Poetry*, became the central figure in *The Dunciad*, the satire which Pope brought out in 1728. It was revised in 1729, and in 1743 a new version appeared, in which another enemy, Colley Cibber, took the place of Theobald. The last major works were the *Essay on Man* and the *Moral Essays*, philosophical verses which were published between 1733 and 1735, but Pope also produced a series of satires, *Imitations of Horace*, between 1733 and 1738, while his celebrated *Epistle to Dr Arbuthnot*, in which he savagely attacked many of his critics and former friends, appeared in 1735. He published a considerable quantity of other verse and some prose, but these writings are of minor interest only. It would appear that Pope was an unpleasant, vindictive person, but he had many friends as well as enemies, and the vigour of his satire was in tune with the spirit of the times, and far less exceptionable than it might appear today. That vigour, his wit, and the facility of his verse have retained for him an important place in the history of English literature.

Porter, Katharine Anne (1890–1980) The American writer Katharine Anne Porter was born in Indian Creek, Texas. She published her first volume of short stories, *Flowering Judas*, in 1930; further collections, *Pale Horse, Pale Rider* and *The Leaning Tower*, appeared in 1939 and 1944 respectively. The *Collected Short Stories*, published in 1965, won both the National Book Award and a Pulitzer Prize. Her major work was the allegorical novel, *Ship of Fools*, which came out in 1962. She also produced a number of essays, including *The Never-Ending Wrong*, an assessment of the Sacco and Vanzetti case, which was published in 1977.

Portrait of a Lady, The A novel by Henry James, first published in 1881. Set in Europe, it tells of Isabel Archer, a young American girl, who, having been wooed by others, chooses the wastrel Gilbert Osmond.

Portrait of the Artist as a Young Man, A An autobiographical novel by James Joyce, on themes which he developed further in *Ulysses*. It was first published between 1914 and 1915.

Potter, Beatrix (1866–1943) Helen Beatrix Potter was born in London. She became famous as the author of the 'Peter Rabbit' books, a series of twenty-three short tales and nursery rhymes for children. The first of them, *The Tale of Peter Rabbit*, was published at her own expense in 1893, but from the third book onwards they were issued by a commercial publisher, and with great success. The stories are enhanced by her own illustrations, and new editions have recently been prepared in which the reproduction of the original artwork has been greatly improved.

Pound, Ezra (1885–1972) The American poet Ezra Weston Loomis Pound was born in Hailey, Idaho, and educated at Hamilton College, Pennsylvania. He taught for a short period at a college in Indiana, but in 1908 left for Europe. In that year he published in Italy his first book of poems, *A Lume Spento* (*With Tapers Quenched*). For several years he lived in London, and during this period, with Richard Aldington, the American poet Hilda Doolittle and F.S. Flint, he founded the Imagist school of poetry, which rejected Romanticism and placed emphasis on direct images rather than symbolism, and on the use of experimental rhythms and, indeed, subjects. He published a number of collections, including *Personae* and *Exaltations*, which both appeared in 1909, and *Ripostes*, in 1914. He edited *Des Imagistes: An Anthology*, published in 1915, which contained work by James Joyce, T.S. Eliot and Wyndham Lewis, as well as poems by himself, Aldington, Doolittle and Flint. He was later largely to abandon the doctrine of Imagism in favour of an even greater freedom of expression and a stricter use of traditional verse forms. He married in 1914, and it was at this time that he began work on his major achievement, the epic series of poems known as the *Cantos*, the first three of which appeared in 1917. *Lustra* was published in 1916, *Quia Pauper Amavi* in 1919, and *Hugh Selwyn Mauberley* in 1920. In the following year he moved to Paris, where he was welcomed into the literary and artistic circles of the day, and while there he gave Eliot considerable assistance and advice on the composition of *The Waste Land*. From 1925 he lived at Rapallo, in Italy, resuming work on the *Cantos*, volumes of which

Ezra Pound, an admirer of Mussolini, giving the fascist salute on his return to Italy from America where he had stood trial on a charge of treason and been judged insane.

appeared in 1926, 1930, 1934 and 1937. An admirer of Mussolini, he made a number of pro-Axis broadcasts during World War II, and in 1945 he was arrested and sent by the American army authorities to detention in Pisa, where he produced the *Pisan Cantos*, eventually published in 1948. Towards the end of 1945 he was taken back to the United States to stand trial for treason, but was judged to be insane, and was confined in a mental institution until 1958. On his release, he returned to Italy, where he lived for the remainder of his life. Although inevitably tarnished by his wartime activities, his reputation slowly recovered as the importance of his work was more widely recognized. Further volumes of *Cantos* were published in 1955 and 1959, and the last poems in the sequence appeared in 1970. Pound also published, especially during the 1920s and 1930s, translations from the Italian, versions from the Chinese, and several volumes of literary criticism. His poetry has never achieved wide popularity; it is not, perhaps, immediately approachable, and it undoubtedly makes considerable demands upon the reader, in its content and style, and especially in the breadth of its cultural references. Nevertheless, it is widely agreed that his work had the most profound influence on contemporary and later poets, and that it was he who, with consummate mastery, charted the whole course of modern poetry.

Powell, Anthony (1905–) The English novelist Anthony Dymoke Powell was born in London and educated at Eton and Oxford. He published his first novel, *Afternoon Men*, in 1931. A number of other novels followed, including *What's Become of Waring?*, which appeared in 1939, before his literary career was interrupted by World War II. In 1948 he published *John Aubrey and His Friends*, and then returned to fiction in 1951 with *A Question of Upbringing*, which was the first of his sequence of novels known as *A Dance to the Music of Time*, in which he produced a portrait of his own generation, both tragic and humorous. The twelfth and final volume in the series, *Hearing Secret Harmonies*, was published in 1975. Among the other works which he has published since are four volumes of memoirs under the collective title *To Keep the Ball Rolling*. A novel, *The Fisher King*, appeared in 1986.

Power and the Glory, The A novel on the theme of good and evil by Graham Greene, first published in 1940.

Powys, John Cowper (1872–1963) The eldest of the three Powys brothers, who were all writers, John Cowper Powys was born in Derbyshire, England, and educated at Cambridge. His early works consisted of poetry and philosophical essays; he brought out a remarkable *Autobiography* in 1934, and a biography of *Rabelais*, with newly translated extracts from the works, appeared in 1948. However, he was regarded as primarily a novelist, especially after the publication in 1929 of *Wolf Solent* and, in 1932, of his best-known work, *A Glastonbury Romance*. Almost all of his books were long and wide in scope, and in later life he became increasingly concerned with the mystic. Among his other works of fiction are *Weymouth Sands* (1934), the Welsh historical novels, *Owen Glendower* and *Porius: A Romance of the Dark Ages* (1940 and 1951 respectively), and the imaginative *Atlantis* (1954).

Powys, Llewellyn (1884–1939) The youngest of the Powys brothers, Llewellyn Powys was born in Dorchester, England, and educated at Cambridge. He published a novel, *Apples Be Ripe*, in 1930, and a fictionalized autobiography, *Love and Death*, in 1939, but was best known for his collections of sketches and essays. These included *Ebony and Ivory*, which appeared in 1923, *Glory of Life*, in 1934, and *A Baker's Dozen*, published posthumously in 1941.

Powys, T.F. (1875–1953) Theodore Francis Powys was born and educated and lived almost all his life in Dorsetshire, England. Like his brothers he was always concerned with the meaning of life and with matters of the spirit, and these interests were reflected in his work. He published several collections of short stories, including *The Left Leg*, in 1923, and *Bottle's Path*, in 1946, and also wrote a number of novels, the best known of which is the allegorical *Mr Weston's Good Wine*, which appeared in 1927.

Pratt, E.J. (1883–1964) Edwin John Pratt was born in Newfoundland and educated in St John's and Toronto. He published a number of volumes of poetry, including *Newfoundland Verse*, which appeared in 1923, and *Collected Poems*, in 1944. *Brébeuf and His Brethren*, which appeared in 1940, was a long verse narrative about Jesuit missionaries murdered by Iroquois Indians, while *Towards the Last Spike*, published in 1952, told of the building of the Canadian Pacific Railway.

Prescott, William Hickling (1796–1859) The American historian William Hickling Prescott was born in Salem, Massachusetts, and educated at Harvard. His first published writings were essays on literary subjects, but in 1826 he decided to begin work on a major project, *The History of Ferdinand and Isabella*, which was published twelve years later. It was immediately successful, and he consolidated his reputation with the publication of his *History of the Conquest of Mexico* in 1843 and a *History of the Conquest of Peru* in 1847. He turned next to the *History of Philip II*, the Spanish king, but failing eyesight and health prevented him from completing the work, and only the first three volumes, two in 1855 and the third in 1858, were published.

Prévost, Abbé (1697–1763) Antoine-François Prévost was born in Artois, France, and educated by the Jesuits. After serving in the army, he became a priest in 1726, lived in England from 1728 to 1734, and then returned to France. He published a number of romances, some histories and several translations from the English, but he is remembered chiefly as the author of the novel *Manon Lescaut*, published in 1731, and later turned into an opera by Massenet.

Pride and Prejudice A novel by Jane Austen, first published in 1813. The story of the five Bennet sisters, and especially of Elizabeth Bennet and the proud Mr Darcy.

Priestley, J.B. (1894–1984) The English novelist John Boynton Priestley was born in Bradford, Yorkshire, and educated at Cambridge. He published a number of books of essays and literary criticism before his third novel, *The Good Companions*, became a bestseller when it was published in 1929. *Angel Pavement* followed in 1930. He was also an extremely successful playwright, and his theatrical works range in style as widely as his many novels, from the 'Time' plays, such as *Dangerous Corner*, produced in 1932, and *Time and the Conways*, in 1937, to the farcical comedy *When We Are Married*, seen in 1938, and the allegorical *Johnson Over Jordan*, in 1939. His vast output also included autobiographical works, travel books and collections of his wartime broadcasts.

Priestley, Joseph (1733–1804) Born in Yorkshire, England, Joseph Priestley became a Presbyterian minister. He wrote several books on theological and educational subjects, and in *An Essay of the First Principles of Government*, published in 1768, set forth his radical political views. His most important works, however, were on chemistry, in which field his discoveries, including the existence of oxygen, were of prime importance. His *Experiments and Observations on different Kinds of Air* appeared in six volumes between 1774 and 1786. His unpopular support of the French Revolution forced him to leave England in 1794, and he spent the last years of his life in the United States.

Prime Minister, The A novel by Anthony Trollope, the fifth in the 'Palliser' series, first published between 1875 and 1876.

Prince and the Pauper, The An historical novel for children by Mark Twain, first published in 1882.

Prince, The A political treatise by Niccolò Machiavelli, written in 1513.

Princess Casamassima, The A novel by Henry James, first published in book form in 1886. It tells of the tragedy of Hyacinth Robinson, an orphan caught up in a social revolutionary movement.

Prior, Matthew (1664–1721) The son of a Dorsetshire joiner, Matthew Prior was educated at Westminster School and Cambridge. In 1687 he and his friend Charles Montagu produced the satire *City Mouse and Country Mouse*, and the prominence which this brought him resulted in a career as a politician and diplomat, the success of which was ended by a change of government in 1715. He was impeached and imprisoned for two years; during this period he wrote some of the poems included in a collection which was published in 1718. He is noted as the author of lyrics which have a lightness of touch and considerable charm.

Pritchett, V.S. (1900–) Victor Sawdon Pritchett was born in Ipswich, England. He published the first of several novels in 1929, and has also written in many other genres, including autobiography, travel and literary criticism, but it is for his short stories that he is best known. The first collection, *The Spanish Virgin and other stories*, appeared in 1932, and it has been followed by many others. In 1985 he published *A Man of Letters*, consisting of essays and critical studies. He was knighted in 1975.

Private Papers of Henry Ryecroft, The A novel about an unsuccessful writer by George Gissing, first published in 1903.

Professor, The Charlotte Brontë's first novel, inspired by her own experiences at the Pension Héger in Belgium. It was published posthumously in 1857.

Prometheus Bound The second in a trilogy of plays by Aeschylus, probably written about 460BC. The other plays, *Prometheus the Fire-Bringer* and *Prometheus Unbound*, are no longer extant.

Prometheus Unbound A verse drama by Percy Bysshe Shelley, first published in 1820.

Proust, Marcel (1871–1922) Born and educated in Paris, Marcel Proust was the son of a professor of medicine and a mother of Jewish birth. In his twenties he became a popular figure in the literary *salons* of the French capital. He contributed to the *Revue Blanche*, and wrote a number of stories of romance in high society which were published in 1896 as *Les plaisirs et les jours* (later translated as *Pleasures and Regrets*), and some literary parodies, mostly written in this period, appeared in 1919 under the title *Pastiches et mélanges*. His enthusiasm for John Ruskin's art critism resulted in the translation of several of Ruskin's works, and in the closing years of the 1890s he devoted much of his energy to the defence of Alfred Dreyfus, the French army officer wrongly accused of betraying his country. In 1902 Proust's health began to fail, and he lived thereafter almost as a recluse. About 1895 he had begun work on his masterpiece, the long and complex sequence of novels known collectively as *A la recherche du temps perdu* (best known in English as *Remembrance of Things Past*). He had almost completed the entire work when he published the first volume in the series, *Du côté de chez Swann*, in 1913, at his own expense. It was quite favourably received, but it was the next volume, *L'ombre des jeunes filles en fleurs*, awarded the prix Goncourt in 1918, which firmly established his reputation. Two more instalments were published in 1921, and the final three appeared posthumously, as did a study of Saint-Beuve. *A la recherche du temps perdu* is an immensely detailed work, filled with deep psychological characterizations, and Proust's analytical approach had a lasting influence on twentieth-century literature. Since the novels are firmly based on his own experience

Marcel Proust, dressed as a soldier, strikes a jaunty pose. He compared his major work *A la recherche du temps perdu* to the structure of a cathedral.

of life, early critics accused him of a vision which was focussed too narrowly on the trivial society of the *salons,* and for some years his homosexuality, clearly indicated in his novels, was a further barrier to full acceptance of his true value. A more enlightened view is taken nowadays, and the profundity of his psychological insight, the fascinations of his portrait of a bygone age, and the general importance of his work are widely recognized.

proverb A term used to describe a short popular saying expressing a generally accepted truth, often in metaphorical style. The seventeenth-century writer James Howell defined proverbs as possessing 'shortness, sense and salt'. Proverbs have been known since the earliest times, and many collections have been made.

Provok'd Wife, The A comedy by John Vanbrugh, first performed in 1697. He followed it with *The Provok'd Husband,* but did not live to finish this play, which was completed by Colley Cibber and presented in 1728.

publishers The business of publishing, as a trade separate from those of bookselling and printing, is of comparatively recent existence. Before the invention of printing, authors were their own publishers, issuing their works in manuscript form. Printers then became publishers and booksellers, but gradually the bookseller began to assume the functions of a publisher, and, although he might himself own printing facilities, often sub-contracted the work of producing copies of the book to a printer who took no other part in the publication. This was true until the nineteenth century, when the first modern publishers were seen, taking responsibility for the procurement of suitable works, editing them where necessary, deciding on the form of their presentation and the number of copies to be printed and bound by firms specializing in such work, and distributing the finished articles to independent booksellers rather than themselves selling direct to the public. With the growth of education and international communications, the publishing business has not only expanded enormously but has become increasingly complex; what was once a somewhat leisurely occupation, suitable for gentlemen with literary leanings, has become a highly commercial enterprise which can survive only by combining management and accounting skills of the highest order with the ability to find and produce books which will sell in adequate quantities. Both in the United States and Britain, where publishers generally split between them the world-wide English-speaking markets, the recent tendency has been for a rise in huge conglomerates of publishing firms which dominate the trade. Nevertheless, large numbers of small independent firms continue to enter the field and many of them manage to survive. In the early days of publishing, authors were frequently unscrupulously exploited by their publishers, but nowadays pressure from authors' organizations has resulted in fairer terms and a more general recognition that the writer who produces the publisher's raw material is a labourer worthy of his hire.

Puck of Pook's Hill A book for children by Rudyard Kipling, published in 1906.

Pudd'nhead Wilson A novel by Mark Twain, set in Missouri at the time of slavery. Wilson is a lawyer who solves a case of mistaken identity involving two boys, with tragic consequences for both. It was first published in 1894.

Pulitzer Prizes Joseph Pulitzer, an American newspaper proprietor, who died in 1911, left in his will the sum of $500,000 to provide annual prizes awarded to American citizens for works in the fields of the novel, the drama, poetry, American history and biography, journalism and music. The literary awards have been won by almost all the distinguished (and inevitably some undistinguished) American writers of the twentieth century.

Joseph Pulitzer left half a million dollars in his will to provide annual prizes to American writers.

Punch, or the London Charivari *Punch,* the foremost British humorous magazine, was founded in 1814. Thackeray, Tom Hood and Tenniel were among the earliest of the many celebrated contributors whose prose and poetry have appeared in its pages, alongside the work of virtually all the most successful British comic cartoonists.

Purchas, Samuel (*c.*1575–1626) Born at Thaxted, Essex, England, and educated at Cambridge, the Reverend Samuel Purchas compiled a number of volumes on travel, using the work of earlier writers. He published *Purchas, his Pilgrimage; or, Relations of the World and the Religions observed in all Ages* in 1613, *Purchas, his Pilgrim* in 1619, and *Hakluytus Posthumus or Purchas his Pilgrimes, contayning a History of the World in Sea Voyages and Lande Travells, by Englishmen and others* in 1625.

Purgatorio, The The second part of Dante's *Divine Comedy*. The poet is guided by Virgil through Purgatory, where those who delayed their repentance wait to expiate their sins. It is divided into seven terraces, corresponding to the Seven Deadly Sins, and the climb from them towards Paradise is steep and difficult.

Pushkin, Alexander(1799–1837) The Russian poet Alexander Sergeyevich Pushkin was born in Moscow and educated at a lyceum near St Petersburg. He began work in the ministry of foreign affairs, and in 1820 published his first long poem, *Ruslan and Ly'udmila*. Soon after this, an 'Ode to Liberty' which he had written displeased the authorities in St Petersburg, and as a punishment he was transferred to a position in Kishinev, in southern Russia. While there he brought out three more long works, *The Prisoner of the Caucusus, The Fountain of Bakhchisarai* and *Gipsies*. In 1824 he resigned from his post and returned to his father's home at Pskov. The following year saw the publication of his tragedy in blank verse, *Boris Godunov*, later adapted as an opera by Mussorgsky, and at this period he also wrote a number of shorter, lyrical poems.

Alexander Pushkin by Hippius.

Poltava, a narrative poem, appeared in 1828, and in 1832 he completed his masterpiece, the verse drama *Eugene Onegin*, which later supplied the story for Tchaikovsky's best-known opera. He wrote other dramatic pieces and poetry in a lighter vein, and from 1830 onwards published a number of prose stories, including *The Queen of Spades*, also to be used by Tchaikovsky for an opera. He had married Natalia Goncharov in 1832, and five years later, convinced that the Baron Georges d'Anthès, who had married Natalia's sister, was paying attentions to his wife, he challenged the Baron to a duel, and died from the wounds he received. He remains among the most eminent of Russian poets.

Pye, Henry James (1745–1813) Henry James Pye was born in London and educated at Oxford. He published several collections of verse which had little merit, and his appointment in 1790 as Poet Laureate, which was almost certainly a reward for his political activities, was greeted with a derision that was maintained for the rest of his life.

Pym, Barbara (1913–80) The English novelist Barbara Mary Crampton Pym was born in Shropshire and educated at Oxford. She wrote a number of novels, including *Some Tame Gazelle*, published in 1950, *Excellent Women*, in 1952, *A Glass of Blessings*, in 1958, and *Quarter in Autumn*, in 1977. Two further novels and *A Very Private Eye*, based on her diaries and letters, have appeared posthumously. Her satirical view of her middle-class characters has gained her many admirers, and her reputation has risen considerably in recent years.

Pygmalion A comedy by G. Bernard Shaw, first performed in 1913 and published in 1916. It formed the basis for the popular musical *My Fair Lady*.

Pynchon, Thomas (1937–) Born in Long Island, New York, and educated at Cornell University, Thomas Pynchon published his first novel, *V*, in 1963. He followed the considerable critical success of this long and complex allegorical story with *The Crying of Lot 49*, which appeared in 1966, and in 1973 he won the National Book Award with *Gravity's Rainbow*. In 1984 he published a volume of short stories, *Slower Learner*.

Q

Quarles, Francis (1592–1644) The English poet Francis Quarles was born in Essex and educated at Cambridge. He published a large amount of poetry, much of it based on biblical subjects, as was his best-known and extremely popular work, *Emblems*, published in 1635.

Quartos, Shakespearian The Quarto editions of Shakespeare's works, so-called in reference to their size, were printed during the playwright's lifetime, the first being issued in 1594. They contain eighteen of the plays. These editions were based, however, on actors' memories of the lines, and are consequently often unreliable, in contrast with the more accurate Folio editions.

Queen, Ellery The American writers and cousins Frederic Dannay (1905–82) and Manfred Lee (1905–71) collaborated on some thirty-five crime novels and many short stories, using the joint pseudonym Ellery Queen. Their first book, *The Roman Hat Mystery*, was published in 1929. They founded *Ellery Queen's Mystery Magazine* in 1941. They also wrote as Barnaby Ross.

***Queen of Spades*, The** A story by Alexander Pushkin, first published in 1834. It tells of a young man's love for a girl whose guardian, an old countess, is reputed to know the secret of winning at cards.

***Quiet American*, The** A novel, set in Vietnam, by Graham Greene, first published in 1955.

Quiller-Couch, Arthur (1863–1944) Born in Bodmin, Cornwall, and educated at Oxford, the English writer Arthur Thomas Quiller-Couch was best known under the pseudonym Q. He became Professor of English Literature at Cambridge in 1912. His first book, a novel called *Dead Man's Rock*, was published in 1887, and was followed by many works in a variety of genres, including novels and short stories. His collections of lectures, *On the Art of Writing* and *On the Art of Reading*, enjoyed a considerable success when they were published in 1916 and 1920 respectively. He also compiled several anthologies, and was the first editor of *The Oxford Book of English Verse*, which appeared in 1902. He was knighted for political services in 1910.

R

Rabelais, François (*c.*1494–*c.*1553) The French writer François Rabelais was born at Chinon. There is little certainty about the events of his early life, but he is known to have become a monk, first in the Franciscan order and later in the Benedictine, and then a priest, and in 1530 he qualified in medicine at Montpellier. Two years later he settled in Lyons and there began his literary career by editing various classical works on medical subjects. In about 1533 he brought out the first volume in the series of vigorous, comic and often obscene books about the giants Gargantua and Pantagruel. Although *Pantagruel* was the first to appear, it was in fact the second in the

sequence, and the introductory volume, *Gargantua*, was published about a year later. For both books Rabelais used the pseudonym Alcofribas Nasier, an anagram of his name. The second volume of *Pantagruel* (that is, the third in the series) came out in 1546, and some chapters of volume four in 1548. The books appear to have aroused the wrath of the authorities, and Rabelais spent some time in exile in Rome, returning to France in 1550. The complete version of *Pantagruel, Part iii* appeared in 1552, and in the following year Rabelais is believed to have died. A final volume was published posthumously in 1563, but some authorities have doubted whether it was in fact written by Rabelais. Although the reputation of the books is that of an uproariously bawdy satire, their author's erudition is beyond question, and he provides not only a vivid portrait of the age, taking his characters from every walk of life, but also a kind of compendium of all the knowledge of the time.

Racine, Jean (1639–99) The great tragic dramatist Jean Racine was born at La Ferté Milon in northern France and educated by the Jansenists at Port Royal, where he began to write poetry. By his early twenties he had secured the patronage of the King, Louis XIV, and had embarked on his career in the theatre. His first play to be produced, *La Thébiäde*, was presented by Molière's company at the Palais Royal theatre in 1664, and was well received, although it is now counted as the poorest of his works. *Alexandre le Grand* followed in 1665, and with it Racine consolidated his position as a successful playwright. He was to continue to use classical themes as his source material. The first of his major works, *Andromaque*, appeared in 1667, and was followed by his only comedy, *Les plaideurs*, which was loosely based on *The Wasps* by Aristophanes. It was a failure at its first performance in 1668, but was presented again a few weeks later and found favour with Louis XIV, whose approval sealed its success. Racine returned to the tragic vein, and in the next nine years produced a series of works of the highest quality, beginning with *Britannicus*, which appeared in 1669. In the following year he presented *Bérénice*, at the same time as Corneille produced a rival piece with the same title and subject, both enjoying similar success, although later generations were to judge Racine's piece much the greater. Next came *Bajazet*, a play set in seventeenth-century Turkey, which appeared in 1672, *Mithridate*, in 1673, and *Iphigénie*, in 1674, *Phèdre*, the tragedy which many critics believe to be his masterpiece, received its first

Jean Racine, depicted by his son Jean-Baptiste.

performance in 1677, and was a disaster. It was an age of great rivalry among dramatists – Racine was always in contention with Corneille for recognition as the foremost tragedian of the day – and a playwright of little ability, Pradon, had also written a piece called *Phèdre*; the two plays were presented at the same time, and Pradon's was adjudged the finer. This failure resulted in a long silence from Racine. By now he was, however, comparatively wealthy, and he married, fathered seven children, and continued to bask in the friendship of Louis XIV. He also became reconciled with the evangelical Jansenists of Port Royal, who saw the theatre as evil, and from whom he had become alienated during the period of his earlier successes. It was not until 1689 that, turning to the Bible for inspiration, he produced *Esther*. It was enormously successful, and two years later came his last major drama, *Athalie*, which again took a biblical theme. But this play, although it is now widely considered to be second only to *Phèdre* among his tragedies, met with no public approval. He wrote nothing more, apart from a few poems. Limited by the conventions of French classical drama, and, if

his work may be compared with that of Shakespeare, lacking the latter's enormous range, poetic majesty and sheer humanity, his plays are little seen in the English-speaking world. Nevertheless, Racine ranks as the greatest of French tragedians and holds an honoured place in the history of literature.

Radcliffe, Ann (1764–1823) The English novelist Mrs Ann Radcliffe, née Ward, was born in London. She married at the age of twenty-three, and then began to write, publishing five novels and some travel books. Her fiction – she was a mistress of Gothic horror novels – was immensely popular. Her best-known books are *The Romance of the Forest*, which appeared in 1791, *The Mysteries of Udolpho*, in 1794, and *The Italian*, in 1797.

Rainbow, The A novel by D.H. Lawrence, set in the English Midlands, and concerned with the relationships within the marriages of the Brangwen family. It was first published in 1915.

Raine, Kathleen (1908–) The poet Kathleen Jesse Raine, who was born in London and educated at Cambridge, published her first volume of verse, *Stone and Flower*, in 1943. She has published three autobiographical works and many other volumes of poetry, including her *Collected Poems*, which appeared in 1981.

Raj Quartet, The A sequence of four novels by Paul Scott, consisting of *The Jewel in the Crown*, *The Day of the Scorpion*, *The Towers of Silence* and *A Division of the Spoils*. They were first published in one volume in 1976, and later formed the basis of the television serial, *The Jewel in the Crown*.

Raleigh, Walter (*c*.1552–1618) The famous British explorer Walter Raleigh (or Ralegh) was born in Devon and educated at Oxford, which he left without taking a degree. He became a soldier and a courtier, and soon found favour with Queen Elizabeth, who granted him many lucrative offices and knighted him in 1584. In that year, and again in 1587, he organized unsuccessful expeditions to establish settlements in Virginia. Replaced in the Queen's favour by the Earl of Essex, he retired in 1589 to Ireland, where Elizabeth had granted him substantial estates. There he met Edmund Spenser, whom he helped to gain royal patronage for the publication of *The Faerie Queen*. Expeditions against the Spanish followed, and then in 1592, for marrying one of her maids of honour without the Queen's consent, he was imprisoned in the Tower of London, where he remained until one of his piratical expeditions returned home with rich prizes. He retired to another estate in Dorset until 1595, when he set out on a voyage to South America in search of El Dorado. In the following year he commanded the force which captured

ABOVE: The title-page to Raleigh's *The History of the World*.

RIGHT: Sir Walter Raleigh with his eldest son, Walter, *c.*1602, after his return from Cadiz and the Azores.

Cadiz, and in 1597 he sailed with Essex to the Azores. Soon after the accession of James I, he was accused of treason and condemned to death, but the sentence was not carried out at once. He was confined in the Tower until 1616, when he was freed in order to make another journey of exploration to the Orinoco River. His failure to bring back the promised gold angered James, and he was executed in 1618. Raleigh wrote a number of poems of considerable quality, and a somewhat fictionalized account of his first voyage to South America, *The Discoverie of Guiana*, appeared in 1596. During his long imprisonment he began *The History of the World*, but completed only one volume, which was published in 1614.

Ralph Roister Doister A play by Nicholas Udall, believed to be the earliest English comedy, first performed in about 1552.

Ramsay, Allan (1686–1758) The poet Allan Ramsay was born in Lanarkshire, Scotland. He became a wig-maker and later a bookseller and the proprietor of a circulating library. He published a number of collections of Scottish poetry, including verses by himself and other contemporaries as well as work dating from before 1600. In 1725 he produced a pastoral play in verse, *The Gentle Shepherd*, which enjoyed great success.

Rand, Ayn (1905–) The American novelist Ayn Rand was born in St Petersburg, Russia. She emigrated to the United States in 1926 and became a naturalized citizen in 1931. She is noted for two major novels, *The Fountainhead*, which appeared in 1943, and *Atlas Shrugged*, in 1957. She also wrote some non-fiction, including *For the New Intellectual: The Philosophy of Ayn Rand*, published in 1961.

Randolph, Thomas (1605–35) Born in Northamptonshire, England, Thomas Randolph was educated at Westminster and Cambridge. He wrote poetry in both English and Latin and a number of slight pieces for the stage, including *Amyntas, or The Impossible Dowry* and *The Muses's Looking-Glass*, both printed in 1638.

Rape of Lucrece, The A long poem by William Shakespeare, in rhyme royal, first published in 1594.

Rape of the Lock, The A humorous, mock-heroic poem by Alexander Pope, first published in 1712, and later revised and expanded.

Rasselas, Prince of Abyssinia, The History of A moralistic romance by Samuel Johnson, first published in 1759, and somewhat similar in style to Voltaire's *Candide*.

Rattigan, Terence (1911–77) Educated at Harrow and Oxford, Terence Mervyn Rattigan achieved his first success as a playwright with *French Without Tears*, which appeared in 1936. His other plays, almost all of which were very popular, included *While the Sun Shines*, in 1943, *The Winslow Boy*, in 1946, and *Ross*, in 1960. *Playbill*, produced in 1948, consisted of two contrasting one-act plays, *The Browning Version* and *Harlequinade*, while the two plays which made up *Separate Tables*, in 1954, were closely linked. He was knighted in 1971.

Raven, The The poem which made Edgar Allan Poe famous when it was first published in a newspaper in 1845.

Rawlings, Marjorie Kinnan (1896–1953) The American writer Marjorie Kinnan Rawlings was born in Washington, DC, and educated at the University of Wisconsin. She became a journalist, and published her first novel, *South Moon Under*, in 1933. She is remembered for *The Yearling*, which appeared in 1938 and was awarded the Pulitzer Prize.

Razor's Edge, The A novel by W. Somerset Maugham, concerned with Indian mysticism. It was first published in 1944.

Read, Herbert (1893–1968) Herbert Edward Read was born in Yorkshire, England, and educated at Leeds University. He published his first volume of poetry, *Songs of Chaos*, in 1915, and many other collections were to follow. He wrote a novel and some autobiographical works, and was a noted literary and art critic.

Reade, Charles (1814–84) The English dramatist and novelist Charles Reade was born in Oxfordshire and educated at Magdalen College, Oxford, later qualifying as a barrister. His first literary successes were on the stage, particularly with the comedy *Masks and Faces*, which was produced in 1852, and with *Peg Woffington*, in 1853. He became equally well known as a novelist when *It's Never Too Late* was published in 1856. From this time onwards he produced large numbers of novels and plays, sometimes adapting the novels for the stage or turning the plays into novels. In 1861 his best-known work, the novel *The Cloister and the Hearth*, was published, and was immediately successful, partly because its content was thought at the time to be somewhat scandalous. Reade was considered by his contemporaries to be a writer of the highest quality, but nowadays even *The Cloister and the Hearth* is little read.

Recruiting Officer, The A comedy, one of George Farquhar's best plays, first presented in 1706.

Red Badge of Courage, The The celebrated novel of the American Civil War by Stephen Crane, first published in 1895.

Redgrove, Peter (1932–) The English poet and novelist Peter William Redgrove was educated at Cambridge. His first volume of poetry, *The Collector and other poems*, was published in 1960. A number of other volumes have appeared, and he has won many awards for his verse. *A Man Named East and other New Poems* appeared in 1985. His novels, among them *In the Country of the Skin*, which appeared in 1980, could be described as prose poems.

Reeve, Clara (1729–1807) Born in Ipswich, England, Clara Reeve was a prolific writer, producing many novels and collections of verse. She enjoyed a huge popular success in 1877 with her carefully restrained Gothic novel, *The Champion of Virtue*, which in subsequent editions was renamed *The Old English Baron*.

Relapse, The or Virtue in Danger A classic of Restoration comedy by John Vanbrugh, first produced in 1696.

Religio Medici A religious tract by Sir Thomas Browne, first published without the author's consent in 1642, and revised by him in the edition of 1643.

Remarque, Erich Maria (1898–1970) The German author Erich Maria Remarque was born at Osnabrück, Germany, and drafted into the army in 1916. He became famous with the publication in 1929 of *Im Westen Nichts Neues* (*All Quiet on the Western Front*). He followed this novel with a sequel, *Der Weg Zurück* (*The Road Back*), which appeared in 1931, and produced a number of other books, including *Flotsam* (*Arc de Triomphe*) in 1946.

Renaissance, The The Renaissance (literally 'the rebirth') is the term given to the revival of interest in the arts which began in Italy in the fourteenth century and gradually spread throughout Europe. The influence of this movement was not confined to literature, music and the fine arts, but affected the whole development of civilization, so that the Renaissance became a broad dividing line between the Middle Ages and the times which are considered to form the modern age.

Renault, Mary (1905–83) Mary Renault was the pseudonym of the English novelist Mary

Challans, who was born in London and educated at Oxford. She wrote a large number of successful books, but established a particular reputation for the brilliance with which she reconstructed the ancient world in such novels as *The Last of the Wine*, published in 1956, *The King Must Die* and *The Bull from the Sea*, which appeared in 1958 and 1962, and the later trilogy based on Alexander the Great.

Rendell, Ruth (1930–) The English crime writer Ruth Barbara Rendell published her first book, *From Doon with Death*, in 1964. She has followed it with a number of highly literate stories, including *Painted Devil*, in 1965, *Some Lie and Some Die*, in 1973, *The Speaker of Mandarin*, in 1983, and *Talking to Strange Men*, in 1987.

***Republic*, The** One of the most celebrated of the dialogues of Plato, concerned with justice and an ideal political state. It was written in the fourth century BC.

Restoration literature The period immediately following 1660, when England returned to the monarchical system and Charles II came to the throne, is known as the Restoration. The removal of the restrictions which had obtained during the Commonwealth resulted in a particularly rich period in the theatre, where such playwrights as Congreve, Wycherley, Vanbrugh and Farquhar were to produce the witty and often bawdy plays known as Restoration comedy. Other major writers of the period include Dryden, Pepys, Bunyan and Locke.

***Return of the Native*, The** A novel by Thomas Hardy, telling the story of Damon Wildeve and the women in his life. It was first published in 1878.

Rhinoceros A 'Theatre of the Absurd' play by Eugène Ionesco, first presented in 1959.

rhyme royal A rhyming scheme in which three different rhymes are used in the ten-syllabled seven-line stanzas, the first for lines one and three, the second for lines, two, four and five, and the third for lines six and seven, i.e. *a*,*b*,*a*,*b*,*b*,*c*,*c*. This form was first used by Chaucer.

Rhys, Jean (*c.*1890–1979) The novelist Jean Rhys was born in Dominica in the West Indies. She came to England, and went on the stage for a short period before marrying and going to live in Paris. Her first book, published in 1927, was *The Left Bank: Sketches and Studies of Present-Day Bohemian Paris*. She then published some novels, the fourth of which, *Good Morning, Midnight*, appeared in 1939. A long silence was broken in 1966 with the publication of her remarkable novel *The Wide Sargasso Sea*, which brought about a great revival of interest in her work. Two collections of short stories and a volume of autobiography followed.

Rice, Elmer (1892–1967) The American playwright Elmer Rice, whose family name was originally Reizenstein, was born in New York and trained as a lawyer. His first play, *On Trial*, was a huge success when it was presented in 1914, but it was with *Street Scene*, in 1928, for which he was awarded a Pulitzer Prize, that his reputation was fully established. His other plays, almost all of which carried a forceful social message, include *We, the People*, in 1933, *Judgement Day*, in 1934, and *American Landscape*, in 1939.

Rich, Adrienne (1927–) Born in Baltimore and educated at Radcliffe College, Massachusetts, Adrienne Cecile Rich published her first volume of verse, *A Change of World*, in 1951. Other collections have included *The Diamond Cutters and other poems*, in 1955, *Snapshots of a Daughter-in-Law: Poems 1954-1962*, in 1963, and *Your Native Land, Your Life*, in 1986. She has also written two plays and published a number of feminist essays.

Rich, Barnabe (*c.*1540–1617) A professional soldier all his life, Barnabe Rich wrote a number of pamphlets on a variety of subjects, including conditions in the army, Ireland and the evils of tobacco. He also produced several romances, including *Riche his Farewell to Militarie Profession conteining verie pleasaunt discourse fit for a peaceable tyme*, which appeared in 1581. This collection of eight stories included one which became the basis of Shakespeare's *Twelfth Night*.

***Richard II*, King** An historical play by William Shakespeare, probably first seen in 1595. It appeared in print in 1597. The play portrays the weak King Richard, who is overthrown by the positive Henry Bolingbroke. Another major character is the elder statesman, John of Gaunt.

***Richard III*, King** An historical play by William Shakespeare, probably first seen in 1591. It appeared in print in 1597. The play shows the ruthless and scheming Duke of Gloucester, who finally succeeds to the throne, becoming Richard III, by the murder of the 'little Princes in the Tower'. It ends with his death at the Battle of Bosworth Field.

Richardson, Dorothy, M. (1873–1957) The English novelist Dorothy Miller Richardson was born in Berkshire. She published two works on Quaker subjects before bringing out *Pointed Roofs* in 1915, the first in a sequence of twelve novels, collectively known as 'Pilgrimage'. She is noted as one of the first writers to use the 'stream of consciousness' technique.

Richardson, Henry Handel (1870–1946) Henry Handel Richardson was the pseudonym of Ethel Florence Lindesay Richardson. Her first novel, *Maurice Guest*, was published in 1908. Although she lived most of her life in England, she is regarded as an Australian writer, for she was born and educated in Melbourne, and the three novels, published between 1917 and 1929, which form the trilogy 'The Fortunes of Richard Mahony' are set in Australia.

Richardson, Samuel (1689–1761) Often regarded as the author of the first work of fiction in English which can truly be called a novel, Samuel Richardson was born in Derbyshire, England, and after a comparatively brief education was apprenticed to a London printer. In 1721 he married his master's daughter and set up his own printing house. The six children of the marriage all died in infancy and his wife also died, in 1731. In 1733 he married again, and fathered an additional six children, of whom four daughters survived. His business was very successsful, and by 1754 he had become Master of the Stationers' Company, Printer of the Journals of the House of Commons and Law-Printer to the King, and he continued to run his printing-house until his death. He had always been a story-teller and was well-accustomed to

An illustration from a 1784 edition of *Clarissa*.

putting his words on paper. In 1733 he had published *The Apprentice's Vade-Mecum*, and his version of Aesop's *Fables* appeared in 1739. It was then that two bookseller friends suggested that he might prepare a book whch would help its readers in the composition of their correspondence by giving examples of letters on a variety of subjects concerned with everyday life, together with some moral guidance. He set to work and soon realized that the epistolary form would be ideal for the telling of a story which had long been in his mind. The result was *Pamela; or, Virtue Rewarded*, which was written in the space of two months and published in two volumes in 1740. It was immediately successful, not only in England, but also in Europe, and particularly in France, where all Richardson's works came to be greatly admired. He had not, however, neglected his friends' suggestion, and *Letters Written to and for Particular Friends, Directing the Requisite Style and Form to be Observed in Writing Familiar Letters* appeared a few weeks later. *Pamela* was rapidly imitated and parodied, notably in *An Apology for the Life of Mrs Shamela Andrews*, which is attributed to Fielding, and Richardson was spurred to continue his story in two further volumes, published in 1741. Three years passed before he began to write his second novel, *Clarissa; or, the History of a Young Lady*. The first two volumes appeared in 1747 and the remaining five in 1748. Although not as popular as *Pamela*, it was extremely well received. The seven volumes of his third and last novel, *The History of Sir Charles Grandison*, were published in 1753 and 1754. All three of these major works were published anonymously, but his authorship of them was not otherwise hidden. In the following year he produced *A Collection of the Moral and Instructive Sentiments Contained in the Histories of Pamela, Clarissa, and Sir Charles Grandison*, and in 1755 a further volume appeared, *The Paths of Virtue Delineated; or, the History in Miniature of the Celebrated Pamela, Clarissa Harlowe, and Sir Charles Grandison, Familiarised and Adapted to the Capacities of Youth*. He wrote nothing else of significance, but worked on revisions of the novels, trying always to reduce their inordinate length, and continued his copious correspondence. He had acquired many friends in the literary world, whom he had been in the habit of entertaining at his second home in Fulham, then a village on the outskirts of London, and his sympathetic treatment of his heroines had also brought him the admiration of his women readers. Although *Pamela* has claims to be the first true novel in English, it would perhaps be fairer to describe Richardson, along with Defoe and Fielding, as one of those who developed the form in an innovative and influential way. His particular contribution was his detailed and analytic approach to the realistic depiction of ordinary people, coupled with the ability to weave his highly moral sentiments into his narrative so that they formed an integral part of the story.

Richler, Mordecai (1931–) Born and educated in Montreal, Mordecai Richler published his first novel, *The Acrobats*, in 1954. Subsequent works include *A Choice of Enemies*, in 1957, *The Apprenticeship of Duddy Kravitz*, in 1959, *Cocksure*, in 1968, *St Urbain's Horsemen*, in 1971, and *Joshua Then and Now*, in 1980. He has also written essays and books for children.

Richter, Conrad (1890–1968) The American novelist Conrad Michael Richter was born in Pennsylvania. He wrote many novels, the best known of which are his trilogy *The Trees*, published in 1940, *The Fields*, in 1946, and *The Town*, which won the Pulitzer Prize in 1950.

Riding, Laura (1901–) Laura Riding, née Reichenthal, was born in New York and educated at Cornell University. She has published volumes of poetry, including her *Collected Poems*, which appeared in 1938, a novel, and some literary criticism. For many years she was closely associated with the poet Robert Graves, and with him wrote *A Survey of Modernist Poetry*, published in 1927.

Rights of Man, The A long and influential political essay by Thomas Paine, the two parts of which appeared in 1791 and 1792. In it Paine defends both the French and the American revolutions and constitutions.

Rilke, Rainer Maria (1875–1926) The German poet Rainer Maria Rilke was born in Prague. He published his first volume of poetry in 1894, but it was in 1905, with *Das Stundenbuch* (*The Book of Hours*), that his true ability was seen. In fact he invented a new kind of lyric poetry, which he called an 'object poem' and which sets out to encapsulate the essential nature of a physical object. His *Neue Gedichte* (*New Poems*) appeared in two volumes in 1907 and 1908, and in 1923 he brought out *Die Sonette an Orpheus* (*Sonnets to Orpheus*). He published many other volumes of both poetry and prose, the latter including *Die Aufzeichnungen des Malte Laurids Brigge* (*The Notebook of Malte Laurids Brigge*), which was a prose equivalent of his *New Poems*.

Rimbaud, Arthur (1854–91) The French poet Jean Arthur Rimbaud was born in the Ardennes. He spent much of his life as a vagabond, and was always in revolt against authority. As a youth he ran away from home (his third attempt to do so)

at the age of seventeen, and attracted the attention of the poet Paul Verlaine when he sent him the manuscript of his poem 'Le bateau ivre', which was later seen as of immense influence in the Symbolist movement. His relationship with Verlaine lasted for two years, ending when Verlaine attempted to murder him. He went to Germany, and in 1875 began wanderings which took him to the Far East, back to Europe, to the Mediterranean, and eventually to Abyssinia, where be became a successful merchant dealing in coffee, perfume, gold and ivory. He had ceased writing poetry when he was nineteen, and the only work which he published himself was the prose poem *Une saison en enfer*, which appeared in 1873. But in 1886 Verlaine, who believed Rimbaud to be dead, published a collection of his work under the title *Les illuminations*, which caused a sensation in literary circles by the innovative nature of its contents.

Ring and the Book, The A very long narrative poem by Robert Browning, first published between 1868 and 1869. It was based on the story of an unhappy marriage which ended in the murder of the wife's family and the execution of the husband, events which took place in Rome in the seventeenth century.

Rip Van Winkle The celebrated story by Washington Irving, in which Rip Van Winkle sleeps for twenty years and wakes to a greatly changed world. It was first published in 1820.

Rivals, the A comedy by Richard Brinsley Sheridan, in which his great comic creation Mrs Malaprop appears. It was first performed in 1775.

Robbe-Grillet, Alain (1922–) The innovative French writer Alain Robbe-Grillet was born in Brest, and trained as a statistician and agronomist. His first published work was *Les gommes* (*The Erasers*), which appeared in 1953. Other novels include *Le voyeur* (*The Voyeur*), in 1955, and *La jalousie* (*Jealousy*), in 1957. In 1970 he published *Projet pour une révolution à New York* (*Project for a Revolution in New York*). His very influential book of literary criticism, *Pour un nouveau roman* (*Towards a New Novel: Essays on Fiction*), appeared in 1963.

Robbins, Harold (1912–) Harold Robbins was born and educated in New York. He published his novel *The Dream Merchants* in 1949, and has since gone on to become one of the most successful purveyors of popular fiction in the world. Other novels include *79 Park Avenue*, in 1955, *The Carpetbaggers*, in 1961, *The Betsy*, in 1971, and *The Storyteller*, in 1986.

Robbins, Tom (1936–) The American writer Tom Robbins describes himself as 'a student of art and religion who dropped out to write fiction'.

His whimsical novels have become a cult among young people. *Another Roadside Attraction* was published in 1971, *Even Cowgirls Get the Blues* in 1976, *Still Life with Woodpecker* in 1980, and *Jitterbug Perfume* in 1984.

Robertson, Thomas William (1829–71) The English dramatist Thomas William Robertson was born in Newark-on-Trent. He became an actor but turned to writing plays, in which he attempted to bring a new note of realism to the theatre. He had his first success in 1864 with *David Garrick*. Other plays followed, among them *Society*, first seen in 1865, and *Caste*, in 1867.

Robertson, William (1721–93) Born in Midlothian, Scotland, and educated at Edinburgh University, the Presbyterian minister William Robertson wrote a number of successful histories, beginning with *History of Scotland during the Reign of Queen Mary and of King James VI*, which was published in 1759, and continuing with *History of the Reign of the Emperor Charles the Fifth*, in 1769, *History of America*, in 1777, and *Disquisition which the Ancients had of India*, in 1791.

Robinson, E.A. (1869–1935) The American poet Edwin Arlington Robinson was born in Maine and educated at Harvard. He published his first volume of poetry, *The Torrent and the Night Before*, in 1896. Many more selections of his verses appeared, and in 1922 he was awarded the Pulitzer Prize for his *Collected Poems*, winning it again in 1924 for *The Man Who Died Twice*. His large output included an Arthurian trilogy in blank verse, consisting of *Merlin*, *Lancelot* and *Tristram*, published between 1917 and 1927.

Robinson, Lennox (1886–1958) Esmé Stuart Lennox Robinson was born in County Cork, Ireland. His play *The Clancy Name* was produced in 1911 at the Abbey Theatre, Dublin, of which he had become manager in 1910, a position which he held until 1914, and again from 1919 to 1923, thereafter acting as its director. He wrote a great many plays, including *The Whiteheaded Boy*, first seen in 1920, and books on the theatre.

Robinson Crusoe, The Life and strange and surprising Adventures of The celebrated story of the castaway Robinson Crusoe and his friend Man Friday, by Daniel Defoe, first published in 1719.

Rob Roy A novel, set in 1715, by Sir Walter Scott, first published in 1817.

Rochester, The Earl of (1647–80) John Wilmot, who became the second Earl of Rochester on the death of his father in 1658, was born in Ditchley and educated at Oxford. He was a poet of the Metaphysical school, and also wrote a number of witty, biting satires. His work suffered from censorship for many years because of his frankness in writing of sexual matters.

Roderick Hudson Henry James' first novel, published in book form in 1876.

Roderick Random, The Adventures of A picaresque novel by Tobias Smollett, first published in 1748.

Roethke, Theodore (1908–63) The American poet Theodore Roethke was born in Saginaw, Michigan, and educated at the University of Michigan and Harvard. A first collection of poetry, *Open House*, was published in 1941. His fourth book, *The Waking* won the Pulitzer Prize in 1953, and three more volumes were to follow. He taught English at Washington University, and his lectures and essays, *On the Poet and His Craft*, were published posthumously in 1965.

Roget's Thesaurus A thesaurus is defined as a treasury of knowledge, but the term has come to be used almost exclusively for a dictionary of words arranged in groups according to their meaning. Dr Peter Mark Roget's *Thesaurus of English Words and Phrases* was first published in 1852, and several revisions of the work have appeared since.

Rolfe, Frederick William (1860–1913) The eccentric English writer Frederick William Rolfe, who also called himself both Baron Corvo and Father Rolfe (he had, in fact, been rejected for the priesthood), wrote stories for the *Yellow Book*, and in 1904 published his most successful novel, *Hadrian the Seventh*. This was followed in 1905 by *Don Tarquinio: A Kataleptic Phantasmatic Romance*. Other novels were brought out posthumously.

Romantic Movement, The In the late eighteenth century and the early half of the nineteenth century, as far-reaching political revolutions were taking place in many parts of the world, a parallel change occurred in literature. The Romantic Movement was a revolt against the restrictions of the classical style; its adherents believed in the importance of imagination, the free expression of emotion and the beauty of life and nature. A list of the Romantic writers would be enormously long, but they can perhaps be represented by such early adherents as Wordsworth, Scott, Rousseau, Hugo and Schiller.

romantic novels This genre has been in vogue throughout the twentieth century, although there are many earlier examples. The romantic novel tells a simple love story, often largely divorced from reality, and with no pretensions to be anything but escapist literature. Nevertheless, special skills are involved in the writing of these romances, and those authors, such as Barbara Cartland, who are practised at the craft can achieve enormous sales.

Romany Rye, The A semi-autobiographical novel of gypsy life by George Borrow, first published in 1857. It was a sequel to *Lavengro*.

Romeo and Juliet A tragedy by William Shakespeare, probably first performed about 1595 and printed in 1597. It tells of the 'star-cross'd lovers' whose love is doomed by the enmity between their families.

Romola A novel, by George Eliot, set in fifteenth-century Florence, and first published in 1863.

rondeau A verse form consisting of ten or thirteen lines, in which two rhymes only are used and the opening words of the first line are repeated twice as a refrain.

Ros, Amanda (1860–1939) Amanda McKittrick Ros, born Anna Margaret McKittrick, was an Irish novelist who, with such works as *Delia Delaney*, which was published in 1898, gained a well-deserved reputation as the world's worst novelist.

Rose and the Ring, The A fairy-story by William Makepeace Thackeray, first published in 1855.

Rosenberg, Issac (1890–1918) The Jewish poet Isaac Rosenberg was born in Bristol, England, of Russian extraction. He trained at the Slade School of Art, and in 1912 published a collection of verse, *Night and Day*. A second volume, *Youth*, appeared in 1915. He was killed in action during World War I, and in recent years has been seen as one of the finest of the War Poets, especially, perhaps, because he speaks of the horror of war without attempting to glorify it as a noble, heroic enterprise.

Rose Tattoo, The A comedy by Tennessee Williams, first presented in 1950. It is about a Sicilian woman and her search for love.

Ross, Martin (1862–1915) Martin Ross was the pseudonym of Violet Martin, who, in collaboration with her cousin Edith Somerville, wrote a number of books, the best known of which are the three collections of humorous stories about an Irish resident magistrate. The first of these, *Some Experiences of an Irish R.M.*, appeared in 1899.

Rossetti, Christina (1830–94) The poet Christina Georgina Rossetti was born in London. She began writing at an early age, and in 1847 a privately produced edition of her *Verses* appeared. In 1850 she contributed poems to *The Germ*, and in 1862 published *Goblin Market and other poems*, which established her reputation. This was followed in 1866 by *The Prince's Progress and other poems*, and in 1870 came *Commonplace*, a work in prose, while *Sing-Song*, a book of verse for children, appeared in 1872. She then suffered a period of severe illness, and no other major work appeared until 1881, when a volume of poetry, *A Pageant and other poems*, was published. From this time onwards her writings, both in prose and poetry, were increasingly concerned with religious themes, typified by *Time Flies: a Reading Diary*, a mixture of moralistic verse and prose readings for each day of the year, which was published in 1885. *New Poems* appeared posthumously in 1896. She is remembered as a lyric poet of the highest quality.

Rossetti, Dante Gabriel (1828–82) The painter and poet Dante Gabriel Rossetti, whose baptismal names were Gabriel Charles Dante, was born in

Self-portrait by Dante Gabriel Rossetti, dated 1870 and (*below*) a portrait of his younger sister, the poet Christina Rossetti, with their mother.

London, the elder brother of Christina Rossetti. He was educated at King's College School and then studied painting. With Millais and Holman Hunt he founded the Pre-Raphaelite Brotherhood. Like his sister, he began to write in his youth, and he contributed poems, which included 'The Blessed Damozel', to *The Germ* in 1850. He married in 1860, and when his wife died two years later he buried with her all the manuscripts of his unpublished poems, and during the following years concentrated on painting. In 1869 he published a number of poems in *The Fortnightly Review*. He was then persuaded to retrieve the verses from his wife's grave, and in 1870 his *Poems* appeared, which included the series of sonnets known as 'The House of Life'. A further volume of *Poems* was published in 1881, and his *Ballads and Sonnets*, which came out in the same year, contained the second instalment of 'The House of Life'. He also published translations from early Italian poets and verses by François Villon. During his lifetime he was accused of immorality in his writings, a charge which seems ludicrous today. At his best he produced poetry of considerable emotional power.

Rossetti, William Michael (1829–1919) The brother of Dante Gabriel and Christina Rossetti, William Michael Rossetti was born in London and educated at King's College School. He became an art critic, prepared editions of Blake, Whitman and Shelley, produced a verse translation of Dante's *Inferno*, and edited various letters and papers of the Rossetti family.

Rostand, Edmond (1868–1918) Born in Marseilles, the French dramatist Edmond Rostand saw his first play, *Les romanesques*, produced in 1894. In 1895 came *La princesse lointaine*, and in 1897 *La Samaritaine*. Later the same year the triumphant first performance of his most famous play, the verse drama *Cyrano de Bergerac*, took place. Sarah Bernhardt, who had appeared in *La Samaritaine*, found one of her more famous parts in his *L'aiglon*, presented in 1900.

Rosten, Leo (1908–) The humorous writer Leo Calvin Rosten was born in Poland. He had a major success with *The Education of H*y*m*a*n K*a*p*l*a*n* in 1937, and followed it with several more books about the same character.

Roth, Philip (1933–) The American novelist Philip Milton Roth was born to an Orthodox Jewish family in New Jersey and educated at Bucknell University, Pennsylvania, and the University of Chicago. He has since taught at a number of universities, including that of Chicago. In 1959 he published *Goodbye, Columbus*, consisting of the title novella and five short stories, and this

An early illustration by Laurence Housman to *Goblin Market*, by Christina Rossetti.

wom him the National Book Award. In 1962 his first important novel, *Letting Go*, was published, to be followed in 1969 by *When She Was Good*. Great popular success came in 1969 with the publication of *Portnoy's Complaint*, a novel which became famous because it dealt so frankly with the subject of masturbation, but the fantasy *The Breast* which appeared in 1972, was less successful. He later embarked on a series of novels concerned with a successful Jewish novelist, Nathan Zuckerman: these are *The Ghost Writer*, which appeared in 1979, *Zuckerman Unbound*, in 1981, *The Anatomy Lesson*, in 1983, and *The Prague Orgy*, in 1985. A major novel, *The Counterlife*, appeared in 1986. Roth is seen as one of the most important present-day novelists, especially in his portrayal of Jewish life and thought in contemporary America.

Roth, Robert (1920–) Robert Roth has been Professor of Philosophy at Fordham University, in the Bronx, since 1970. He has published many books on philosophy and theology, including *American Religious Philosophy*, which appeared in 1967, and *A Philosophical Exploration*.

Roughing It An autobiographical account by Mark Twain of his experience in the American West in the 1860s, first published in 1872.

Rousseau went to Notre Dame to place the manuscript of his *Dialogues* on the high altar, with the inscription 'An offering entrusted to Providence'. He found the door to the choir shut and abandoned the idea.

Rousseau, Jean-Jacques (1712–78) The French philosopher Jean-Jacques Rousseau was born in Geneva and educated privately. He lived a largely unsettled life, but became famous in 1750 when his *Discours surs les sciences et les arts* won first prize in a major competition. He fled first to Switzerland and then to England a dozen years later when his writings had made him unpopular with the French authorities, both secular and clerical. Meanwhile, he had written more philosophical treatises, and in 1760 had published his famous novel, *Julie, ou la nouvelle Héloise*, which was hugely successful. A second work of fiction, *Emile*, appeared in 1762. The famous *Confessions* and the supplemental work, *Les rêveries du promeneur solitaire*, were written in the last years of his life and published posthumously between 1781 and 1788.

Rowe, Nicholas (1674–1718) Probably born in Bedfordshire, England, Nicholas Rowe was trained as a lawyer, but, inheriting a fortune, decided to become a playwright. His first play,

The Ambitious Stepmother, was produced in 1700, and he followed it with a number of other tragedies, mostly on historical subjects. He was appointed Poet Laureate in 1715, translated the Roman poet Lucan, and edited Shakespeare's plays, dividing the plays into acts and scenes and adding some stage directions.

Rowlandson, Mary (*c*.1635–78) In 1676 Mary Rowlandson, née White, and her three children were abducted by Indians from the town of Lancaster, Massachusetts. After being ransomed, she wrote an account of her experiences, *The Soveraignty and Goodness of God, Together with the Faithfulness of His Promises Displayed; Being a Narrative of the Captivity and Restauration of Mrs Mary Rowlandson*. It was published posthumously in 1682.

Rowley, William (*c*.1585–1626) Nothing is known of the early life of the English dramatist William Rowley, but by 1614 he was established as a comic actor. He collaborated with such dramatists as Middleton, Dekker, Webster and Heywood, and was solely responsible for at least four plays, still extant, which are *A New Wonder, A Woman Never Vext, A Match at Midnight, A Tragedie called Alls Lost by Lust*, and *A Shoomaker a Gentleman with the Life and Death of the Cripple that stole the Weathercock at Paules*.

Roxana, or The Fortunate Mistress A romantic novel by Daniel Defoe, first published in 1724.

Rubáiyát of Omar Khayyám, The A collection of four-lined verses, known as *rubais* or quatrains, by a Persian poet of the twelfth century. The familiar translation is by Edward Fitzgerald, and first appeared in 1859.

Runyon, Damon (1884–1946) Born in Kansas, Alfred Damon Runyon left school to fight in the Spanish-American War, and then became a journalist. He is famous as the author of a number of short stories, set mostly among low-life characters in New York, and told exclusively in the present tense and with a mock solemnity in the use of slang. The best known of his collections is *Guys and Dolls*, published in 1932, and later to become a successful musical.

Rural Rides A book of essays by William Cobbett, describing the situation of the English countryside at that time, first published in book form in 1830.

Rushdie, Salman (1947–) Ahmed Salman Rushdie was born in Bombay and educated at Rugby and Cambridge. His first book, published in 1975, was *Grimus. Midnight's Children* won the Booker Prize in 1981, and *Shame* appeared in 1983. He is a practitioner of Magic Realism.

Ruskin, John (1819–1900) Born in London of Scottish parents, John Ruskin attended King's College, London, and Christ Church, Oxford,

John Ruskin, art theorist and social critic. He attempted to find the solution to many social problems through his approach to art, which he expressed in his writing.

published in 1865, which was concerned both with literature and with the place of women in society. He wrote over fifty works of various kinds, and exerted a very considerable influence, not only on the art, architecture and social structure of his times, but also on literature, in which field his prose was seen as a model of elegance and lucidity.

Russell, Bertrand (1872–1970) Bertrand Arthur William Russell, later to become the 3rd Earl Russell, was born in Monmouthshire and educated at Cambridge. He was both mathematician and philosopher and published widely in these fields, as well as producing political studies, short stories and some volumes of autobiography. A pacifist, he was imprisoned for refusing to fight in World War I, and during

Bertrand Russell, the philosopher and mathematician.

but his main education came from his parents and from his frequent travels as a boy and youth. After publishing essays on architecture and art in various magazines, he brought out his first book, *Modern Painters*, in 1843. The second volume of this work appeared in 1846, and was followed in 1849 by *The Seven Lamps of Architecture*, and in 1851 by the first volume of *The Stones of Venice*. 1851 also saw the publication of his story for children, *The King of the Golden River*. The second and third volumes of *The Stones of Venice* came out in 1853, and the third and fourth volumes of *Modern Painters* in 1856. He became a popular lecturer, and published many collections of his lectures and essays, turning increasingly for his subjects from art and architecture to issues of the day and an idealistic theory of socialism. One of the most successful of these books was *Sesame and Lilies*,

the last twenty years of his life compaigned vigorously against nuclear weapons. His most important books include *Principles of Mathematics*, which appeared in 1903, *Principia Mathematica*, which was written jointly with Professor A.N. Whitehead and came out in 1910, *Our Knowledge of the External World as a Field for Scientific Method in Philosophy*, in 1914, *An Inquiry into Meaning and Truth*, in 1940, and *Human Society in Ethics and Politics*, in 1954. He also published a number of works intended for more popular consumption, such as *The ABC of Atoms*, which appeared in 1923, *The ABC of Relativity*, in 1925, *A History of Western Philosophy*, in 1945, and *The Wisdom of the West*, in 1959. He was awarded the Nobel Prize for Literature in 1950.

Russell, George William (1867–1935) The Irish poet George William Russell, who used the pseudonym AE, was born in County Armagh. He published his first poetry, *Homeward: Songs by the Way*, in 1894, and followed it with many more. His poetic drama, *Deirdre*, which had been performed at the Irish National Theatre in 1902, was published in 1907. He was also a journalist, and wrote widely on political themes.

Ruth A novel about the redemption of a 'fallen woman' by Mrs Gaskell, first published in 1853.

Rymer, Thomas (1641–1713) Born in Yorkshire and educated at Cambridge, Thomas Rymer become Historiographer Royal in 1692 and was then directed to write his *Foedera*, a record of England's international agreements from 1100 onwards. Fifteen volumes were published during his lifetime, and the work was continued by other hands after his death. Rymer wrote many other books, including a notorious attack on Shakespeare and Jonson in *A Short View of Tragedy*, published in 1693.

S

Sackville-West, Vita (1892–1962) The Hon. Victoria Mary Sackville-West was born in Kent, at Knole, one of the great 'stately homes of England'. She published a number of books on poetry, including the long poem *The Land*, which appeared in 1926, several novels, the best known of which is *All Passion Spent* (1931), and books on a variety of non-fiction subjects, including biographies and gardening manuals.

Sacred Fount, The A short novel by Henry James, one of the least successful of his works, first published in 1901.

Sade, The Marquis de (1740–1814) Comte Donatien Alphonse François de Sade, who gave his name to the sexual deviation known as sadism, was born in Paris. He wrote several books with explicit sexual details. These include *Les infortunes de la vertu* (*The Adversities of Virtue*), published in 1787, *Les crimes de l'amour* (*Crimes of Passion*), in 1788, *Justine*, in 1791, and *Juliette*, in 1798. He spent much of his life in prison for sexual offences, occupying his time in writing – one work produced in this way was *Les 120 journées de Sodom* (*One Hundred and Twenty Days of Sodom*), which was written on a roll of paper thirty-nine feet long.

saga Originally used to describe the Norwegian and Icelandic narratives in prose dating from the Middle Ages, the term also refers to legends handed down through the ages by word of mouth. More recently the word has been applied to almost any long novel, especially as instanced in the 'family saga', a domestic story covering more than one generation.

Sagan, Françoise (1935–) The French writer Françoise Quoirez uses the pseudonym Françoise Sagan. She wrote her first novel, *Bonjour, Tristesse*, at the age of eighteen, and it was published in 1954. *Un certain sourire* (*A Certain Smile*) appeared in 1956 and *Aimez-vous Brahms* in 1959. Other novels, short stories and screenplays have followed.

Saint-Exupéry, Antoine de (1900–44) Antoine Marie Roger de Saint-Exupéry was born in Lyons, France. He became a pilot, and published his first novel, *Courrier-Sud* (*Southern Mail*) in 1929. Two years later he produced *Vol de nuit* (*Night Flight*). His autobiography, *Terre des hommes* (*Wind, Sand and Stars*), appeared in 1939. He was killed during World War II.

Saint Joan A play by G. Bernard Shaw, first performed in 1923. It presents Joan of Arc as a down-to-earth peasant girl, never understood by either her friends or her foes.

Saint-John, Perse (1887–1975) Perse Saint John was the pseudonym of Marie René Auguste Alexis Saint-Léger Léger, who was born in Guadaloupe. After completing his education at the universities of Paris and Bordeaux, he entered the diplomatic service. He published his first volume of verse, *Eloges*, in 1911. His long poem *Anabase*, which appeared in 1924, was later translated by T.S. Eliot as *Anabasis*. After the fall of France in 1940 he lived in the United States. His volumes of poetry included *Exile*, in 1942, *Chronique*, in 1960, and *Oiseaux* (*Birds*), in 1962. He was awarded the Nobel Prize for Literature in 1960.

St Ronan's Well A novel by Sir Walter Scott, satirizing contemporary Scottish society, first published in 1823.

Saintsbury, George (1845–1933) George Edward Bateman Saintsbury was born in Southampton, England, and educated at Oxford. He became a literary critic and an authority on both French and English literature, on which subjects he published a number of books. These ranged from studies of individual writers to more general works, such as *A Short History of French Literature*, published in 1882, and *A History of Criticism*, which appeared between 1900 and 1904.

Saki (1870–1916) Hector Hugh Munro, who used the pseudonym Saki, was born in Burma. He became a journalist, and then made a considerable reputation with his witty short stories, the first volume of which, *Reginald*, was published in 1904. Other selections included *The Chronicles of Clovis*, in 1911, and *Beasts and Super-Beasts*, in 1914. He also wrote two novels and three plays.

Salinger, J.D. (1919–) Jerome David Salinger was born in New York City and educated at New

York and Columbia universities. Having published a number of short stories, in 1951 he produced *The Catcher in the Rye*, a first novel narrated in the first person by teen-aged Holden Caulfield. It captured the spirit of post-war adolescent rebellion, and became not only an international bestseller but a cult book among younger readers. Salinger has been unable to repeat its success. *Franny and Zooey* appeared in 1961, and *Raise High the Roof-Beam Carpenters, and Seymour: an Introduction*, in 1963. Both consisted of two long short stories, concerned with an eccentric family. While neither of these two publications is without merit, equally neither can be described as outstanding in quality.

Sallust (86–34BC) Gaius Sallustius Crispus was born in central Italy. He became a Roman politician, an adherent of Julius Caesar, whose part he takes in his historical writings. These consist of *The Catiline Conspiracy* and *The Jugurthine War*, both of which are still extant, and the *Histories*, an account of Rome from 78 to 67 BC, of which only fragments have come down to us.

Samson Agonistes A tragedy, largely in blank verse, by John Milton, first published in 1671. It tells of the last days of Samson, as a prisoner of the Philistines.

Sand, George (1804–76) Madame Amandine Lucile Aurore Dudevant, née Dupin, used the pseudonym George Sand when, after separating from her husband, she began to write. She produced a vast number of novels, and had almost as many lovers, including Alfred de Musset and Chopin. Her books, especially those with a country background, exercised great influence on such diverse writers as Dostoevsky, Elizabeth Barret Browning and George Eliot.

Sandburg, Carl (1878–1967) The American poet Carl August Sandburg was born in Galesburg, Illinois. His education was extremely limited, but he became a journalist, and began to publish poetry in magazines. His first collection, *Chicago Poems*, appeared in 1916, and was followed by many more. His *Collected Poems*, published in 1950, won him a Pulitzer Prize. He wrote a number of books for children and compiled two collections of folksongs in *The American Songbag*. In 1926 he published, in two volumes, *Abraham Lincoln: The Prairie Years*, and the work was completed in 1939 with the four volumes of *Abraham Lincoln: The War Years*, for which he was awarded a second Pulitzer Prize.

Sanditon A novel by Jane Austen, written in 1817, the year of her death, and not completed.

Santayana, George (1863–1952) The philosopher George Santayana was born in Madrid, but went to the United States from the age of nine and was educated at Harvard. His first published work was poetry, but between 1905 and 1906 he produced the five volumes of his *The Life of Reason; or the Phases of Human Progress*, which remained his major work. He published many collections of essays and lectures, and studies of the characters of various nationalities of men.

Sappho (7th-6th centuries BC) The Greek poet Sappho was born on the island of Lesbos. She wrote lyric verse, and although much of her poetry no longer exists, some fragments have been retrieved from ancient papyri. She has been regarded as the high priestess of Lesbian love.

Sargeson, Frank (1903–82) Born in Hamilton, New Zealand, Frank Sargeson trained as a lawyer. He published a first volume of short stories, *Conversations with my Uncle*, in 1936, and *The Stories of Frank Sargeson* appeared in 1973. He also wrote the novels *I Saw in my Dream*, published in 1949, and *Sunset Village*, in 1973.

Sartor Resartus: The Life and Opinions of Herr Teufelsdröckh A philosophical and partly autobiographical work by Thomas Carlyle, first published in book form in 1836.

Sartre, Jean-Paul (1905–80) Jean-Paul Sartre was born in Paris and educated at the Ecole Normale Supérieure and in Berlin. He was a teacher until the outbreak of World War II, during which he was active in the French resistance movement, but by 1938 he had already produced a novel, *La Nausée (Nausea)*, and after the war he devoted himself to writing. He was a novelist, a playwright, a biographer and literary critic, and, perhaps most importantly, a philosopher of the

Jean Paul Sartre spoke briefly to the crowd at a silent demonstration in Paris in 1961 pleading for an end to the seven-year war in Algeria.

left wing. Among his novels were the three volumes of *Les chemins de la liberté* (*The Roads to Freedom*), which were published between 1947 and 1950; his plays included *Les mouches* (*The Flies*), first presented in 1943, *Huis Clos* (*In Camera*), in 1945, and *Les mains sales* (*Dirty Hands*), in 1948; he wrote biographies of Baudelaire, Genet and Flaubert, and in 1948 published *Qu'est-ce-que la littérature?* (*What is Literature?*). His most important philosophical books were *L'être et le néant* (*Being and Nothingness*), which appeared in 1943, and *Critique de la raison dialectique* (*Critique of Dialectical Reason*), in 1960. He was the leading exponent of the philosophy of Existentialism, which stresses the individuality and importance of each human being and the responsibility which each of us bears for our individual development, and his influence on twentieth-century thought and on literature has been very considerable. In his thinking and in his work he was always supported by his lifelong companion Simone de Beauvoir. He was awarded the Nobel Prize for Literature in 1964, but refused to accept it.

Sassoon, Siegfried (1886–1967) The English poet Siegfried Lorraine Sassoon was born in London and educated at Cambridge. During World War I he began to write poetry, which was first published in 1917 and 1918 in *The Old Huntsman* and *Counter-Attack*. Several more collections were to follow over the next decades. He also published, between 1928 and 1936, the three autobiographical novels which were later grouped together as *The Complete Memoirs of George Sherston*.

satire Originally limited to compositions in verse, including drama, which ridicule subjects that the author considers to be foolish, the term satire is also applied to prose writings of a similar nature. Satires are frequently allegorical, and may also use parody. Authors who have written in this vein are too numerous to mention, but have existed in every age, from Juvenal and Horace to Chaucer, from Dryden, Swift and Pope to Byron, and, in more recent times, to Evelyn Waugh and Joseph Heller.

Satyricon A work of fiction by the Latin author Petronius, written about the middle of the first century AD. It presents a bawdy picture of life in Rome at the time of the Emperor Nero.

Savage, Richard (*c*.1697–1743) Little reliable information is available concerning the early life of the poet Richard Savage. In 1727 he was accused of murder, but escaped punishment, but he ended his days in prison for debt. He wrote two plays and published satires and other poems, including his best-known work, *The Wanderer*, which appeared in 1729.

Sayers, Dorothy, L. (1893–1957) Dorothy Leigh Sayers was born and educated in Oxford. She published *Whose Body?*, the first of her novels to feature the amateur detective Lord Peter Wimsey, in 1923, and, with such books as *Clouds of Witness*, which appeared in 1926, *The Unpleasantness at the Bellona Club*, in 1928, and *The Nine Tailors*, in 1934, soon established herself as one of the best writers in this genre. She also wrote a number of religious works, and in 1943 published her cycle of plays, *The Man Born to be King*, which had been extremely successful when broadcast between 1941 and 1942. In her last years she produced translations of Dante's *Inferno* and *Purgatorio*, but did not complete the *Paradiso*.

Scannell, Vernon (1922–) The English poet Vernon Scannell was born in Lincolnshire and educated at Leeds University. He published his first volume of verse, *Graves and Resurrections*, in 1948, and several more selections have followed, including *New and Collected Poems 1950-1980*, which appeared in 1980, and *Funeral Games and other poems*, in 1987. He has also produced some novels and an autobiography.

Scarlet Letter, The A novel by Nathaniel Hawthorne, first published in 1850. Set in seventeenth-century New England, it tells of Hester Prynne, condemned as an adulteress to wear the scarlet letter A.

Scenes of Clerical Life Three stories by George Eliot, which were first published in *Blackwood's Magazine* in 1857, appeared in book form, in two volumes, in 1858.

Schiller, Friedrich von (1759–1805) Johann Christoph Friedrich von Schiller was born at Marbach, Germany, and educated as a military doctor. In 1781 he published at his own expense his first play *Die Räuber* (*The Robbers*), which caused a sensation by a highly dramatic approach to its anti-authoritarian theme, and established him as the leader of the Romantic movement in Germany. The plays which followed were *Kabale und Liebe* (*Intrigue and Love*), presented in 1784, and the blank verse tragedy *Don Carlos*, in 1787. Then came his masterpiece, *Wallenstein*, in 1799, and four more plays were to follow: *Maria Stuart*, in 1800, *Die Jungfrau von Orleans* (*The Maid of Orleans*), in 1801, *Die Braut von Messina* (*The Bride of Messina*) in 1803, and *Wilhelm Tell*, in 1804. Schiller wrote much poetry of the highest quality, and in 1797 and 1798 he and his friend Goethe published jointly collections of their verse. He was also a notable historian, publishing accounts of the Revolt of The Netherlands, in 1788, and of the Thirty Years War, between 1791 and 1793, and producing works on philosophical and literary subjects and a number of translations.

His output in his all-too-short life was considerable, and of a standard which ranks him second only to Goethe in the history of German literature.

Schnitzler, Arthur (1862–1931) The Viennese-born playwright Arthur Schnitzler was educated as a doctor of medicine. He first attracted attention in the theatre with his seven one-act *Anatol* plays, produced in 1898, but is chiefly remembered for *Reigen* (more familiarly known under its French title, *La ronde*), which was first seen in 1920, and which for many years was considered scandalous. He also wrote novels and short stories.

School for Scandal, The A comedy by Richard Brinsley Sheridan, first performed in 1777, in which a web of intrigue entangles the good and bad brothers, Charles and Joseph Surface, the flirtatious Lady Teazle and her elderly husband, Sir Peter.

Schopenhauer, Arthur (1788–1860) The German philosopher Arthur Schopenhauer was born in Danzig and educated at the University in Göttingen. He published a number of books and essays, but his principle work was *Die Welt als Wille und Vorstellung* (*The World as Will and Idea*), first published in 1819, and subsequently revised.

Schiller's anti-authoritarian dramas helped inspire German liberals in the 1848 revolution.

He saw the will to live as essentially evil, and the world and all religion as illusory.

Schreiner, Olive (1862–1920) Olive Emilie Albertina Schreiner was born in South Africa. An early feminist, she achieved instant success with her novel, *The Story of an African Farm*, when it was published in 1883 under the pseudonym Ralph Iron. She wrote other novels and some works of non-fiction, including *An English South African's View of the Situation*, which appeared in 1899, and *Women and Labour*, in 1911.

Schulberg, Budd (1914–) The American writer Budd Wilson Schulberg was born in New York City and grew up in Hollywood. He published his first novel, *What Makes Sammy Run?* in 1941. *The Harder They Fall* followed in 1947 and *The Disenchanted* in 1950. His screenplay of *On the Waterfront* won an Academy Award for the best screenplay and story in 1954.

science fiction A genre covering both novels and short stories which are almost always set in the future, and which envisage tremendous changes, particularly in technological advances (spaceships and interplanetary travel are commonplace). In many works placed under this heading, the scientific element is scarcely present, and these books are better described as fantasy. Early practitioners include Jules Verne and H.G. Wells, and prominent among present day writers are Brian Aldiss, Isaac Asimov, Ray Bradbury, Arthur C. Clarke, Ursula Le Guin, Michael Moorcock and Kurt Vonnegut, Jr.

Scott, Duncan Campbell (1862–1947) Born in Ottawa, Duncan Campbell Scott was educated in Quebec. He published his first volume of poetry, *The Magic House*, in 1893. It was followed by other collections, and he also published a number of short stories.

Scott, Paul (1920–78) The English novelist Paul Mark Scott was born in London. He was an officer in the Indian Army during World War II, and many of his novels were set in India and based on his personal observations. After the war he worked as a publisher and literary agent, and brought out his first novel, *Johnny Sahib*, in 1952. Several more novels followed, including *The Alien Sky*, in 1958, and *The Chinese Love Pavilion*, in 1960. His major achievement was the tetralogy 'The Raj Quartet', consisting of *The Jewel in the Crown*, which appeared in 1966, *The Day of the Scorpion*, in 1968, *The Towers of Silence*, in 1971 and *A Division of the Spoils*, in 1975. These books, later adapted into the television series, *The Jewel in the Crown*, portray the last days of British rule in India. Scott continued the story, after Independence, in *Staying On*, which won the Booker Prize in 1977.

Scott, Walter (1771–1832) The Scottish novelist Walter Scott was born and educated in Edinburgh, and trained as a lawyer. His first published works were translations from the German, and were followed by an anthology, *Minstrelsy of the Scottish Border*, which appeared in three volumes between 1802 and 1803. Two years later he brought out *The Lay of the Last Minstrel*, a long poem which immediately achieved such great popularity that he decided to embark on a career as a writer. He began his novel *Waverley*, but abandoned it for the time being in favour of *Marmion*, a narrative in verse which was published in 1808 and was even more successful than *The Lay of the Last Minstrel*. By this time he had begun his partnership in the printing firm of John Ballantyne & Co. Several more long poems followed, including *The Lady of the Lake*, but in 1814 he returned to *Waverley*, completing and publishing it in the space of a few weeks. From this time on until his death a new book, or two, or even three, appeared every year. These include the three novels which some critics believe to be his finest, *The Antiquary* and *Old Mortality*, both published in 1816, and *The Heart of Midlothian*, in 1818. Among other familiar titles are *The Bride of Lammermoor* and *Ivanhoe*, both of which came out in 1819, *Kenilworth*, in 1821, *Redgauntlet*, in 1824, and *The Talisman*, in 1825. He had been created a baronet in 1820, he lived well at Abbotsford, and, although Ballantyne & Co. had been through periods of financial difficulty, he was at the height of his success as a popular and respected author, but in 1826 he suffered two terrible blows: his wife, whom he had married in 1797, died; and his London publisher, Constable, with which Ballantyne & Co. had become

Portrait of Sir Walter Scott by the famous painter and sculptor Sir Edward Landseer. Scott did much to impress on the world the romantic image of Scotland.

'The Captain of Knockdunder'. An evocative illustration by George Cruikshank to Scott's *The Heart of Midlothian*. It captures the essence of the Jacobite era.

inextricably involved, collapsed, and Scott found himself personally repsonsible for debts of more than a hundred thousand pounds. For the remainder of his life he worked to reduce this sum, and soon after his death the whole amount had been paid. The many works which belong to this period include *Woodstock*, published in 1826, and a nine-volume *Life of Napoleon*, in 1827, from which date he acknowledged for the first time his authorship of his books. Among others were *The Fair Maid of Perth*, in 1828, *Anne of Geierstein*, in 1829, and an uncompleted *History of Scotland*, the first two volumes of which appeared in 1829 and 1830. He also wrote for the theatre, as he had done earlier, and produced two plays in 1830. In the same year he published a new edition of his poems and his *Letters on Demonology and Witchcraft*. In 1831 he began to suffer more acutely from the ill-health which had plagued him for some time, but nevertheless completed two more novels, *Count Robert of Paris* and *Castle Dangerous*. This unflagging industry undoubtedly hastened his death. Scott's works are not much read nowadays – even the romances such as *Ivanhoe* seem more ponderous than lively – but in his time he enjoyed not only the widest popularity but tremendous literary prestige. Many nineteenth-century novelists modelled their work on his, especially if they were writing historical novels, a genre which he may not have invented, but which he certainly developed as no previous writer had done. His influence on fiction in general has been immense.

Scriblerus Club, The A group of writers, of whom the most prominent were Swift and Pope, which existed to raise the standards of literature. *The Memoirs of Martinus Scriblerus*, a satire published in 1741, was largely the work of John Arbuthnot, also a member of the Club.

Seagull, The The first of the four great plays by Anton Chekhov. It was a failure when presented in 1895, but was very successfully revived in 1898.

Sea-Wolf, The A novel by Jack London, based on his early experiences at sea and first published in 1904.

Secret Agent, The A colourful novel by Joseph Conrad, in which the secret agent Verloc is pitted against a group of anarchists, with tragic results. It was first published in 1907.

Seeger, Alan (1888–1916) Born in New York, the American poet Alan Seegar began to write poetry while still at Harvard. In 1912 he went to live in France, and was killed during World War I. His *Collected Poems* appeared in 1916.

Seferis, George (1900–71) Georgios Stylianou Seferiades, who was born in Smyrna and educated in Athens, was a Greek poet and diplomat. He used the pseudonym George Seferis. His first volume of poems, *I strofi* (The Turning Point), was acclaimed when it appeared in 1931. Many other books followed, including *I sterna* (The Cistern), in 1932, the long poem *Kikhli* (Thrush), in 1947, and *Poiímata 1924–1955* (Poems 1924–1955), in 1969. He brought new life to Greek poetry, and was awarded the Nobel Prize for Literature in 1963.

Seifert, Jaroslav (1910–) The Czech poet Jaroslav Seifert was born in Prague, and worked as a journalist until 1950. His first volume of poems, *City in Tears*, was published in 1920. He has produced some thirty volumes of verse, mostly with highly political themes. These include *On Wireless Waves*, in 1925, *The Nightingale Sings Wrong*, in 1926, and *Switch Off the Lights*, in 1938. He was awarded the Nobel Prize for Literature in 1984.

Seneca (c.3BC–AD65 The Roman philosopher and tragedian Lucius Annaeus Seneca was the son of a rhetorician of the same name. He wrote a number of works in prose, including *Physical Investigations*, as well as volumes of moral essays. His plays, remarkable for their bombastic style, included *Thyestes*, *Phaedra* and *Oedipus*.

Senghor, Léopold Sédar (1906–) The proponent of the theory of Negritude, Léopold Sédar was born in Joal, Senegal, and studied in Paris. He sat in the French National Assembly from 1946 to 1959, and became President of Senegal, a position which he held from 1960 to 1980. He published *Nations et voie africaine du socialisme* (*On African Socialism*) in 1961, but in the literary world is best known for his poetry, which includes *Chants d'ombre* (*Shadow Songs*), which appeared in 1945, *Hosties noires* (*Black Offerings*), in 1948, *Ethiopiques*, in 1956, *Nocturnes*, in 1961, and *Lettres d'hivernage* (*Winter Letters*), in 1973.

Sense and Sensibility A novel by Jane Austen which tells of the Dashwood sisters, Elinor and Marianne, and the young men with whom they are in love. It was first published in 1811.

Sentimental Journey, A A discursive fictional account by Laurence Sterne of Parson Yorick's journeyings in France. Based on his own travels, it was first published in 1768.

Service, Robert William (1874–1958) The Canadian poet and novelist Robert William Service was born in Preston, England. He went to Canada in 1905, and in 1907 published *Songs of a Sourdough*, which included the famous ballads 'The Shooting of Dan McGrew' and 'The Cremation of Sam Mcgee'. He brought out other volumes of verse, and also wrote novels and autobiographical works.

sestina A complex verse form, originating in medieval Italian and Provençal poetry, and consisting of six stanzas, each of six lines, to which is added a final three-line stanza. The six words used to end the lines in the first verse are also used to end the lines in the remaining five verses, but they appear in a different order each time; they are also all included in the concluding three-line stanza. Sestinas were originally written exclusively in blank verse, but later poets have used rhyme. Swinburne, who was largely responsible for the revival of the form in English, produced a number of examples, including a celebrated double sestina, 'The Complaint of Lisa'.

Seven Against Thebes, The A tragedy by Aeschylus, concerned with the struggle for the kingship of Thebes. It was first performed in 467BC.

Seward, Anna (1747–1809) The 'Swan of Lichfield', as Anna Seward is sometimes called, was born at Eyam, Derbyshire, England. She wrote several volumes of poetry and a poetical novel, *Louisa*, which had a marked success at the time. Sir Walter Scott admired her work, but it is now largely forgotten.

Shadow of a Gunman, The Sean O'Casey's first successful play, presented at the Abbey Theatre,

Dublin, in 1923. It is a tragedy, concerned with the conflict between the Irish Republican Army and the Black and Tans.

Shadwell, Thomas (*c.*1642–92) Born in Norfolk, England, Thomas Shadwell was educated at Cambridge, but left without taking a degree. His first play was *The Sullen Lovers, or the Impertinents*, presented in 1668, and he went on to write many more successful plays, including *Epsom Wells*, in 1972, and *The Squire of Alsatia*, in 1688. He quarrelled with Dryden, and both men wrote satires against one another. He succeeded Dryden as Poet Laureate and Historiographer Royal in 1688.

Shaffer, Peter (1926–) Peter Levin Shaffer, the English playwright, was born in Liverpool and educated at Cambridge. His first major success was *Five Finger Exercise*, a family drama produced in 1958. He followed it with a number of other theatrical triumphs, including the double bill *The Private Ear* and *The Public Eye*, in 1962, *The Royal Hunt of the Sun*, in 1964, *Equus*, in 1973, *Amadeus*, in 1979, and *Yonadab*, in 1985.

Shakespeare, William (1564–1616) The son of John Shakespeare, a well-to-do tradesman and farmer, William Shakespeare was born in Stratford-on-Avon, Warwickshire. He is believed to have been educated at the local grammar school. In November 1582, when he was sixteen, he was married to Anne Hathaway, and their first child, Susanna, was born in the following spring. The twins, Hamnet and Judith, were born about twenty-one months later. In 1584 he was forced to leave Stratford, possibly for poaching offences, but there is no certainty as to where he went or how he was occupied during the next eight years. At some time during that period he went to London and began to work in the theatre, first as an actor but soon as a playwright. The dates of the writing and earliest production of his plays are often in doubt, so the details which follow can be regarded as approximate only. It is believed that *The Contention of York and Lancaster* (later to become known as Parts 2 and 3 of *Henry VI*) appeared in 1591, and was followed the next year by *Henry VI*, Part 1. From mid-1592 until 1594 the London theatres were closed for many months, and it has been suggested that he travelled in Europe during this period. If so, his time abroad did not prevent him from writing, for the poem *Venus and Adonis* appeared in 1593, and the plays *Richard III* and *The Comedy of Errors* are also thought to belong to this year. When the theatres reopened, he was established as a member of the theatrical company known as the Lord Chamberlain's Men, and 1594 saw not only *Titus Andronicus, The Taming of the Shrew, Love's*

Mr. WILLIAM
SHAKESPEARES
COMEDIES,
HISTORIES, &
TRAGEDIES.
Publiſhed according to the True Originall Copies.

LONDON
Printed by Iſaac Iaggard, and Ed. Blount. 1623.

This engraving by Droeshout appeared in the first edition of Shakespeare's plays in 1623. It is one of two authenticated portraits of the poet, the other appears opposite.

Labours Lost (which some scholars have believed to be Shakespeare's earliest play, dating it in 1591) and *Romeo and Juliet*, but also the poem *The Rape of Lucrece*, while in 1595 came *A Midsummer Night's Dream, The Two Gentlemen of Verona* and *King John*. His son Hamnet died in 1596, in which year his father acquired a coat of arms and the status of a gentleman and is believed to have written *Richard II* and *The Merchant of Venice*. By this time Shakespeare was becoming wealthy, and in 1597 he purchased New Place, a large house in Stratford. The theatres were again closed for a period, and only Part 1 of *Henry IV* is attributed to this year, to be followed by Part 2 and *Much Ado About Nothing* in 1598, the year in which the Globe Theatre was built. He was still acting at that time, for we know that in 1598 he took part in Ben Jonson's play *Every Man in his Humour*. His next plays were *Henry V, Julius Caesar, The Merry Wives of Windsor, As You Like It,*

Hamlet, Twelfth Night, Troilus and Cressida and *All's Well that Ends Well*. Queen Elizabeth I died in 1603, and the theatres were closed once more, but on the accession of James I the Lord Chamberlain's Men became the King's Men, the most favoured theatrical troupe of the time – partly, no doubt, because of the qualities of their resident playwright. *Othello* and *Measure for Measure* both appear to have received their first performances towards the end of 1604, but it is not certain whether *Macbeth* was produced before them or after, while *King Lear* belongs to either 1605 or 1606. Even more doubt surrounds the dates of *Antony and Cleopatra, Coriolanus, Timon of Athens, Pericles, Cymbeline, The Winter's Tale* and *The Tempest*, but all these plays seem to belong to the years between 1610 and 1611. Although working in an age when collaboration among playwrights was commonplace, Shakespeare appears in the main to have eschewed this kind of work. However, *Timon of Athens* was probably partly the work of Thomas Middleton, while *Henry VIII* was almost certainly written with John Fletcher, and Shakespeare may himself

LEFT: This portrait of Shakespeare by an unknown artist and the one on the facing page are the only authenticated portraits of the poet.

BELOW: Shakespeare's birthplace at Stratford-on-Avon.

have had a hand in Fletcher's *Two Noble Kinsmen*. In 1609 a book called *Shakespeares Sonnets, never before Imprinted* was published. It contained one hundred and fifty-four sonnets, and, apart from providing some of the most beautiful verses in the English language, it has given scholars throughout the last three centuries cause for unending speculation concerning the identities of Mr W.H., 'the onlie begetter of these insuing sonnets', to whom the volume was dedicated, and of the Dark Lady referred to in them. In about 1610 Shakespeare left London, and thereafter lived in retirement at Stratford, where he died on the 23rd April (a day which is also popularly supposed to have been his birthday). William Shakespeare is unquestionably the greatest playwright the world has ever known, and the power and beauty of his work survives whatever may be done to it in the way of bizarre interpretations and despite the best efforts of some teachers to make the plays a penance for their young pupils. The verse at its best is incomparable, the dramatic technique strong, and, perhaps most important of all, the characters are truly representative of all humanity. No other writer before or since has so fully captured the human soul in all its variety and set it down so that it speaks to every generation in terms which are instantly recognizable.

Shape of Things to Come, The A novel of the future by H.G. Wells, first published in 1933.

Shaw, G. Bernard (1856–1950) George Bernard Shaw was born in Dublin, where he went to school until he was fifteen. He and his family moved to London in 1876 and before long he had begun to write. His first works were novels, serialized at the time in various minor periodicals; they included *Cashel Byron's Profession*, which appeared in book form in 1886. Shaw then became a journalist, writing on literature, art and music for a number of papers and magazines, and began to build a reputation. In 1892 his first play, *Widowers' Houses*, was produced. It was not particularly successful, but Shaw had found his métier, and between then and his death in 1950 wrote more than fifty plays, establishing himself as the major playwright of the twentieth century. Among them were *Mrs Warren's Profession*, which was not seen publicly until 1925 because of censorship problems. *The Devil's Disciple*, in 1897, *Caesar and Cleopatra*, in 1898, *Man and Superman* and *Major Barbara*, both in 1905, *The Doctor's Dilemma*, in 1906, *Pygmalion*, in 1916, *Heartbreak House*, in 1920. *Back to Methuselah*, in 1921, and *Saint Joan*, which many critics believe to be his masterpiece, in 1923. He also published a number of books in which he

put forward his strongly-held views, championing Wagner and Ibsen respectively in *The Quintessence of Ibsenism* and *The Perfect Wagnerite*, and campaigning unceasingly for socialism – he was an early and enthusiastic member of the Fabian Society – as in *Socialism for Millionaires*, which came out in 1901, and *The Intelligent Woman's Guide to Socialism and Capitalism*, in 1928. He lectured widely and with great success, and his wisdom and wit gave him the reputation of a minor prophet, partly because he was never afflicted with self-doubt and therefore spoke with authority on any subject that interested him. He was listened to with respect, even if some of his hobby-horses, such as the need to reform English spelling, seemed to many ordinary people to verge on eccentricity. He married Charlotte Payne-Townshend in 1898; it was a happy but apparently asexual partnership, and it is doubtful whether his love for the actresses Ellen Terry and Mrs Patrick Campbell,

George Bernard Shaw. A member of the Fabian Society from its foundation in 1883. Shaw wrote widely on politics, socialism and economics, but his fame rests on his plays.

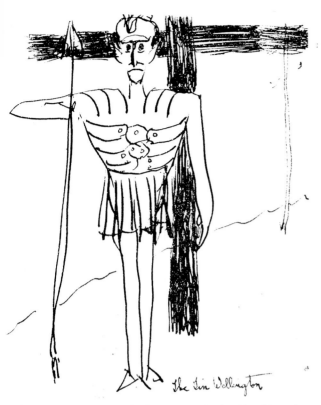

Shaw's own drawing of a Roman soldier for *The Black Girl*. Typically, he says of it 'My own drawings, which I offer rather as a warning than an example, suggest the pretentious futility of Cheltenham, not the pride of Rome'.

with both of whom he carried on a lively correspondence, was more than Platonic. Shaw believed firmly that there were only two great playwrights in English literature – Shakespeare and himself – and he was clearly inclined to place himself in the higher position. He was undoubtedly a great man of the theatre – a master of technique, an imaginative creator of character, superbly accomplished in the cut and thrust of his dialogue and in his humour, and he made (and still makes) his audiences think. However, it must be said that he was an inveterate preacher, and virtually every one of his plays contains a message (which he often reinforced in the lengthy 'Prefaces' to them). There is no reason why the theatre should not be used as a platform for the author's views, but, brilliantly and dramatically though Shaw presented his arguments, the didactic quality of the work is sometimes obtrusive. It is not unfair to say that at his worst he can be a bore; but at his best (which is fortunately more often) he is magnificent. He was awarded the Nobel Prize for Literature in 1925.

Shelley, Mary Wollstonecraft (1797–1851) Mary Wollstonecraft Shelley, the second wife of Percy Bysshe Shelley, was born in London. Before their marriage, while she was in Switzerland with Shelley and Byron, a suggestion that members of the party should write a story of the supernatural resulted in her novel *Frankenstein, or the Modern Prometheus*. It was published in 1818. She wrote a number of other novels, as well as short stories, biographies and travel books, and, after Shelley's death edited his poems and other writings.

Shelley, Percy Bysshe (1792–1822) Born at Field Place, near Horsham, England, Percy Bysshe Shelley was the eldest child of a Member of Parliament. He was educated at Eton, where he became known as 'Shelley the Atheist', and at University College, Oxford. Having previously published a number of short novels and poems at his own expense, in 1811 he was expelled from his college for having written, together with T.J. Hogg, a pamphlet, *The Necessity of Atheism*. He went to London, and a few months later eloped with a Miss Harriet Westbrook to Scotland, where they were married. For the next three years they moved from place to place, while Shelley concerned himself with a variety of campaigns on causes ranging from vegetarianism to politics. In 1813 they were in London, where Harriet gave birth to their first child, a daughter, and in this year he published his first important volume of verse, *Queen Mab*. The marriage was near to disintegration, and in 1814, although Harriet was again pregnant, he left for Switzerland with Mary Wollstonecraft Godwin, with whom he had fallen in love, and her stepsister, Claire Clairmont. He had been living on an allowance made to him jointly by his father and father-in-law, but early in 1815 the death of his grandfather, Sir Bysshe Shelley, brought him financial independence. He and Mary set up home near Windsor, and it was here that he wrote *Alastor, or the Spirit of Solitude*, which established his reputation as a major poet. In 1816 he went again to Switzerland, this time with Byron as well, and soon after returning to London he was able to marry Mary, following the suicide of Harriet, who drowned herself in the Serpentine, the lake in London's Hyde Park. At this time he wrote a number of pamphlets and essays and some poetry, including *The Revolt of Islam*, published in 1818. In that year he and Mary and their two tiny children, together with Claire Clairmont and the daughter whom she had borne to Byron, left England for Italy, where Shelley was to spend the rest of his life and to write his most enduring poetry. 1819 was for him a year of great creativity, and he not only produced many poems, including the 'Ode to the West Wind', 'To a Skylark' and the long work *The Witch of Atlas*, but also completed his two great poetic dramas, *Prometheus Unbound* and *The Cenci*. Despite a lack of success in getting his work published, he continued to write, both in prose and in verse, and his *Defence of Poetry* was composed in 1821. The death of Keats in Rome inspired him to write *Adonais*, and his attraction to a young Italian girl resulted in *Epipsychidion*. In 1822 he finished another drama, *Hellas*, and began his last major work, *The Triumph of Life*. In July he, a friend, Lieutenant Edward Williams, and a cabin-boy were all drowned when their small schooner, the *Ariel*, was caught in a sudden storm off Viareggio, near Livorno. Seen in his lifetime as a revolutionary and a libertine, and sometimes still regarded as the typical romantic poet who ignores all the conventions of society in pursuit of his Muse, Shelley was a man of considerable culture and great independence of mind. He was also one of the greatest of all lyric poets.

The lyrical poet Shelley, painted by Amelia Curran in 1819, a few years before he drowned.

Shepard, Sam (1943–) Playwright, novelist, short story writer and actor, the American Samuel Shepard Rogers uses the name Sam Shepard. Among his many publications are *La Turista*, which appeared in 1968, *Five Plays: Chicago, Icarus's Mother, Red Cross, Fourteen Hundred Thousand and Melodrama Play*, in 1967, *Mad Dog Blues and other plays*, in 1971, *Angel City and other plays*, in 1976, and *Fool for Love and other plays*, in 1984. His plays are usually concerned with the destruction of the American Dream, and he is regarded as one of the most important of contemporary American dramatists.

Shepheardes Calendar, The A collection of twelve eclogues, one for each month of the year, by Edmund Spenser. The subjects range from love to religion and the public disregard of poetry. The poems were first published in 1579.

Shepherd's Calendar, The A volume of pastoral poetry by John Clare, the 'peasant poet', containing much of his best verse. It was first published in 1827.

Sheridan, Richard Brinsley (1751–1816) Thomas Sheridan was an actor; his wife, Frances, was a novelist and playwright. Their son, Richard Brinsley Butler Sheridan, was born in Dublin and educated at Harrow. After leaving school at seventeen, for the next seven years he continued his education privately, wrote plays, poetry and pamphlets, fought two duels with a Major Mathews, who had been an importunate suitor of Elizabeth Ann Linley, and himself married Miss Linley, first in a clandestine ceremony and later openly. He then moved to London, and early in 1775 his comedy, *The Rivals* was produced with great success at Covent Garden. Before the year was out his farce, *St Patrick's Day, or the Scheming Lieutenant*, and *The Duenna*, a comic opera, had also appeared, and both had been equally well received. In 1776, in partnership with his father-in-law, the composer Thomas Linley, and a Dr Ford, he bought David Garrick's half-share of Drury Lane Theatre and became its manager. *A Trip to Scarborough*, which was a revised version of Vanbrugh's *The Relapse*, was presented in 1777, and was followed in the same year by his masterpiece, *The School for Scandal*. It was a triumph, and made him a great deal of money, which he spent as fast as it came in, or faster. In 1779 he presented *The Critic*, a farce which, although it was successful, virtually marked the end of his career as a playwright. Only one more play was to come – the tragedy, *Pizarro*, which appeared twenty years later. He continued to manage his theatre, he and his partner having bought the other half-share in 1778, but he had ambitions as a politician. He

A portrait in pastels of the brilliant comic writer Sheridan by John Russell. His sparkling wit made him a fine parliamentary orator and a popular member of fashionable Regency society.

entered Parliament in 1780, soon rising to hold a number of minor government offices, and his speech on the subject of Warren Hastings, the Governor of India who was impeached for corruption, was hailed as an outstanding piece of oratory. His Parliamentary career continued to flourish when his party, the Whigs, were in power, and he included the Prince Regent among his intimate and eminent friends. His life was not easy, however. In 1791 Drury Lane was condemned as unsafe and had to be rebuilt at vast cost. In the following year his wife died, and in his distress he took to gambling and accrued large debts. He remarried in 1805. A fire at Drury Lane in 1809 necessitated a second rebuilding, and then he quarrelled with the Prince Regent, failed in 1812 to be elected to Parliament, and in the following year was arrested for debt. He spent the remainder of his life in penury. *The Rivals* and *The School for Scandal* are still performed today, and their glittering wit and humour rank them as the finest English comedies of the eighteenth century.

Sherriff, R.C. (1896–1975) Robert Cedric Sherriff was born in Kingston-upon-Thames, England. He is best known for his World War I play, *Journey's End*, first produced in 1929. He wrote a number of other plays, including *St Helena*, in 1934, and *Home at Seven*, in 1950, some novels, and an autobiography, *No Leading Lady*.

Sherwood, Robert (1896–1955) Robert Emmet Sherwood was born in New York. His first successful play was *The Road to Rome*, which was presented in 1927, while *The Petrified Forest* made him famous in 1935. Three of his plays, *Idiot's Delight*, produced in 1936, *Abe Lincoln in Illinois*, in 1938, and *There Shall Be No Night*, in 1940, all won Pulitzer Prizes. He also won a Pulitzer Prize for his political study, *Roosevelt and Hopkins*, published in 1948.

She Stoops to Conquer, or The Mistakes of a Night A romantic comedy by Oliver Goldsmith in which two young blades mistake a private country house for an inn, and believe that the irascible Mr Hardcastle, owner of the house, and his pretentious wife are the innkeepers. It was first produced in 1773.

Ship of Fools An allegorical novel by Katherine Ann Porter, first published in 1962.

Shirley A novel by Charlotte Brontë, set in Yorkshire in the early nineteenth century and much concerned with the local wool industry. It was first published in 1849.

Shirley, James (1596–1666) The English dramatist James Shirley was born in London and educated at both Oxford and Cambridge. After some years as a priest and then a schoolmaster, he went to London and began a career as a dramatist. His first play, *Love Tricks*, appeared in 1623, and he followed it with *The Maides Revenge*, in 1626. During the next twenty years he wrote some forty plays, both tragedies and comedies, and also published some volumes of poetry.

Shoemaker's Holiday, The A comedy by Thomas Dekker, first presented in 1599.

Sholokov, Mikhail Alexandrovich (1905–84) The Russian novelist Mikhail Alexandrovich Sholokov was born in the village of Veshenskaya in the Don region. He received little formal education. He published his first books, *Tales of the Don* and *The Azure Step*, both of which were collections of short stories, in 1925 and 1926. He achieved great success in 1928 with the novel *The Quiet Don* (published in English in two volumes, *And Quiet Flows the Don*, which appeared in 1934, and *The Don flows Home to the Sea*, in 1940). His second novel, *Virgin Soil Upturned*, came out in 1931, but he did not live to complete his third, *They Fought for the Fatherland*. He was awarded the Nobel Prize for Literature in 1965.

Shropshire Lad, A A group of sixty-three poems, the best-known work of A.E. Housman, first published at the poet's own expense in 1896.

Shute, Nevil (1899–1960) The English novelist Nevil Shute Norway took up an aeronautical career after completing his education at Oxford. He published his first novel, *Marazan*, in 1926, and went on to write a great many bestsellers, including *The Chequer Board*, which appeared in 1947, *No Highway*, in 1948, *A Town Like Alice*, in 1949, *In the Wet*, in 1953, and *On the Beach*, in 1957.

Siddharta A novel by Hermann Hesse, first published in 1922. Its mysticism made it a cult book in the 1960s.

Sidney, Sir Philip (1554–86) The English poet, soldier and statesman Philip Sidney was born at Penshurst, Sussex, and educated at Shrewsbury School and Christ Church, Oxford. He attended the court of Queen Elizabeth I and spent several years in Europe, often as Elizabeth's representative, but by 1578 was back in England, and wrote a masque, *The Lady of the May*, for the Queen's entertainment. In 1580, having incurred her displeasure, he retired from the court, and it was at this time that he wrote his *Arcadia*, a romance in prose and poetry, completed in 1581 but subsequently revised. He also produced *An Apologie for Poetrie* (sometimes called *The Defence of Poesie*) and the sequence of sonnets and songs, *Astrophel and Stella*. Restored to favour, he returned to the court, and was knighted in 1583. Spain was at this time an enemy, and Sidney, hankering after a military life, proposed to sail with Francis Drake in 1585 on a punitive expedition to the Spanish coast. Instead, he was sent to the Netherlands, where he became Governor of Flushing. In July 1586, he led a raid on Axel, and later that month, in another action, received a bullet wound in the thigh (and characteristically refused a cup of water, giving it to a dying soldier with the words, 'Thy need is greater than mine.'). His wound became infected, and a month later he died. His work was not published until after his death, when it became apparent that he was among the best poets of his era.

Silas Marner A novel by George Eliot, telling of the weaver of Raveloe, despised as a miser, and of his adopted daughter Eppie. It was first published in 1861.

Silent Spring A work by the American writer Rachel Carson, published in 1963, in which she attacked the indiscriminate use of chemicals in farming.

Sillitoe, Alan (1928–) Born in Nottingham, the English writer Alan Sillitoe received little formal education. He published a book of poetry, *Without Beer or Bread*, in 1957, and in the following year brought out his bestselling novel, *Saturday Night and Sunday Morning*. He has published other novels, among them *Down from the Hill*, which appeared in 1984, and several collections of short stories, including *The Loneliness of the Long Distance Runner*, in 1959. He is also a poet, and *Sun Before Departure: Collected Poems 1974–82*, published in 1984, and *Out of the Whirlpool*, in 1987, are recent volumes.

Simenon, Georges (1903–) The crime-writer Georges Simenon was born and educated in Liège, Belgium. He has written well over two hundred novels, some eighty of which feature his detective Inspector Maigret. Among his latest books to appear in English are *The Couple from Poitiers*, in 1985, and *The Outlaw*, in 1986. He has also produced a number of autobiographical works, including *Intimate Memoirs*, published in 1984.

Simon, Neil (1927–) Neil Simon was born in New York City. He had his first success in the theatre in 1961 with *Come Blow Your Horn*, which he has followed with a number of brilliant plays, including *Barefoot in the Park*, first seen in 1963, *The Odd Couple*, in 1965, *Plaza Suite*, in 1968, *The Prisoner of Second Avenue*, in 1973, *California Suite*, in 1980, and *Biloxi Blues* and the female version of *The Odd Couple*, both in 1985. He has also written musicals and a number of screenplays.

Simpson, Louis (1923–) The poet Louis Aston Marantz Simpson was born in Jamaica and, after being educated there, went on to Columbia University. An academic, he has taught at the universities of California and New York. He published his first volume of poetry, *The Arrivistes: Poems 1940–1949*, in 1949, and has followed it with several more volumes, including *At the End of the Open Road: Poems*, which appeared in 1963 and won a Pulitzer Prize. He has also written a novel and a play and a number of works of literary criticism.

Sinclair, Upton (1878–1968) The American novelist Upton Beall Sinclair was born in Baltimore and educated at the College of the City of New York and Columbia University. He became, and remained, an ardent socialist, and in 1906 founded a socialist colony in Englewood, New Jersey. In that year, too, he published his most famous book, *The Jungle*, a novel in which he exposed the conditions then prevailing in the Chicago stockyards. The book resulted in an investigation into the meat-packing industry and the passing of the first Federal laws relating to food purity. Many of his other novels were equally designed to draw attention to aspects of society which offended him. For instance, he attacked capitalism in *The Metropolis*, in 1908, religion in *The Profits of Religion*, in 1918, the corruption of the Press in *The Brass Check*, in 1919, and the oil scandals of the period in *Oil*, in 1927. Between 1940 and 1953 he wrote a series of eleven novels centred on the character of Lanny Budd; one of these, *Dragon's Teeth*, published in 1942, was awarded a Pulitzer Prize. He also produced some works of non-fiction, including *A Personal Jesus, A Biography*, which appeared in 1952, and *The Autobiography of Upton Sinclair*, in 1962.

Singer, Isaac Bashevis (1904–) Born in Radzymin, Poland, and educated at the Rabbinical Seminary in Warsaw, Isaac Bashevis Singer emigrated to the United States in 1935, where he became a journalist, contributing to the Yiddish newspaper, *The Jewish Daily Forward*. He writes in Yiddish, and his first work to be translated into English was the novel *The Family Moskat*, which appeared in 1950. In 1953 he attracted much attention with his celebrated short story 'Gimpel the Fool', which later became the title piece of a collection. In his subsequent fiction he has become noted and greatly admired for the skill with which he explores the deep mysteries of faith through the medium of simple stories about simple people, often taking the material from folk-tales. His novels include *Satan in Goray*, which appeared in 1955, *The Magician of Lublin*, in 1960, *The Slave*, in 1962, the two-volume work, *The Manor* and *The Estate*, in 1967 and 1969, *Enemies: A Love Story*, in 1972, *Shosha*, in 1978, and *The Penitent*, in 1984. Among his many collections of short stories are *Gimpel the Fool*, published in 1957, *The Seance*, in 1968, *Passions*, in 1976, and *The Image and other stories*, in 1986. His autobiography, *Love and Exile*, appeared in 1984. He was awarded the Nobel Prize for Literature in 1978.

Singleton, Adventures of Captain A story of adventures in exotic settings by Daniel Defoe, first published in 1720.

Sir Charles Grandison Samuel Richardson's third novel, written to form a contrast with his earlier books, *Pamela* and *Clarissa*, and telling the story of 'a Good Man'. It was first published in 1754.

Sir Launcelot Greaves, The Life and Adventures of A novel by Tobias Smollett, first published in 1762. It is the story of a man driven by love to a state of insanity.

Sister Carrie Theodore Dreiser's first novel, published (but suppressed as immoral) in 1900, and reissued in 1912. It is the story of a girl and her rise to stardom, and of the decline of her wealthy protector.

Sitwell, Edith (1887–1965) The English poet Edith Louisa Sitwell was born in Scarborough, Yorkshire, and educated privately. Her first volume of poetry, *The Mother and other poems*, appeared in 1915, and was followed by several others. In 1923 she produced the astonishing *Façade*, with music by William Walton, which brought her some notoriety, but she achieved her greatest success during World War II with such volumes of verse as *Street Songs*, published in 1942, and *The Song of the Cold*, in 1945. Her eccentric dress and controversial attitudes made her a public figure during her last decades. She was created a Dame in 1954.

Sitwell, Osbert (1892–1969) Sir Francis Osbert Sacheverell Sitwell, brother of Edith Sitwell, was born in London and educated at Eton. He published several volumes of verse, novels, short stories and essays, and, most notably, his five volumes of autobiography, *Left Hand, Right Hand!*, *The Scarlet Tree*, *Great Morning*, *Laughter in the Next Room* and *Noble Essences*, published between 1944 and 1950.

Sitwell, Sacheverell (1897–) The third member of the literary family, brother of Edith and Osbert, Sacheverell Sitwell was educated at Eton. He published several volumes of verse, beginning with *The People's Palace*, in 1918, and wrote books on many subjects, including art and architecture, music and travel, and also produced some works of fiction.

Skeat, W.W. (1835–1912) Walter William Skeat was born in London and educated at Cambridge. He became an expert on Middle English, and published editions of many early works of literature, including *Piers Plowman* and all of Chaucer's writings. Between 1879 and 1882 he brought out an *Etymological English Dictionary*, considered to be a major work.

Skelton, John (*c*.1460–1529) Little is known with certainty of the early years of the English poet John Skelton. He wrote many satires, including *Colyn Cloute*, a diatribe against the clergy, while *The Tunnynge of Elynoure Rummynge* described a group of drunken women at a local inn. *The Garlande of Laurell* was an allegory in which he celebrated his own eminence as a poet, and *A Ballade of the Scottysshe Kynge* records the English victory over the Scots at Flodden. His verses are not far removed from doggerel, but have considerable vigour.

Sketches by Boz Charles Dickens' first published articles, consisting of pictures of contemporary life, which appeared in a number of different periodicals, and led to the commissioning of *The Pickwick Papers*. They were published in book form between 1836 and 1837.

Small House at Allington, The A novel by Anthony Trollope, the fifth in the Barsetshire series, first published in 1864.

Smart, Christopher (1722–71) The English poet Christopher Smart was born in Kent and educated at Cambridge, where he won the Seaton poetry prize on five occasions. In 1752 he went to London and began to work in journalism, but also published a volume of poetry, *Poems on Various Occasions*. By 1756 he had developed religious mania and was confined in an asylum, where he wrote his best-known work, a long poem entitled *A Song to David*, published in 1763. A later religious poem, *Jubilate Agno*, did not appear until 1939.

Smiles, Samuel (1812–1904) Born in Scotland and trained as a doctor at Edinburgh University, Samuel Smiles gave up medicine to write, and published a large number of popular biographies. He is best known for his moralizing book *Self-Help*, which appeared in 1859.

Smith, Adam (1723–90) A native of Kirkcaldy, Scotland, Adam Smith was educated at Glasgow University and Oxford. In 1759 he published his *Theory of Moral Sentiments*, which gained him considerable recognition, and then in 1776 came his major work, the *Inquiry into the Nature and Causes of the Wealth of Nations*. This book was immensely influential and is, indeed, one of the most important expositions of economic theory ever written.

Smith, Captain John (1579–1631) John Smith, born in Lincolnshire, England, was an adventurer and sailor who, after travelling widely (his experiences included being sold as a slave in Tartary), emigrated in 1606 to Virginia, where he is said to have been saved from death by the Indian princess Pocohontas. He wrote *The General History of Virginia, New England and the Summer Isles*, which was published in 1624.

Smith, Logan Pearsall (1865–1946) The American literary critic and bibliographer Logan Pearsall Smith was born in Milville, Pennsylvania, and educated at Harvard and Oxford. In 1895 he published a collection of short stories, *The Youth of Parnassus*. His first major work, *The Life and Letters of Sir Henry Wotton*, appeared in 1907, to be followed by *Songs and Sonnets* in 1909. In later years he brought out a series of what might be termed commonplace books called *Trivia*, collected together in 1933 as *All Trivia*. His autobiography, *Unforgotten Years*, was published in 1938.

Smith, Stevie (1902–71) Stevie Florence Margaret Smith was born in Hull, England. She published a novel, *Novel on Yellow Paper*, in 1936, and followed it with a volume of verse, *A Good Time Was Had by All*, in 1937. Two other novels appeared, but her reputation was that of a poet, and she published several more collections, including *Not Waving but Drowning*, in 1957.

Smith, Sydney (1771–1845) At his father's insistence, Sydney Smith, who was born in Essex, England, and educated at Oxford, became a clergyman, although he would have preferred a legal career. He was one of the founders and the first editor of *The Edinburgh Review*, and contributed to it regularly for nearly thirty years. In 1808 he published ten essays on Catholic emancipation under the title of *Peter Plymley's Letters*, and various other polemical essays and letters appeared. He was a man of great wit, and his sermons and lectures drew large crowds. In 1850 his widow published his *Elementary Sketches of Moral Philosophy*.

Smith, Wilbur (1933–) The South African novelist Wilbur Addison Smith was educated in Natal and at Rhodes University. After some years as a businessman, he turned to writing when his first book, *When the Lion Feeds*, was spectacularly successful in 1964. He has produced many bestselling novels since then, including *Eagle in the Sky*, in 1974, *Men of Men*, in 1981, *Angels Weep*, in 1984, and *Power of the Sword*, in 1986.

Smollett, Tobias (1721–71) Tobias George Smollett was born in Dumbartonshire, Scotland. After leaving Glasgow University he was apprenticed to a surgeon, but left Scotland at the age of eighteen, having written a tragedy, *The Regicide*, which he tried in vain to persuade someone to present. He joined the Navy as a surgeon's mate, but by 1744 was practising as a surgeon in London's Downing Street. In 1746 he published a poem, 'The Tears of Scotland', attacking the Duke of Cumberland's treatment of the Scots after Culloden, which brought him considerable acclaim, and followed it with two political satires, *Advice* and *Reproof*. He then turned to fiction, and his picaresque novel, *The Adventures of Roderick Random*, appeared in two volumes in 1748. It was instantaneously successful, and although it was published anonymously, Smollett was not backward in acknowledging it to be his. A second novel, on similar lines, *The Adventures of Peregrine Pickle*, came out in 1751, and also enjoyed large sales. It was followed in 1753 by *Ferdinand Count Fathom*, a novel with a much stronger plot than its predecessors, an unpleasant central character and a number of incidents which qualify it, at least in part, as a horror novel. It was not very well received, and although the earlier books had made Smollett successful, he was a lavish spender, and the failure of *Ferdinand Count Fathom* placed him in financial difficulty. During the next few years he attempted to recoup his fortunes by engaging in a variety of literary activities, including translating Cervantes and Voltaire, launching new periodicals, preparing and partly writing a *Universal History*, and at last achieving some success in the theatre with his patriotic play, *The Reprisal, or the Tars of Old England*, which was presented by Garrick in 1757. In 1760 he was sent to the Marchelsea prison for a libellous piece he had written about Admiral Sir Charles Knowles. For his periodical *The British* he wrote another novel, *The Adventures of Sir Launcelot Greaves*, which was published in book form in 1761, with little acclaim. Two years later his only daughter died. His own health was poor, and he and his wife decided to leave for Europe, visiting France and Italy and spending a long period on the French Riviera. They returned to England in 1765, and in the following year he published *Travels through France and Italy*, in which he displayed again the acerbic side of his nature that had already been apparent in his fiction. He visited Edinburgh, where he was fêted in literary circles, but in 1768 was back in London, and

Tobias Smollett, noted for his caustic wit and acerbic prose, painted not long before his death.

shortly thereafter published *The History and Adventures of an Atom*, a coarse and bitter satire on the government of Britain during the previous twelve years. His health deteriorated, and in 1769 he left England again, settling near Livorno. In 1770 he wrote *The Expedition of Humphrey Clinker*, which is generally considered to be his finest achievement. It is gentler in tone than his earlier works, telling in epistolary style of a journey to Scotland and back, during which an assortment of adventures befall the members of the Bramble family and Humphrey Clinker is finally revealed for the estimable character he really is. It was published in 1771, a short while before its author's death. Smollett's work is vigorous, full of acid humour, and marked by keen observation. He has been accused of a predeliction for cruelty and squalor in his writings, but in this he was perhaps simply reflecting one side of the age that he lived in. The direct quality of his prose, his depth of characterization and the construction of his plots give him a major place in the development of the English novel.

An illustration to *Humphrey Clinker* by Cruikshank.

Snow, C.P. (1905–80) Charles Percy Snow was born in Leicester, England, and educated at Leicester University College and Cambridge. He published his first novel, *Death Under Sail*, a detective story, in 1932. Other novels appeared and then in 1940 he began a sequence known as 'Strangers and Brothers', completed in 1970. It consisted of eleven novels narrated by the barrister Lewis Eliot, the best known of which was *Corridors of Power*, published in 1963. He also wrote other novels, biographies and literary studies. He was knighted in 1957 and created Baron Snow of Leicester in 1964. He was married to the writer Pamela Hansford Johnson.

Soldiers, Three A collection of stories, set in India, by Rudyard Kipling, first published in 1888.

Solzhenitsyn, Alexander Isayevich (1918–) The Russian writer Alexander Isayevich Solzhenitsyn was born in Kislovodsk and educated at the University of Rostov-on-Don. He fought in the Russian army during World War II, and in 1945 was sent to a labour camp for his criticisms of Stalin. Released in 1953, he became a teacher, and in 1962 published a novel, *One Day in the Life of Ivan Denisovich*, which described a labour camp in stark detail. He next brought out a volume of short stories, *Matrena's House*. The novels *Cancer Ward* and *The First Circle* appeared in 1968 and 1969 respectively, both being published in the West but not in Russia. In 1970 he was awarded the Nobel Prize for Literature. *The Gulag Archipelago*, the immensely long catalogue of Russian prison camps, with details of those confined in them, was published between 1973 and 1975, and resulted in his expulsion from Russia. He settled in the United States, and has since published several books,

The exiled Soviet writer Alexander Solzhenitsyn was awarded the Nobel Prize for Literature in 1970.

including the novel *August 1914*, which appeared in 1971, a volume of autobiography, *The Oak and the Calf*, in 1975, and a trilogy of plays – *The Love Girl and the Innocent*, in 1969, and *Victory Celebrations* and *Prisoners*, both in 1983. His reputation in the West is immensely high, but although he is undoubtedly a major writer, his popularity might well have been considerably less had he not been seen as a victim of the Soviet suppression of dissidents.

Somerville, E. (1858–1949) Edith Denone Somerville collaborated with her cousin, Violet Martin (who used the pseudonym Martin Ross) on a number of books, the best known being the amusing stories about an Irish resident magistrate. The first of these collections, *Some Experiences of an Irish R.M.*, appeared in 1899.

Song of Myself A poem by Walt Whitman, which sets out his philosophy of life. It was first published in *Leaves of Grass* in 1855.

Songs of Innocence and Experience A collection of poems by William Blake. *Songs of Innocence* appeared in 1789, and a new edition was published in 1795 together with (in the same volume) the *Songs of Experience*, which included 'Tyger! Tyger! burning bright'.

sonnet A poem consisting, in English versions, of fourteen decasyllabic lines. The two main forms are the Petrarchan and the Elizabethan or Shakespearian sonnet. The former uses the rhyming scheme a b b a a b b a for the first eight lines, then introduces a break in the thought and employs two or three different rhymes in the final six lines; the latter form is rhymed a b a b c d c d e f e f g g. The sonnet form has been widely used by poets writing in English since the sixteenth century.

Sonnets by Shakespeare First published in 1609, the one hundred and fifty-four poems which make up Shakespeare's *Sonnets* were probably written in the last decade of the sixteenth century. Apart from their matchless beauty, they have provided scholars with a number of unsolved mysteries: who was Mr W.H., to whom the collection is dedicated and to whom the majority of the verses are addressed? who was the rival poet referred to in sonnets 80 to 86? and who was the Dark Lady of sonnets 127 to 152?

Sonnets from the Portuguese A sequence of poems by Elizabeth Barrett Browning, first published in 1850. Despite the title, they are not in fact translations.

Sons and Lovers D.H. Lawrence's first important novel, published in 1913. Partly autobiographical, it tells of Paul Morel's relationships with his mother, with the shy Miriam, and with Clara, a married woman.

Sophie's Choice A novel by William Styron, first published in 1979. It concerns the relationship between an American Jew and a Polish Catholic girl who is a survivor from a concentration camp.

Sophocles (495–406 BC) In chronological terms the second of the great Greek tragedians, Sophocles was born near Athens, thirty years after Aeschylus and fifteen years before Euripides. Apart from his career as a dramatist, comparatively little is known of his life, but he is believed to have been prominent in civic affairs and may have travelled abroad frequently as a representative of Athens. He was apparently appointed as a general under the Athenian leader Pericles during the Samian War of 440 to 439BC. He wrote over a hundred plays, beginning with the *Triptolemus*, and much poetry besides, but only seven of his tragedies still exist: *Oedipus the King*, *Oedipus at Colonus*, *Antigone*, *Electra*, *Trachiniae*, *Ajax* and *Philoctetes*. In 468BC he defeated Aeschylus in the annual contest for tragic poets. It was one of his few such victories, but, whatever the judges may have thought, his work was always more popular than that of his two main rivals. He drew his subjects from legends and stories of the past, many being concerned with the fall of Troy, and was admired not only for the depth of his characterizations, which, while idealized, were less stereotyped than those of Aeschylus, but also for the sheer dramatic content of his plays, in which respect he outshone both Aeschylus and Euripides. He was the first dramatist to put three actors on the stage, in addition to the chorus, and is also said to have broken the tradition of the times that dramatists should always act in their own plays.

Sordello A long narrative poem by Robert Browning, about an Italian troubadour of the Middle Ages. It was first published in 1840.

Sound and the Fury, The One of the most important of William Faulkner's novels, evocatively portraying the decline of the American South. It was first published in 1929.

Soupault, Philippe (1897–) The French poet and novelist Philippe Soupault was born in Chaville and educated at the Sorbonne. His first volumes of verse, *Aquarium* and *Rose des vents* (*Rose of the Winds*), published in 1917 and 1920 respectively, showed a Dadaist influence. He then turned to surrealism, and *Les champs magnétiques*, which he wrote in collaboration with André Breton, and which appeared in 1920, is regarded as the first surrealist work of literature. His novels include *Les frères Durandeau* (The Durandeau Brothers), published in 1924, *Le nègre* (*The Negro*), in 1927, *Les moribonds* (*The Dying*), in 1934, and *Le temps des assassins* (*Age of Assassins*) in 1945.

Southerne, Thomas (1660–1746) The dramatist Thomas Southerne was born and educated in Dublin. His first play, *The Persian Prince, or the Loyal Brother*, appeared in 1682. After a period in the army, he returned to a career as a dramatist, and his *The Fatal Marriage, or the Innocent Adultery* was extremely successful when presented in 1692. He wrote several other plays, many of them, like the two mentioned, based on works of fiction by other writers.

Southey, Robert (1774–1843) Born in Bristol, England, Robert Southey was educated at Westminster and Oxford, where he met Samuel Taylor Coleridge. Together they planned an ideal society and wrote *The Fall of Robespierre*, a drama published in 1794. *Poems* by Southey and Robert Lovell appeared in 1795, and Southey's epic poem *Joan of Arc* came out in 1796. By this time he had married Edith Fricker, whose sisters Sara and Mary had married Coleridge and Lovell respectively. In 1795 he had been abroad, and his *Letters written during a Short Residence in Spain and Portugal* resulted. He now went back to Portugal, intending to write a history of that country. Returning to England in 1801, he went to the Lake District, where he lived for the rest of his life. He wrote prodigiously and published many collections of verse, long poems, biographies (notably his *Life of Nelson*, which appeared in 1813), editions of other poets' works, essays and histories, including a *History of Brazil*. He was appointed Poet Laureate in 1813. His work is not now greatly admired, although he is remembered for such ballads as 'The Battle of Blenheim' and 'The Inchcape Rock'.

Southwell, Robert (*c.*1561–95) The Jesuit poet Robert Southwell was born in Norfolk, England, and educated in France. In 1586 he returned to Protestant England as a Roman Catholic priest, and was captured, tortured, imprisoned and finally hanged. While in prison he wrote much poetry, including *St Peter's Complaint with other poems*, and this and other works were published posthumously. He was beatified in 1929 and canonized in 1970.

Soyinka, Wole (1934–) The Nigerian poet, playwright and novelist Wole Soyinka was educated in Ibadan and at Leeds University. In 1958 his first play, *The Swamp Dwellers* was produced in London, and his first novel, *The Interpreters*, came out in 1965. He has published altogether some twenty books, including other novels, volumes of verse and philosophy, and a work describing his experiences as a political prisoner, *The Man Died*. Among his plays are *Kongi's Harvest*, seen in 1965, *Jero's Metamorphosis*, in 1973, and *Opera Wonyosi*, in 1978. A bitter opponent of colonialism, apartheid and corruption in high places, he is probably Black Africa's best-known writer. He was awarded the Nobel Prize for Literature in 1986.

Spanish Fryar, The A play by John Dryden, first presented in 1681.

Spanish Tragedy, The The most famous of Thomas Kyd's plays, first performed in 1592. The unmasking of its villains by the hero, Hieronimo, provided Shakespeare with the idea for 'The Mousetrap', the play within a play in *Hamlet*.

Spark, Muriel (1918–) A native of Edinburgh, Muriel Sarah Camberg married S.O. Spark in 1938. She published her first volume of poetry, *The Fanfarlo*, in 1952. After bringing out some volumes of literary criticism, she turned to fiction, and her first novel, *The Comforters*, appeared in 1957. Many other novels have followed, including *The Prime of Miss Jean Brodie*, in 1962 (which was very successfully adapted for the stage), *The Mandelbaum Gate*, in 1965, *Loitering with Intent*, in 1981, and *The Only Problem*, in 1984. She has also published many short stories, and these were collected in *The Stories of Muriel Spark* in 1987.

Spectator, The A daily paper started by Richard Steele and Joseph Addison in March, 1711, and continued until December in the following year. Addison, who regularly contributed essays, brought the paper out again for a short period in 1814. The present-day *Spectator*, a weekly magazine, was founded in 1828.

Spencer, Herbert (1820–1903) The English philosopher Herbert Spencer was born in Derby and was largely self-educated. After working for the London and Birmingham Railway, he became a journalist in 1848, and in 1850 published the first of his books, *Social Statics*, following it in 1855 with *Principles of Psychology*. His major work was a series of books in which he expounded his theories of evolutionary philosophy, *First Principles*, *Principles of Biology*, *Principles of Ethics* and *Principles of Sociology*, the first volume of which was published in 1862 and the last in 1896.

Spender, Stephen (1909–) Stephen Harold Spender was born in London and educated at Oxford, where he became friendly with W.H. Auden and Louis MacNeice. He published his first volume of poetry, *Nine Experiments*, in 1928, and followed it with *Twenty Poems*, in 1930. Several other collections of verse appeared, and in 1955 he brought out his *Collected Poems 1928–1953*. He has also written a play, *Trial of a Judge*, short stories and novels. His wide range of non-fiction includes literary criticism, autobiography and works on politics and travel, while – mostly in collaboration with others – he has prepared a considerable number of translations from the

German, the French and the Spanish. For a time he was co-editor of the literary magazine *Horizon*, and later of *Encounter*. His *Journals 1939–83* appeared in 1985. He was knighted in 1983.

Spengler, Oswald (1880–1936) The German writer Oswald Spengler was born at Blankenburg in the Harz Mountains and educated at the universities of Munich and Berlin. His most striking work was *Der Untergang des Abendlandes* (*The Decline of the West*), published in two volumes in 1918 and 1922, in which he compared modern Western society with great civilizations of the past, noting similar symptoms of decay in each. His other books included *Der Mensch und die Technik* (*Man and Technics*), which appeared in 1931, and *Jahre der Entscheidung* (*Hour of Decision*), in 1934.

Spenser, Edmund (*c.*1552–99) The poet Edmund Spenser was born in London and educated at the Merchant Taylors' School and at Pembroke Hall, Cambridge. His first verses, which were translations from Petrarch and the French poet Du Bellay, were published in 1569 in an

The title-page of the 1611 edition of *The Faerie Queen*.

anthology, *Theatre for Worldlings*. Ten years later, after a period as secretary to the Bishop, he published *The Shepheardes Calendar*, which he dedicated to Sir Philip Sidney. In 1580 he became secretary to Lord Arthur Grey of Wilton, and went with him to Ireland, where Lord Grey spent two years in suppressing a rebellion with much violence and bloodshed. When Grey returned to England, Spenser remained in Ireland, becoming clerk to the council of Munster, and some time afterwards was granted three thousand acres of land and the castle of Kilcolman in County Cork as a reward for his part in the earlier campaign. He settled there and devoted himself to writing, working on his masterpiece, *The Faerie Queene*, the great poem which he had begun before leaving England. In 1589 Sir Walter Raleigh visited him and persuaded him to come to London, where the first three books of *The Faerie Queene* were published. The work was immediately successful, and Spenser was received at Queen Elizabeth's court and acclaimed as the finest poet of his age. He stayed in London for a year and then returned to Kilcolman, but not before arranging the publication of a pastoral elegy, *Daphnaida*, and a volume of short poems, *Complaints, Containing sundrie small Poemes of the Worlds Vanitie*. In 1595 he was back in London. In the meantime he had married Elizabeth Boyle, and he now published his *Amoretti*, a sequence of love sonnets, and the *Epithalamion*, regarded as the finest of his shorter works, in which he recorded his joy at the marriage. *Colin Clouts Come Home Againe*, which told of his earlier visit to the capital and return

An illustration by Walter Crane to Spenser's *Canto IX*. Crane's work, which is noted for its decorative borders and graceful calligraphy, skilfully complements the archaic lyrical verse of Edmund Spenser.

to Ireland, also appeared, and in 1596 he brought out the three remaining books of *The Faerie Queene*, his elegy for Sir Philip Sidney, *Astrophel*, the *Prothalamion* and *Fowre Hymns*. In this year he also wrote a *View of the Present State of Ireland*, but encountered censorship and was not able to publish it. In September, 1598, he was appointed sheriff of Cork. A month later his house and all his possessions were burned by rebels, and although he escaped without personal harm, when he came to London in December of that year it was to plead with the Queen for a new approach to the problem of maintaining the peace in Ireland. A few weeks later he was dead. He had been regarded as the greatest writer of the era, had received, at various times, the patronage of such eminent men as the Earl of Leicester and the Earl of Sussex, and had been smiled upon by the Queen herself. Nevertheless, he felt himself ill-rewarded, since his estates in Ireland had provided little more than a home, and, far from amassing a fortune from his published work, he might have been buried in a pauper's grave had not the Earl of Essex paid for his funeral in Westminster Abbey. For almost four centuries, however, he has been honoured as one of the finest of all English poets, and his reputation is undiminished today.

Spillane, Mickey (1918–) The American thriller writer Frank Morrison Spillane was working for a publisher when he decided that he could write a better book than those on which he was working. He published *I, the Jury* in 1947, and produced six more enormously successful 'tough-guy' stories featuring his 'private eye', Mike Hammer. A long silence followed, and then he began to write again and brought out a further series of stories notable for their violence and explicit sexual content.

Spinoza, Benedict de (1632–77) The Dutch philosopher Benedict Baruch de Spinoza was born in Amsterdam. Brought up as an Orthodox Jew, he was greatly influenced by the writing of Descartes, and his outspoken pantheistic views caused his expulsion from the commonwealth of Israel in 1656. In 1670 he brought out his *Tractatus theologico-politicus*, but little of his work was published during his lifetime, and his major book, *Ethics*, appeared posthumously in 1677, along with the uncompleted *Tractatus politicus*.

Spoils of Poynton, The A short novel by Henry James. It was first published in the *Atlantic Monthly* as *The Old Things*, but appeared under the present title in book form in 1896.

spoonerism The Reverend W.A. Spooner, who lived from 1844 to 1930 and was Warden of New College, Oxford, is celebrated for his frequent accidental transposition of the initial letters or sounds of neighbouring words, as when he announced a hymn as 'Kinquering Congs their titles take'. Properly called a 'metathesis', such an error is usually known as a 'Spoonerism'.

Spoon River Anthology, The A collection of verse epitaphs in which Edgar Lee Masters portrayed a small imaginary community in Illinois. It was first published in 1915.

Spring, Howard (1889–1968) The novelist Howard Robert Spring was born in Cardiff, Wales. He became a journalist, and later achieved considerable success with a number of popular novels, including *O Absalom!*, first published in 1938 (republished as *My Son, My Son!*) and *Fame is the Spur*, which appeared in 1940.

Stalky & Co A collection of partly autobiographical stories by Rudyard Kipling about a group of schoolboys, first published in 1899.

stanza Poems are often divided into stanzas, groups of lines in which each such group follows similar metrical and rhyming patterns. The term is often loosely used to describe any section of a poem separated from the lines preceding and following it.

Stead, Christina (1902–83) The Australian writer Christina Ellen Stead was born and educated in Sydney. Her first book, a collection of short stories, *The Salzburg Tales*, was published in 1934. She married an American, and many of her subsequent novels, which reflect both her feminist views and her strongly left-wing politics, were set in the United States, including her best-known work, *The Man who loved Children*, which appeared in 1940.

Steele, Richard (1672–1729) Born in Dublin and educated at the Charterhouse and Christ Church, Oxford, Richard Steele became a soldier and rose to the rank of captain. In 1701 he published *The Christian Hero*, a prose tract which brought him the favour of William III, and thereafter he turned to literature. His first play, a comedy called *The Funeral*, was successfully produced in 1701, and he followed it with two other plays. Then, in 1709, he founded *The Tatler*, in which enterprise he was assisted by his friend Joseph Addison, whom he had first met at school. The essays which the two of them wrote, although Addison's were the finer, set a high standard for this form of literature. *The Tatler* was succeeded by *The Spectator*, *The Guardian* and a number of other short-lived periodicals. Steele also published a number of pamphlets on political subjects. Meanwhile, he had become a Member of Parliament, and on the accession of George I he was given many appointments – among them Surveyor of the Royal Stables, Deputy-Lieutenant of Middlesex, Governor of the Royal Company of Comedians – and in 1715 he was knighted. *The Conscious Lovers*, a new comedy and his most popular work for the stage, was produced in 1722. Financial problems dogged him, and in 1724 he left public life and wrote no more.

The masthead of *The Tatler*.

Steffens, Lincoln (1866–1936) The journalist Joseph Lincoln Steffens was born in San Francisco and educated at the universities of California, Berlin, Heidelberg, Leipzig and Paris. He edited a number of periodicals, but became famous for his hard-hitting articles, two series of which, attacking corruption in city and state governments, were published as *The Shame of the Cities* and *The Struggle for Self-Government*. His *Autobiography* appeared in 1931.

Stein, Gertrude (1874–1946) The American writer Gertrude Stein was born in Pennsylvania and educated at Radcliffe College and Johns Hopkins University. In 1902 she went to Paris and lived there for the rest of her life, sharing her home from 1907 with her friend Alice B. Toklas. She became a well-known literary figure, and provided what might almost be described as a club for such expatriate writers as Ernest Hemingway and Sherwood Anderson and for artists such as Picasso and Matisse. In 1909 she published *Three Lives*, long stories about three women, and in 1914 came a volume of verse, *Tender Buttons*. *The Making of Americans*, published in 1925, was an exceptionally long work based on her own family. Her best-known book, *The Autobiography of Alice B. Toklas* (which was in fact a volume of her own memoirs), appeared in 1933, and she followed it with other reminiscences in *Everybody's Autobiography*, in 1938, *Paris France*, in 1940, and *Wars I Have Seen*, in 1945. Among her other works was a play, *Four Saints in Three Acts*, published in 1929 and produced in the United States five years later. Her work was highly individual, much given to repetition – 'a rose is a rose is a rose' – and to unpunctuated prose in the 'stream of consciousness' style.

Steinbeck, John (1902–68) John Ernest Steinbeck was born in Salinas, California, and educated at Stanford University. He published his first novel, *Cup of Gold*, about the pirate Henry Morgan, in 1929. He then began to write about the farming communities which provided him with the characters for so many of his novels. A collection of stories, *The Pastures of Heaven*, appeared in

John Steinbeck, Nobel Prize-winning author and rugged sportsman, at the Whaler's Festival, Sag Harbor, Long Island, New York in 1966.

1932, and the two novels *To a God Unknown* and *Tortilla Flat*, in 1933 and 1935 respectively. *In Dubious Battle*, the story of a strike in the Californian fruit industry, followed in 1936. He was well established as a writer by this time, but his reputation soared in 1936 with the publication of the short novel, *Of Mice and Men*, in which he presented a sympathetic portrait of two itinerant farm workers. After another volume of short stories, *The Long Valley*, he published in 1939 his most successful book, *The Grapes of Wrath*, which won the Pulitzer Prize. Many more novels were to follow, but he never managed to achieve as fine a book as *The Grapes of Wrath*, although *The Wayward Bus*, in 1947, and the family saga, *East of Eden*, in 1952, both sold in large quantities. He also wrote a number of non-fiction books, including *The Log of the Sea of Cortez*, in 1951, and a collection of his despatches as a war correspondent during World War II, published in 1958 as *Once There Was a War*. He was awarded the Nobel Prize for Literature in 1962.

Stendhal (1783–1842) Marie Henri Beyle, who used the pseudonym Stendhal, was born and educated in Grenoble, France. He went to Paris, and in 1800 followed Napoleon to Italy, where he was a witness at the Battle of Marengo, thereafter joining the army, in which he served for two years. This visit was the beginning of a long love affair with Italy, where he spent a large part of his life. From 1806 to 1814 he held an important position in the commissariat, but after Napoleon's defeat exiled himself to Milan. In 1814 he published his first book, on Haydn and Mozart, and this was followed by a number of works on a variety of subjects, including a history of painting in Italy, an essay on love, travel books and studies of Racine and Shakespeare. His first novel, *Armence*, appeared in 1827, and then in 1830 came *Le rouge et le noir, chronique du XIXe siècle* (*The Red and the Black, a Chronicle of the Nineteenth Century*). Although it was later regarded as a classic, it received little attention at the time, and it was not until 1839, when he brought out *La Chartreuse de Parme* (*The Charterhouse of Parma*), that he achieved any real measure of popular success. At the time of his death he left a great many unfinished manuscripts, including a number of autobiographical works. Stendhal had a great influence on the novel in France, and has been much admired as a forerunner of both the exponents of realism and the analytical school of writers.

Stephen, Leslie (1832–1904) The son of Sir James Stephen and brother of Sir James Fitzjames Stephen, both of whom were writers, Leslie Stephen was born in London and educated at

Eton and Cambridge. He wrote a large number of essays on a variety of subjects, including mountaineering, and edited the *Cornhill Magazine* from 1871 to 1872, after which he became the editor of the *Dictionary of National Biography*. In 1876 he published his major work, *The History of English Thought in the Eighteenth Century*. *The Science of Ethics*, which appeared in 1882, was also highly regarded at the time as an important contribution to philosophical history. He was knighted in 1902. He was the father of Virginia Woolf.

Stephens, James (1882–1950) A native of Dublin, James Stephens was an ardent campaigner for the independence of Ireland and the revival of Erse. His first volume of poetry, *Insurrections*, appeared in 1909. Many more collections of verse were to follow, but it was his fantasy novel, *The Crock of Gold*, which brought him great success when it appeared in 1912. He published a number of other novels and many short stories, and later became a popular broadcaster.

Stern, Richard Martin (1915–) The American novelist Richard Martin Stern published his first book, *The Bright Road to Fear*, in 1958. Many successful novels have followed, a number of them with a major disaster of some kind as the central theme. They include *Suspense*, which appeared in 1959, *Cry Havoc*, in 1963, *The Tower*, in 1973, *Flood*, in 1979, and *Wildfire*, in 1985.

Sterne, Laurence (1713–68) Born in Dublin and educated at Cambridge, Laurence Sterne became a clergyman. He lived as a country parson in Yorkshire, in charge of the two parishes of Sutton-in-the Forest and Stillington, for some twenty years before publishing the first two volumes of *The Life and Opinions of Tristram Shandy* in 1759. It was sensationally successful, and he became so much of a celebrity that even a collection of his sermons, published in 1760 as *The Sermons of Mr Yorick*, sold in huge quantities (though it must be admitted that, in Yorkshire at least, he had a reputation as an excellent preacher). He was presented with an additional living at Coxwold in Yorkshire, where he installed himself, his wife and his daughter – his many other children having all been stillborn. His marriage appears to have been less than happy, and his life was enlivened with many flirtations and amours. The extra income he now received allowed him not only to write but also to travel. A further four volumes of *Tristram Shandy* appeared in 1761, but his health had deteriorated – he suffered from tuberculosis – and in the following year he left England with his wife and daughter for the warmth of France, where he was much fêted in literary circles. He spent two

and a half years in the south of France, before returning briefly to England for the publication of the seventh and eighth books of *Tristram Shandy* in 1765. Later in the year he went back to France, visited his family, who had remained there during his trip to London, and then began a tour of France and Italy, which was later to provide material for his other major work, *A Sentimental Journey*. The final volume of *Tristram Shandy* came out in 1767. At the beginning of the following year he published the two volumes of *A Sentimental Journey through France and Italy* (although the journey does not in fact progress beyond Lyons, and it can only be surmised that he had intended to add further volumes had he lived). Having seen them through the press, he died in London in March. An early skit, *The History of a Warm Watch-Coat*, was published posthumously in 1769. Laurence Sterne was a writer of enormous originality. *Tristram Shandy* is a vast, sprawling, exuberant book, full of diversions from the main story, which itself is so

The writer and divine Laurence Sterne captured in classical pose by the famous portrait artist Sir Joshua Reynolds.

amorphous as to be almost impossible to summarize; it presents a gallery of the most engaging characters, including Tristram himself, his father Walter, his Uncle Toby, Corporal Trim and Parson Yorick; it is bawdy and sentimental, and it overflows with ironic wit and humour, the jokes often extending to the way the book is set out and to such devices as leaving a page blank so that the reader may draw his own picture of the Widow Wadman, who has designs upon Uncle Toby; on yet another level, it parodies all other fiction of its period. It can fairly claim to be the first truly comic novel in English, and Sterne is also seen as the father of the 'stream of consciousness' form of writing. The writers of the twentieth century who have used the 'stream of consciousness' technique have done so with great deliberation and care; it seems more likely that Sterne simply wrote down whatever thoughts came into his head. Fortunately, his genius was such that, whether by accident or design, he produced in *Tristram Shandy* a work of unique quality.

Stevens, Wallace (1878–1955) The American poet Wallace Stevens was born in Reading, Philadelphia, and educated at Harvard, after which he became a journalist and then an insurance lawyer, working in that capacity for the rest of his life. He began to publish his verse in the American magazine *Poetry*, and in 1923 brought out his first collection, *Harmonium*, which attracted considerable attention. Many other volumes of verse were to follow, including *Ideas of Order*, in 1936, *The Man With the Blue Guitar*, in 1937, *Parts of a World*, in 1942, and, in the same year, the book which many critics consider his masterpiece, *Notes Toward a Supreme Fiction*. *Esthétique du mal* appeared in 1945, *Transport to Summer* in 1947, *The Auroras of Autumn* in 1950, and his *Collected Poems* in 1954. *The Necessary Angel*, published in 1951, was a collection of essays, and *Opus Posthumous*, in 1957, combined poems and His work was acclaimed with a Pulitzer Prize and two National Book Awards.

Stevenson, Robert Louis (1850–94) A native of Edinburgh, Robert Louis (originally spelt Lewis) Balfour Stevenson was educated at Edinburgh University. He had originally intended to follow his father in a civil engineering career, but his fragile health forced him to abandon the idea. Instead he studied law, and was called to the bar in 1875. He did not practise, but travelled in Europe, and in 1878 and 1879 published his first books, *An Inland Voyage* and *Travels with a Donkey in the Cevennes*. In 1876, while in France, he had met Mrs Fanny Osbourne, and in 1879 he travelled to California to be with her. His

travels and the year he spent in the Napa Valley were described in *The Amateur Emigrant* and *The Silverado Squatters*. After her divorce he married Fanny, and they returned to Scotland in the autumn of 1880. His health was still poor, and he visited Switzerland on two occasions for that reason, but settled in the south of France in 1882. Meanwhile, he had begun his collaboration with W.E. Henley, which resulted in the production of four undistinguished plays, and had also published his collection of essays for young readers, *Virginibus puerisque*. More importantly, he had started work on his adventure story *The Sea-Cook*, which was later to become famous under the more familiar title, *Treasure Island*, first published in 1883. In the following year, after a severe illness, he left France and set up home in Bournemouth, on England's south coast. A number of works appeared in this period, including *A Child's Garden of Verses*, in 1885, and *The Strange Case of Dr Jekyll and Mr Hyde*, which, when it was published in 1886, enhanced the

A perceptive portrait by Sir William Blake Richmond of R.L. Stevenson, whose *Treasure Island* was first conceived to amuse his stepson.

popularity brought to him by *Treasure Island*. He scored another success in the same year with the publication of *Kidnapped*. His father died in 1887, and he set out, with his mother, his wife and his stepson, on a two-and-a-half-year journey, via the United States, Honolulu and the leper colony at Molokai, to Samoa, which was to be his last home. In the meantime he had completed *The Master of Ballantrae*, which was published in 1889, and had collaborated with his stepson, Lloyd Osbourne, in the first of the three works which they wrote together, a farcical romance entitled *The Wrong Box*, which also appeared in 1889. Before settling in Samoa, he went briefly to Australia, and there, upset by what he had seen at Molokai, published in 1890 *Father Damien: an Open Letter to the Rev. Dr Hyde of Honolulu*, in which he vehemently defended Father Damien and his efforts to help the lepers. In Samoa his health improved for a time; he was happy, and well enough to write a number of books, including *Catriona*, the sequel to *Kidnapped*, which was published in 1893, as was *Island Night's Entertainments*, a collection of three tales. In 1892 he had begun the book which many critics consider to be his masterpiece, *Weir of Hermiston*; he was still working on it on the day he died, and it was published in its uncompleted state in 1896. Stevenson has been accused of not taking his work seriously enough and of wasting his talent on popular romances. He was in fact more than merely a writer of adventure stories for boys, and such critical comments ignore his careful and graceful use of the language, the deeper meanings that can be found in much of his writing, and his sheer charm. In any case, it is perhaps sufficient to be 'Tusitala', as they called him in Samoa — 'the story-teller' — when he told stories so well.

Stoker, Bram (1847–1912) A native of Dublin, Abraham Stoker, after spending some years as a civil servant, became private secretary to the actor, Sir Henry Irving. He wrote several novels and short stories, including the classic tale of vampirism, *Dracula*, which was published in 1897.

Stone, Irving (1903–) The novelist Irving Stone, whose family was originally Tennebaum, was born in San Francisco and educated at the universities of California and South California. He wrote a number of detective stories before achieving considerable success with his fiction-alized biography of Vincent Van Gogh, *Lust for Life*, published in 1934. He has followed it with similar novels based on famous persons, including *The Agony and the Ecstasy* (Michelangelo), in 1961, *The Passions of the Mind* (Freud), in 1971, and *The Origin* (Darwin), in 1980.

Stones of Venice, The An architectural study, first published in three volumes between 1851 and 1853, in which John Ruskin not only examined the architecture of Venice, but also presented his views on the relationship between workers and employers.

Stoppard, Tom (1937–) One of the most highly regarded and successful of contemporary British dramatists, Tom Stoppard, who changed his original family name, Straussler, to that of his stepfather, was born in Czechoslovakia. His first play, *A Walk on Water*, was seen on television in 1963, but it was with *Rosencrantz and Guildenstern are Dead*, presented in 1966, that he had his first major success. Many other plays have followed, including *Jumpers*, in 1972, *Travesties*, in 1974, and *The Real Thing*, in 1982. He has written many plays for radio and television, notably *Squaring the Circle: Poland 1980–81*, which was seen on the small screen in 1984. His work is marked by great wit and verbal dexterity.

Story of Rimini, The A poem by Leigh Hunt, telling the story of Paolo and Francesca, first published in 1816.

Stout, Rex (1886–1975) Rex Todhunter Stout wrote a number of straight novels, including *How Like a God*, published in 1929, and *Forest Fire*, in 1933, before beginning a long series of mysteries with *Fer-de-Lance*, which appeared in 1934. Other books in this vein included *The League of Frightened Men*, in 1935, *Some Buried Caesar*, in 1939, *Murder by the Book*, in 1951, and *The Doorbell Rang*, in 1966. His detective was Nero Wolfe, the gourmet who solved all the crimes without stirring from his chair.

Stow, John (c.1525–1605) The antiquary and historian John Stow was a London tailor. In 1561 he published his first book, *The Woorkes of Geffrey Chaucer, newly printed with divers addicions whiche were never in printe before*, and four years later brought out his *Summarie of Englyshe Chronicles*. He edited and published a number of ancient histories, but his most important work was the *Survey of London*, published in 1598, which gives a fascinating picture of the capital in Elizabethan times.

Stowe, Harriet Beecher (1811–96) Harriet Elizabeth Beecher was born in Connecticut, the daughter of a Congregational minister. In 1832 she went with her father to Cincinnati and taught in the theological seminary there, of which he was head. In 1836 she married Calvin Ellis Stowe. Her first book, *The Mayflower*, a collection of stories and sketches, was published in 1843. She became passionately interested in the question of slavery, and her celebrated *Uncle Tom's Cabin* was serialized in *The National Era* and published

135,000 SETS, 270,000 VOLUMES SOLD.

UNCLE TOM'S CABIN

FOR SALE HERE.

AN EDITION FOR THE MILLION, COMPLETE IN 1 Vol., PRICE 37 1-2 CENTS.
" " IN GERMAN, IN 1 Vol., PRICE 50 CENTS.
" " IN 2 Vols., CLOTH, 6 PLATES, PRICE $1.50.
SUPERB ILLUSTRATED EDITION, IN 1 Vol., WITH 153 ENGRAVINGS.
PRICES FROM $2.50 TO $5.00.

The Greatest Book of the Age.

A contemporary advertisement for Uncle Tom's Cabin.

in book form in 1852. It was sensationally successful, and undoubtedly converted many of its readers to the anti-slavery cause. She continued to write prolifically, producing poems, essays, and a number of other novels, including *The Minister's Wooing*, which appeared in 1859. Nowadays *Uncle Tom's Cabin* is regarded as condescending in its often sentimental portrayal of Blacks, and the expression 'Uncle Tom-ism' is used critically to describe similar attitudes; nevertheless, in its day the book was a powerful and influential indictment of slavery.

Strachey, Lytton (1880–1932) Giles Lytton Strachey was born in London and educated at Liverpool University and Cambridge. He wrote for many periodicals and became a member of the Bloomsbury Group. In 1912 he published *Landmarks in French Literature*, and in 1918 came *Eminent Victorians*, his irreverent portraits of Cardinal Manning, Florence Nightingale, Dr Arnold and General Gordon. It was very successful, although more recently its value has been questioned. The rather more sympathetic biography, *Queen Victoria*, appeared in 1921, and in 1928 he brought out *Elizabeth and Essex: A Tragic History*.

stream of consciousness A term originally coined by the American philosopher William James to describe thought processes, and used in literature for the device by which a writer transcribes a character's thoughts in a literal style, often without punctuation and in all their natural confusion and lack of logical sequence. Laurence Sterne is sometimes said to have been the first novelist, in *Tristram Shandy*, to use the technique, but it is in the twentieth century that it has become prevalent, with James Joyce as its most noted exponent. The long section at the end of Joyce's *Ulysses*, presenting Molly Bloom's thought, is a perfect example.

Streetcar Named Desire, A A drama by Tennessee Williams, concerned with the moral and mental destruction of Blanche DuBois, a fading Southern belle. It was first presented in 1947.

Strickland, Agnes (1796–1874) Born in Suffolk, England, Agnes Strickland began her literary career with verse, but soon turned to royal biography and produced *The Lives of the Queens of England*, published in twelve volumes between 1840 and 1849. This was followed by the eight-volume *Lives of the Queens of Scotland*, between 1850 and 1859, a single book on *Bachelor Kings of England*, in 1861, and *Lives of the Last Four Stuart Princesses*, in 1872.

Strindberg, August (1849–1912) The Swedish writer Johan August Strindberg was born in Stockholm and educated briefly at Uppsala University. He worked as a teacher and an actor before turning to journalism. In 1879 he published *The Red Room*, a collection of bitter sketches of literary life in which his celebrated misogyny was evident. His play *Master Olof* was produced in 1878, and in the next decade he brought out two comedies, a number of novels and a volume of autobiography. His powerful drama, *The Father*, was presented in 1887, and in the following year came his best-known play, *Miss Julie*. Many more theatrical works followed, including a number of historical dramas, *The Dance of Death*, in 1901, and *The Ghost Sonata*, in 1907. His plays always had a profound psychological content, and both audiences of the period and the authorities found them so strong as to be shocking and even offensive. His personal life was unhappy; none of his three marriages lasted for long, and he suffered several attacks of mental derangement. Less than successful in his lifetime, his works, despite his pessimism and his anti-feminism, are now seen to have been of major importance in the history of modern drama, and he has had considerable influence on many later playwrights.

Struwwelpeter A cautionary tale for children, known in English as *Shock-Headed Peter*, by Heinrich Hoffmann, first published in 1847.

sturm und drang A term (literally 'storm and stress') used for many works in the German Romantic movement led by Goethe, Schiller and Herder. *Sturm und Drang* was the title of a melodrama by Friedrich Maximilian von Klinger, which gave its name to the movement.

Styron, William (1925–) Born in Newport News, Virginia, and educated at Duke University, William Styron published his first novel, *Lie Down in Darkness*, in 1951. His view of the Korean War resulted in a novella published in 1952. His next important work was *Set This House on Fire*, which appeared in 1960, and two major novels followed: in 1967 came *The Confessions of Nat Turner*, which won a Pulitzer Prize, about the revolt of a band of slaves in 1831; and in 1979 *Sophie's Choice*, in which he examined the relationship of an American Jew and a survivor from the Nazi concentration camps.

Suckling, John (1609–42) The English poet John Suckling was born in Middlesex to a well-to-do family and educated at Cambridge. He travelled in Europe and saw service as a soldier in Germany. A favourite at the court of Charles I, he was knighted in 1630. His later activities as a confirmed Royalist forced him into exile in France, where he is said to have committed suicide. He wrote three plays, of which *Aglaura* and *The Goblins* were both presented in 1638, while *Brennoralt, or the Discontented Colonel* was seen in 1639. The plays contained a number of lyrics, and it is largely on these verses that his reputation as a poet is based.

Sumer is icumen in The name, taken from its opening line, by which a thirteenth-century poem is known. It is believed to be the earliest lyric in English.

Summoned by Bells An autobiography in verse by John Betjeman, first published in 1960.

Sun Also Rises, The A novel by Ernest Hemingway, set in France and telling of the frustrated love between Lady Brett Ashley and the impotent Jake Barnes. It was first published in 1926, when it established Hemingway's reputation.

Suppliants, The Usually regarded as the oldest of the plays of Aeschylus which are still extant, *The Suppliants* was probably written about 490BC. It concerns the fifty daughters of Danaus and their attempts to avoid marriage with the fifty sons of their uncle, Aegyptus.

Surrey, Henry Howard, Earl of (c.1518–47) The son of the Duke of Norfolk, Henry Howard was cousin to both Anne Boleyn and Catherine Howard, and a courtier of Henry VIII. Although his early reputation was that of a wise and sober young man, he later spent a number of periods in prison for various misdemeanours, and was finally beheaded for treason. While in prison he wrote most of the poetry for which he is renowned. This was published after his death, together with works by Sir Thomas Wyatt, as *Songs and Sonettes written by the Ryght Honorable Lorde Henry Howard Late Earle of Surrey, and Other*. He also translated *The Aeneid* into blank verse, the first known use in English of this form.

Surtees, Robert Smith (1803–64) Born in Durham, England, Robert Smith Surtees became a journalist, and in 1832 founded *The New Sporting Magazine*, to which he contributed the pieces published in 1838 as *Jorrocks's Jaunts and Jollities*. The success of these humorous sketches prompted him to write many more books in similar vein, including *Mr Sponge's Sporting Tour*, which appeared in 1853, and *Mr Facey Romford's Hounds*, in 1865.

Swedenborg, Emanuel (1688–1772) The Swedish theosophist, philosopher and scientist Emanuel Swedberg was born in Stockholm and educated at Uppsala University. His surname was changed to Swedenborg when his family was ennobled in 1718. He worked as an engineer, but gradually became deeply concerned in spiritual matters and claimed to have received the word of God in the form of visions. In 1763 he published *Divine Love and Wisdom*, in which he set forth his views, and this and other works led to the founding of a Christian sect, the Swedenborg Society, which is still active.

Swift, Graham (1949–) The English novelist Graham Swift published his first novel, *The Sweet-Shop Owner*, in 1980, and followed it in 1981 with *Shuttlecock*. A volume of short stories, *Learning to Swim*, appeared in 1982, and he then produced the novel, *Waterland*, which, when it was published in 1983, established him as one of the leading novelists in England today.

Swift, Jonathan (1667–1745) The satirist Jonathan Swift was born in Dublin and educated at Kilkenny School and Trinity College, Dublin. He became secretary to a distant relative, Sir William Temple, but returned to Ireland in 1694 and was ordained and given a small living at Kilroot, near Belfast. He went back to Temple two years later, and in 1697 wrote *The Battle of the Books*, on the subject of whether ancient or modern writers are the greater. It was not published until 1704, at which time his satire *The Tale of a Tub* also appeared. In the meantime he had returned to Dublin, where he was attached to St Patrick's Cathedral, and began to write a series of pamphlets on political and religious themes. He visited London frequently and met many leading writers of the day, including the playwright William Congreve whom he had first

ABOVE: An illustration from *Gulliver's Travels*.

RIGHT: Jonathan Swift painted by Charles Jervas, *c*.1718.

known at school, and Addison and Steele. His comic attack on an astrologer, *The Vindication of Isaac Bickerstaff Esq.* appeared in 1709, and in the following year he began his *Journal to Stella*, a series of letters addressed to Esther Johnson, whom he had first met when she was a child, and her friend Rebecca Dingley, in which he described in detail his daily life in London and his literary and political activities. Pamphlets on a number of subjects continued to appear, and in 1714 they were particularly concerned with attacks on the Whigs. In that year he joined the Scriblerus Club, of which other prominent members were Pope, Gay and Arbuthnot, but the fall from power of his Tory friends led him to return to Ireland in August, where he took up his duties as Dean of St Patrick's, a position to which he had been appointed in 1713. He was soon involved in Irish affairs, and his anger against

the Whigs and their Irish policies found vent in the *Drapier's Letters*, published in 1724, which caused an uproar and succeeded in preventing an unscrupulous exploitation based on the Irish currency. Swift, who had believed he was doomed to obscurity, was very much in the public eye again, and two years later came *Travels Into Several Remote Nations of the World*, more familiarly known as *Gulliver's Travels*. He had been working on it for more than a decade, and it was written with high indignation against the follies of mankind, but was so entertaining that for generations readers have ignored the bitterness of the satire and enjoyed the book for its charm and humour. In 1729 he published *A Modest Proposal for Preventing the Children of Poor People from being a Burden to their Parents or the Country*, in which he suggested ironically that such children should be fattened and eaten.

A Complete Collection of Polite and Ingenious Conversation, which appeared in 1738, and his *Directions to Servants*, in 1745, were equally satirical. His vast output, which had also included much verse, was virtually over. In 1742 he became incapable of managing his affairs, declined into dementia, and lingered for three years before his death in 1745. He did not marry – unless there is truth in the story that he was secretly married in 1716 to his Stella – and the virulence of much of his writing suggests a difficult, cantankerous character. Yet he was greatly loved by the people of Dublin, and was mourned by his friends. Whatever kind of human being he was, his position as a stylist and as the pre-eminent satirist cannot be challenged.

Swinburne, Algernon (1837–1909) The English poet Algernon Charles Swinburne was born in London and educated at Eton and Oxford. In 1860 he published two verse dramas, *The Queen Mother* and *Rosamund*, and five years later attracted considerable attention with a verse tragedy, *Atalanta in Calydon*. His *Poems and Ballads*, published in 1866, became extremely popular, despite savage attacks from critics who considered them immoral. His next major poetic works were *Song of Italy*, which appeared in 1867, and *Songs Before Sunrise*, in 1871. He wrote a number of other verse plays, including the

A cartoon of Swinburne by Alfred Bryan.

trilogy *Chastelard*, *Bothwell* and *Mary Stuart*, and also produced two novels, only one of which, *Love's Cross-Currents*, was published in his lifetime. His literary criticism was of a high standard and had considerable influence – especially the *Note on Charlotte Brontë*, which appeared in 1877, and the two Shakespeare volumes, *Study of Shakespeare*, in 1880, and *The Age of Shakespeare*, in 1909. Among the many other collections of his verse were two more volumes of *Poems and Ballads*, in 1878 and 1889, *Tristram of Lyonesse*, in 1882, *A Century of Roundels*, in 1883, and *Miscellanies*, in 1886. His work is now often considered to be over-romantic and lush, but in his day he was seen as a poet who brought a new freedom in the use of imagery and in the intensity of the emotional content of his verses, while his revival of such forms as the rondeau and the ballade demonstrated his ability as an imaginative verse technician.

Swiss Family Robinson, The A story by Johann David Wyss of a family marooned on a desert island, first published in two volumes in 1812 and 1813.

Sword of Honour A trilogy of novels by Evelyn Waugh, consisting of *Men at Arms*, *Officers and Gentlemen* and *Unconditional Surrender*, first published between 1952 and 1961. Set during World War II, they tell the story of Guy Crouchback.

Sybil, or The Two Nations A novel by Benjamin Disraeli, the second in the trilogy of which the other books are *Coningsby* and *Tancred*. It was first published in 1845.

Sylvia's Lovers A novel by Mrs Gaskell, set during the Napoleonic Wars and first published in 1863.

Symonds, John Addington (1840–93) Born in Bristol, England, John Addington Symonds was educated at Harrow and Oxford. He published several collections of poetry and essays and wrote literary biographies of Shelley, Sir Philip Sidney, Ben Jonson, Walt Whitman and others. His major work was *Renaissance in Italy*, published in seven volumes between 1875 and 1886.

Symposium, The A dialogue by Plato describing a banquet at which Socrates, Aristophanes and others discuss love. It was from this work that the concept of Platonic love was derived.

Synge, J.M. (1871–1909) The Irish dramatist Edmund John Millington Synge was born near Dublin and educated at Trinity College, Dublin. After some years of travel in Europe, he went to the Aran Isles in 1898, and there wrote a series of portraits of the islanders, published in 1907 under the title *The Aran Islands*. He had earlier written two one-act plays, *The Shadow of the Glen* and *Riders to the Sea*, which were produced in

1903 and 1904 respectively, and he then became a director of the Abbey Theatre, Dublin, where his three-act play *The Well of the Saints* was presented in 1905. It was considered offensive, and the early performances in 1907 of his next play, *The Playboy of the Western World*, were interrupted by demonstrations, although its quality was later recognized and it became the most popular of his works. A farce, *The Tinker's Wedding*, was seen in the same year. In 1909 he published *Poems and Translations*. His last work, the play *Deirdre of the Sorrows*, was all but completed by the time of his death, and was first performed in 1910.

T

Tacitus (*c*.55–*c*.120) Nothing is known of the birth and early years of Cornelius Tacitus, and very little of his later life, yet he is regarded as the most eminent of Roman historians. Five of his works are still extant: his *Dialogue on Orators*, a *Life of Agricola*, a survey of *Germany*, and his most important writings, the *Histories* and the *Annals*. These last-mentioned books provide a history of Rome from AD14 to AD98 but are incomplete, since of the original manuscripts more than half have not survived.

Tale of a Tub, A A comedy by Ben Jonson, first performed in 1633.

Tale of a Tub, A A satire by Jonathan Swift, on corruptions in religion and learning, first published in 1704.

Tale of Two Cities, A A novel by Charles Dickens, set in London and Paris at the time of the French Revolution. It was first published in 1859.

Tales from Shakespeare A collection by Charles and Mary Lamb in which they told the stories of twenty of Shakespeare's plays for the benefit of young readers. It was first published in 1807.

Talisman, The An historical novel by Sir Walter Scott, set in the Holy Land during the Crusades, first published in 1825.

Tamburlaine the Great A tragedy in blank verse by Christopher Marlowe, probably first performed about 1597. It tells of Tamburlaine, the Scythian shepherd-chieftain who becomes a tyrannical monarch and conqueror.

Taming of the Shrew, The A comedy by William Shakespeare, in which Petruchio comes from Verona to Padua and woos and tames the shrew Katharina. It was probably first performed about 1592, and first printed in 1623.

Tam O'Shanter A poem by Robert Burns in which Tam is pursued by witches. It was first published in 1791.

Tancred A novel by Benjamin Disraeli, first published in 1847. It is the third part of the trilogy begun by *Coningsby* and *Sybil*.

Tarkington, Booth (1869–1946) Newton Booth Tarkington was born in Indianapolis and educated at Princeton. His first novel, *The Gentleman from Indiana*, was published in 1899, and was followed by the very successful romance, *Monsieur Beaucaire*, in 1900. He wrote some thirty other novels, including *The Magnificent Ambersons*, which appeared in 1918, and *Alice Adams*, in 1921, both winning Pulitzer Prizes. He also produced many short stories, essays and plays.

Tasso, Torquato (1544–95) The Italian poet Torquato Tasso was born at Sorrento. A precocious child, he had become renowned for his learning by the age of eight. In 1562 he brought out a poem, *Rinaldo*, which received great acclaim, and his next important work was a pastoral play, *Aminta*, which was very successful when presented in 1573. *Gerusalemme Liberata* (*Jerusalem Delivered*), an epic poem which appeared in 1581, is considered to be his masterpiece. He also wrote a number of odes and a tragedy, *Torrismondo*.

Tate, Allen (1899–1979) John Orley Allen Tate was born in Winchester, Kentucky, and educated at Vanderbilt University, Nashville. He published his first poetry, *Mr Pope and other poems*, in 1928, and it was followed by other volumes, including his *Collected Poems*, in 1977. He held the chair in poetry at the Library of Congress from 1934 to 1944. He also wrote a novel, *The Fathers*, as well as biographies of *Stonewall Jackson* and *Jefferson Davis*, and his several works of literary criticism were highly regarded.

Tate, Nahum (1652–1715) Born in Dublin and educated at Trinity College, Dublin, Nahum Tate published his first book of poems in 1677. He wrote a great deal of poetry and was appointed Poet Laureate in 1692, but is chiefly remembered, with ridicule, for his theatrical pieces, which consisted mainly of absurdly altered versions of works by the Elizabethan dramatists.

Tatler, The A periodical, appearing three times weekly, founded by Richard Steele, to which he and Addison contributed. The first number appeared in April, 1790, and it continued until January, 1711.

Taylor, Edward (*c*.1644–1729) Born in Leicester, England, Edward Taylor emigrated to Massachusetts in 1668, attended Harvard, and subsequently became a pastor and physician. He did not wish his poetry to be published, and it was not until 1937 that his work became known and he was revealed as a metaphysical poet of great distinction. Most notable are his religious poems, *Sacramental Meditations*.

Taylor, Elizabeth (1912–75) The English writer Elizabeth Taylor published her first novel, *At Mrs Lippincote's*, in 1945, and rapidly established a reputation for the elegance of her style and her meticulous observation of middle-class life. She wrote a number of other novels, the best known of which is *A Wreath of Roses*, which appeared in 1950, and also published several collections of short stories.

Taylor, Jeremy (1613–67) The English divine Jeremy Taylor was born in Cambridge, where he went to the university, taking holy orders in 1633. He became chaplain to Archbishop Laud and chaplain in ordinary to Charles I, and ended his life as Bishop of Dromore. He published several volumes of sermons and wrote many devotional books, the most notable of which were *The Rule and Exercise of Holy Living*, which appeared in 1650, *The Rule and Exercise of Holy Dying* in 1651, and *The Golden Grove: or a Manuall of Daily Prayers and Letanies*, in 1655. He is also remembered for his plea for tolerance, *A Discourse of the Liberty of Prophesying*, published in 1646.

Tempest, The A play by William Shakespeare, usually taken to be the last play of which he was the sole author. The exiled Duke of Milan, Prospero, lives on an island with his daughter Miranda and his servants Ariel, the spirit, and Caliban, the monster. The action develops when a shipwreck brings his usurping brother Antonio to the island. It was first presented in 1611, and published in 1623.

Tenant of Wildfell Hall, The The second novel by Anne Brontë, said to contain a fictional portrait of her brother Branwell. It was first published in 1848.

Tender is the Night A novel by F. Scott Fitzgerald, first published in 1934. It tells the story of a young American psychiatrist who falls in love with one of his patients, marries her, and is eventually corrupted by her wealth.

Tenniel, John (1820–1914) The illustrator and cartoonist John Tenniel was born in London. He worked for *Punch* for more than fifty years, for most of them as the magazine's chief cartoonist. He illustrated many books, most notably *Alice in Wonderland* and *Through the Looking Glass*. He was knighted in 1893.

Tennyson, Alfred (1809–92) The English poet Alfred Tennyson was born in Lincolnshire. He was educated first at a local grammar school, then by his father, and finally at Cambridge. His earliest published work appeared in 1827, along with verses by his brother Charles, in *Poems by Two Brothers*, and in 1830 he brought out *Poems, Chiefly Lyrical*, which, although several critics treated it harshly, revealed that a new young poet of great talent had arrived. At the end of 1832 a further volume of *Poems* appeared, containing, among other pieces, 'The Lady of Shalott', 'The Lotus Eaters', 'The Drama of Fair Women' and 'Œnone'. A few months later the sudden death of his close friend Arthur Hallam, who was later to be commemorated in *In Memoriam*, affected him deeply, and another blow fell in 1837 when the Tennysons were dispossessed of both their Lincolnshire home and the larger part of their income, which meant a postponement of his planned marriage to Emily Sellwood. In 1842 he published a two-volume collection of *Poems*, which contained revised versions of his earlier works and much that was new; with it his reputation was established, and he made the acquaintance of leading writers of the day, such as Dickens, Carlyle, and Elizabeth Barrett. Nevertheless, his financial difficulties continued, and he also had periods of poor health. *The Princess* appeared in 1847, and in 1850 came *In Memoriam A.H.H.*, which was not only a collection of elegies for Arthur Hallam, brought together in one long poem, but a statement of faith. It was extremely successful, and Tennyson was at last able to

A romantic image of the lyrical poet Tennyson by Samuel Laurence. His poetry reflects Victorian values and morality.

marry his Emily, and in the same year was appointed Poet Laureate in succession to Wordsworth. He wrote his 'Ode on the Death of the Duke of Wellington' in 1852 and 'The Charge of the Light Brigade' in 1854, by which time he had settled with his family at a house called Farringford in the Isle of Wight. *Maud* appeared in the following year and was another success, despite unfavourable reviews, and then in 1859 he published the first four sections of *Idylls of the King*, which brought him his greatest popular triumph, selling ten thousand copies in the first four weeks. He published further instalments in 1869, 1871 and 1872 and finally completed it in 1885. A dedicatory poem for the *Idylls*, in memory of the late Prince Albert, was published in 1862 and resulted in an audience with Queen Victoria, who admired him greatly and saw him regularly from that time on. Various other poems had appeared, including 'Enoch Arden', in 1864, and he then began to write verse dramas; none of these enjoyed much success, however, with the exception of *Becket*, when it was revived by Henry Irving and Ellen Terry in the year after Tennyson's death. *Ballads and other poems* was published in 1880, by which time he was living at a house called Aldworth in Surrey, and in 1884 he at last accepted the baronetcy which had been offered twice before, and became Baron Tennyson of Aldworth and Farringford. Three other major collections were still to appear: *Tiresias and other poems*, in 1885, *Demeter and other poems*, in 1889, and *The Death of Oenone and other poems*, in 1892, shortly after his death. The reputation which he enjoyed during his lifetime has not survived intact, and much of his narrative poetry has been dismissed as second-rate, but his lyrics are still greatly admired for their beauty and their atmospheric qualities.

Terence (*c*.190–159BC) The Roman playwright Publius Terentius Afer is said to have been born a slave in Carthage, but he was educated by his master Terentius Lucanus, whose name he later adopted. His first play, the *Andria*, was seen in 166BC, and he produced five more comedies before setting out on a voyage to Greece, from which he never returned. His work was largely based on earlier Greek models, but he brought to it an unprecedented depth of characterization, and was also much admired for the purity of his style.

Teresa, St (1515–82) Teresa de Cepeda was born at Avila, Spain, and at the age of eighteen became a Carmelite nun. She was subject to visions, and on the orders of her superiors wrote an account of them, as well as two treatises on mystical religion, *El camino de la perfección* (*The Way of*

Perfection) and *El castillo interior* (*The Castle of the Soul*). She founded a new, strict sect of the Carmelites, and wrote a history of the convents she founded. She was canonized in 1622.

Tess of the D'Urbervilles Sub-titled 'A Pure Woman', this novel by Thomas Hardy tells of the tragic life of Tess Durbeyfield, whose early seduction by the heartless Alec D'Urberville leads her at last to the hangman's rope. Often considered Hardy's finest novel, it was bitterly attacked as immoral when it was first published in 1891.

Thackeray, William Makepeace (1811–63) The son of a civil servant, Thackeray was born in Calcutta and educated at the Charterhouse and Trinity College, Cambridge. He then trained as a lawyer, purchased and edited a periodical, *The National Standard*, and, when it failed, spent a period studying art in Paris – he was later to illustrate much of his own work, including *Vanity Fair*. Before returning to London he was married in Paris to Isabella Shawe. He then took up a career as a journalist, contributing particularly to *Fraser's Magazine*, for which he wrote *The Yellow-plush Papers*, in 1837 and 1838, *Catherine*, in 1839, and *A Shabby Genteel Story*, in 1840. In 1836 he

William Thackeray, painted in dissolute repose by F.Stone, *c*.1839. Despite personal tragedy and an unrestrained lifestyle, he wrote outstanding satirical novels.

had published a small volume of sketches, *Flore et Zephyr*, but now, in 1840, came his first lengthy publication in book form, *A Paris Sketch Book*, by M.A. Titmarsh (Thackeray was much given to the use of pseudonyms, and Michael Angelo Titmarsh was the one he favoured most often). It was followed in 1841 by *The History of Mr Samuel Titmarsh and the Great Hoggarty Diamond*. At about this time his wife, who had given birth to three daughters, lost her sanity, a condition from which she never recovered. He continued to write prolifically, and in the next few years produced *Fitzboodle's Confessions and Professions*, *The Luck of Barry Lyndon* and *The Irish Sketch Book*. *Punch* had been founded in 1841, and soon after its first appearance he became a contributor, and it was in its pages that *The Diary of C. Jeames de la Pluche*, the *Snob Papers* (later called *The Book of Snobs*) and his parodies, *Punch's Prize Novelists*, appeared. His work so far had been largely of a comic nature, but in 1847 *Fraser's Magazine* published under his own name the first instalment of *Vanity Fair*, the novel which was to become his most popular and celebrated work. As each monthly part came out, ecstatic praise was

'Mrs Rawdon's departure from Paris', an illustration from Thackeray's *Vanity Fair*, the story of the adventuress Becky Sharp and her virtuous friend Amelia.

heaped on the book. The critical enthusiasm was not entirely reflected in the sales, but Thackeray was suddenly famous, and it was clear that he must continue as a novelist. *The History of Pendennis* followed in the years 1848 to 1850, *The History of Henry Esmond* in 1852, and *The Newcomes* between 1853 and 1855. He had also become a popular lecturer, both in Britain and in the United States, and collections of his lectures, *The English Humourists of the Eighteenth Century* and *The Four Georges*, later appeared in print. A totally different kind of book appeared in 1854; *The Rose and the Ring, A Fireside Pantomime for Great and Small Children* was a charming, burlesque fantasy which had its origins in drawings he had made for some of his young friends. In 1857 he stood for Parliament but failed to be elected by sixty-five votes. His next major novel was *The Virginians*, which appeared between 1857 and 1859, and in the latter year he became the first editor of *The Cornhill Magazine*. His last four works appeared in its pages: *Lovel the Widower*, a story which he had previously written in dramatic form as *The Wolves and the Lamb*, but which he had failed to get produced; *The Roundabout Papers*, a series of essays; the novel *The Adventures of Philip*, which was serialized between 1861 and 1862; and his last book, *Denis Duval*, which appeared between 1860 and 1863 but was uncompleted at the time of his death. Thackeray also wrote a number of ballads and poems, but it is as a novelist that he is remembered. It is perhaps unfortunate that, whereas no single Dickens novel can be said to overshadow the others, Vanity Fair is the one book by Thackeray that everyone knows, for all his serious work has a great deal to offer.

Theatre of the Absurd A term applied to a number of works for the stage by such playwrights as Ionesco, Beckett, Pinter, Albee and Genet, which seek to show the absurdity of the world and the incomprehension and despair with which humanity tries to cope with it. The Theatre of the Absurd frequently presents apparently meaningless situations, almost unidentified characters, and a complete lack of conventional exposition and development of the story.

Theocritus (*c*.308–*c*.240BC) The Greek poet Theocritus was born in Sicily and is credited as having been the first to write verses in the pastoral vein. Very little is known of his life, but he is believed to have visited the island of Cos, where some of his bucolic poems are set, and to have spent much of his life in Egypt. The existing poems are divided into three main groups, the *Bucolics* (set in the countryside) and the *Mimes* (set in towns), the *Epics* and the *Lyrics*.

Theroux, Paul (1941–) The American writer Paul Theroux, who lives in London, England, was born in Medford, Massachusetts. His first novel, *Waldo*, was published in 1967, and since then he has brought out many works of fiction, including the novels, *Jungle Lovers*, in 1971, and *O-Zone*, in 1986, and collections of short stories. He became celebrated in 1975 with the publication of *The Great Railway Bazaar*, an account of a journey by train from London to Tokyo and back, and he followed it with a similar record of a train journey to southern Argentina, *The Old Patagonian Express*, which appeared in 1979.

These Twain A novel by Arnold Bennett, the third in his 'Clayhanger' series, first published in 1916.

Thespis (Sixth century BC) Thespis, who came from Icaria, in Attica, Greece, is often considered to have been the originator of tragedy in the theatre, since he is believed to have been the first writer to separate one actor from the chorus, to become the 'answerer'. From his name the term 'Thespian' is derived, used to refer to the art of drama or to an actor.

Thiong'o, Ngugi Wa (1938–) Formerly known as James T. Ngugi, the Kenyan-born novelist Ngugi Wa Thiong'o was educated at the universities of Makerere and Leeds. His first novel, *Weep Not, Child*, was published in 1964, since when he has produced *The River Between*, in 1965, *A Grain of Wheat*, in 1967, and *Devil on the Cross* originally written in Kikuyu), in 1982.

Thomas, D.M. (1935–) Donald Michael Thomas was born in Cornwall, England, and educated at Oxford. He published his first poetry, *Two Voices*, in 1968, and a number of other volumes have appeared since, including his *Selected Poems*, in 1983. He has also translated the poetry of Akhmatova and Pushkin from the Russian. His novels include *The Flute Player*, in 1979, *Birthstone*, in 1980, *Ararat*, in 1983, *Swallow*, in 1984, *Summit*, in 1987, and, most notably, *The White Hotel*, which established his reputation when it appeared in 1981.

Thomas, Dylan (1914–53) The poet Dylan Marlais Thomas was born and educated in Swansea, Wales. After leaving school he worked as a journalist, and published a first volume of poetry, *Eighteen Poems*, in 1934. It was followed in 1936 by *Twenty-Five Poems*, and in the same year he married Caitlin Macnamara. *The Map of Love*, which appeared in 1939, contained a selection of both poetry and prose. The autobiographical sketches, *Portrait of the Artist as a Young Dog*, came out in 1940. During World War II he worked for the British Broadcasting Corporation, and then, in 1946, published *Deaths and Entrances*. His earlier poetry had been quite well received,

but it was this book which brought him a much wider public and greater popular success than he had had before, and his fame was increased by gossip about his Bohemian lifestyle and wild carousals. *In Country Sleep and other poems* came out in 1952, as did his *Collected Poems 1934–1952*. The remainder of his works appeared posthumously; these included a volume of previously unpublished verse and the collection of short stories, *Adventures in the Skin Trade*, both appearing in 1955. He built a considerable following in the United States, and it was there, on his fourth visit, that he died, shortly after taking part in a performance of *Under Milk Wood*, the poetic drama which presents portraits of the inhabitants of a small Welsh village, and which has become his best-known work. Intended to be read rather than staged, it was broadcast by the B.B.C. shortly after his death, but successful theatrical presentations have also taken place. Hostile critics have accused Dylan Thomas of obscurity and – despite the Welsh bard-like richness of his language – of a lack of emotional involvement, a fault attributed to his habit of meticulous revision. He was also charged, especially in *Under Milk Wood*, with sentimentality, but at his best he produced some excellent poems, and his work can truly be said to have 'helped to change the shape and significance of the universe', as he said good poetry should.

Thomas, Edward (1878–1916) Philip Edward Thomas was born in London and educated at Oxford. His early publications were in prose and included a novel, biographies and books about the countryside. A meeting with the American poet Robert Frost turned his mind to poetry, and some examples of his verse were published under the pseudonym Edward Eastaway. He was killed in action during World War I, and his *Collected Poems* did not appear until 1920, since when his work has been much admired.

Thomas, R.S. (1913–) The Reverend Ronald Stuart Thomas was born in Cardiff, Wales, and educated at University College, Bangor. He published his first volume of poetry, *The Stones of the Field*, in 1946, but did not attract attention until his fourth collection, *Song at the Year's Turning*, appeared in 1955. Several more volumes have followed, establishing him as a pastoral poet whose work reflects the Welsh country parishes in his charge.

Thomas à Kempis (*c.*1380–1471) Thomas Hammerken, who was born at Kempen, near Düsseldorf, Germany, took the name by which he is generally known, Thomas à Kempis, from his native town. He became a monk, and wrote a large number of religious tracts and other edifying works. He is remembered principally for his *De Imitatione Christi* (*The Imitation of Christ*), one of the most widely read books ever written on the Christian way of life.

Thompson, Francis (1860–1907) The English poet Francis Thompson was born in Lancashire and trained for the priesthood at Ushaw College, but having no vocation he turned first to medicine and then to literature. He suffered constantly from ill health, exacerbated by an addiction to opium. His first volume of *Poems*, published in 1893, contained his best-known work, 'The Hound of Heaven'. He brought out *Sister Songs* in 1885 and *New Poems* in 1897, and also wrote some biographies and essays.

Thomson, James (1700–48) Born in Roxburghshire, Scotland, James Thomson was educated at Edinburgh University. He wrote a number of tragedies and collaborated with David Mallet in a masque, *Alfred*. The song 'Rule Britannia', which was included in the masque, is believed to be by Thomson. His best-known work was the four-part poem *The Seasons*, published between 1726 and 1730.

Thoreau, Henry David (1817–62) A native of Concord, Massachusetts, Henry David Thoreau was educated at Harvard. After a short period as a teacher, he decided to become an author and lecturer, supplementing his income by working as a surveyor. He published his first book, *A Week on the Concord and Merrimack Rivers*, which described a boating expedition he had undertaken with his brother, in 1839. He became a disciple of the transcendentalist movement, and lived for some time in Ralph Waldo Emerson's house. In 1845 he built himself a hut on the shore of Walden Pond, near Concord, and set out to prove his belief that it was possible to live a totally independent life at the cost of comparatively little labour. For two years he grew his crops, occasionally undertook various small jobs, and devoted himself to the study of the animals, birds, fish and plants of the area. Few men have ever communed so deeply with Nature as he did, but the keenness of his observations, though those of an ordinary man rather than a scientist, were never marred by sentimentality. *Walden; or, Life in the Woods*, his account of his experiment, embodying his philosophy and written with great insight and in a polished style which sometimes approached the poetic, was published in 1854, and has since become recognized as a major work of literature. From 1847 onwards he travelled in New England and Canada, became much involved in the issues of slavery and of the individual's rights in opposition to those of the State, and wrote

The title-page of an early edition of *Walden*.

extensively. No other major works appeared during his lifetime, however (although mention should be made of the essays 'On the Duty of Civil Disobedience' and 'Life Without Principle'), and *The Maine Woods*, *Cape Cod* and *A Yankee in Canada* were all published posthumously, in 1863, 1865 and 1866 respectively. Collections of his verse also appeared. During the last years of his life he had been working on his *Journals*, which Emerson had originally encouraged him to write, and these were eventually seen in print, in fourteen volumes, as late as 1906. Thoreau's reputation rests principally on *Walden*, but his doctrine of the importance of the individual, as revealed in all his works, has been very influential.

Three Clerks, The A partly autobiographical novel by Anthony Trollope, first published in 1858.

Three Musketeers, The The historical novel by Alexandre Dumas, relating the adventures during the reign of Louis XIII of France of Athos, Porthos and Aramis, and of their Gascon friend D'Artagnan. It was first published between 1844 and 1845.

Three Sisters, The A drama by Anton Chekhov, presented in 1901 and centred around the attempts of the sisters Olga, Masha and Irina to prevent their sister-in-law from dispossessing them.

Through the Looking-Glass The second of the 'Alice' stories by Lewis Carroll, in which Alice is involved in a fantastic game of chess. It was first published in 1871.

Thubron, Colin (1939–) A descendant of John Dryden, Colin Thubron was born in London. After a period in publishing, he travelled widely and wrote five books about the Middle East. In 1983 his account of a journey across Russia, *Among the Russians*, was widely praised as an outstanding travel book. He has also received considerable critical acclaim for his novels, which include *A Cruel Madness*, published in 1984.

Thucydides (c.460–c.399BC) Comparatively little is known of the life of Thucydides, the Greek historian. He was an Athenian, and became a naval commander during the Peloponnesian War between Athens and Sparta, which lasted from 431 to 404BC, but from 423BC until his death he lived in Thrace. There he wrote his *History* of the war, which is noted for its careful attention to historical facts.

Thurber, James (1894–1961) James Grover Thurber was born in Columbus, Ohio, and educated at Ohio State University. After working for the US government in Washington and Paris, he became a journalist, and in 1927 joined the staff of *The New Yorker*, in which most of his work

James Thurber. His work comments satirically on modern American middle-class life.

first appeared. He excelled both as a humorous writer and as a cartoonist (his simple sketches of dogs and his savagely funny drawings of women were especially renowned), and in both genres he had a distinctive style which brought him an immense following. His first major work was *Is Sex Necessary?*, written in collaboration with E.B. White, which came out in 1929. He published a great many collections of short pieces, including *The Owl in the Attic, and Other Perplexities*, which appeared in 1931, *The Seal in my Bedroom*, in 1932, *The Middle Aged Man on the Flying Trapeze*, in 1935, *Let your Mind Alone*, in 1937, *Fables for Our Time and Famous Poems Illustrated*, in 1940, *My World — and Welcome to It!*, in 1942, and *The Beast in Me, and Other Animals*, in 1948. A second collaboration resulted in the successful comedy, *The Male Animal*, written with Elliot Nugent and produced in 1940. The autobiographical *My Life and Hard Times*, published in 1933, was equally comic, and he also wrote *The Years with Ross*, which came out in 1959, about the time he spent on *The New Yorker*. His most celebrated piece was the short story 'The Secret Life of Walter Mitty', which first appeared in 1942 and was later to be translated to the screen with Danny Kaye in the leading role.

Time Machine, The An early work of science fiction by H.G. Wells. It was his first novel, published in 1895.

Timon of Athens A play by William Shakespeare, telling the bitter story of a man who, deserted by his friends, turns misanthrope. Believed to have been written in collaboration with Thomas Middleton, it was probably seen for the first time about 1607, and was printed in 1623.

Tin Drum, The The most famous of the novels by Günter Grass, first published in 1959.

'Tis Pity She's a Whore A tragedy by John Ford on the theme of incest. It was first presented in 1633.

Titus Andronicus A tragedy by William Shakespeare, concerned with the terrible and intemperate revenge that Titus, a Roman general, takes upon his enemies. It was probably written about 1590, being one of Shakespeare's earliest plays, and was printed in 1594.

To a Skylark A lyrical poem by Percy Bysshe Shelley, written in 1820.

To Autumn The celebrated poem by John Keats, first published in 1820.

Tobacco Road A novel by Erskine Caldwell of decadence in the American Deep South, first published in 1932.

To Kill a Mocking Bird The bestselling novel by Harper Lee, first published in 1960. It tells of a father and his two motherless children, and is set in America's South.

Tolkien, J.R.R. (1892–1973) John Ronald Reuel Tolkien was born in Birmingham, England, and educated at Oxford. He became Professor of English Language and Literature at Oxford, and published a number of books on Middle English and also several volumes of verse. In 1937 he produced a book for children, *The Hobbit*, out of which developed the trilogy known as 'The Lord of the Rings', which appeared in 1954 and 1955. These stories of his fantasy world, Middle Earth, became immensely popular. A further volume about Middle Earth, *The Silmarillion*, appeared posthumously in 1977.

Tolstoy, Leo (1828–1910) Count Leo Nikolaevich Tolstoy was born to a family of the Russian nobility in a large country house, Yasnaya Polyana, near Toula in Central Russia. His mother died when he was three and his father when he was six, and he was brought up by aunts. At the age of fifteen he went to the University of Kazan, but having studied Eastern languages, law, religion and history, left in 1847 without taking a degree. After some months he joined the army, and it was then that he began to write. His first book, *Childhood*, appeared in 1852 in the magazine *Contemporary*, and before long *The Landlord's Morning* and *Boyhood* had also been published. In 1854 he took part in the siege of Sebastopol during the Crimean War, and his *Tales from Sebastopol*, which came out in 1855 and

Tolstoy was an influential factor in the social restlessness that swept Russia before the 1917 revolution.

1856, won him wide acclaim, and a command from Czar Nicholas that he should no longer serve in the front line, for fear that such a talent might be lost. *Youth*, completing the semi-autobiographical trilogy begun with *Childhood* and *Boyhood*, was published in 1857, and *Family Happiness* appeared in 1859. During the next four years he made three journeys abroad and also spent some time at the family estate, where, aware of changing attitudes, he freed all the serfs and started a school for the local peasants. In 1859 he published *Three Deaths*, and in 1863, a year after his marriage to Sophia Behrs, *The Cossacks* appeared. He now began both *War and Peace* and *Anna Karenina*, the former appearing in serial form between 1864 and 1869 and the latter between 1873 and 1877. Although Turgeniev, some ten years his senior, had been ready with his praise for *Tales from Sebastopol*, the attitudes of the two men had differed widely, and had led in 1864 to a violent quarrel; in 1878, however, convinced that he was dying, Tolstoy engineered a reconciliation. At this point religion and philosophical questions began increasingly to occupy his mind, and his next works reflected both his fervent Christianity and his growing socialist beliefs; these books included his auto-biography, *My Confessions*, published between 1879 and 1882, a number of short moral tales, and the novels *The Death of Ivan Ilyich*, in 1886, and *The Kreutzer Sonata*, in 1889. His socialism had persuaded him to renounce his estates in 1888, to work for the relief of famine during 1891 and 1892, and in 1895 to campaign on behalf of an oppressed sect, the Doukhobors. In support of their cause he wrote *Resurrection*, which was published in 1899 and resulted in his excommunication two years later because of the strong attack on the Orthodox Church which it contained. A last novel, *Hadji Murad*, appeared in 1905. In 1910 he decided to leave Yasnaya Polyana, and set out on a journey which ended suddenly with his death at Astapovo. Tolstoy's reputation as the greatest of all Russian novelists rests on the two great books, *War and Peace* and *Anna Karenina*. *War and Peace* is an epic story – a huge and colourful tapestry which provides a complex picture of the Russian nobility at the time of the Napoleonic wars, and gives us unforgettable characterizations in Peter Bezouchov, Prince André and Natasha Rostov; *Anna Karenina*, which some critics believe to be Tolstoy's finest book, is a superb study of an unhappy marriage, with the most profound insight into Anna herself, her husband Karenin, her lover Count Wronsky, and the secondary characters, Kitty Cherbatzky and Levine.

Tom Jones, The History of Henry Fielding's masterpiece was first published in 1749. The novel, one of the earliest examples in English of the genre, tells the story of a foundling who suffers many vicissitudes before finally overcoming his enemies.

Tom Sawyer, The Adventures of A novel by Mark Twain, telling of the adventures of young Tom Sawyer and his friend, the ebullient Huckleberry Finn. It was first published in 1876.

Tom Thumb, A Tragedy A farcical play by Henry Fielding, first presented in 1730.

Tono-Bungay A novel by H.G. Wells, centring on a quack inventor of a patent medicine, first published in 1909.

To the Lighthouse A novel, first published in 1927, by Virginia Woolf, in which she used effectively the 'stream of consciousness' technique. It is set mainly in the Hebrides and explores the relationships of the Ramsay family.

Tourgée, Albion W. (1838–1905) The novelist and politician Albion Winegar Tourgée was born in Ohio and educated at the University of Rochester, but left his studies to fight in the Civil War, after which he became involved in politics in the American South, where he was accused of corruption. He wrote a number of novels, including *'Toinette*, published in 1874, *Figs and Thistles* and *A Fool's Errand*, considered to be his best work, both in 1879, *Brick Without Straw*, in 1880, *John Eax and Mamelon*, in 1882, and *Hot Plowshares*, in 1883.

Toynbee, Arnold (1889–1975) Arnold Joseph Toynbee, nephew of the social reformer Arnold Toynbee, was born in London and educated at Winchester and Oxford. He became Professor of Byzantine and Modern Greek Language, History and Literature at London University. He published a number of works on historical and political subjects and several travel books, but his most important work was *A Study of History*, published in twelve volumes between 1934 and 1961.

tragedy A term used to describe a serious play which ends in the downfall or death of the central character or characters, or in disaster of some kind. There is often a moral element in tragedy, and in the early days of drama the principal character was frequently subject to the vengeance of the gods for some major misdemeanour. More recently, the unhappy ending is brought about directly by the character's own failings and actions.

Tragic Muse, The A novel by Henry James, about Lady Agnes Dormer and her concern for the future of her three children. It was first published in book form in 1890.

transcendentalism A philosophy developed by Ralph Waldo Emerson which was based on such premises as 'God is in every man', 'Nature is the incarnation of thought' and 'the purpose of life seems to be to acquaint man with himself'. Thus, every accepted religion was inadequate, since all human achievement was divine and each person could communicate directly with the Deity. The mystic character of the philosophy extended into the transcendentalist approach to social and economic questions, while the emphasis on self-sufficiency and the glories of Nature, epitomized in Thoreau's *Walden or Life in the Woods*, were profoundly influential.

Traveller, or a Prospect of Society, The A poem by Oliver Goldsmith, based on his travels in Europe, first published in 1764.

Travels Through France and Italy A malicious but entertaining account by Tobias Smollett of his journeys abroad between 1763 and 1765, first published in 1766.

Travels with a Donkey in the Cevennes An early book by Robert Louis Stevenson, charmingly describing his tour in southern France with the donkey Modestine. It was first published in 1879.

Traven, B. (c.1882–1969) The real name and identity of the mysterious B. Traven, about whom so little was known in his lifetime, and who was at one time thought to have been Berick Traven Torsvan, born in Chicago, has in recent years been revealed as Albert Otto Max Feige, born in Swiebodzin, Poland, of German origins. His first stories were published in Berlin, and in 1925 his novel, *The Death Ship* won him considerable fame. He then went to live in Mexico, and it was there that he wrote most of his novels and stories, including his best-known work, *The Treasure of Sierra Madre*, which appeared in 1935.

Treasure Island The perennially popular adventure story by Robert Louis Stevenson, originally entitled *The Sea-Cook*, in which young Jim Hawkins thwarts the villainous Long John Silver and eventually finds the lost treasure. It was first published in book form in 1883.

Treatise of Human Nature, A David Hume's major work of philosophy, first published in three volumes between 1739 and 1740.

Trevelyan, G.M. (1876–1962) The English historian George Macaulay Trevelyan was born in Stratford-upon-Avon and educated at Harrow and Cambridge. He published a number of books on English history and a major trilogy on Garibaldi, but is remembered chiefly as the author of *English Social History*, which became a bestseller when it was published in 1944.

Trevor, William (1928–) Born in County Cork, Ireland, and educated at Trinity College, Dublin,

William Trevor Cox has published a great many novels and short stories under the name William Trevor. His first book, *A Standard of Behaviour*, was published in 1956, and among his other novels, set mainly in Ireland, are *The Old Boys*, which appeared in 1964, *The Children of Dynmouth*, in 1976, and *Fools of Fortune*, in 1983. *The News from Ireland and other stories* appeared in 1986. He has also written several plays.

Trial, The A novel by Franz Kafka, first published in 1925, in which he was concerned with his constant theme of the individual in conflict with a faceless, irrational and all-powerful bureaucracy.

Trilby A novel by George du Maurier about an artist's model, Trilby O'Ferrall, who becomes a famous singer when under the hypnotic influence of the sinister Svengali. It was first published in 1894.

Trilling, Lionel (1905–75) The literary critic Lionel Trilling was born in New York City and educated at Columbia University. His first book was a study of *Matthew Arnold*, published in 1938, and a similar work on *E.M. Forster* appeared in 1943. His important work, *The Liberal Imagination*, came out in 1950, and *Sincerity and Authenticity* was warmly praised on its appearance in 1972.

triolet A verse form which uses two rhymes only in an eight-line stanza. The first line is repeated again in the fourth and seventh lines, and the second line is repeated in the eighth.

Trip to Scarborough, A A play by Richard Brinsley Sheridan, with music and songs, based on Vanbrugh's *The Relapse*. It was first presented in 1777.

Tristram of Lyonesse A poem by Algernon Swinburne, first published in 1882.

Tristram Shandy, The Life and Opinions of A long and leisurely humorous novel by Laurence Sterne. The story-line is vague, and of less importance than the numerous lengthy asides, flashbacks, jokes and parodies by which it is constantly interrupted. Apart from Tristram Shandy himself, the book introduces the memorable characters Uncle Toby and his servant, Corporal Trim. It was first published in nine volumes between 1759 and 1767.

Troilus and Cressida A tragedy by William Shakespeare, probably first performed in 1602, and printed in 1609. It tells the love story of Troilus and Cressida against a background of the siege of Troy.

Troilus and Criseyde A long poem by Geoffrey Chaucer, written somewhere between 1385 and 1390. It takes a highly moral attitude to the familiar story of the Greek lovers.

Trollope, Anthony (1815–82) The English novelist Anthony Trollope was born in London and

The Warden was the first book of the Barsetshire Chronicle series.

educated at Harrow and Winchester. After his father became bankrupt, his mother, Frances Trollope, supported the family by her writing, and his brother Thomas also became a successful author. Anthony Trollope's early years were unsettled, and he was constantly in trouble of some kind. He was no scholar, and obtained his first junior clerkship in the Post Office by the use of influence rather than by passing an examination. In 1841, however, he was transferred to Ireland, where he married three years later, and from that time began to build a successful career and, despite a somewhat dilatory approach to his work — he regularly took time off to indulge his passion for hunting — rose to a position of some eminence as a Post Office inspector, in which capacity he travelled widely. He is credited, incidentally, with the invention of the pillarbox as a receptacle for letters. Meanwhile, he had published his first three books, *The Macdermots of Ballycloran*, *The Kellys and the O'Kellys* and *La Vendée*, in 1847, 1848 and 1850, all without success, and had then gone on to bring out the first of his chronicles of Barsetshire, *The Warden*, in 1855, and *Barchester Towers*, in 1857, two books which established his reputation. *Doctor Thorne*, the third of the series, was published in 1858, and the fourth, *Framley Parsonage*, which appeared in 1861, set the seal on his popularity. He completed the sequence with *The Small House at Allington*, in 1864, and *The Last Chronicle of Barset*, which he firmly believed to be his best book, in 1867. His other major series of novels, the six Palliser books, which had a political theme, began in 1864 with *Can You Forgive Her?* and was completed in 1880 with *The Duke's Children*. In 1867 he retired from the Post Office, stood unsuccessfully for Parliament, and thereafter, apart from his travels to Australia and South Africa, devoted himself to writing, including journalism – he had helped to establish the *Fortnightly Review* in 1865, and he edited the *St Paul's Magazine* from 1867 to 1870. He produced well over fifty books in all, including volumes of short stories, biographies, literary studies, and travel books, in addition to the novels, the best of which include, as well as the Barsetshire and Palliser series, *The Bartrams*, in 1859, *Orley Farm*, in 1862, *The Way We Live Now*, in 1875, *The American Senator*, in 1877, and *Dr Wortle's School* and *Ayala's Angel*, both in 1881. His *Autobiography*, published posthumously in 1883, revealed that between 1859 and 1879, he had made close on £70,000 from his writing, a very considerable sum indeed for those days, and also described how, even while he was working for the Post Office, he had trained himself to produce three thousand words every day in a three-hour period early in the morning. Out of fashion for a time, his work has become greatly admired in recent years, and those who enjoy his lifelike characterizations, his brilliant evocation of the Victorian middle-class scene and his cleverly constructed plots may well wonder that so controlled and almost mechanical a method of writing should have produced work which, despite an occasionally over-mannered style, retains the vivacity and charm of its singularly acute observation.

Trollope, Frances (1780–1863) The mother of Anthony Trollope, Frances Milton married Thomas Trollope in 1809. After spending some years in America, the family returned to England, and when her husband was forced to flee to Belgium to escape bankruptcy, Frances Trollope turned to writing, publishing in 1832 her highly critical *Domestic Manners of the Americans*, which was hugely successful in Europe but aroused great anger in the United States. She went on to write similar studies of a number of European nations, and also produced several novels, the most popular of which, such as *The Vicar of Wrexhill*, published in 1837, successfully exploited her aptitude for comedy.

Trumpet Major, The A novel by Thomas Hardy, set during the Napoleonic wars and telling of the rivalry between John Loveday, the trumpet major, and his brother Bob, both of whom love Anne Garland. It was first published in 1882.

Ivan Turgeniev

Turgeniev, Ivan Sergeevich (1818–83) Born in Orel, Russia, the son of a nobleman, Ivan Sergeevich Turgeniev was educated at the University of St Petersburg. While he was still a student there, two of his poems were published in the periodical *Contemporary Notes*. He studied further at Berlin University, and in 1843 published, at his own expense, a long poem 'Parasha'. He then began to write short stories which were published in various magazines. Many of them pointed to the evils of the system of serfdom prevalent in Russia, and these were later collected under the title *A Sportsman's Sketches*. He went to Paris in 1847, and while there wrote a number of plays, the most popular of which is *A Month in the Country*, first seen in 1850. In that year he returned to Russia, and although he continued to write short stories, he now began work on the series of major novels which place him alongside Tolstoy and Dostoevsky as one of the three great nineteenth-century Russian masters of prose. In the remaining years of his life he travelled often and spent long periods abroad, making the acquaintance of most of the leading writers of the time in Western Europe, where his work was much admired and was, indeed, better known than that of either Tolstoy or Dostoevsky. The first of his novels, *Rudin*, was published in 1858, and in a period of considerable productivity he followed it with *A House of Gentlefolk*, in 1858, the powerful *On the Eve*, in 1859, and *First Love*, in 1860. *Fathers and Sons*, probably his best-known work, which is concerned with the revolt of a young student, Bazarov, against the reactionary aristocratic Russian régime, appeared between 1860 and 1861, and next came *Smoke*, between 1865 and 1866. His last novel, *Virgin Soil*, was published in 1877, five years before his death in Paris.

Turner, Frederick Jackson (1861–1932) The American historian Frederick Jackson Turner was born at Portage, Wisconsin, and educated at Wisconsin and Johns Hopkins Universities. He became an academic, teaching at Wisconsin University and Harvard. His most notable works were *The Frontier in American History*, published in 1920, and *The Significance of Sections of American History*, which appeared in 1932 and won him a posthumous Pulitzer Prize.

Turn of the Screw, The A short and chilling novel by Henry James, in which the narrator, a governess, strives to save her young charges, Miles and Flora, from the ghosts of the evil Peter Quint and his paramour, Miss Jessel. First published in 1898, it was later to become the basis for an opera by Benjamin Britten.

Tutuola, Amos (1920–) The Nigerian writer Amos Tutuola was born in Abeokuta. His first book to appear in print was *The Palm-Wine Drinkard*, in 1952. It was well received, and he went on to write a number of other books, including *My Life in the Bush of Ghosts*, which appeared in 1954, *Abaiyi and His Inherited Poverty*, in 1967, *The Witch Herbalist of the Remote Town*, in 1980, and *Pauper, Brawler and Slanderer*, in 1987.

Twain, Mark (1835–1910) Samuel Langhorne Clemens was born in Florida, Missouri. He received little formal education, became a journeyman printer, travelling right across the United States, and then worked on the river steamboats which plied the Mississippi, qualifying as a pilot in 1859. The outbreak of the Civil War in 1861 ended this career, and in the following year he set out with his brother for Nevada, where he tried his hand at journalism, and adopted his pseudonym, Mark Twain, from the cry of the riverboat sailors who sounded the depth of the river passages. He moved to San Francisco, and there met Bret Harte and worked with him on a local newspaper. His first real success came with his comic sketch, *The Celebrated Jumping Frog of Calaveras County*, which first appeared in 1865 in the *Saturday Press* and was used as the title story in a volume published in 1867, a book which immediately established him as a leading humorist. He attracted sufficient attention for a San Francisco paper to finance a voyage to the Mediterranean, which resulted in *The Innocents Abroad*, which was highly successful when it was published in 1869. He became, for a brief period, editor of a Buffalo newspaper, and then married, settled in New England, and devoted himself to

Huckleberry Finn

writing books. In 1872 he brought out an account of his experiences in Nevada, *Roughing It*, and next came a novel, *The Gilded Age*, written in collaboration with Charles Dudley Warner, which he then dramatized, while in 1876 he published his classic story, largely based on his own boyhood, *The Adventures of Tom Sawyer*. A tour in Germany was recorded in *A Tramp Abroad*, in 1880, and an earlier visit to England – he had become greatly in demand as a lecturer on both sides of the Atlantic – inspired him to write his story of the young Edward VI and the beggar boy Tom Canty, *The Prince and the Pauper*, which came out in 1882, while the following year saw the publication of the autobiographical *Life on the Mississippi*. At this period Twain became chief partner in the publishing firm Charles L. Webster & Co., and it was under this imprint that he published *The Adventures of Huckleberry Finn*, the sequel to *Tom Sawyer*. The joyous Huck Finn is one of the most engaging characters in literature, and his story is generally agreed to have been its author's masterpiece. *A Yankee at the Court of King Arthur* followed in 1889, and a novel, *The American Claimant*, in 1892. His publishing firm collapsed into bankruptcy in 1894, and for the next few years he struggled to pay off his debts. *Pudd'nhead Wilson*, another novel of the Mississippi, came out in 1894, *Personal Recollections of Joan of Arc*, an historical romance, in 1896, and another volume of travel sketches, *Following the Equator*, in 1897. He also tried to follow up his earlier success with *Tom Sawyer Abroad*, in 1894, and *Tom Sawyer Detective*, in 1896. A collection of tales and sketches, *The Man that Corrupted Hadleyburg*, was published in 1900, but thereafter he produced little of importance, partly, no doubt, because of family sadnesses – his wife died in 1904, and only one of his daughters survived him. Nevertheless, he continued to lecture and to write essays on a variety of subjects, and in 1906 he began the first instalments of his autobiography. Mark Twain's reputation is not simply that of a great humorist, or even of a chronicler of bygone days on the Mississippi; he was also a realist, and although he has sometimes been accused of sentimentality, the darker vein of bitter observation is often apparent, especially in his later work; even more importantly, he was an innovator – the first American writer truly to find a native tongue and to sweep away the obfuscation of the traditional writers of his time, replacing it with a sharp, economical style which reflected the characteristic ebullience of his nation.

Twelfth Night A comedy by William Shakespeare, in which various complications ensue when Viola, disguised as a young man, courts the Lady Olivia on behalf of Duke Orsino. The play introduces three of Shakespeare's finest comic creations, Sir Toby Belch, Sir Andrew Aguecheek, and the absurd and conceited Malvolio. It was first presented about 1601 and published in 1623.

Two Gentlemen of Verona A comedy by William Shakespeare, first seen about 1594 and printed in 1623. It is concerned with the loves and the misunderstandings between the two gentlemen, Valentine and Proteus, and their ladies, Julia and Silvia.

Two Noble Kinsmen, The A drama believed to have been written jointly about 1613 by John Fletcher and William Shakespeare.

Two on a Tower A somewhat melodramatic novel by Thomas Hardy, first published in 1882.

Tyndale, William (*c.*1495–1536) Believed to have been born in Gloucestershire, William Tyndale was educated at both Oxford and Cambridge. A cleric, he spent much of his life in conflict with the ecclesiastical authorities of the time, and was finally strangled and then burnt as a heretic. He wrote a number of Protestant tracts, but is remembered for his translation into English of the Bible, consisting of the New Testament and some chapters of the Old Testament. This work was substantially used in the subsequent preparation of the Authorized Version.

Typee, or a Peep at Polynesian Life Herman Melville's first novel, based on his experiences in the Marquesas Islands, and concerned with the adventures of two young sailors, Tommo and Toby. It was first published in 1846.

Tyrannick Love, or the Royal Martyr A drama about St Catherine by John Dryden, first presented in 1669.

U

Udall, Nicholas (1504–56) Born in Southampton and educated at Winchester and Oxford, Nicholas Udall became a schoolmaster. In later life he took charge first of Eton College and then of Westminster School. He lived a somewhat turbulent existence, and was at various times in serious trouble with the authorities. He translated Erasmus, Terence and others and wrote a number of plays, being chiefly remembered for *Ralph Roister Doister*, which was probably first presented in 1553 and is counted as the first comedy to be written in English.

Ulysses A novel by James Joyce, in which Stephen Dedalus and Leopold Bloom and his wife Molly are seen in a Dublin Odyssey. The whole action takes place during a single day, and ends within Molly Bloom's mind in a long chapter using the 'stream of consciousness' technique. The novel is experimental in its construction and its use of language and literary devices. Joyce's masterpiece, it was first published in Paris in 1922, but as a result of censorship was not freely available in the United States and Britain until 1937.

Uncle Silas A novel of murder and terror by Sheridan Le Fanu, first published in 1864.

Uncle Tom's Cabin The novel by Harriet Beecher Stowe which aroused anti-slavery emotion when it was published between 1851 and 1852. Its characters include Uncle Tom himself, Eliza, Little Eva and Topsy (who 'wasn't born, but growed').

Uncle Vanya A play by Anton Chekov presenting the comic and pathetic figure of the eponymous character, who has wasted his life in triviality. It was first performed in 1900.

Under Milk Wood: A Play for Voices The first performance of this evocation of a small Welsh town, Llareggub ('Bugger all' spelt backwards), took place in New York just before the death in 1953 of its author, Dylan Thomas.

Under the Greenwood Tree A romantic novel by Thomas Hardy, with a rural setting, telling the love story of Dick Dewy and Fancy Day. It was first published in 1872.

Undertones of War, The Edmund Blunden's classic account, in prose and verse, of his experiences as a soldier during World War I. It was first published in 1928.

Under Western Eyes A novel by Joseph Conrad. Concerned with Russian revolutionaries, it was first published in book form in 1911.

unities, the The unities of action, place and time were a dramatic convention based on comments in Aristotle's *Poetics*. They decreed that a play should have a single plot, that it should take place in one location, and that the timespan of the action should occupy no more than twenty-four hours (and preferably only twelve). The rules were never rigidly observed in the English theatre but retained their dominance elsewhere, particularly in France, until they were swept away by the Romantic movement.

Updike, John (1932–) The American writer John Hoyer Updike was born in Pennsylvania and educated at Harvard. He worked for *The New Yorker*, and in 1958 published a volume of verse, *The Carpentered Hen and Other Tame Creatures*, which appeared in England as *Hoping for a Hoopoe*. A novel, *The Poorhouse Fair*, and a collection of short stories, *The Same Door*, followed in 1959, and in 1960 he produced the bestselling novel, *Rabbit, Run*, which looked at the lives of Harry and Janice Angstrom in a small American town. He was later to complete their story in *Rabbit Redux*, which appeared in 1971, and *Rabbit is Rich*, in 1981. Meanwhile he had published a new collection of short stories, *Pigeon Feathers and other stories* in 1962, and then came *Centaur*, in which he explored the life of a schoolmaster and his relationship with his son. Published in 1963, it won the National Book Award. Since that time he has brought out several more collections of poetry, including *Telephone Poles*, in 1965, *Midpoint and other poems*, in 1969, *Tossing and Turning*, in 1977, and *Facing Nature*, in 1985. Among his volumes of short stories are *The Music School*, which won the O. Henry Award in 1966, *Museums and Women and other stories*, in 1972, and *Problems and other stories*, in 1979. He has also written a play, *Buchanan Dying*. His other major novels include *Couples*, in 1968, describing the sexual interplay between young marrieds in Tarbox, a Massachusetts town which has also featured in other books, *Marry Me*, in 1976, *The Coup*, in 1979 (in which he deserted his usual milieu to tell the story of a deposed African dictator), *The Witches of Eastwick*, in 1984, and *Roger's Version*, in 1986. Working in a powerful, if somewhat mannered, prose, he has captured more effectively than any other writer the essence of ordinary people in contemporary America, observing with a shrewd and sometimes satiric eye their attempts to come to terms with changing values and the stresses of modern life (and particularly the new sexual freedoms).

Uris, Leon (1924–) The novelist Leon Marcus Uris was born in Baltimore. He served in World War II, and published his first book, *Battle Cry*, in 1953. *Exodus*, which appeared in 1958 and was a fictionalized version of the founding of Israel, was immensely successful. Among the bestselling novels he has written since are *Mila 18*, published in 1961, *QB VII*, in 1970, *Trinity*, in 1976, and *The Hai*, in 1984.

Urn Burial An archeological treatise by Sir Thomas Browne, first published in 1658. Otherwise called *Hydriotaphia*, it develops into a sermon on Christianity.

Urquhart, Thomas (1611–60) The son of Sir Thomas Urquhart of Cromarty, Thomas Urquhart was educated in Aberdeen, Scotland. He travelled widely, serving the Royalist cause, and was knighted by Charles I in 1641. In 1652 and 1653 he published a genealogy which traced his family back to Adam, a curious tract about a lost jewel which turns out to be a missing manuscript, and a treatise on the need for a universal language. He is chiefly remembered for his translations of the works of Rabelais, two volumes of which appeared in 1653 and a third, posthumously, in 1693.

Utopia Thomas More's celebrated work, written in Latin and first published in 1516. Utopia, which means 'Nowhere land', is a country in which all are equal, education is universal and complete freedom exists in regard to religion.

V

Vallejo, César (1892–1938) The Peruvian poet César Abraham Vallejo was educated at the University of Trujillo and studied law. His first book was *Los heraldos negros* (*The Black Heralds*), published in 1918. It was followed in 1922 by a volume of short stories, *Escalas melografiadas* (*Musical Scales*), and a collection of poems, *Trilce*. In the following year he published a novel, *Fabula salvaje* (*Savage Story*), and then went to Europe. He was expelled from France as a militant Marxist in 1930 and went to Spain, returning to Paris two years later. In 1931 he published a novel, *El tungsteno* (*Tungsten*), and his *Poemas humanos* (*Human Poems*) appeared in 1938.

Vanbrugh, John (1664–1726) The architect and playwright John Vanbrugh was born in London. He went to France to study art, became a soldier while he was there, and was later arrested on a charge of espionage. He spent four years in a French prison, and, during his imprisonment he turned to writing for the theatre. When he returned to England his comedy *The Relapse, or Virtue in Danger* was produced in 1696, and was hugely successful. He followed it in 1697 with *The Provok'd Wife*, and among his other plays is

The Confederacy, first seen in 1705. Thereafter he devoted himself to architecture, designing Castle Howard, Blenheim Palace, and a number of other buildings. He was knighted in 1714.

Van der Post, Laurens (1906–) Laurens van der Post was born in South Africa and educated in Bloemfontein. His first novel, *In a Province*, was published in 1934, and he has since produced many others, including *A Bar of Shadow*, in 1952, *Flamingo Feather*, in 1955, and *A Far-Off Place*, in 1974. He has also written a number of travel books and studies of South Africa, such as *Venture to the Interior*, which appeared in 1952, *The Lost World of the Kalahari*, in 1958, and *Creative Art in Primitive Man*, in 1956.

Van Dine, S.S. (1888–1939) Willard Huntington Wright, who was born in Charlottesville, Pennsylvania, and educated at Harvard, used the pen name S.S. Van Dine for the crime stories he wrote. A literary, art, drama and music critic, he published a number of books under his own name, including *Songs of Youth*, in 1913, *What Nietzsche Thought*, in 1914, and *The Future of Painting*, in 1923. The first of his mysteries featuring his detective Philo Vance was *The Benson Murder Case*, which appeared in 1926. Among the others were *The Scarab Murder Case*, in 1930, *The Dragon Murder Case*, in 1935, and *The Powwow Murder Case*, in 1939.

Van Druten, John (1901–57) Born in London and educated at London University, John William Van Druten became a naturalized American citizen in 1944. He scored a great success with his first drama, *Young Woodley*, produced in 1928, and thereafter wrote many successful plays, including *After All*, in 1929, *The Voice of the Turtle*, in 1943, *I Remember Mama* (adapted from the book by Kathryn Forbes), in 1944, *Bell, Book and Candle*, in 1950, and *I Am a Camera* (adapted from Christopher Isherwood's Berlin stories), in 1951. He also wrote a number of novels.

Vanity Fair William Makepeace Thackeray's most famous novel, set at the time of the Napoleonic wars, and telling the story of the adventuress Becky Sharp and her gentler friend Amelia Sedley. It was first published in book form in 1848.

Vargas Llosa, Mario (1936–) Jorge Mario Pedro Vargas Llosa was born in Arequipa, Peru, and educated in Bolivia and Lima. His first published work was a play, *La huida del Inca* (*The Escape of the Inca*), which appeared in 1952. His first novel, *La cuidad y los perros* (translated as *The Time of the Hero*) enjoyed a wide success when it was published in 1963. Among his other novels are *La casa verde* (*The Green House*), which came out in 1966, *Conversación en la catedral* (*Conversation in the Cathedral*), in 1969, and *La tía Julia y el escribidor*

(*Aunt Julia and the Scriptwriter*) in 1977. He has also written short stories, essays and literary criticism.

Vaughan, Henry (1622–95) The metaphysical poet Henry Vaughan was born in Wales, and he and his twin brother Thomas both studied at Oxford. He then became a doctor of medicine, practising in Breconshire, and is believed to have fought for the Royalist cause during the Civil War. In 1646 he published his first volume of poetry, *Poems, with the Tenth Satyr of Juvenal Englished*, and it was followed in 1651 by *Olor Iscanus* (*The Swan of Usk*), both books containing love poems and translations from the Latin. *Olor Iscanus*, which had been completed by 1645, was published without his consent, probably because since writing the verses he had, under the influence of George Herbert, undergone a religious conversion. In 1650 he brought out his major work, *Silex Scintillans: or Sacred Poems and Pious Ejaculations*, which demonstrated in their style not only his debt to Herbert but also his admiration of John Donne. His next book, *The Mount of Olives: or Solitary Devotions*, appeared in 1652, and two years later he published *Flores Solitudinis*, consisting of prose translations of various devotional works, together with a life of Paulinus of Nola. He also translated *Hermetical Physick* and *The Chymists Key*, both by **Henricus Nollius**. His last publication, which appeared in 1678, was *Thalia Rediviva; The Pass-Times and Diversions of a Country Muse*, which included poems by his twin brother in addition to his own.

Vega Carpio, Lope de (1562–1635) The Spanish playwright and poet Lope Felix de Vega Carpio was born in Madrid and educated there and at the University of Alcalá de Henares. He went on an expedition to the Azores, and in 1588 sailed with the Armada against England, but then devoted himself to an extraordinarily prolific career as a dramatist. According to his own account, by 1632 he had written fifteen hundred plays on immensely varied subjects – the total may have been considerably higher. Of these, fewer than a third have survived. He is regarded as the father of the Spanish drama, having not only brought a regular form to the genre but set a fine example in the construction of his plots. He also produced a vast amount of poetry, including pastorals, sonnets and odes.

Vein of Iron A novel by Ellen Glasgow about a Virginia family, first published in 1935.

Venetia A novel by Benjamin Disraeli, first published in 1837.

Venice Preserv'd, or a Plot Discovered A tragedy in blank verse by Thomas Otway, first presented in 1682.

Venus and Adonis A poem by William Shakespeare, first published in 1593. It tells of the unrequited love of the goddess for the handsome youth, and of his death while hunting.

Verne, Jules (1828–1905) Born in Nantes, Jules Verne began his literary career by writing librettos for comic operas, but soon turned to the novels of imaginary journeys for which he became famous, and which are regarded as early examples of science fiction. These include *A Journey to the Centre of the Earth*, which appeared in 1864, *Twenty Thousand Leagues under the Sea*, in 1869, and *Around the World in Eighty Days*, in 1872. He is credited with having foreseen many modern scientific developments, but it has to be said that his imagination was of a higher calibre than his science.

Very, Jones (*c*.1813–80) The poet Jones Very was born in Salem, Massachusetts, and educated at Harvard. He was afflicted by religious mania, and for a period was confined in an asylum. In 1839 he published *Essays and Poems*, and a further volume of poetry was published posthumously in 1883.

Vicar of Wakefield, The A novel by Oliver Goldsmith recounting the misfortunes and final vindication of the parson Dr Primrose. It was first published in 1766.

Victory A dramatic novel by Joseph Conrad, set in the East Indies on the island of Samburan, first published in 1915.

Vidal, Gore (1925–) The American writer Gore Vidal was born in West Point, New York, and educated at the University of New Hampshire. After serving in World War II, he published his first novel, *Willawaw*, in 1946. His third work of fiction, *The City and the Pillar*, brought him fame when it appeared in 1948, at least in part because of its frank homosexual theme. A number of other novels followed, including *Dark Green, Bright Red*, in 1950, and *The Judgment of Paris*, in 1952. A play, *The Best Man*, was presented in 1960, and two years later he published his first collection of essays, *Rocking the Boat*. His essays have also appeared in *Reflections of a Sinking Ship*, in 1962, *Matters of Fact and Matters of Fiction*, in 1977, and *Pink Triangle and Yellow Star and Other Essays*, in 1982. He has also produced a number of satirical works, including *Washington DC*, which came out in 1964, and the controversial novel *Myra Breckinridge*, published in 1968. The novel *Lincoln*, a recreation of nineteenth-century history in the United States, was published in 1984 and is his most ambitious work to date. A travel book, *Vidal in Venice*, appeared in 1985. His reputation is that of a particularly sharp-eyed observer of contemporary America.

Vile Bodies A satirical novel of London society by Evelyn Waugh, first published in 1930.

Village, The A long poem by George Crabbe, realistic rather than romantic in its view of country life. It was first published in 1783.

villanelle A verse form consisting, usually, of five three-line stanzas, in which only two rhymes are used throughout, one for the first and third lines, and the other for all the second lines. The first and third lines of the first stanza are repeated alternately as the last line of the second, third, fourth and fifth stanzas. The villanelle is completed by a four-line stanza, in which the last two lines repeat again the first and third lines of the first stanza.

Villette A novel by Charlotte Brontë, first published in 1853. It reflects the author's experiences as a governess in Belgium, but also contains some elements of the supernatural.

Villon, François (1431–63, or later) Little is known of the early life of the French poet François Villon, except that he was educated at the University of Paris, becoming Master of Arts in 1452. He appears to have lived violently and criminally: several times he suffered banishment or imprisonment, and once he was condemned to death, although the sentence was commuted to banishment. This last brush with the law took place in 1463, after which there is no clear record of his subsequent life. He may have died soon after or have lived to as late as 1489. He wrote two major works, known as the *Petit testament* and the *Grand testament*, the former being completed in about 1456 and the latter in 1461. They consist of poetry, mainly in stanzas of eight octosyllabic lines, but also contain ballades and rondeaus. The *Grand testament*, in which the poet often laments his wasted life, contains the 'Ballade des dames du temps jadis' with the celebrated repeated line 'Mais où sont les neiges d'antan?' ('Where are the snows of yesteryear?'). Some other short poems have survived, but some critics have doubted whether they can authentically be attributed to Villon. He is regarded as the most important of all the French medieval poets, not so much because of any innovation in his verse forms, but because of the depth of emotion and personal involvement which he brought to his work, and because of the outstanding beauty of many of his best poems.

Virgil (70–19BC) Publius Vergilius Maro was born near Mantua and educated in Cremona, Milan and Rome. His pastoral poems, the *Eclogues*, were first published about 37BC. Modelled on Greek pastorals, they already showed an individuality of tone, and he developed his personal style in the *Georgics*, which were composed during the next seven years, and in which he again took rural life as his subject, demonstrating his great affection for his native land. For the rest of his life, residing quietly in Campania, he worked on his great epic poem, the *Aeneid*. Having finished it, he set out for Greece, intending to revise the work while there, but the Emperor Augustus persuaded him to return to Italy, and shortly afterwards he died. He had left instructions that the *Aeneid* and any other unpublished writings were to be burnt, but fortunately Augustus overruled that wish. Virgil was greatly admired during his lifetime, and if all that remained of his work had been the *Eclogues* and the *Georgics* he would still be regarded as a poet of outstanding quality, but the *Aeneid*, which tells the story of Aeneas after the fall of Troy, his wanderings and his founding of Rome, is one of the world's finest epics. It raised him to the position of the greatest of all Roman poets, and one of the most important in all literature.

Virginian, The The famous novel of the American West by Owen Wister, first published in 1902. It can be considered the prototype for the thousands of Westerns which have appeared since.

Virginians, The A novel by William Makepeace Thackeray, first published between 1857 and 1859. It is a sequel to *The History of Henry Esmond*.

Vittoria A novel by George Meredith, set in Italy during the revolution of 1848 and 1849, first published in 1867.

Vivian Grey Benjamin Disraeli's first novel, and the first volume in the trilogy completed by *Alroy* and *Contarini Fleming*. It was published between 1826 and 1827.

Volpone, or The Fox A comedy by Ben Jonson, in which greed and double-dealing are the main elements. It was first performed about 1605.

Voltaire (1694–1778) François-Marie Arouet, who used the pseudonym Voltaire, was born in Paris and educated by the Jesuits. His literary career began with a drama, *Oedipe*, successfully performed in 1718. He wrote numerous other plays, the best of which was probably *Zaïre*, which appeared in 1832, and two long poems, *La Henriade*, an epic on the subject of Henry of Navarre, and *La Pucelle*, an anti-religious work, but he is remembered chiefly as the witty and often vituperative author of satirical and moralistic essays, letters and other works. Notable among these were the *Lettres sur les anglais*, inspired by a visit to England, in which he attacked the institutions of France, the two novels, *Zadig*, published in 1747, and the celebrated *Candide*, which appeared in 1759.

Vonnegut, Kurt (1922–) Kurt Vonnegut, Jr. was born in Indianapolis and educated at the universities of Cornell, Chicago and Tennessee. During World War II he was captured in battle by the Germans and interned at Dresden, where he witnessed the destruction of the city by Allied bombers, an event which affected him deeply. He published his first novel, *Player Piano*, in 1952, and followed it in 1959 and 1963 with the satirical science fiction novels, *Cat's Cradle* and *The Sirens of Titan*. A collection of short stories, *Welcome to the Monkey House*, appeared in 1968. His reputation was already high when in 1969 he produced *Slaughterhouse-Five or The Children's Crusade*, which reflected his Dresden experiences and became something of a cult book, especially among younger readers. Since then he has published several more novels, including *Between Time and Timbuktu*, in 1972, *Wampeters, Foma and Granfalloons*, in 1974, *Slapstick*, in 1976, *Jailbird*, in 1979, *Palm Sunday*, in 1981, and *Galapagos*, in 1985. His work is intelligent, witty and purposeful.

W

Wain, John (1925–) The English writer John Barrington Wain was born in Stoke-on-Trent and educated at Oxford. His first novel, *Hurry On Down*, was published in 1953, and like much other work of the period reflected the new social attitudes which had followed World War II. He has since published numerous novels, some volumes of poetry, an autobiography and a biography of Samuel Johnson. He published a volume of reminiscences, *Dear Shadows*, in 1986.

Waiting for Godot A seminal allegorical play in which the tramps Vladimir and Estragon wait vainly for the arrival of the mysterious Godot. This outstanding example of the Theatre of the Absurd by Samuel Beckett was first presented in the original French in Paris in 1953, and received its première in English in 1955.

Waiting for Lefty A play about a taxi-drivers' strike by Clifford Odets, first performed in 1935.

Walcott, Derek (1930–) The poet and playwright Derek Alton Walcott, regarded as perhaps the most important of contemporary West Indian writers, was born in St Lucia and educated at the University of the West Indies. His first publication was *Twenty-Five Poems*, in 1948. Several other collections of verse have appeared since, including *In a Green Night: Poems 1948-1960*, which was widely acclaimed when it came out in 1962. He has written a large number of plays, among which are *Henri Christophe: A Chronicle*, first seen in 1950, and *O Babylon!*, in 1976. He is the founder of the Trinidad Theatre Workshop.

Walden, or Life in the Woods The influencial account of the two years which Henry Thoreau spent in living a simple, self-sufficient life and studying Nature. It was first published in 1854.

Waley, Arthur (1889–1966) Arthur David Schloss, who later adopted his mother's family name, was born in Kent, England, and educated at Rugby and Cambridge. He became celebrated as a translator and interpreter of Chinese and Japanese literature. Among his best-known publications are the English versions of *A hundred and seventy Chinese Poems*, which appeared in 1918, and *The Tale of Genji*, published in six volumes between in 1925 and 1933.

Walker, Alice (1944–) The Black poet, novelist and critic Alice Walker was born in Eatonton, Georgia. She has published several volumes of poetry, including *Once, Revolutionary Petunias, Goodnight, Willie Lee, I'll See You in the Morning* and, most recently, *Horses Make a Landscape Look More Beautiful*. Her first novel, *The Third Life of Grange Copeland*, appeared in 1970, and her next, *Meridian*, in 1976. The novel *The Color Purple*, published in 1983, brought her wide acclaim; it won a Pulitzer Prize and the National Book Award, and became a very successful film. Also in 1983 she brought out *In Search of Our Mother's Garden: Womanist Prose*. A volume of short stories, *In Love and Trouble*, appeared in 1984.

Wallace, Edgar (1875–1932) The extremely prolific English thriller writer Richard Horatio Edgar Wallace was born and educated in London. He became a journalist and published his first book, *Songs*, in 1895. He wrote plays, a very large number of crime stories, the most famous of which was probably *The Four Just Men*, published in 1905, and between 1905 and 1911 produced a series of books, set in Africa, about his character Sanders of the River. At the time of his death he was in Hollywood, working on the script of the movie *King Kong*.

Wallace, Irving (1916–) The novelist Irving Wallace, whose family name is Wallechinsky, was born of Russian Jewish parents and brought up in Wisconsin. He published hundreds of short stories and worked in Hollywood, before publishing his first novel, *The Fabulous Originals*, in 1955. *The Chapman Report*, which appeared in 1960, was a major success, and has been followed by many more novels, of little literary merit but immense popular appeal, including *The Miracle*, in 1984, *The Seventh Secret*, in 1986, and *The Celestial Bed*, in 1987.

Wallace, Lew (1827–1905) Lewis Wallace was born in Indiana, studied law, and then joined the army at the beginning of the American Civil War, eventually rising to the rank of major-

general. After leaving the army he returned to the law, served for a period as minister in Turkey, and took to writing. He published a number of novels, but is remembered solely for his popular *Ben-Hur: A Tale of the Christ*, which appeared in 1880.

Waller, Edmund (1606–87) Born in Coleshill. Buckinghamshire, the English poet Edmund Waller was educated at Eton and Cambridge. He was a Member of Parliament for most of his life, except for a period before and during the Commonwealth, which, as a Royalist, he spent in exile. The author of the familiar 'Go, lovely rose', he wrote a considerable quantity of poetry, of which the main collections were *Poems*, in 1645, and *Divine Poems*, in 1685.

Walpole, Horace (1717–97) A Londoner by birth, Horace Walpole was educated at Eton and Cambridge. After making the grand tour he was a Member of Parliament for close on twenty years, but was always much involved in the world of letters and established his own printing press, on which many of his essays and other works were produced. In 1764 he published *The Castle of Otranto: a Gothic Story*, which was not only the prototype of the Gothic novels of terror and the supernatural but may also be considered to mark the beginning of the Romantic movement in England. Among his other works were a tragedy, *The Mysterious Mother*, presented in 1768, and three historical accounts, *Historic Doubts on the Life and Reign of King Richard the Third*, published in 1760, and *Memoirs of the Last Ten Years of the Reign of King George II* and *Memoirs of the Reign of King George III*, both of which appeared posthumously, in 1822 and 1845 respectively.

Walpole, Hugh (1884–1941) The novelist Hugh Seymour Walpole was born in New Zealand and educated at Cambridge. He published his first novel, *The Wooden Horse*, in 1909, following it in 1910 with *Maradick at Forty* and in 1911 with one of his most admired stories, *Mr Perrin and Mr Traill*. He wrote a great many novels, the most successful of which were *Rogue Herries* and the three subsequent volumes of 'The Herries Chronicle', written between 1930 and 1933. He was knighted in 1937.

Walton, Izaak (1593–1683) Born in Stafford, England, Izaak Walton became an ironmonger, but retired in 1644 and spent the rest of his life in leisurely pursuits and in writing. He had already completed a biography of John Donne, which appeared in 1640, and was later to publish lives of Henry Wotton, George Herbert, Richard Hooker and Bishop Sanderson. He is remembered for his great classic *The Compleat Angler*, which is not only a treatise on fishing but also a compendium of anecdotes, discussions of other rural sports, songs and discourses on the countryside. It was first published in 1653, but Walton continued for the next quarter of a century to produce revised and much expanded editions.

War and Peace The great novel by Leo Tolstoy of three Russian aristocratic families at the time of the Napoleonic wars, first published between 1863 and 1869.

War of the Worlds, The A prophetic novel by H.G. Wells, in which Earth is invaded by Martians. It was first published in 1898.

Ward, Mrs Humphry (1851–1920) Mary Augusta Arnold, granddaughter of Dr Arnold of Rugby and niece of the poet Matthew Arnold, was born in Tasmania. In 1872 she married Thomas Humphry Ward, who became an author and art critic, and soon began to write herself, producing articles, a book for children and other works before publishing her most successful novel, *Robert Elsmere*, in 1888. Her subsequent fiction often dealt with social and moral themes, and she was a campaigner in the field of education.

Warden, The The earliest of Anthony Trollope's Barsetshire novels, first published in 1855.

Warner, Sylvia Townsend (1893–1978) The English poet and novelist Sylvia Townsend Warner was born in Harrow. Her first collection of verse, *The Espalier*, appeared in 1925, and was followed by several others. Her most memorable novel is probably *Lolly Willowes*, a story of a spinster who becomes a witch, published in 1926. She also brought out several collections of short stories.

Warren, Robert Penn (1905–) Born in Guthrie, Kentucky, Robert Penn Warren was educated at the University of California and at Yale, Harvard and Oxford. His first book, published in 1929, was a biography, *John Brown, The Making of a Martyr*. In 1936 he brought out *XXXVI Poems*, and the novel *Night Rider* appeared in 1946. In the same year he produced his most famous book, *All the King's Men*, which was centred upon a corrupt Southern politician. It was awarded a Pulitzer Prize and became a bestseller. A volume of short stories, *The Circus in the Attic*, was published in 1948, and other novels have included *World Enough and Time*, in 1950, *Band of Angels*, in 1955, *Wilderness*, in 1961, and *Flood*, in 1964. He has also written essays and literary criticism, has taught at various universities, and for a time was co-editor of the *Southern Review*. He is a noted poet. *Brother to Dragons*, a volume of verse which appeared in 1953, won a Pulitzer Prize and the National Book Award. Among his other poetry collections are *Or Else*, which came out in 1974, *Now and Then: Poems*, in 1978, and *Being Here: Poetry 1977-1980*, in 1980.

Warton, Thomas (1728–90) Both Thomas Warton's father and his brother were Professors of Poetry at Oxford, and he himself held the chair in Poetry from 1757 to 1767. He was born in Basingstoke and educated at Oxford, and became well-known as a literary critic and a poet. His collected *Poems* appeared in 1777, and in 1785 he was appointed Poet Laureate. His major work was *The History of English Poetry*, published in three volumes between 1774 and 1781.

Washington, Booker T. (1856–1915) Booker Taliaferro Washington was the son of a white man and a Black slave and was born on a plantation in Virginia. By his own efforts he succeeded in obtaining an education at the Hampton Normal and Agricultural Institute. Later he organized a school for Blacks in Alabama, and became widely known as a speaker on behalf of his people. He published a number of books, including *The Future of the American Negro*, in 1899, *Working with the Hands*, in 1904, and *The Negro in Business*, in 1907. His best-known book is his autobiography, *Up From Slavery*, which appeared in 1901.

Washington Square A novel by Henry James, telling of a determined father's efforts to keep his heiress daughter from marrying a wastrel. It was first published in 1881.

Wasps, The A satirical comedy by Aristophanes, first seen in 422BC, in which a litigious Athenian is eventually converted to become a student of music and literature.

Waste Land, The A poem by T.S. Eliot, divided into sections called 'The Burial of the Dead', 'A Game of Chess', 'The Fire Sermon', 'Death by Water' and 'What the Thunder Said'. The poem, which is accompanied by Eliot's 'Notes', is seen as an expression of post-war disillusionment. It was first published in 1922.

Watch and Ward A novel by Henry James, first published in book form in 1878. It tells of the growing love of Roger Lawrence for his ward, Nora.

Water Babies, The A highly moral tale for children by Charles Kingsley. It tells the story of the little chimney sweep Tom, who falls into a river and joins the water babies who live there. It was first published in book form in 1863.

Watsons, The A novel by Jane Austen, uncompleted at the time of her death.

Watts, Isaac (1674–1748) Born in Southampton and educated at the Nonconformist Academy at Stoke Newington, Isaac Watts became a minister, and in later life devoted himself to writing. He produced educational and theological works, but is chiefly remembered for his religious poetry, including such hymns as 'O God, our help in ages past' and 'When I survey the wondrous Cross'.

Waugh, Evelyn (1903–66) The novelist Evelyn Arthur St John Waugh was born in North London and educated at Lancing College and Oxford. He became a schoolmaster, and then in 1928 published his amusing first novel, *Decline and Fall*, which was immediately successful. In 1930 he was received into the Roman Catholic Church. His career as a novelist continued with *Vile Bodies*, which appeared in 1930, *Black Mischief*, in 1932, *A Handful of Dust*, in 1934, and the satire on journalism, *Scoop*, in 1938. During World War II he served in the Royal Marines. His most serious work, *Brideshead Revisited*, later to become a successful television serial, appeared in 1945, and was followed in 1948 by his satirical squib about Californian funeral rites, *The Loved One*. His trilogy 'Sword of Honour', about an English officer during World War II, began in 1952 with *Men at Arms* and continued with *Officers and Gentlemen*, in 1955, and *Unconditional Surrender*, in 1957. His last major work was *The Ordeal of Gilbert Penfold*, a semi-autobiographical novel about the mental breakdown of a famous novelist, which appeared in 1957. He published a number of other works, including travel books, and his revealing *Diaries* were published posthumously. As a man, Evelyn Waugh was irascible, right-wing and old-fashioned in his attitudes; as a novelist, he was not only a witty and irreverent satirist, particularly adept at capturing the absurdity of the society in which he lived, but also a writer, in his more serious moments, of considerable sensitivity, and always an impeccable stylist.

Waverley Sir Walter Scott's earliest novel, set against a background of the Jacobite rebellion of 1745 and first published in 1814.

Waves, The A novel by Virginia Woolf, first published in 1931, and telling of the lives of six friends.

Way of All Flesh, The A novel of the Victorian middle-class world by Samuel Butler, first published in 1903.

Way of the World, The William Congreve's comedy of manners about the intrigue surrounding the lovers Mirabell and Millamant. It was first presented in 1700.

Wealth of Nations, Inquiry into the Nature and Causes of the An extensive and influential survey of the whole subject of political economy by Adam Smith, first published in 1776.

Webb, Mary (1881–1927) Gladys Mary Meredith was born in Shropshire. She married Henry Bertram Law Webb in 1912. She wrote a number of novels, including *Gone to Earth*, which was published in 1917, and *Precious Bane*, a story of country people, which appeared in 1924 and was satirized by Stella Gibbons in *Cold Comfort Farm*.

Webster, John (*c.*1578–*c.*1634) Very little is known of the life of the English dramatist John Webster. He collaborated with many other playwrights of the day, including Thomas Dekker, John Fletcher and John Ford, but several of these joint works have been lost, and we do not know how much of those that have survived was written by Webster. If such plays represented all of his work, he would not be worthy of a prominent place in the history of literature, for few of them have much literary value. However, he was the sole author of three plays which are still extant. *The Devil's Law Case* is an undistinguished work, but the other two, *The White Devil* and *The Duchess of Malfi*, both of which were written between 1609 and 1612, may be considered as among the major tragedies of the Elizabethan period. They were largely ignored after their early performances until Charles Lamb drew fresh attention to their quality at the beginning of the nineteenth century, since when they have been much admired and frequently revived. The plots of the two plays are almost excessively violent, abounding in foul deeds and bringing the curtain down on the deaths of all the major characters, but, although the construction of both plays can be faulted, their characterizations and dramatic power are strong enough to overcome these faults, and their poetry enhances the emotions of terror and pity which they evoke.

Webster, Noah (1758–1843) Born at West Hartford, Connecticut, and educated at Yale, Noah Webster published his first book, *A Grammatical Institute of the English Language*, between 1873 and 1875. It was enormously successful, selling more than a million copies a year. Other philological works appeared, and in 1807 he began to prepare *An American Dictionary of the English Language*, which was published in two volumes in 1828. He brought out a revised and expanded edition shortly before his death, and many revisions have appeared since. *Webster's Dictionary* stands beside *The Oxford Dictionary* as one of the two great lexicons of the English language.

Wedgwood, C.V. (1910–) Cicely Veronica Wedgwood was born in Northumberland and educated privately and at Oxford University. Her first published work was *Strafford*, which appeared in 1935, and this was followed by her history of *The Thirty Years War*, in 1938. She has written many other historical and literary studies, including *William the Silent*, in 1944, *Seventeenth Century Literature*, in 1950, and her three-part history of the English Civil War, *The King's Peace*, *The King's War* and *The Trial of Charles I*, published between 1955 and 1964. She was created a Dame in 1968.

Weil, Simone (1909–43) The social philosopher and mystic Simone Weil was born in Paris. During World War II she worked with the French Resistance. Her first work to be published in English was *The Iliad: or, The Poem of Force*, which appeared in 1945. Her major book, *La pesanteur et la grâce* (*Gravity and Grace*), which reflected her mystic experiences, came out in 1952. Other posthumous publications were her spiritual autobiography, *L'attente de Dieu* (*Waiting for God*), in 1951, and *L'enracinement* (*The Need for Roots*), in 1952.

Weir of Hermiston A novel by Robert Louis Stevenson which he was working on at the time of his death. The uncompleted story, about the conflict between a diehard father and his liberal-minded son, was published in 1896.

Weiss, Peter (1916–82) Peter Ulrich Weiss was born at Potsdam, Germany. Nazi persecution forced him into exile and he eventually settled in Sweden. He published three novels, *Der Schatten des Körpers des Kutschers* (*The Shadow of the Body of the Coachman*), in 1960, *Abschied von den Eltern* (*The Leavetaking*), in 1962, and *Fluchtpunkt* (*Exile*), in 1966. He is best known, however, as a playwright, and in this genre his works include *Die Ermittlung* (*The Investigation*) and the celebrated *The Persecution and Assassination of Jean-Paul Marat as Performed by the Inmates of the Asylum of Charenton Under the Direction of the Marquis de Sade*. Usually known as *Marat/Sade*, this play contrasts the ideal of individualism and revolution against a background of insanity.

Well-Beloved, The A novel by Thomas Hardy, centred upon a sculptor's obsession with perfection in art and in women. It was first published in 1892.

Wells, H.G. (1866–1946) Herbert George Wells was born in Kent, England, and educated at the Royal College of Science and at London University. After a period as a teacher, he began to write for various periodicals, and published his first novel, *The Time Machine*, in 1905. This was the first of his many highly successful books in the science fiction genre, which he may be said to have pioneered in England, and which he also used as vehicles for his socialist views. These early works include *The Island of Dr Moreau*, which appeared in 1896, *The Invisible Man*, in 1897, *The War of the Worlds*, in 1898, and *The First Men in the Moon*, in 1901. He also produced a large number of novels set in the middle-class society of his day, among which were *Love and Mr Lewisham*, in 1900, *Kipps* (later to become the musical *Half a Sixpence*), in 1905, *Ann Veronica* and *Tono-Bungay*, both in 1909, and *The History of Mr Polly*, in 1910. These books established him

'Mr H.G. Wells penetrates the unknown', a cartoon by Claud Fraser.

as a very popular writer who not only told entertaining stories but mirrored the social upheavals of the time – *Ann Veronica*, for instance, takes the emancipation of women as its theme. *Mr Britling Sees It Through*, which appeared in 1916, was a novel of England during World War I, but although Wells continued to write fiction, his later work in this genre was less successful, and he was to produce only one more major novel – *The Shape of Things to Come*, published in 1933 and later triumphantly transferred to the screen. Meanwhile, he had also published several volumes of short stories, such as *The Country of the Blind, and other stories*, which appeared in 1911, and a number of non-fiction works in which he looked forward to the future and again expounded his theories of socialism. In 1920 he brought out *The Outline of History, Being a Plain History of Life and Mankind*, and this long volume became a bestseller and brought him a new reputation as a popular historian and philosopher. He followed it with many books of a similar nature, including *A Short History of the World* (which he said was designed to be read as a novel), in 1922, *The Science of Life*, the three volumes of which came out between 1929 and 1930, *The Fate of Homo Sapiens*, in 1939, and *The New World Order*, in 1940. In 1934 he published his *Experiment in Autobiography*, which included much interesting material on his literary and socialist friends. His last book, *Mind at the End of its Tether*, published in 1945, was deeply pessimistic in tone. He was a very prolific writer, and the full list of his books is immensely long. His reputation has faded somewhat since his death, but he had considerable influence on public opinion in his day, and his novels are still readable, as is his *Outline of History*. He married in 1891 and for a second time in 1895, but was noted as a womanizer. His many affairs included the much-publicized involvement with the writer Rebecca West, by whom he had a son Anthony West.

Welty, Eudora (1909–) The American novelist and short story writer Eudora Welty was born in Jackson, Mississippi, and educated at the universities of Wisconsin and Columbia. She published her first collection of short stories, *A Curtain of Green*, in 1941, and was immediately accclaimed as a writer with an impeccable sense of style and atmosphere. She used a limited canvas, almost always confining herself to the southern states of America, but painted her pictures with great delicacy and the most telling effect. Her next book was a fantasy, *The Robber Bridegroom*, which appeared in 1942, and then a second volume of stories, *The Wide Net*, came out in 1943. Her first full-length novel, *Delta Wedding*, which told the story of a week in the lives of the Fairchilds of Shellmound Plantation in the Mississippi Delta, appeared in 1946, and greatly enhanced her reputation. *The Golden Apples*, published in 1949, and *The Bride of the Innisfallen*, in 1955, were further collections of stories, while her other novels were *The Ponder Heart*, in 1954, *Losing Battles*, in 1970, and, in 1972, *The Optimist's Daughter*, which was awarded a Pulitzer Prize.

Wesker, Arnold (1932–) The playwright Arnold Wesker was born and educated in London. He worked at a variety of occupations before his play *Chicken Soup with Barley* was produced in 1958 and gained him recognition as one of the most interesting dramatists to emerge after World War II. The play was based on his own experiences as a member of a Jewish family in London's East End, and covers the period from the 1930s to the 1950s. It was followed by *Roots*, the story of a girl who returns to her family from London and comes to realize that her own sophistication is as corrupt as their ignorance. The play which completes the trilogy, 'I'm Talking

About Jerusalem', looks at the disillusion of a couple filled with idealism for the honesty of rural life and defeated by the demands of modern society. Wesker's first play, *In the Kitchen*, was eventually performed in 1961, and it confirmed Wesker's place as a leader in the realistic school of domestic drama which became popular at that time. He has written several plays since, the best known of which is *Chips with Everything*, a social commentary on the young men who had been conscripted into National Service. He has also published essays, including *Distinctions*, in 1985, and short stories, and has been responsible for many major screenplays.

Wesley, Charles (1707-88) The eighteenth child of the Rector of Epworth, Charles Wesley was educated at Westminster and Oxford, where, with his brother John, he became one of the leaders of the Methodist movement. Both the brothers wrote a large number of hymns, but those of Charles, which include 'Jesu, Lover of my soul', 'Love Divine, all loves excelling' and 'Hark! the herald angels sing', have remained the most popular.

West, Morris (1916–) The Australian novelist Morris Langlo West was born in Melbourne and educated at the university there. He published his first novel, *Gallows on the Sand*, in 1955, and had his first major success in 1959 with *The Devil's Advocate*. Many other bestselling novels have followed, including *The Shoes of the Fisherman*, which appeared in 1963, *Harlequin*, in 1974, and *Cassidy*, in 1987.

West, Nathanael (1903–40) Nathan Wallenstein Weinstein, who was born in New York and educated at Brown University, Rhode Island, adopted the pseudonym Nathanael West. He went to Paris, where he wrote his first novel, *The Dream Life of Balso Snell*, which was published in 1931. The satire on pretentious intellectuals, as exemplified in its central character, was extremely broad, and the book is little read nowadays. Returning to America, he became a journalist, and in 1933 produced the much more memorable *Miss Lonelyhearts*, in which he portrayed a newspaper man who writes as an 'agony aunt', and whose involvement with his correspondents leads to his murder. He then went to Hollywood to become a scriptwriter, and his experiences there resulted in two novels, *A Cool Million*, published in 1934 and now largely forgotten, and his second major work, *The Day of the Locust*, a brilliant, if vicious, exposé of Hollywood in fictional form, which appeared in 1939. He was killed in an automobile accident at far too early an age. None of his novels was particularly successful during his lifetime, but both *Miss*

Lonelyhearts and *The Day of the Locust* have been widely admired since for their acerbic pictures of the febrile society in which he lived and the backgrounds against which they take place.

West, Rebecca (1892–1983) Cicely Isabel Fairfield was born in Ireland and educated in Edinburgh. She became an actress and later a journalist, writing under the name of Rebecca West and becoming an early apostle of feminism. In 1912 she met H.G. Wells, with whom she embarked on a long affair, and to whom she bore a son, Anthony West. She published her first novel, *The Return of the Soldier*, in 1918, and followed it with many others, including *The Fountain Overflows*, in 1956, and *The Birds Fall Down*, in 1966. She was a successful novelist, but also wrote many works of non-fiction. It was her book on Yugoslavia, *Black Lamb and Grey Falcon*, published in two volumes in 1941, which set the seal on her reputation, while her study of a number of traitors, *The Meaning of Treason*, was extremely successful when it was published in 1949, after she had attended the Nuremberg trials. She was made a Dame in 1959.

Westward Ho! A novel of the English struggle against the Spanish Armada by Charles Kingsley, first published in 1855.

Weyman, Stanley John (1855–1928) The English novelist Stanley John Weyman was born in Shropshire and educated at Oxford. He was called to the bar in 1881, and practised law before publishing his first novel, *The House of the Wolf*, in 1889. An historical romance set in France, it was followed by many others in similar vein, the best known of which was *Under the Red Robe*, which appeared in 1894.

Wharton, Edith (1862–1937) Edith Newbold Jones was born in New York City and educated privately. In 1885 she married Edward Wharton, and it was as Edith Wharton that her first stories and poetry appeared in *Scribner's Magazine*. In 1902 she published an historical novel, *The Valley of Decision*. It made little impression, but her next book, *The House of Mirth*, signalled the arrival of a novelist of importance. In 1907, in which year *The Fruit of the Tree* appeared, the Whartons moved to France, where Edith continued to live after her divorce in 1913. Meanwhile she had published in 1911 another major work, the sombre novel *Ethan Frome*. It was followed by a number of other novels, some set in France and others in the United States, including the very successful *The Age of Innocence*, which came out in 1920 and won the Pulitzer Prize, and *The Mother's Recompense*, in 1925. *The Old Maid*, which was later dramatized and filmed, was one of a collection of novellas published in 1924 under

the title *Old New York*. She also published many volumes of short stories, some verse, a number of travel books and an autobiography, *A Backward Glance*. Edith Wharton's work, in which her chief characters often found themselves in conflict with the society in which they lived, has often been compared with that of her friend Henry James.

What Maisie Knew A novel by Henry James, telling of a young and innocent girl caught up in her parents' marital merry-go-round. It was first published in 1897.

White, Gilbert (1720–93) The English naturalist Gilbert White was born in Selbourne, Hampshire, and educated at Oxford. He entered the Church, and from 1761 was curate at Farringdon, near his birthplace, and later at Selbourne itself. He spent much of his life in observation of the countryside in which his parish was set, and in 1789 published his *Natural History and Antiquities of Selbourne*, still popular for its acute and detailed study of Nature and landscape, for the charm of its somewhat haphazard construction, and for the simple excellence of its writing.

White, Patrick (1912–) The Australian novelist Patrick Victor Martindale White was born in London and educated at Cambridge, but has lived in Australia since 1946. He published his first novel, *Happy Valley*, in 1939. Two other novels followed before he produced the first of his major works, *The Tree of Man*, in 1955, and the second, *Voss*, in 1957. These two long accounts of early days in Australia won him very considerable acclaim. Many other novels have appeared since, including *Riders in the Chariot*, in 1961, *The Vivisector*, in 1970, and *The Twyborn Affair*, in 1979. In 1986 he brought out *Memoirs of Many in One*, which purports to be by its central character, Alex Xenophon Demirjian Gray. He has also published collections of short stories, plays and a volume of autobiography. He was awarded the Nobel Prize for Literature in 1973.

White, T.H. (1906–64) Terence Hanbury White, who was educated at Cambridge, became a teacher. He published his first novel, *Loved Helen*, in 1926, and followed it with *Farewell Victoria*, in 1933. *The Sword in the Stone*, the first volume of his Arthurian trilogy, appeared in 1939, and the second and third volumes, *The Witch in the Wood*, and *The Ill-Made Night*, came out in 1940 and 1941. The three books were republished in a revised form and with additional material as *The Once and Future King*, in 1958, and in 1977 a final section of the story, *The Book of Merlyn*, was retrieved from the author's papers. He wrote a number of other novels, including *Mistress Masham's Repose*, published in 1946, and *The Goshawk*, in 1951.

White, William Hale

White, William Hale (1831–1913) Born in Bedford, England, William Hale White was trained for the Nonconformist ministry, but found he had no vocation, and became a civil servant. In 1881 he published *The Autobiography of Mark Rutherford, Dissenting Minister*, and followed this novel in 1885 with a sequel, *Deliverance*. Using the pseudonym of Mark Rutherford, he published a number of other novels, the most notable of which was *The Revolution in Tanner's Lane*, which appeared in 1881. He also produced volumes of essays, translations of Spinoza and a biography of John Bunyan.

White Company, The An historical romance, set in the fourteenth century, by Arthur Conan Doyle, first published in 1891.

White Devil, The A tragedy of intrigue, adultery and murder by John Webster, first produced about 1608. Its full title is *The White Devil: or the Tragedy of Paolo Giordano Ursini, Duke of Brachiano, with the Life and Death of Vittoria Corombona the famous Venetian Courtezan*. Set in sixteenth-century Italy, its most notable characters are the wicked brother and sister, Flamineo and Vittoria.

White Fang A novel by Jack London, first published in 1905. Like *The Call of the Wild*, it is set in the far North, and tells of the dog White Fang, who is three parts wolf and who responds, in London's own words, to 'the call of the tamed'.

White Goddess, The Subtitled 'a historical grammar of poetic myth', this study by Robert Graves suggests that poetry is essentially inspired by the feminine side of human nature. It was first published in 1948.

White Jacket; or the World in a Man-of-War A realistic novel of the sea by Herman Melville, first published in 1850.

White Peacock, The D.H. Lawrence's first novel, set in rural England and largely concerned with Lettie Beardsall and the two rival aspirants for her hand. It was published in 1911.

Whitman, Walt (1819–92) The son of a farmer and carpenter, Walt Whitman was born in West Hills, Long Island. His education was rudimentary, and at an early age he became an errand-boy. Subsequently he worked in a printing business, and for a brief period as a teacher. In 1836 he founded, and for three years ran, a local newspaper, *Long Islander*. He wrote for various journals, and from 1842 to 1847 was editor first of the New York paper, *Aurora*, and then of the Brooklyn *Eagle*. In 1848 he went to New Orleans, where he was employed by the *Crescent*. He returned to New York in the following year, much impressed by his travels, which had opened his eyes to the glories of Nature, and was soon greatly influenced by Emerson and the doctrines of transcendentalism, with their emphasis on the divinity of human life and the overwhelming importance of love. Although he had become a rebel against society, he worked conventionally in Brooklyn as a builder and vendor of small houses, but he continued to write. In 1855 he had a small collection of poems printed, which he called *Leaves of Grass*. It attracted little attention until Emerson wrote in high praise of it, when it became widely read. A revised and expanded version appeared in 1856, and was followed in 1860 by a third edition, to which a large amount of new material had been added. In 1862 he went to Washington to become a government clerk, but also acted as a volunteer nurse in army hospitals during the Civil War, and from his experiences came *Drum Taps*, a volume of verse which was published in 1865, and the *Sequel to Drum Taps*, which appeared shortly after. These two collections, which were incorporated into later editions of *Leaves of Grass*, contained some of his finest poems, including his elegies for Abraham Lincoln. A large section of the American public, including many critics, considered his work to be immoral, especially since the poems called 'Calamus' were

The American poet Walt Whitman with Nigel and Catherine Jeanette Cholmely-Jones in 1887.

seen as homosexual in theme, but he had received adulatory comments from English reviewers, and his reputation in his own country had gradually grown, enabling him to publish other works with some success, and to continue to produce new editions of *Leaves of Grass*. In 1871 he brought out his prose attack on political corruption, *Democratic Vistas*. Two years later he suffered a stroke, and he spent the remainder of his life quietly in Camden, New Jersey. In 1875 he published *Memoranda during the War*, and in 1876 a new version of *Leaves of Grass* was accompanied by *Two Rivulets*, containing both prose and verse. *November Boughs* appeared in 1888, and a complete edition of his works, which included his apologia, *A Backward Glance O'er Travelled Roads*, was published in 1889. His last book, *Goodbye, My Fancy*, appeared in 1891. Whitman's poetry has been accused of a lack of careful construction, but few writers have been his equal in the celebration of Nature and the joy of life. His work has a depth of feeling and a strength which override any weakness of form. A true prophet of democracy, he is the greatest American poet of his age, and his influence is much in evidence in the work of present-day writers.

Whittier, John Greenleaf (1807–92) The Quaker poet John Greenleaf Whittier was born in Haverhill, Massachusetts, and educated at the Haverhill Academy. He became a journalist (and was later to help in the founding of the *Atlantic Monthly*), and in 1831 published his first book, *Legends of New England*, which consisted of both prose and verse. He became a politician and an ardent Abolitionist, and produced many works on anti-slavery themes, including his first collection of lyrics, *Poems written during the Progress of the Abolition Question in the United States*, published in 1837. A large number of volumes of poetry followed, and his reputation was firmly established with the publication in 1866 of *Snow Bound*, describing his farmstead home during the winter.

Widowers' Houses A play by G. Bernard Shaw, first presented in 1892, in which he attacked the evils of slum landlords.

Wiesel, Elie (1928–) Born in Szighet, Romania, Elie Wiesel received a Jewish religious education. He was deported to a Nazi concentration camp in 1944, but survived, and after World War II attended the Sorbonne in Paris. A journalist and academic, he has published a number of novels including *La nuit* (*Night*) and *Les portes de la forêt* (*the Gates of the Forest*), which appeared in 1958 and 1964 and both of which reflected his wartime experiences. Among other novels are *L'aube* (*Dawn*), which came out in 1960, *Le jour* (*The Accident*), in 1962, *Les Juifs du silence* (*The Jews of Silence*) in 1966, and *Le mendiant de Jerusalem* (*A Beggar in Jerusalem*), in 1968. He was awarded the Nobel Peace Prize in 1986.

Wilbur, Richard (1921–) The American poet Richard Purdy Wilbur was born in New York City and educated at Amherst college, Massachusetts, and Harvard. He published his first volume of poetry, *The Beautiful Changes*, in 1947. Many other collections have appeared, including several for children. *Things of This World*, which came out in 1956, was awarded both the National Book Award and the Pulitzer Prize. He has also published verse translations of plays by Molière.

Wilcox, Ella Wheeler (1850–1919) Born in Wisconsin, Ella Wheeler Wilcox published her first book, *Drops of Water*, in 1872. She produced nearly forty volumes of her saccharine, worthless verses. The condemnation in 1883 of one of the collections, *Poems of Passion*, as immoral, naturally added to her sales. She also published two volumes of autobiography.

Wilde, Oscar (1854–1900) Oscar Fingal O'Flahertie Wills Wilde was born in Dublin. His father was a distinguished surgeon, and his mother had established some reputation as a writer of both prose and verse under the pseudonym Speranza. He distinguished himself as a scholar at Trinity College, Dublin, and then went on to Magdalen College, Oxford, where he became the leader of the aesthetic movement. In 1882 he published a volume of *Poems*, and in the same year, already famous as a wit and as the principal target of the satire in the Gilbert and Sullivan comic opera, *Patience*, he went on a lecture tour of the United States. He married Constance Lloyd in 1884. *The Happy Prince*, a collection of fairy stories, appeared in 1888, and his novel, *The Picture of Dorian Gray*, was serialized in *Lippincott's Magazine*, in 1890, enjoying great success and causing considerable scandal – it was considered shocking not simply because it portrayed a monster of depravity, but because Wilde had treated his theme so lightly, embellishing it with the most sparkling of epigrams. In the following year *Dorian Gray* appeared in book form, and Wilde also published *Lord Arthur Savile's Crime and other stories*, a further selection of fairy stories, *A House of Pomegranates*, a collection of literary reviews, *Intentions*, and *The Soul of Man Under Socialism*, which had been inspired by Bernard Shaw. Meanwhile his plays *Vera*, produced in 1883, and *The Duchess of Padua*, in 1891, had both been failures, but in 1892 he had the first of his great theatrical successes with *Lady Windermere's Fan*. It was followed in 1893 by *A Woman of No Importance*, and in 1895 by *An Ideal Husband*. All three plays had serious themes and presented fascinating pictures of Victorian high society; their entertainment value was enhanced by the wit with which they were liberally laced (including many of the best epigrams from *Dorian Gray*). 1895 also saw the first production of his masterpiece, *The Importance of Being Earnest*, the farcical comedy in which he gave full rein to his wit, and in which he created Lady Bracknell, one of the two finest comic parts for women in the history of drama (the other being Sheridan's Mrs Malaprop). Earlier he had written, in French, the play *Salomé*. The Lord Chamberlain had refused to grant a licence for its performance in England – it was presented in Paris, with Sarah Bernhardt in the leading role, in 1896, and was later to become the basis for the Richard Strauss opera – but a translation by Lord Alfred Douglas had appeared in 1894. The Marquess of Queensbury, Lord Alfred's father, strongly disapproved of his son's friendship with Wilde, who further aroused Queensbury's enmity, in 1895, by publicly insulting him and subsequently suing him for criminal libel. The trial was an utter disaster for Wilde, who was convicted of homosexuality and sent to prision. While serving his sentence, he wrote a statement in his own defence, *De Profundis*, a part of which was published in 1905, while *The Ballad of Reading Gaol*, which appeared in 1898, told of the degradation that he suffered. Released in 1897, he spent the rest of his life in France, and died in Paris. Arriving once in New York he said, 'I have nothing to declare but my genius'. If only in *The Importance of Being Earnest*, Oscar Wilde's genius lives on.

Wilder, Thornton (1897–1975) The novelist and playwright Thornton Niven Wilder was born in Madison, Wisconsin, and educated at Yale, in Rome, and at Princeton. His first novel, *The Cabala*, was published in 1926, and in the following year he achieved immediate fame with his second, *The Bridge of San Luis Rey*, which was awarded a Pulitzer Prize. *The Woman of Andros* and *Heaven's My Destination* followed in 1930 and 1934 respectively. His first major success in the theatre came in 1938 with *Our Town*, which also won a Pulitzer Prize, and which, like his earlier one-act plays, *The Happy Journey from Trenton to Camden* and *The Long Christmas Dinner*, broke with many conventions in its construction and style of presentation. It was followed in 1942 by the even more experimental *The Skin of Our Teeth*, which won him a third Pulitzer Prize. A major novel, *The Ides of March*, came out in 1948, and *The Matchmaker*, a revision of his earlier *The Merchant of Yonkers*, gave him another theatrical triumph in 1954 (and later became the musical *Hello, Dolly!*). He published two more novels, *The Eighth Day*, in 1967, and *Theophilus North*, in 1973.

William of Malmesbury (*c*.1095–*c*.1143) The historian William of Malmesbury, noted for the readable and accurate nature of his work, spent most of his life as a monk in Malmesbury, Wiltshire, England. He produced five major works *Gesta Rerum Anglorum* and *Historia Novella*, which were histories of England from 449 to 1120 and from 1128 to 1142 respectively. *Gesta Pontificum Anglorum*, a history of the Church in England from 597 to 1125, a life of St Dunstan and a history of the antiquities of Glastonbury.

William of Newburgh (*c*.1136–*c*.98) A canon of the Augustinian priory of Newburgh in Yorkshire, William of Newburgh wrote a history of England from 1066 to 1198, known as *Historia Rerum Anglicarum*. It was largely derived from other works, but was notable for its impartiality.

William of Occam (*c*.1300–*c*.49) William of Occam (or Ockham) was born in Ockham, Surrey, England. He rose to eminence in the Franciscan order and was renowned as a theologian. He wrote a number of philosophical works, and his

This caricature of Oscar Wilde by Carlo Pellegrini was first published in 1844 in the magazine *Vanity Fair*.

teaching that it is wrong to generalize from universal realities was summed up in his dictum 'entities must not be unnecessarily multiplied', a phrase which is known as 'Occam's razor'.

Williams, Roger (c.1604–84) The founder of Rhode Island, Roger Williams was born in London and educated at Cambridge. He emigrated to New England in 1931, incurred the wrath of the Massachusetts authorities by his libertarian views, and set up a colony at Providence, Rhode Island, in 1636. He established religious freedom there, and worked for harmony with the native Indians. In 1643 he published *A Key into the Language of the Indians of America*, and his other writings, mostly political tracts, included *The Bloudy Tenent of Persecution for the Cause of Conscience*, an attack on Puritan religious intolerance, which appeared in 1644.

Williams, Tennessee (1911–83) Thomas Lanier Williams, known as Tennessee Williams, was born in Columbus, Mississippi, and educated at the universities of Washington and Iowa. His early works as a dramatist, the one-act plays called *American Blues* and the full-length *Battle of Angels*, were unsuccessful when presented in 1939 and 1940 respectively, although many critics recognized the promise in them. He then went to work in Hollywood, and perfected his craft to such an extent that in 1944 he established his reputation with *The Glass Menagerie*, a family drama set in St Louis. Its success was followed by an even greater triumph with the production in 1947 of *A Streetcar Named Desire*, the tragic story of Blanche DuBois, which remains his best-known play and for which he was awarded a Pulitzer Prize. Next came *Summer and Smoke*, the comedy *The Rose Tattoo*, and the experimental *Camino Real*. Another major work, *Cat on a Hot Tin Roof*, appeared in 1955, and this study of a family in disintegration won him a second Pulitzer Prize. He wrote many more plays, almost all distinguished by their highly-charged atmosphere, among them *Sweet Bird of Youth*, seen in 1959, and *Night of the Iguana*, in 1962. His other publications included several collections of short stories, some poetry, the short novel, *The Roman Spring of Mrs Stone*, which appeared in 1950, and a volume of *Memoirs*, in 1975.

Williams, William Carlos (1883–1963) Poet, novelist, short story writer and essayist, William Carlos Williams was born in Rutherford, New Jersey, and educated in Europe and at the University of Pennsylvania, where he qualified as a doctor of medicine. After further study in New York and Leipzig, he practised as a pediatrician in Rutherford, and also pursued a career as an author. At university he had met Ezra Pound and Hilda Doolittle, and his first volume of *Poems*, published privately in 1909, placed him in the Imagist school, although he was later to move away from this approach. More selections of poetry appeared, including *The Tempers*, in 1913, *Kora in Hell*, in 1920, *Spring and All*, in 1922, *The Collected Early Poems*, in 1938, and *The Collected Later Poems*, in 1950, the last-named volume winning the National Book Award. His poetry was popular, since it was simple and direct in style. Between 1946 and 1958 he brought out his major poetic work, *Paterson*, a long portrait in free verse of life in a modern American city. *Pictures from Breughel*, published in 1963, was a later selection. *The Great American Novel* and *In the American Grain*, which came out in 1923 and 1925 respectively, were collections of essays. He also wrote plays and published a number of volumes of short stories and several novels, tha latter including the trilogy made up of *White Mule*, which appeared in 1937, *In the Money*, in 1940, and *The Build-Up*, in 1952. His *Autobiography* was published in 1951.

Williamson, Henry (1895–1977) The English novelist Henry Williamson was born and educated in London. After service in World War I he became a journalist, and published in 1921 *The Beautiful Years*, the first novel in the four-volume sequence 'The Flax of Dreams'. He devoted much of his writing life to a related group of fifteen partly autobiographical novels, published between 1951 and 1969, collectively known as *A Chronicle of Ancient Sunlight*, covering some seventy years in the life of the writer Philip Maddison. He is probably best known, however, for his series of nature stories, including *The Peregrine's Saga*, in 1923, *Salar the Salmon*, in 1935, and the most popular of them all, *Tarka the Otter*, which made his name in 1927.

Wilson, Angus (1913–) Angus Frank Johnstone Wilson was born in South Africa and educated at Westminster and Oxford. His first two books were collections of short stories, *The Wrong Set*, which appeared in 1949, and *Such Darling Dodos*, in 1950. Their wit and meticulous style immediately gained recognition. A novel, *Hemlock and After*, came out in 1952, and many other works of fiction have appeared since, including *Anglo-Saxon Attitudes*, in 1956, *The Old Men at the Zoo*, in 1961, and *No Laughing Matter*, in 1967. Wilson has also published several volumes of literary criticism, and his *Reflections in a Writer's Eye* came out in 1986. He was knighted in 1980.

Wilson, Edmund (1895–1972) Born in Red Bank, New Jersey, and educated at Princeton, Edmund Wilson became a journalist after overseas service during World War I. He was editor of *Vanity*

Fair, and contributed regularly to *The New Yorker* and *The New Republic*. He published a novel, *I Thought of Daisy*, in 1929, and his collection of short stories, *Memoirs of Hecate County*, was well received when it appeared in 1946. However, he is thought of primarily as a prolific and distinguished essayist and literary critic of the left wing. *Axel's Castle*, a survey of symbolism in literature, and *The Boys in the Back Room*, on contemporary Californian writers, both appeared in 1931. Among other works of literary criticism are *Triple Thinkers*, in 1938, *The Wound and the Bow*, in 1941, and *Patriotic Gore: Studies in the Literature of the American Civil War*, in 1962. Wilson's polemical writings include *Travels in Two Democracies*, contrasting the United States and Russia, which was published in 1936, and *To the Finland Station*, a review and history of socialist thinking, in 1940. He also published some volumes of autobiography, and after the death of F. Scott Fitzgerald, whom he had met at Princeton and who was a close friend, he edited two volumes of Fitzgerald's work, the unfinished novel, *The Last Tycoon*, and the miscellaneous writings published as *The Crack-Up*.

Wilson, John (1785–1854) The Scottish critic John Wilson was born in Paisley and educated at Glasgow University and Oxford. He published a volume of poetry, *The Isle of Palms*, in 1812, and later brought out more verse, three novels, and collections of stories and sketches. However, his principal work was as a prolific contributor to *Blackwood's Magazine*, in which he praised Shelley, Wordsworth, Byron and Scott, but vilified Keats, Leigh Hunt and Hazlitt.

Winesburg, Ohio A collection of stories about a small American town which established Sherwood Anderson's reputation when published in 1919.

Wings of the Dove A novel by Henry James, published in 1902, describes how Kate Croy has love and wealth within her grasp and loses both.

Winsor, Kathleen (1919–) Kathleen Winsor worked as a journalist before producing *Forever Amber*, the historical novel which, at the time it was published in 1944, was considered daring. Subsequent novels have included *Star Money*, in 1950, *The Lovers*, in 1952, *Wanderers Eastward, Wanderers West*, in 1965, and *Jacintha*, in 1983.

Winterset A play in blank verse by Maxwell Anderson, based on the Sacco and Vanzetti case and first produced in 1935.

Winter's Tale, The A play by William Shakespeare in which, before all ends happily, Leontes, King of Sicily, believes his wife Hermione and daughter Perdita to be dead as a result of his unfounded mistrust. It was first performed in 1611 and published in 1623.

Winthrop, John (1588-1649) The Puritan leader John Winthrop was born in Suffolk and educated at Cambridge, becoming a prominent lawyer. He emigrated to Massachusetts in 1630, and was Governor of the Puritan colony there for twelve years. He kept a *Journal*, which was published in 1826 as *The History of New England from 1630 to 1649*. It is regarded as one of the most important documents in the early history of settlement in America.

Winthrop, Theodore (1828–61) A lawyer born in Connecticut and educated at Yale, Theodore Winthrop spent much of his life travelling in Europe and the United States. He wrote a number of books about his journeys and also some novels, the best known of the latter being *John Brent*, which was published in 1862. He was killed during the Civil War, and all his works appeared posthumously.

Wise, John (*c*.1652–1725) A militant campaigner for the independence of individual churches, John Wise was born in Roxbury, Massachusetts, and educated at Harvard. He became a minister of the church at Ipswich. He published a pamphlet, *The Churches Quarrel Espoused*, in 1710, and followed it with *A Vindication of the Government of New England Churches*, in 1717, and *A Word of Comfort to a Melancholy Country* in 1721.

Wister, Owen (1860–1938) Born in Philadelphia and educated at Harvard, Owen Wister became a lawyer, but soon decided to devote himself to writing. Having spent some years in Arizona and New Mexico, he set many of his books in the West, and achieved great success in 1902 with his classic story *The Virginian*. His other novels include *Lady Baltimore*, which appeared in 1906, and he also wrote biographies of U.S. Grant and Washington and a tribute to his friend Theodore Roosevelt.

Wither, George (1588–1667) The Hampshire-born poet and satirist George Wither was educated at Oxford. His satires, *Abuses Stript and Whipt* and *Wither's Motto: Nec habeo, nec careo, nec curo*, published in 1611 and 1621 respectively, both earned him periods in prison. His secular poetry appeared notably in *The Shepherd's Hunting*, in 1615, *Fair-Virtue, The Mistress of Phil' Arete*, in 1622, and *Britain's Remembrancer*, in 1628, while his religious verse was published in *Hymnes and Songs of the Church*, in 1623, and *Haleluiah: or Britain's Second Remembrancer*, in 1641.

Wives and Daughters A novel by Mrs Gaskell, first published in 1866, and concerned with life in a small country town.

Wodehouse, P.G. (1881-1975) Pelham Grenville Wodehouse was born in Guildford, England, and educated at Dulwich College. He worked in a bank, but soon turned to writing, producing stories for boys' magazines and later contributing to *Punch* and the *Strand Magazine*. His first novel, *The Pothunter*, appeared in 1902, and in 1917 his most memorable Edwardian characters, Bertie Wooster and Jeeves, made their first appearance in a collection of short stories. His vast output of humorous novels and stories brought him immense popularity, and admiration not only as a master of comic writing but as a remarkably economic and careful stylist. He was also the author of a large number of successful musical comedies, and many of his books were adapted for the stage. During World War II he was captured by the Nazis and later broadcast, at their behest, to America, an action which lost him much sympathy. However, the British forgave him, and he was granted a knighthood in 1975. He spent the last decades of his life in the United States, becoming an American citizen in 1955.

Wolcot, John (1738–1819) The English satirist John Wolcot, who wrote under the pseudonym Peter Pindar, was born in Devonshire, and became a doctor of medicine and a priest. After spending some years in Jamaica, he returned to England and between 1782 and 1786 published a considerable number of savage satirical verses, in which he attacked such subjects as the painters of the day in *Lyric Odes to the Academicians*, George III in several works, including *The Lousiad*, and James Boswell in *An Epistle to James Boswell* and *Bozzy and Piozzi*.

P.G. Wodehouse in his study. He wrote about Edwardian upper-class society.

Wolfe, Charles (1791–1823) An Irish poet, Charles Wolfe was born in County Kildare and educated at Trinity College, Dublin. He became a priest, and had some reputation at the time as a poet, but is remembered nowadays only for his verses on 'The Burial of Sir John Moore', published in 1817.

Wolfe, Thomas (1900–38) The novelist Thomas Clayton Wolfe was born in Asheville, North Carolina, the son of a stone-cutter, and educated at the University of North Carolina. Graduating in 1920, he decided to become a dramatist, and entered Harvard in 1923 to study play-writing there. His early plays, *Welcome to Our City* and *Mannerhouse*, did not sell, and he took a position teaching English at New York University. In 1930 his great novel *Look Homeward, Angel* was published after Maxwell Perkins, the celebrated editor, had succeeded in cutting the enormous manuscript to manageable size. Highly autobiographical, the story of the boyhood and youth of Eugene Gant was immediately successful, despite the fact that some critics accused it of lack of discipline. The second long novel, *Of Time and the River*, which appeared in 1935, continued Eugene Gant's fictional biography. In the same year he brought out a collection of short stories, *From Death to Morning*, and in 1936 published *The Story of a Novel*, an account of how he came to be a writer and his experiences in writing. He visited Nazi Germany, and was much upset by what he saw. The last months of his life were also disturbed by a quarrel with Perkins and various lawsuits. He died of an infection after a bout of pneumonia. Two novels were published posthumously, *The Web and the Rock*, in 1939, and *You Can't Go Home Again*, in 1940, and again these were autobiographical, although the central character was now called George Webber. An unfinished novel, *The Hills Beyond*, came out in 1941. Noted for his exuberant, vigorous prose, his work was in some ways akin to that of Melville, and his influence can still be seen today.

Wolfram von Eschenbach The greatest of the early German poets, Wolfram von Eschenbach is believed to have been born towards the end of the twelfth century. He left two major works, the epic poems *Parzival* (in which he expanded the story as told by Chrétien de Troyes) and *Willehalm*. Still extant also are his *Titurel*, a story of the Holy Grail, and his *Wächterlieder* (or *Tagelieder*), poems for lovers who are called by the nightwatchman to separate at dawn.

Wollstonecraft, Mary (1759–97) Born in London, Mary Wollstonecraft was a teacher and governess. In 1787 she published an essay, *Thoughts on the*

Education of Daughters, and in the following year a novel, *Mary, a Fiction, A Vindication of the Rights of Man* came out in 1790, and her best-known work, *A Vindication of the Rights of Woman*, in 1792. Following her liaison with the American writer Gilbert Imlay, to whom she bore a daughter, she married William Godwin, and died shortly after the birth of her daughter Mary, who was to become the wife of Percy Bysshe Shelley.

Woman in White, The A novel of mystery by Wilkie Collins, first published in 1860.

Woman of No Importance, A A play of London high society by Oscar Wilde, first performed in 1893.

Women in Love A novel by D.H. Lawrence, first published in the United States in 1920. It describes the relationships between the sisters Ursula and Gudrun Brangwen and their lovers Rupert Birkin and Gerald Crich.

Wood, Anthony à (1632–95) The English antiquary Anthony à Wood was born and educated in Oxford. In 1674 his history of Oxford University, originally written in English, was published in Latin as *Historia et Antiquitates Universitatis Oxoniensis*. His major work, *Athenae Oxoniensis: an Exact History of the Writers and Bishops who have had their Education in the University of Oxford from 1500 to 1690, to which are added the Fasti, or Annals for the said time*, which appeared between 1691 and 1692, contained matter that offended the authorities, and he was expelled from the university in 1693.

Wood, Mrs Henry (1814–87) Ellen Price was born in Worcester, England. She married Henry Wood in 1836. After writing anonymously for various periodicals, she published her most famous book, *East Lynne*, in 1861, and thereafter produced a large number of novels, which, although forgotten now, were very popular at the time. She became the owner and editor of the *Argosy* magazine, in which many of her stories appeared.

Woodforde, James (1740–1803) The Reverend James Woodforde was born in Somerset, England, and educated at Oxford. He kept a diary, covering the years 1758 to 1802, detailing his life as a curate in Somerset and as Rector of Weston Longeville in Norfolk. *The Diary of a Country Parson* was published between 1924 and 1931, and has achieved a wide readership for its portrait of Woodforde's times, and in particular for its descriptions of gargantuan meals.

Woodlanders, The A novel by Thomas Hardy, first published in 1887, about the relationships of Grace Melbury, Edred Fitzpiers, whom she marries, and Giles Winterbourne, whom she loves.

Woodstock A novel by Sir Walter Scott, first published in 1826. It is set in 1651, during the Civil War, and is concerned with the search by Cromwell's men for the defeated King Charles II, who takes refuge in the royalist household of Woodstock.

Woolf, Leonard (1880–1969) Born in London of Jewish extraction and educated at Cambridge, Leonard Sidney Woolf worked in the Ceylon Civil Service before returning to England in 1911. In the following year he married Virginia Stephen, and in 1913 and 1914 published two novels, *The Village in the Jungle* and *The Wise Virgins*. He became a prominent member of the Bloomsbury Group, and with his wife founded the Hogarth Press in 1917. Most of his writings thereafter were on left wing political themes, and include *Economic Imperialism*, which appeared in 1920, and *Principia Politica*, in 1953. His five volumes of autobiography, *Sowing, Growing, Beginning Again, Downhill all the Way* and *The Journey not the Arrival Matters*, published between 1960 and 1969, have been much admired.

Woolf, Virginia (1882–1941) Adeline Virginia Stephen was born in London. Her mother died when she was thirteen; she suffered a breakdown, and from that time on her mental health was precarious, her periods of derangement intensified by the strain of her writing. In 1904, after her father's death, she and her brothers Thoby and Adrian and her sister Vanessa (who later married Clive Bell) lived in a house in Bloomsbury, and the literary *salons* which they hosted there resulted in the formation of the Bloomsbury Group. Its members included J.M. Keynes, David Garnett, Roger Fry and Lytton Strachey. An engagement to Strachey came to nothing, and in 1913 she married Leonard Woolf. She had already become a regular contributor to *The Times Literary Supplement*, and in 1915 she published her first novel, *The Voyage Out*. She and her husband founded the Hogarth Press in 1917, and its first publication was *Two Stories* – 'The Mark on the Wall' by Virginia and 'Three Jews' by Leonard. Her next novels were *Night and Day*, which appeared in 1919, and *Jacob's Room*, in 1922, the main character in the latter based in part on her brother Thoby, who had died in 1906. *Jacob's Room* was the first of her works in which she employed the innovative style for which she became famous, and the principles of which she set out in her celebrated essay 'Mr Bennett and Mrs Brown', attacking Arnold Bennett's realistic approach. *Mrs Dalloway* followed in 1925, in which year she also published a collection of essays, *The Common Reader* (a second series of these was to appear in 1932). *To the Lighthouse* came in 1927. By this time she was widely recognized as one of the most important novelists of the twentieth century, and her readership was considerably widened with the very successful publication in 1933 of *Orlando*, a fantasy covering four centuries and involving a change of sex for the central character. The story had been inspired by her intimate friend Vita Sackville-West, and in it she again demonstrated the beauty and poetic nature of her prose style. Her novel *The Waves* was published in 1931, and her next book was *Flush:A Biography*, in 1933, which told of the romance of Elizabeth Barrett and Robert Browning as seen through the eyes of Elizabeth Barrett's dog. Another two novels were still to come: *The Years*, in 1937, and *Between the Acts*, in which her experimental approach was further developed, published shortly after her suicide by drowning in 1941. Among her other publications were a story for children and a biography of the painter Roger Fry, while a collection of short stories and several volumes of essays appeared posthumously. Already acclaimed during her lifetime, Virginia Woolf has gained in stature since her death, and her admirers have by no means been confined to the feminists, in whose canon she occupies a place of considerable prominence (she wrote two notable feminist tracts, *A Room Of One's Own*, published in 1929, and *Three Guineas*, in 1938). She is now seen as one of the most influential of writers, and the contribution she made to the development of the modern novel, by her exploration of the 'stream of consciousness' technique, her masterly use of imagery, and her oblique and impressionistic approach to narrative, cannot be underestimated.

Woolson, Constance Fenimore (*c*.1840–94) A greatniece of James Fenimore Cooper, Constance Fenimore Woolson was born in Claremont, New Hampshire. She wrote sketches of the American Lake country and of the Old South, and also produced a number of novels, including *Anne*, published in 1882, and *Horace Chase*, in 1894.

Wordsworth, Dorothy (1771–1855) The companion of her poet brother William, for whom she kept house for most of her life, Dorothy Wordsworth was born at Cockermouth, not far from Grasmere, where she and William were to make their home. She wrote some poetry herself, but her main literary efforts were devoted to a series of *Journals* and accounts of journeys which she and her brother made. These have provided invaluable information for the biographers of William Wordsworth and for students of his work.

Wordsworth, William (1770–1850) Born at Cockermouth, Cumberland, the great English poet William Wordsworth was educated at Cambridge.

LEFT: The picturesque garden of Monks Cottage in Sussex, home of Virginia Woolf for fifty years.

BELOW: Terraced gardens at Cockermouth near Grasmere in Cumbria, the birthplace of the Wordsworths.

He published his first poem, 'An Evening Walk', in 1793, and a second, 'Descriptive Sketches', in 1794. It was at that time that he and his sister Dorothy decided to set up house together, and a timely legacy not only allowed them to do so, but gave him the financial freedom to devote himself to poetry. While he was living in Dorset, he met Samuel Taylor Coleridge, and in 1797 he and Dorothy moved to Somerset in order to be near to Coleridge and his family. In the following year the joint production of the two poets, *Lyrical Ballads*, was published, Wordsworth contributing fifteen poems, including 'We Are Seven' and 'Lines above Tintern Abbey'. Several expanded editions of the volume followed, and contained, in addition to new poems by Wordsworth, such as 'Ruth' and the pastoral 'Michael', a 'Preface' in which he expounded his theories of poetry, the language of which, he argued, should be simple rather than ornate. After a tour of Germany in 1798 and 1799, which produced among other work the 'Lucy' poems, the Wordsworths settled at Grasmere in the Lake District, where he worked on *The Excursion*. At this period he was writing prolifically; among the poems he produced are 'Lines on Westminster Bridge', composed while on the way to France in 1802, 'Highland Girl' and 'The Solitary Reaper', the last two both inspired by a journey to Scotland in 1803. In 1802 he married Mary Hutchinson, by whom he had five children, two of whom died in childhood. Dorothy continued to live with them. *Poems in Two Volumes*, which appeared in 1807, included the ode on 'Intimations of Mortality' and sonnets and lyrics which are among his best-known work. In addition to the legacy already mentioned, he had received in 1805 repayment of a debt which had been owed to his father, and his wife had also brought him some money, but frugal though Dorothy was as a housekeeper, the Wordsworths lived in near-poverty until he was appointed stamp-distributor for the County of Westmoreland in 1813, a post which brought him an annual income of £500. *The Excursion*, a long philosophical poem in nine books in which he expressed his views on the nature of human beings and the society in which they live, including reflections on the French Revolution and a plea for the education of children, was published in 1814; it was the first published part of a huge project, 'The Recluse', which he had been planning for many years. It was never completed, although a second instalment, *The Prelude*, on which he had begun work as early as 1799, appeared posthumously in 1850. *The Excursion* was savaged by the critics, and his next works, all of which had been written

William Wordsworth, Poet Laureate and one of the greatest English Romantic poets, portrayed in chalk by Benjamin Haydon in 1818.

several years earlier, fared equally badly; these were *The White Doe of Rylstone*, published in 1815, and *Peter Bell* and *The Waggoner*, both of which came out in 1819. From this time on, however, his reputation began to grow. *Sonnets on the River Duddon*, published in 1820, was followed in 1822 by *Ecclesiastical Sonnets* and *Memorials of a Tour on the Continent*. After a long interval, he brought out *Yarrow Revisited*, in 1835, and *Poems chiefly of Early and Late Years*, in 1842. In 1843 he was appointed Poet Laureate. Coleridge, Southey, Scott and Wordsworth are regarded as the first generation of English Romantic poets, and there is little doubt that Wordsworth is the greatest of these four.

Works and Days A poem attributed to Hesiod, the Greek author, probably written in the eighth century BC. Concerned with the life of a farmer, it became a model for later pastoral works.

Wotton, Henry (1568–1639) The diplomat and poet Henry Wotton was born in Kent and educated at Oxford. He spent many years abroad on various missions and ambassadorships, and was knighted in 1603 by James I. In 1624 he published *The Elements of Architecture*, which was a paraphrase from the work of Marcus Vitruvius Pollio. The few poems which he wrote were published posthumously in 1651 in a book called *Reliquiae Wottonianiae*.

Wouk, Herman (1915–) After completing his education at Columbia University, Herman Wouk, who was born in New York City, became a radio script writer. He published his first novel, *Aurora Dawn*, in 1947, and the following year brought out *The City Boy*. He achieved a huge success in 1951 with *The Caine Mutiny*, which won a Pulitzer Prize. Other novels have followed, including *Marjorie Morningstar*, in 1955, *Youngblood Hawke*, in 1962, *The Winds of War*, in 1971 and *Inside, Outside*, in 1985.

Woyzeck A drama by Georg Büchner, inspired by the author's involvement in the politics of the time. It was not published until some forty years after the author's death in 1837, and received its first performance in 1913.

Wright, Richard (1908–60) The Black writer Richard Wright was born in Natchez, Mississippi. Self-educated, he worked at a number of jobs in Memphis before moving to Chicago. He joined the Communist party in 1936, but renounced his membership in 1944, as he later recorded in his essay in the symposium *The God That Failed*. His first published work was a collection of short stories, *Uncle Tom's Children*, which appeared in 1938, and in 1940 he brought out *Native Son*, a novel in which a Black youth called Bigger Thomas is befriended by a white family, accidentally kills the daughter, and embarks on a chain of self-aggrandizing lies before being tried and condemned to death. This powerful book established him as the leader of the generation of Black writers which was to emerge fully after World War II. He followed it in 1941 with the historical survey, *Twelve Million Black Voices*, and his impressive and outspoken autobiography, *Black Boy*, appeared in 1945. *White Man, Listen!* was a collection of lectures, published in 1957, and he also wrote critical books on Ghana and Franco's Spain. In addition to *Native Son*, he produced three other novels: *The Outsider*, which came out in 1953, *The Long Dream*, in 1958, and *Land Today*, published posthumously in 1961.

Wrinkle in Time, A An outstanding volume of poetry by Madeleine L'Engle, first published in 1962.

Wuthering Heights The powerful novel by Emily Brontë, first published in 1847. It tells of the destructive passion of the vengeful Heathcliff for Catherine Earnshaw, and the consequences which follow for their families.

Wyatt, Thomas (1503–42) The English poet Thomas Wyatt was born in Kent and educated at Cambridge. He was at the court of Henry VIII and went on many official missions to foreign countries. He was knighted in 1537. Many of his love poems, consisting of sonnets, rondeaus and lyrics, were published in 1557, together with the work of other writers, in a miscellany called *Songes and Sonnets*. He also prepared versions of the Penitential Psalms, which appeared in 1549 as *Certayne Psalms drawen into English meter by Sir Thomas Wyat Knyght*. He is credited with having pioneered the sonnet form in English.

Wycherley, William (1641–1716) Born in Shropshire, William Wycherley was educated in France and at Oxford. He then studied law, but quickly turned to the theatre, and his comedy *Love in a Wood, or St James's Park* was given its first performance probably early in 1671. *The Gentleman Dancing Master*, was probably presented in 1671, and was followed in 1675 by his masterpiece, *The Country Wife*. Often condemned since by prudish critics for its bawdiness, it is full of zest and witty characterizations. His last play was *The Plain Dealer*, which was probably first seen in 1676, and which is almost as fine as *The Country Wife*. *Love in a Wood* had earned him the patronage of the Duchess of Cleveland, mistress to Charles II, and royal favours might have followed if he had not secretly, and to the king's displeasure, married the Countess of Drogheda in 1680. A year later the Countess died, and for the remainder of his life Wycherley was hounded by debtors, spending seven years in the Fleet prison, and his financial troubles continued even after James II had released him from prison and granted him a pension. He married again at the age of seventy-five, apparently with the principal intention of disinheriting a nephew.

Wycliffe, John (*c*.1330–84) The Yorkshire-born cleric John Wycliffe was educated at Oxford. He campaigned against what he saw as the corruption of the Church and the Pope, attacked the doctrine of transubstantiation, and was eventually forced to retire to his living at Lutterworth in Leicestershire. He instigated the first complete translation of the Bible into English, and the two versions which appeared in the 1380s are associated with his name, although he may have done comparatively little of the translation himself.

Wylie, Elinor Morton Hoyt (1885–1928) The American novelist and poet Elinor Morton Hoyt Wylie was born in Somerville, New Jersey. Between 1921 and 1928 she published four volumes of poetry and four novels – *Jennifer Lorn*, *The Venetian Glass Nephew*, *The Orphan Angel* and *Mr Hodge and Mr Hazard*.

X

Xenophon (*c*.430-352BC) The Greek historian and miscellaneous writer Xenophon was born in Athens. He spent much of his life as a soldier, fighting for both Athens and Sparta. He left a number of works, which include the *Anabasis*, an account of an expedition against the Persian king Ataxerxes II, the *Hellenica*, a history covering the period 411 to 362BC, tracts on horsemanship and hunting, some recollections of Socrates, and a romantic and philosophical work, the *Cyropaedia*, which purports to be a life of the Persian king Cyrus but contains much that is wholly imaginative.

Y

Yeats, W.B. (1865–1939) William Butler Yeats was born in Dublin, the son of a distinguished artist. He was educated in London, and then, when his family returned to Ireland, studied art for a three-year period beginning in 1884. During that time he began to contribute poems and articles to various magazines, and decided on a literary career. In 1888 Oscar Wilde gave him much encouragement and introduced him to literary circles in London. His first volume of verse *The Wanderings of Oisin*, was published in 1889, and was followed by a series of prose works, *Fairy and Folk Tales, Tales from Carleton, John Sherman and Dhoya*, published between 1889 and 1891. *The Countess Cathleen*, a verse drama, appeared with other poems in 1892, and *The Celtic Twilight*, a collection of sketches and essays, in 1893. A second play, *The Land of Heart's Desire*, was performed in 1894. He was now established in the vanguard of the new Celtic movement, and his position was confirmed in 1895 with his collected *Poems*. *The Secret Rose*, consisting of Irish legends and containing both poetry and prose, came out in 1897, and in 1899 he published a new selection of verse, *The Wind among the Reeds*. At this point he became interested in the establishment of an Irish theatre, and his association with Lady Gregory led some years later to the founding of the Abbey Theatre in Dublin, where much of his dramatic work was produced, including the one-act plays *Cathleen ni Houlihan* and *On Baile's Strand*, which were on the opening bill in 1907. During the next years he wrote prolifically, producing many new volumes of poetry, among them *The Green Helmet and other poems*, in 1910, *Poems Written in Discouragement*, in 1913, *Responsibilities: Poems and a play*, in 1914,

An etching of William Butler Yeats by Augustus John.

and *The Wild Swans at Coole*, in 1917. At the same time he was writing plays and essays, and also taking an increasing part in Irish politics. In 1917, having previously proposed in vain to the Irish nationalist Maud Gonne, he married Georgie Hyde-Lees, and his new wife had a profound effect on his work. She had paranormal gifts, and through her 'automatic writing' he came to discover a system of symbolism for which he had been seeking. The results were seen in the many volumes of poetry which followed, such as *Michael Robartes and the Dancer*, published in 1920, which contained many poems inspired by the uprisings in Ireland, 1including 'Easter 1916' and 'The Second Coming', and *The Tower*, in 1928. Meanwhile he had received many honours, including the award of the Nobel Prize for Literature in 1923, and had become a member of the Irish Senate, in which he sat from 1922, when it was formed, until 1928. Later collections included *Words for Music Perhaps and other poems*, in 1932, *New Poems*, in 1938, and *Last Poems and Plays*, which appeared posthumously in 1940. In addition to his large output of poetry, plays and essays, he had undertaken in his long career much other literary work; he had, for instance, edited the works of Blake and *The Oxford Book of Modern Verse*, translated the Oedipus plays of Sophocles, and written several volumes of autobiography; he had encouraged younger writers such as Ezra Pound and Edith Sitwell; he had also made a number of lecture tours, and, in his later years, had become a successful broadcaster. Yeats was not merely the most gifted poet that Ireland has ever produced, but one of the greatest writing in any language in the twentieth century.

Yellow Book, The A literary periodical published in London by John Lane between 1894 and 1897. Among the authors whose work appeared in it were Arnold Bennett, Max Beerbohm, John Buchan, Ernest Dowson, Henry James, Richard Le Gallienne and W.B. Yeats, while the artists who contributed included Aubrey Beardsley, John Sargent, Walter Sickert and Wilson Steer.

Yonge, Charlotte M. (1823–1901) The English writer Charlotte Mary Yonge was born in Hampshire. She was an extremely prolific writer, and, after publishing no fewer than five novels in 1841, produced well over a hundred other works, including books for children, among them *The Little Duke*, which appeared in 1854, histories and educational works. Her chief fame was as a novelist, and her best-known work of fiction was *The Heir of Redclyffe*, published in 1853.

Young, Edward (1683–1765) Born near Winchester, England, and educated at Oxford, Edward Young was a poet and playwright, and much later in life became a clergyman. After publishing some poetry, he began to write for the theatre, and his plays *Busiris* and *Revenge* were produced in 1719 and 1721 respectively. Between 1725 and 1728 he brought out a number of satires, collected in 1728 as *Love of Fame, the Universal Passion*. His most famous work, *The Complaint, or Night Thoughts on Life, Death and Immortality* (known generally as *Night Thoughts*), a long gloomy and strongly didactic poem in nine books, was published between 1742 and 1745, and became immensely popular throughout Europe. His tragedy *The Brothers* was performed in 1753.

Z

Zangwill, Israel (1864–1926) The Jewish writer Israel Zangwill was born in London and educated at London University. He became a teacher and then a journalist, but the publication in 1892 of *Children of the Ghetto* confirmed him in a career as an author. He followed the success of this book with a number of others, including *Ghetto Tragedies*, in 1893, *Dreamers of the Ghetto*, in 1898 and *Ghetto Comedies*, in 1907, in which he provided sketches of contemporary English Jewry and glances at Jewish history. He also had a considerable success in the theatre with such plays as *Merely Mary Ann* and *The Melting Pot*.

Zola, Emile (1840–1902) Emile Edouard Charles Antoine Zola was born in Paris and educated in Aix and Marseilles. His first book, *Contes á Ninon*, appeared in 1864, but it was his novel, *Thérèse Raquin*, published in 1867, which brought him to public attention. He was to become the leader of the French school of naturalism, and, although many of his books were very successful, he suffered harsh criticism and was always regarded as a highly controversial writer. He devoted most of his life to the production of a vast series of novels in which he told the story of the Rougon-Macquart family and painted a picture of French society during the second empire (1852–70), and especially of the middle and working classes. Among the twenty volumes in the series, which were published between 1871 and 1893, are *L'assommoir*, *Nana*, *Germinal* and *La terre*. He turned next to a trilogy of romances based on three cities, *Lourdes*, *Rome* and *Paris*, which appeared between 1894 and 1898. In 1898, when France was in turmoil over the Dreyfus case (in which a Jewish army officer was accused of treason), he wrote his famous article 'J'accuse', denouncing the enemies of Dreyfus. Prosecuted for libel, he went to England, where he worked on the first of a new group of novels on the themes of population, work, truth and justice. These were *Fécondité*, published in 1899, *Travail*, in 1901, and *Vérité*, which dealt with the Dreyfus case, in 1903. The fourth book, *Justice*, was planned but not written, for he was asphyxiated by fumes from a faulty flue. After his death he was granted the praise which he had not received during his life.

Zorba the Greek The celebrated novel by Nikos Kazantzakis, first published in 1943. It was later made into a highly successful film starring Anthony Quinn.

Zuckmayer, Carl (1896–1977) The German playwright Carl Zuckmayer was born at Nackenheim. His first published work was a comedy, *Der Fröhliche Weinberg* (*The Happy Vineyard*), which appeared in 1925. *Der Hauptmann von köpenik* (*The Captain of Köpenik*), seen in 1932, was a satire on Prussian militarism. He fled from the Nazis to Austria, and eventually to the United States, where he became an American citizen. His best-known play was *Des Teufels General* (*The Devil's General*), first produced in English in 1962. He also wrote essays and several screenplays, including, in 1930, that of *The Blue Angel*.

Zuleika Dobson A novel by Max Beerbohm, set in the University of Oxford in the 1890s, first published in 1911.

Examples of various forms of verse
(*Explanations can be found in the main text*)

ALEXANDRINE

Extract from
Ode to the Pious Memory of Mrs Anne Killgrew

What can we say to excuse our second fall?
Let this thy Vestal, Heaven, atone for all!
Her Arethusian stream remains unsoil'd,
   Unmixt with foreign filth, and undefil'd;
Her wit was more than man, her innocence a child.

JOHN DRYDEN

The final line in this short extract is an alexandrine, having twelve syllables in contrast with the other lines, which are decasyllabic.

BLANK VERSE

Extract from *Julius Caesar*

This was the most unkindest cut of all;
For when the noble Caesar saw him stab,
Ingratitude, more strong than traitors' arms,
Quite vanquish'd him: then burst his mighty heart;
And, in his mantle muffling up his face,
Even at the base of Pompey's statue,
Which all the while ran blood, great Caesar fell.
O! what a fall was there, my countrymen;
Then I, and you, and all of us fell down,
Whilst bloody treason flourish'd over us.
O! now you weep, and I perceive you feel
The dint of pity; these are gracious drops.

WILLIAM SHAKESPEARE

The lines are iambic pentameters.

HEROIC COUPLETS

Extract from *The Prologue* to *The Canterbury Tales*

Whan that Aprille with his schowres swoote
The drougt of Marche hath perced to the roote,
And bathed every veyne in swich licour,
Of which vertue engendred is the flour; —
Whan Zephirus eek with his swete breethe
Enspired hath in every holte and heethe
The tendre croppes, and the yonge sonne
Hath in the Ram his halfe cours i-ronne,
And smale fowles maken melodie,
That slepen al the night with open eye,
So priken hem nature in here corages: —
Thanne longen folk to gon on pilgrimages.

GEOFFREY CHAUCER

HEROIC VERSE

Man

Know then thyself, presume not God to scan,
The proper study of mankind is man,
Placed on this isthmus of a middle state,
A being darkly wise, and rudely great:
With too much knowledge for the stoic's pride,
He hangs between; in doubt to act, or rest;
In doubt to deem himself a God, or beast;
In doubt his mind or body to prefer;
Born but to die, and reasoning but to err;
Alike in ignorance, his reason such,
Whether he thinks too little or too much:
Chaos of thought and passion, all confused;
Still by himself abused or disabused;
Created half to rise and half to fall;
Great lord of all things, yet a prey to all;
Sole judge of truth, in endless error hurled:
The glory, jest, and riddle of the world!

ALEXANDER POPE

LYRIC

Going to the Wars
Tell me not, Sweet, I am unkind,
   That from the nunnery
Of thy chaste breast and quiet mind
   To war and arms I fly.

True, a new mistress now I chase,
   The first foe in the field;
And with a stronger faith embrace
   A sword, a horse, a shield.

Yet this inconstancy is such
   As thou too shalt adore;
I could not love thee, Dear, so much,
   Loved I not Honour more.

RICHARD LOVELACE

RHYME ROYAL

The Love Unfeigned

O yonge fresshe folkes, he or she,
In which that love groweth with your age,
Repeyreth hoom from worldy vanitee,
And of your herte up-casteth the visage
To thilke god that after his image
Yow made, and thinketh al nis but a fayre
This world, that passeth sone as floures fayre.

And loveth him, the which that right for love
Upon a cros, our soules for to beye,
First starf, and roos, and sit in hevene a-bove;
For he nil falsen no wight, dar I seye,
That wol his herte al hoolly on him leye.
And sin he best to love is, and most meke,
What nedeth feyned loves for to seke?

GEOFFREY CHAUCER

RONDEAU

In After Days

In after days when grasses high
O'er-top the stone where I shall lie,
  Though ill or well the world adjust
  My slender claim to honour'd dust,
I shall not question nor reply.

I shall not see the morning sky;
I shall not hear the night-wind sigh;
  I shall be mute, as all men must
    In after days!

But yet, now living, fain would I
That some one then should testify,
  Saying – 'He held his pen in trust
  To Art, not serving shame or lust.'
Will none? – Then let my memory die
    In after days!

HENRY AUSTIN DOBSON

SESTINA

I saw my soul at rest upon a day
  As a bird sleeping in the nest of night,
Among soft leaves that give the starlight way
  To touch its wings but not its eyes with light;
So that it knew as one in visions may,
  And knew not as men waking, of delight.

This was the measure of my soul's delight;
  It had no power of joy to fly by day,
Nor part in the large lordship of the light;
  But in the secret moon-beholden way
Had all its will of dreams and pleasant night,
  And all the love and life that sleepers may.

But such life's triumph as men waking may
  It might not have to feed its faint delight
Between the stars by night and sun by day,
  Shut up with green leaves and a little light;
Because its way was as a lost star's way,
  A world's not wholly known of day or night.

All loves and dreams and sounds and gleams of night
  Made it all music that such minstrels may,
And all they had they gave it of delight;
  But in the full face of the fire of day
What place shall be for any starry light,
  What part of heaven in all the wide sun's way?

Yet the soul woke not, sleeping by the way,
  Watched as a nursling of the large-eyed night,
And sought no strength nor knowledge of the day,
  Nor closer touch conclusive of delight,
Nor mightier joy nor truer than dreamers may,
  Nor more of song than they, nor more of light.

For who sleeps once and sees the secret light
  Whereby sleep shows the soul a fairer way
Between the rise and rest of day and night,
  Shall care no more to fare as all men may,
But be his place of pain or of delight,
  There shall he dwell, beholding night as day.

Song, have thy day and take thy fill of light
  Before the night be fallen across thy way;
Sing while he may, man hath no long delight.

ALGERNON SWINBURNE

SONNET

(1) The Elizabethan or Shakespearian sonnet

Sonnet 116

Let me not to the marriage of true minds
Admit impediments. Love is not love
Which alters when it alteration finds,
Or bends with the remover to remove:
O, no! it is an ever-fixed mark,
That looks on tempests and is never shaken;
It is the star to every wandering bark,
Whose worth's unknown, although his height be taken,
Love's not Time's fool, though rosy lips and cheeks
Within his bending sickle's compass come;
Love alters not with his brief hours and weeks,
But bears it out even to the edge of doom.
  If this be error and upon me proved,
  I never writ, nor no man ever loved.

WILLIAM SHAKESPEARE

Examples of various forms of verse

(2) The Petrarchan sonnet

On first looking into Chapman's Homer

Much have I travelled in the realms of gold,
    And many goodly states and kingdoms seen;
    Round many western islands have I been
Which bards in fealty to Apollo hold,
Oft of one wide expanse had I been told
    That deep-brow'd Homer ruled as his demesne:
    Yet did I never breathe its pure serene
Till I heard Chapman speak out loud and bold:
Then felt I like some watcher of the skies
    When a new planet swims into his ken;
Or like stout Cortez, when with eagle eyes
    He stared at the Pacific — and all his men
Look'd at each other with a wild surmise —
    Silent, upon a peak in Darien.

JOHN KEATS

TRIOLET

When first we met, we did not guess
That Love would prove so hard a master;
Of more than common friendliness
When first we met we did not guess,
Who could foretell the sore distress,
This irretrievable disaster,
When first we met? — we did not guess
That Love would prove so hard a master.

ROBERT BRIDGES

VILLANELLE

A dainty thing's the Villanelle.
    Sly, musical, a jewel in rhyme,
It serves its purpose passing well.

A double-clappered silver bell
    That must be made to clink in chime,
A dainty thing's the Villanelle;

And if you wish to flute a spell,
    Or ask a meeting 'neath the lime,
It serves its purpose passing well.

You must not ask of it the swell
    Of organs grandiose and sublime —
A dainty thing's the Villanelle;

And, filled with sweetness, as a shell
    Is filled with sound and launched in time,
It serves its purpose passing well.

Still fair to see and good to smell
    As in the quaintness of its prime,
A dainty thing's the Villanelle;
It serves its purpose passing well.

W.E. HENLEY

List of principal authors referred to
(Arranged chronologically by date of birth)

Homer ? Eighth century BC
Aeschylus 525-456 BC
Sophocles 495-406 BC
Euripides 480-406 BC
Aristophanes c.448-380 BC
Aristotle 384-322 BC
Cicero 106-43 BC
Virgil 70-19 BC
Augustine, St 354-430
Alfred, King 849-900
Abelard, Peter 1079-1142
Dante, Alighieri 1265-1321
Petrarch 1304-74
Boccaccio, Giovanni 1313-75
Gower, John c.1330-1408
Chaucer, Geoffrey c.1340-1440
Caxton, William c.1422-91
Villon, François 1431-?63
Erasmus 1466-1536
More, Thomas 1478-1535
Rabelais, François c.1494-c.1553
Ascham, Roger 1515-68
Montaigne, Michel de 1533-92
Gascoigne, George c.1537-77
Cervantes, Miguel de 1547-1616
Spenser, Edmund c.1552-99
Raleigh, Walter c.1552-1618
Sidney, Philip 1554-86
Kyd, Thomas 1558-94
Chapman, George c.1559-1634
Bacon, Francis 1561-1626
Vega Carpio, Lope de 1562-1635
Drayton, Michael 1563-1631
Marlowe, Christopher 1564-93
Shakespeare, William 1564-1616
Nashe, Thomas 1567-1601
Alabaster, William 1567-1640
Donne, John 1572-1631
Jonson, Ben 1572-1637
Marston, John c.1575-1634
Webster, John c.1578-c.1634
Fletcher, John 1579-1625
Massinger, Philip 1583-1640
Beaumont, Francis 1584-1616
Ford, John 1586-c.1640
Hobbes, Thomas 1588-1679
Herrick, Robert 1591-1674
Herbert, George 1593-1633
D'Avenant, William 1606-68
Corneille, Pierre 1606-84
Milton, John 1608-74
Butler, Samuel 1613-80
Marvell, Andrew 1621-78
Molière 1622-73
Vaughan, Henry 1622-95
Bunyan, John 1628-88
Dryden, John 1631-1700
Locke, John 1632-1704
Pepys, Samuel 1633-1703
Racine, Jean 1639-99
Behn, Aphra 1640-89

Wycherley, William 1641-1716
Otway, Thomas 1652-85
Defoe, Daniel 1660-1731
Swift, Jonathan 1667-1745
Congreve, William 1670-1729
Addison, Joseph 1672-1719
Steele, Richard 1672-1729
Farquhar, George 1678-1707
Bolingbroke, Henry 1678-1751
Gay, John 1685-1732
Berkeley, George 1685-1753
Pope, Alexander 1688-1744
Richardson, Samuel 1689-1761
Chesterfield, Lord 1694-1773
Voltaire 1694-1778
Franklin, Benjamin 1706-90
Fielding, Henry 1707-54
Johnson, Samuel 1709-84
Hume, David 1711-76
Rousseau, Jean-Jacques 1712-78
Sterne, Laurence 1713-68
Gray, Thomas 1716-71
Walpole, Horace 1717-97
Smollett, Tobias 1721-71
Kant, Immanuel 1724-1804
Goldsmith, Oliver 1728-74
Burke, Edmund 1729-97
Cowper, William 1731-1800
Macpherson, James 1736-96
Gibbon, Edward 1737-94
Paine, Thomas 1737-1809
Boswell, James 1740-95
Bentham, Jeremy 1748-1832
Goethe, Johann Wolfgang
  von 1749-1832
Burns, Robert 1750-96
Sheridan, Richard Brinsley 1751-1816
Chatterton, Thomas 1752-70
Burney, Fanny 1752-1840
Godwin, William 1756-1836
Blake, William 1757-1827
Schiller, Friedrich von 1759-1805
Cobbett, William 1763-1835
Edgeworth, Maria 1767-1849
Wordsworth, William 1770-1850
Scott, Walter 1771-1832
Coleridge, Samuel Taylor 1772-1834
Southey, Robert 1774-1843
Austen, Jane 1775-1817
Lamb, Charles 1775-1834
Hazlitt, William 1778-1830
Stendhal 1783-1842
Irving, Washington 1783-1859
Hunt, Leigh 1784-1859
Audubon, John James 1785-1851
De Quincey, Thomas 1785-1859
Peacock, Thomas Love 1785-1866
Byron, George, Lord 1788-1824
Cooper, James Fenimore 1789-1851
Shelley, Percy Bysshe 1792-1822
Clare, John 1793-1864

Keats, John 1795-1821
Carlyle, Thomas 1795-1881
Heine, Heinrich 1797-1856
Balzac, Honoré de 1799-1850
Pushkin, Alexander 1799-1837
Hood, Thomas 1799-1845
Macaulay, Thomas Babington 1800-59
Newman, John Henry 1801-90
Dumas, Alexandre 1802-70
Martineau, Harriet 1802-76
Hugo, Victor 1802-85
Beddoes, Thomas Lovell 1803-49
Bulwer-Lytton, Edward 1803-73
Borrow, George 1803-81
Emerson, Ralph Waldo 1803-82
Hawthorne, Nathaniel 1804-64
Disraeli, Benjamin 1804-81
Andersen, Hans Christian 1805-75
Browning, Elizabeth Barrett 1806-61
Mill, John Stuart 1806-73
Longfellow, Henry Wadsworth 1807-82
Whittier, John Greenleaf 1807-92
Poe, Edgar Allan 1809-49
Gogol, Nikolai 1809-52
Darwin, Charles 1809-82
FitzGerald, Edward 1809-83
Tennyson, Alfred, Lord 1809-92
Holmes, Oliver Wendell 1809-94
Fuller, Margaret 1810-50
Musset, Alfred de 1810-57
Gaskell, Elizabeth 1810-65
Thackeray, William Makepeace 1811-63
Stowe, Harriet Beecher 1811-96
Dickens, Charles 1812-70
Browning, Robert 1812-89
Reade, Charles 1814-84
Trollope, Anthony 1815-82
Brontë, Charlotte 1816-55
Thoreau, Henry David 1817-62
Brontë, Emily 1818-48
Marx, Karl 1818-83
Turgeniev, Ivan Sergeevich 1818-83
Froude, J.A. 1818-94
Kingsley, Charles 1819-75
Eliot, George 1819-80
Whitman, Walt 1819-92
Ruskin, John 1819-1900
Melville, Herman 1819-91
Brontë, Anne 1820-49
Baudelaire, Charles 1821-67
Flaubert, Gustave 1821-80
Dostoevsky, Fyodor 1821-81
Burton, Richard 1821-90
Arnold, Matthew 1822-88
Parkman, Francis 1823-93
Patmore, Coventry 1823-96
Collins, Wilkie 1824-89
Rossetti, Dante Gabriel 1828-82
Meredith, George 1828-1900
Ibsen, Henrik 1828-1906
Tolstoy, Count Leo 1828-1910

List of principal authors referred to

Dickinson, Emily 1830-86
Rossetti, Christina 1830-94
Alcott, Louisa M. 1832-88
Carroll, Lewis 1832-98
Stephen, Leslie 1832-1904
Morris, William 1834-96
Butler, Samuel 1835-1902
Twain, Mark 1835-1910
Gilbert, W.S. 1836-1911
Swinburne, Algernon 1837-1909
Howells, William Dean 1837-1920
Adams, Henry Brooks 1838-1918
Harte, Bret 1839-1902
Daudet, Alphonse 1840-97
Zola, Emile 1840-1902
Hardy, Thomas 1840-1928
Hudson, W.H. 1841-1922
Mallarmé, Stéphane 1842-98
James, William 1842-1910
James, Henry 1843-1916
Hopkins, Gerard Manley 1844-89
Nietsche, Friedrich Wilhelm 1844-1900
Bridges, Robert 1844-1930
Jeffries, Richard 1848-87
Strindberg, August 1849-1912
Maupassant, Guy de 1850-93
Stevenson, Robert Louis 1850-94
Moore, George 1853-1933
Rimbaud, Arthur 1854-91
Wilde, Oscar 1854-1900
Shaw, G. Bernard 1856-1950
Conrad, Joseph 1857-1924
Jerome, Jerome K. 1859-1927
Doyle, Arthur Conan 1859-1930
Housman, A.E. 1859-1936
Chekhov, Anton 1860-1904
Barrie, James 1860-1937
Henry, O. 1862-1910
Wharton, Edith 1862-1937
Kipling, Rudyard 1865-1936
Yeats, W.B. 1865-1939
Wells, H.G. 1866-1946
Bennett, Arnold 1867-1931
Galsworthy, John 1867-1933
Pirandello, Luigi 1867-1936
Gorky, Maxim 1868-1936
Masters, Edgar Lee 1868-1950
Belloc, Hilaire 1870-1953
Crane, Stephen 1871-1900
Synge, J.M. 1871-1909
Proust, Marcel 1871-1922
Dreiser, Theodore 1871-1945
Beerbohm, Max 1872-1956
Powys, John Cowper 1872-1963
Russell, Bertrand 1872-1970
Colette 1873-1954
De la Mare, Walter 1873-1956
Chesterton, G.K. 1874-1936

Anderson, Sherwood 1874-1941
Frost, Robert 1874-1963
Churchill, Winston 1874-1965
Maugham, W. Somerset 1874-1965
Rilke, Rainer Maria 1875-1926
Mann, Thomas 1875-1955
London, Jack 1876-1916
Cather, Willa 1876-1947
Hesse, Hermann 1877-1962
Stevens, Wallace 1878-1955
Masefield, John 1878-1967
Sandburg, Carl 1878-1967
Sinclair, Upton 1878-1968
Forster, E.M. 1879-1970
O'Casey, Sean 1880-1964
Woolf, Leonard 1880-1969
Wodehouse, P.G. 1881-1975
Joyce, James 1882-1941
Woolf, Virginia 1882-1941
Milne, A.A. 1882-1956
Kafka, Franz 1883-1924
Williams, William Carlos 1883-1963
Lawrence, D.H. 1885-1930
Lewis, Sinclair 1885-1951
Pound, Ezra 1885-1972
Brooke, Rupert 1887-1915
Jeffers, Robinson 1887-1962
Sitwell, Edith 1887-1965
O'Neill, Eugene 1888-1953
Anderson, Maxwell 1888-1959
Eliot, T.S. 1888-1965
Chandler, Raymond 1888-1959
Kaufman, George S. 1889-1961
Pasternak, Boris 1890-1960
Miller, Henry 1891-1980
MacLeish, Archibald 1892-1982
West, Rebecca 1892-1983
Stein, Gertrude 1894-1946
Thurber, James 1894-1961
cummings, e.e. 1894-1962
Huxley, Aldous 1894-1963
Priestley, J.B. 1894-1984
Hartley, L.P. 1895-1972
Wilson, Edmund 1895-1972
Williamson, Henry 1895-1977
Graves, Robert 1895-1986
Fitzgerald, F. Scott 1896-1940
Blunden, Edmund 1896-1974
Faulkner, William 1897-1962
Wilder, Thornton 1897-1975
Garcia Lorca, Federico 1898-1936
Brecht, Bertolt 1898-1956
Hemingway, Ernest 1899-1961
Coward, Noël 1899-1973
Nabokov, Vladimir 1899-1977
Borges, Jorge Luis 1899-1986
Wolfe, Thomas 1900-38
Hughes, Richard 1900-76

Malraux, André 1901-76
Steinbeck, John 1902-68
West, Nathanael 1903-40
Orwell, George 1903-50
Waugh, Evelyn 1903-66
Day-Lewis, C. 1904-72
Isherwood, Christopher 1904-86
Greene, Graham 1904-
Singer, Isaac Bashevis 1904-
Sartre, Jean-Paul 1905-80
Snow, C.P. 1905-80
Koestler, Arthur 1905-83
Sholokov, Mikhail Alexandrovich 1905-84
Powell, Anthony 1905-
Warren, Robert Penn 1905-
Betjeman, John 1906-84
Beckett, Samuel 1906-
MacNeice, Louis 1907-63
Auden, W.H. 1907-73
Wright, Richard 1908-60
Spender, Stephen 1909-
Welty, Eudora 1909-
Williams, Tennessee 1911-83
Durrell, Lawrence 1912-
White, Patrick 1912-
Camus, Albert 1913-60
Wilson, Angus 1913-
Thomas, Dylan 1914-53
Bellow, Saul 1915-
Burgess, Anthony 1917-
Solzhenitsyn, Alexander 1918-
Lessing, Doris 1919-
Salinger, J.D. 1919-
Scott, Paul 1920-78
Larkin, Philip 1922-86
Amis, Kingsley 1922-
Vonnegut Jr, Kurt 1922-
Heller, Joseph 1923-
Mailer, Norman 1923-
Baldwin, James 1924-
Vidal, Gore 1925-
Fowles, John 1926-
Grass, Gunter 1927-
Garcia Marquez, Gabriel 1928-
Plath, Sylvia 1932-63
Naipaul, V.S. 1932-
Updike, John 1932-
Wesker, Arnold 1932-
Roth, Philip 1933-
Soyinka, Wole 1934-
Stoppard, Tom 1937-